American Orators
Before
1900

American Orators Before 1900

CRITICAL STUDIES AND SOURCES

EDITED BY
Bernard K. Duffy and
Halford R. Ryan

GREENWOOD PRESS

NEW YORK
WESTPORT, CONNECTICUT
LONDON

Library of Congress Cataloging-in-Publication Data

American orators before 1900.

Bibliography: p.
Includes indexes.
1. Oratory—United States—History. 2. Orators—
United States—Biography. 3. Speeches, addresses, etc.,
American—History and criticism. 4. Oratory—United
States—Bibliography. 5. Orators—United States—
Biography—Bibliography. 6. Speeches, addresses, etc.,
American—Bibliography. I. Duffy, Bernard K. II. Ryan,
Halford Ross.
PN4055.U5A4   1987   815'.009   86-33610
ISBN 0-313-25129-0 (lib. bdg. : alk. paper)

Library of Congress Catalog Card Number: 86-33610
ISBN: 0-313-25129-0

First published in 1987

Greenwood Press, Inc.
88 Post Road West, Westport, Connecticut 06881

Printed in the United States of America

The paper used in this book complies with the
Permanent Paper Standard issued by the National
Information Standards Organization (Z39.48-1984).

10 9 8 7 6 5 4 3 2 1

For Sue
    Elizabeth
    Cheryl
    Shawn

CONTENTS _____

ACKNOWLEDGMENTS ─────────

We want to thank those persons who helped us to bring this book to completion.

Marilyn Brownstein, humanities editor at Greenwood Press, encouraged us to develop a companion volume to *American Orators of the Twentieth Century: Critical Studies and Sources*, and aided us in the beginning of our work. Mildred Vasan, politics and law editor, helped us once the project was underway. Beverly Miller, copy editor, lent her expertise when the manuscript was assembled and Lisa Reichbach, production editor, oversaw the final production of the book. Our work reflects their professional guidance.

Bernard Duffy's colleagues in the English Department at Clemson University offered a great deal of encouragement. G. William Koon, the department head, and Robert A. Waller, dean of the College of Liberal Arts, approved a sabbatical leave during which part of this book was completed. Pearl Parker and Kim Hunter of the departmental secretarial staff typed portions of the manuscript.

Halford Ryan thanks John Elrod, dean of the College, Washington and Lee University, for supporting a Glenn Grant to do research in the Beecher Family Papers, Yale University.

We are grateful to the Speech Communication Association, the American Political Science Association, and the Society for the History of the Early American Republic for carrying a call for contributors in their respective publications.

We especially thank the authors of the entries. These scholars, representing the disciplines of speech, history, political science, government, and religion, accommodated themselves to a uniform style and format appropriate to the nature of the entries in this book. We hope that those who use this book will appreciate their achievements, as we do.

INTRODUCTION —————————

This book is about American oratory before 1900. Its companion volume, *American Orators of the Twentieth Century: Critical Studies and Sources*, focuses on twentieth-century speakers. In both works, we take oratory to be discourse that treats the constitutional, social, theological, moral, and political concerns of the American people in a free and open society. This sense of oratory has been inherited from the earliest period of the nation's history. The social significance of speeches in the past has endured, although the style of oratory has changed. Oratory remains a vibrant force in American society, and historically important speeches articulate with undiminished eloquence many of the beliefs and values to which modern orators still appeal. The study of public address inevitably demonstrates the continuity of the past and the present.

There are many ways to examine American religion, politics, and culture. Among the most fascinating windows to the past are contemporary speeches. Because they are fragments of historical moments, one frequently finds in them an unvarnished truth that would otherwise remain hidden beneath the veneer of popular history. This book concerns the speeches and speakers who helped guide the nation. Although speeches are often ephemeral, some because they addressed political or other pragmatic matters of a transitory nature, others because they may not have been committed to paper, many have survived and become part of the legacy of the nation's birth and development. The religious fervor, political wrangling, social unrest and upheaval, as well as the most sublime thoughts regarding the nature of the human spirit, are all recorded in the nation's speeches. More than reflect American society, these speeches embody it.

In his famous encomium of speech, Isocrates holds that speech is responsible for the development of civilization. The history of oratory in the United States affirms the importance of oral discourse as an influence on culture. The spoken word shaped the institutions of the new society and expressed a distinctive national character. As American society embraced its version of Greek democracy, it also renewed the Greek oral tradition and implanted the basic precept that democracy is impossible without free speech. Unlike the written word, the spoken word excluded no one either as an audience or as a participant in the great continuous social and political dialogue into which every generation of Americans is born.

Oratory in the new land, like much else, assumed a character peculiar to its new environment. Lawrence Buell in *New England Literary Culture* reminds us of oratory's importance in American letters. As well as being the pragmatic instrument for erecting the nation's political and social institutions, and really because of this fact, oratory came to occupy a position of great importance in the nation's literature. Buell points out, "The early national sense of literary inferiority did not extend to the area of public speaking." Oratory flourished in both religion and politics.

The history and culture of the United States have been shaped by orators, particularly those before the twentieth century. American public address during this period reflected the nation's struggle to achieve cultural and political independence. Pulpit preaching expressed the diversity of American religious experience, and ceremonial oratory celebrated the freedoms that became a national birthright. Among the fifty-five orators discussed in these pages are the nation's leading intellectuals, patriots, preachers, and politicians. Not all spoke in support of noble causes. Not all achieved their aims or were considered eloquent, but all influenced the American polity.

John Cotton and Jonathan Edwards imprinted on their generations and subsequent ones a national religious fervor and practice. The religious beliefs of Americans were periodically revived by the speaking of such preachers as Phillips Brooks, Theodore Parker, William Ellery Channing, Dwight L. Moody, Charles Finney, DeWitt Talmage, and Henry Ward Beecher. By their preaching, they transformed the Puritan God of doctrine and damnation into a God of feeling and love. If the relationship between humans and God was spelled out in the Scriptures, colonial Americans eventually realized that their relationship to the state needed to be written down in a constitution. Not content with Parliament's assertion that the unwritten British constitution was, in effect, what Parliament said it was, patriotic speakers such as James Otis, Sam Adams, and Patrick Henry fired the first salvo of the Revolution. They ignited their rhetoric with incendiary condemnations of Parliament and king long before the first gunpowder was fired at the redcoats. After the colonists talked themselves into a revolution, the founding fathers delineated the need of a written constitution. Such leading figures as Alexander Hamilton, John Adams, George Mason, and Benjamin Franklin lent their voices, although sometimes from different perspectives, at critical moments during the creation of the nation. Debate continued to play an important role in the formation and adoption of the Constitution in convention, and the contest between Patrick Henry and James Madison in Virginia's ratification convention affirmed the importance of debate as a tool to decide what the constitutional text did or did not mean.

Debate figured prominently in the golden age of American oratory from 1820 to 1865. The great senatorial triumvirate—Daniel Webster, Henry Clay, and

John C. Calhoun—spoke for their sectional interests on the great issues of the day, the tariff and the slavery question. Senators Thomas Hart Benton and Stephen Douglas added their voices to the fray, and although Douglas won the series of debates against Abraham Lincoln in the Illinois senatorial contest, the Little Giant lost the greater plum of the presidency. The Compromise of 1850 gathered the great orators for the last peaceful adjustment of differences by debate. By 1860, positions had become so polarized that oratory could not readily bring the sections to compromise. The oratory of southerners such as William Yancey, Robert Toombs, and Lucius Lamar—who north of the Mason-Dixon line were known as fire-eaters—or the more patrician Jefferson Davis, did not ameliorate the situation. On the other hand, the vice-president of the Confederacy, Alexander Stephens, tried futilely with his rhetoric to stem the tide of secession in Georgia. Of course, the accusing finger could just as easily be pointed at the abolitionists, among them William Lloyd Garrison, Joshua Giddings, Wendell Phillips, and Charles Sumner, for fomenting discord and disaffection. The Civil War finally settled the dispute.

Yet the age witnessed other issues, not so momentous perhaps as to be settled by a war, but important enough to evoke memorable rhetoric. Red Jacket's oratory poignantly portrayed the Indian's slow demise at the white man's hand. Famed abolitionist Frederick Douglass pricked the conscience of one generation of Americans, and Booker T. Washington spoke tirelessly for aims that were only partially fulfilled in the nineteenth century. Neither were the demands that women be given the right to vote acted upon until the early twentieth century, but the women's suffrage movement grew strong in the arms of its founders Susan B. Anthony, Sarah and Angelina Grimké, Elizabeth Cady Stanton, Lucy Stone, and Sojourner Truth.

Many of the speakers considered in this book made reputations as occasional orators, although they were equally well known as deliberative, forensic, or religious speakers. Henry Ward Beecher, the clergyman, and Daniel Webster, the great senatorial debater and courtroom advocate, were among the orators whose virtuosity led to their acclaim as public encomiasts. A mix of entertainment and inspiration, Fourth of July speeches revealed oratorial pyrotechnics that often competed successfully with the fireworks. More sublime were such epideictic addresses as those delivered by Edward Everett and Abraham Lincoln at Gettysburg, although Lincoln's infinitely briefer, if less representative, speech, when judged by nineteenth-century standards, has become an enduring model of the genre. Audiences in the lyceum circuit were well entertained and edified by the loquacity of Mark Twain and Ralph Waldo Emerson, who joined the company of such famous after-dinner speakers as James Russell Lowell and Robert Green Ingersoll, the great agnostic and perhaps the best speaker of them all.

The contributors to this book have used the case study for their entries because we believe it is the best methodology to reveal the rhetorical relationship of the speaker, the speech, and the audience. Each entry opens with a brief introduction that places the orator in historical perspective, with particular emphasis on the person's oratorical training, the causes the speaker espoused, the general effects of the orator's rhetoric, and whether the figure contributed significantly to the theory and practice of the art of persuasive address. The core of each essay is a critical examination of each person's speaking. Based on a close and careful reading of speech texts, this exegesis is often supported by illustrative quotations from the speeches. The entry also explicates other important elements. As appropriate, each essayist considers rhetorical topics, such as the preparation of speeches, persuasive techniques, style, and delivery skills. Whenever possible, the critics assess a speaker's impact on the American social, legal, and political scene and discuss causes and movements that influenced or were influenced by the speaker's oratory. Each essay closes with a summative evaluation of the orator's contribution to or detraction from American values and democracy.

Following the critical rhetorical essay is a section entitled "Information Sources," which is intended as a valuable research aid, especially for those just beginning to investigate an orator's rhetoric. Under the heading "Research Collections and Collected Speeches," each essayist identifies and discusses resources germane to the speaker. The books, anthologies, and collected works in which complete and authoritative speech texts may be found are listed; these collections are source coded with abbreviations so that each speech text can be located readily. In "Selected Critical Studies," each writer places pertinent critical essays, case studies, and theses and dissertations that shed significant light on the related speech activities of the orator. In "Selected Biographies," each essayist delineates the works that illuminate the speaker's persuasive practices. The entry closes with a helpful "Chronology of Major Speeches." The sources of many of these speeches are coded to the speech texts, which were listed in Research Collections and Collected Speeches. These major speeches are discussed in the entry and represent the core materials of the essay.

As an added convenience to researchers, a Glossary of Rhetorical Terms has been appended. The glossary explains the meanings of classical and technical speech terms, as well as modern rhetorical terminology, that may not be encountered in general parlance.

There is also a brief exposition of standard sources in public address, a subject index, an index to the speakers and speeches discussed in this book, and a Contributors List. The list describes the scholarly interests of those who contributed to this book and also serves as an additional research tool. Researchers may wish to contact the appropriate scholar in order to delve deeper into the research materials on a speaker.

Two principles guided our selection of speakers. Within space constraints, we attempted to match with a list of speakers, whose numbers were more than could be totally treated in the book, scholars who were best equipped and qualified to write the entry. The other side of that consideration was the necessity for the existence of enough speech texts, enough critical studies and secondary works, and enough scholarly interest in an individual orator to justify that speaker's being represented. Therefore four general classes of speakers have been included in this book. For presidents of the United States, we included those who were orators, without regard to their executive abilities. The other presidents were excluded, not because they did not merit rhetorical attention but for the pragmatic reasons discussed. Second, we endeavored to include great congressional speakers who eloquently addressed the important issues of their days. Individuals from the House of Representatives and the Senate figure prominently in the list of legislative orators. Third, we tried to include a variety of voices from more ordinary Americans who did not attain elevated offices but whose voices were nevertheless heard and heeded. A panoply of people is thus represented: suffragists, abolitionists, secessionists, spokesmen for civil rights, and encomiasts. Fourth, we included from a spectrum of religious figures those we felt were most representative or significant.

We hope that this book will prove useful to all who consult it and that it will both stimulate and guide future research on the important and fascinating topic of American political oratory before 1900.

American Orators
Before
1900

JOHN ADAMS
(1735–1826), second president of the United States

John Adams graduated from Harvard University at the age of twenty. His public service career began before his Revolutionary activities in the Massachusetts Colony. He successfully defended John Hancock against charges of smuggling in 1768 and in 1770 successfully defended the British soldiers involved in the shootings known as the Boston Massacre.

In 1774, Adams was elected delegate from Massachusetts to the Continental Congress and again attended sessions from February through June 1776. He was a member of the committee to draft the Declaration of Independence and delivered eloquent orations in the Congress advocating the adoption of the declaration.

In 1789, Adams was elected the first vice-president of the United States and presided over the inaugural session of the U.S. Senate from April to September. In 1793, he was reelected vice-president. In 1796, Adams defeated Thomas Jefferson and was elected to the nation's highest office. Allegations of fraud arose concerning specific votes in Pennsylvania and Maryland; however, there were no provisions in the law or by Congress related to false votes. Some hypothesize that Jefferson was actually the winner of the presidential election of 1796.

In responding to the crisis with France in 1798, Adams appointed George Washington commander in chief of the armed forces. In October 1800, Adams became the first occupant of the yet-unfinished president's house in Washington, D.C. In December, he was defeated by Jefferson in the presidential election. Before leaving office, Adams appointed John Marshall chief justice of the U.S. Supreme Court.

Adams spent the next few years preparing his autobiography. Part I was completed in 1805 and part II in 1807. In 1819, Adams published the collected edition of *Novanglus and Massachusettensis*, editorials written prior to the Revolutionary War in Braintree, Massachusetts. His editorials in this volume (*Novanglus*) reflect some of his best rhetorical efforts. Adams died on July 4, 1826, the same day as Thomas Jefferson and fifty years to the day of the signing of the Declaration of Independence.

JOHN ADAMS AS PUBLIC COMMUNICATOR

Much of John Adams's public speaking was recorded after he was elected president of the United States. Prior to that date, he concentrated his rhetorical efforts on writing editorials in newspapers and letters to his family and confidants. In the pamphlet, *Braintree Instructions*, Adams wrote, "We further recommend the most clear and explicit assertion and vindication of our rights and liberties to be entered on the public records, that the world may know, in the present and all future generations, that we have a clear knowledge and a just sense of them, and, with submission to Divine Providence, that we never can be slaves.''

On July 3, 1776, Adams wrote to his wife, Abigail, ''Yesterday, the greatest Question was decided, which ever was debated in America, and a greater perhaps, never was or will be decided among Men. A resolution was passed without one dissenting Colony 'that these united Colonies are, and of right ought to be free and independent states, and as such, they have, and of Right ought to have full Power to make War, conclude Peace, establish Commerce, and to do all the other Acts and Things, which other States may rightfully do.' '' Through the medium of letters, Adams summarized his perspectives on government, Great Britain, the colonies, and independence. In a letter to John Winthrop, dated June 23, 1776, Adams stated, ''It is said, that such a Declaration, will arouse and unite Great Britain. But are they not already aroused and united, as much as they will be? Will not such a Declaration arouse and unite the Friends of Liberty, the few who are left, in opposition to the present system?''

Adams regretted the fact that there were no public records of his speeches made to the Continental Congress. Many of these sessions were carried on in secret. Adams biographer Mellen Chamberlain reports, ''There were no congressional reporters in those days [1774–1778]. The members were pledged to secrecy. The journals are neither full or accurate, and even John Adams's own diary fails us at some of the most critical and interesting points.'' Thus, records of John Adams's speaking before his rise to public office as vice-president, and later president, are imcomplete, with some of the significant speeches lost because they were not recorded during sessions of the Congress and not written down by Adams.

Written transcripts of Adams's speeches were not made until he was elected president. As president, his Inaugural Address summed his studies of other governments and his devotion to the independence of the United States. In this speech, Adams addressed the claims of fraud in the election of 1796. He stated, ''If an election is to be determined by a majority of a single vote, and that can be procured by a party through artifice or corruption, the Government may be the choice of a party for its own ends, not of the nation or the national good.'' Concerning Adams's Inaugural Address, Alexander Hamilton wrote, ''The outset [of Adams's presidency] was distinguished by a speech which his friends lamented as temporising. It had the air of a lure for the favor of his opponents at the expense of his sincerity.''

To fulfill his constitutional obligation, Adams delivered an annual speech in each year of his presidency. He presented them on the following dates: November 22, 1797, December 8, 1798, December 3, 1799, and November 22, 1800. These are the only speeches delivered and recorded during his presidency. The paucity of public speeches delivered by Adams during his administration might be attributed to his apparent apprehension of speaking in public. In a letter to Henry Merchant on September 17, 1789, Adams confessed, ''It [public speaking] gave me a Pain in my Breast, which was not only troublesome for the time, but dangerous for the future." In the same letter he continued, "My present office not only obliges me to a constant and loose attention of Mind, but to continual Reading and Speaking, which has again affected, . . . as it used to, and raises many doubts how long I shall continue to go on." In his later years, Adams continued to write about public speaking. In a letter to William Wirt on January 23, 1819, Adams declared, "Oratory, Mr. Wirt, as it consists of expressions of the countenance, graces of attitude and motion, and intonance of voice, although it is altogether superficial and ornamental, will always command admiration, yet it deserves little veneration. Flashes of wit, coruscations of imagination and gay pictures, what are they? Strict truth, rapid reason and pure integrity are the only essential ingredients of sound oratory."

Even as president, Adams preferred writing correspondence to giving speeches. Although no specific motivation for this preference can be determined, one might certainly include his expressed apprehension of public speaking as one possible factor. In letters published in *A Selection of Patriotic Addresses to the President of the United States*, he continually expressed his views on the United States, the development of its government, and his role in its growth. Responding to the grand jurors of Columbia County, New York, Adams wrote, "We know that our government, whether we call it elective or representative, depends for its existence on the purity of our elections, unbiased by foreign influence and untainted by corruption." Answering a query from the inhabitants of Providence, Rhode Island, he declared, "The honor of our nation is now universally seen to be at stake, and its independence in question, and all America appears to declare, with one heart and one voice, a manly determination to vindicate both." Writing to the New Hampshire legislature, Adams reported, "Every old republic has fallen before it. If America has not spirit and sense enough to learn wisdom from the example of so many republican catastrophies passing in review before her eyes, she deserves to suffer, and most certainly will fail." Finally, in writing to the mayor, alderman, and the citizens of Philadelphia, Adams concluded, "I am but one of the American people, and my fate and fortune must be decided with theirs."

Perceptions of Adams's skills as an administrator and orator varied. In 1800, Hamilton wrote, "Not denying to Mr. Adams's patriotism and integrity, and even talents of a certain kind, I shall be deficient in candor, were I to conceal the conviction, that he does not possess the talents adapted to the *Administration* of Government, and that there are great and intrinsic defects in his character, which unfit him for the Office of Chief Magistrate." In his eulogy for John Adams and Thomas Jefferson, Daniel Webster contended, "The eloquence of Mr. Adams resembled his general character, and formed, indeed, a part of it. It was bold, manly and energetic; and such the crisis required." In an anonymous biography written in approximately 1800, the author stated, "He [John Adams] was pre-eminently distinguished as a pleader and counselor. Consistently with the honor of his country—with the principles of justice in apportion to popular invective and prejudice,'' he saw to his professional duties.

Adams in his correspondence reveals aspects of his private character. In his letter to Henry Merchant, on September 17, 1789, Adams continued to lament his disdain for public speaking: "There is more confinement in my present situation in any that I have been in for these thirty years; and another Evil is come upon me, under which I suffered formerly, but from which I have been wholly relieved during my absence from America—Public Speaking." In assessing his own skills as a public servant, Adams wrote to Dr. Thomas on February 2, 1796, "I pray that my Country may take from me all temptation to remain in office before the approach of old age shall take from me the capacity of doing any thing but mischief to the Public and dishonor to my character." Addressing James Warren, Adams wrote on December 22, 1778, "Modesty is a Virtue, that can never thrive in public. Modest Men! is there such a thing remaining in public life?"

Adams delivered his last speech at his home in August 1821. The cadets of West Point, stationed in Boston, devoted a day to visiting with Adams in Quincy. In this speech Adams stated, "There is no real glory in this world or any other but such as arises from wisdom and benevolence. There can be no solid glory among men but that which springs from equity and humanity; from the constant observance of prudence, temperance, justice, and fortitude. Battles, victories, and conquests, abstracted from their only justifiable object and end, which is justice and peace, are the glory of fraud, violence, and usurpation." Adams concluded this brief speech by stating, "That I may not fatigue you with many words, allow me to address every one of you in the language of a Roman dictator to his master of the horse, after a daring and dangerous exploit for the safety of the country: 'Macte virtute esto.' "

It is difficult to assess Adams's skills as an orator; there are conflicting perspectives from his contemporaries and historians. The transcriptions of his speeches, recorded as president, reveal an orator able to reason logically, appease perceived enemies, rally the support of his followers, and meet most commonly accepted standards for acceptable substance and form. However, most of Adams's rhetorical efforts were in written form. From his editorials in the newspapers to his correspondence with family members and contemporaries, these rhetorical artifacts of Adams reveal a competent, persuasive, and dedicated public servant. In 1813, Thomas Jefferson, usually an adversary of Adams, wrote a lasting tribute to him: "He was the pillar of its [the Declaration of Independence] virtue on the floor of Congress, its ablest advocate and defender against the multifarious assaults it encountered." Adams was a major force in persuading other delegates to adopt the declaration, in making the Continental Congress strive for independence, in negotiating the financial security of the new nation, in negotiating a treaty with Great Britain to end the Revolutionary War, in developing relations for the United States with the rest of the world, and in initiating the democratic form of government, first as vice president and then as president.

INFORMATION SOURCES

Research Collections and Collected Speeches

Researchers interested in John Adams's rhetoric can rely heavily on the resources of the Massachusetts Historical Society, Boston. Scholars interested in the communication strategies of Adams in the pre-Revolutionary, Revolutionary, and post-Revolutionary periods in U.S. history will find an abundance of primary and secondary source materials and large collections of correspondence there. These letters include both those written by John Adams and original letters written to him. All letters referred to in this essay can be located in the Massachusetts Historical Society. Additionally, the library holds a wealth of material related to the colonial period and the development of the Revolutionary War. Close to Boston, in Quincy, scholars can visit the John Adams home.

Another place to find research materials on Adams is the Library of Congress, Washington, D.C. Although most of Adams's presidential papers were destroyed during the War of 1812, there remains a great deal of primary and secondary sources available in the Adams and Jefferson Buildings of the Library of Congress.

Adams, Charles Francis. *The Works of John Adams: Second President of*   *WJA*
    the United States. 10 vols. Boston: Little, Brown, 1856.

Bremer, Howard. *John Adams: 1735–1826: Chronology-Documents-Bio-*   *CDB*
    graphical Aids. Dobbs-Ferry, N.Y.: Oceana Publications, 1967.

A Compilation of the Messages and Papers of the Presidents, 1789–1897.   *CMP*
    Edited by James D. Richardson. Washington, D.C.: Library of Congress, 1899.

A Selection of Patriotic Addresses to the President of the United States.   *ASP*
    Edited by John W. Folsom. Boston: John W. Folsom, 1798.

The Founding Fathers, John Adams: A Biography in His Own Words. Edited   *TFF*
    by James Bishop Peabody. New York: Newsweek, 1973.

Selected Critical Studies

Bezayiff, David. "Legal Oratory of John Adams: An Early Instrument of Protest." *Western Journal of Speech Communication* 40 (1976): 63–71.

Chaly, Ingerborg. "John Adams and the Boston Massacre: A Rhetorical Reassessment." *Central States Speech Journal* 28 (1977): 36–46.

Hamilton, Alexander. *Letter from Alexander Hamilton, Concerning the Public Conduct and Character of John Adams, esq., President of the United States*. New York: George F. Hopkins, 1800.

Howe, John R. *The Changing Political Thought of John Adams*. Princeton: Princeton University Press, 1966.

Kurtz, Stephen G. *The Presidency of John Adams: The Collapse of Federalism, 1795–1800*. Philadelphia: University of Pennsylvania Press, 1957.

Rogers, Jimmie. "John Adams' Summation Speech in Rex v. Wemms, *et al*: A Delicate Act of Persuasion." *Southern Speech Communication Journal* 34 (1973): 134–44.

Selected Biographies

Anonymous. *Biography of John Adams.* c. 1800. Located in the Massachusetts Historical Society.

Butterfield, L. H. *The Adams Papers: Diary and Autobiography of John Adams.* 4 vols. New York: Atheneum, 1964.

Chamberlain, Mellen. *John Adams: The Statesman of the American Revolution.* Boston: Houghton Mifflin, 1968.

Hutson, James H. *John Adams and the Diplomacy of the American Revolution.* Lexington: University of Kentucky Press, 1980.

Sanders, Frederick K. *John Adams Speaking: Pound's Sources for the Adams Cantos.* Orono: University of Maine Press, 1975.

Shaw, Peter. *The Character of John Adams.* Chapel Hill: University of North Carolina Press, 1976.

Wesbster, Daniel. *Discourse in Commemoration of the Lives and Services of John Adams and Thomas Jefferson, Delivered in Faneuil Hall, Boston.* Boston: Cummings, Hilliard and Company, 1826.

CHRONOLOGY OF MAJOR SPEECHES

See "Research Collections and Collected Speeches" for source codes.

Inaugural Address, Philadelphia, Pennsylvania, March 4, 1797; *CDB*, pp. 26–32; *CMP*, pp. 228–32; *TFF*, pp. 353–58; *WJA*, 9:105–11.

Speech to both Houses of Congress, Philadelphia, Pennsylvania, May 16, 1797; *WJA*, 9:111–19.

First State of the Union Address, Philadelphia, Pennsylvania, November 22, 1797, or November 23, 1797 (there are conflicting reports as to the exact date of this speech); *CMP*, pp. 250–54; *CDB*, pp. 39–43; *WJA*, 9:121–26.

Second State of the Union Address, Philadelphia, Pennsylvania, December 8, 1798; *CMP*, pp. 271–75; *CDB*, pp. 67–71; *WJA*, 9:128–34.

Third State of the Union Address, Philadelphia, Pennsylvania, December 3, 1799; *CMP*, pp. 289–92; *CDB*, pp. 72–76; *WJA*, 9:136–40.

Fourth State of the Union Address, Washington, D.C., November 22, 1800; *CMP*, pp. 305–8; *CDB*, pp. 77–78; *WJA*, 9:143–47.

Address to the Cadets of West Point, Quincy, Massachusetts, August 1821; *WJA*, 10:419–20.

JOHN QUINCY ADAMS
(1767–1848), sixth president of the United States

_____ MICHAEL G. MORAN

Ambassador to major courts of Europe, twice member of Congress, secretary of state under James Monroe, first Boylston Professor of Rhetoric and Oratory at Harvard College, respected lawyer, outspoken critic of slavery, supporter of a strong federal government, sixth president of the United States, John Quincy Adams lived a long, useful life during which he debated most of the central issues of his day. Viewing himself as a member of the second generation of Americans enjoying the benefits of the Constitution, Adams worked all his life to strengthen this document while enlarging its influence in American life by extending its protections to the disenfranchised, especially slaves. Although *Lectures on Rhetoric and Oratory*, which collected his Harvard Boylston lectures, was derived from classical rhetorical theory and practice, it was the first major rhetoric written in the United States and demonstrated his interest in the subject. Adams was indeed a man of vision who used his considerable literary and oratorical skills to place himself at the center of most important political debates of his time.

The son of John Adams, the third president, John Quincy Adams was one of the best-educated and most experienced statesmen of his time. When only eleven, he accompanied his diplomat father first to France, where he continued his education, and later to Spain, Amsterdam, and Russia before returning to Quincy, Massachusetts, to prepare for and then to enter Harvard, from which he graduated Phi Beta Kappa and second in his class. After taking his degree, he studied law with Theophilus Parsons and then opened a Boston law practice in 1790 before being appointed Washington's minister to the Dutch Republic in 1794 and being elected as a Federalist to the U.S. Senate in 1803. After he split from the Federalists and lost his seat, Madison appointed him ambassador to Russia. In 1814 he served on the American peace committee at Ghent, and during the following year he became Monroe's secretary of state in which capacity he negotiated the Adams-Onis Treaty, which ceded to the United States East and West Florida, established its claims to the Oregon Territory, and helped frame the Monroe Doctrine. On March 4, 1824, Adams was inaugurated the sixth president of the United States after narrowly defeating Andrew Jackson in a runoff election in the House. After being defeated by Jackson in 1828, he was elected to the House of Representatives in 1830, where he energetically served until his death eighteen years later.

ADAMS AS POLITICAL ORATOR

Because Adams spoke throughout his long career, his oratory addressed numerous specific issues and included examples of the three classical genres: deliberative, judicial, and epideictic. Three common threads unified many of his important public pronouncements: he argued for a stronger Union, for a broader interpretation of the constitutional powers of the federal government, and for the rights of all Americans to petition Congress.

Adams addressed the need for a strong Union in his first significant speech, his Harvard graduation address, "The Importance and Necessity of Public Faith in the Well-Being of the Nation," delivered on July 16, 1787, when he was barely twenty, and published the following year in the *Columbian Magazine* by Jeremy Belknap. In this speech Adams turned what could have been a set declamation into a major statement supporting his ambassador father's attempts to strengthen the nation in order to negotiate a trade agreement with Britain. In particular, young Adams argued that most of the nation's current problems— Shays's Rebellion, the scarcity of money, the upsurge of luxury and dissipation, the bonds of Union being relaxed—could be traced to a common root, the inability of the nation to establish national credit because many argued that it should not pay its foreign debts incurred during the Revolutionary War. Although his friends and family appreciated his nervous delivery, two Boston newspapers that reviewed the speech criticized Adams. Both accused him of being favored because of his father's influence, and one sniffed that another student, Nathanael Freeman, was the superior orator.

Adams often used his epideictic oratory to drive home the need for national unity. For instance, on December 22, 1802, in Plymouth, Massachusetts, he delivered the "Oration at Plymouth" in commemoration of the landing of the Pilgrims in which he argued for the many connections individuals had to their fellow citizens, to their ancestors, to their species, and to their children. All of these natural connections, he noted, worked to bind a people into a nation, and he took this particular occasion to eulogize the Pilgrim fathers in order that their virtues inspire his audience to strengthen the "national Union." Adams used other epideictic speeches such as *"The Jubilee of the Constitution,"* a speech the New York Historical Society invited him to deliver on April 30, 1839, to celebrate the fiftieth anniversary of Washington's inauguration, for similar purposes, to give his audiences a sense of their nation's glorious past in order to encourage them to create an equally glorious future.

Because he was a minority president elected by the House of Representatives after narrowly losing both the popular and electoral vote to Andrew Jackson, Adams's major presidential addresses are notable for their careful defensiveness, especially the later ones in which he was forced to defend his floundering trade policies before an increasingly disgruntled Congress. Two of his presidential speeches, however, stand out as historically important because they advanced the concept of internal improvements, the argument that the federal government possessed and should use constitutional powers to improve the physical, intellectual, and moral well-being of its citizens. In his Inaugural Address of March 4, 1825, he reintroduced this idea—which he had supported many years before while serving in the Senate—but he took it up most fully in his first State of the Union address on December 6, 1825, which was one of his few major presidential addresses in which he was not directly defending himself against the attacks of his Jacksonian opponents. In this address, he outlined a broad, innovative plan to improve the nation and the human condition by building a series of national roads and canals, by equipping a scientific expedition to circumnavigate the globe, by establishing a uniform set of weights and measures, and by founding a national university, which never reached fruition. Knowing that these ideas were unpopular with his congressional opponents, he used various strategies to argue his case, including principle—that government had a moral obligation to better the lives of its citizens—historical precedent—that ancient civilizations were remembered for their great achievements—and analogy—that other contemporary governments were benefiting from such projects. Although Adams never fully implemented his ambitious programs, he introduced to American political debate the issue of the federal government's responsibilities to improve the condition of its citizens.

The first State of the Union address also offers insight into the care with which Adams prepared and delivered his presidential oratory. After drafting the speech himself, he solicited but did not always accept the criticisms of his cabinet when revising both content and style. Completing the first draft on November 22, he read it initially to his secretary of the treasury, Richard Rush, who warned Adams that the sections on internal improvements would not be well received by other members of the administration. On the next day, he read the draft to the entire cabinet, only to have Henry Clay and James Barbour criticize the improvements section. Adams, however, was willing to make only stylistic changes, and after reading the offending section to the group again, he finally convinced his associates to withdraw their objections. On November 28, he read the speech to Attorney General William Wirt and received his support. Following the tradition of Jefferson, Adams had his speech delivered before Congress by another speaker, in this case Matthew St. Clair Clarke, clerk of the House, who took one hour to read what it had taken Adams an hour and a half to present before his cabinet.

Although never a radical abolitionist, later in his career Adams became one of the foremost critics of slavery, and much of his most important oratory, both legislative and judicial, addressed this issue. His most significant antislavery speeches in the House cannot be separated from his battles to rescind the gag rules, a series of congressional rulings that disallowed resolutions, discussions, or debates on the slavery issue. This forced Adams to use complicated parliamentary maneuvers, for which he became famous, to gain the floor to debate the slavery issue. Because of his single-minded efforts to fight slavery and the gag rules, the press attacked him for being a mad old man, especially since he constantly brought to the floor resolutions, which were consistently tabled, to abolish slavery and because he regularly placed himself in danger of being censured by the proslavery members of the House. One of his most significant statements on slavery was his address before the House of Representatives on May 25, 1836, in which he first fully enunciated the doctrine of Congress's constitutional powers to emancipate slaves in time of war, a principle that Lincoln used thirty years later in the "Emancipation Proclamation." The speech, which Adams considered one of his best, was particularly impressive because he delivered it extempore, although he later wrote out from memory the expanded and clarified version published in the *Appendix to the Congressional Globe*. In this speech, Adams argued from principle—that Congress possessed certain powers of war, particularly the powers to interfere in the internal workings of an enemy's government, that find their ultimate justification in the laws and usages of nations—and precedent—that slaves had been freed in the past during times of war, as when Great Britain, during the Revolutionary War, had invited slaves to join the royalist cause and then refused to return them after defeat. The speech also demonstrated Adams's considerable parliamentary skill because the gag rules forced him to work his condemnation of slavery into his qualified support of a resolution framed by southern members to lend financial assistance to citizens of Georgia and Alabama suffering from Indian attacks. By arguing that he could justify to his constituents such aid only on the principle of Congress's war powers, he positioned himself to attack slavery on the same principle.

One of Adams's most bitter battles against the gag rules took place during the debate in the House over the issue of annexing Texas into the Union. In his speech on the right of people to petition, delivered on the floor of the House between June 16 and July 7, 1838, Adams again demonstrated his ample abilities as an impromptu speaker who combined wit, charm, perseverence, and intelligence to expose the dangers of the gag rules; to support the rights of all Americans, including slaves and women, to petition the House; and to refuse control of the House to a minority of slave state representatives and their sympathizers.

Although the ostensible issue under discussion was the annexation of Texas, the issues that Adams brought to the floor concerned freedom of speech and petition and the question of slavery. The Committee of Foreign Affairs chaired by Benjamin Chew Howard of Maryland, which was heavily weighted in favor of slavery and annexation, had tabled numerous petitions and resolutions against annexation that had been referred to it by the House, thus preventing debate on slavery, the primary issue of those against annexation. An astute parliamentarian, Adams used this state of affairs to criticize the common strategy of automatically tabling all antislavery petitions. His complex argument relied on strategies such as reading sample petitions from citizens groups and state legislatures against annexation and slavery; upholding principles of freedom of speech and debate as well as the universal right to petition Congress; and accusing the committee and the proslavery administration of bringing odium down upon themselves for supporting a "system of suppression." Because of the tenacity with which he argued his cause, the Speaker of the House at one point ruled him out of order for not confining himself to the issue under debate, and this ruling was supported by a vote of 115 to 36, an indication of the hostility that Adams faced when arguing against slavery.

Adams's most important argument in the cause against slavery was given before the Supreme Court on February 24 and March 1, 1841. In his brief, Adams spoke on behalf of illegally enslaved blacks of the schooner *Amistad* who had mutinied against their Spanish captors, killed several of them, and then made their way from Cuba to Long Island where they were captured by Lieutenant Thomas R. Gedney of the U.S. Coast Guard. The government then had to decide what to do with them. For abolitionists, the *Amistad* case became a cause célèbre, especially since Secretary of State John Forsyth, a Georgia slaveholder, wanted to return the blacks as slaves to their Spanish captors. But to win their case, the abolitionists realized that they needed a lawyer with a national reputation, so Lewis Tappan and Ellis Gray Loring asked Adams to become assistant counsel to Roger Baldwin when the case went before the Supreme Court. Adams had many reasons to refuse, but his conscience, which had always found slavery abhorrent, demanded that he argue the case.

As the case unfolded, Adams listened in court to the arguments of Attorney General Henry Gilpin and Baldwin. Writing and rewriting his brief, he could not organize his arguments. After court recessed on February 23, he rushed to the Library of Congress to reread James Madison's speech on the dual condition of slaves as both persons and property. By the next day, when he rose to speak for four and a half hours, plus four hours more on March 1, all his thoughts came together in one of the great pieces of American forensic oratory and one of the key arguments in the long battle against slavery.

Adams's primary strategies in his brief were to apply the principles of universal justice to the *Amistad* case and to expose the logical fallacies and contradictions in the arguments and assumptions of Calderon, the Spanish minister demanding the return of the blacks as slaves, and of Secretary Forsyth, who was abetting Calderon in this action. By demanding that justice be served, Adams argued convincingly that the blacks, because they had legal possession of the schooner when it reached Long Island, were due all the protections of natural, international, and American law and could not be removed from the U.S. legal system and turned over to Spain. Neither the secretary of state nor the president had this power. By exposing the fallacies in the various arguments of Calderon and Forsyth, Adams convinced the justices that the *Amistad* blacks could not be viewed as human beings who could be tried for mutiny and murder on the one hand and as chattel, like coffee or sugar, to be returned to their rightful owners on the other. The historical importance of Adams's brief was that it successfully exposed, in the highest court in the land, the great contradiction in the proslavery position. It also helped lay the groundwork for affording equal protections and rights under law for all Americans.

By the close of his life, Adams was known among his supporters as Old Man Eloquent because of his great skills as a speaker. Arguably one of our best-educated statesmen, he brought to his oratory wide reading and learning, as well as a highly developed literary sense. If his speeches too often smell of the lamp, they also express a powerful moral vision of what the young nation could and should become. His advocacy of a strong union that protected all Americans, especially slaves, places his body of oratory among the most significant but neglected of the nation.

INFORMATION SOURCES

Research Collections and Collected Speeches

Researchers of Adams's oratory can rely on the resources of the Adams Papers collected in the Massachusetts Historical Society, Boston. These are available on microfilm. There is, however, no complete collection of his speeches, although some of them have been reprinted or published in modern editions. For some material, researchers can rely on *The Congressional Record* and nineteenth-century publications cited in the critical studies.

American Eloquence: A Collection of Speeches and Addresses. Edited by   AE
    Frank Moore. 2 vols. New York: Appleton, 1895.
Appendix to Gales and Seaton's Register of Debates. Vol. 2. Washington,   ARD
    D.C.: Gales and Seaton, 1825.
Appendix to the Congressional Globe. Vols. 2–3. Washington, D.C.: Blair   ACG
    and Rives, 1836.
Diary of John Quincy Adams. Vol. 2. Edited by David Grayson Allen.   DJQA
    Cambridge: Harvard University Press, 1981.
John Quincy Adams 1767–1848: Chronology, Documents, Bibliographical   JQA
    Aids. Edited by Kenneth V. Jones. Dobbs Ferry, N.Y.: Oceana
    Publications, 1970.

Selected Critical Studies

Banninga, Jerald L. "John Quincy Adams' Address of July 4, 1821." *Quarterly Journal of Speech* 53 (1967): 44–49.
———. "John Quincy Adams' Doctrine of Internal Improvements." *Central States Speech Journal* 20 (1969): 286–93.
———. "John Quincy Adams on the Right of a Slave to Petition Congress." *Southern Speech Communication Journal* 38 (1972): 151–63.
———. "John Quincy Adams on the War Powers of Congress." *Central States Speech Journal* 19 (1968): 83–90.
Rahskopf, Horace G. "John Quincy Adams: Speaker and Rhetorician." *Quarterly Journal of Speech* 32 (1946): 435–41.
Tade, George T. "The Anti-Texas Address: John Quincy Adams' Personal Filibuster." *Southern Speech Journal* 30 (1965): 185–98.

Selected Biographies

Bemis, Samuel Flagg. *John Quincy Adams and the Foundations of American Foreign Policy*. New York: Knopf, 1949.
———. *John Quincy Adams and the Union*. New York: Knopf, 1956.

Hargraves, Mary W. M. *The Presidency of John Quincy Adams.* Lawrence: University Press of Kansas, 1985.

Hecht, Marie B. *John Quincy Adams.* New York: Macmillan, 1972.

CHRONOLOGY OF MAJOR SPEECHES

See "Research Collections and Collected Speeches" for source codes.

"The Importance and Necessity of Public Faith in the Well-Being of the Nation," Cambridge, Massachusetts, July 16, 1787; *DJQA*, pp. 258–63.

"Oration at Plymouth," Plymouth, Massachusetts, December 22, 1802; *AE*, pp. 251–57.

Inaugural Address, Washington, D.C., March 4, 1825; *JQA*, pp. 22–27.

First State of the Union address, Washington, D.C., December 6, 1825; *ARD*, pp. 2–8.

Speech on the war powers of Congress, Washington, D.C., May 25, 1836; *ACG*, pp. 447–51.

Speech on the right of people to petition," Washington, D.C., June 16–July 7, 1838; New York: Arno Press, 1969.

"The Jubilee of the Constitution," New York, April 30, 1839; New York: Samuel Coleman, 1839.

Argument of John Quincy Adams, before the Supreme Court of the United States, Appellants, vs. Cinque, and Others, Africans, Captured in the Schooner Amistad, by Lieut. Gedney, Washington, D.C., February 24, March 1, 1841; rpt. New York: Negro Universities Press, 1969.

SAMUEL ADAMS
(1722–1803), father of the American Revolution

_____ MICHAEL DENNIS MCGUIRE

Samuel Adams was born in Boston, September 16, 1722, into the family that gave the United States its second and sixth presidents. Adams was very much a part of this important colonial, Revolutionary, and early American family. His cousin John, later second president of the United States, greatly admired Samuel, who already was well established and respected in public life by the time John became politically active. Samuel Adams's father, also named Samuel, was a minister in Boston and hence a man of some social influence and stature. From this fact, two important consequences seem to have followed. First, although son Samuel elected not to pursue the ministry, to the disappointment of his parents, he was what some biographers have called a pure Puritan—a man who longed for the clarity of the world of Cotton Mather or Jonathan Edwards. Second, father Samuel habitually held one or another public office in Boston, having been, at different times, tax collector, constable, selectman, member of the general court, and even hogreeve. He was a founding member of the Caucus Club and an active, influential figure in Boston civic affairs and politics. Young Samuel was accustomed to life with political opportunities and duties alike.

The Boston Adamses were not wealthy, however, and neither father nor son was competent at business. Indeed, they went bankrupt together once running a brewery, and young Adams already had accomplished the feat alone scarcely a year before the brewery episode occurred. When young Samuel attended Harvard for his education, he was compelled to work for part of his support. Nonetheless, at Harvard, where young men were ranked by importance of family, Samuel was ranked fifth of fifty-two (biographers differ about the class size, not the rank). Thus although the Boston Adamses lacked massive, liquid assets, they inhabited a sizable estate and had recognized influence. Samuel Adams graduated Harvard with his A.B. in 1740 and three years later received his Master of Arts degree offering a thesis suggestive of his future: "Whether It Be Lawful to Resist the Supreme Magistrate, If the Commonwealth Cannot Otherwise Be Preserved." The colonial governor and officials of the Crown reportedly slept through his presentation—testament to their interest in the colonists and, sadly, to Samuel Adams's mediocre speaking skills.

Like his father before him, Samuel Adams occupied a variety of public offices, paid and unpaid. He was clerk at the city-owned Boston market, city scavenger, and eventually a tax collector who was perpetually short in his accounts— ultimately by over 7,000 pounds. Adams never achieved wealth and is said to have flaunted his poverty. Neighbors often rendered aid to Samuel Adams's family. He was popular with the people, as well as with the patricians.

SAMUEL ADAMS AS POLITICAL REVOLUTIONARY

Samuel Adams was the most important individual figure influencing the course of American colonial politics away from any possible reconciliation with England. When General Gage gained control in the colonies, he offered amnesty to anyone repentent except Samuel Adams and John Hancock. In pre-Revolutionary England, as in the colonies—especially New England—Samuel Adams was perceived as the intellectual and political force behind independence. Two observations and one disclaimer should precede this examination of Adams's rhetoric. First, Adams was among the first to believe in and argue for independence from England. While others still were concerned with achieving representation in Parliament or with coercing concessions from the Crown, Adams favored, advocated, and maneuvered for independence. He was the first recorded advocate of the total separation of the colonies from all ties with England. Second, Adams's Revolutionary rhetoric was of a type not always thought of as revolutionary. With his advocacy, Adams confronted and solved the tricky rhetorical dilemmas of needing to persuade Americans—loyal English subjects—to revolution, while not appearing, to them or to the British, to be too extreme too soon.

A great deal of his rhetorical activity therefore took two forms. Samuel Adams wrote hundreds of pages of letters to editors of newspapers and signed them with such names as "Candidus," "Vindex," and "A Chatterer." Besides the safety of anonymity such letters afforded, they may have served as a barometer of public opinion for Adams, who was shrewd enough to attend to the reactions they elicited. Second, Adams maintained a truly voluminous correspondence with leaders of the Revolution and with sympathetic British parties. While many of his correspondents were famous—Franklin, Washington, Hancock, and Britons Chatham, Barre, Rockingham—many were the Committees of Correspondence and other political groups, such as the Caucus Clubs of Boston, important to Adams's personal, political standing. His handling of committees and the Caucus Clubs led some to call him the inventor of machine politics. That pejorative assessment nonetheless acknowledges Adams's skill at persuading political groups to support him and his policies in an era of fierce competition and tremendous uncertainty owing partly to the absence of a stable, uniform governmental or political tradition other than the one being rejected. These two observations show Adams's reliance on written rhetoric—a reliance one may attribute either to his own lack of great voice and delivery skills, to the difficulty of reaching an audience as vast as his by speech, or to both. All knowledgeable scholars have conceded, as contemporary reports such as those by John Adams compel one to, that Samuel Adams was a mediocre speaker who rose to eloquence rarely, if ever. He was thorough, systematic, and competent; he was rarely inspired and never theatrical. This essay is confined to Adams's Revolutionary career; it will not attempt to treat his later work drafting the Articles of Confederation or serving as governor of Massachusetts. Adams is best remembered and known for his Revolutionary rhetoric, and there is enough accomplishment there for the most demanding critic of rhetorical careers.

The earliest internationally read evidence of Samuel Adams's talents and leadership was "The True Sentiments of America," published in January 1768. The text pretended to be a letter to Massachusetts's agent in London, Dennys

De Berdt, but it was patently for him to relay to England's ministry and population. It was also published in the *Boston Gazette* on April 4, 1768. Adams submitted the letter to the General Court of Massachusetts on January 6, 1768, and over a week was spent reviewing and debating the precise wording of arguments before the letter was adopted and dispatched to be published. Adams wrote in reaction against the revenue acts that Parliament had just passed and sent to the colonies, and he established the framework that rhetoric followed for the next few years, until Samuel Adams reframed it. Adams began by observing that numerous new tax laws had arrived in the colonies, but "as the people of this province had no share in the framing of those laws, in which they are so deeply interested, the House of Representatives, who are constitutionally entrusted by them, as the guardians of their rights and liberties, have thought it their indispensable duty, carefully to peruse them; and having so done, to point out such matters in them as appear to be grievous to their constituents, and to seek redress."

The unfairness of taxation without representation emerged in Adams's opening sentence. Yet here the argument was based on, and continued to elaborate, "fundamental rules of the constitution . . . which [British subjects] are all *equally* entitled to, in all parts of his Majesty's extended dominions." The constitution was the sole basis for the power of any governing legislature, said Adams. In a passage presaging the truth while hiding it, Adams observed: "When we mention the rights of the subjects in America, and the interest we have in the British constitution, in common with all other British subjects, we cannot justly be suspected of the most distant thought of independency on Great Britain." The rumors were abroad in England that there were those in America, Massachusetts especially, who wanted to separate from the mother country. Adams said "the colonies would refuse it if offered to them," knowing that their happiness and security lay in their connections with England.

This happiness in the connection is based on the constitution, however, which Adams put beyond amendment by man, and which had not been attended to as concerns the colonies. Accordingly, Adams argued:

It is the glory of the British Constitution that it hath its foundation in the law of God and nature. It is an essential natural right that a man shall quietly enjoy and have the sole disposal of his own property. The right is adopted into the Constitution. This natural and constitutional right is so familiar to the American subjects that it would be difficult, if possible, to convince them that any necessity can render it just, equitable, and reasonable, in the nature of things, that Parliament should impose duties, subsidies, talliages, and taxes upon them, internal or external, for the sole purpose of *raising a revenue*. The reason is obvious; because they cannot be represented, and therefore their consent cannot be constitutionally had in Parliament.

The rights guaranteed by the constitution did not stem from that document, according to Adams. The "law of God" is the basis, and there are "natural" rights that no mere Parliament could amend or revoke. One among those rights is to be represented in a governing body with taxation powers. That right stems from one's prerogative to enjoy all benefits from one's property. Adams acknowledged Parliament's right to use taxes to regulate commerce but not to raise revenue, the constitutional crisis then confronting England and the colonies. Adams communicated the true sentiments of the colonies to England, and the following month, February 1768, he communicated Massachusetts's sentiments to the other colonial assemblies.

Adams's message of February 11 to the speakers of other houses of representatives in the colonies declared as its intention "to communicate their [Massachusetts's] mind to a sister colony upon a common concern." Already organizing, Adams pointed out that "it seems necessary that all possible care should be taken, that the representations of the several assembly upon so delicate a point should harmonize with each other." But Samuel Adams was singing lead as he presented a summary of his "True Sentiments" as published in England for the other colonial assemblymen to consider and endorse. "The House have humbly represented to the ministry, their own sentiments that His Majesty's high Court of Parliament is the supreme legislative Power over the whole Empire: That in all free States the Constitution is fixed; & as the supreme Legislative derives its Power & Authority from the Constitution, it cannot overleap the bounds of it without destroying its own foundation." Adams observed that the colonists, "who acknowledge themselves bound by ties of allegiance," were entitled to all constitutional rights. But most important remains "an essential unalterable right in nature, ingrafted into the British Constitution, as a fundamental Law & ever held sacred & irrevocable by the Subjects within the Realm, that what a man has honestly acquired is absolutely his own, which he may freely give, but cannot be taken from him without his consent." Adams concluded his appeal to other colonies by explaining that enemies of the colonies have described them as "factious, disloyal, and having a disposition to make themselves independent of the Mother Country," which he denied to the English in "True Sentiments." He finally claimed not to be attempting to lead the other colonies and that he had confidence in the success of their combined appeals to the king for redress of their shared grievances.

Over the next eighteen months, relations between the colonies, especially Massachusetts, and England worsened. Colonial administrators wrote distraught letters of protest to England, accusing the people of Boston of insurrection and violence. Governor Bernard was among the authors of such letters to respond, to which the assembly selected Samuel Adams, who published "An Appeal to the World" on October 16, 1769. The full, lengthy title of the appeal explained that it was "a vindication of the town of Boston from many false and malicious aspersions" cast upon it by Governor Bernard, General Gage, and others. In the "Appeal" Adams used rhetorical techniques not evident in his earlier rhetoric. He presented legally grounded, judiciously reasoned appeals to the English and to his fellow colonial representatives. Even forgetting the obligatory compliments to the king, Adams struck an almost conciliatory note or posture in his earlier rhetoric. In this document, he took pains to make his "Appeal to the World" a memorable, sarcastic review of incompetent, dishonest colonial officials. Adams reviewed for pages an incident the governor had complained of in which a group of boys paraded through Boston with a horn and a drum. The governor had elaborated how threatened several commissioners and their families had felt. Of the parade Adams asked:

"What possible harm can there be in that? Why, among other houses they passed by the Council-Chamber when he was sitting in council: and did they stop to insult the governor and council? Such a circumstance would doubtless have embellished his Excellency's Narrative. Their passing by, however, carried the Air of an insult, tho' in all likelihood, the unlucky boys might not know that his Excellency was there.—But they assembled before Mr. Paxton's house, and lest it should be forgot, his lordship [recipient of Bernard's letter] is reminded that Mr. Paxton is "a *Commissioner!*" And did they do Mr. Paxton any injury? Yes truly; "they huzzza'd," and went off.

Adams used a series of quotations such as these from Bernard's letter to dismiss the governor's allegations of insurrection as the fantasies of a paranoid.

"Appeal to the World" was not confined to sarcasm or accusations of foolishness against colonial governors. Adams presented a detailed review of letters of Governor Bernard to show that the governor had misrepresented some events and blatantly lied, even in contradiction to official documents of his own council, about others. These demonstrations were argued tightly over facts, so that the impression of total refutation was achieved. Additionally Adams pointed out clearly any fallacies of reasoning or argument the governor had committed. In one example, Adams showed the governor having shifted an argument of the colonists against particular, incompetent administrators as if it were an argument against the legal, constitutional process that appointed them, so that the colonists appeared not unhappy but disloyal. However, a sarcastic tone prevailed throughout his "Appeal" and was reinforced by one of Adams's favorite devices in printed rhetoric, the frequent use of underscore to call attention to a word or phrase. For example, Adams said that when it came to rumor, "the governor believed *or pretended to believe* every Word of it, till he had the *mortifying* Sight of the true contents of this *very important* Paper."

All of Samuel Adams's Revolutionary rhetoric revealed four particular characteristics. First, he developed arguments relying on two different strategies. His confirmative arguments, those made when he was on the offensive, speaking for the affirmative, were based on lines of constitutionality or legality, and he further grounded principles of the British constitution in the laws of God and nature. He stood squarely with God and the British constitution and against the Parliament, which tampered with both. Second, in refutational argument, Adams seized on specific phrases, evidence, or inferences of his opposition to make them appear foolish, illogical, or dishonest. He brought to bear meticulous attention to details of logic and evidence in his arguments and was no less thorough in refutation than in confirmation. Third, his style in affirmation was the style of a plain man, perhaps a Puritan, trying merely to make evident the principles God and nature endorse for human society. His language in such rhetoric was almost completely without ornament, as if he wanted his arguments to convince, not persuade. Finally, the Samuel Adams arguing refutation (and, incidentally, this was the Adams who wrote anonymous and pseudonymous articles attacking the British) was a stylish, self-conscious rascal given to exaggerative techniques like underlining quoted words he demeaned for sarcastic effect.

Ironically, Samuel Adams' most famous and widely reprinted speech almost certainly was not his work, although it was, and still is, attributed to him and was translated into French and German, as well as receiving wide circulation in England and the English-speaking colonies. The speech, entitled "American Independence," which was published in London in 1776, was identified by its title page as "An *ORATION* delivered at the State House in PHILADELPHIA to a very numerous AUDIENCE on THURSDAY the 1st of AUGUST, 1776; By SAMUEL ADAMS, Member of the **** ********** the General CONGRESS of The ****** ****** of AMERICA." [I have imitated the printer's peculiar capitalizations, boldface, and asterisks.] The speech is completely faithful to Adams's rhetoric in invention and style; but historical arguments suggest strongly that it cannot have been Adams's work, as his descendant-biographer William Wells showed in 1865. But it is also difficult to imagine a motive for this Piltdown; certainly it was not to slur Adams, already known in England as the biggest troublemaker in the colonies, nor can it be supposed that someone published it to increase Adams's reputation. In any case, this document remains the world's strongest impression of Adams's rhetoric.

This famous speech reads like a triumphant announcement and celebration of the American Declaration of Independence. Adams reviewed the spuriousness of England's claims that it was entitled to raise revenue in the colonies by taxes on account of having had to pay for wars against the French and Indians—wars, we are told, based purely on the quarrel between two Crowns and never involving any claim of the American colonists—wars to which, moreover, the colonists had contributed mightily in men and materials, as Adams always argued. The argument was as detailed and accurate as Adams's other works, where it often is made. And in a passage mocking the English—a famous passage containing a description of the English usually attributed to Bonaparte—the speech used Adams's skill with invective, rhetorical question, and sarcasm and even his penchant for underlining for emphasis: "Men who content themselves with the semblance of truth and a display of words talk much of our obligations to Great Britain *for protection*! Had she a *single eye* to *our* advantage? A nation of shopkeepers are very seldom so disinterested." The speech exhorted Americans to follow God, saying, "*He who made all men* hath made the truths necessary to human happiness obvious to *all*." Adams's characteristic appeal to the laws of nature and God was followed by the equally typical interpretation that those laws support everything good—colonial—and formerly British: "Our forefathers threw off the yoke of Popery in religion; for you is reserved the honor of levelling the popery of politics." There is perhaps the finest single concise statement of Adams's argument for the laws of God and nature taking precedence over the decisions of any human parliament—a parliament in this case transformed rhetorically into a pope, falsely interpreting the laws of God and suppressing (religious) freedom. In this speech, the very concept of royalty was derogated blatantly, not characteristic of the pre-Revolutionary Adams, as a fraud and sham to enslave people against God's will, by which all are equal except in distribution of mental and physical talents or powers. The speech went on to argue the independence in fact of the colonists, relying on the same sorts of evidence so amply marshaled by Edmund Burke in his speech "On Conciliation." The basic message seemed to be that the colonists had outgrown England and no longer would submit to its will. If the enigmatic Samuel Adams's greatest claim to rhetorical fame is a speech he did not write, it is at least one that asserts his principles well and that he never renounced.

INFORMATION SOURCES

Research Collections and Collected Speeches

Most of Samuel Adams's surviving papers and letters can be found in the New York Public Library, as well as in the collection edited by Cushing. In addition, scholars studying Samuel Adams can find work at the Harvard College Library, Cambridge; the Massachusetts Historical Society, Boston; and the Massachusetts Archives at Columbia Point, Boston. Only the possibly spurious one of Adams's speeches has been reprinted widely; I have indicated common sources for it below. Wells's three-volume biography includes full and partial texts of speeches and writings by Adams, including the speech he argues is not truly Adams's work and some not in Cushing's fine collection.

Adams, Samuel. *The Writings of Samuel Adams.* Edited by Harry A. Cush-   WSA
    ing. 4 vols. 1904; rpt. New York: Octagon Books, 1968.
The Library of Oratory. Edited by Chauncey M. Depew. 15 vols. New   LO
    York: E. R. Du Mont, 1902.
Wells, William V. *The Life and Public Services of Samuel Adams.* 3 vols.   LPS
    Boston: Little, Brown, 1865.

Selected Critical Studies

Beach, Stewart. *Samuel Adams: The Fateful Years, 1764–1776.* New York: Dodd, Mead, 1965.
Canfield, Cass. *Samuel Adams's Revolution.* New York: Harper & Row, 1976.
Davidson, Philip. *Propaganda and the American Revolution, 1763–1783.* Chapel Hill: University of North Carolina Press, 1941.
Miller, John C. *Sam Adams: Pioneer in Propaganda.* 1936; rpt. Stanford: Stanford University Press, 1966.

Rich, Andrea L., and Smith, Arthur. *Rhetoric of Revolution: Samuel Adams, Emma Goldman, Malcolm X*. Durham, N.C.: Moore Publishing Co., n.d.

Weatherly, Michael. "Propaganda and the Rhetoric of the American Revolution." *Southern Speech Journal* 36 (1971): 352–63.

Selected Biographies

Chidsey, Donald Barr. *The World of Samuel Adams*. New York and Nashville: Thomas Nelson, 1974.

Hosmer, James K. *Samuel Adams*. 1885; rpt. Cambridge, Mass.: Riverside Press, 1887.

CHRONOLOGY OF MAJOR SPEECHES

Address to the Sons of Liberty, Boston, March 18, 1769; *LPS*, 1: 247–49.

"The Rights of the Colonists," Boston, November 20, 1772; *WSA*, 2: 350–59; *LPS*, 1: 502–09.

Addresses to the people of Pennsylvania, Philadelphia, February 3 (and others), 1776; *WSA*, 3: 261–66; *LPS*, 2: 360–63, 349–52.

"American Independence," Philadelphia, August 1, 1776; *LPS*, vol. 3, appendix 1, pp. 407–22; *LO*, 2: 312–32.

FISHER AMES
(1758–1808), congressman from Massachusetts

ANTHONY HILLBRUNER

Just as the ultraliberal movement that led to the American Revolution was the making of such a great speaker as Patrick Henry and such a skillful publicist as Tom Paine, so too its antithesis, the thermidorian trend of the later eighteenth century, which fostered the ultraconservative movement, was the making of Fisher Ames as an orator and political theorist. As a Tory spokesman, Ames was part of the reactionary thrust untouched by the French liberalism that had influenced Thomas Jefferson and the Enlightenment in the United States. Ames thus was against all "men of the new order" and was part of the antiegalitarian movement of the time. The reactionary forces had been influenced by the inherent aristocracy of the later John Adams and by Alexander Hamilton, who advocated government by "the rich, the wise and the well born."

Ames became a power in the movement because he had all the requisites of the persuasive orator. Clever, intelligent, and precocious, his rhetoric had the firm foundation of knowledge based on his scholarly nature, which, even in his youth, focused on wide reading and writing. At thirteen, he was already attending Harvard College, where, coveting eloquence, he gave declamations in the debating society and studied classical models, as well as the poetry of Shakespeare and Milton. At sixteen, Ames received his degree and almost immediately began teaching school in New England. His active intellect, however, soon tired of that profession, and he decided upon a law career. A short time later in 1781, at the age of twenty-three, he began the practice of law. In 1785, he turned to politics and was elected to the state legislature in Massachusetts. Soon Ames's fellow legislators, impressed by his suasive potency sent him to the state convention, which was meeting at that time to ratify the U.S. Constitution. It was here that his political career began and his oratorical power grew, manifesting itself first in an effective address about biennial elections. Again it was his rhetorical skill at the convention, as well as a remarkable series of essays written during Shays's Rebellion in 1786–1787, that gave him his reputation as a great orator and publicist. This success, in addition to his Calvinism and Tory political theory enabled him to be elected to Congress as a Federalist congressman in December of the same year. He remained in the House throughout Washington's administration, supporting it always with his votes and speech making.

Ames left Congress at the end of his term in 1797 because of ill health and spent the last decade of his life in virtual retirement. He was still admired as a thinker and orator and thus was selected to deliver the eulogy on Washington three years after leaving the House. He declined the presidency of Harvard in 1804, however, and pleading ill health spent his declining years at his home in Dedham. He died there at the age of fifty on July 4, 1808, on the same date, if not the same year, as did his great antagonist, Thomas Jefferson.

AMES AS POLITICAL THEORIST AND PUBLICIST

Although Ames's political career in Congress was a short one, lasting only from 1788 to 1798, in his active years he was considered one of the greatest Federalist thinkers and spokesmen of his time. This was predicated not just on his speech making but on his writings as well. In both, his Tory political theory was copiously present. Content with the familiar and habitual and believing that the future should be akin to the past, his philosophy made almost any change in society undesirable. Ames's views reflected a Calvinistic strain, focusing on the evil nature of man whose main aim was to gain wealth and fame by any means. This commitment to Toryism comprised his philosophy and therefore served as the basis for his Federalist political views, which he expressed in his rhetoric.

To Ames, the ideal of Federalism was a religion to be defended with all the ardor of a moralist; those who derided it, he believed, were children of the devil. His firm commitment to the Calvinistic doctrine of the elect was synonymous with the doctrine of success; it made him preeminent in the sociopolitical radical Right, a movement that swept aside French liberal thought that had brought on the American Revolution. Ames became one of the leaders of that movement, which subjected the ideals of democratic equality to sharp attack. This, then, was the thermidorian antithesis by which the counterdefense by antidemocratic forces began their offensive. The movement was the Essex Junta.

The movement's rhetorical tactic was similar to the activism that had made the case for the American Revolution. In his activism, Ames stood arm in arm with two leaders of the movement, John Adams, who supported the stake-in-society views of Samuel Harrington rather than equity; and Alexander Hamilton, who in his antagonism asserted that "the people is a great beast." These leaders of the movement were part of the Essex Junta and were conspicuous for their British sympathies. They strongly defended the established conservative pattern of economic, political, and social arrangements while articulating a vehement antagonism to the French Revolution and its lauding of alleged Jacobinism at home.

Ames's rhetoric focused on a society in which the aristocracy—with its continued restriction of the suffrage to substantial property owners—would rule. The future, too, would be improved by a strong case for revealed religion. Founded on the evil nature of man, Ames's Federalist theory, with its doctrine of the elect, meant that the masses should be ruled by a rod of iron. His theory thus focused on a coercive sovereignty rather than on a democracy. The latter was a government of the worst and would lead to despotism or worse, anarchy. These were the views of the Essex Junta on which Ames focused his acerbic rhetoric throughout his lifetime.

As a publicist, Ames was a Federalist who presented his views with a great fertility of imagination in cogent essays as well as in forceful oratory. The "quintessence of government," he wrote in his essay, "Phocian," was "to protect property and its rights." Furthermore, "where property is safe by rules and principles there is liberty." Ames also condemned democracy in a series of six articles published in *The Palladium* under the rubric "Equality." He began by castigating the "men of the new order," particularly Tom Paine, whose doctrine, which proclaimed "to all men that they are free and equal," was most pernicious because it suggested that the present generation was equal politically to past generations. Using irony and sarcasm—his most potent instruments of emotional proof—Ames wrote that "this generation being equal to the last owes no obedience to the institutions; and being wiser owes them not even deference." Ames therefore did not accept the terminable compact, the Jeffersonian ideal that gave true equality to the people. Instead it was liberty that was most important in American life. Ames went much further in "Equality No. 2" when he wrote that the democrats who supported equality were wrong because "all the rights and equality they admire are destitute of any rational security" and "are subversive of all true liberty." This led to his condemnation of majority rule, stating sardonically that the people, "having an unlimited right to act as they please, whatever they please to act is a rule. Thus virtue itself, thus, public faith, thus, common honesty are no more than arbitrary rules which the people have as yet, abstained from rescinding." The way to curb these was to consider the rights of the individual that "are to be exercised," he wrote in "Equality No. 6," "with due regard to the rights of others; they are fast tied to restrictions, and are to be exercised within certain reasonable limits." This view of the rights of the minority was not just a Federalist one. Jefferson also accepted it, as was seen in his First Inaugural and his addresses to the Indians.

It was as a Federalist orator, the Oracle of the Tie-Wig School, that Ames was the most influential voice of the Essex Junta, and Congress was the stage where most of his rhetoric was presented. As a political theorist, Ames was the complete conservative ideologue. As a Federalist politician, however, he was much more pragmatic in his oratory, and this was aided by his delivery and rhetorical style. When he rose to speak, he made a striking appearance. Above middle height, he was well proportioned and held himself almost militarily erect. His regular features—with a forehead that was neither too broad nor too high— were complemented by a well-formed mouth and mild blue eyes. His voice aided in the delivery of his often caustic speeches, being distinguished by a mellifluent quality that made for pleasant listening and thus added to his ethos. His rhetorical style, too, was effective. Stemming from his personal belief that he was one of the elect, his style was cynical and sarcastic. Full of generalities, it was fluent and emotionally moving, particularly in its ironic and sardonic vein. In his role as a leader of the antiegalitarian movement, Ames's acerbic use of antagonism was therefore effectively expressed in his appeals to *pathos*.

Yet early in his congressional career, when he spoke on the apportionment bill, Ames appeared to favor equal rights and equal power. Moreover, he was much less emotional and much more logical when he argued, "Before the Constitution was formed our rights were equal; and can it be believed that compact has made them less? Men equal in rights assented to a Government which preserves them equal in power. Thirty thousand citizens residing where they may, must possess equal rights and powers equal to thirty thousand in any other part of the Union.'' Such a clear statement, with its analogical reasoning, seems to be a direct contradiction of the emotional outbursts about the inequality of man seen in his writings. Why the metamorphosis? Why did he also declare, ''To determine what is right some principle must be ascertained. That first principle is equality; it is another name for justice. That which is the right of the people, therefore, is the duty of government.'' The conclusion Ames came to in this address is still another anomaly when he said, ''The principle upon which this tax is founded . . . is that the duty is expected to fall equally upon all.'' Such views about the connections of equality to power, justice, and economics would be encountered more likely in the rhetoric of Paine or Jefferson, Ames's arch political rivals, rather than in the usual oratory of this shrill Jeremiah of that radical Right, antiequality movement, the Essex Junta. It can only be concluded that Ames had his reasons for these many deviations from his conservative social theory and that these probably were based on the realistic practice of most politicians. Ames was astute enough to alter his ideological stance when the times appeared to warrant it.

Ames was a prolific speaker, but today he is known for two addresses that gave him his reputation as one of the greatest orators of his time. The first, his deliberative speech, ''On the British Treaty,'' also popularly known as Jay's treaty, was delivered in the middle of his oratorical career; the other, an address of the epideictic genre, was the eulogy on Washington delivered at its end.

A lengthy discourse, running some thirty pages of printed text, ''On the British Treaty'' was delivered in the House of Representatives April 28, 1796. At issue was the treaty that had been set in 1794. It had been ratified by President Washington, who sent it to the House so that the needed appropriations might be made to carry it into effect. The treaty met with almost universal denunciation, but Ames supported it with such efficiency that Dr. Priestly called it the most bewitching piece of eloquence he had ever heard. It swept the congressmen so off their feet that one of them asked for a delay in the vote because Ames's emotional rhetoric was too eloquent to allow them to be dispassionate. Another observer indicated that he had heard Lord Chatham and Pitt the Younger, as well as Edmund Burke and Charles James Fox, speak in the British Parliament, but he said that Ames, in this address was the equal of them all.

As a vehement Jeremiah, Ames was most effective when he used the syndrome of blame in his oratory. Nevertheless, he could be eloquent when he used praise in his speeches, as in his most moving public address, the eulogy on Washington. In it, Ames gave due reverence and praise to Washington for his great contributions as a general and as president. In addition to these accolades, however, another significant concept surfaced in the address, one that had been the core of many of his condemnations, the egalitarian ideal. In keeping with the use of praise, so important in the epideictic genre, equality now was viewed as an aid to that most significant of Washington's views, the archetype of liberty. Toward the development of this viewpoint, Ames noted in the eulogy that the chief "duty and care of all governments is to protect the rights of property and the tranquility of society." Although these could be accomplished only by the acceptance of the libertarian ideal, this ideal could be fulfilled and put into practice only through education, laws, and habits. Even more important, Ames said, was that liberty also depended "on an almost equal diffusion of property," as well as being founded "on morals and religion." Washington, Ames asserted with fulsome praise, was the true repository of all these virtues. Nor were "the honors paid to this great patriot excessive, idolatrous or degrading to freemen who are all equal." These commendations of Washington, he said, were highly deserved even in an egalitarian republic. Ames's eloquence in the eulogy became legendary not only for its epideictic hymn of praise but even more so because he used the occasion for deliberative persuasion. In the discourse, then, he effectively utilized the great authority of Washington to fortify his own theory of the function of government in the American Republic.

Even here, however, Ames's elitist activism and antagonism were not completely erased. Rather, it appeared to be a realistic recognition that the antithetical ideas he had used so frequently had not completely attained their ends. But while his acerbic oratory had not halted irrevocably the developmental march of democratic egalitarian change, it nevertheless had helped arrest it to some extent.

The ultraconservative movement of which Ames had been such an integral part and of which he had been a rhetorical godfather did not end with him. It was pursued after his death in 1808 by John Adams and Alexander Hamilton, both part of the Essex Junta, who continued to voice Ames's views. Quiescent during the heyday of Jefferson and Madison, the antidemocratic egalitarian spirit had its resurgence after the War of 1812, when ultraconservative ideology, as propounded by Joseph Story and Chief Justice John Marshall, began to hold sway again. It was only when Andrew Jackson heralded the Age of the Common Man that the Federalist Tory theories of Ames lost some of their significance and were placed in limbo, at least for a while. Nevertheless, the political theory of Fisher Ames, based on his Puritanism and coupled to the Yankee vision of success, has not died. It has been evident in the late twentieth-century in the radical Right movement. The sociopolitico spirit of the Oracle of the Tie Wig School lives on.

INFORMATION SOURCES

Research Collections and Collected Speeches

Ames, Fisher. *Works of Fisher Ames*. Edited by T. Kirkland. Boston: T. B.   WFA
　　Wait and Co., 1809.
————. *Works of Fisher Ames*. Edited by Seth Ames, Boston: Little, Brown,   WFA
　　1854.

Annals of the Congress of the United States Vol. 3 Compiled by Joseph   *ACUS*
    Gales, Sr. Washington, D.C.: Gales and Seaton, 1834.
Debates and Proceedings of the Congress of the United States. Vol. 3.   *DPCUS*
    Washington, D.C.: Gales and Seaton, 1849.
Modern Eloquence. Vol. 11. Edited by Thomas B. Reed. New York: Amer-   *ME*
    ican Law Book Co., 1903.

Selected Critical Studies

Bowers, Claude B. *Jefferson and Hamilton.* Boston: Houghton Mifflin, 1925.
Hillbruner, Anthony. " 'Fisher Ames.' In The Concept of Equality in the Speeches of
    Selected Speakers between the Revolutionary War and the Civil War." Ph.D.
    dissertation, Northwestern University, 1953.
————. "Fisher Ames and Equality." *Western Speech* 19 (1955): 185–93.

Selected Biographies

Ames, Seth, introd. *Works of Fisher Ames* by Fisher Ames. Edited by Seth Ames.
    Boston: Little, Brown, 1854.
Eubank, Henry. "Notices of the Life and Character of Fisher Ames." In *The Influences
    of Democracy.* Edited by Henry Eubank. London: John W. Parker, West Strand,
    1835.

CHRONOLOGY OF MAJOR SPEECHES

See "Research Collections and Collected Speeches" for source codes.

Speech on biennial elections, Boston, January 1783; *WFA*, 2: 3–8.

Speech on apportionment bill, Washington, D.C., December 19, 1791; *DPCUS*, 3: 254–62.

Speech on Madison's commercial resolutions, Washington, D.C., January 3, 1794; *WFA*, 2: 8–37.

Speech on the British Treaty, Washington, D.C., April 28, 1796; *WFA*, 37–71; *ME*, 11: 43–76; *WBO*, 1: 156–67.

Eulogy on Washington, Boston, Massachusetts, February 8, 1800; *WFA*, 2: 71–88.

SUSAN B. ANTHONY
(1820–1906), suffragist

_____ ALLEN H. MERRIAM

Susan Brownell Anthony personified the quest for social and political reform in nineteenth-century America. From her earliest public speeches in support of temperance and the abolition of slavery through fifty years of promoting woman's suffrage, Anthony became one of the most zealous advocates of social change in U.S. history. Spurred by a close working relationship with Elizabeth Cady Stanton, Anthony devoted most of her adult life to lecturing, touring, organizing meetings, lobbying state legislatures, testifying before congressional committees, attending political conventions, circulating petitions, and writing letters and articles in support of a constitutional amendment granting women the right to vote. By her own estimate, the indefatigable native of Rochester, New York, averaged between seventy-five and one-hundred lectures per year during the forty-five-year span from 1852 to 1897. A founder of the National Woman Suffrage Association in 1869, she was president of the National American Woman Suffrage Association from 1892 to 1900. Anthony interviewed five U.S. presidents and made four trips to Europe, speaking at international women's conferences in London in 1899 and Berlin in 1904. She was the central figure in a well-publicized trial in 1873, disrupted the 1876 Centennial Exposition by reading the "Declaration of Rights for Women," and helped organize during the 1893 Chicago World's Fair the World Congress of Representative Women, which attracted nearly 150,000 people during a week-long celebration of womanhood. Between 1868 and 1870, she edited a feminist newspaper, the *Revolution*, which had as its motto: "Men, their rights and nothing more; women, their rights and nothing less." She also assumed a major role in editing the definitive *History of Woman's Suffrage*, which eventually filled six volumes and over 5,000 pages. For the sheer output of her propagandistic efforts and the profound significance of the political reform she espoused, Anthony represents an important voice in the history of American public address.

ANTHONY AS ORATOR

Although she never had any formal training in public speaking, several factors contributed to Anthony's development as an advocate. Her Quaker parentage and early years in upstate New York imbued her with a deep devotion to sexual egalitarianism and social action. Her father, Daniel Anthony, held liberal beliefs in matters of religion and politics, and the family home was frequented by noted reformers of the day, including William Lloyd Garrison, Wendell Phillips, William Ellery Channing, and Frederick Douglass. As a young woman, Anthony supported temperance and abolitionist causes. Her first public speech, delivered March 1, 1849, was at a village supper in Canajoharie, New York, sponsored by the Daughters of Temperance. Anthony's several years as a teacher at the Canajoharie Academy offered experience in public communication, as did

Quaker religious practices, which encourage women to speak at meetings. In promoting liberal ideas of racial and sexual equality, Anthony and her feminist colleagues challenged the widespread nineteenth-century assumption that no woman, let alone a respectable spinster, should debate political issues from a public platform. She was eight years old at the time of the first public speech by a woman in America, traditionally acknowledged to be Frances Wright's July 4, 1828, oration in New Harmony, Indiana. Anthony's resolve to oppose discrimination was no doubt intensified in 1852 when, upon rising to speak at a temperance rally, she was rebuked by the chairman: "the sisters were not invited here to speak, but to listen and to learn."

That same year Anthony and her new friend Elizabeth Cady Stanton determined to combine their energies in the cause of women's rights. For the next half-century, they frequently traveled, wrote, and lectured together. And as often happens with pairs in history (Plato and Aristotle in Greek philosophy, Bach and Handel in baroque music, Gandhi and Tagore as twin souls of modern India), Anthony and Stanton shared a common idealism despite complementary differences in orientation and style. Anthony emphasized the need for economic independence and sought to mesh feminism with the emerging trade union movement; Stanton concentrated on sexual liberation and a woman's sovereignty over her own body. In her final four decades, Anthony focused almost exclusively on the suffrage movement, whereas Stanton linked women's issues to a widely based program of political reform and attacks on religious fundamentalism. And Anthony the organizer stood in contrast to Stanton the stylist. Often the two collaborated in composing resolutions and speeches, with Anthony usually supplying the facts, statistics, and arguments and Stanton putting them into rhetorical form. Said Anthony: "Mrs. Stanton is my sentence maker, my pen artist."

Never fully comfortable with the demands of speech composition, Anthony normally spoke extemporaneously or from brief notes. She adapted readily to group discussion and impromptu speaking situations and was quite effective in welcoming delegates to conventions, describing the logistics of rallies, and offering appropriate remarks at public meetings. "But a sustained speech was, is and always will be an impossibility," she commented in 1899. Despite misgivings about her oratorical ability, Anthony spent many years on the professional lecture circuit. Beginning in 1857, she worked for four years as a paid organizer of the American Anti-Slavery Society, traveling and speaking extensively on behalf of abolition. During the early 1870s, she was in the employ of the New York Lyceum Bureau, Star Course, and the Dime Lecture Course series. Between 1876 and 1888, she was under contract intermittently with the Slayton Lyceum Bureau, lecturing and writing pamphlets, articles, and letters in support of women's rights. Much of Anthony's career was financed by contributions and donations supplemented by income derived from lecturing.

While early in her career Anthony relied heavily on emotional appeals and vivid language in denouncing the evils of drunkenness and the horrors of slavery, it was as a crusader for woman's suffrage after the Civil War that she made her greatest contribution to American political discourse. Anthony's suffrage rhetoric, when condensed to its essence, offers a classic case of syllogistic reasoning. If one grants her major premise (women are persons) and her minor premise (persons in a democracy have the right to vote), then one cannot escape her logical conclusion that women therefore have the right to vote. Although overly naive in assuming that voting was the answer to nearly all social problems, Anthony never waivered from her fundamental position that "in the ballot lies the supreme source of power."

Probably nowhere else did Anthony argue woman's suffrage more forcefully than in her "Constitutional Argument" speech delivered about forty times in the spring of 1873. Facing trial for having voted in the 1872 election, Anthony barnstormed throughout upstate New York seeking to influence public opinion and thereby the jury's verdict. Anthony based her case directly on constitutional principles, especially the Fourteenth Amendment, ratified in 1868, which states that "all persons born or naturalized in the United States . . . are citizens," and the Fifteenth Amendment, ratified in 1870, which declared that "the right of citizens of the United States to vote shall not be denied." Eloquently defending the right to vote as "inalienable" and "God-given," Anthony espoused "the great principle of equal rights to all" in order to produce "a harmonious union and a homogeneous people." Echoing James Otis that "taxation without representation is tyranny," she applied the Jeffersonian doctrine of individual liberty to all persons: "It was we, the people, not we the white male citizens, nor we, the male citizens, but we, the whole people who formed this Union."

Most lawyers and politicians at the time, who, of course, were male, would not agree with Anthony's contention that since the state legislature had not passed laws expressly denying the vote to women, they therefore were enfranchised. Had it worked, that clever strategy of arguing a presumption could have changed American society. Indeed, if Judge Ward Hunt had not unilaterally found Anthony guilty by interpreting the fourteenth Amendment as applying only to males or if the Supreme Court had not upheld his decision in a similar case involving Frances Minor in 1875, the battle for woman's suffrage might have been won then and there. Such a development would have made Anthony's "Constitutional Argument" speech one of the most momentous turning points in the history of American political rhetoric. But woman's suffrage had to await ratification of the nineteenth Amendment in 1920, forty-seven years after Anthony's trial and fourteen years after her death.

Anthony's suffrage speeches reflected a strong reliance on logical argumentation. Her reasoning was primarily deductive, emanating from general principles such as that discrimination is wrong, that the denial of political rights destroys economic and moral well-being, and that individual freedom is a natural right. Her evidence took many forms: statistics ("In New York alone, there are over 50,000 . . . women receiving less than fifty cents a day"); quotations ("Alexander Hamilton said one hundred years ago, 'Give to a man the right over my subsistence, and he has power over my whole moral being' "); comparisons (often of the plight of women to the degradation of blacks under slavery); and historical allusions appealing to patriotic emotions ("With man, woman shared the dangers of the Mayflower on a stormy sea, the dreary landing on Plymouth Rock, the rigors of New England winters, and the privations of a seven years' war"). Anthony relied heavily on quotations from the Declaration of Independence and the U.S. Constitution to establish the legal basis for political liberties.

Anthony's speeches included a strong emphasis on the economic plight of women, attributable to their financial dependence on men. In "Suffrage and the Working Woman," Anthony attacked "the false theory . . . that woman is born to be supported by man." She claimed that women must be educated for financial self-sufficiency because women significantly outnumber men, making it mathematically impossible for every woman to have a supportive husband, not to mention those women who choose "not to be ruled." The United States, she prophesied in "Homes of Single Women," was entering an "epoch of single women." Declaring in her popular and oft-repeated "Social Purity" lecture that "independence is happiness," Anthony decried the "sickly sentimentalism which counts the woman a heroine and a saint for remaining the wife of a drunken, immoral husband." Promulgating the need for legal recognition of a wife's equal share in the assets of a marriage, she assumed that "whoever controls work and wages, controls morals." Elaborating on this view, which is good Marxist doctrine, in her "Woman Wants Bread" lecture given many times throughout the United States and Europe, Anthony argued that the disfranchisement of women made them a "degraded class of labor" for "there never was, there never can be, a monopoly so fraught with injustice, tyranny and degradation as this monopoly of sex, of all men over all women."

One of Anthony's most dramatic gestures in propagating the suffrage message occurred July 4, 1876, during ceremonies in Philadelphia celebrating the one-hundredth anniversary of the Declaration of Independence. A festive event honoring the centennial took place in front of Independence Hall with numerous male dignitaries, including Emperor Dom Pedro of Brazil and acting U.S. Vice-President Thomas Ferry on the platform. Denied a place on the program or even admission to the ceremony for a suffragist delegation, Anthony gained access to the proceedings with a reporter's pass. Immediately following the reading of the Declaration of Independence, Anthony and several accomplices moved to the podium and distributed copies of a "Declaration of Rights for Women," which she and Matilda Joslyn Gage had posed. To complete the upstaging of the celebration, Anthony then mounted the nearby musicians' stand and, in the symbolic shadow of the Liberty Bell, read aloud the Declaration, turning the milling crowd into an attentive audience. Quoting Abigail Adams's assertion that women "will not hold ourselves bound to obey laws in which we have no voice or representation," she identified the suffragists' demand: "We ask justice, we ask equality, we ask that all the civil and political rights that belong to citizens of the United States be guaranteed to us and our daughters forever." Although many Americans no doubt shared the opinion of *New York Tribune* editor Whitelaw Reid who decried this "discourteous interruption" and "disregard of order," the centennial episode represented one of the notable acts of militancy in the nineteenth-century suffrage crusade.

Photographs of Anthony with her high-neck dresses, hair pulled tightly in a bun behind her head, and thin-rimmed glasses suggest a staid and rather austere appearance. She was an introspective person who admitted to occasional feelings of depression and suffered from problem teeth and strabismus, an eye defect. But she also possessed wit and quickness of mind, as evident in her use of satire and sarcasm in refuting critics of the revolutionary doctrine that women should share equally with men in political rights. For example, Harper recounted a confrontation with an abolitionist who told her, "You are not married, you have no business discussing marriage," to which she retorted: "Well, Mr. Mayo, you are no slave, suppose you quit lecturing on slavery." In 1884, during a hearing with U.S. senators, she facetiously stated the antisuffrage assumption that "women are not people," to which Senator George Edmunds countered with "Angels," prompting Anthony to reply: "Yes, angels up in heaven or else devils down here." With compelling logic, spiced with biting humor, she once told a predominantly male audience: "Do you not see that so long as society says a woman is incompetent to be a lawyer, minister, or doctor, but has ample ability to be a teacher, that every one of you who chooses this profession tacitly acknowledges that he has no more brains than a woman?"

Assessments of Anthony's effectiveness as an orator vary. Harper wrote of her well-modulated voice, distinct enunciation, and pure and unexaggerated language, while Dorr praised Anthony's clear contralto voice and fine economy of words. An 1890 evaluation cited by Twitchell, however, described her speaking style as "angular in gesture and uncouth in phraseology." Most critics tend to agree that, as a platform performer, Anthony was generally inferior to other nineteenth-century feminists such as Anna Dickinson, Ernestine Rose, Anna Shaw, Elizabeth Stanton, and Lucy Stone. Anthony's real strengths lay in her strong organizational abilities, logical precision in framing arguments, and keen lobbying skills. There is no evidence that she was familiar with the rhetorical theory of her day, nor did she contribute to it.

Although she died in 1906 with her lifelong goal unattained, history has treated Anthony kindly in recognizing her as a major propagandist for the uplift of women. Despite deficiencies as an orator, she exerted considerable impact on American society through more than fifty years of intense devotion to social reform. Her bust stands in the Hall of Fame of Great Americans in New York City. With Stanton and Lucretia Mott, she is portrayed in Adelaide Johnson's sculptured monument in the Capitol in Washington, D.C. Her life inspired a motion picture by Encyclopaedia Britannica Films and a two-act opera, "The Mother of Us All," with words by Gertrude Stein and music by Virgil Thomson, first performed in 1947. The subject of an ill-fated silver dollar issued by the U.S. Mint in 1979, she remains a stimulus to scholarship, as seen in the creation of the Susan B. Anthony Center for Women's Studies at the University of

Rochester. Certainly her most fitting memorial is the nineteenth Amendment to the U.S. Constitution, often called the Anthony amendment. The crusade to open American democracy to women formed the consuming passion of her oratorical career.

INFORMATION SOURCES

Research Collections and Collected Speeches

Rhetorical critics should be aware that the extant texts of Anthony's speeches are, in most cases, not verbatim transcripts but the result of editorial compilations based on notes and newspaper reports. Anthony's Scrapbooks, which fill thirty-three volumes in the Rare Book Room of the Library of Congress, Washington, D.C., include programs of conventions, leaflets, announcements of lectures, abstracts of speeches, and clippings of newspaper reports of her political and personal activities. The Anthony papers at the Schlesinger Library, Radcliffe College, Cambridge, Massachusetts, and the Susan B. Anthony Library of the Los Angeles Public Library also contain valuable resources for research. The most useful resource on Anthony's rhetoric is Ida Harper's three-volume biography, the appendix of which includes the texts of seven speeches.

American Forum; Speeches on Historic Issues, 1788–1900. Edited by Ernest   *AF*
    J. Wrage and Barnet Baskerville, New York: Harper & Row, 1960.
Anthology of Public Speeches. Edited by Mabel Platz. New York: H. W.   *APS*
    Wilson, 1940.
Congressional Record. January 25, 1887, vol. 18, pt 1.   *CR*
Elizabeth Cady Stanton—Susan B. Anthony: Correspondence, Writings,   *ECS-SBA*
    Speeches. Edited by Ellen Carol DuBois. New York: Schocken
    Books, 1981.
Harper, Ida Husted. *Life and Work of Susan B. Anthony.* 2 vols. 1898–   *LW*
    1899; rpt., New York: Arno and the New York Times, 1969.
Outspoken Women; Speeches by American Women Reformers, 1635–1935.   *OW*
    Edited by Judith Anderson. Dubuque, Iowa: Kendall/Hunt, 1984.
Stanton, Elizabeth Cady, Susan B. Anthony, Matilda J. Gage, and Ida H.   *HWS*
    Harper. *History of Woman's Suffrage.* 6 vols. 1881–1922; rpt., New
    York: Collectors Editions, 1971.

Selected Critical Studies

Berman, Ruth F. "A Critical Evaluation of the Speeches of Susan B. Anthony." Master's
    thesis, University of Wisconsin, 1947.
Coleman, Ronald G. "A Historical Survey of the Rhetorical Proofs Used by the Women
    Speakers of the Suffrage Organizations: 1869–1919." Ph.D. dissertation, Case
    Western Reserve University, 1968.
Grim, Hariett E. "Susan B. Anthony, Exponent of Freedom." Ph.D. dissertation, Uni-
    versity of Wisconsin, 1938.
McDavitt, Elaine E. "Susan B. Anthony: Reformer and Speaker." *Quarterly Journal of
    Speech* 30 (April 1944): 173–80.

O'Connor, Lillian M. F. *Pioneer Women Orators: Rhetoric in the Ante-Bellum Reform Movement*. New York: Columbia University Press, 1954.
Riegel, Robert E. *American Feminists*. Lawrence: University Press of Kansas, 1963.
Trent, Judith S. "Susan B. Anthony and Martha W. Griffiths: Two Speaking for Equal Rights." Paper presented at the annual meeting of the Central States Speech Association, Milwaukee, Wisconsin, April 4, 1974.
Twitchell, Doris Yoakum. "Susan B. Anthony." In *A History and Criticism of American Public Address*. Vol. 3. Edited by Marie Katherine Hochmuth. New York: Longmans, Green, 1955.

Selected Biographies

Anthony, Katherine. *Susan B. Anthony: Her Personal History and Her Era*. New York: Doubleday, 1954.
Bryan, Florence H. *Susan B. Anthony: Champion of Women's Rights*. New York: Julian Messner, 1947.
Dorr, Rheta Childe. *Susan B. Anthony: The Woman Who Changed the Mind of a Nation*. New York: Frederick A. Stokes, 1928.
Harper, Ida Husted. *The Life and Work of Susan B. Anthony*. 3 vols. Indianapolis: Hollenbeck Press, 1898–1909.
Lutz, Alma. *Susan B. Anthony: Rebel, Crusader, Humanitarian*. Boston: Beacon Hill, 1959.

CHRONOLOGY OF MAJOR SPEECHES

See "Research Collections and Collected Speeches" for source codes.

"Address to Congress," adopted by Eleventh National Woman's Rights Convention, New York, May 10, 1866; *LW*, 2: 968–71.

"Suffrage and the Working Woman," given many times between the 1860s and the 1890s; *ECS-SBA*, pp. 139–45.

"Woman Wants Bread, Not the Ballot," given many times between 1870 and 1890; *LW*, 2: 996–1003.

"Constitutional Argument," given about forty times in New York State, spring 1873; *APS*, 691–93; *ECS-SBA*, 152–65; *HWS*, 2: 630–47.

"Social Purity," given many times but first in Chicago, March 14, 1875; *LW*, 2: 1004–12.

"Declaration of Rights for Women," Philadelphia, July 4, 1876; *HWS*, 3: 31–34.

"Homes of Single Women," given many times, including in October 1877; *ECS-SBA*, pp. 146–51.

Address to the U.S. Senate Select Committee on Woman Suffrage, Washington, D.C., March 7, 1884; *CR*, March 7, 1884, 998–1002; *AF*, 318–32.

"The Demand for Party Recognition," Kansas City, Kansas, May 4, 1894; *LW*, 2: 1015–21; *OW*, 11–16.

HENRY WARD BEECHER
(1813–1887), pulpit orator

_____ HALFORD R. RYAN

Whenever an important oration was delivered in the mid-nineteenth century, Henry Ward Beecher seemed to be the orator on the platform or in the pulpit. He was aptly described as a stump speaker who stumbled into the pulpit. Whether propounding religion in his famous Plymouth Church in Brooklyn, New York, or pounding at slavery from abolitionist platforms, or celebrating the flag-raising ceremonies at Fort Sumter in 1865, or exuberantly extolling American virtues in lecture halls at home and abroad, Beecher spoke for the United States. He was the vox populi.

Beecher was born into a quintessential American family. His father was Lyman Beecher, an important Presbyterian preacher, and his famous sibling was Harriet Beecher Stowe, the author of _Uncle Tom's Cabin_. His first pastorate after graduation from Amherst College and Lane Theological Seminary was at Lawrenceburg, Indiana. After two years there, he moved to Indianapolis (1839–1847) and then to the Plymouth Church, which he served for forty years until his death in 1887. Although Beecher's oratory is the subject of this essay, it should be noted that he edited two important national journals, the _Independent_ and the _Christian Union_, through which he propagated his reformist views, and he published twenty-four books. Lyman Beecher was partly responsible for Henry's melding the pulpit with the platform, sacred Protestantism with secular politics. Henry Ward Beecher's oratorical prowess depended on his ability to bring the power of pulpit preaching to the public platform and the principles of public persuasion to the pulpit. His persuading and preaching earned him an exalted place in the history of American oratory and ranked him as one of the most important preachers in the United States.

BEECHER AS PREACHER AND PERSUADER

Except for that of the bar, the Reverend Beecher seemed to succeed in all of the genres of oratory. As a man of public stature, he often spoke as an encomiast. He delivered eulogies of some of the most important Americans in his generation: Charles Sumner, Wendell Phillips, and Ulysses S. Grant. Although these encomia deal on the surface with the famous decedents, Beecher often paid himself indirect compliments when discussing their (his) role in the antislavery movement, their support of the Civil War, and their vindication in final victory. Beecher did rise to epideictic eloquence in his eulogy of Abraham Lincoln on April 23, 1865. In his introductory remarks, Beecher chose an appropriate text from Deuteronomy that related how Moses was led by God to the top of Mount Pisgah where he was allowed to see the Promised Land but was not allowed to enter it. Beecher extended that analogy in reviewing Lincoln's life with the sorrowful irony that Lincoln was not allowed to taste the final fruits of his presidency. Although much of Beecher's speech is maudlin by twentieth-century standards, he did manage to speak in a simple sentence Lincoln's greatness for all Americans: "He was a man from the common people who never forgot his kind."

Beecher also excelled as a lecturer. It has been estimated that Beecher received during his lifetime over $400,000 in lecture fees. Audiences were delighted in the self-congratulatory ideas in his lecture on "Puritanism," were enlightened by his exposes in "The Wastes and Burdens of Society," in which he showed his audiences that school children often had less air to breath per cubic foot than criminals did in prison, and were extolled in the obviously patriotic lecture "The Reign of the Common People." These lectures were among Beecher's most famous and successful, and they were repeated on demand throughout his oratorical career.

Beecher's oratorical *persona* was adopted into the vernacular of the Victorian era. "Beecher's boats," an allusion to the biblical fisher-of-men image, referred to the ferries that plied people between Manhattan and Brooklyn on Sundays for Plymouth Church. "Beecher's Bibles" referred to a public relations scheme he hit upon to aggrandize his *ethos*. As Bloody Kansas became bloodier in 1856, Beecher preached that rifles there would do the abolitionists more good than Bibles. He joined a movement to send rifles to Kansas and even persuaded Plymouth Church to send additional rifles and as many Bibles. To conservative Christians, "Beecher's Bibles" was a parody of his *persona* as a clergyman, but the abolitionists, with whom Beecher had cast his lot, used the phrase to praise his willingness to act upon his own rhetoric. Accordingly Plymouth Church was known as the Church of the Holy Rifles.

It was at Plymouth Church that Beecher established his reputation as the nation's preacher in the mid-nineteenth century. He was called to Plymouth because of his oratorical successes in Indiana and because leading members of the rising gentry in Brooklyn wanted a minister who could build a church by attracting crowds through the dynamism of a powerful preaching style. During his years in Indianapolis, Beecher had tested and coalesced the major themes of his oratorical career: reform, antislavery, and liberalizing the Christian religion. These themes met some of the needs of Victorian Americans, and Beecher brought them to fruition in the Plymouth pulpit. As a speaker for reform, he stressed women's rights, better national government, and, to a lesser degree, temperance. He was vocal in the woman's movement, was a close ally of Susan B. Anthony, and lectured widely on that subject throughout his career. Beecher was active in the formation of the Republican party because it took a stand against the extension of slavery in the territories. He supported its candidate, John Frémont, in 1856; he invited Abraham Lincoln to the East for his famous address at Cooper Institute in New York in 1860; and he campaigned for Lincoln in 1860 and 1864 from the platform and pulpit. Early in the war, however, Beecher criticized Lincoln in the *Independent* for not grounding the war on emancipation rather than on Lincoln's avowed premise of saving the Union. He was heartened by the president's Emancipation Proclamation, although it could have come earlier in Beecher's opinion. The president was evidently not too perturbed by Beecher's broadsides because he invited the preacher to deliver an address at the flag-raising ceremonies at Fort Sumter.

The one issue on which Beecher spoke from secular and sacred daises, and which forever identified him in the public's mind as an orator of the first rank, was his antislavery crusade. Beecher drew some notice in 1846 for a series of sermons he delivered in Indianapolis against slavery. Although he did not at that time suggest any viable solutions to the problems in the South, he did gain some prominence (or perhaps notoriety) for using the Christian pulpit to discuss secular matters at a time when preachers avoided the subject as divisive or as inappropriate sermonic material.

Beecher penned some thoughts for a speech sometime in the 1850s that reflected his thinking and rhetoric on antislavery. In a classical *partitio*, he first delineated those factors that did not contribute to the growing sectional conflict: it was not from business, not a conflict of political ideas, not religion, or social conflict; rather, it was "*the radical diversity* of the ideas *North and South upon Labor*! [italics in original]." He then outlined three logical consequences of that root cause: ill treatment of slaves, moral apostasy, and an idea that is similar to the main themes in Abraham Lincoln's "House Divided" speech and Henry Seward's "Irrepressible Conflict" speech. Beecher wrote: "Theory of freedom and slavery are utterly *irreconcilable*. A community cannot long hold both. You cannot believe in despotism in our distinction and in democracy in the others [italics in original]."

Beecher delivered a famous impromptu speech at a protest meeting, May 30, 1856, against the caning of Senator Charles Sumner by Preston Brooks. Beecher was spotted in the crowd, and the audience would not be satisfied until he addressed them. He compared Brooks's caning to the bludgeoning of a sleeping woman or the braining of a blind man. Warming to his subject, he smote the South: "There he sat, the scholarly Senator, unarmed, with anything save the pen. Ah! there you have it! The symbol of the North is the pen. The symbol of the South is the bludgeon. [Tremendous applause.]."

A most impressive rhetorical tour de force in the nineteenth century was Beecher's speaking swing through England and Scotland in the early fall of 1863. His congregation sent him to England and the Continent for a six-month rest in early June, and Beecher brushed aside preliminary suggestions that he speak for northern interests while on vacation. Upon his return from the Continent to England in September, Beecher, who had come under increased pressure from his friends and associates to speak out, conferred with Charles Francis Adams, the U.S. ambassador to Great Britain, and subsequently Beecher decided on a speaking tour, which was arranged by the English Emancipation Society. While official British government policy toward the North and South was neutral, in fact it tilted toward the South. For a variety of reasons—economic, political, and social—the ruling classes of Great Britain sympathized with the South, whereas the disenfranchised lower classes favored the northern antislavery cause.

Consequently Beecher courageously faced agitators and opponents who mingled with his otherwise sympathetic audiences. Moreover, as Lionel Crocker demonstrated in his superb analysis of newspaper coverage of Beecher's tour, while the press printed his remarks, the speech texts were juxtaposed to critical editorial reviews. These, however, did not reflect the enthusiastic reception given to Beecher by the common Englishman and Scotsman.

The estimated effect of Beecher's speeches on British public opinion has waxed and waned. His contemporaries believed he had singlehandedly turned public opinion toward the North at a critical juncture in the war. Beecher received a hero's welcome upon return to New York, and he was at pains to give himself considerable credit for his apparent victory. Oliver Wendell Holmes, writing in the *Atlantic Monthly*, proclaimed additional plaudits for the tour: "it has been to lift him from the position of one of the most popular preachers and lecturers, to one of the most popular men in the country." On the other hand, recent critics correctly observe that events of July 4, 1863—the fall of Vicksburg and the failure of Lee at Gettysburg—more than Beecher's oratory demonstrated to the British government that the South probably would not win the war, that the propaganda value of the Emancipation Proclamation placed southern sympathizers in the untenable position of being proslavery, that the *Trent* affair fortunately receded from public prominence, and that Lord Russell's seizure of Confederate steam rams being built in England occurred before Beecher's tour began. Therefore, they argue, Beecher's influence on official British policy was not as mighty as believed by his contemporaries. Although their analysis is well taken, the point is that Beecher's American audiences thought their hero had accomplished an oratorical coup for the North, and their belief helped to brighten Beecher's already luminous stardom.

The basic rhetorical stance Beecher took in his speeches at Manchester, Glasgow, Edinburgh, Liverpool, and London, October 9–20, 1863, was that the South stood for slavery and the North represented the Union, which favored emancipation. This polarization demonstrated to his British audiences that to favor the South was to succor slavery. He argued the point effectively, as at Liverpool: "They have gone off declaring that the Union in the hands of the North was fatal to slavery.[Loud applause.]."

Henry Ward Beecher was capable of theatrics on a grand scale. Perhaps no other speech exhibited such patriotic pablum and orotund oratory as his "Raising the Flag over Fort Sumter," delivered in Charleston, South Carolina, on April 14, 1865, by invitation of President Abraham Lincoln. Much of the speech was unfortunately an exuberant epideictic oration of the most pedestrian kind, the hackneyed Fourth of July genre. In that vein are these examples of Beecher's purple patches of prose: "Ruin sits in the cradle of treason. Rebellion has perished. But there flies the same flag that was insulted"; No more war. "No more accursed secession. No more slavery, that spawned them both"; "No North, no West, no South, but the United States of America." What made the speech noteworthy, however, was his utilization of two rhetorical devices, which are perhaps more appropriate to pulpit oratory but nevertheless functioned effectively for his secular audience. Beecher realized that his celebrating the victory of the North would perforce alienate the vanquished South, yet he sought in his address to reconstitute both peoples. So he used the techniques of victimization and scapegoating. He allowed that the ordinary southerner had been duped by the southern aristocracy into committing its treason. The scapegoat, derived from ancient Hebrew thought, figuratively bore the sins of the people so that they could be sanctified; thus, by selecting the southern patricians as the scapegoat, Beecher rhetorically cleansed the plebians so that they could reenter the Union with their treasonous sins purified. For having victimized the common man, Beecher rhetorically drove the patricians into the wilderness with loathsome metaphorical lashes: "an aristocracy as intense, proud, and inflexible as ever existed . . . obsequious to the people for the sake of governing them . . . [they] ran in the blood of society like a rash not yet come to the skin; this political tapeworm, that produced nothing, but lay coiled in the body, feeding on its nutriment . . . [so that] slaves worked that gentlemen might live at ease." He then spoke his rhetorical coup de grace: "the war was set on by the ruling class, the aristocratic conspirators of the South. They suborned the common people with lies, with sophistries, with cruel deceits and slanders. . . . I charge the whole guilt of this war upon the ambitious, educated, plotting, political leaders of the South. They have shed this ocean of blood. They have desolated the South. They have poured poverty through all her towns and cities." With the southern aristocrat as victimizer figuratively driven from the Union, Beecher asked his audience, and the rest of the nation, to reinstate the southern common man quickly and fully: "But for the people misled, for the multitudes drafted and driven into this civil war, let not a trace of animosity remain . . . Recall to them the old days of kindness. Our hearts wait for their redemption. All the resources of a renovated nation shall be applied to rebuild their prosperity, and smooth down the furrows of war." Although Beecher spoke at Fort Sumter in terms reminiscent of Lincoln's recent Second Inaugural Address, "to bind up the nation's wounds," his rhetoric could not quell the political reality of Reconstructive tendencies that gained ground after Lincoln's assassination, which ironically occurred on the same day as Beecher's speech in Charleston. Nevertheless, the *New York Times* termed Beecher's address a success and noted that it was "delivered in his matchless, eloquent and effective manner."

Although Beecher represented northern sentiments at Fort Sumter, he addressed the problems inherent in reconciling and reconstructing the Union in an evenhanded pronouncement on behalf of the South. The mounting problem was coalesced when General Lee was appointed president of Washington College, now Washington and Lee University, in the late summer of 1865. The approbation of the vanquished South was countered by the opprobrium of the victorious North on Lee's acceptance of the position. Beecher entered the fray by preaching "Conditions of a Restored Union" from the Plymouth pulpit on October 29, 1865. Never one to mince words, he addressed Lee's case directly: "When his history is impartially written, it can never be covered up that in an hour of great weakness he committed himself wickedly to the cause of rebellion. . . . And when the war ceased, and he laid down his arms, who could have been more modest, more manly, more true to his own word and honor than he was?'' Beecher skillfully played on the Christian concept of the call and capped his argument with a practical consideration in two rhetorical questions: ''And when he was called to the presidency of a college, must he not accept it? Must he not do something for a living?'' He then applied his principle of Christian charity to counter northerners who would castigate all southern civilian and military leaders: ''And I tell you we are not making friends, nor helping the cause of a common country, by raising the names of eminent Southern men, one after another, into the place of bitter criticism. It is not generous.'' The arrangement of this speech was noteworthy because he used the method of residues to refute possible objections to his position and to counter his opponents' points: (1) against those who called for the immediate adjustment of southern beliefs and attitudes, he employed a medical analogy to sustain his stance, ''Now we are to remember that convalescence is often slower and longer than the run of the disease itself''; (2) against those who mistrusted the motives of southerners in rejoining the Union, Beecher believed it was not ''wise or Christian for us to distrust the sentiments of those in the South that profess to be desirous, once again, of concord and of union''; and (3) in response to those who wanted more of a ''spirit of humility on the part of the South,'' he accurately observed that the South was devastated enough—should Christians want more? This sermon demonstrated Beecher's ability to place a pressing political problem in a Christian context wherein religious values could function to solve a secular crisis.

Beecher's speech preparation was consistently inconsistent over his oratorical career. For practically fifty years, he used a variety of methods with no apparent regard for purpose or occasion. Sometimes he wrote sermons on six-by-eight-inch pieces of paper; often these would run to sixty or seventy pages of notes. He divided his Thanksgiving sermon for November 28, 1839, into three parts and used subheading numbers for his points; then he drew his own stylized hand with pointed finger to indicate important points. His early patriotism was evident in the words he underlined: ''In its *authors*—its *spirit*—its object is *American* [italics in original].'' At other times, he outlined his thoughts, and some of these outlines were decidedly more skeletal than others that had more complete phrases and sentences. Neither was it unusual for him to orate in an impromptu or extempore fashion. Beecher seemed to compose his speeches and sermons in apparent haste because his handwriting is often incomplete, sometimes illegible, and usually difficult to read. This may help to explain why he did not rely extensively on notes when he gave a speech. For some of his addresses, though, he did take more care in their textual appearance and presentation. In preparing his Brooklyn Rink speech, October 22, 1884, in favor of presidential candidate Grover Cleveland, he wrote a detailed draft. The problem with this draft, or any other draft written by Beecher, is that he often strayed widely from his notes as he spoke. In this address, he ad-libbed extensively and deleted great chunks of prepared materials. But with an orator's sense of the dramatic, he did deliver some eloquent, and sarcastic, lines almost as he prepared them. Beecher wrote:

What a salutary reform will Mr. Blaine make! He would not allow Mr. Dudley to forsake his pension bureau in W. [Washington] and go teach the people to bow down to the Golden Calf—would he? He would not allow Congress to donate land to speculator Rail Road would he? He would not allow huge railroad corporations to cheat the government of its dues, would he? He would seize the great transcontinental R. R. by the throat and help Thurman and Edmunds to drag it to a settlement—wouldn't he!

In comparison, Beecher actually said:

What would Mr. Blaine do for reform? He would not allow Mr. Dudley to forsake the Pension Bureau in order to teach the people to worship the golden calf—Would he? [Laughter.] He would not allow Congress to donate lands to railroads. Would he? [Renewed laughter.] He would seize the Pacific Railroads by the throat and help Thurman and Edmunds to drag them to settlement. Wouldn't he? [Great laughter.]

Beecher did make some emendations on his drafts, but these seemed to be of the second-thought variety in which he changed words or phrases just written. In my research of Beecher's papers, I found no speeches or sermons that went through more than one draft. Beecher probably knew from experience that he would not pay close attention to his notes as he delivered his addresses and therefore did not bother with superfluous speech work. This inference is supported by Beecher's own evaluation of his sermons. In "Henry Ward Beecher: Analysis of Own Sermons," December 27, 1847, he noted that his delivery was better than his organizational content: "The reception is good; the execution very incomplete but thorough; but *effect* by delivery very solemn. This is possible with a sermon extremely faulty in respect to its absolute rhetorical formation to produce nevertheless strong effect [italics in original]."

Beecher preached religion but not theology. He broke with the coldness of Calvinism, the preaching of dogma, the portrayal of an avenging God. Rather, he sermonized the warmth of a romantic Christianity that suited emerging Victorian values of his era. He opened to his audiences a kind God who loved humanity here and now. He stressed a religion of the heart and feelings, and the orator in him was thus able to tap the *pathos* implicit in a romanticized secular and sacred God. He even designed the Plymouth pulpit so that he was physically thrust into the congregation. This augmented his preaching a humanistic religion over a formal theology.

Beecher was responsible for adjusting Darwin's theory of evolution to Christianity and Christianity to the challenges to doctrine by evolutionary and scientific ways of thinking. In 1885, he preached six successive sermons, which were telegraphed to the leading newspapers of the day, on the meaning and impact of evolution to Christianity. Against the fundamentalist bigotry of the times,

Beecher believed that evolution threatened neither the religious nor moral teachings of the Bible. For instance, in "The Two Revelations," May 31, 1885, Beecher argued that the scientific revelations of evolution did not hinder but indeed helped individuals become better Christians. He castigated ministers who attacked evolution with "grimace and shallow ridicule and witless criticism" of enacting "the very feats of the monkey in the attempt to prove that the monkey was not their ancestor." As for the fear that evolution attacked the bedrock tenets of theology, Beecher countered: "the whole Christian world for two thousand years, since the completion of the canons, has been divided up like the end of a broom into infinite splinters, quarreling with each other as to what the book did say, and what it did mean." Rather, Beecher maintained that evolution would bolster religion. He told his Plymouth congregation that "religion is the condition of man's nature as toward God and his fellow-man." Evolution, then, would aid the individual to understand better God's design for mankind and for the individual to realize a fuller humanity on earth. This sermon was one of Beecher's better-organized addresses. He listed two objections against evolution that he answered (he asserted that "faith that can be unsettled by the access of light and knowledge had better be unsettled") and then developed seven arguments on why Christians should accept evolution as an aid to their religious beliefs. Beecher also stressed the theme of how evolutionary tenets could improve man's religious state in "Divine Providence and Design" delivered on June 28, 1885. Just as evolution was unfolding and revealing the materialistic world, its method was allowing people to reach greater possibilities in realizing God: "In this direction, it may be, we shall find a philosophy of miracle, of powers of faith, of prophecy, of a human control of matter which allies exalted manhood to the creative power of God. Such an augmented power of the human soul was unquestionably taught by Jesus." With regard to the impact of evolutionary findings on the Christian religion, Beecher's preaching and theology prevailed then as well as now: individuals need not sacrifice their intellects in order to be believing Christians.

Beecher evidently delivered his speeches and sermons effectively, yet a detailed analysis of his skills is difficult to delineate. Because Beecher spoke before the advent of sound and film and because contemporary reports, though effusive in his praise, were relatively unresponsive to the niceties of delivery, one can paint only a partial portrait of his *pronuntiatio*. Most sources agree that Beecher spoke in a rich baritone-to-bass-pitched voice, that he managed it melodiously, and that he easily addressed all 2,500-plus parishioners in his Plymouth Church. He realized the impact of powerful gestures and used his expressive facial visage to evoke the range of pathetical appeals. His bearing and erect posture on the platform communicated his presence to the people. In fact, some critics hold that Beecher's forte was playing to the hilt Henry Ward Beecher. He used pantomime in the pulpit to illustrate his points, he practiced and preached that the orator-preacher should address audiences conversationally, and he evidently had effective eye contact. This is inferred because he often spoke without notes, or if he had a manuscript, he relied on it sparingly. Consequently he was capable of delivering the caustic or humorous ad-lib remark (which is difficult for some speakers to exercise effectively because their attention is focused on their speech manuscripts rather than on their audiences' responses). Many of Beecher's printed speech texts indicate various kinds of audience reactions, and it is clear that Beecher played to them subsequently in his speech. For instance, at the emotionally charged Liverpool, England, speech on slavery in the United States, delivered on October 16, 1863, Beecher timed his ad-lib remarks to gain the goodwill of the audience: "In the first place I am ashamed to confess that such was the thoughtfullness—(interruption)—such was the stupor of the North—(renewed interruption)—you will get a word at a time; to-morrow will let folks see what it is you don't want to hear . . . (Applause and uproar)." For a campaign speech for Grover Cleveland—Beecher was a nominal Republican, but he supported the reform-minded Cleveland over James Blaine—Beecher effectively used humor in his rhetorical repartee:

Why, then, is it that I am now opposed to the organized movement of the Republican party? That is a significant question. For, gentlemen, I have never fed on official pap. (Laughter and applause.) I have never asked a favour for myself, nor could one be given me. I would not take a seat in the Senate of the United States, even if I could get it, and I fear that I am too good a man to get it. (Great laughter.)

Lionel Crocker quoted an incident at a lecture Beecher was giving where he rolled out a pompous period, "the voice of the people is the voice of God"—to which a drunk in the audience responded, "The voice of the people is the voice of a fool"—to which Beecher calmly retorted, to the crowd's great delight, "I said the voice of the people, not the voice of one man."

In preaching the gospel of love, Beecher may have carried the doctrine too far. The summer sex scandal of 1875 titillated Victorian sensibilities because it involved America's greatest preacher, Beecher himself. He allegedly seduced in 1855 the wife of a prominent parishioner of Plymouth Church, but the episode was hushed by the aggrieved husband in order not to harm Beecher's career. He was not so lucky the next time. In 1872, incriminating letters were leaked to the newspapers about Beecher's alleged seduction of a Mrs. Tilton, the wife of Beecher's colleague who was the editor of the religious journal the *Independent*, in 1868. The evidence in the case was biased from all of the principals, and the issues were confused and confusing. Beecher was finally acquitted in a criminal trial. So great was their esteem for him that his congregation raised $100,000 to help him pay his legal expenses. The Beecher-Tilton affair was important because it demonstrated the power of Beecher's established *ethos* on the age and on his congregation. His church, the community, and Victorian America rallied to his defense because they refused to believe that their symbol of Christian love and piety could stoop to sordid sexual imbroglios. To reject Beecher would in effect be to deny their identification with the man and his message, to deny his personal magnetism with the people. While the historical verdict acquitted him, the contemporary verdict is that Beecher probably did seduce at least Mrs. Tilton. Although the ordeal sapped the sixty-two-year-old man's strength and finances, it did not materially affect his position as America's minister until after his death.

If there is a key to understanding Beecher, it may well be that he was an orator first and a minister second. He did not visit the sick, did not make house calls, and knew the names of only wealthy people in his congregation. As his career developed, it seemed increasingly to be the case that public oratory was his profession and preaching his job. He was most unministerial. He thrived on being a controversial figure, on being a vocal advocate of causes and positions that would bring him personal acclamation, and on being a sought-after spokesman for Victorian values. Whether on the platform or in the pulpit, he conceived people to be an audience gathered to hear Henry Ward Beecher talk. Much of his rhetoric was personal aggrandizement. Yet through his oratorical career, he made a lasting impression on Victorian America. Robert Ingersoll, known as the Great Agnostic and a contemporary of Beecher, paid him a lasting compliment: "I think Mr. Beecher has liberalized the English-speaking people of the world." For forty years as a peripatetic preacher and secular speaker, Beecher never disappointed his audiences.

INFORMATION SOURCES

Research Collections and Collected Speeches

The Reverend Beecher's speech and sermon materials are located in the Beecher Family Papers, Sterling Library, Yale University, New Haven, Connecticut. The collection consists of speech outlines, sermon notes and notebooks, speech and sermon manuscripts, newspaper texts of addresses, printed editions, and pamphlet-like copies of speeches. About 200 sermons are arranged and accessible by biblical text, although many of these are undated; there are some 180 undated sermons arranged in a rough alphabetical order; and about 100 speeches exist, many fragments and many undated. A number of his lectures were delivered numerous times, and a record exists of time and place for some of them. Also included are T. J. Ellinwood's stenographic reports of Beecher's oratory. Some of these reports were edited by Beecher for later publicaton.

American Public Addresses: 1740–1952. Edited by A. Craig Baird. New   APA
    York: McGraw-Hill, 1956.
American Rebellion: Report of the Speeches of the Rev. Henry Ward Beecher.   AR
    London: Sampson Low and Son, 1864.
Henry Ward Beecher Papers, Beecher Family Papers, Sterling Library, Yale   HWBP
    University, New Haven, Conn.
Beecher, Henry Ward. *Patriotic Addresses.* New York: Fords, Howard, and   PA
    Hulbert, 1887.

―――. *Lectures and Orations by Henry Ward Beecher*. Edited by Newell   *LO*
Dwight Hillis. New York: Fleming H. Revell, 1913.

Sermons in American History. Edited by DeWitte Holland. Nashville: Abing-   *SAH*
don Press, 1971.

Selected Critical Studies

Crocker, Lionel. "Henry Ward Beecher." In *A History and Criticism of American Public
Address*. Edited by William Norwood Brigance. New York: McGraw-Hill, 1943.

―――. "Henry Ward Beecher and the English Press of 1863." *Speech Monographs* 6
(1939): 20–43.

―――. "Henry Ward Beecher at Fort Sumter, April 14, 1865." *Southern Speech
Communication Journal* 27 (1962): 273–83.

―――. "Lincoln and Beecher." *Southern Speech Communication Journal* 26 (1960):
149–59.

Holmes, Oliver Wendell. "The Minister Plenipotentiary." *Atlantic Monthly* 13 (1864):
106–12.

Oliver, Robert T. *History of Public Speaking in America*. Boston: Allyn and Bacon,
1965.

Selected Biographies

Clark, Clifford E., Jr. *Henry Ward Beecher*. Urbana: University of Illinois Press, 1978.

McLoughlin, William G. *The Meaning of Henry Ward Beecher*. New York: Alfred A.
Knopf, 1970.

Waller, Altina L. *Reverend Beecher and Mrs. Tilton*. Amherst: University of Massachusetts Press, 1982.

CHRONOLOGY OF MAJOR SPEECHES

See "Research Collections and Collected Speeches" for source codes.

Thanksgiving sermon, Indianapolis, Indiana, November 28, 1839; *HWBP*, ser. 2, box
52, folder 68.

Analysis of own sermon, n.p., December 27, 1847; *HWBP*, ser. 2, box 55, folder 256.

Sectional conflict speech, n.p., c. 1850s; *HWBP*, ser. 2, box 55, folder 260.

Speech at Sumner protest meeting, Broadway Tabernacle, New York, May 30, 1856;
New York Times, May 31, 1856, p. 1.

Series of speeches on slavery, Manchester, Glasgow, Edinburgh, Liverpool, and London,
October 9–20, 1863; *AR*, pp. 1–109; *PA*, pp. 437–573.

"Raising the Flag over Fort Sumter," Charleston, South Carolina, April 14, 1865; *PA*,
pp. 676–97.

Eulogy on Abraham Lincoln, Brooklyn, New York, April 23, 1865; *LO*, pp. 263–83;
PA, pp. 701–12.

"Conditions of a Restored Union," Brooklyn, New York, October 29, 1865; *PA*,
pp. 713–35.

"Eloquence and Oratory," Philadelphia, Pennsylvania, 1876; *LO*, pp. 128–56.

Speech at Brooklyn Rink, Brooklyn, New York, October 22, 1884; *LO*, pp. 284–311.

"The Two Revelations," Brooklyn, New York, May 31, 1885; *APA*, pp. 160–8.

"Divine Providence and Design," Brooklyn, New York, June 28, 1885; *SAH*, pp. 271–81.

Beecher delivered the following public lectures throughout his career in a number of places:

"Puritanism," *LO*, pp. 11–42.

"The Reign of the Common People," *LO*, pp. 94–127.

"The Wastes and Burdens of Society," *LO*, pp. 43–93.

THOMAS HART BENTON
(1782–1858), U.S. senator from Missouri
MICHAEL CASEY and THOMAS H. OLBRICHT

Throughout his thirty-year Senate career (1820–1850), Jacksonian democracy lay at the heart of Thomas Hart Benton's oratory. Benton was able to advance and sustain his political career by delivering and publishing his speeches. He studied briefly at the University of North Carolina where Blair's *Lectures* were taught, and when he started his law practice in Tennessee, he studied elocution to improve his speaking ability. At some point he also studied Cicero's rhetorical theory. He was enamored with the grand potential of the West and moved to St. Louis in 1815, becoming a protégé of the city's premier lawyer, eventually copying his speaking style. Through hard work and study, Benton quickly surpassed his mentor. Timothy Flint, a Presbyterian missionary, said Benton was unsurpassed at the bar despite his labored and florid style because he possessed the passion necessary for the frontier. In 1818 Benton became a newspaper editor and through his paper spread his visionary political views. Because of his high visibility as a lawyer and newspaper editor, he successfully won the U.S. Senate seat when Missouri attained statehood in 1820. Benton was well prepared for his Senate duties and became a skillful advocate for western causes.

BENTON AS A SENATORIAL RHETOR

Benton's work as a politician was just as important as that of his better-known colleagues—Henry Clay, Daniel Webster, and John Calhoun—though he was not as effective an orator as they in the Senate chamber. Because of his western and agrarian political interests, Benton's oratory differed markedly from the classical aristocratic styles of the eastern and southern establishments. He was a classic deliberative orator who, true to Aristotle's description, concerned himself with the future, the good, and the expedient. Nevertheless, the genesis of his rhetoric was a rhetorical vision of restoring a perfect past that would usher in the glorious political destiny of the United States.

This rhetorical vision had profound implications for his oratory and caused him to deviate sharply from standard classical prescriptions on speaking. To Benton, the past was the key to the future, an idea that recurs in his oratory. His grandiose vision of the West and Jacksonian America sprang from his own version of the ideals of Thomas Jefferson. This basic theme with all its variants cuts across all the political issues for which Benton fought: direct presidential elections, the destruction of the U.S. Bank, hard money, the central railroad, free public lands, and his defense of the Union. According to Benton's daughter, Jefferson's Louisiana Purchase awakened him to the possibilities of the West and helped him lay aside his English and eastern seaboard training. Benton saw Jefferson as the epitome of democratic ideals, and he believed that his own political purpose was to finish the revolution the founding fathers began, to labor "to preserve their work," and to do "justice to the PEOPLE who sustain such men.'' Individual rights, liberty, and the original intentions of the framers of the Constitution constituted a perfect political system. The ensuing chaos, or political problems of the country, were caused by a drifting from the primordial Constitution and the intentions of its framers by incorrect political legislation. Jackson, as he embodied Jeffersonian ideals, had captured the essence of the Constitution, and the country, by following Jefferson's and Jackson's ideals, could solve all its political problems.

Benton saw himself as a spokesperson for ''the people'' who upheld the primordial Constitution and legitimated it. ''Benton and the people, Benton and democracy are one and the same, sir,'' captured in a line Benton's vision, though his best biographer, William Chambers, thinks that the quotation is apocryphal. His Senate speech for the direct election of the president on January 30, 1824, has some of the key aspects of Benton's rhetorical vision. He objected to the electoral college since it was the ''favorite institution of aristocratic republics and elective monarchies'' and violated democratic ideals. Although the Constitution provided for electors, Benton argued that it violated the intention of the Constitution because electors could vote for whomever they wanted. According to Benton, ''the only effectual mode of preserving our government from the corruptions which have undermined the liberty of so many nations'' was to let the people elect the president. He esteemed ''the incorruptibility of the people'' to choose ''the best man for President.'' The will of the people and democracy were inherently perfect and upheld the Constitution as the means of solving America's political problems.

Benton's concept of the people and democracy rested clearly upon a vision of the West and working-class interests because what was best for that region was best for the people. The West, if it could participate fully in the political process, would ultimately fulfill the destiny of the United States. Benton repeatedly offered bills to the Senate to open up the public lands of the West by selling them at a fair price to settlers. In his public lands Senate speech on May 26, 1826, Benton argued that the inflated prices and unfair government regulation of the land kept people from moving west and slowed the nation's manifest destiny: ''The course of emigration is from East to West because it began in the East, and to accomplish the purposes of God, must end in the West.'' When the Mississippi region was settled and the Rocky Mountains passed, people would reach the Pacific Ocean, and ''the circumambulation of the globe will be completed.'' This rhetorical vision placed him ahead of his time on this and other issues. In 1849, before a usable steam engine was built, he proposed a bill for a national central highway so that a railroad could be built from St. Louis to the Pacific. Benton said in his February Senate speech for the bill that this was Jefferson's idea when he purchased the Louisiana Territory. Jefferson realized that all Western nations from Phoenicia to the present had sought trade with India and ''that wealth and power followed it, and disappeared upon its loss.'' Benton argued that roads were necessary for great empires and compared the project to the roads of the Roman empire because ''their magnificence—their grandeur" was "an example worthy of . . . imitation." This road to India through the West would "revive upon its line all the wonders we read about—and eclipse them. . . . A long line of cities will grow up. Existing cities will take a new start. . . . It is our destiny to give it . . . now, and hereafter, for thousands of years to come."

Benton gave similar speeches about the railroad in ceremonial and educational settings late in his career. In one of his most famous speeches, "There Is East: There Is India," delivered in St. Louis on October 17, 1849, at a national railroad convention, Benton said that the building of the steam car by the genius of science meant a fulfilling of Columbus's dream of "putting Europe and Asia into communication." After pushing for the railroad, he proposed carving a giant statue of Columbus out of a Rocky Mountain peak with his arm pointing to the West and saying to the passengers, "There is East: there is India!" Although his idea never was adopted by Congress, it was enthusiastically received by western audiences and foreshadowed later building of railroads across the West. His vision played well in western settings, but in Washington among friends as well as opponents, he was regarded as a wild visionary with impractical ideas.

Benton's restoration of Jeffersonian ideals also extended to advocacy of the gold standard and his war against the U.S. Bank. His greatest fame came from the advocacy of these views, earning him the nickname of Old Bullion. Several times Benton proposed bills to replace paper currency with hard money—gold and silver. In his Senate speech "Divorce of the Government from Banks," he argued, "To restore the currency of the constitution to the federal government— to re-establish the great acts of 1789 and of 1800—declaring that the revenues should be collected in gold and silver coin only. . . . I am for this restoration. . . . I am for carrying back this government to the solidity projected by its founders." This restoration of the past would bring "healing on its wings . . . safety to the government, and blessings to the people." In 1834 in his first speech on the "Revival of the Gold Standard," Benton claimed that when paper money took the place of hard money, "the whole edifice slid, at once, from the solid rock of gold and silver money, on which its founders placed it, into the troubled and tempestuous ocean of a paper currency." The paper money advocates or the U.S. Bank had also undervalued gold to keep hard money at a disadvantage to paper money. Benton complained that gold needed to be valued correctly, and he acknowledged that "the great apostle of American liberty (Mr. Jefferson)" said that "the value of gold was a commercial question, to be settled by its value in other countries." Again Benton's plans meant restoring a pure Jeffersonian past to solve the political problems of the time. The Second U.S. Bank was Benton's primary target in this speech and others. In his February 2, 1831, speech "Against the United States Bank," he objected to the bank because its power resided in a "remote and narrow corner of the Union, unconnected by any sympathy" with the West, where the "natural power of the Union—the power of numbers" would reside before the term of a proposed renewal charter would expire. Besides hurting the West by drawing off its wealth to the East, the bank made wealthy capitalists richer while it hurt small capitalists. Appealing to class prejudices, Benton claimed: "It is injurious to the laboring classes, because they receive no favors and have the price of the property they wish to acquire raised to the paper maximum." Benton, like other Jacksonians, tried to align the poorer classes of the East with the agrarian interests of the West to overcome the Whig establishment of the East.

This rhetorical vision of restoring Jeffersonian ideals had a dramatic impact on Benton's argumentation, his adaptation to audiences, and his speaking style. Benton primarily used argument by example, including those of Jefferson and the Constitution's framers. He also used stories from Greece, Rome, and England that upheld democratic principles of his vision of the West. For example, on January 25, 1825, Benton wanted Congress to appropriate funds to build and protect a road from Missouri to New Mexico that would extend 150 miles beyond the United States into Mexican territory to take advantage of growing trade between the United States and Mexico. Because of the unusual request to build a federal road on foreign territory, Benton found it "necessary to lay a foundation of facts" in his speech for the request. Benton's key argument was historical precedents or examples of past federal roads. His most important example came from Thomas Jefferson. In a conversation with Benton, Jefferson told Benton that in his last term as president, a federal road was built from Georgia to New Orleans through Spanish territory. He told Benton the maps of the road were in the Library of Congress. Benton found the statute book containing the laws on the road, read them to Congress, and then showed them the volume of maps he found as Jefferson had instructed him. The surprised senators passed Benton's bill. Benton's speeches were usually massive compilations of charts, tables, and historical examples that were painstakingly researched. He thought the facts of a case alone would persuade, particularly the historical precedents that showed proposed legislation was just the same as a Jeffersonian ideal. The ideals of Jefferson or the Constitution as cast in a rhetorical vision of the West could be repeated at any time in history. Therefore Benton felt he needed only to bring forward a historical precedent of the proposed legislation to prove its worth. This is an unusual case in which a rhetorical vision was made persuasive not by dramatic narrative but by the presentation of facts.

Because of these assumptions, Benton deliberately rejected the Ciceronian tradition. He believed his speeches differed from the prescriptions of the rhetoricians. He thought people were intelligent and attracted to practical proposals. To address the public, "I concluded that of the six parts of the regular oration, four parts might be thrown away: that I could dispense with all except the facts, and the application of the facts, cemented and enforced by reason. . . . My speeches were stripped of ornament, stinted on phrases, and crowded with material." His speeches were extraordinarily long. Some were delivered over two or three days. Most, especially those delivered early in his career, were ineffective in the Senate chamber. When he spoke, the chamber frequently emptied, and the galleries cleared. Many senators rustled papers or yawned whenever he paused to find needed documents. Daniel Webster commented on a speech against the bank that it was in Benton's usual style; he said a lot about the bank in a vague manner. Benton was always laborious with his documents.

Benton in the earlier part of his career at times cared little about the immediate audience in Washington, appealing instead to the larger audience, the people. Nineteenth-century America was a print culture. Although Benton did not make the best use of the oral word, he was a master of using the print medium to spread his speeches to larger audiences in the West. Most of his congressional speeches were printed into the official records, and he became angry when they were not printed accurately. Most were also reprinted as pamphlets to be distributed to wider audiences. Much like modern-day politicians who care little for the immediate context as they address the mass audience of the media, Benton did not mind if no one listened in the Senate because he was appealing to the larger audience, the people, who would bring political pressure to bear on Congress. He reprinted his speeches for bills on the selling of public lands despite the rejections of the bill because of their effect on the public.

His appeal to the people was not something his fellow politicians could ignore. John Quincy Adams when president complained that Benton's 1826 public lands speech excited and encouraged the hope in the West that land could be extorted from the government for nothing. Benton printed his speech in pamphlets and distributed it all over the country as he went home to Missouri. Adams grumbled that Benton made himself "amazingly popular" in the West by his speech and that the minds of the people on the subject were all debauched. Daniel Webster knew Benton's first speech in 1831 against the bank renewal charter was intended for print and circulation, so he and the Whig party planned a published reply. Benton knew that this speech would have little effect on the Senate; his proposal to stop the bank charter was defeated. Instead, he later reported in *Thirty Years View*: "it was a speech to be read by the people—the masses . . . and was conceived and delivered for that purpose; and was read by them; and has been complimented since, as having crippled the bank, and given it the wound of which it afterwards died."

The U.S. Senate on March 28, 1834, passed the famous resolution censoring President Jackson for ordering the removal of federal deposits from the Second U.S. Bank. Benton immediately promised to press for expurgation of the vote of censure. On three occasions, he tried unsuccessfully to pass the expunging resolution, finally succeeding on the fourth. Benton printed his unsuccessful speeches. His first speech in 1835 was designed not to influence the Senate, which still consisted of the members who censored Jackson; instead Benton hoped to influence the elections of 1836. He timed his second speech for the expunging resolution before the 1836 elections. His third and final speech on January 12, 1837, when the resolution was finally passed, was one of his most famous speeches, mainly a eulogy of Jackson's presidency as a new golden age or primordium where the ideals of the Constitution were realized or restored. Jackson's ideals were enduring and incorruptible by history, and Benton thought his own speech on Jackson would appeal to Americans of all ages.

Benton utilized the print medium effectively. His long-time friend, newspaper editor Francis Blair, believed that Benton's earliest printed speeches were better than their oral delivery. Benton sometimes presented an entire table of financial figures. His presentation of facts was most effective in the print medium and very dull and difficult to comprehend when delivered orally. His restoration archetype fit the print medium. It communicated the idea that Jeffersonian ideals were permanent throughout time. Just as the printed words on the page give the psychological impression of permanency, as Walter Ong noted, Benton's message and communication medium recreated the ideals of the Jeffersonian and made it appear that Jacksonian democracy was perfect and immune to the relativism of history and political problems. The message fit the medium and also adapted well to the audience to which Benton spoke.

Situations, however, are not stable. Benton, the Jacksonian, remained a senator long after Jacksonian democracy. He encountered new political problems, and his style shifted as his political circumstances began to change. Increasingly he found himself in disagreement with his fellow Democrats on many issues. The expansionist tendencies of westerners and many Democrats began to go beyond what Benton desired. He also became more seriously entangled in the political consequences of the Texas question. Texas had won its independence in 1836 from Mexico, and American settlers, many from Missouri, had moved there. Expansionists wanted the United States to annex Texas and extend the Texas border to the Rio Grande, territory still held by the Mexican government. President John Tyler negotiated a treaty with Texas for annexation to the Rio Grande, and John Calhoun made the treaty a test case over whether southern slave interests would be protected by the federal government. Benton led the opposition to the treaty in the Senate. In his May 1844 Senate speech against the treaty, Benton argued that the United States was overstepping the historical precedent and trying to take land that rightfully belonged to Mexico. "Now the real Texas . . . never approached the Rio Grande except near its mouth! while the upper part was settled by the Spaniards and the great part of it in the year 1694—just one hundred years before La Salle first saw Texas!" He implied that Mexico's claim to Texas through the Spanish settlement of Texas was one hundred years prior to the U.S. claim to Texas through the French settlement of the Louisiana Territory. To annex territory that had always been Spanish or Mexican was an outrage to Mexico. Benton gave a detailed reconstruction of the events that led the South to work for annexation. American fears that Texas would be seized by Britain were unfounded, and Benton saw the matter as a political ploy by Tyler to keep the presidency. Benton also shockingly announced that he would not support the extension of slavery into new territories, a complete change from his all-out proslavery position of 1829 that roused bitter opposition to Benton by Calhoun and other southern senators. Benton had earlier won many battles in the Senate with a West-South coalition, but now it was dead. He offered a counterbill that required negotiation with Mexico and hoped it would cool the ardor of the slavery question. After a brutal personal attack by Senator George McDuffie of South Carolina, Benton gave an electrifying impromptu reply to McDuffie on June 15, 1844, on Texas and disunion, attacking Calhoun and Tyler for raising the Texas issue. "Disunion is at the bottom of" the Texas problem. "Under the pretext of getting Texas into the Union, the scheme is to get the South out of it" into a separate "confederacy." Benton saw the southerners and the Texas question as a threat to his rhetorical vision. The American democracy and Jeffersonian ideals would be destroyed by disunion. This outweighed the slave question and even outweighed annexing Texas. Francis Blair described the speech as "more vehement in manner and unsparing in expression than any I have heard from Benton." This was the beginning of a shift in Benton's speaking tactics.

From that point on, Benton was on the defensive. Many of his constituents were supporters of the defeated annexation treaty. Benton was barely reelected in 1844, but he continued to find himself voting against his fellow Democrats and Missourians in the 1840s. The Missouri State legislature in March 1849 passed the Jackson resolutions that declared Missouri's support for the slave-holding states against "northern fanaticism" and instructed Missouri congressmen to "act in conformity" with them. The resolutions were designed to kill Benton politically. From May to early November, Benton toured Missouri making speeches with his appeal to the people of Missouri. His most famous speech of the tour was given at Jefferson City on May 26, 1849. Benton blamed the Jackson resolutions on Calhoun, claiming they were part of an elaborate plot by Calhoun to divide the Union. In his conclusion Benton uttered an oft-quoted phrase, which he repeated in later speeches: "Now I have them [Calhoun and the South], and between them and me, henceforth and forever, a *high wall and a deep ditch*! and no communication, no compromise, no caucus with them." The five-month tour was wild and rancorous. Benton went into slaveholding towns under threats on his life. A war of words in pamphlets and newspapers ensued. Benton's biographer, William Chambers, reports that Benton's enemies called him "renegade, traitor, abolitionist, apostate, liar." One person even called him a "God dam'd liar." At Fayette, Missouri, the crowd began "braying, whistling, yelling, and groaning" as he walked to the stand. Within fifteen minutes, "the insulters were cowed." Francis Blair described Benton putting on a fight against the local politicians like a great bear surrounded by a yelping pack of whelps. "He slaps one down on this—another on that—and grips a third with his teeth, then tosses him with his snout." Benton's speaking clearly came alive while defending his convictions against hostile crowds. This carried over even to the Senate chamber. He now spoke without notes and with such emotion that the galleries were packed. Blair, who once preferred reading Benton's speeches, now thought his printed speeches were not comparable to his oral delivery. He saved some of his best oral speeches for the great debate over the

Compromise of 1850. The different territories gained in the Mexican War, especially California, now wanted statehood. New Mexico and Texas were about to start a "private little" war over their shared border. The slave question worsened because the questions of how far to extend slavery and what to do about runaway slaves could not be settled. Henry Clay proposed a compromise on these questions that finally came out of a committee headed by Clay and was labeled the omnibus bill. Clay in his speech for the bill had counted on his fingers five "gaping wounds" that the bill would heal. Benton sarcastically replied in his anti-compromise speech delivered on June 10, 1850, that if Clay had more fingers and even toes on his hand, he might come up with more points. The "problem" did not exist. The bill simply was five old bills "altered just enough to spoil each, then tacked together, and christened a compromise, and pressed upon the Senate as a sovereign remedy for calamities which have no existence." The questions also were unrelated, and Benton urged that the omnibus bill be rejected and that each question be debated individually. William Seward thought the satire and ridicule directed at Clay and the committee helped Benton make a powerful onslaught on the bill as he delivered the speech. Although Benton faced great opposition, the speech brought laughter and cheers from his audience. The omnibus bill was defeated, and the Senate took up the issues one by one and passed them on that basis. These were Benton's last efforts at senatorial rhetoric. The Missouri opposition was too well organized and despite his speaking tour of 1849, Missouri was proslavery. He was defeated in the 1850 election.

It is difficult to assess Benton's delivery. The descriptions are extremely biased because of the bitter partisan politics: friends praised him too much and enemies ridiculed him too quickly. He clearly read massive amounts of material in his early speeches, but, as he fought for the survival of his political ideas, he switched to an extemporaneous delivery. A New York congressman described Benton in 1828 as a handsome man. He thought Benton's delivery was accurate and distinct and that his words flowed sensibly and fluently, always in a soft, winning tone, except when he was angry; then no one could speak and look more terrible. In 1832 a hostile journalist said Benton thundered in a roaring voice as he lifted his arms, and he had a horrible jumble of newspapers and documents on his table. In contrast, a friendly journalist believed his style was trenchant and elevated. In 1836 an anti-Jackson man gave what is probably an accurate assessment: that Benton was a powerful first-rate orator who spoke with ease, grace, and elegance. The English traveler Sarah Mytton Maury commented later that Benton delivered a speech with much dignity; he was rarely excited, his movement and gestures were expressive, and his speech deliberate.

Benton in his long career in the Senate became an effective advocate for Western interests and Jacksonian democracy. When he delivered them, his speeches were relatively ineffective in the Senate because they were too long, and Benton tended to read copiously from documents. But these same qualities made his speeches effective pamphlets and built a national audience for Jackson's political platform, forcing the Whigs to come to terms with his arguments. Most recognized that Benton could take political issues and put them into language that the common people understood. His grand rhetorical vision was one his western constituents shared, and it eventually propelled the United States into its present status. As a politician, Benton deserves to be remembered with Clay, Webster, and Calhoun. As an orator, he was not their equal because he refused to follow classical rhetorical prescriptions used by the aristocratic segments of American society. Still he had an eloquence and a rhetorical effectiveness based on a rhetorical vision of restoring Jeffersonian ideals. Benton embodied the strengths and weaknesses of Jacksonian democracy.

INFORMATION SOURCES

Research Collections and Collected Speeches

Many of Benton's papers and presumably all of his speech manuscripts were lost in 1855 when his house in Washington burned. Two important collections of Benton papers do exist at the Missouri Historical Society, St. Louis, Missouri, and at the Missouri State Historical Society, Columbia, Missouri, respectively. Benton's letters and manuscripts are scattered all over the country in various collections of papers of Benton's political contemporaries. The greatest collection of these papers can be found at the Library of Congress, Washington, D.C. Most of Benton's Senate speeches are preserved in published congressional records. Many are also accessible in Benton's two-volume political history of Congress, *Thirty Years View*. Many of Benton's speeches printed as individual pamphlets can be found in various libraries across the country. Several of Benton's campaign speeches in Missouri are available in Missouri newspapers at the Missouri State Historical Society.

Annals of the Congress of the United States. 1819–1824.	AC
Benton, Thomas Hart. *Thirty Years View: or A History of the Working of the American Government for Thirty Years, from 1820 to 1850*. 2 vols. New York: Appleton, 1854, 1856.	TYV
Congressional Globe. 1833–1850.	CG
Jefferson Inquirer (Jefferson City, Mo.).	JI
Register of Debates in Congress, 1824–37.	RD
World's Greatest Orations. Edited by David J. Brewer. St. Louis: Ferd P. Kaiser, 1900.	WGO

Selected Critical Studies

Bierbaum, M. Eugene. "Thomas Hart Benton's Union Speaking in Missouri." *Southern Speech Journal* 34 (1968–1969): 115–25.

Hunter, Charles F. "Thomas Hart Benton: An Evaluation." *Quarterly Journal of Speech* 30 (1944): 279–85.

Lewis, Thomas R. "Thomas Hart Benton's Analysis of His Audience." *Quarterly Journal of Speech* 35 (1949): 441–47.

Mattis, Norman W. "Thomas Hart Benton." In *A History and Criticism of American Public Address*. Edited by Marie Hochmuth. New York: Longmans, Green, 1955.

Seelen, William E. "Thomas Hart Benton's Expunging Speech: An Analysis of the Immediate Audience." *Speech Monographs* 8 (1941): 58–67.

Selected Biographies

Chambers, William Nesbet. *Old Bullion Benton: Senator from the New West*. Boston: Little, Brown, 1956.

Frémont, Jessie Benton. "Biographical Sketch of Senator Benton in Connection With Western Expansion." In John Charles Freemont, *Memoirs of My Life*. Chicago and New York: Belford, Clarke, 1887.

Smith, Elbert B. *The Magnificent Missourian*. New York: Lippincott, 1958.

CHRONOLOGY OF MAJOR SPEECHES

See "Research Collections and Collected Speeches" for source codes.

Speech on election of president, Washington, D.C., January 30, February 2, 3, 1824; *AC*, 18th Cong., 1st sess., pp. 168–204; *TYV*, 1: 37–41.

Speech on road to New Mexico, Washington, D.C., January 25, 1825; *RD*, 18th Cong., 2d Sess., pp. 342–48; *TYV*, 1: 41–44.

Speech on sale of public lands, Washington, D.C., May 26, 1826; *RD*, 19th Cong., 1st sess. pp. 720–49.

Against the U.S. Bank, Washington, D.C., February 2, 1831; *RD*, 21st Cong., 2d sess., pp. 46–78; *WGO*, pp. 425–29.

"Revival of the Gold Standard," Washington, D.C., March 21, 22, 1834; *RD*, 23d Cong., 1st sess., pp. 1073–1105; *TYV*, 1: 436–58.

First expunging speech, Washington, D.C., February 27, 1835; *RD*, 23d Cong., 2d sess., pp. 631–60; *TYV*, 1: 529–49.

Second expunging speech, Washington, D.C., March 18, 1836; *RD*, 24th Cong., 1st sess., pp. 877–933; *TYV* 1: 645–9.

Third expunging speech or "The Political Career of Andrew Jackson," Washington, D.C., January 12, 1837; *TYV*, 1: 719–31; *WGO*, pp. 411–25.

"The Divorce of the Government from Banks," Washington, D.C., September 22, 1837; *CG*, 26th Cong., 1st sess., appendix, pp. 119.

Against Texas Annexation treaty, Washington, D.C., May 16, 18, 20, 1844; *CG*, 28th Cong., 1st sess., Appendix, pp. 474–86; *TYV*, 2: 600–13.

"Texas or Disunion," in reply to McDuffie, Washington, D.C., June 15, 1844; *TYV*, 2: 613–16.

"Highway from the Mississippi to the Pacific Ocean," Washington, D.C., February 7, 1849; *CG*, 30th Cong., 2d sess., pp. 470–74.

Union speech, Jefferson City, Missouri, May 26, 1849; *JI*, May 26, 1849.

Union speech, Fayette, Missouri, September 1, 1849; *JI*, October 6, 1849.

"There Is East: There Is India," St. Louis, Missouri, October 17, 1849; *WGO*, pp. 429–30.

Anti-compromise speech, Washington, D.C., June 10, 1850; *CG*, 31st Cong., 1st sess., pp. 1173, Appendix, pp. 676–84; *TYV*, 2: 749–65.

PHILLIPS BROOKS
(1835–1893) Episcopal rector and bishop
THOMAS H. OLBRICHT and MICHAEL CASEY

Phillips Brooks was among the foremost American preachers of his era and was widely acclaimed beyond his denomination in both the United States and England. He served on numerous governmental, cultural, and educational boards and received recognition as a capable administrator.

Brooks first came to the attention of his Harvard classmates as a writer of essays that he read in their rooms. They recalled his mature thinking, word choice, and clarity. In his junior year, he received the Bowdoin Prize for his essay, "The Teaching of Tacitus Regarding Fate and Destiny." Courses in elocution were offered at both Harvard and Virginia Theological Seminary, where Brooks received his theological training between 1856 and 1859, but he rejected elocution as mechanical and unnatural. Even then he sought a personal style. He did not aspire to notoriety as a orator, but his persistence and facility at writing foreshadowed his later acclaim as a preacher inasmuch as he wrote the majority of his sermons.

Although Brooks relished his pastoral duties, he served the church foremost through his intense proclamation of the faith. His sermonic skills surfaced immediately upon accepting a rectorship, that of the Church of the Advent in Philadelphia (1859–1861). As news of his speaking ability spread, the crowds increased weekly. Through pulpit exchanges, others witnessed his prowess. Soon the premier Episcopal church in Philadelphia, Holy Trinity, called him (1861–1869). His majestical rhetoric became known throughout the Northeast, and in another decade he accepted a ministry in Boston, where his fame grew nationally and internationally as rector of Trinity Church (1869–1891). He spent much time in travel and preached outside the United States, including before Queen Victoria in 1879. His influence spread through the publication of sermons. The earliest volume, *The Purpose and Use of Comfort*, appeared in 1878 and sold 25,000 copies in the first printing. At the time of his death in 1893, he was bishop of Massachusetts and the most respected American Protestant minister.

PHILLIPS BROOKS AS A PREACHER AND HOMILETICIAN

The characteristics of Brooks's preaching most frequently commented on were the intensity and rapidity of delivery, the clarity and eloquence of style, and his penetrating insight into the concerns, anxieties, and aspirations of humankind.

People who heard Brooks for the first time almost to a person reported that they were unprepared for his intensity and his speaking rate of 215 words per minute. His intensity derived from his complete submersion into the task at hand. This was obvious both in voice and body. He usually began in a subdued tone but soon increased the volume in a rising crescendo that converged with an increasing bodily tension, rising and falling with the demands of the ideas. His voice was melodic but not noteworthy. Brooks stood in one spot behind the podium and gestured infrequently with his right hand. The result was not as it might seem, since the whole of his body responded and converged with his voice and content. He seldom looked at the audience. His eyes were either glued to the manuscript or lifted toward the sounding board above his head. Regardless, the total effect electrified the congregation and resulted in a search of heart and a buoyancy of the spirit.

Brooks attributed the clarity and eloquence of his style to painstaking writing. The finished product was a thirty-page manuscript that he read at the rate of a page a minute. Before moving to Boston, Brooks wrote almost all his sermons. After that time, his addresses became so numerous that sometimes he resorted to extensive outlining, which he carried to the speaker's stand but seldom used. The ideal to him was, however, the manuscript sermon. He made it clear in his *Lectures on Preaching* that cogency, systematic thought, and elevated language resulted from writing. He therefore wrote sermons until the end of his career. Sometimes Brooks's listeners preferred the extempore, but he feared that inadequate preparation would lead to laziness. His sermons were rich in metaphor, sometimes one running through the whole sermon, as in "The Candle of the Lord." His language was elevated; it eschewed the commonplace but also intellectualistic or technical theological terms. His incoming correspondence made it clear that his word craftsmanship appealed to persons of all socioeconomic levels. It was fresh and alive yet elevated. He seldom, however, depicted experiences in highly descriptive and emotive words in the manner of Robert Ingersoll.

Brooks's sermons invariably commenced with a text. He was careful in text selection. Only in a few cases can the biblical scholar charge misapplication. Sometimes the direction in which Brooks moved was more metaphorical than literal. In most instances the text served as a launching pad for the sermon theme. After a paragraph or two, the text receded into the background. Long explications of singular texts are almost nonexistent. From his correspondence, it is clear that Brooks read commentaries, but detailed exposition based on the results of such reading never surfaced in the sermons. Scriptures in addition to the text were frequently cited in the body of the sermon but never explicated at length. Though Brooks read much, he seldom quoted anyone, whether Biblical exegete, theologian, biographer, or novelist. The results of such reading appear, but only infrequently did he identify speakers. Brooks counseled infrequent quoting on the grounds that most quoting is undigested. By far the predominant amplification in Brooks's sermons involved careful and insightful scrutiny of human anxiety and inadequacy yet aspiration to improvement, hope, and belief. Brooks's analysis of the human situation could be compared with the phenomenological method of Edmund Husserl, but the presuppositions and rigor differed. Brooks's analysis eschewed philosophical sophistication but captivated intellectuals and the uneducated alike. Many letters to him attested that they left the church having been immersed in self-inspection yet affirmed, challenged, and inspired to improve their morality and service. It is clear that Brooks achieved his goal of lifting his congregation to a new vision of and commitment to the Christian faith.

As the Civil War wound down, the twenty-eight-year-old rector of Holy Trinity in Philadelphia preached a sermon titled "The Eternal Humanity" on June 12, 1864. The war had highlighted man's inhumanity to man. A further cloud on the horizon was the publication of Darwin's *Origin of the Species* in 1859. In Darwin's version, man is the most developed and complicated of the animal species, evolving morally as well as biologically. Brooks set out to challenge this wave of pessimism regarding human nature.

The sermon focused on Revelation 12:13 "I am Alpha and Omega, the Beginning and the End, the First and the Last." From the eternal character of Christ as human-divine, Brooks posited an ontological origin for man who is made in the image of Christ. Christ is the Alpha in that there has always been "a Divine Human in the Godhead." He is likewise the Omega in that "the ascended Saviour speaking or acting still is the same genuine humanity which He had worn on earth." In this fresh, creative manner, Brooks developed the fourth-century doctrine that God is eternally Father, Son, and Spirit. This affirmation does not set aside the necessity of the atonement. An arm grows properly on its own unless broken and then needs a remedy. So man bears the image of Christ the eternal God-man until such time as his life becomes distorted and broken. At that time, the cross of Christ addresses his brokenness and sets him on the right track again.

What are the implications of eternal humanity for the human plight? Brooks answered plainly by a rhetorical question: "What if the type of this life I live were part and parcel of the everlasting Godhead?" Man is situated ontologically in the one who himself is the God-man. This ontological status, however, does not prevent man from distorting the image he bears. It declares his worth; it sets before him his prospects. Brooks now addressed "the tendencies of modern science towards a depreciation of what has always been considered the unshared honor of humanity." He set out the claims of Darwinism but did not refute details. Rather he contrasted Darwinian ontology with a Christ ontology. He rejected the charge that human origins are located in the material universe and argued that they are situated in Christ: "In Him I find the eternal pattern after which my nature was to be fashioned."

Brooks's rhetorical strategy in this sermon was sound as well as profound. He gathered up age-old Christology, reclothed it in fresh terminology, and applied it to the gloomy prognostication for humanity of the Civil War years. His auditors shared enough of his presuppositions to hear him out. The freshness and clarity of his ideas went a long way toward affirming his congregation in the eternal prospects for humanity. He did not confront the opponent head on but engineered an end run and, in the eyes of the congregation, victoriously crossed the goal line.

While the body of Abraham Lincoln lay in Philadelphia, April 23, 1865,

Brooks delivered his Lincoln address. He focused on character, "the only destiny or fate" of humankind. He highlighted Lincoln's growing up among men and things, not words and theories. He identified his character in his work—hence for Brooks his health—and in his intellect, which according to Brooks cannot be separated from his moral nature. He refrained from discussing whether Lincoln was an intellectual. No one "can tell you today whether the wise judgments that he gave came most from a strong head or a sound heart."

These characteristics opposed another character, that of southerners who espoused Old World feudalism, a way that depreciated labor and despised it: "The one was ready to state broad principles, of the brotherhood of man, the universal fatherhood and justice of God . . . the other denied even the principles." For Brooks a clash of such characteristics was inevitable regardless of whether the approach of the northern abolitionists was viable. It was inevitable "that a great wrong asserting itself vehemently should arouse to no less vehement assertion the opposing right." Lincoln, according to Brooks, opposed the wrong almost single-handed. He was the man God prepared for the task since his life and person was the result of free life and institutions. Brooks ended the speech singling out those Lincoln touched and those who persisted in atrocities and, in anticipation, that the challenge of Lincoln by his death furthered the cause for which he stood. He closed by reading the Gettysburg Address.

The address centered around a theme. Brooks made only one reference to Lincoln's body lying in the city. It was the man's cause that captured Brooks's attention. The speech moved unerringly to its goal: calling men to rightness and liberty with Lincoln as model. It was coherent, discrete, and forceful.

"The Candle of the Lord," which Brooks preached on several occasions, is noteworthy for the manner in which the imagery of candle, light, and fire pervaded the entire address. The text was from Proverbs 20:27: "The Spirit of man is the candle of the Lord." Brooks's interpretation demanded that the human soul has a natural affinity for the fueling of God's goodness just as a candle sustains a flame. The soul therefore has an ontology, but not self-sustained as with Plato. It draws its fire and its purpose from God. Brooks moved in the direction of Emerson and Wadsworth, but he stopped short. The human soul transcends matter not independently but so as to be fired by God. The question of whether Brooks has misused this text is appropriate. The New International Version of the bible translates the proverb, "The lamp of the Lord searches the spirit of man." But the idea is biblical in that man is an instrument through whom God carries out his work and service. Brooks came quickly to the point that some men light up a community or a room. Those who do sustain the flame from God. The human scandal is that many fail to open their lives to the flame. The power of this famous sermon lies in the metaphor, which serves as the rallying point for both theology and application. While the sermon addressed the individual, it did so more obliquely than in "The Eternal Humanity." As Phillips matured, his sermons contained less direct exhortation.

Brooks gave the sermon "The Young and Old Christians" in 1871, not long after he began his ministry at Trinity Church, Boston. In it he sought to articulate more clearly his perspective on the central doctrines of the Christian faith, which he defined as "God's being, God's care, Christ's incarnation, Christ's atonement, immortality." Brooks took his text from Deuteronomy 33:16 in which he envisioned an old Moses reminiscing over his experience as a young man at the burning bush. This interpretation is in some measure fanciful, but it exhibited Brooks's typical employment of texts. He used texts not so much as proof but as an imaginative prolegomenon to the theme, in this case the religious proclivities of the young and the old. He did so because "we hear all around us now-a-days a great impatience with the prominence of dogma—that is, of truth abstractly and definitely stated—in Christianity." In the sermon he developed the view that young Christians are inclined to hold doctrines uniformly and conceptualize them crudely and dogmatically. Older Christians, in contrast, have learned to flesh out doctrines in life. Objections as the young perceive doctrine are well taken. Persons mature in the faith are much more diverse in outlook because they have incorporated and tailored doctrine for the circumstances of their lives. As as example he cited the apostles who, from his perspective, were much alike when they first met the Lord. But after they had been with the Lord for several months, they flowered as individuals. The mature Christian is the one who recognizes and welcomes "individual difference of thought and feeling and actions."

This sermon has a prolegomenon to Brooks's broad churchmanship. In it he embraced the standard doctrines of the Christian faith but not in a dogmatic sense, recognizing that when incorporated into life, they become different for different persons. The approach and strategy of the sermon was good, particularly effective for the indifferent or to one offended by doctrine. The narrow-minded would not be won over, but because of Brooks's reputation, they were a minority at Trinity. In "The Symbol and the Reality," preached at Trinity in 1878, Brooks applied the same strategy to rites and ceremonies, liturgy, and the apostolic succession. The purpose of these are not for their own sake or to make the church exclusive and mechanical but to bring the believer closer to God. Likewise in "The Mitigation of Theology," October 27, 1878, Brooks addressed the change adumbrated by the desire "to escape from the severer, stricter, more formal, more exacting statements of truth and duty, and to lay hold of the gentler, more gracious, more spiritual, more indulgent representations of God and what He asks of man." Brooks openly identified with the change but cautioned that this change in itself would not bring anyone closer to God. In this sermon more than in others, Brooks provided the historical backdrop for his remarks, commenting on Puritan theology of a generation ago. He found good even there because of its vision of "the sacredness of duty and the awfulness of life," which any theology must maintain. The newer theology can contribute to the faith only if it underpins the "everlasting need of moral struggle, of patient watchfulness over ourselves, or resolute faith with ourselves and of humble prayer to God, and of brotherly devotion to our brethren which alone makes us truly men.'' In this last sermon, Brooks seemed to speak to the avant-garde of the congregation but whether successfully seems questionable because these characteristics likely were no more a high priority with them than was doctrine. But no doubt he affirmed and concretized the convictions of the majority.

In 1883 Brooks went to England. His fame went ahead of him, and large crowds attended his services in several different churches. One might suppose that a somewhat different rhetorical strategy would be demanded, but it is difficult to detect differences. As usual, Brooks made no reference to local situations or customs. In fact, for the most part, he read sermons already written and preached in Massachusetts. His assumption was that humanity and human needs are essentially universal. The assumption was apparently correct, at least in respect to England. He received the same rave notices there as in Boston. His sermon "The Sufficient Grace of God,'' preached at St. Marks Church, London, June 3, 1883, was developed in the typical manner. He distinguished between the person who envisions God as a powerful magistrate and the one who perceives him as the pervasive source of power. He delineated a church that focused on the prerogatives of God at its disposal from one that is "a vital union by love and obedience.'' The praiseworthy believer, the commendable church, is that for whom the grace of God is sufficient. The same may be observed in regard to the sermon "Gamaliel,'' a favorite with Brooks preached at Temple Church, London, July 1, 1883. The sermon was somewhat different from others in that it focused on one individual, but the content made the same points on broad churchmanship characteristic of Brooks in this period. Gamaliel was commended because he upheld the search for truth: "He who is seeking anywhere for truth loses the true spirit of his search if he forbids any other man to seek for truth anywhere else.'' Gamaliel served as a premier model because he was a man "of wise and generous toleration.'' Brooks's latitudinarianism also showed itself in his declaration that Gamaliel "must somewhere, sometime—if not here, than beyond—have come to the truth and to the Christ himself.'' The sermon was one of great power, and Brooks obviously employed the textual account of Gamaliel in an exemplary manner.

Brooks's sermons pertaining to the church calendar do not differ in structure and refer even less to the climate of the time. He addressed perennial foundation points for the church through the ages and therefore apparently envisioned that his remarks transcended place and time. We shall examine three of these on Christmas, Trinity Sunday, and Easter. These sermons are undated but were probably preached in the 1880s in Trinity Church, Boston.

For his Christmas Eve sermon, Brooks took his text from Luke 2:7: "Because there was no room for them in the inn.'' One might expect since the incarnation was the center of Christian doctrine for Brooks that his sermon would focus on some aspect of how God became man. But he apparently took seriously the growing loss of appetite for doctrine from the divine prospective and focused on the propensity of humans, Christians or not, to crowd God out of their lives. Men generally are overfull: "Every chamber of the intellect, from garret to cellar, is preengaged. Science, morals and physics, politics, history, art—all these are with us and must be royally fed and lodged." He ended with a plea: "Let us give up our lives to Him and beg that He will rule them."

In "A Trinity-Sunday Sermon," Brooks became more doctrinal in the traditional sense, but the trinity he presented was one of revelation or salvation, not essence in the manner of the fourth-century Greek fathers. Even the trinity, for Brooks, was human related. But then a trinity of revelation is more New Testament than one of essence. The three are revealed to humanity by their work or action. God is creator, Christ redeemer, and the Holy Spirit the sanctifier. All pertain to human salvation but are not three salvations, just as a child's education extended over twenty years with many different teachers is nevertheless one. Toward the end of the sermon, Brooks attacked certain deviant views. These have theological names, but Brooks, as is typical, avoided the technical vocabulary. For him the bottom line is that each of the three be divine: "That is our faith in the Trinity,—three Persons and one God." For Brooks's congregation, these remarks were entirely appropriate, and persons accustomed to more traditional formulations should not have been alienated.

In "An Easter Sermon," Brooks took his text from Revelation. He did not come to the text immediately but utilized "He that liveth, and was dead" throughout the sermon. Theological beginning points differ. In the past two decades under the influence of Wolfhardt Pannenberg and Jurgen Moltmann, the resurrection had surfaced as the foundation for Christology. But Brooks was more interested in the divine-human image of man in the present, not the future of man adumbrated by the resurrection. The outcome of the resurrection must be not an item in a creed but a vital life-changing event: "Oh that everything dead and formal might go out of our creed, out of our life, out of our heart today. He is Alive! Do you believe it? . . . Oh if we could only lift up our heads and live with Him."

Brooks preached the sermon "Foreign Mission" in Boston, January 20, 1889, only four years prior to his death. The pattern of the sermon remained the same. The foundations for missions, according to Brooks, are that the church needs to take its message of life and salvation, and the ends of the world desire that it should come, though it is only half-conscious of its need. In a somewhat longer section than normal, in the middle of the sermon, Brooks took to task past failures of the Puritans to engage in missions. Of note were the efforts of Eliot with the Indians but little other than that. He felt the failure to carry the gospel to the native Americans caused the Puritans to turn inward and carry on inconsequential, if not damaging, intramural disputes. He cited with approval the early nineteenth-century mission efforts originating in Williamstown, Massachusetts. Those who still resisted he compared with the Jews of the biblical period. Brooks only on occasion engaged in negative analysis of the past and present, usually only briefly to move on to positive motivations and theology.

Brooks was one of the most highly regarded pulpit ministers of his age. He believed that truth should be mediated through personality. He himself was a case in point. Because of his life of high principles, community and educational service, and a distaste for grappling in petty disputes, he exuded high credibility with most persons, the only reservation being his broad churchmanship among those less ecumenical. The intensity of delivery as a manifestation of belief provided the other dimension of his ethos. He eschewed autobiographical references in his sermons, as he made clear in his *Lectures on Preaching*. He revealed little of either his outer or inner history. Though he knew most of the important people of the United States and Europe, without exception he avoided any indication of these acquaintanceships in sermons. The truth Brooks heralded pertained to the central Christian beliefs, found in some measure in the Scriptures and mediated through mainstream Christian history and particularly as fleshed out in the lives of those who enthusiastically embraced the faith.

Some changes may be discovered in Brooks's sermons but the same modus operandi and person are apparent throughout his career. It is difficult to pick up a sermon of Brooks, early or late, and not discover a continuity in style and approach. Some earlier sermons were more doctrinal in the traditional sense, though developed from Brooks's fresh perspective, and more cogent and direct, exuding the exuberance of youth. The more mature sermons drew on more aspects of human experience, rallied around a central theme, but were more diffuse. They still elicited action from the auditors but with less direct exhortation. It has been said that as Brooks matured, his own emotional response became increasingly obvious. The great preachers in the late nineteenth century occupied much space on the front page. Phillips Brooks received more than his share.

INFORMATION SOURCES

Research Collections and Collected Speeches

The most extensive collection of Brooks's sermons, letters, school records and compositions, his journal, and notebooks may be found in Houghton Library, Harvard University. Other collections of lesser magnitude are located at the University of Southern California, Los Angeles, and the Boston Athenaeum. Of the 814 numbered sermons, approximately two-thirds remain. Four hundred may be found in the Harvard collection. Two hundred are found in the ten-sermon volumes. The manuscripts for these sermons presumably were employed in typesetting and subsequently destroyed. The other sermons are either widely scattered or lost. In a letter to William Stevens in 1881, Brooks mentioned that many of his sermons had been destroyed. The Houghton collection also contains 585 outlines, work sheets, and lecture notes. The ten-volume set of sermons was reprinted as many as six times and later issued in a series of volumes. Brooks selected the sermons for the first five volumes; those of the last five were probably made by his brothers. The ten-volume collection is as follows, all published by E. P. Dutton & Company, New York:

The Purpose and Use of Comfort, 1878.   PUC
The Candle of the Lord, 1881.   COL
Sermons Preached in English Churches, also London, 1883.   SPE

Twenty Sermons, 1886, later *Visions and Tasks*.
The Light of the World, 1890.
The Battle of Life, 1893.   *BOL*
Sermons for the Principal Festivals and Fasts of the Church Year, edited   *PFF*
    by John Cotton Brooks, 1895.
New Starts in Life, 1896.   *NSL*
The Law of Growth, 1902.
Seeking Life, 1904.
Addresses by Phillips Brooks. Philadelphia: Henry Altemus, n.d.   *APB*
    For a complete listing of other individual addresses and collections see:
Albright, Raymond W. *Focus on Infinity A Life of Phillips Brooks*. New York: Macmillan,
    1961.
Lectures on Preaching. London: H. R. Allenson, 1895.

Selected Critical Studies

Cunningham, Raymond J. "From Preachers of the Word to Physician of the Soul: The
    Protestant Pastor in 19th Century America." *Journal of Religious History* 3 (1965):
    327–46.
Ensley, Francis Gerald. "Phillips Brooks and the Incarnation." *Religion in Life* 20 (1951):
    350–61.
Hance, Kenneth G. "Elements of the Rhetorical Theory of Phillips Brooks." *Speech
    Monographs* 5 (1938): 16–39.
Hochmuth, Marie, and Norman W. Mattis. "Phillips Brooks." In *A History and Criticism
    of American Public Address*. Edited by William Norwood Brigance. New York:
    McGraw-Hill, 1943.
McLeon, N. Bruce. "The Preaching of Phillips Brooks: A Study of Relevance versus
    Eternal Trust." *Religion in Life* 34 (1964): 50–67.
Politzer, Jerome R. "Theological Ideas in the Preaching of Phillips Brooks." *History
    Magazine of the Protestant Episcopal Church* 33 (1964): 157–69.

Selected Biographies

Albright, Raymond W. *Focus on Infinity: A Life of Phillips Brooks*. New York: Mac-
    millan, 1961.
Allen, Alexander V. G. *Life and Letters of Phillips Brooks*. 2 vols. New York: E. P.
    Dutton, 1900.
————. *Phillips Brooks 1835–1893: Memories of His Life with Extracts from his Letters
    and Note-Books*. London: Hodder and Stoughton, 1908.
Lawrence, William. *Life of Phillips Brooks*. New York: Harper & Brothers, 1930.

CHRONOLOGY OF MAJOR SPEECHES

It is not now possible to date all of Brooks's major addresses, especially the more
famous ones he preached on many occasions, since the manuscripts were thrown away.
"The Eternal Humanity," Holy Trinity Church, Philadelphia; June 12, 1864, *BOL*,
pp. 310–26.

Abraham Lincoln address, Philadelphia, April 23, 1865; *APB*, pp. 140–65.

"The Candle of the Lord"; *COL*, pp. 1–21.

"The Young and Old Christians," Trinity Church, Boston, 1871; *COL*, pp. 39–59.

"The Symbol and the Reality," Trinity Church, Boston, 1878; *PUC*, pp. 282–98.

"The Mitigation of Theology," October 27, 1878; *NSL*, pp. 337–56.

"The Sufficient Grace of God," St. Marks Church, London, June 3, 1883; *SPE*, pp. 112–33.

"Gamaliel," Temple Church, London, July 1, 1883; *SPE*, pp. 243–64.

Christmas Eve sermon; *PFF*, pp. 72–84.

Trinity Sunday sermon; *PUC*, pp. 228–46.

Easter sermon; *PUC*, pp. 210–27.

Foreign mission sermon, Boston, January 20, 1889; *BOL*, pp. 346–62.

JOHN C. CALHOUN
(1782–1850), spokesperson for the South and the Union
_____ WILLIAM LYON BENOIT and ALEXANDER MOORE

John Caldwell Calhoun was born on March 18, 1782, near Abbeville, South Carolina. After studying at Moses Waddell's Academy at Willington, South Carolina, he graduated with honors from Yale in 1804. Although he was to present a commencement speech at Yale on "The Qualifications Necessary to Constitute a Perfect Statesman," illness prevented him. He entered Judge Tapping Reeve's law school in Litchfield, Connecticut, and completed his legal studies in Charleston in the offices of Henry De Saussure and Timothy Ford. He then entered practice with George Bowie in Abbeville. Calhoun's first public speech presented a local committee resolution protesting the _Chesapeake_ affair in June 1807. A short while later that year, at the age of twenty-five, he was elected to the South Carolina legislature. He married Floride Bonneau Calhoun (his second cousin) on January 8, 1811.

Calhoun served South Carolina and the rest of the nation in a variety of important capacities in the next four decades. He was a member of the U.S. House of Representatives from 1811 to 1817, secretary of war from 1817 to 1824, and a presidential candidate in 1824 and 1844. When he could not win the election in 1824, he settled for the vice-presidency, a post he held from 1825 to 1833. He resigned this office on December 28, 1832, in a dispute with President Andrew Jackson over the nullification controversy. He was elected to the Senate, where he remained from 1833 to 1843. He served as President John Tyler's secretary of state from 1844 to 1845, returning to the Senate in March 1845 until his death on March 31, 1850.

CALHOUN, DELIBERATIVE ORATOR

Although Calhoun is best known as the South Carolina "nullifier" and as an apologist for southern slavery, he spoke on virtually every topic of importance in the antebellum era, including the War of 1812, banking and the economy, commerce, internal improvements, and territorial expansion. In general, Calhoun advocated the interests of South Carolina and the South first and the Union of sovereign states second.

Calhoun was a nationalist in his early career, especially when he perceived the interests of the South and the Union to be united. One of his earliest legislative triumphs stemmed from his maiden speech in South Carolina against the British. Upon his arrival at Washington as a member of the House of Representatives, Speaker Henry Clay appointed him to the Foreign Affairs Committee. Calhoun introduced the bill declaring war on England on June 3, 1812, which President James Madison signed into law on June 18. On December 12, he took the floor in reply to Virginia Congressman John Randolph, who opposed a resolution to raise an army. While countering several of Randolph's specific objections (among them, that the country was not prepared, that war was expensive and dangerous, and that the United States should not wage war against the country of Locke and Newton), Calhoun maintained that "war, in our country, ought never to be resorted to but when it is clearly justifiable and necessary; so much so, as to not require the aide of logic to convince our understandings, nor the ardor of eloquence to inflame our passions" but the United States must not abandon "our own commercial and maritime rights, and the personal liberties of our citizens in exercising them."

In 1816, after the war, Calhoun advocated three important legislative programs: incorporation of a national bank, the tariff of 1816, and transportation improvements. Speeches on these topics dwelled on how they could strengthen and unify the nation. Calhoun argued in his speech of February 26, 1816, on the bill to charter the national bank that "a national bank would be favorable to the administration of the finances of the Government" and that its establishment would eliminate the "disorders in the national currency." In a speech on the tariff bill, Calhoun adverted that "the security of a country mainly depends on its spirit and its means; and the latter principally on its moneyed resources." Protection was necessary for the growing manufacturing interests. In the speech on transportation improvements, he declared that "the strength and political prosperity of the republic are [intimately] connected with" transportation improvements. All three passed, although President Madison vetoed the last in 1817.

A fifteen-year hiatus in his public speaking career began when he accepted an appointment as secretary of war under President James Monroe (1817–1825). Subsequently he was vice-president, first during John Quincy Adams's presidency.

Although he advocated the tariff of 1816, Calhoun opposed subsequent tariffs that favored northern industry at the expense of southern agriculture. This was his view of the woollens bill of 1817, an important measure of the Adams administration, which had passed the House and was tied in the Senate. As president of the Senate, he could have abstained from voting and the bill would have been defeated. Instead he voted against it, a demonstration of principle taken against the advice of some of his political allies.

He next served as vice-president during Andrew Jackson's first term. Both Democrats, Calhoun initially supported Jackson's administration but soon became alarmed at the president's notions of the role of the federal government and the actions he pursued to further these ideas. The North refused to let the tariff issue rest, passing the tariff of 1828, the "tariff of abominations" to many southerners. Calhoun authored the "South Carolina Exposition and Protest," anonymously at first since he still cherished presidential ambitions, which declared the 1828 tariffs unfair and unconstitutional, advanced the theory of nullification or interposition (that a sovereign state could declare an unconstitutional federal law null and void within that state), and urged citizens of South Carolina to postpone nullifying the tariff of 1828 in order to give Congress ample opportunity to correct its mistake before resorting to the ultimate remedy. If Congress amended the Constitution to make the law constitutional, the state had either to conform or secede from the Union. However, secession was intended only as a last resort. Clearly Calhoun hoped Congress would revise the questionable legislation to conform to the Constitution. The South Carolina legislature endorsed the exposition in December of 1828.

Senator Robert Y. Hayne of South Carolina presented the nullification doctrine in the Webster-Hayne debate of 1830, while Calhoun presided over the Senate, watched approvingly, and openly advised Hayne during his speech. In 1831 he publicly supported nullification as the rift between himself and President Jackson widened. Congress revised the tariff in 1832, but southerners were not satisfied with the changes. The South Carolina Ordinance of Nullification was adopted on November 24, 1832, declaring the tariff of 1828 unconstitutional and therefore null and void in South Carolina. In response, President Jackson issued the Proclamation against the Nullifiers on December 10, 1832. Calhoun sundered his relationship with Jackson and resigned the vice-presidency on December 28, sixteen days after being elected to the U.S. Senate by the South Carolina legislature. Jackson championed the force bill on January 17, 1833, authorizing the president to send troops and ships to states—South Carolina was the only real target—to enforce federal law.

Calhoun spoke for two days, February 15 and 16, on the "bloody bill" as it became known to many. He spurned allegations that South Carolina wished to avoid paying its share of federal revenues and then addressed the issue of his support of the tariff of 1816. Calhoun argued that the purpose of the tariff of 1816 had been to generate revenue, citing as evidence the debt from the War of 1812 and the fact that "it fixed a much higher rate of duties on the unprotected than on protected articles." Since the war debt was virtually discharged in 1833 and there was no current need for additional funds, this new tariff had no purpose but to protect northern manufacturing interests at the expense of southern agriculture. Calhoun claimed that while he had mentioned other benefits from the 1816 tariff, he had supported it as a revenue measure. In 1833, Calhoun declared that a tariff could not be justified for protection alone.

Having differentiated the first tariff from subsequent ones, Calhoun amplified the constitutional ramifications of the tariff. He asked whether it was constitutional for the federal government to impose a tariff for protection: "Has this government a right to impose burdens on the capital and industry of one portion of the country, not with a view to revenue, but to benefit another?" Calhoun answered this question in the negative, but the greater issue was whether the states had the constitutional power to decide this question for themselves. Could South Carolina declare the tariff of 1828 unconstitutional and nullify its effect within its borders?

Calhoun's speech answered "Yes!" The crux of his argument was that "to give to either party [of the constitutional compact] the conclusive right of judging, not only of the share allotted to it, but of that allotted to the other, is to annul the division, and to confer the whole power on the party vested with such right."

It followed that the force bill was tyrannical and punitive. South Carolina had done nothing worthy of punishment. It had merely acted to preserve its reserved powers from the unchecked encroachment of an unconstitutional law.

Calhoun also argued against the provisions of the "bloody bill": "It puts at the disposal of the President the army and navy, and the entire militia of the country." Furthermore, there were no congressional checks on his power, for "the President may, under its authority, incur any expenditure, and . . . create a new national debt." Nor were there judicial checks, for the force bill "authorized the President, or even his deputies, when they may suppose the law to be violated, without the intervention of a court or jury, to kill without mercy or discrimination." Finally, he ridiculed the notion that the Union could be preserved by force: "Force may, indeed, hold the parts together, but such a union would be the bond between master and slave."

When it became clear that the force bill would pass, Calhoun and his supporters left the Senate chamber as the roll call vote began. Clay and Calhoun introduced a compromise bill to reduce tariffs over a ten-year period, which passed on March 1, 1833. Calhoun hastened to South Carolina, in an arduous journey, which impaired his health, and persuaded the legislature to rescind its nullification.

In 1833 President Jackson decided to remove federal funds from the Bank of the United States. When Secretary of the Treasury William Duane refused to do so, Jackson removed him from office and appointed Roger Taney, who complied with Jackson's wishes. The removal of the deposits united the triumvirate of Calhoun, Clay, and Webster in opposition, and Calhoun supported a resolution to censure the president for this action in a speech on January 13, 1834.

He began with a dilemma: "either the intention or the letter [of the bank incorporation act] must prevail—he may select either, but cannot be permitted to take one or the other as may suit his purpose." He then argued that both the president's message to Congress and the debates demonstrated that the intent of the law was to ensure the security of the deposits, but "it is not even pretended that the public deposits were in danger." In fact, it was generally recognized that they were less safe. Hence, the secretary not only failed to follow the law's intent but in fact directly violated it. Impaled on the other horn of the dilemma was Jackson's argument that the letter of the law granted the secretary the power to remove deposits without specifying any limits, for example, only in pursuance of security. Calhoun explained that Secretary Taney did more than remove the monies; he then deposited them in other banks without legal authorization. In fact, the literal wording of the statute permitted only withholding of further deposits, not withdrawing of previous deposits.

Calhoun concluded the legal argument against removal and then, as was his wont, addressed constitutional implications. He stated without hesitation that Jackson's act "is one of the alarming signs of the times which portend the overthrow of the constitution and the approach of despotic power." The president has usurped Congress's constitutional power to regulate the currency and the

Supreme Court's statutory power to judge the Bank of the United States. Calhoun declared that this was "a struggle on the part of the Executive to seize on the power of the Congress, and to unite in the President the power of the sword and the purse." He then reminded his audience of the force bill, "which absorbed all the rights and sovereignty of the States."

On March 28 the Senate voted to censure the president for his actions. Three weeks later, the president protested the censure, causing further outrage. He then sent a more moderate reply, but the Senate passed another resolution denying the president the power to question their actions. Jackson had the final victory on this issue though, for his forces were able to expunge this censure from the records in January 1837.

In addition to the problems of protective tariffs and executive usurpation, Calhoun, the South, and the Union faced another threat—the growing abolitionist movement. Antislavery advocates began distributing inflammatory literature through the U.S. mail and flooding Congress with petitions. On March 9, 1836, Calhoun attempted to stem the flood by proposing a resolution to refrain from receiving their petitions. He addressed the question of whether such action infringed constitutional guarantees of the right of petition.

Calhoun observed that "there must be some point . . . where the right of petition ends, and that of this body begins." The right of petition "cannot be extended beyond the presentation of a petition, at which point the rights of this body commence." Evidence was offered from the Senate rules on reception of petitions, adopted on April 19, 1789, at the Senate's first session, and Thomas Jefferson's comment that "regularly a motion for receiving it must be made and seconded." Calhoun also pointed to certain types of petitions that the British Parliament voted not to receive and a Senate vote not to receive petitions supporting Jackson's removal of deposits. "To receive is to take jurisdiction," Calhoun argued. To receive these petitions is but a short step from accepting their substance, which would endanger the Union. Preservation of the Union "demands that the agitation of this question shall cease *here*—that you shall refuse to receive these petitions, and decline all jurisdiction over the subject of abolition, in every form and shape. It is only on these terms that the Union can be safe." Calhoun's resolution failed to muster sufficient support to pass, but the Senate subsequently adopted a gag rule whereby abolition petitions were received but automatically sent to committee and tabled.

Confiscation of slaves on U.S. ships in the British West Indies—the *Comet* in 1830, the *Encomium* in 1834, and the *Enterprise* in 1835—provided Calhoun another opportunity to denounce abolitionists, this time on an international scale. Slaves had been seized from U.S. vessels forced to dock in the Bahamas and freed by local authorities on the ground that slavery was illegal on British territory. After long negotiation, the British reluctantly agreed to compensate the owners of the first two ships because they landed before slavery was actually abolished in the British colonies, but they refused compensation in the *Enterprise* case.

Calhoun spoke on this issue on March 14, 1840. He did not deny that slavery was illegal on British soil but demonstrated that U.S. ships, where the slaves had been held, were U.S. territory. British refusal to compensate the *Enterprise*'s owners could be justified on but two grounds: "either that her municipal laws are paramount to the law of nations, when they come in conflict; or that slavery . . . is against the law of nations." The former was ipso facto preposterous, and Britain's compensation of the *Comet* and *Encomium* foreclosed the latter possibility.

Calhoun also argued that the British were hypocrites, for they had "hundreds of thousands of slaves in the most wretched condition, held by her subjects in her Eastern possessions. . . . The whole Hindostan, with the adjacent possessions, is one magnificent plantation, peopled by more than one hundred millions of slaves, belonging to a company of gentlemen in England, called the East India Company, whose power is far more unlimited and despotic than that of any Southern planter over his slaves."

In late 1842 Calhoun resigned from the Senate in order to run for president, a course he abandoned in January 1844 due to lack of support. After once refusing the office of secretary of state, he accepted it when Secretary Abel P. Pushur was accidentally killed. His primary task was to bring Texas into the Union, but his treaty failed to pass the Senate, in large part because Texas was perceived as proslavery. It was annexed in 1845 via a joint resolution.

In 1850 President Taylor proposed admitting California to the Union as a free state, which was its preference, and Clay proposed a compromise, later called the Compromise of 1850, to defuse the slavery issue. Calhoun denounced this plan in his last great speech. Too ill to deliver it himself, Calhoun sat silently as Senator James Mason of Virginia read the speech from a manuscript on March 4, 1850.

Calhoun declared that "the Union is in great danger," but "it is a great mistake to suppose that disunion can be effected by a single blow. The cords which bound these States together in one common Union are far too numerous and powerful for that. Disunion must be the work of time. It is only through a long process, and successively, that the cords can be snapped, until the whole fabric falls asunder." He offered statistical comparisons of population, number of states, number of senators, number of congressmen, and votes in the electoral college, each of which had been roughly equal in 1790 but in 1850 favored the North. "The result of the whole is to give the Northern section of predominance in every department of the government." This imbalance would grow as additional states were admitted to the Union.

Recent divisions of major Protestant denominations into northern and southern branches over the slavery question pointed to disunion:

The first of these cords which snapped, under its explosive force, was that of the powerful Methodist Episcopal Church. The numerous and strong ties which held it together, are all broken, and its unity gone. The next cord that snapped was that of the Baptists. . . .

That of the Presbyterian is not entirely snapped, but some of its strands have given way.
. . . The strongest cord, of a political character . . . has fared no better than the spiritual.

The growing imbalance between North and South had not been happenstance but could be traced to three sorts of legislation. The first were the laws that excluded the South from much of the new territories; the Ordinance of 1787 and the Missouri Compromise were examples. The second kind were financial, forcing the South to pay more in tariff duties and receive less in benefits than the North. The third type of legislation took constitutional powers from the states and concentrated them in the federal government.

The speech of March 4, 1850, was the capstone and epitaph of Calhoun's career. It drew together the diverse threads of his important political battles throughout his career: the tariffs, the usurpation of power by the federal government generally (and the executive specifically), and the attacks on slaveholding. His final sentence, appropriately enough, expressed his belief that he had "faithfully done my duty . . . both to the Union and my section."

Calhoun's discourses primarily partook of the deliberative genre. Although he studied law and was admitted to the South Carolina bar in 1808, he apparently viewed law as an entrée to politics and soon abandoned his practice. No forensic speeches have survived. He engaged in relatively little epideictic speaking, and when he did so, he often addressed the important contemporary political issues. Thus he primarily spoke in the legislative assembly. On occasions when he spoke in other forms, such as his adddress to the Memphis Convention, he retained the substance and style of a deliberative orator.

Calhoun was known for his powers of reasoning, generally acknowledged to be quite strong (assuming his premises), and for his great conviction. The passages considered here illustrated, for example, effective use of dilemma. He often argued from principles such as purpose or intent. A fitting description of his style was that he represented logic set on fire. He was not known as an eloquent speaker, as many considered Webster, for example, but striking and compelling nonetheless. Francis Wharton, for example, observed that there is "a distinction between Mr. Calhoun and Mr. Webster . . . that while the eloquence of the one is inherent in his argument, the eloquence of the other is extraneous to it." Calhoun's use of metaphor in his last speech is striking.

It is risky to evaluate the effectiveness of a speech on the basis of subsequent events. As many rhetorical scholars have pointed out, a myriad of factors can influence the events instead of, in spite of, or in support of such discourses, including, for example, the speeches of other orators. However, over the course of the career of such an orator as Calhoun, patterns emerge that encourage the conclusion that his discourses were influential.

Calhoun achieved his best successes early in his career. In the flush of Thomas Jefferson's political revolution of 1800 and the "second war of independence," he spoke for the nation at large. Later, as a defender of southern interests, he spoke for a minority, one that grew even smaller as his career progressed.

Consequently his initiatives were increasingly less successful. Calhoun introduced a bill declaring war on England in 1812, which passed after a great political struggle. Each of the three major bills he advocated in the immediate postwar period—the tariff of 1816, the bank, and internal transportation improvements—passed Congress, although the president vetoed the last. While he was out of the Senate, the "tariff of abomination" passed. When he returned, with the help of Clay, the compromise tariff provided relief to southerners. Although he was unable to halt the passage of the force bill, it was never used against South Carolina. The resolution censuring President Jackson for removing deposits passed, although it was later expunged over Calhoun's strenuous objections. Calhoun's bill restricting abolitionist activities failed to pass, but the Senate adopted a gag rule, receiving but automatically tabling these petitions. The Mexican War was waged against his recommendations. He opposed the Wilmot Proviso, and although it passed the House repeatedly, it never passed the Senate. Nearly on his deathbed, he futilely opposed the Compromise of 1850.

No one possessed sufficient stature and ability to assume Calhoun's mantle. South Carolina senator James Henry Hammond adhered to and extrapolated some of his thoughts. Hammond was regarded by some as the premier spokesman for the South in the generation that followed Calhoun, but he had none of Calhoun's political acumen or his personal character. During and after the Civil War, Calhoun and his thought were stigmatized in the North. His two treatises on government were ignored, but his speeches were frequently anthologized and recognized as historically important, even if they were not intellectually in vogue.

Calhoun was the only statesman of his generation to write formal treaties on political science. His *Disquisition on Government* and *Discourse on the Constitution and Government of the United States* do not rank with the Federalist Papers but are precise, readily available expositions of an important strand of American constitutional thought. Interest periodically revives his writings, particularly his defense of minority rights and his position in support of a pluralistic society, where capital and commercial interests coexist with agrarian ones.

Calhoun usually placed his principles above political expediency. One example concerns his tie-breaking vote as president in the Senate on the tariff bill of 1827. His sincerity and integrity have rarely been impeached, even by opponents, but some of his principles were deeply flawed. His advocacy of human slavery cannot be defended or exonerated, although it can be rationalized on various grounds, for example, he inherited slavery, he did not invent it; he believed that only in such a system could the two races live together; he believed that free blacks suffered more than slaves (he freed one slave who, after attempting to live free, returned and begged Calhoun to reenslave him). He considered slavery part and parcel of the constitutional compromise of the 1780s. However, the gap between Calhoun's philosophical and rhetorical preoccupations with liberty and his defense of human chattel slavery is too great to bridge even for those most sympathetic to his principles. His views on slavery were tragically myopic, for in his speech on the force bill, he declared that "force may, indeed, hold the parts together, but such a union would be the bond between master and slave." He characterized that struggle as one between power and liberty, and "strong as may be the love of power on their side, the love of liberty is stronger still on ours." The state of slavery, the loss of liberty that was reprehensible for free white southerners, was not merely acceptable but preferable for blacks, despite the fact that it is easy to argue that political inequality is a far milder form of slavery than that endured by blacks.

INFORMATION SOURCES

Research Collections and Collected Speeches

Major collections of Calhoun's manuscripts, including personal and political correspondence, exist at the Library of Congress; Clemson University, South Carolina; and the South Caroliniana Library, University of South Carolina, Columbia, South Carolina. His official correspondence as secretary of war and secretary of state resides in the National Archives. The offices of the Papers of John C. Calhoun, a documentary editing project, are located in the Department of History, University of South Carolina. They house photocopies and microfilm copies of all known Calhoun papers and maintain a research facility containing bibliographical, biographical, and historical material concerning Calhoun, including all known versions of Calhoun's speeches. The *Annals of Congress* (Washington, D.C., 1811–1824) and the *Congressional Globe* (Washington, D.C., 1833–1850) contain texts of virtually all of Calhoun's congressional speeches.

Calhoun: Basic Documents. Edited by John M. Anderson. State College,   CBD
    Pa.: Bald Eagle Press, 1952.
Speeches of John C. Calhoun: Delivered in the Congress of the United States   SJC
    from 1811 to the Present Time. New York: Harper and Brothers,
    1843.
The Papers of John C. Calhoun. Edited by Robert L. Meriwether, W. Edwin   PJC
    Hemphill, and Clyde N. Wilson. 16 vols. Columbia: University of
    South Carolina Press, 1959–1984.
The Works of John C. Calhoun. Edited by Richard K. Cralle. 6 vols. 1851.   WJC
    rpt., New York: D. Appleton & Co., 1853–1857.

Selected Critical Studies

Bradley, Bert E. "Refutative Techniques of John C. Calhoun." *Southern Speech Communication Journal* 37 (1972): 413–23.
———, and Jerry L. Tarver. "John C. Calhoun's Argumentation in Defense of Slavery." *Southern Speech Journal* 35 (1969): 163–75.
———. "John C. Calhoun's Rhetorical Method in Defense of Slavery." In *Oratory in the Old South: 1828–1860*. Edited by Waldo W. Braden. Baton Rouge: Louisiana State University Press, 1970.
[Brownson, Orestes A.]. "Life and Speeches of John C. Calhoun." *Brownson's Quarterly Review* 1 (1844): 105–31.
Curry, Herbert I. "John C. Calhoun." In *A History and Criticism of American Public*

Address. Vol. 2. Edited by William Norwood Brigance. New York: Russell & Russell, 1960.

Eubanks, Ralph T. "The Rhetoric of the Nullifiers." In *Oratory in the Old South: 1828–1860*, Edited by Waldo W. Braden. Baton Rouge: Louisiana State University Press, 1970.

Harsha, David A. "John C. Calhoun." In *The Most Eminent Orators and Statesman of Ancient and Modern Times: Containing Sketches of Their Lives, Specimens of Their Eloquence, and an Estimate of Their Genius*. New York: Charles Scribner, 1855.

Hubbell, Jay B. "John C. Calhoun." In *The South in American Literature, 1607–1900*. Durham, N.C.: Duke University Press, 1954.

Oliver, Robert T. "Behind the Word: Studies in the Political and Social Views of the Slave Struggle Orators: I. John Caldwell Calhoun." *Quarterly Journal of Speech* 22 (1936): 413–29.

———. "John C. Calhoun: Prophet of the South." In *History of Public Speaking in America*. Boston: Allyn and Bacon, 1965.

Volpe, Michael. "The Logic of Calhoun's Constitutional Theory." *Southern Speech Communication Journal* 39 (1973): 161–72.

[Wharton, Francis]. "Mr. Calhoun's Parliamentary Eloquence." *United States Magazine and Democratic Review* 16 (1944): 111–30.

Wilson, Clyde N. "John C. Calhoun." In *Antebellum Writers in New York and the South, Dictionary of Literary Biography*. Vol. 3. Edited by Joel Myerson. Detroit: Gale Research, 1979.

Winn, Larry James. "The War Hawks' Call to Arms: Appeals for a Second War with Great Britain." *Southern Speech Communication Journal* 37 (1972): 402–12.

Selected Biographies

Coit, Margaret L. *John C. Calhoun: American Portrait*. Boston: Houghton Mifflin, 1950.

Current, Richard N., ed. *John C. Calhoun*. New York: Washington Square Press, 1963.

[Hunter, Robert M. T.]. *Life of John C. Calhoun, Presenting a Condensed History of Political Events from 1811 to 1843*. New York: Harper and Brothers, 1843.

Meigs, William M. *Life of John Caldwell Calhoun*. 2 vols. New York: Neale Publishing Co., 1917.

Thomas, John L., ed. *John C. Calhoun: A Profile*. New York: Hill and Wang, 1968.

Von Holst, Herman E. *John C. Calhoun*. Boston: Houghton Mifflin, 1882.

Wiltse, Charles M. *John C. Calhoun: Nationalist, 1782–1828*. Indianapolis: Bobbs-Merrill Co., 1944. *Nullifier, 1829–1839*, 1949. *Sectionalist, 1840–1850*, 1951.

CHRONOLOGY OF MAJOR SPEECHES

See "Research Collections and Collected Speeches" for source codes.

Speech on the report of the Foreign Relations Committee, Washington, D.C., December 12, 1812; *CBD*, pp. 101–11; *PJC*, 1:75–86; *SJC*, pp. 9–14; *WJC*, 2:1–13.

Speech introducing the bank bill, Washington, D.C., February 26, 1816; *PJC*, 1:331–39; *WJC*, 2:153–62.

Speech on the new tariff bill, Washington, D.C., April 6, 1816; *CBD*, pp. 125–133; *PJC*, 1:347–57; *WJC*, 2:163–73.

Speech on internal improvements, Washington, D.C., February 4, 1817; *PJC*, 1:398–409; *WJC*, 2:186–96.

Speech on the force bill, Washington, D.C., February 15, 16, 1833; *CBD*, pp. 135–90; *PJC*, 12:45–94; *SJC*, pp. 67–98; *WJC*, 2:197–262.

Speech on the removal of the deposits, Washington, D.C., January 13, 1834; *PJC*, 12:200–25; *SJC*, pp. 122–38; *WJC*, 2:309–343.

Speech on the abolition petitions, Washington, D.C., March 9, 1836; *PJC*, 13:91–110; *SJC*, pp. 197–210; *WJC*, 2:465–90.

Speech on the case of the brig *Enterprise*, Washington, D.C., March 14, 1840; *PJC*, 15:139–57; *SJC*, pp. 378–90; *WJC*, 3:462–87.

Speech to the Memphis convention, Memphis, Tennessee, November 13, 1845; *WJC*, 6:273–84.

Speech on the slavery question, Washington, D.C., March 4, 1850; *CBD*, pp. 297–324; *WJC*, 4:542–73.

WILLIAM ELLERY CHANNING
(1780–1842), preacher and social reformer

J. JUSTIN GUSTAINIS

William Ellery Channing was born into an affluent family in Newport, Rhode Island, on April 7, 1780. He graduated with high honors from Harvard in 1798 and then studied independently for the ministry in Newport and at Harvard, where he served as a regent. He was ordained into the ministry on June 1, 1803, and joined the Federal Street Church in Boston, with which he would be affiliated for the rest of his life. His first published sermon, "The Duties of Children," appeared in 1807, and his first sermon on war was delivered in 1810. He married his cousin, Ruth Gibbs, in 1814 and the following year became embroiled in the rebellion against the institutional Calvinist church, a conflict that led to what is generally regarded to be the most important incident in the history of American Unitarianism—Channing's speech "On Unitarian Christianity," which he delivered in 1819. Channing was an active preacher and essayist for most of his adult life, focusing on the traditionally pastoral topics of religion and philosophy, as well as the less traditional topics of pacifism, slavery, and social justice. He died in Bennington, Vermont, on October 2, 1842.

Most of the scholars who have written about Channing and his work have focused on his theology, his philosophy, or his efforts at social reform. A topic frequently neglected is Channing's rhetoric. This is a particularly unfortunate omission, for without Channing's rhetorical skills, his other efforts would probably have amounted to very little. Channing's influence largely came about as a direct result of his abilities to persuade, from both the pulpit and the secular podium.

Channing is probably best known as one of the founders of Unitarianism in America. His sermon, "On Unitarian Christianity," given May 5, 1819, in Baltimore at the ordination of the Reverend Jared Sparks, was the first broadly circulated articulation of those beliefs that evolved into what became known as Unitarianism. The sermon is also considered Channing's most important public speech. The address, which was heard by ministers who had come from all over the East and later read by countless others, did not advance any ideas that had not been the subjects of sermons for years. But by stating these ideas on such a public occasion, before such a large audience, and in such eloquent terms, Channing gave them the impact of doctrine. In the sermon, Channing stated how Unitarians came to their beliefs and what the central doctrines were. He refuted the major attacks made by the Calvinists, such as the argument that Unitarians were making too much use of reason and individual interpretation when it came to Scripture. The doctrines Channing articulated included those of the oneness of God, as opposed to the notion of the Holy Trinity; the single nature of Jesus, in contrast to the argument that he had two natures, those of God and man; the possibility of individual atonement for sin; and the nature of human piety. The sermon cemented Channing's reputation as one of the foremost Unitarian thinkers in the United States.

Another movement for which Channing is considered a major inspiration is transcendentalism. Along with fellow New England transcendentalists Ralph Waldo Emerson and Theodore Parker, Channing was dismayed to find that much of American Protestantism, especially Calvinism, had evolved into a system for defending and perpetuating the political status quo—a system that allowed oppressive legislation, discouraged the exercise of free speech, and tolerated the continued existence of slavery. Channing attacked Calvinism's repressive doctrines on December 7, 1826: "Religion, in one or another form, has always been an engine for crushing the human soul. But such is not the religion of Christ. If it were, it would deserve no respect." Channing's rhetoric, on this and other occasions, was a rhetoric of liberation. He spoke out against intellectual narrow-mindedness and in favor of free thinking and was an inspiration to many young New England intellectuals, especially Theodore Parker.

Channing was also one of the major voices for social reform. He believed that the poverty, drunkenness, and dirt that seemed to be the lot of many occupying the lowest rungs of the socioeconomic ladder were neither desirable nor inevitable. Although he did not attempt to influence legislation, believing that what he called collective action was essentially futile, he did try to influence his listeners to see that social reform was possible on a one-to-one basis. If each of them fed one hungry mouth, he reasoned, the world would be a better place. Channing also took a stand against what he regarded as the single greatest social evil of his day, slavery. His standing as a theologian and intellectual added considerable prestige to his antislavery message. His speeches, sermons, and essays had considerable influence on the abolitionist views of Charles Sumner.

Another cause with which Channing allied himself was pacifism. He believed that war resulted from "contempt for human nature; on the long, mournful habit of regarding the mass of human beings as machines, or as animals having no higher use than to be shot at and murdered for the glory of the chief." He gave a number of well-received sermons against war and openly opposed the War of 1812.

Channing's rhetorical training was largely informal; there was no program in rhetoric at Harvard while he was a student there. He was active in the school's public speaking clubs, but most of his knowledge of rhetorical theory came from reading. Hugh Blair's *Rhetoric and Belles Lettres* was standard in the Harvard curriculum; by all accounts, Channing was strongly influenced by it, although he interpreted Blair's dictums very conservatively, unlike Emerson, who took the same ideas and applied them in much more imaginative ways. Channing was familiar with many of the classical rhetorical theorists, including Plato, Demosthenes, Cicero, and Longinus. He read Sheridan's *A Course of Lectures on Elocution*, Campbell's *A Philosophy of Rhetoric*, and Whately's works on rhetoric and logic. Channing's own rhetorical theory was a blend of all of these, but the strongest influence remained Blair.

Just as Channing rebelled against Calvinist theology, so too did he oppose what he saw as the dominant characteristics of Calvinist preaching. He depicted

Calvinist preachers as eschewing a common, everyday language, which could be readily understood by all, in favor of a rhetorical style that had little to do with the way most people actually spoke. This approach, he felt, was less concerned with communication between minister and congregation than it was with elitist literary theory. He also contended that the Calvinists were overly dependent on models.

Although Channing had his own ideas about the proper rhetorical style to be employed by a preacher, he saw several dilemmas that the preacher faced. On the one hand, he believed, one should use a style that was plain, but not pedestrian, for maximum communicability; however, too plain a style runs the risk of robbing the audience of the use of its imagination. Second, although Channing did believe in the age-old rhetorical canon of audience adaptation, he also thought it ill advised to pander to an audience, to compromise one's message for the sake of acceptance. The third dilemma involved eloquence versus dignity and reason. Channing saw no contradiction between plainness and eloquence. He thought the preacher could and should strive for eloquence without becoming turgid, but this must be done only within the bounds of dignity and reason. The message must not be lost behind a screen of well-chosen words and phrases. Channing thus adopted what might be called a moderately plain style. He stressed simplicity and ease of comprehension. His typical approach to rhetoric was to begin with a statement of his purpose, followed by a brief forecast of the points he wished to develop, followed in turn by a discussion of each point, and concluding with a brief summary and direct appeal to the audience for action. Channing was, at base, a pragmatist. He knew that the desirable result of his sermons, whether the theme was how to live a more Christian life or how to end slavery, was action. He understood the dichotomy represented by the cases of two great classical orators, Demosthenes and Cato. When the Greek Demosthenes spoke, people were awestruck by his eloquence; when Cato spoke to the ancient Romans, urging them to wage war against Carthage, the reaction among audience members was to march. Channing was not interested in rhetoric for its own sake. For him, it was a means to an end.

Channing avoided exaggeration, excessive generalization, and high-flown figures of speech. He was especially careful about his use of metaphor. He had criticized the Calvinists for choosing metaphors outside the audience's experience. He tried to avoid epigrams, sentimentality, and floridity. He also refused to pepper his speeches and sermons with Latin phrases—a hallmark of many other preachers who liked to display their education from the pulpit. There is little wit or humor in Channing's rhetoric. Although not generally pompous, he was a serious man who took his work, and his rhetoric, seriously.

Judging from the available commentaries, it seems clear that Channing was one of the best-received public speakers of his day. Several accounts have been written of audiences listening to Channing's sermons and speeches in rapt, utter silence, punctuated only by bursts of frantic applause. Once he had reached his prime as a speaker, he never failed to have a profound emotional impact on his audiences. People would leave the church or lecture hall weeping with joy, smiling with rapture, or shaking their heads in awe and wonderment. Their reactions were due in no small part to Channing's delivery. Establishing precisely what factors in his speech making allowed him to achieve these effects is not easy, but it is possible to isolate four areas for discussion: his sincerity, his voice, his eye contact, and his use of notes.

Channing's notion of sincerity in public speaking may well prove confusing to the modern reader. It seemed so simple a concept to account for much of his success, but Channing believed it was the essential ingredient of public speaking. He deplored artifice and theatricality. He believed that if an emotion was felt by a speaker, it would be communicated in the rhetoric; if the emotion was not present, it could not and should not be counterfeited. He once cautioned a young minister, "On no account, in your public services, try to exhibit by look or tone any emotion which you do not feel. If you feel coldly, appear so. The sermon may be lost, but your own truthfulness will be preserved." Channing was not explicit about the process by which the sincere emotion felt by the orator is transmitted to the audience; he believed it just happened. One aspect about which he was clear is the necessity of prior preparation—not of gestures or intonations but of text. In his sermon, "Charge at the Ordination of the Rev. John Sullivan Dwight," he advised the new minister, "Write with earnestness, and you will have little difficulty in preaching earnestly. . . . The fire which is to burn in the pulpit, must be kindled in the study."

Channing's sincerity was always evident to his audiences, and one of the most powerful mechanisms for conveying that sincerity was his voice. Because of his abhorrence of theatrical speaking, he did not use his voice to bludgeon his listeners with its force. Several who heard Channing speak described his voice as musical and melodious, and Channing himself wrote that this was an important quality in a speaking voice. Beyond the intent to be musical, Channing's use of his voice was apparently quite spontaneous. He had no special techniques on which he would rely to produce particular effects. He sometimes deliberately spoke in a very soft voice in order to make his listeners concentrate on what he was saying, but his basic reliance was on his own sincerity and the belief that all the vocal technique he needed would flow from his conviction and feelings.

Another important component of Channing's delivery was the way he used his eyes. He made effective use of eye contact and was also able to use his eyes to express the emotions applicable to the ideas he was presenting. Ralph Waldo Emerson is said to have observed that Channing's works should not be printed for dissemination beyond the time and place they were spoken; he believed that without Channing's gaze to give them life, they would lose a great deal.

Channing was able to make effective use of his eyes, though he always spoke from notes. His preparation was so thorough that he rarely had to refer to his manuscript, but it was always before him. He admired those who could speak extemporaneously and tried the approach himself occasionally when speaking in small country churches. But he was never able to deliver one of his major addresses or sermons without having the complete text in front of him.

Although Channing's approach to rhetoric was often more instinctive than studied, it is nonetheless possible to discuss the ways he used forms of proof to support his arguments. These can be analyzed in terms of the traditional Aristotelian division of ethical, logical, and pathetic proofs.

Aristotle's concept of *ethos* refers to the persuasive power to be gained from an audience's perception of a speaker's character. Although there is nothing to suggest that Channing ever attempted coldly to exploit the credibility he had with his hearers, the fact remains that his *ethos* was high. He was widely known as a man of humility, piety, and learning. His appearance gave him the look of an ascetic—he was small, verging on emaciation, and had a piercing gaze. Indeed, the ill health that contributed to his thinness may have helped his credibility as well. As a result of a rigorous program of self-denial begun during his youth, Channing had suffered from digestive and circulatory problems since he was nineteen years old. He did not attempt to capitalize on his illnesses, but his audiences knew that he was often in poor health and that he frequently gave sermons and speeches when unwell. The perception on the part of his listeners of a man giving his all to them when, by rights, he should be home in bed added enormously to Channing's credit.

Unlike his *ethos*, Channing's use of the logical forms of rhetorical proof does not lend itself to easy characterization. It is safe to say that he often employed logic in his sermons and speeches, which is more than could be said for many of his peers in the ministry. The prominent approach to homiletic rhetoric at the time seems to have been directly descended from Jonathan Edwards's well-known Puritan sermon, "Sinners in the Hands of an Angry God." It was widely felt among ministers that the primary goal of a good sermon was the evocation of strong emotion. Although Channing certainly did not abandon the use of emotion in his rhetoric, neither did he rely on it to the exclusion of reason. He wrote, "To rule over passive minds, to dictate to those who will not inquire and judge, seems to me a low ambition, a poor dominion."

Although Channing did not restrict himself to one form of logical proof, he favored the use of induction, the drawing of generalized conclusions from an examination of one or more specific instances. Channing believed in the universal application of particular insights, whether they were drawn from experience, intuition, faith or conscience. In this, Channing was influenced by the work of the eighteenth-century moralist Richard Price, who had developed a hierarchical arrangement for logical proofs. The first among these was immediate consciousness or feeling. In short, Price, and Channing, believed that an audience will grant that the things they feel to be true in a particular case may be generalized to a host of other cases. Such an approach naturally lends itself to the use of argument by analogy, and it is thus unsurprising that this type of inductive argument was one of Channing's favorites.

He was also capable of using deductive argument—applying general precepts to draw conclusions about individual situations. Channing did make occasional use of formal syllogisms and the more subtle enthymeme form. In such arguments, the major premise would often come from some central article of religious faith shared by Channing and his listeners, based on their understanding of Scripture.

Channing often combined his use of logic with emotional appeals. Although he abhorred the emotional excesses in the pulpit carried out by the Calvinists and others, he nonetheless recognized that most people are frequently governed by their feelings. Unlike the Calvinists, whose most common appeal to emotion involved fear, Channing concentrated on the more positive feelings of humanity, brotherhood, duty, justice, progress, and love. His emphasis on love is well illustrated by his 1821 sermon, "The Evidences of Revealed Religion," in which he described what he saw as the most important characteristic of Jesus Christ: "Love to man as man, love comprehending the hated Samaritan and the despised publican, was a feature which separated Jesus from the best men of his nation and the world."

As is frequently the case with skilled orators, Channing's speeches and sermons were astute combinations of the three forms of proof: ethical, logical, and emotional. This is clearly seen in his speech, "The Present Age," given before the Mercantile Library Company in Philadelphia on May 11, 1841. The ethical appeal came from the audience's view of Channing's character. If they did not think well of him, he would not have been invited to speak. His arguments in the speech frequently took the form of the deductive argument from principle, as when he said:

The grand doctrine, that every human being should have the means of self-culture, of progress in knowledge and virtue, of health, comfort, and happiness, of exercising the powers and affections of a man, this is slowly taking its place as the highest social truth.

Channing also made effective use of emotional appeal in the speech, especially when discussing the subject of slavery:

[Benevolence] remembers the slave, pleads his cause with God and man, recognizes in him a human brother, respects in him the sacred rights of humanity, and claims for him, not as a boon, but as a right, that freedom without which humanity withers and God's child is degraded into a tool or a brute.

Channing placed himself foursquare in opposition to slavery and in the process inspired the opposition of others. In his lifetime, he inspired many—Unitarians, transcendentalists, philosophers, social reformers, and abolitionists. He was one of the great men and orators of his age.

INFORMATION SOURCES

Research Collections and Collected Speeches

The American Unitarian Association Historical Society Library, Harvard Divinity School, Cambridge, Massachusetts, contains copies of some of Channing's sermons and letters, as well as letters written to him by such notables as Horace Mann, Joseph Tuckerman, and Elizabeth Peabody. The Channing Collection at Meadeville Theological Seminary, Chicago, includes many complete sermons and fragments of sermons by Channing, some of which were never published. Also in the collection are several hundred personal notes and memoranda by Channing, mostly undated. The Rhode Island Historical Society, Providence, has a Channing Autograph Collection, consisting of letters to Channing by well-known contemporaries, including John Quincy Adams, Lord Holland, Henry Clay, and John C. Calhoun. The Library of Congress also has a collection of Channing letters.

Channing, William E. *The Works of William E. Channing, D.D.* 4th ed. 6   WWEC
    vols. Boston: James Munroe and Company, 1845.

————. *Memoir of William Ellery Channing, with Extracts from His Cor-*   MWEC
    respondence and Manuscripts. 6th ed. 3 vols. Boston: Crosby and
    Nichols, 1854.

————. *Unitarian Christianity and Other Essays.* Edited by Irving H. Bar-   UCOE
    tlett. New York: Liberal Arts Press, 1957.

————. *Discourses on War.* 1903; rpt., New York: Garland Publishing,   DOW
    1972.

Selected Critical Studies

Buell, Lawrence. "The Unitarian Movement and the Art of Preaching in 19th Century
    America." *American Quarterly* 24 (1972): 166–90.
Edrich, Mary W. "The Channing Rhetoric and 'Splendid Confusion.' " *Emerson Society
    Quarterly* 57 (1969): 5–12.
Hochmuth, Marie. "William Ellery Channing, New England Conversationalist." *Quart-
    erly Journal of Speech* 30 (1944): 429–39.
Toulouse, Teresa Andrea. "The Aesthetic of Persuasion: Plain Style and Audience in
    John Cotton, Benjamin Colman, and William Ellery Channing." Ph.D. diss.
    Harvard University, 1980.

Selected Biographies

Brown, Arthur W. *Always Young for Liberty: A Biography of William Ellery Channing.*
    Syracuse: Syracuse University Press, 1956.
Edgell, David P. *William Ellery Channing: An Intellectual Portrait.* Boston: Beacon
    Press, 1955.
Rice, Madeline Hooke. *Federal Street Pastor: The Life of William Ellery Channing.* New
    York: Bookman Associates, 1961.

CHRONOLOGY OF MAJOR SPEECHES

See "Research Collections and Collected Speeches" for source codes.

"On Unitarian Christianity," sermon at the ordination of Jared Sparks, Baltimore, Maryland, May 5, 1819; *WWEC*, 3:59–103; *UCOE*, pp. 3–38.

"The Evidences of Revealed Religion," lecture given as part of the Dudleian Lecture Series, Harvard University, Cambridge, March 14, 1821; *WWEC*, 3:105–36; *UCOE*, pp. 60–85.

"Charge at the Ordination of the Rev. John Sullivan Dwight," ordination sermon given at the Second Congregational Church, Northampton, Massachusetts, May 20, 1840; *WWEC*, 5:297–316.

"The Present Age," speech delivered before the Mercantile Library Company, Philadelphia, May 11, 1841; *WWEC*, 6:147–82.

HENRY CLAY
(1777–1852), legislative leader

CARL R. BURGCHARDT

Compared to Daniel Webster and John C. Calhoun, Henry Clay was ill prepared to join the great oratorical triumvirate of the nineteenth century. Clay's
formal education consisted of only three years in a rural schoolhouse, yet his
magnetic personality, powerful intellect, and public speaking prowess overcame
his educational deficiencies to put him on an equal footing with the other rhetorical giants of his age. Nonetheless, his lack of systematic study in oratory
and the other arts marked his career strongly and influenced his discourse. Clay
learned to orate by observing the public discourse around him and by practical
experience, circumstances that contributed to the lifelong pragmatic quality of
his rhetoric.

After completing his schooling, Clay was fortunate to read law under several
distinguished attorneys in Richmond, Virginia. His association with George
Wythe and Robert Brooke gave him access to the most stimulating minds of
Richmond society. Here Clay was exposed continually to a high level of campaign
rhetoric, legislative sessions, and court trials. In addition, he honed his speaking
skills in the local debating society, a practice he continued when he moved to
Lexington, Kentucky, to pursue a legal career in 1797.

Clay first attained widespread prominence as a speaker in the law courts. His
pragmatic commonsense appeals were well suited to the frontier legal system,
and his eloquence and charisma often attracted large, excited audiences. His
speeches from the hustings added to his renown as a speaker. By 1803 Clay
was regarded as a promising political candidate, and he was elected to the
Kentucky Assembly. Once again, his abilities as an orator won him recognition,
so much so that he was selected to fill the unexpired terms of two U.S. senators,
once in 1806 and again in 1810.

Even at the national level, Clay impressed his colleagues with his political
and rhetorical abilities. When he was elected to the U.S. House of Representatives
in his own right in 1810, he was immediately elected Speaker. He elevated this
office from one of mere ornament to a powerful leadership position, and rhetoric
was the tool he used to forge the transformation. He often stepped down from
the chair to deliver speeches on controversial issues. After leaving the House in
1825, Clay finished his legislative career in the Senate during two intervals.
Although he professed to disdain public speaking outside the courtroom and
legislature, over the course of his career, he delivered numerous rousing addresses
during speaking tours and political campaigns. These occasions elicited an out-
pouring of public adulation few other orators could match. Because of a loyal
national following, Clay was a frequent candidate for president, but he failed to
translate his personal popularity into enough votes at the national level. While
he never obtained his most cherished prize of the presidency, his rhetoric was
perfectly attuned to the voters of Kentucky, who gave him unwavering support
on nearly all of his positions.

HENRY CLAY: THE GREAT PACIFICATOR

Clay's greatest historical contribution was his battle to preserve the Union in the face of unprecedented divisiveness, and several of his most important orations were devoted to moderation and compromise. His first role as a mediator occurred during the 1820–1821 debate over the Missouri Compromise, where, according to reports, he argued convincingly for compromise at a critical juncture in the proceedings. His efforts at mediation earned him the title of the Great Pacificator, a role he played again in 1833 during the crisis over nullification. When South Carolina nullified the hated tariffs of 1828 and 1832 and Andrew Jackson threatened to enforce compliance, Clay proposed to reduce gradually the repugnant rates, thus helping to avert secession. In Clay's speech of February 25, 1833, he refuted objections to the compromise proposal and advocated an honorable solution for both sides. In answering the charge that his recent support for reduced tariff rates was motivated by political ambition, Clay stated, "Yes, I have ambition; but it is the ambition of being the humble instrument, in the hands of Providence, to reconcile a divided people; once more to revive concord and harmony in a distracted land—the pleasing ambition of contemplating the glorious spectacle of a free, unified, prosperous, and fraternal people!''

As slavery replaced the tariff as the most divisive national issue, Clay strove to develop a compromise position that would minimize conflict. He attempted to isolate and silence the ultra-abolitionists while at the same time placating more moderate factions. In his speech before the Senate on February 7, 1839, Clay stated, "I am, Mr. President, no friend of slavery. The searcher of all hearts knows that every pulsation of mine beats high and strong in the cause of civil liberty.'' On the other hand, he recognized the South's right to maintain slavery without interference and condemned immediate emancipation as impracticable and dangerous to the nation. Clay also gave a memorable speech concerning slavery on October 1, 1842, at Richmond, Indiana. A Quaker abolitionist named Mendenhall stepped forward from the large, pro-Clay audience and presented him with a petition to free his slaves. Clay repeated his arguments of 1839, stating the practical difficulties of immediate emancipation. The only rational solution to the problem of slavery, Clay asserted, was gradual emancipation coupled with colonization. He then asked Mendenhall if he was prepared to raise the large sum of money necesssary to support Clay's slaves if he should free them. He ended the speech by advising Mendenhall to "go home, and mind your own business, and leave other people to take care of theirs. Limit your benevolent exertions to your own neighborhood . . . and you will be a better and wiser man than you have this day shown yourself.''

By 1847 Clay realized that the Mexican War, with its potential to acquire vast new tracts of land, would upset the political balance between proslavery and antislavery factions. On November 13, 1847, in Lexington, Kentucky, Clay criticized the "unnatural war'' and opposed the annexation of Mexican territory for the purpose of extending slavery. He argued that the United States already possessed abundant unsettled land and asked, "Ought we not to be satisfied with such a country?" His warning about the Mexican territory, however, was not heeded, and in 1850 he faced the task of advocating a compromise over slavery and the settlement of the new territory. He delivered a major address in support of his eight compromise resolutions on February 5 and 6. Clay attempted to move the antagonists away from questions of inflexible principle to questions of political expediency. He aimed to strike a compromise by granting tangible benefits to each side. At the same time, he made patriotic appeals and reminded both factions that they had a mutual interest in preserving the Union. Throughout the speech, he urged reason and moderation. He staunchly denied the right of any state to secede from the Union, and he predicted that secession would inevitably lead to a ghastly war. In the moving conclusion of the address, Clay pleaded with his colleagues to "pause at the edge of the precipice, before the fearful and disastrous leap be taken into the yawning abyss below, from which none who ever take it shall return in safety."

The public response to Clay's speech was overwhelmingly positive, and initial support for his plan mounted quickly. Clay himself believed his oration "produced a powerful and salutary effect in the country and in Congress." Although this address did not win immediate approval of the compromise package, it provided a starting point for subsequent debate. Clay personally spoke more than seventy times during the discussion. The cumulative effect of his speaking was to help create a favorable climate for the eventual passage of the compromise as separate bills.

Although Clay justifiably earned the sobriquet of the Great Pacificator, he began his career as a firebrand, and a surprising number of his speeches were combative. He was a major spokesman for advocating the War of 1812. In fact, Josiah Quincy thought that "Henry Clay was the man whose influence and power more than any other produced the war of 1812." Clay delivered one of his most powerful speeches for war in the House on December 31, 1811. He argued that the United States must increase its preparedness for war because England's violation of America's neutral rights and impressment of seamen were intolerable. In answer to the question, "What are we to gain by war?" he responded: "What are we not to lose by peace? Commerce, character, a nation's best treasure, honor!" Clay mesmerized the House with this address; even his opponents admitted his persuasive power. The speech was printed and widely circulated and discussed. Moreover, it served as the blueprint for the war hawks' entire persuasive campaign; Clay's followers echoed the tone and substance of his arguments, which proved to be successful in bringing war with England. Once the war was underway, Clay had to defend his policy against the bitter attacks of Josiah Quincy and the Federalists. In Clay's speech of January 8–9, 1813, "The New Army Bill," he supported a measure to raise additional troops. He argued that the reasons for the war were just and honorable, explained why no peace agreement had been reached, and pleaded to prosecute the war vigorously until U.S. grievances had been satisfied. He concluded the address with a strong emotional appeal: "In such a cause, with the aid of Providence, we must come out crowned with success; but if we fail, let us fail like men, lash ourselves to our gallant tars, and expire together in one common struggle, fighting for FREE TRADE AND SEAMEN'S RIGHTS." The speech, which caused some in the audience to weep, bolstered Clay's status as a national leader and influenced public opinion significantly. The enlistment bill passed the House on January 14 by a decisive margin.

Aside from the War of 1812, Clay participated in other important foreign policy debates, such as his support for the recognition of the emerging republics in South America. His best speech in this debate occurred on March 24–25, 1818, when he moved that funds be appropriated to send a minister to the United Provinces of Rio de La Plata. He argued the United States should support "the glorious spectacle of eighteen millions of people, struggling to burst their chains and to be free." But, significantly, he also argued that recognition would lead to economic and political advantages for the United States in the areas of trade and security. Although he was not immediately successful in 1818, supporters and opponents alike noted that Clay's rhetoric excited public interest on the topic. His March 24–25 speech was also translated into Spanish and read before the revolutionary armies, which made Clay a hero in South America. Finally, this speech was significant because it contained nearly all of the arguments that he would use in subsequent addresses. In 1820 the House voted to support Clay's resolution to recognize the revolutionary governments. Some commentators believe that Clay's oratory pushed Monroe and Congress into an early policy of recognition. Along the same lines, Clay supported the Greek rebellion against the Turks. In his speech of January 23, 1824, he argued for Daniel Webster's proposal to appropriate money to send an agent to Greece. Clay taunted his opponents by stating the only reason to avoid recognizing Greece was a cowardly fear of Europe: "Are we so humbled, so low, so debased, that we dare not express our sympathy for suffering Greece; that we dare not articulate our detestation of the brutal excesses of which she has been the bleeding victim, lest we might offend some one or more of their imperial and royal majesties?" The House refused to pass the resolution, but Clay's speech was thought to be eloquent, and it appealed to his constituents in the West.

A substantial portion of Clay's rhetoric was delivered, directly or indirectly, in opposition to Andrew Jackson, his political nemesis. The enmity began early. Clay gave a forceful speech on January 20, 1819, supporting resolutions of censure for Jackson's activities in the Seminole War of 1818. He argued that Jackson had exceeded his orders by unjustifiably seizing Spanish towns and executing prisoners. Clay warned the nation that the elevation of Jackson for his deeds "will be a triumph of the principle of insubordination, a triumph of the military over the civil authority, a triumph over the powers of this House, a triumph over the Constitution of the land. And I pray most devoutly to Heaven, that it may not prove, in its ultimate effects and consequences, a triumph over the liberties of the people." The House defeated the censure resolutions soundly, but Clay lost more than a single vote with this speech because he alienated President Monroe. Furthermore, the January 20 speech began a series of unsuccessful battles against Jackson and his supporters, who never forgave Clay for the attack. On December 26, 1833, Clay presented to the Senate his resolutions censuring Andrew Jackson for his policy of removing funds from the Bank of the United States and depositing them in "pet" banks. Clay made two major arguments in the oration: "the president has assumed a dangerous power over the treasury of the United States, not granted to him by the Constitution and the laws; and . . . the reasons assigned for the act, by the Secretary of the Treasury, are insufficient and unsatisfactory." Moreover, he viewed Jackson's actions as the "premonitory symptoms of despotism." After three months of acrimonious debate, the resolutions of censure passed in the Senate. Jackson's forces tried for several years to have the censure expunged from the record. Finally, they were successful, an event that Clay viewed as an outrage and a national tragedy. On January 16, 1837, Clay argued it was unconstitutional to desecrate the Senate journal, and he attacked Jackson as a dictator: "Must we blot, deface, and mutilate the records of the country to punish the presumptuousness of expressing an opinion contrary to his own?"

Not all of Clay's rhetoric was combative, reactive, or devoted to compromise. He did have a constructive, domestic program, the American system, which called for a prosperous, self-sufficient nation, protected by tariffs, and unified by internal improvements and economic cooperation among regions. Several presidents, however, including Monroe, doubted that Congress had constitutional authority to implement internal improvements, such as roads and canals. In March 1818, Clay disputed Monroe's contention. Although he respected the sovereignty of the states, Clay appealed on March 7 for a flexible interpretation of the Constitution, which could meet the future needs of the nation: "Every man who looks at the constitution, in the spirit to entitle him to the character of an American statesman, must elevate his views to the height which this nation is destined to reach in the rank of nations." Despite Clay's eloquence, he failed to obtain the desired national policy. However, he continued to appeal for his domestic program, and on March 30 and 31, 1824, he delivered a victorious speech in favor of increased tariffs, which became a classic statement of protectionist arguments. Clay contended that the economic troubles of 1824 were caused by inadequate foreign markets for U.S. agricultural and industrial products, and he proposed to develop a vigorous home market through the introduction of a protective tariff. He appealed to the patriotism of all regions, but particularly the South, to establish a truly "American system" for the ultimate benefit of all. The tariff, said Clay, "is the cause of the country, and it must and will prevail. It is founded in the interests and affections of the people. It is as native as the granite deeply imbosomed in our mountains."

Unlike many of his contemporaries, Clay did practically no ceremonial speaking. However, two of his epideictic speeches were recorded and celebrated. The first occurred on December 10, 1824, when Clay, as Speaker, welcomed the

Marquis de Lafayette to the House of Representatives. More significant was Clay's "Valedictory" to the Senate, delivered on March 31, 1842, to a crowded Senate chamber and galleries. Clay looked old and tired, and his voice trembled with emotion as he stated that he had always tried to operate from pure motive throughout his career, and he had never wished to offend anyone. He concluded with the following benediction: "May the most precious blessings of heaven rest upon the whole Senate and each member of it, and may the labours of every one redound to the benefit of the nation and to the advancement of his own fame and renown. And when you shall retire to the bosom of your constituents, may you receive the most cheering and gratifying of all human rewards—their cordial greeting of 'Well done, good and faithful servant.' " The speech was so moving that, in the words of Senator Oliver Smith, "many manly cheeks were suffused with tears." Clay's "Valedictory" proved his effectiveness in the genre, but he much preferred legal and deliberative oratory, which had an immediate, obtainable goal. Just as his life had been shaped by practical experience, so his rhetoric eschewed the speculative and ornamental. In fact, Clay often became impatient with abstract, theoretical discussions during debates. He rarely referred to philosophical, classical, or literary sources in his speeches. His rhetoric was straightforward, grounded in common sense and appeals to probability.

Textual authenticity is particularly a problem with Clay's speeches because one of his trademarks was a lack of care in preserving his oratory. Since Clay delivered his speeches extemporaneously from notes, manuscripts are rare. Even when Clay was asked to provide accurate manuscripts for publication, he declined, saying, "As for myself I care very little about it." Clay usually relied on news reporters to furnish published versions of his speeches. Clay or editors revised some of the reports after the fact, but for the most part the available texts of his speeches are running accounts. Such reports probably are accurate on organization and major arguments, but the precise word choice is suspect. This makes a detailed analysis of Clay's style problematical. He was generally satisfied with the reports of his speeches that appeared in the *Washington National Intelligencer*, and this publication is the source for many collections of his speeches.

Clay once remarked to Senator Oliver Smith that he believed greatness in oratory was founded on preparation: "I seem to speak off-hand, so does Mr. Webster; yet we both speak with preparation, and never without it on important subjects." Despite this observation, Clay did not develop a reputation among his peers for meticulous preparation or research. There is no doubt that he often relied on his wit and sharp intellect to avoid the tedium of overpreparation, but his key speeches usually display thorough research and thought. Most of the materials for Clay's speeches came from his personal experience, from the Constitution and other public documents, from popular magazines and newspapers, and from personal correspondence and conversation. Clay's prepared speeches were organized clearly, with a discernible introduction, body, and conclusion. He developed a central theme in each speech, and the main points were usually separated by clear transitions. He often provided strong previews and summaries. The chronological method of organization was used frequently. His arguments were developed systematically and were adapted well to the particular audience. Most of his speeches advocated policy propositions; these were well supported by evidence. Clay relied especially on historical examples, appeals to authority, and historical and legal precedent. He used both inductive and deductive logic. His arguments were most often based on causality, historical and figurative analogies, and enthymemes. A good deal of his argument was refutation, which underscores the fact that Clay usually spoke in debates.

Throughout his career, Clay struggled against negative public perceptions about his character. Because of a profligate youth, he had the reputation of being a drunkard, gambler, and adulterer, among other things. Perhaps more damaging, however, was the charge that he had made a corrupt bargain with President Adams in 1824 to secure a cabinet post. Clay spent the rest of his life denying this allegation, as well as the accusation that he was motivated solely by political ambition. For the most part, however, Clay entered each speaking situation with a positive reputation based on his high public office and oratorical ability. He often exploited this by referring to his length of service, his legislative accomplishments, and his wisdom and experience. He sometimes pointed out the sacrifices he had made or was willing to make for his country. He often played for sympathy by discussing his frail health. Frequently he asked for the help and mercy of God. He portrayed himself as a humble man, one who regretted that he must disagree with his esteemed colleagues. He sometimes claimed to be the national spokesman for union, liberty, justice, democracy, and the Constitution.

Clay also made overt emotional appeals based on the positive values of patriotism, duty, and public welfare. He appealed frequently to fear of future dangers to the nation, such as economic problems or dissolution of the Union. He often questioned the courage, honor, and patriotism of his opponents, a practice that brought him public criticism, as did his tendency to use sarcasm, irony, and invective during his debate exchanges. Clay had a quick wit and a fine sense of humor, although it was displayed more in conversations, social events, and the give and take of debate than in his famous set speeches.

Clay's style was direct, forceful, and clear. His metaphors and similes were simple and unaffected but powerful. He often used vivid description, parallelism, and personification. Rhetorical questions were especially prominent. Most of his sentences were of the simple type, although he varied type and length. He used many one-syllable words. His precise language probably reflected his legal profession. Clay's discourse is almost austere when compared to the grandiloquent oratory of his peers. In general, Clay disapproved of ornament for its own sake. His direct, simple language was better suited for compromise than the rhetoric of display and self-aggrandizement.

One of the most frequent comments made about Clay is that his power as an orator cannot be gauged accurately from reading his speeches. Audiences reacted warmly to his physical presence. He was not regarded as particularly handsome, but his appearance was striking. He had an engaging smile, and his face mirrored his emotions. Clay gestured frequently while speaking. He used his entire body and also objects, such as his glasses or snuffbox, to underscore a point. His greatest asset, however, was his voice, which imbued even mundane passages with vibrancy. Listeners were impressed with the "melody," "strength," "compass," "power," and "fulness" of Clay's voice. It varied from "soft as a lute" to "full as a trumpet" and from a deep bass to a falsetto. He spoke clearly at a quick but deliberate pace, and he varied volume and rate. He could make himself heard before large audiences, even in outdoor settings. His delivery had a conversational quality, and he devoted less attention to polished pronunciation and enunciation than some of the other celebrated speakers of his day. Clay once remarked to a friend that nature had "singularly favored me by giving me a voice peculiarly adapted to produce the impressions I wished in public speaking." Although some accused Clay of histrionics, most observers were impressed with the naturalness of his delivery. Clay usually spoke with "visible emotion" or a state of "physical fever." He became totally immersed in the act of speaking, which may account for the impression of sincerity, earnestness, and spontaneity that were so frequently reported. Clay's method of delivery was extemporaneous. He usually outlined his speeches using terse notes. Since Clay did not use a manuscript, he concentrated his gaze on the audience the entire time. Many noted Clay's direct eye contact, which made each individual in the audience feel that he was addressing them personally.

Clay's significance as a political leader was founded on his oratory, and the record of the major debates and legislation of his age can be found in his rhetoric. Clay addressed the War of 1812, the recognition of the South American republics, the protective tariff, the Bank of the United States, disposition of public lands and surplus revenues, the slavery question, the issue of national expansion, the Mexican War, and, finally, the Compromise of 1850. He was a founder of the Whig party and the political idol of hundreds of thousands of loyal followers for forty years. Given these impressive accomplishments, why is Clay's rhetoric not more widely acclaimed? Why is he currently not accorded the same status as Webster and Calhoun? One of the major reasons is that his speeches were directly linked to practical political problems of the day; the themes of his discourse do not continue to inform and inspire. He was not a philosopher, a political theorist, or a literary stylist. As Lincoln aptly put it, "All his efforts were for practical effect. He never spoke merely to be heard." Clay genuinely did not seem to care about his historical standing, for he did not revise and polish his speeches for publication; thus, no single passage or phrase from Clay's rhetoric lives on in the popular memory. Since he was cast in the role of the compromiser, it was difficult for him to stand for strong moral principles, something we tend to prize in oratory. Moreover, a compromiser is not revered by partisans from either side of a conflict. One of the most prominent criticisms of Clay was he did not stand for anything other than his own political advancement, that he was an opportunist who changed positions to suit political exigencies.

There is certainly a measure of truth to this charge, but there is also a unifying theme in Clay's rhetoric. As he wrote in 1844, "If anyone desires to know the leading and paramount object of my public life, the preservation of this Union will furnish him the key." Political compromise, Clay believed, was vital to making democracy work and preserving the Union. He can be criticized for lacking conviction about political questions, but this same flexibility and tolerance made him ideally equipped to play an important role in his nation's history. Given the fact that Clay devoted much of his life to preserving the Union, he used the rhetorical methods best suited to his objectives. The principled speakers for radical abolitionism and radical secessionism no doubt used methods appropriate for their purposes, but the goal of preservation required a subtler art, one that Henry Clay mastered.

INFORMATION SOURCES

Research Collections and Collected Speeches

Annals of Congress	*AC*
Clay, Henry. *Life and Speeches of the Honorable Henry Clay*. Edited by Daniel Mallory. 2 vols. New York: Robert P. Bixby and Company, 1843.	*LS*
———. *The Papers of Henry Clay*. Edited by James F. Hopkins. 8 vols. Lexington: University of Kentucky Press, 1959–1984.	*P*
———. *The Works of Henry Clay*. Edited by Calvin Colton. 10 vols. New York: G. P. Putnam's Sons, 1904.	*W*
Congressional Globe.	*CG*
Niles' Weekly Register.	*NWR*
Register of Debates.	*RD*

Selected Critical Studies

Gunderson, Robert Gray. "The Magnanimous Mr. Clay." *Southern Speech Communication Journal* 16 (1950): 133–40.

Lightfoot, Alfred. "Henry Clay and the Missouri Question, 1819–1821." *Missouri Historical Review* 61 (1967): 143–65.

Oliver, Robert T. "Behind the Word: III. Clay." *Quarterly Journal of Speech* 23 (1937): 409–26.

———. *History of Public Speaking in America*. Boston: Allyn and Bacon, 1965.

Parker, E. G. "Henry Clay as an Orator." *Putnam's Monthly Magazine of American Literature* 3 (1854): 493–502.

Peck, Charles H. "The Speeches of Henry Clay." *Magazine of American History* 16 (1886): 58–67.

Sinzinger, Richard A. "A Rhetorical Analysis of Henry Clay's Speeches on the South American Revolutions between 1817 and 1820." Ph.D. dissertation, Case Western Reserve University, 1968.

———. "Henry Clay, Master Propagandist for the Latin American Revolutionists." *Communication Quarterly* 18 (1970): 27–32.

Winn, Larry James. "The War Hawks' Call to Arms." *Southern Speech Communication Journal* 37 (1972): 402–12.

Wrage, Ernest J. "A Critical Study of the Speaking and Speeches of Henry Clay." Ph.D dissertation, Northwestern University, 1941.

———. "Henry Clay." In *A History and Criticism of American Public Address*. Edited by William Norwood Brigance. New York: Russell and Russell, 1960.

Selected Biographies

Eaton, Clement. *Henry Clay and the Art of American Politics*. Boston: Little, Brown, 1957.

Mayo, Bernard. *Henry Clay*. 1937; rpt., n.p.: Archon Books, 1966.

Schurz, Carl. *Henry Clay*. 2 vols. 1915; rpt., New York: Frederick Unger Publishing Co., 1968.

Van Deusen, Glyndon G. *The Life of Henry Clay*. Boston: Little, Brown, 1937.

CHRONOLOGY OF MAJOR SPEECHES

See "Research Collections and Collected Speeches" for source codes.

Speech on additional military force, Washington, D.C., December 31, 1811; *AC*, 23:596–602; *LS*, 1:222–29; *NWR*, 1:332–34; *P*, 1:602–9; *W*, 6:35–41.

New army bill address, Washington, D.C., January 8, 9, 1813; *AC*, 25:659–76; *LS*, 1:240–58; *P*, 1:754–73; *W*, 6:53–70.

Speech on internal improvements, Washington, D.C., March 7, 1818; *AC*, 31:1164–80; *P*, 2:448–64.

Speech on the South American states, Washington, D.C., March 24–25, 1818; *AC*, 32:1474–1500; *LS*, 1:321–47; *P*, 2:512–39; *W*, 6:138–62.

Speech on the Seminole War, Washington, D.C., January 20, 1819; *AC*, 23:631–55; *LS*, 1:365–89; *P*, 2:636–60; *W*, 6:181–204.

Speech on Greece, Washington, D.C., January 23, 1824 (often listed erroneously as January 20); *AC*, 41:1170–77; *LS*, 1:432–39; *P*, 3:603–11; *W*, 6:246–53.

Speech on tariff, Washington, D.C., March 30–31, 1824; *AC*, 42:1962–2001; *LS*, 1:440–82; *P*, 3:683–727; *W*, 6:255–94.

Address to Lafayette, Washington, D.C., December 10, 1824; *LS*, 1:484–85; *P*, 3:893–94; *RD*, 1:3–4; *W*, 6:297–98.

Compromise tariff speech, Washington, D.C., February 25, 1833; *LS*, 2:122–38; *RD*, 9:729–42; *W*, 6:552–67.

Speech on the removal of the deposits, Washington, D.C., December 26, 30, 31, 1833; *CG*, 1:54–57, 65–67, 71–72; *LS*, 2:145–90; *RD*, 10:58–94; *W*, 7:576–620.

Speech on the expunging resolution, Washington, D.C., January 16, 1837; *LS*, 2:264–78; *RD*, 13:429–40; *W*, 8:46–60.

Abolition address, Washington, D.C., February 7, 1839; *CG*, 7: appendix, 354–59; *LS*, 2:355–75; *W*, 8:140–59.

Valedictory address, Washington, D.C., March 31, 1842; *CG*, 11: appendix, 376–77; *LS*, 2:562–68; *W*, 9:353–58.

Mendenhall speech, Richmond, Indiana, October 1, 1842; *LS*, 2:595–600; *NWR*, 63:134–35; *W*, 9:385–90.

Mexican War speech, Lexington, Kentucky, November 13, 1847; *NWR*, 73:197–200; *W*, 3:60–69.

Speech on the compromise resolutions of 1850, Washington, D.C., February 5–6, 1850; *CG*, 19: appendix 1, 115–27; *W*, 3:302–45.

TOM CORWIN
(1794–1865), orator for lost causes

———————————————————————————— J. JEFFERY AUER

Some orators are long remembered because they fought a good fight and won. But many who fought equally well for causes that were lost are forgotten. As Vernon Louis Parrington wrote in *Main Currents in American Thought*, "Lost causes have a way of shrinking in importance in the memory of later generations, and the historian must go back to the days before their overthrow and view them in the light of their hopes. . . . Communing with ghosts is not unprofitable to one who listens to their tales."

Tom Corwin was such a ghost. He was one of America's leading and most colorful orators in the decades before the Civil War and the champion of three lost causes. First, Corwin was a Whig, and ultimately his party died of acute indecision. But in its prime, his eloquence supported it. On the campaign circuit for forty years, he was the acknowledged king of the stump, elected Warren County, Ohio, prosecuting attorney (1818–1828); to the Ohio legislature (1821–1823, 1829–1830); congressman (1830–1840); governor of Ohio (1840–1842); senator (1844–1850); and congressman (1858–1861). In congressional debate, he was called the terror of the House and was second to none as party spokesman, judged even by his severest critic as the equal of Henry Clay and Daniel Webster. In every election from 1830 to 1850, he was beseiged by requests for campaign support by Whigs from Iowa to New York, and when the old Whigs rallied to the new Republican party, Corwin joined with Lincoln and was returned to Congress in 1858 and 1860. In opposing President Polk and the Mexican War in 1847, he fought for peace and against America's first imperialist venture. He failed to stop manifest destiny, but he presaged Franklin Roosevelt's 1933 good neighbor policy in Latin America. Finally, almost to the attack upon Fort Sumter, as chairman of the House Committee of Thirty-three, he continued a lifelong argument for compromise. The leading men of both parties gave him their profoundest attention, but it was too late. "I cannot comprehend the madness of the times. Southern men are theoretically crazy. Extreme Northern men are practical fools," he wrote Lincoln on January 16, 1861. "I think, if you live, you may take the oath." With quixotic justice, Lincoln appointed Corwin minister to Mexico, 1861–1864, and charged him to outwit his Confederate counterpart, which he did.

CORWIN AS POLITICAL ORATOR

Tom Corwin was a product of the midwestern frontier where, in the early decades of the nineteenth century, all public issues were debated in popular assemblies and decided by popular vote. Consequently western politics in the era of the rise of the common man was not speculative but active. Distinguished foreign visitors observed that the only instrument for advancement was the force of public persuasion, that speech making was not for display but a practical art for obtaining verdicts in law courts, winning votes for office, and controlling legislative assemblies. Thus, fame came to the men who excelled as spellbinders and storytellers and who could lace their speeches with poetry and philosophy, history and humor. As extant texts and contemporary descriptions of his speeches reveal, Corwin drew illustrations constantly from Milton, Shakespeare, Bacon, and Bunyan; Caesar, Napoleon, William of Orange, and Washington; and the prophets Abraham, Moses, Joshua, and Daniel. He practiced creating sentences that imitated Johnson, Gibbon, and Carlyle and was often found reading speeches by great British orators before taking the floor for an effort of his own. Above all, he was famed for his use of humorous stories, self-satire, and telling sarcasm and ridicule. Frequently newspaper advertisements for Corwin's stump speeches promised that audiences would not only learn but laugh. For him the horse laugh became the handmaiden of horse sense.

One of the consequences of this approach to oratory for popular western audiences was that it supplemented persuasion with education and entertainment. Essentially unlettered citizens in Ohio, Indiana, Illinois, and the Michigan Territory were lusty laughers and responded to witty anecdotes and humorous sallies, occasional flights of fancy, high-flown imagery and hyperbole, and even a superfluency of speech. The courthouse attracted forensic performances, not legal distinctions. In a campaign year after the crops were in, they traveled by wagons to follow their favorite orators from town to town. Often they gathered in a grove of trees and listened while the orator rampant spoke from the top of a freshly cut stump.

It was in the rollicking fanfaronade of 1840, when the Democrats were sung and stung to death by the Whigs, that stump speakers emerged as a significant force in U.S. politics. One of the most effective was Corwin, heading the Ohio Whig ticket for governor of Ohio after a decade in Congress. He described his labors in a November 20, 1840, letter to Senator John Crittenden: "I have made more than *one hundred* regular *orations* to the people this summer. . . . I have, *first & last* addressed at least seven hundred thousand people, men, women, children, dogs, negroes & Democrats inclusive."

However accurate his estimate may have been, there was contemporary evidence that for twenty-two of these speeches, his average audience was 8,500. On a typical occasion, as in Wilmington, Newark, Bataavia, or Clinton, there would be a spectacular parade, then an outdoor rally under party banners, surrounded by replica log cabins and real hard cider barrels, and with rousing campaign songs interspersing the bursts of oratory that climaxed with Corwin's. What did the speakers say? Before the campaign, Corwin wrote, on February 26, 1840, to South Carolina congressman Hugh Legare that President Van Buren's misrule made "the whole *people feel* rather than *think* that they have been cajoled, cheated & *fooled*." And his speeches eloquently depicted the administration's sins, described its scandals, and appealed to the latent prejudices of the poor, self-reliant, and aggressive frontier democrats. But he studiously avoided promising anything more specific than general reform and "great *amend-*

ments in the administration of public affairs.'' Instead, in this campaign and in others, the stump speaker tended to an exaggerated and declamatory style, verbose and intumescent, replete with florid and fanciful images, and in spacious, rhythmical, and vivid language. In short, he was demonstrative rather than deliberative.

Fashions in oratory change, as do the times, and the ascendancy of the stump speaker, and Tom Corwin, the unparalleled exemplar, was in the frontier political climate of the 1830s and 1840s. But when facile speakers from the Midwest found that even effete easterners responded to smaller doses of this same style, they carried it to Washington and into the national forum. A prime example was Corwin's "Reply to General Crary,'' the speech in the House on February 15, 1840, that launched the presidential campaign of William Henry Harrison and in hundreds of thousands of copies became the favorite Whig campaign document.

The occasion was created by Democratic members who regularly disparaged Harrison's intellect and military leadership qualities in the belief that if they destroyed in House debate the popular legends about the old hero's War of 1812 battle of Tippecanoe exploits, they would undermine his ballot box appeal. Thus, a debate on the National Road Convention became an attack upon Harrison by young Isaac E. Crary of Michigan, who bore the honorary title of general in the local militia. Tom Corwin replied, in a speech that was both a point-by-point refutation of Crary's charges and a direct attack on Crary and the militia experiences that presumably qualified him as an expert on battlefield tactics. It was roisterous ridicule, combining, said Kentucky congressman Garrett Davis, "the invective of Junius with the humor and satire of Don Quixote,'' while *New York Tribune* editor Horace Greeley called it unequaled "for wit, humor, and withering yet good-natured sarcasm.'' John Quincy Adams, who wrote in his diary that Corwin "reminded me of Apollo skinning Marsysas,'' referred to the victim a few days later in House debate as "the late General Crary.''

There were occasions when Corwin demonstrated great prowess in invention and disposition, handling arguments and supporting evidence forcefully, as in his 1822 Ohio Assembly speech "Against Corporal Punishment,'' his 1834 House speech "On the Public Deposits,'' or his 1848 Senate speech "On the Clayton Compromise.'' But even in these speeches there were traces of the stump style: anecdotal argument, strong imagery, and, above all, humor as a persuasive device.

By the time Corwin took his seat in the Senate in March 1845, the state of Texas had virtually taken its place in the American flag, and a war was to be fought to keep it there. In a mandate against "Polk, Texas, and eternal slavery,'' the Ohio legislature instructed its senators to vote against annexation, and over the next two years Corwin battled against manifest destiny, the Mexican War, and President Polk. In the end he lost but only after the most vigorous parliamentary attacks, culminating in his great speech of February 11, 1847, "On the

Mexican War,'' widely thought to have been the most extensively republished text of any other speech in Congress for the preceding twenty years.

One of the driving forces of U.S. history in the nineteenth century was the belief that a divine providence had given the United States a manifest destiny to spread over the continent. President James K. Polk offered destiny a helping hand by creating a situation that he asked Congress to resolve in May 1846 by declaring war on Mexico. Whigs were in opposition for many reasons— some purely partisan, others because they believed the U.S. forces had invaded Mexican territory in a war of conquest by a strong nation against its weaker neighbor, and that the addition of territory would lead to new states that would ensure southern domination of Congress, the extension of slavery, and, ultimately, a civil war over the sectional controversy. At least some Whigs accepted each of these arguments, and it was left to Tom Corwin's leadership to weave them all into a speech opposing the war by attacking a bill to provide Polk with funds to carry it to a conclusion. He commanded attention not only for his known oratorical abilities and his ethical standing with his colleagues but also because many Whigs considered him a leading candidate for their presidential nomination in 1848. The speech thesis was set out early: unless the unjust war was terminated with an immediate and honorable peace, the existence of the nation was at risk. For two and a half hours, he argued that all of history condemned excessive executive power and unjust war; that manifest destiny had been the excuse for every empire since Alexander's; and that ''should we prosecute this war another moment, or expend one dollar in the purchase or conquest of a single acre of Mexican land, the North and South are brought into collision on a point where neither will yield.'' Although there were many even among his opponents in the Senate audience who regarded the speech as Corwin's finest, and it was praised by Whigs nationally and by antislavery forces and was widely reprinted in newspapers and in pamphlet editions, its cause was lost. The final vote, twenty-nine to twenty-four, subjected to analysis by party and section, revealed that the Mexican War was as much the child of northern support for manifest destiny as of any alleged southern slavocracy conspiracy. But the result only confirmed Corwin's fear that the slavery issue would be resolved by civil conflict, and to prevent this by sectional compromise became the third great cause of his political life.

In his ''Whig Strategy Speech'' at a Carthage, Ohio, party gathering, September 18, 1847, Corwin confronted his personal dilemma: to urge any policy that would maintain the Union was to be Whig first, antislavery later; but to urge any measure to contain or abolish slavery was to be Free-Soiler or antislavery first and last. Corwin was a Whig. Thus he recommended, first, that his party believe in the Wilmot Proviso, precluding slavery from any territories that might be acquired from Mexico, but put it aside as so inflammatory that it could end the Union; second, that the party, already being antiwar, now become antiexpansion and thus preclude the question of extending slavery; but, third, that if the Senate refused to forgo new territories, then the party must apply the Wilmot Proviso to them. Attractive as it was to some, the strategy was doomed, as was the party, by an inability to reconcile antislavery and disunion, and in 1852 it died.

By 1858 Corwin wrote to a cousin that he was plunging again into "that turbid water, politics—amongst the monsters, big and little, that swim in that sea of troubles." In "Views on Political Questions," at Morrow, Ohio, August 7, he spent two and a half hours updating the "Whig Strategy Speech" position on the Wilmot Proviso by implicitly endorsing popular sovereignty: "do not let the territory become slave and the people will not be apt to apply for admission to the Union with a slave constitution." It was not shift enough for the ultras, but the moderate Republicans knew the strength of vintage Corwin oratory to be their best chance of winning the old Fillmore Whigs to their cause, and they nominated him to Congress. In his acceptance speech, August 18, 1858, Corwin said he no longer feared the dissolution of the Union because the rejection of the proslavery Kansas Lecompton Constitution undoubtedly "convinced the South of the will of the people of the North." But, the old compromiser added, the North should now propose only "generous but magnanimous persuasion, and mild conciliatory measures."

Safely elected, Corwin turned to aid his new party with more than fifty speeches in the Ohio State elections of 1859 and many more in Indiana, Illinois, and New York. In New York City alone he spoke four times: in Lamartine Hall, Brooklyn Musical Hall, Cooper Institute, and Henry Ward Beecher's church. Each was important for Corwin and the Republican cause, but the speech at Cooper Institute paved the way for Abraham Lincoln four months later by introducing New Yorkers to the principles of western Republicanism. His audience of more than 3,000 was expectant, for a letter written to a New York friend had been published in the *New York Times* a few days earlier. "I have been constantly on the stump," he wrote, *"fighting the heresies of Republicanism and the humbugs of Democracy.* The former, I trust, in Ohio, are thoroughly expunged from the creed of that party, and the latter, I hope, are somewhat damaged." Tom Corwin spoke at the invitation of the party and was introduced by the man who was to head the New York delegation to the 1860 national convention.

The Republican doctrine that Congress possessed the power to legislate on slavery in the territories was developed, as Lincoln would do later, by reading the historical record of supporting opinions by men of all parties, including the Democrats, down to 1854. Corwin called the Douglas doctrine of popular sovereignty, tied to the repeal of the Missouri Compromise, an occasion when Congress "pulled down the dyke and let loose the waters of bitterness all over the land." The Fugitive Slave Law he justified, in the face of some audience dissent, but won applause by saying, "If you do not like the Constitution of your country only two alternatives remain—have it changed, leave the country and go to Morocco. We can change it whenever we please." Referring to himself as "the only representative alive on the face of the earth of the old Whig party," he saw to it that Whiggish elements of western Republicanism were well exposed:

retrenchment of federal expenditures, curbing of southern filibustering, free public lands, and abolition of polygamy, which he called the Utah offspring of popular sovereignty. He concluded with an appeal for citizens to vote and an Edmund Burke–like appeal for representatives to vote independently of their narrow section, and for "the whole people of the United States." When Lincoln spoke at Cooper Institute four months later, he would be new to New York, but his philosophy would not.

In 1860 Corwin was a delegate to the Republican convention and supported Lincoln on the final poll. Then he took to the campaign trail, barely speaking in his own district where he was easily reelected but traveling to ten states for dozens of speeches in each. Everywhere he played the role of the last of the living Whigs, assuring his conservative friends that they could live with the Republican platform and trust Lincoln. He had known Lincoln since early days in Congress, not only as a fellow Whig but a companion in opposing the Mexican War, and the two thought alike on such issues as the Dred Scott decision, John Brown's raid, the Fugitive Slave Law, and Douglas's popular sovereignty. In Lincoln's home state, he spoke in nine cities and in Springfield with Lincoln in his audience. It was Corwin's last appearance as a stump speaker, a specialized field of oratory in which he had no peer. He was, as Robert Ingersoll called him, "King of the Stump."

After the election there came a lame duck session of the Thirty-sixth Congress, and in both houses there was a last late effort at conciliation and compromise. Inevitably Tom Corwin was named chairman of the Select Committee of Thirty-three, one member from each state. After a moving speech by a humorless Corwin, characterized by Carl Schurz as "the last pathetic gasp of the policy of compromise," the cotton state men voted down the committee proposals to admit New Mexico as a slave state, urge the repeal of personal liberty laws, and adopt a constitutional amendment forever protecting slavery where it existed. In the Senate the Crittenden Compromise was defeated by the Republicans, and so was its resubmission by the Washington Peace Conference. In one more try, Corwin fashioned a proposed thirteenth amendment, promising that no future Congress should have the power to abolish or interfere with slavery anywhere. Both houses approved it, Buchanan rushed to sign it, and at the last minute Lincoln inserted in his Inaugural Address a specific approval of it. The Corwin amendment was rejected by the New England states, and ratification came only in Maryland and Ohio but after the firing on Fort Sumter.

It must be concluded that more than any other American political leader before William Jennings Bryan, Tom Corwin was guilty of advocating the right causes at the wrong times in history. But Clio records that the ultimate triumph of right causes comes only after the devoted advocacy of some men in wrong as well as in right times. Few Americans mourned the death of Corwin's beloved Whig party, yet it held the Union together for forty years and contributed to the Republican party not only many of its leaders, including Abraham Lincoln, but much of its political philosophy. Few Americans today would give back the

Southwest to the Mexicans, yet the moral position of the nation today is undoubtedly on the side of Corwin, not Polk. Few Americans today believe that the Corwin amendment compromise might have prevented the Civil War, yet there is a tradition of respect for sincere men of peace. But whatever the judgment of history upon the causes that Corwin championed, the evidence is overwhelming that his advocacy of them was persuasive.

INFORMATION SOURCES

Research Collections and Collected Speeches

The only extant papers of Corwin are in the Library of Congress—about 3,000 patronage and routine business letters when secretary of the treasury from 1850 to 1853. But in two dozen manuscript collections of contemporaries, from Salmon P. Chase to Gideon Welles, valuable material is in the Library of Congress and historical libraries of Cincinnati, Cleveland, Columbus, Fremont, Lebanon, Miami, and Oberlin, Ohio; Boston, Massachusetts; and Madison, Wisconsin. There is no published biography. Thus, memoirs and diaries of many contemporaries and biographies of some are important sources. The *Congressional Globe* gives texts for House and Senate speeches; and Washington printers, such as Towers and Gales & Seaton, published many in pamphlet form for public and party distribution. Contemporary newspapers give accounts of Corwin's extensive campaign speaking.

Corwin, Tom. *Life and Speeches of Thomas Corwin*. Edited by Josiah   LSTC
    Morrow. Cincinnati: W. H. Anderson & Co., 1896.
———. *Speeches of Thomas Corwin, with a Sketch of His Life*. Edited by   STCS
    Isaac Strohm. Dayton: Wm. F. Comly & Co., 1859.

Selected Critical Studies

Auer, J. Jeffery. "Tom Corwin: 'King of the Stump.' " *Quarterly Journal of Speech*
    30 (1944): 47–55.
———. "Tom Corwin: 'Men Will Remember Me as a Joker!' " *Quarterly Journal of*
    Speech 33 (1947): 9–14.
———. "Lincoln's Minister to Mexico." *Ohio State Archeological and Historical Quarterly* 59 (1950): 115–28.
———. "A Northern Whig and the Southern Cause." *Southern Speech Journal* 16 (1950):
    15–39.
———. "Cooper Institute: Tom Corwin and Abraham Lincoln." *New York History* 32
    (1951): 399–413.
———. "Tom Corwin's Reply to General Crary." *Central States Speech Journal* 30
    (1979): 369–73.
Bochin, Hal. "Tom Corwin's Speech against the Mexican War: Courageous but Misunderstood." *Ohio History* 90 (Winter 1981): 33–54.
Pendergraft, Daryl. "Thomas Corwin and the Conservative Republican Reaction, 1858–
    1861." *Ohio State Archeological and Historical Quarterly* 57 (1948): 1–23.

CHRONOLOGY OF MAJOR SPEECHES

See "Research Collections and Collected Speeches" for source codes.

"Against Corporal Punishment," Ohio General Assembly, Columbus, Ohio, December 18, 1822; *LSCT*, pp. 139–47; *STCS*, pp. 51–67.

"On the Public Deposits," U.S. House, Washington, D.C., April 14, 1845; *LSCT*, pp. 149–88.

"Reply to General Crary," U.S. House, Washington, D.C., February 15, 1840; *LSCT*, pp. 246–63; *STCS*, pp. 253–81.

"On the Mexican War," U.S. Senate, Washington, D.C., February 11, 1847; *LSCT*, pp. 277–314; *STCS*, pp. 326–88.

"Whig Strategy Speech," Carthage, Ohio, September 18, 1847; *Lebanon* (Ohio) *Western Star*, September 24, 1847.

"On the Clayton Compromise," U.S. Senate, Washington, D.C., July 22, 1848; *LSTC*, pp. 324–58; *STCS*, pp. 404–61.

"Views on Political Questions," Morrow, Ohio, August 6, 1858; *Cincinnati Daily Gazette*, August 7, 1858.

Acceptance speech, Lebanon, Ohio, August 18, 1858; *Columbus Ohio State Journal*, August 19, 1858.

Cooper Institute speech, New York, November 3, 1859; *New York Daily Tribune*, November 4, 1859; *New York Times*, November 4, 1859.

Report of Committee of Thirty-Three, U.S. House, Washington, D.C., January 31, 1861; *LSTC*, pp. 457–77.

JOHN COTTON
(1584–1652), influential Puritan minister

CELESTE MICHELLE CONDIT

John Cotton, the most broadly influential Puritan preacher in New England's first two decades, was born in Derby, England, in 1584. He was schooled in the rhetorical tradition after the standard curriculum of the day at Trinity College, Cambridge, and later at Emmanuel College. At age twenty-eight, this lawyer's son became minister of St. Botolph's in Boston, England, serving 1,500 communicants. For twenty years, he kept this post in spite of his thorough-going nonconformity to the rules and doctrines of the Anglican church. In 1632, however, he was faced with a summons to the high court, and he fled to the American colonies.

In Massachusetts, Cotton was immediately appointed teacher of the Boston church. For almost twenty years, this important post allowed him to be extremely active in molding the Massachusetts way. Through his thrice-weekly preaching and the rhetorical battles concerning Roger Williams, Ann Hutchinson, and the Westminster Assembly, he shaped and defended Congregationalism and supported a transitional form of theocracy. By today's standards, Cotton's sermons often seem both tedious and wrong, but his rhetorical skill in knitting together the early American communities and in forging halfway positions among virulent opposing beliefs and practices makes him one of the giants of the earliest American orators.

JOHN COTTON AS MINISTER AND POLITICAL PREACHER

Cotton's preaching career began at the Puritan Emmanuel College where he was noted for an elegant, ornamental, yet scholarly style. In 1609, however, a religious experience converted him to the use of the Puritan plain style and format that pervade his nearly forty volumes of sermons and writings. In his discourse, Cotton provided the standard statement of a scriptural text and then explored doctrine in segments that were often tedious. He laboriously "opened" the document, often offering several meanings for each word in the text, supported by quotations from Scriptures. These sections and the "reasons" that followed them varied from clear, deductive statements to self-serving, niggling, or even bizarre interpretations. It was his concluding applications that often shone. Although he did not often refer to daily life or morality, he offered elegant general prescriptions and rationales for the Puritan community's mode of life.

Cotton's style, like that of many other American Puritans, relied heavily on concrete metaphors and examples from the natural world—analogies to rain and sun, to farming and gardening, or to family relationships. These simple descriptions gave force and clarity to his complex doctrines. He was, however, repetitive, making his discourse clear but often dull. Cotton's popularity, then, derives not from stylistic effect but from the raw power generated by the fact that Cotton spoke, through his doctrines, to the passionate political issues in the community of his day.

Cotton's preaching in England was his least explicitly political, but perhaps most politically important, for in this period he was concentrating on the doctrinal issues that separated him from the existing power of the Anglican church with its ties to the hereditary aristocracy. A collection of sermons from this period indicates his interests and the doctrines he preached. In the sermons of *Christ the Fountaine of Life* (delivered between 1612 and 1632), Cotton emphasized that human beings could not save themselves from death; only Christ had that power. Cotton urged that one could gain the love of Christ only through self-debasement, indicating that "this shall you ever finde to be the frame of the spirit of a Christian, the more deeply he affects Christ, the more inwardly he loathes himself . . . as an unclean and abominable thing." As a consequence of this debasement of self, Cotton demanded the complete subjection of will and thought, declaring that "God leaves us not one thought free, nor are we willing to have any thought free." For Cotton, then, that crucially controversial word of his day, *liberty*, did not mean freedom to do as we would but the ability to be free of fear and "sinne" by trusting in Christ.

Cotton's English sermons also virulently attacked an older religious and political enemy, the Roman Catholic church. Finally, they disclosed the doctrine behind Cotton's lifelong political practice—that of balance or the middle way. Cotton noted that "God couples every grace with another grace, that they may poyse one another."

The English sermons laid the doctrinal and psychological foundations of Cotton's career. Although they did not fully address the American issues, they established the platform for those concerns. The bridging sermon came in his departure blessing to American colonizers in Southampton in 1630.

In "God's Promise to His Plantation" (1630), Cotton provided warm reassurance for the departing Puritans, who faced a 3,000-mile journey across a wild ocean to wilder, unknown lands. He assured the apprehensive colonists that God chooses the places for his people and protects them. Moreover, in a rhetorical tour de force, he provided a compelling justification for their departure, an explanation that avoided alienating the English authorities. He also supplied England, and the morally apprehensive colonists, a defense of their right to take possession of the Indians' lands. In return for the temporal gifts of the Indians, the English would offer the gifts of the spirit. He concluded with a charge for the emigrants to seek God in their new home.

This animative justification was to apply to Cotton himself only two years later. As the most successful institutional representative of the Puritan movement, he could hardly be expected to escape the increasing pressure to conformity. He was summoned to the high court in 1632. He chose to go to America to seek God's plantation.

In every strand, Cotton's American preaching reflected this belief that the colonists were "God's Plantation." As a consequence, Cotton necessarily interwove church and state and, in his sermons, doctrine and politics. His most extravagant series of sermons, the American round of preaching on the Psalms of Solomon, "A Brief Exposition on Canticles," delivered perhaps in 1641 in Boston, illustrates this interweaving. The Psalms are themselves lyrical and sensual. Cotton took full advantage of this appeal, beginning with the exhortation that "every chast spouse of Christ, whether Church or Christian soule, longeth for the kisses of Christ's mouth, not for a single kisse, but for kisse upon kisse," continuing through the desire to "teach virgins to lay down all carnall congresse, bashfulness, and to attend to the savoury and sweet invitement of Christ Jesus" and flinching not even at "My beloved put his hand by the hole of the door, and my bowels were moved by him" (*BEPOBC*, pp. 1, 8, 131). Cotton used this only partly disembodied ardor to pronounce a relationship between church and state that was interdependent yet a middle way between "Independency" and "Uniformity." He argued that magistrates must "submit to Christ" but that they have different duties from ministers (and Cotton eventually suggested they should not have civil power to punish doctrinal offenses, as opposed to the situation in England). He described the magistrates as the "walls" of the church of Christ, while ministers served as the "doors." He concluded that, with these complementary powers, "it is a great advancement to the beauty and comeliness of a church state, when people and magistrates do both consent together to purge the whole countrey, even to the utmost borders of the Churches, from corruption in religion."

These doctrines on church and state were challenged throughout Cotton's American reign. Soon after he arrived, he was faced with the attack from "Independency" in the figure of Roger Williams, a pious radical who urged, in the interests of purity, complete renunciation of the English church and total separation of church and state in America. Williams wandered among the church towns of Massachusetts Bay, facing greater official hostility the more successful he was in his unofficial "prophesying."

As a consequence of Cotton's belief in the efficacy of persuasion, the Boston "teacher" sought to convince Williams of his errors privately rather than to bring civil penalties. Eventually, however, in May 1635 disciplinary proceedings began that resulted in Williams's banishment in the winter of 1636. The public laundry on this issue was not aired until ten years later, when, in 1644, an angry Williams issued *The Bloudy Tenant of Persecution*, accusing Cotton of religious persecution and urging liberty of conscience. Cotton replied to this momentous document with *The Bloudy Tenant Washed and Made White in the Bloud of the Lamb* (1647). Several interchanges followed. In them, Cotton maintained that he did not urge persecution for conscience but that if a Christian were "admonished" (argued with) and still did not conform, the person was not resisting for reasons of conscience but from recalcitrance. Once someone knew the good reasons, they were bound to follow God's law. He saw this not as persecution for conscience but as persecution of one who is "sinning against his owne conscience." Cotton admitted fallibility on the part of the admonishers but not in "fundamental" matters. He thus sought his middle way, defending the act of purging the community of religious dissenters but without denying the right to discuss and argue, within certain bounds.

Although the public documents on the controversy over liberty of conscience were not created until ten years after Williams left Massachusetts Bay colonies, Cotton had to deal with the immediate consequences of the turmoil in the bay. To do this, he went to Salem in 1636 to preach a healing sermon. After demonstrating his goodwill through a confession of his own errors, he worked to reestablish the unity necessary for the survival of the community. In his most significant treatment of the issues of works and grace, he emphasized that although the people might have differences over works, in spirit or grace they shared the covenant with God. Cleverly he indicated that to know that one was in the covenant required that one be "afflicted with the sense of your own unrighteousness," a rhetorical strategy that tended to humble the listeners so that they might not self-righteously challenge each other's faith. He concluded by building a bulwark against separation, urging that the Lord's command was not to separate from the unclean but to help them to become clean. Skillfully, then, Cotton applied abstract doctrine to heal the community's wounds and to help preserve the community at Massachusetts Bay.

It was not long, however, until the community was again threatened by dissension. Although the dispute engendered by Ann Hutchinson was bred by tensions between city and surroundings, classes and genders, it was expressed as a dispute over grace and revelation. For two years, in 1637 and 1638, the community chose sides, debated, and held courts and synods to deal with a growing rift, for which John Cotton was in part responsible. He and John Wheelwright (Hutchinson's brother-in-law) were the only preachers in the colony to emphasize a doctrine of grace over works, defining a doctrine of works in very broad terms. Essentially Cotton preached that pious behavior did not lead to election, nor did it serve as a sufficient sign that one was elect. The indwelling of the spirit was the only true sign of grace; hence sanctification was not a sign of justification. Hutchinson took this doctrine a bit further. Whereas Cotton always emphasized the hearing of the word through preaching as the main vessel of conversion and grace, Hutchinson suggested a private communion with God was sufficient, and ultimately she claimed personal revelations from God. While Cotton's doctrine threatened the tidy relationship between good public behavior and the Christian community, Hutchinson threatened the existence of the church itself.

After private counseling, public trial, and church hearing, Hutchinson and others were banished, excommunicated, and punished for their claims. Throughout, Cotton played his careful middle-ground suit. As the "teacher" of Hutchinson, he worked cautiously and diligently to reform her, to clarify his own positions, and to protect her from prosecution and punishment. Ultimately, however, Hutchinson did not compromise and find a middle way. Her banishment was important to the community, to Cotton, and eventually even to England.

As Charles I faltered and the chance for reform in England improved, the Puritan churches in New England began to hope that the Massachusetts way would become the model for all of England. To present this model in the best possible light, among other things, they had to respond to the suspicion, fostered by the Williams and Hutchinson cases, that Cotton's American "Congregationalism" led to separatism and constant schism. The most important document on the issue was probably Cotton's *The Keys to the Kingdom of Heaven* (1644), sent to England as a response to the Westminster Assembly. The tract defended the American churches against the charge of separatism and Brownism but urged the appropriateness of their nonhierarchical relationships among churches and communities. Cotton specified that the ministers and elders had authority, but the people retained their power and liberty through a series of checks on the elders. These themes were reflected in Cotton's sermons of the time.

In his preaching, Boston's teacher attacked the Catholic church with vehemence. Cotton's American and English audiences would have found this attack convincing and used it as a ground of common identification. However, Cotton pointedly made an analogy between the Anglican church and that of Rome, noting that "we believe in no visible church but congregations." Thus, his denunciation of the Roman church could be read as applying equally to the Anglicans. Cotton thereby defended the New England way by a covert attack upon that of old England.

In the "Seven Vials," Cotton warned further that the mercy and patience of God is limited—reforming actions could not be delayed forever. Additionally, he responded to the issues raised by the Hutchinson and Williams controversies, pointedly emphasizing, for example, that private revelations were outdated. The voice of God could be heard with certainty only when it was validated through public preaching. Thus, Cotton justified the American way, attacked the Anglicans, and attempted to unify the colonists by dissolving past "errors," all through a consolidation of power in the preachers.

Ironically, the political and social turmoil that created hope for reform in England also brought an escalating challenge to the church powers in America. Cotton was forced into increasingly severe efforts to protect the "holy commonwealth" from the intensifying dissent that was sprouting at home. The Anabaptists were the most severe threat, but Presbyterians, Quakers, and others were to challenge the right of the elect to control both church and state in Massachusetts Bay. In what was probably his last published sermon, "The Covenant of God's Free Grace," in 1644, Cotton demonstrated the polarization that resulted from what has been called the growing tribalism of the Puritans. He discussed the means of receiving grace, indicating the preeminent importance of ancestry. He commented that if you had not come from an elect family or at least lived with an elect family, that "I confess then thy condition is so much the more to be pitied." He closed the net by emphasizing the ultimate inadequacy of piousness or works for achieving grace; God had already chosen the elect. Other documents by Cotton in the period showed increasing severity toward the challenging outsiders. He supported severe punishments for those who disturbed his holy community with their "unGodly" views. Ultimately he had to drop his middle way on "persecution for conscience" because he could not "admonish" the Anabaptists, who denied the entire tradition from which Cotton's admonishments were reasoned.

Gradually, as America grew, it left Cotton's enforced middle way and holy community for a diverse community that countenanced a variety of ways. Consequently, by modern standards, Cotton's preaching, powerful as it was, failed not only of beauty and forcefulness of reason but also of political adequacy. Nonetheless, it was arguably Cotton's ability to step lightly between contending factions that preserved the Massachusetts colony at a time when it was threatened by the Anglicans abroad and the separatists at home. Moreover, Cotton's theology, because it recognized the place of argument (admonishment), acknowledged the power and liberty of the brethren and praised a local model over any monolithic power; it not only knit together a community in a wilderness, helping it to survive and prosper, but also created a "plantation" model in which republican forms could sprout.

INFORMATION SOURCES

Research Collections and Collected Speeches

Cotton's sermons and writings are available fairly widely, but some relevant American documents are contained at the Massachusetts Bay Historical Society, Boston, and Prince Collection of the Boston Public Library.

Cotton, John. *A Brief Exposition with Practical Observations Upon the Whole Book of Canticles.* London: TR and EM, 1655.   BEPOBC

———. *Christ the Fountain of Life: or Sundry Choyce Sermons on Parts of the Fifth Chapter of the First Epistle of St. John.* London: Robet Ibbison, 1651.   CFL

———. *The Covenant of God's Free Grace.* London: for John Hancock, 1645.   CGFG

———. *An Exposition upon the Thirteenth Chapter of the Revelation.* London: MS, 1655.   ETCR

Depew, Chauncey M. *The Library of Oratory: Ancient and Modern.* Vol. 2. New York: E. R. DuMont, 1902.   LO

Emerson, Everett H. *God's Mercie Mixed with His Justice.* Gainesville, Fl.: Scholar's Facsimiles and Reprints, 1958.   GMMJ

Potter, David, and Thomas, Gordon L. *The Colonial Idiom.* Carbondale: Southern Illinois University Press, 1970.   CI

Ziff, Larzer. *John Cotton on the Churches of New England.* Cambridge: Belknap Press of Harvard University Press, 1968.   JCOCNE

Selected Critical Studies

Habegger, Alfred. "Preparing the Soul for Christ: The Contrasting Sermon Forms of John Cotton and Thomas Hooker." *American Literature* 41 (1969): 342–54.

Rosenmeier, Jesper. "The Teacher and the Witness: John Cotton and Roger Williams."
William and Mary Quarterly ser. 3, 25 (1968): 408–31.

Toulouse, Teresa. " 'The Art of Prophesying': John Cotton and the Rhetoric of Election."
Early American Literature 19 (1984–1985): 279–300.

Selected Biographies

Emerson, Everett H. *John Cotton*. New York: Twayne Publishers, 1965.

Ziff, Lazarus. *The Career of John Cotton*. Princeton: Princeton University Press, 1962.

CHRONOLOGY OF MAJOR SPEECHES

See "Research Collections and Collected Speeches" for source codes.

"Christ the Fountain," St. Botolph's, Boston, England, circa 1624; *CFL*.

"God's Promise to His Plantation," Southampton, England, 1630; *LO* pp. 1–12.

"A Sermon Deliver'd at Salem, Massachusetts," June 1636; *JCOCNE*, pp. 41–68.

"An Exposition upon the Thirteenth Chapter of the Revelation," Boston, New England, 1639–1640; *ETCR*.

"A Brief Exposition on Canticles," Boston, New England, circa 1641; *BEPOBC*.

"Vial I," Boston, circa 1641; *CI*, pp. 363–76.

"The Powring out of the Seven Vials," Boston, circa 1642; *CI*, pp. 363–76.

"The Covenant of God's Free Grace," Boston, circa 1644; *CGFG*.

JEFFERSON DAVIS
(1808–1889), president of the Confederacy

For twenty-four years after the Civil War, Jefferson Davis stood as a living symbol of the lost cause. Maligned by a false story of his trying to escape Union custody disguised as a woman, imprisoned at Fortress Monroe and placed in chains, denied pardon and stripped of citizenship, he was to many southerners the personification of a martyred Old South. However, he was still an awkward topic of discussion for many of his past constituency, tainted as he was by the shame of defeat. Indeed, it was not until the mid–1880s that Davis received any significant regional adulation. Frequently considered a tragic figure, Davis is even now a controversial persona, with the one general agreement being that he was, in his better moments at least, a skillful orator.

JEFFERSON DAVIS AS A REGIONAL SPOKESMAN AND ORATOR

Reservations have been expressed by some Davis scholars, but the general consensus has been that he did have strengths as an orator: he was endowed with a pleasing voice; he was brilliant as a debater; his thoughts were always effectively organized and tightly reasoned; he could achieve an inspiring, moving, and literary style; he was capable of motivating with forceful and emotional rhetoric; that in general, however, his rhetoric was not ornamented or his delivery impassioned. Even Edward Pollard, Davis's most persistent detractor, praised his speaking, claiming Davis had "an eloquence . . . without parallel in his time," adding that his public address compared "with the best models in history of public and deliberative discourse." However, Pollard said Davis's style was not florid; it "rejected all extravagances" and "had none of that rhetorical excess which has disfigured so many American statesmen." Dallas Dickey added the observation that Davis was the "debater type," and Varina Davis, Jefferson Davis's second wife, called her husband's style "plain," arguing that he deliberately developed a less ornamented rhetoric and an extemporaneous and audience-directed delivery.

Mrs. Davis's statement reinforces the idea that her husband was instinctively a debater but not a persuader, that his goal was triumph in argument as opposed to persuasive eloquence. This thesis could explain another judgment made by Pollard: "His eloquence was haughty and defiant, and his manners singularly imperious. He spoke as one who would not brook contradiction." Larry Winn, who examined Davis's Civil War speaking to build and sustain Confederate morale, suggested that the Confederate president's speaking was effective with those who already supported him but was probably ineffective with those he most needed to persuade. In debate Davis could be arrogant. Examples of this weakness can be found in the Henry Clay–Davis confrontation over the Compromise of 1850; Davis showed the aging Kentucky senator little respect. However, Davis could also be human, emotional, and moving, as suggested by a series of speeches delivered in 1864 when military operations were going badly for the Confederacy. According to Clement Eaton, Davis "did not . . . lack passion, but he was stoical and self-controlled, and failed to express it until nearly the end of the war."

Born June 3, 1808, in a log cabin in Christian County, Kentucky, less than a hundred miles from Lincoln's birthplace, the future Confederate president was named Jefferson Finis Davis. Later the family moved to Mississippi, where Jefferson and an older brother, Joseph, eventually established themselves as well-to-do planters, leaving their yeoman origins and assuming attitudes and values of the Old South, Bourbon, planter aristocracy. Before all of this, however, Davis attended West Point, received a commission, served seven years at posts in the Midwest, saw action in the Black Hawk War, and married Sarah Knox Taylor, daughter of Zachary Taylor. Sarah soon died of malaria. Then for ten years Davis remained a widower, throwing himself into clearing Brierfield, his Mississippi plantation. In February 1845, at age thirty-six, he married Varina Howell of Natchez and settled into a developing political career.

In November 1845, Davis was elected to the U.S. House of Representatives, where he spoke for, among other issues, President Polk's declaration of war against Mexico, a war that brought a brief recess to Davis's political career. Elected to command a Mississippi regiment, the young colonel of volunteers marched into Mexico, serving under the generalship of his former father-in-law, Zachary Taylor. In one important battle, against significantly greater odds, Davis's regiment routed a Mexican charge, thus becoming the "heroes of Buena Vista." Returning to Mississippi, Davis found himself so highly regarded that Governor Albert Gallatin Brown appointed him to the unexpired term of a recently deceased senator. Then in July 1848, the Mississippi legislature returned Davis to the U.S. Senate for a full term. Thus he was positioned in the national forum at a time when attention focused sharply on newly acquired western territories. At the heart of these considerations was slavery—whether the institution would be extended westward and, if so, by what method. Davis had much to say on these and other regional issues, and he quickly became a major spokesperson for the South as the nation moved inexorably toward disunion.

Between 1848 and 1851, Davis frequently became a defender of southern slavery. He took every opportunity to attack abolitionists, believing they sought no social good, only political power. Liberally paternalistic toward his own slaves, the Mississippian felt the Negro was better off in the South under slavery than as a northern freeman in bondage to a harsh industrial system. But Davis most enjoyed discussing slavery from a legalistic perspective, arguing that the institution itself and the movement of slaves to federal territories were constitutionally protected. He could accept a sovereign state outlawing slavery, but he judged unconstitutional all actions by the federal government to restrict the institution in a sovereign state or in a territory. To provide a methodology for settling future North–South disputes, Davis advocated a basic change in the federal legislative process. Following John Calhoun's proposal for a system of "concurrent majorities," the Mississippian suggested that "in one branch of the Congress the North and in the other the South should have a majority of representatives." By such a system, he noted, no federal legislation could pass that did not have the support of both sections.

In September 1851, Davis left the Senate to accept the Mississippi Democratic party's nomination for governor. He ran against Henry S. Foote, who was supported by the state's Union Democrats and Whigs. A majority of the state's electorate, fearing secessionist fever, had by now turned in favor of the Compromise of 1850, and these voters viewed Davis as a disunionist. In truth he was not, but he could not escape the label. He lost this contest and retired for a period to the seclusion of Brierfield but did not remain out of the political scene for long, receiving a request to join Franklin Pierce's cabinet. The Mississippian served four years as secretary of war, accruing for this effort more acclaim than he garnered for any other service of his career, with the exception of his leadership during the battle of Buena Vista. Historian Clement Eaton had high praise for Davis's secretary of war tenure, calling his leadership "innovative," "efficient," and marked by "high standards." Clement also credited Davis with numerous improvements in the U.S. military, advances that may have worked against the Mississippian between 1861 and 1865. Davis's influence over Pierce's domestic policies, however, may have been far more important than this service to the War Department. Clement labeled Davis the "power behind the throne," noting that on one occasion the secretary of war was called the "de facto president." This influence became most significant when it instigated Pierce's support of the Kansas-Nebraska bill, legislation that effectively nullified the "permanent solution" that the Compromise of 1850 was supposed to have established.

Following Davis's tenure as secretary of war, he was reelected to the Senate, arriving back in these chambers in time to be active in the final round of sectional debates leading to southern secession. Davis was not a disunionist, at least not in the sense that he took every opportunity to threaten or advocate southern withdrawal. Nevertheless, he did remain unbending in his constitutional arguments protecting slavery. In the summer of 1858, an illness led Davis to seek the coolness of New England, and his trip to and from Portland, Maine, provided opportunity for one of the senator's most significant speaking tours. Two of these addresses were of particular importance: a speech presented in Boston's Faneuil Hall, October 12, 1858, and his New York City Palace Garden discourse, delivered a week later. Both speeches avoided any fire-eating tone and actually drew some criticism back home for "placating the Yankees." The southern senator seemed bent on explaining to the North once and for all the South's position on slavery and states' rights, but he tried to keep the mood of these discourses friendly and constructive. In Faneuil Hall, Davis shifted blame for disunionist sentiment to the abolitionists, charging their rhetoric with keeping secessionist fires burning. He also reviewed his arguments concerning the constitutionality of slaves as property, and he reminded his audience that Massachusetts had its own history of standing for states' rights and local political autonomy. In addition, Davis appealed to the economic interests of his auditors, arguing that agriculture was vital to southern agriculture and thus vital to northern manufacturing. In New York he again charged that southerners were not the real disunionists, summarized his position relative to federal control of slavery in the territories, repeated his contention that only a sovereign state could restrict slavery within its boundaries, characterized the entire sectional dispute as motivated by a grasp for power, and attacked the idea that there was a "higher law" than the Constitution—all while still maintaining a conciliatory and positive tone.

This tone, however, did not last long, for either Davis or for northerners who had applauded the warmth of his rhetoric. In October 1859, John Brown's raid at Harpers Ferry generated extreme passions on both sides of the Mason-Dixon line, and Davis was appointed to a Senate committee investigating charges of abolitionist complicity in the event. Although the committee found no grounds for such allegations, Davis used this occasion to intensify his own rhetoric. Still, in March 1860, he made one more legislative attempt, placing before the Senate seven resolutions containing the heart of his states' rights arguments. The resolutions ran in sharp opposition to Stephen A. Douglas's popular sovereignty proposal and thus played a role in priming the Democratic party for its shattering 1860 convention. After the Democrats split and named three nominees, Davis worked with others of his party in an attempt to select a compromise candidate. But these efforts did not succeed, and on November 6, 1860, the Republican, Abraham Lincoln, became the nation's sixteenth president. Nevertheless, says Clement Eaton, Davis still tried "to put the brake on the momentum toward secession," attempting to steer Mississippi toward more moderate reactions. However, all of this was to no avail. On December 20, 1860, South Carolina seceded, and during January 1861, states in the Lower South, including Mississippi, followed suit. Davis' farewell to the Senate was delivered on January 21, with the Mississippian now saying he supported the actions of his state.

In February 1861, in Montgomery, Alabama, Davis was inaugurated president of the Confederacy's provisional government; and a year later, in Richmond, he went through a second inauguration, this time as president of the permanent government. Neither of the speeches delivered on these occasions was among his best. In Montgomery he spoke only briefly but maintained the moderate tone he had established just prior to secession. The Confederacy only wanted peaceful coexistence with the North, he said, but the South still should be prepared to fight for its freedom, and southern people should be ready to sacrifice. This Montgomery audience was confident and jubilant, but at the Richmond inaugural, the crowd was more somber. It was raining, and news had just arrived of the surrender of 15,000 Confederate troops at Fort Donelson. Davis tried to be inspirational, charging that such defeats simply required more heroics from southern people. Admitting recent losses, he reasoned, however, that the South could depend on God as its protector, since the deity was always on the side of right.

Davis's public discourses appear not to have been a vital factor during much of his tenure as president of the Confederacy. Instead his relationships with his generals, his cabinet, and the state governors seem to have consumed the vast majority of his energy and to have been more critical to the war's outcome. Nevertheless, on at least one significant occasion, Davis tried to meet the Confederacy's problems with public speaking. Sherman had taken advantage of indecisiveness in the Army of Tennessee and followed defeat at Chickamaugua in 1863 with the invasion of Georgia in 1864. This Union offensive proved embarrassing to Davis, since he and Georgia's Governor Brown had engaged in several disputes over deployment of Georgian troops. When Sherman's forces threatened Atlanta, Brown even advised Davis relative to precise troop movements, advice that Davis curtly rejected. Thus when Joseph Johnston failed to hold northern Georgia and when Johnston's replacement, John B. Hood, lost Atlanta, Brown felt justified in saying, "I told you so."

With Confederate morale running low, with desertions climbing to an all-time high, with Alabama and South Carolina fearful Sherman would turn in their directions, and with Brown demanding termination of the war by negotiation, Davis visited the Middle South to rally the Army of Tennessee and the peoples of Georgia, Alabama, and South Carolina. Speaking in Macon, Montgomery, Augusta, and Columbia, Davis developed the following arguments: that although the loss of Atlanta was regrettable, there had been nothing more he personally could have done to save the city; that with renewed dedication—and particularly with the return of deserters to their units—the Army of Tennessee would drive Sherman back into Kentucky and beyond; that this was no time for armchair generals to criticize responsible Confederate leaders; and that absolutely no considerations should be given calls for negotiation with the enemy. More important than all this was the tone of these speeches. Gone was the arrogance of which Pollard complained, replaced by an emotional plea that southerners rally to the cause, that women help by shaming deserters back to duty, that state leaders drop all petty animosities and unify behind the central government, and that talk of negotiation be terminated. It was a desperate, last-effort type of rhetoric, and it abandoned the debater's style for a passion not wholly typical of Davis.

After the war, it took time for Davis to reemerge as a platform figure. Marilyn Miller Thompson, who studied Davis's postbellum speaking, labeled the former Confederate president the "reluctant orator," indicating that the humiliation of defeat and the consequent criticism of his leadership—from both the South and the North—drove the Mississippian from public view. The picture Thompson painted is of a speaker who had to be coaxed back to the podium and who was comfortable only before audiences of admirers. Nevertheless, Davis did regain some platform prominence, delivering twenty ceremonial addresses between

1870 and his death in 1889. Still, twenty speeches in nineteen years seem no great number, and there was a sameness about most of the occasions: memorials to Confederate leaders and soldiers, two meetings of the Southern Historical Society, a Texas State Fair address, reunions of Confederate veterans, one speech to the Mississippi state legislature, and a couple of university addresses. From the rhetoric of these postbellum speeches, Davis gained an image as unyielding, unreconstructed, and unrepentant, attitudes that greatly disturbed the North. His language was seldom bellicose or even arrogant, but he held unrelentingly to old constitutional arguments advanced in his numerous antebellum discourses, claiming on more than one occasion that the nation would eventually recognize the rightness of the Confederate cause.

Davis had weaknesses in platform style and temperament—his haughtiness of tone and his intense debater instincts—but his most profound deficiency may have been his inability to recognize changing values. There was little in his rhetoric, for example, indicating he ever perceived the abolitionist movement as anything other than one side of a political power struggle. The only pure cause he apparently saw was the cause of strict construction constitutionality, and he was able to disregard any evils that ideology might protect. Clément Eaton summed up his judgment of Davis by asserting that he was "an admirable, honorable, but misguided man of exceptional ability and force who accepted the assumptions of his society." Perhaps if his cultural conditioning had been different, he would have found a less controversial place in history.

INFORMATION SOURCES

Research Collections and Collected Speeches

Davis, Jefferson. *Jefferson Davis, Constitutionalist, His Letters, Papers,*   JD
    and Speeches. 10 vols. Edited by Roland Dunbar. New York: J. J.
    Little and Ives Company, 1923.
———. *Speeches of the Hon. Jefferson Davis of Mississippi, Delivered*   SJD
    During the Summer of 1858. Baltimore: John Murphy and Co., 1859.
The Congressional Globe (1846–1961).   CG

Selected Critical Studies

Dickey, Dallas. "Were They Ephemeral and Florid?" *Quarterly Journal of Speech* 32
    (1946): 16–21.
Ellingsworth, Hubert. "The Thwarted Lecture Tour of Jefferson Davis." *Quarterly Jour-*
    nal of Speech 43 (1957): 284–87.
Oliver, Robert T. *History of Public Speaking in America.* Boston: Allyn and Bacon,
    1965.
Richardson, Ralph E. "The Speaking and Speeches of Jefferson Davis." Ph.D. disser-
    tation, Northwestern University, 1950.
Thompson, Marilyn Miller. "Jefferson Davis, The Reluctant Orator: A Study of His

Postwar Speaking (1867–1889)." Master's thesis, Louisiana State University, 1974.

Winn, Larry James. "The Rhetoric of Morale-Building: A Study of Jefferson Davis' Efforts to Build and Sustain Confederate Morale." Master's thesis, Memphis State University, 1970.

Selected Biographies

Eaton, Clement. *Jefferson Davis*. New York: Free Press, 1977.

Davis, Varina. *Jefferson Davis: Ex-President of the Confederate States of America, A Memoir*. 2 vols. New York: Belford Company, 1890.

Pollard, Edward A. *Life of Jefferson Davis, with a Secret History of the Southern Confederacy*. Philadelphia: National Publishing Company, 1869.

Strode, Hudson. *Jefferson Davis: American Patriot, 1808–1861*. New York: Harcourt, Brace and Company, 1955.

———. *Jefferson Davis: Confederate President*. New York: Harcourt, Brace and Company, 1959.

———. *Jefferson Davis: Tragic Hero*. New York: Harcourt, Brace and World, Inc., 1964.

CHRONOLOGY OF MAJOR SPEECHES

See "Research Collections and Collected Speeches" for source codes.

Speech against the Compromise of 1850, Washington, D.C., February 13, 14, 1850; *JD*, 1:263–308.

Faneuil Hall address, Boston, October 12, 1858; *SJD*, pp. 29–39.

Palace Garden address, New York, October 19, 1858; *JD*, 3:332–39.

"Seven Resolutions," Washington, D.C., May 7, 1860; *CG*, 36th Cong., 1st sess., pp. 1937–42.

Farewell to the Senate, Washington, D.C., January 21, 1861; *JD*, 5:40–45.

First Inaugural, Montgomery, Alabama, February 18, 1861; *JD*, 5:49–53.

Second Inaugural, Richmond, Virginia, February 22, 1862; *JD*, 5:198–203.

Speech at Macon, Georgia, September 25, 1864; *JD*, 6:341–44.

Speech at Montgomery, Alabama, October 2, 1864; *JD*, 6:345–47.

Speech at Columbia, South Carolina, October 4, 1864; *JD*, 6:350–56.

Speech at Augusta, Georgia, October 5, 1864; *JD*, 6:356–61.

JOHN DICKINSON
(1732–1808), Pennsylvania politician

SANDRA SARKELA HYNES

For John Dickinson, often called the penman of the American Revolution, public speech was not only an invaluable right, it was the means by which liberty was maintained. Public speech, including written and oral discourse, allowed what Dickinson called "moderation" to exist in government and society. Through discourse, citizens could avoid the weakness of submission to tyranny without resorting to outright rebellion. Dickinson exemplified and advocated this philosophy of social change during the first ten years of the American Revolutionary movement. In petitions, pamphlets, and speeches, Dickinson called on Americans to act in defense of their liberties. Although he is not acknowledged as a great speaker today, many of Dickinson's contemporaries felt otherwise. Benjamin Rush and Charles Thomson praised Dickinson's effectiveness as a speaker. In fact, Thomson claimed Dickinson was the most eloquent speaker in the First Continental Congress. Despite his tremendous influence there, however, Dickinson's support fell apart during the Second Continental Congress. He was not ready for a Declaration of Independence by mid–1776, and he argued against the declaration in a speech that signaled the end of his leadership of the American Revolutionary movement. Several years later, as a delegate to the Constitutional Convention, Dickinson regained some of his influence. His convention speeches, however, were barely an echo of the commanding presence he exhibited from 1764 to 1776.

JOHN DICKINSON'S RHETORIC OF RESISTANCE

Throughout his life, Dickinson advocated a philosophy of social change based on a fundamental value for moderation. He believed that revolution, or abandonment of the existing governmental framework, was unnecessarily reckless. Change was inevitable and desirable, but revolution was not. Thus Dickinson advocated progressive change in government, but he urged caution when it appeared that the constitution, or governmental framework itself, was under attack. Dickinson's moderation also commanded him to act. One could not remain free in a world torn between weakness and evil without fighting against both forces. Appropriate moderate tactics exemplified and advocated by Dickinson included a combination of verbal persuasion and nonviolent coercion.

His first noteworthy statement of this view occurred on May 27, 1764, in a speech before the Pennsylvania Assembly. Benjamin Franklin and Joseph Galloway, leaders of the powerful Quaker party, called for a change in Pennsylvania's government from a proprietary to a royal colony. Dickinson's speech caused a stir in the assembly in part because it was so unexpected. Until this point, Dickinson had been Franklin's spokesman in opposing the proprietor. Then Dickinson demonstrated backbone and conviction as he broke with his powerful former ally, Benjamin Franklin, and with most of his fellow Quakers, by speaking in an emotionally charged atmosphere against a change in Pennsylvania government. The speech was not primarily a statement of political ideology; it was part of an argument over strategy. However, three ideological positions were stated. First, Dickinson said the liberties guaranteed by the Pennsylvania Charter of Privileges were "founded on the acknowledged rights of human nature." Second, Dickinson feared power. For that reason he said the British ministry could not be trusted. He explained that "power is like the *ocean*, not easily admitting limits to be fixed in it." The third aspect of Dickinson's political ideology apparent in this speech is the fairly radical belief that government could not be changed "without the almost *universal consent of the people* exprest in the plainest manner."

The strategy Dickinson advocated was two-sided. Most of the speech was taken up by a plea for caution in pursuing a change in government. At the same time, however, Dickinson asserted that people must be spirited in defense of their liberties: "With unremitting vigilance, with undaunted virtue, should a free people *watch* against the encroachments of power, and *remove* every pretext for its extension." This was also how Dickinson justified his own action in speaking out against his former allies. As a citizen of a free society, he felt he was morally obligated to speak out: "I shall cheer-full submit to the censure of having been *too apprehensive* of injuring the people of this Province. . . . This truth I am convinced of, that it will be much easier for me to bear the unmerited reflections of *mistaken zeal* than the just reproaches of a *guilty mind*."

Although he was fighting a losing battle in the assembly, Dickinson did everything he could to get his position publicized, even if it meant changing or violating rules of order and alienating former allies. By the time the assembly adjourned, Dickinson had cut ties with his successful past. During that summer, however, he emerged as the spokesman for a new political coalition of dissatisfied Presbyterians, Anglicans, and conservative Quakers, which was finally organized into a slate of assembly candidates called the New Ticket. Publication of Dickinson's assembly speech revealed that all of the arguments that had failed before the assembly were persuasive with Dickinson's new audience. Dickinson's belief in the need for assemblymen to consider "our distrest fellow-subjects" and that the charter could not be "surrendered" without "almost universal consent of the many that fill this Province" surely added to the speech's persuasive impact with those outside the assembly. Dickinson's speech served as a manifesto for opposition to the assembly's petition for a change in government, and he was at the center of a political maelstrom during the summer and fall of 1764. He set forth alternative policies for a new political coalition and enthusiastically attacked Joseph Galloway, his principal opponent. Dickinson became a hero to the Presbyterians as a result. While Dickinson advocated a cool and rational approach to policy making, his own behavior was consistently bold and spirited.

John Dickinson continued his political activity briefly in the Pennsylvania Assembly and as a member of the Stamp Act Congress in 1765. During the winter of 1765–1766, he resumed his rhetorical leadership of Pennsylvania's

New Ticket. His reputation as a radical leader was enhanced during this period by publication of his widely circulated pamphlet opposing the Stamp Act. Despite repeal of the Stamp Act in 1766 and Dickinson's loss in the October 1766 assembly elections, he, and the Presbyterian/Whig party, did not recede from politics. Instead, during the years from 1767 to 1770, this new political force strengthened its organization and acquired mass support. The two men most responsible for the increasing strength of their political faction were Charles Thomson and John Dickinson. Under their leadership, the Whig party coalesced around a drive for nonimportation to stop Parliament from interfering with American home rule. Dickinson's famous "Letters from a Farmer in Pennsylvania" generated support throughout the colonies, but Philadelphia lagged behind.

In an attempt to get Philadelphia merchants to join other colonies in a nonimportation agreement, Dickinson addressed Philadelphia merchants on April 25, 1768. He knew his address would also reach other audiences since it was subsequently printed in the *Journal* and published separately as a broadside. Thus, it was essentially a short restatement of his "Letters from a Farmer," with emphasis on the need for unity. He made a special appeal to the merchants, stating that inconvenience was sometimes necessary to maintain unity and achieve redress of grievances: "I hope, my Brethren, there is not a Man among us, who will not chearfully join in the Measure proposed, . . . nay, even submit to a present Inconvenience for the Sake of Liberty, on which our Happiness, Lives, and Properties depend." But the appeal was not successful, and on June 14 the New York nonimportation agreement collapsed with Philadelphia's failure to join in. When a nonimportation agreement was finally secured the next year, Dickinson's popularity soared. He was a nearly unanimous choice for an assembly seat in 1770. During the next several years, Dickinson maintained his popularity among Presbyterians and artisans but began to build support among conservative Quakers as well. By the time the First Continental Congress convened in 1775, Dickinson was the acknowledged leader of Pennsylvania's resistance movement and was equally respected in Congress. He wrote all but one of the documents issued by the First Congress.

With the eruption of violence on April 19, 1775, at Lexington and Concord, the anti-British movement was forced closer to crisis. Dickinson continued to exert a significant, if not controlling, influence on the Second Continental Congress. He developed a strategy for dealing with Great Britain in the wake of military encounters and explained it in a speech before Congress. He contended that the best approach to reaching an agreeable settlement was to pursue all potential avenues of settlement, including full preparations for war, petitioning the king, and authorizing American agents to work for a negotiated settlement. This strategy, Dickinson said, was like holding an "Olive branch in an armed hand." The strategy should have helped unify the increasingly divided Congress because it had something for everyone, but Dickinson did not use that appeal. Instead he asserted the consistency of his opinion, flattered his opponents, and expressed the hope that he was not wrong. Later in debate over the issue, however, Dickinson warned the Congress that unity was fragile, and he urged Congress not to be too extreme: "If some of Us cannot go as far as others let them not strain us too far—to put us out of breath to discourage Us." The appeal worked, and Dickinson was assigned responsibility for drafting the second petition to the king, often called the "Olive Branch Petition." He was also called in to revise both the drafting committee's and Thomas Jefferson's version of the Declaration of the Causes and Necessities of Taking up Arms, a document that was the most popular piece of the Congress until the Declaration of Independence. These two documents, the second petition and declaration, are the keys to Dickinson's bifold strategy initially advocated in his speech before Congress.

The late summer and early fall of 1775 brought some trouble to Dickinson. New England delegates were anxious for more radical policies and began to woo Franklin. Dickinson, however, successfully defended his own program. The general trend was not one of increasing caution for Dickinson but increasing radicalization of the movement. At the same time, it must be remembered that Dickinson maintained majority support in Congress. So far, New England delegates represented a minority view, but not for much longer. In June 1776, Richard H. Lee introduced the resolution for independence. Dickinson and a few others opposed the resolution, not because they opposed independence but because they felt the timing was poor and the strategic value minimal. Those opposed to independence managed to get a delay in a call for the question. Three committees were established instead. Dickinson was on two of the three committees. He was assigned to draft the Articles of Confederation and to help set up negotiations for an alliance with France. The only committee he was not appointed to was the one to draft a Declaration of Independence.

Before the articles were out of committee, however, the committee drafting a declaration brought the document before Congress. It was debated July 1 and the vote counted the next day. Dickinson delivered a speech against the declaration. The most notable facet of the speech is not Dickinson's timidity but his courage in speaking so plainly against the known majority sentiment. He must have stunned fellow delegates with his forthright acknowledgment of his potential unpopularity: "I might indeed, practise an artful, an advantageous Reserve upon this Occasion. But thinking as I do on the subject of Debate, Silence would be guilt. . . . I must speak, tho I should lose my Life, tho I should lose the Affections of my C[ountrymen]." The situation recalled Dickinson's 1764 speech against royal government, which was also a bold move to stop what he believed was an ill-timed policy and unnecessary change. In this speech, however, Dickinson clearly agreed with the proposed change—that America should be an independent nation—but he objected to the timing of the declaration. In arguments that echoed the June 7–8 debates, Dickinson said Congress should wait until alliances were secure, or at least until responses had been received from foreign countries, before declaring independence. He claimed, "It is treating them with Contempt to act otherwise." Thus, Dickinson urged Congress: "Let Us in the most solemn Manner inform the House of Bourbon, at least France, that we wait only for her

Determination to declare an Independence.'' Dickinson also felt the Articles of Confederation should be complete before declaring independence: ''The Committee on Confederation dispute almost every Article—some of Us totally despair of any reasonable Terms of Confederation. We cannot look back. Men generally sell their Goods to most Advantage when they have several Chapmen. We have but two to rely on. We exclude one by this Declaration without knowing What the other will give.'' Finally, Dickinson was irritated by the fairly sudden change in attitude of many delegates, fostered by the radicals from New England. He ended the speech on a bitter note: ''A worthy Gentleman told Us, that people in this House have had different Views for more than a 12 month. Amazing after what they have so repeatedly declared in this House & private Conversations—that they meant only Reconciliation.''

Dickinson always campaigned for unified resistance. His ability to unite disparate factions in support of a particular issue was one of his greatest strengths. Dickinson sought the same broad-based support for a new American government, but before he had time to gather such support in Pennsylvania, New England congressional delegates pushed through the Resolution for Independence. Dickinson feared this sort of factionalism and apparently believed Pennsylvania would not long exist under the same government as New England. From this point until the end of the year, Dickinson was outspoken and principled to the point of self-destruction. He understood the political reality of an independent America, and he could go so far as to develop alliances and write a Constitution, but the Declaration of Independence was ill timed, and he could not vote for it. When the Pennsylvania Assembly chose new delegates for the Congress, Dickinson was not among them. Wasting no time in Philadelphia, Dickinson set off with his battalion for New Jersey, where he remained until the end of September when he resigned his position.

During the 1780s Dickinson became active again. First he served as president of Delaware and then as president of Pennsylvania, completing a three-year term. In 1787 he served as a delegate to the Constitutional Convention. Dickinson's performance there was a disappointment to himself and observers. His delivery was uninspiring, which has probably been a factor in his current reputation as a poor speaker. Furthermore, he was unable to present several speeches he prepared due to illness. The content of the speeches reveals Dickinson tried to draft a compromise plan of government much as he drafted the documents of the Stamp Act Congress in 1765. If he had been well enough to attend and speak at more sessions, Dickinson might have recaptured some of the national popularity he achieved as the Pennsylvania Farmer. As it was, his contribution was interesting and constructive but not of great impact. Nevertheless, the ideas and language generated by John Dickinson from 1764 to 1776, so expressive of majority sentiment at the time and so effective in securing unified support of resistance strategies, influenced American political attitudes and language found in important documents from the Declaration of Independence to the U.S. Constitution.

INFORMATION SOURCES

Research Collections and Collected Speeches

Dickinson's personal papers, including drafts of all his known speeches, are located at the Historical Society of Pennsylvania, Philadelphia. Of special interest are the Dickinson Papers, Library Company Collection; the Dickinson Papers, R. R. Logan Collection; the Logan Papers; and the Maria Dickinson Logan Collection.

Dickinson, John. *Political Writings*. 2 vols. Wilmington, 1801.   *PW*
——. *The Writings of John Dickinson*. Edited by Paul Ford. Philadelphia: *WJD*
     Historical Society of Pennsylvania, 1891.
Letters of Delegates to Congress. 5 vols. Edited by Paul L. Smith. Wash-   *LDC*
     ington, D.C.: Library of Congress, 1976.
Hutson, James H. "John Dickinson at the Federal Constitutional Conven-   *JDFCC*
     tion." *William and Mary Quarterly* 40 (1983): 256–82.

Selected Critical Studies

Boyd, Julian. "The Disputed Authorship of the Declaration on the Causes and Necessities
     for Taking Up Arms, 1775." *Pennsylvania Magazine of History and Biography*
     74 (1950): 51–73.
Hooker, Richard. "John Dickinson on Church and State." *American Literature* 16 (1944):
     82–92.
Kaestle, Carl. "The Public Reaction to John Dickinson's 'Farmer's Letters.' " American
     Antiquarian Society, *Proceedings* 78 (1968): 323–59.
Powell, John H. "The Debate on American Independence." *Delaware Notes* 23d ser.
     (1950): 37–62.
——. "John Dickinson's Speech against Independence." *Pennsylvania Magazine of
     History and Biography* 64 (1941): 189–224.

Selected Biographies

Flower, Milton. *John Dickinson: Conservative Revolutionary*. Charlottesville: University
     Press of Virginia, 1983.
Hynes, Sandra Sarkela. "The Political Rhetoric of John Dickinson, 1764–1776." Ph.D.
     dissertation, University of Massachusetts, 1982.
Jacobson, David. *John Dickinson and the Revolution in Pennsylvania, 1764–1776*. Berke-
     ley: University of California Press, 1965.
Powell, John H. "John Dickinson: The Penman of the Revolution." Ph.D. dissertation,
     University of Iowa, 1938.
Stille, Charles. *The Life and Times of John Dickinson*. Philadelphia: Lippincott, 1891.

CHRONOLOGY OF MAJOR SPEECHES

See "Research Collections and Collected Speeches" for source codes.

Speech against royal government, Philadelphia, May 27, 1764; *PW*, 1:1–40; *WJD*, pp. 9–49.

Address to merchants, Philadelphia, April 25, 1768; *WJD*, pp. 409–17.

Strategy speech in Second Continental Congress, Philadelphia, May 23–25(?), 1775; *LDC*, 1:371–83.

Speech against independence, Philadelphia, July 1, 1776; *LDC*, 4:351–58.

Speech(es) at the federal Constitutional Convention, Philadelphia, June 18–19, 29–30, 1787; *JDFCC*, pp. 270–79.

STEPHEN A. DOUGLAS
(1813–1861), U.S. senator from Illinois

DAVID ZAREFSKY

History has not been kind to Stephen A. Douglas. In his own day among the most prominent senators, the most persistent advocate of territorial expansion, and a constant defender of the principles of local self-government, he is today remembered chiefly as a stepping-stone in Abraham Lincoln's career or, worse yet, as an apologist for slavery. Appraising Douglas's public discourse requires placing the man and the speeches in context, for Douglas was preeminently a man of his times.

Stephen Arnold Douglass (he dropped the final *s* from his name in 1846) was born in 1813 in Vermont. At the age of fifteen, he first became entranced by Andrew Jackson; Old Hickory would remain his hero throughout his life. In 1830 he began his westward migration, first to the Burned-Over district of Canandaigua, New York, where he attended school and studied law. In 1833 he moved farther west, arriving finally at the central Illinois town of Jacksonville. He taught school in nearby Winchester and the following year obtained his license to practice law.

Douglas had developed an avid interest in politics, which quickly competed with his legal career for his attention. He spoke for the Democrats at rallies, followed election campaigns closely, and held a succession of public offices. Beginning in the mid–1830s, he served as state's attorney, a member of the Illinois legislature, register of the land office at Springfield, secretary of state for Illinois, and a judge of the Illinois Supreme Court—the last position obtained after a successful court packing attempt to dilute Whig strength on the court. In 1842 he was elected to the U.S. House of Representatives where, as an ardent supporter of expansion, he was named chairman of the Committee on Territories. He assumed the same position in the Senate, to which he was elected in 1846.

Douglas was considered a serious presidential candidate beginning in 1852. In 1856 he threw his support to James Buchanan, probably in order to block the renomination of the unpopular Franklin Pierce. In 1860 he won the nomination of a divided Democratic party. Following his defeat, he was a staunch defender of the Union and opponent of secession, until his life ended abruptly in June 1861, at the age of forty-eight.

DOUGLAS AS POLITICAL ADVOCATE

Of Douglas's early speaking career, relatively little is known. Texts are difficult to find since it was not the custom to transcribe campaign speeches. He earned the sobriquet "The Little Giant" during the mid–1830s for his strident denunciation of the Whigs. He is first known to have encountered Lincoln in debate during the fall of 1839, when each man was supporting his party's candidate for president in the upcoming election. In this encounter, ironically, Lincoln appealed to anti-Negro attitudes by alleging that Douglas's candidate,

Martin Van Buren, favored suffrage for free blacks. When Douglas denied the charge, Lincoln produced Van Buren's official campaign biography to subtantiate it. Douglas replied that anyone who could write such a book thinking that it would help Van Buren's chances in Illinois must be a fool, flung the book out into the audience, and thereby dismissed the charge. This rough-and-tumble approach to argument, with apparent disregard for logic and evidence, was not uncommon.

The Little Giant was an early advocate of the Mexican War, which he saw as a means toward national expansion, the ultimate goal being to make the "area of liberty," the United States, as great as the North American continent itself. In a speech in the House in May 1846, he developed an elaborate historical argument to support the dubious American claim to the Rio Grande as the national boundary, demanded consistency in policies toward Texas and Oregon, and impugned the patriotism of opponents of the war—the characteristic combination of defense and attack that would mark his later speeches on the slavery question.

Douglas played a major role in the Compromise of 1850, proposing to break a deadlock by dividing the omnibus bill into several separate bills that could be passed by floating majorities. Douglas's role, however, was played largely behind the scenes and was masked by his effusive praise of Henry Clay's stewardship of the compromise. He did speak in the Senate in June 1850 against a clause that would prevent territorial legislatures from acting with respect to slavery. In this speech, Douglas developed two arguments that would be standard themes in his later oratory. One was the argument from comparison: people who were competent to legislate on all other "rightful subjects of legislation" must be presumed to be competent to legislate with respect to Negroes. The other was the liquor analogy that Douglas used to support his later contention that "friendly local legislation" was a prerequisite for slavery, notwithstanding the *Dred Scott* decision. The analogy was simple: local restrictions could effectively prevent a tavern keeper from doing business, notwithstanding his constitutional right to take his property there. If territories had the power to forbid the importation of one species of property (liquor), then they should have the power to forbid the importation of another (slaves).

The zenith of Douglas's speaking career began when he introduced the Kansas-Nebraska bill in January 1854. On March 3 he delivered a major address, concluding the debate on the bill with a comprehensive review of the arguments. The bill, he said, was essential to promote white migration to the West. The main issue, as he saw it, was between the principles of the Missouri Compromise and those of the Compromise of 1850. Denying popular folklore that regarded the Missouri Compromise as a sacred compact, Douglas insisted that its principles had been superseded by those of 1850 and proposed only to acknowledge this fact in 1854. Moreover, he argued that the principles of 1850 were actually a return to those of the Revolution, an early use of a specious comparison that would figure prominently in his speeches from 1858 to 1860. After maligning his opponents, Douglas predicted that the Kansas-Nebraska Act would be popular not just in the South but also in the North because of its appeal to the principle of self-government.

In this last prediction, Douglas proved to be profoundly mistaken. The act, though passed by Congress and signed by President Pierce, evoked intense opposition in the North, so much so that Douglas himself said that he could travel from Washington to Chicago by the light of his own effigy. The act's passage also reawakened the political interest of Abraham Lincoln, who had withdrawn from politics in 1849 after a single term in the House of Representatives.

Douglas spoke during the fall of 1854 in an attempt to vindicate his position. Although he refused to debate Lincoln (who had become the leader of the anti-Nebraska Whigs), they each spoke at the state fair in what was a debate in fact if not form. The Little Giant was surprised when a coalition of anti-Nebraska Whigs and Democrats passed over James Shields for the U.S. Senate, choosing instead the renegade Lyman Trumbull, to whom Lincoln had thrown his support in order to break a deadlock. This episode, however, was a portent of the weakness of Douglas's popular-sovereignty views in the North, a weakness that he moved to repair later in the decade.

In the *Dred Scott* case, decided in March 1857, the Supreme Court held that Congress had no power to regulate slavery in the territories. This decision undercut Douglas's popular sovereignty, for how could a territorial legislature, a *creature* of Congress, exercise powers denied to its creator?

Douglas greeted this decision initially with silence, but three months later he delivered a speech in Springfield in which he tried to reconcile popular sovereignty with *Dred Scott*. The court decision, he held, dealt only with an abstract property right; friendly local legislation (the prerogative of the territorial legislature) was needed to make it meaningful.

Popular legend has it that Douglas improvised this crucial distinction between abstract and concrete rights in response to a shrewd dilemma posed by Lincoln in one of their debates and that the theory repaired Douglas's political standing in the North while exposing his vulnerability in the South. Neither part of this legend is correct. Douglas had propounded his theory a full year before the debates; Lincoln was reasonably sure how his opponent would reply at Freeport. And Douglas's view was initially supported by many in the South as well as by the newspapers of the Buchanan administration. What really threatened Douglas's stature in the South was his break with Buchanan over the Lecompton Constitution.

The story of the drafting of this document, by which Kansas would enter the Union as a slave state, is complex. Suffice it to say that the Lecompton instrument was a legal but clearly unrepresentative expression of the will of the people of Kansas. Douglas denounced it as a violation of popular sovereignty; he was criticized in the South for supporting popular sovereignty only when its consequence was freedom.

Douglas's opening speech was delivered in the Senate on December 9, 1857.

Noting that Buchanan had not advocated Lecompton but indicated only that he would sign a bill if Congress passed it, the senator tried to put the best possible construction on the president's acts and motives. He then attacked the Lecompton Constitution, primarily because only the slavery clause—not the entire document—would be submitted for a referendum. That was a sham, Douglas insisted, much like an election in which Napoleon allegedly told his troops that they could vote as they pleased, but if they voted against him, they would be shot. Why was the entire constitution not submitted to vote, when all the parties involved had understood that there would be a referendum? Because, Douglas asserted, of fear that the voters of Kansas would reject it. That was a clear violation of popular sovereignty, and he could not endorse it. Nor would Douglas be satisfied if the slavery clause were rejected by such a method, for the real issue was procedure and not the disposition of any individual section of the constitution. It was in this context that he made the famous remark, later to be quoted out of context against him, that he "care[d] not whether [the slavery clause] is voted down or voted up."

As Buchanan explicitly endorsed Lecompton, declared its passage to be a party measure, and employed the patronage against Douglas and other recalcitrants, the enmity between the senator and the president deepened. In his closing address of the Lecompton debate on March 22, 1858, Douglas excoriated the administration. Although his health was weak and his cause was lost, he delivered a clear and forthright statement of his position. Arguments from history established the sanctity of the popular sovereignty principle; the key question was whether the Lecompton Constitution embodied that principle. Douglas's answer was no because many Kansans had been defrauded from voting for convention delegates and because the constitution itself was not to be submitted to popular vote. The nature of the slavery clause per se was not central to his objections, nor was the dispute about whether the constitution could be amended before the self-proclaimed seven-year probationary period. The key fact was that the instrument was not wanted by the people of Kansas, as was dramatically demonstrated by the results of a nonbinding referendum in January, at which it had been decisively rejected.

Lecompton caused Douglas's southern position to erode, but it made him popular in the North, caused many Republicans such as Horace Greeley to consider popular sovereignty as an effective means to their own end, and made him appear virtually unstoppable in his quest for reelection. His challenger, Abraham Lincoln, was a leading Illinois Whig but a relative unknown outside the state, while he, the incumbent, chairman of the Senate Committee on Territories, strode the stage.

Lincoln had opened the campaign with the "House Divided" speech accepting the Republican nomination. Stuck in Washington until Congress adjourned, Douglas opened fire in a speech given in Chicago on July 9, 1858. He portrayed the "house divided" doctrine as leading inevitably to abolitionism, a radical and unrespectable program, especially among the swing voters of central Illinois.

In contrast, the principle of popular sovereignty would allow the nation to remain forever, yet divided "as our fathers made it," half slave and half free. With this blast, repeated in speeches in Bloomington and Springfield, Douglas had his challenger on the run. Having difficulty in drawing his own crowds, Lincoln began following Douglas on the campaign trail to inherit his audiences. Partly to forestall this practice, the incumbent reluctantly agreed to a series of seven debates against his challenger, extending from mid-August to mid-October.

Douglas maintained the initiative in the opening debates. He lambasted the "house divided" doctrine, portrayed Lincoln's position as being in conflict with that of the founding fathers and of the revered Henry Clay, defended the theory of popular sovereignty, and accused Lincoln of conspiring with Trumbull to take over the two major parties and convert them to abolitionism, solely to enhance their personal political fortunes. Even the famous Freeport question was answered forthrightly and so effectively that Lincoln dropped the matter in rebuttal.

Douglas's argument remained basically the same throughout the debates, and the grueling campaign began to take its toll on his health. Lincoln, on the other hand, hit his stride in the last few debates by developing the moral argument that slavery was wrong, remonstrating Douglas for the seeming amorality of his "don't care" position, and yet reconciling his moral claim with Illinoisans' distaste for immediate abolition by saying that the "public mind" would be convinced that slavery was in the "course of ultimate extinction" if it were kept out of the territories, since it must expand or die.

Large crowds, from 2,000 to 20,000, attended the debates. People arrived early in the day for the three-hour discussions in the afternoon. In the end, the debates probably changed few votes. In the Senate race, Lincoln won in the popular vote, but Douglas carried enough legislative districts to win reelection. Of special interest, he captured most of the swing counties of central Illinois.

Douglas returned to the Senate, but even in the aftermath of his electoral triumph, he was on the defensive. Southerners, enraged by his Lecompton position and the publicity given to his Freeport doctrine, stripped him of the chairmanship of the Committee on Territories. Growing numbers of northerners, meanwhile, were becoming uneasy with the apparent moral neutrality of popular sovereignty. Douglas tried to appeal to the South's memories of a common past, to the conservatism of southern Whigs, and to the prospect of acquiring Cuba as a way to subordinate sectional differences to national expansion. It was increasingly necessary, however, to reconcile popular sovereignty with positive protection of slavery for southern audiences and yet also to reduce the moral callousness it conveyed to northerners. That combination of results required ambivalence that was difficult to sustain, as is evident in three of Douglas's rhetorical efforts during 1859. First, in June he wrote a letter to Dubuque editor J. B. Dorr specifying that he would accept the 1860 presidential nomination only on a popular-sovereignty platform—an apparent effort to reassure northern Democrats that he had made no substantial concessions on his recent southern trip.

Second, in early September, he embarked on a speaking tour in Ohio, speaking in Columbus, Cincinnati, and Wooster in behalf of Democratic candidates. Since Lincoln was also speaking in the state, the Ohio canvass in many respects was a replay of the Lincoln-Douglas debates. In the Columbus speech, for example, Douglas attributed to the Republicans an activist intention to abolish slavery, drawing his evidence from Lincoln's "house divided" speech and William Henry Seward's proclamation of an "irrepressible conflict." He then argued that this view put the Republicans at odds with the founding fathers, who waged the Revolution in order to establish popular sovereignty. Indeed, the Republicans, by denying the right of territorial inhabitants to govern themselves in all respects, were akin to the Tories who had defended taxation without representation. The founding fathers, Douglas insisted, understood the question better, and the country should be left as they made it, divided between free and slave states. Douglas also began to argue that the Republicans and southern fire-eaters were essentially similar, differing only as to when they would have the government intervene in what ought to be a local matter. All of these themes were natural extensions of the 1858 debates, but Douglas did make some concessions to his Ohio audiences. He referred to popular sovereignty as "self-government" and euphemized slavery as "local and domestic concerns."

As the Columbus speech reflects, Douglas—like Lincoln—was increasingly preoccupied with discerning the intentions of the founding fathers. His third major rhetorical effort of 1859—a lengthy article in the September issue of *Harper's*—spoke to this need. Douglas argued that the Revolution had been fought for the principle of popular sovereignty, that territories were virtually the same as states, and that Congress could confer to the territorial legislatures powers it could not exercise itself. It is unlikely that the article attracted a large readership, but it did evoke hostile editorials in southern papers, which insisted that the South would be satisfied with nothing less than affirmative moves to protect the peculiar institution.

As 1860 arrived, Douglas felt the extremes pressing against the middle ground. He would go into the Democratic convention with support of a majority of the delegates but fewer than the two-thirds needed for the nomination. He received the nod for the presidency only after many of the southerners had withdrawn and nominated John C. Breckinridge. In the campaign, Douglas became the first candidate to campaign actively for the office. He delivered speeches throughout the country, appealing always for compromise and moderation and noting the common interest of Republicans and fire-eaters in conspiring against the will of the people.

In Iowa, for example, Douglas attributed current discontent entirely to congressional attempts to regulate the slavery issue, he equated Republicans and Tories, and he attributed to the Republicans an abolitionist design. The Republican claims to a higher morality Douglas ridiculed; they implied "that George Washington signed a league with hell when he put his name to the Constitution." In Raleigh he stressed the same themes and added that the split in the Democratic party was the result of a conspiracy by the Republicans and fire-eaters to exclude the middle ground. He also defended the Freeport doctrine by insisting that climate was the ultimate determinant of whether the people of a territory wanted slavery, notwithstanding the abstract right promulgated in the *Dred Scott* decision. In Montgomery he again alleged the existence of a conspiracy to break up the Union and called on "every good citizen to frustrate the scheme." In Chicago he attacked Seward and Lincoln as extremists who secretly favored social equality for the Negro but were unwilling to say so publicly. He appealed to the Compromise of 1850 and its principle of congressional noninterference, and he repeated the same conspiracy charge.

What is noteworthy about Douglas's 1860 campaign, aside from its novelty, was its national scope. The Little Giant did not neglect the South, though he had no chance to win there. Moreover, he delivered strong appeals for the preservation of the Union. Although he "would regard the election of Lincoln as a great calamity, to be avoided by all honorable means by patriotic men," as he said in Raleigh, still he insisted that the election of any president by constitutional means was not sufficient reason for secession. To take such a step would be treason; as for traitors, Douglas would "hang them higher than Haman." His southern campaign was intended less to block Lincoln's election (which Douglas had decided was certain even before he began his second tour of the South) than to urge a Unionist vote, and in this goal he succeeded: The combination of Lincoln, Douglas, and Bell outpolled Breckinridge in the southern states. Yet the southern tour profoundly alarmed Douglas; he had heard rumors of a southern conspiracy to stage a coup d'état and install Breckinridge in the president's chair by force. In his Chicago speech, he exclaimed that he thought the country was in greater danger than ever before and that only a strong appeal to union would enable it to surmount the deadly combination of northern and southern sectionalism. Douglas's advocacy of Union in the face of his own impending defeat in 1860 is commonly judged an act of high statesmanship, and yet it only made explicit what had been among his transcendent principles throughout his career.

The Little Giant's final rhetorical effort returned him to Illinois in an attempt to rally northwestern Democrats, among whom there had been some talk of letting the errant southern states go in peace. On April 25, 1861, he addressed the Illinois legislature in the Hall of Representatives at Springfield. Noting that he had held out for compromise as long as possible, Douglas explained that the question now was a simple one: wait for the enemy to carry out its boast to destroy the government of our fathers or rally to its defense? The evidence did not justify rebellion; secession was prompted merely by the loss of a presidential election. Drawing an analogy to the passions surrounding the French Revolution and making a special appeal to the Midwest's economic interest in keeping control of the Mississippi River, Douglas pleaded with Illinoisans to submerge partisanship and argued that unanimous support for the war was the shortest path to peace.

The following week, in Chicago, Douglas was even more explicit. Insisting that the slavery question and Lincoln's election were merely pretexts employed by a disunion conspiracy, he put the question: "Are we to maintain the country of our fathers, or allow it to be stricken down by those who, when they can no longer govern, threaten to destroy?" On this question there was no middle ground: "Every man must be for the United States or against it. There can be no neutrals in this war, *only patriots—or traitors.*" Ironically, the man who for a decade had sought a middle ground against the extremes, only to see that ground disappear, now rallied his countrymen by insisting that it was gone. The Chicago address was the Little Giant's last. His health was poor; he developed a case of acute rheumatism and died on June 3, admonishing his young sons to support the laws and obey the Constitution of the United States.

From this survey of his career, Douglas's basic political principles can be discerned. First, he was an ardent nationalist. He believed in manifest destiny and was committed to the expansion of U.S. territory in the Southwest, the Northeast, and through the acquisition of Cuba. Territorial expansion was both a good in itself—in that it spread the blessings of liberty—and a means to subsume sectional or partisan disputes with a transcendent appeal.

Second, Douglas was committed to popular sovereignty, which he regarded as self-government at the local level. Originally this commitment was an expedient; the vexed question of slavery could be removed from the halls of Congress and sectional division could be avoided by remanding the issue to the inhabitants most directly affected, whose decisions would be determined by climate in any case. As his views came under attack, however, he gradually elevated popular sovereignty to the status of principle, treating it as a procedural kind of morality. It was in that context—a belief that procedure was more important than results—that Douglas could maintain that he "don't care" whether slavery "is voted down or voted up." Douglas located the power of self-government in communities, not individuals. From this perspective, freedom was not the condition of an individual not in slavery; it was the prerogative of the community to accept or reject the peculiar institution within its own domain.

Douglas defended this procedural standard of morality consistently, with one notable exception. Incensed by the practice of polygamy in Utah Territory, he proposed in 1857 that Congress revoke that territory's enabling act. Lincoln seized on the discrepancy between what Douglas would do in Utah and Kansas as proof that popular sovereignty was not genuine and as support for the specious claim that Douglas secretly plotted to extend slavery into Kansas.

Third, Douglas abhorred sectionalism. He condemned the Republican party because its appeal was sectional; he insisted that the test of a doctrine's validity was its ability to be promulgated anywhere in the nation. Until the late 1850s, his appeal to the Democrats was his stature as a national political figure. But he did not regard personal popularity as the way to transcend sectionalism; he saw that task achieved only by fidelity to the Constitution in all its particulars. The heart of the problem with the extremists, he insisted, was that they marked out certain sections of the Constitution that they found embarrassing or no longer relevant.

Certain conclusions also can be drawn with respect to Douglas's rhetorical method. To be sure, he was a gifted orator. He identified himself with the public; he was direct and forthright. And yet there was a sophistic quality to his argumentation. Even a sympathetic biographer accused him of twisting logic and misrepresenting the opposition, though convincing his immediate audiences. Harriet Beecher Stowe heard him speak in 1856; she was overwhelmed by his clarity, his gestures, and his forceful voice, yet she and Horace Greeley agreed that Douglas magnified quibbles, engaged in special pleading, and seemed deliberately to confuse his listeners.

The sophistic quality of Douglas's argument reflects in part his tendency to evade the burden of proof and to place his adversary on the defensive. From his early days as state's attorney in Illinois, he had extracted the maxim, ''Admit nothing, and require my adversary to prove everything material to the success of his cause.'' Employing this maxim, Douglas constantly engaged in refutation of his opponent's remarks. It was a common practice in his later years for him to take Lincoln's ''House Divided'' speech or Seward's ''irrepressible conflict'' speech as a text and then deliver a blistering refutation. As a consequence of this stance, it was clear what Douglas opposed. Except at the most general level, however, it was often unclear what he supported. One searches his speeches in vain, for example, for a statement of his own view about the morality of slavery. Somewhat less persuasive were his often hairsplitting distinctions, which, opponents charged, were invoked to work himself out of a jam caused by the ambiguity or inconsistency of his own position.

In his treatment of his opponents, Douglas reflected the rough-and-tumble rhetoric of the frontier West. In 1854 he viewed all opponents of the Kansas-Nebraska Act as basically alike. By the late 1850s, he was opposed by different people for different reasons, but he grouped all his opponents together in order to attack them. He viewed the Republican party and the southern fire-eaters as engaged in a coordinated effort to defeat him and repeatedly argued that their platforms were similar. He charged his northern opponents with hypocrisy, insisting that they favored Negro equality but were unwilling to say so directly, swearing to uphold the Constitution and then selectively violating it. Or he argued that the implication of his opponents' position was that the framers of the government were hypocrites, declaring that all men were created equal and then continuing themselves to hold slaves. Moreover, Douglas used generous doses of personal attack, ridicule and reductio ad absurdum in discussing his opponents' views.

As for his own position, Douglas maintained that it was based on principle and hence consistent over time. In fact, his contention was both true and false. On the face of it, Douglas seems to protest too much. His own rhetorical career was marked by the invention of new appeals in response to changed circumstances; he was an opportunist as well as a man of principle. He first supported and then opposed the Missouri Compromise. He first claimed that Congress had the power to legislate regarding slavery in the territories and then later said that the right had been conferred to the territories. He first declared that the issues in the *Dred Scott* case were matters for the Supreme Court to decide and then later held that "friendly local legislation," not the Court's decision, would be dispositive of the case.

In a larger sense, however, Douglas was profoundly correct, but that proved to be his undoing. He consistently asserted the beliefs of the 1840s: the nation was destined to grow and to be great; domestic problems, even slavery, were trivial when seen against the backdrop of national greatness; potentially distracting questions must be removed from the public sphere so that the nation could get on with the work, which would subsume those questions; and the people, blessed by Providence, could confidently assume that things would turn out for the best. In these views, Douglas did not waver, and in espousing them in the halls of Congress, he was truly a man of his time. But he reached the pinnacle of power just when the times were changing, and he did not know it. Neither North nor South remained content with a substantively neutral approach to the question of slavery; neither believed that national growth superseded all other issues; and neither was willing to remove from the public sphere the issue that everyone seemed to care most about. Though gifted in the tactics of politics, Douglas became increasingly out of step with what men viewed as the ends of political action. Though a young man, Douglas was on the scene too late. Only in the last six weeks of his life, when the reality of war swept aside the nuances of popular sovereignty, was there apparent movement in his position. And his stance then, like Lincoln's, was confined to the preservation of the Union. How he would have dealt with what became the larger issues of the war, no one will ever know.

INFORMATION SOURCES

Research Collections and Collected Speeches

The most complete Douglas collection is in the University of Chicago Library, but it consists entirely of incoming correspondence. All of Douglas's major letters have been published in Robert W. Johannsen, ed., *The Letters of Stephen A. Douglas* (Urbana: University of Illinois Press, 1961). Many of Douglas's speeches are elusive, although his speeches in Congress can be found in the *Congressional Globe*, and the texts of the Lincoln-Douglas debates are widely available. Other speeches may be found in individual newspapers, and Douglas material is included in other manuscript collections at the Illinois State Historical Library, Springfield.

Chicago Tribune.	CT
Congressional Globe.	CG
Created Equal? The Complete Lincoln-Douglas Debates of 1858. Edited by Paul E. Angle. Chicago: University of Chicago Press, 1958.	CE

Illinois State Journal.   *ISJ*
Kansas, Utah, and the Dred Scott Decision. Remarks of Hon. Stephen A.   *KUD*
   Douglas, Delivered in the State House at Springfield, Illinois, on
   12th of June, 1857. N.p., n.d.
New York Times.   *NYT*

Selected Critical Studies

Crocker, Lionel. "The Campaign of Stephen A. Douglas in the South, 1860." In *Antislavery and Disunion, 1858–1861: Studies in the Rhetoric of Compromise and Conflict.* Edited by J. Jeffery Auer. New York: Harper & Row, 1963.

Oliver, Robert P. "Practical Politics and the Higher Law: Douglas, Seward, and Lincoln (1850–1865)." In *History of Public Speaking in America.* Boston: Allyn and Bacon, 1965.

Whan, Forest L. "Stephen A. Douglas." In *A History and Criticism of American Public Address.* Edited by William Norwood Brigance. 1943; rpt., New York: Russell and Russell, 1960.

Zarefsky, David. "The Lincoln-Douglas Debates Revisited: The Evolution of Public Argument." *Quarterly Journal of Speech* 72 (1986): 162–84.

Selected Biographies

Capers, Gerald M. *Stephen A. Douglas: Defender of the Union.* Boston: Little, Brown, 1959.

Heckman, Richard Allen. *Lincoln vs. Douglas: The Great Debates Campaign.* Washington, D.C.: Public Affairs Press, 1967.

Jaffa, Harry V. *Crisis of the House Divided: An Interpretation of the Issues in the Lincoln-Douglas Debates.* 1959; rpt., Chicago: University of Chicago Press, 1982.

Johannsen, Robert W. *Stephen A. Douglas.* New York: Oxford University Press, 1973.

Milton, George Fort. *The Eve of Conflict: Stephen A. Douglas and the Needless War.* Boston: Houghton Mifflin, 1934.

Sheahan, James W. *The Life of Stephen A. Douglas.* New York: Harper and Brothers, 1860.

Wells, Damon. *Stephen Douglas: The Last Years, 1857–1861.* Austin: University of Texas Press, 1971.

CHRONOLOGY OF MAJOR SPEECHES

See "Research Collections and Collected Speeches" for source codes.

Defense of the Mexican War, Washington, D.C., May 13, 1846; *CG*, 29th Cong., lst sess., pp. 815–17.

Defense of the Compromise of 1850, Washington, D.C., June 3, 1850; *CG*, 31st Cong., 1st sess., pp. 1114–18.

Kansas-Nebraska Act speech, Washington, D.C., March 3, 1854; *CG*, 33d Cong., 1st sess., appendix, pp. 325–28.

Speech on Kansas, Utah, and the Dred Scott Decision, Springfield, Illinois, June 12, 1857; *KUD*.

Lecompton opening speech, Washington, D.C., December 9, 1857; *CG*, 35th Cong., 1st sess., pp. 14–22.

Lecompton closing speech, Washington, D.C., March 22, 1858; *CG*, 35th Cong., 1st sess., appendix, pp. 194–201.

Speech, Chicago, July 9, 1858; *CE*, pp. 12–25.

Lincoln-Douglas debates, August 21-October 15, 1858; *CE*, pp. 103–37, 139–76, 190–231, 235–75, 285–321, 324–60, 362–402.

Speech, Columbus, Ohio, September 7, 1859; *NYT*, September 8, 1859.

Chicago Campaign Speech, October 5, 1860; *ISR*, October 9, 1860.

Speech to Illinois legislature, Springfield, Illinois, April 25, 1861; *ISJ*, April 26, 1861.

Final speech, Chicago, May 1, 1861; *CT*, May 2, 1861.

FREDERICK DOUGLASS
(1818–1895), race statesman, abolitionist, republican

————————————————————— WALDO E. MARTIN, JR.

As the preeminent nineteenth-century black leader, Frederick Douglass spoke eloquently and profoundly on behalf of his people's full liberation. Although born a slave on Maryland's Eastern Shore, he essentially taught himself how to read and write and eventually escaped to freedom in 1838 and began his phenomenal rise to public acclaim. A significant measure of his prestige and influence derived from the extraordinary power and range of his oratory. Indeed, his superb oratorical abilities and career dovetailed and enhanced his roles as race leader, abolitionist, social reformer, journalist, Republican, and government official.

His rhetorical education began early and initially consisted of imbibing from two basic black rhetorical traditions: the secular art of storytelling and the religious art of preaching. The didactic, direct, emotional as well as rational, and entertainment emphases of these traditions provided a solid beginning. Later, when he became a hired slave in Baltimore, he was able to build on that beginning by observing and participating in debates among the city's free black population, notably as part of the East Baltimore Mental Improvement Society. Earlier, as a young adolescent, he had come across Caleb Bingham's *The Columbian Orator*, which gave him his first formal introduction to rhetoric. Even as a free man, he might return to the lessons he gathered from that text. Most likely, his critical decision to employ oratory as a strategy toward freedom, equality, and justice derived in part from the book's strong initial impact on him. The stress on a natural style, in addition to issues such as emancipation, temperance, and education, on one hand, and grand ideas like liberty, courage, and patriotism, on the other, clearly made a lasting impression on him.

As a free man, Douglass expanded his ongoing rhetorical education and refined his oratorical skills. He not only read widely and attended public lectures shortly upon arriving in the North, but he also continued to speak publicly. In 1841, he joined the Massachusetts Anti-Slavery Society and became a Garrisonian abolitionist. Renown and a modicum of economic security soon came his way as his oratorical prowess accelerated rapidly.

RACE LEADER AS REFORMER AND POLITICIAN

From 1841 to 1849, Douglass espoused the radical, uncompromising principles of his Garrisonian cohorts. In addition to immediate, unconditional emancipation, they argued that the Constitution was a proslavery document and thus that neither it nor political action under it was viable and moral. They denounced the proslavery ties of the religious and business establishment. They vigorously agitated the northern, and national, conscience as a means to convert as many as possible to their beliefs. Their rhetoric rested on a deep commitment to the efficacy of moral suasion as the best means to end slavery. Douglass quickly adopted these and other aspects of Garrisonianism—such as antisabbatarianism and a broad social reform vision—into his evolving personal philosophy.

His early speeches revealed his rapid mastery of reform oratory as well as Garrisonianism. Easily the most important factor in his accelerated rise as an abolitionist orator was his striking ability as an ex-slave to engage his audiences as a prelude to a persuasive indictment of slavery and its corollary, race prejudice. A variety of rhetorical techniques—in combination with his exceptional mind and natural speaking talent—helped him to sway his audiences: humor, sarcasm, ridicule, satire, mimicry, illustrations, and anecdotes. With a sonorous voice, organ-like in pitch and intonation, he soon rose to the forefront among orators of his generation in an age of great oratory. His speeches usually began slowly as he laid out his assumptions and themes, giving particular attention to the personal and experiential dimensions of his outlook. From there, he carefully crafted a clear and factual yet sincere and moving speech. Relying heavily on moral, humane, and ennobling sentiments, as well as an increasingly demonstrative yet natural style, the oration would build to a crescendo. Models of cogent argument, his best speeches artfully combined emotional and rational appeals.

His development as an abolitionist orator was meteoric and dramatic. From 1841 to 1845, he served as a paid lecturer for the Massachusetts Anti-Slavery Society. During his initial year, many observers noted his astonishingly rapid maturation as a speaker. After having begun as an introductory speaker, he soon became a headliner. He immediately came to personify the vital and burgeoning abolitionist tradition of fugitive slave orators whose own life stories enabled them to speak with an authenticity and cogency unmatched by even the best white abolitionists.

Fresh upon the publication of his powerful *Narrative of the Life of Frederick Douglass* in 1845, he went on a successful lecture tour of the British Isles lasting until 1847. His overwhelming reception clearly made him the leading black abolitionist of the day. Everywhere he went, the overflow audiences were enthusiastic. In his "Farewell to the British People," March 30, 1847, he reiterated many of the themes he had hammered away at during his tour: the proslavery character of the U.S. Constitution, northern complicity in southern bondage, legal and customary racism throughout his native land, and proslavery institutions, especially the proslavery church. He excoriated those British Christians who fellowshipped with southern slaveholders. The blatant hypocrisy and immorality of proslavery American churches particularly outraged him. Such institutions forced him to reveal America's "pretensions to republicanism, and expose her hypocritical professions of Christianity; to denounce her high claims to civilization."

Douglass formally broke with the Garrisonians in 1849 for a variety of reasons, including his growing independence and his decision to become a journalist. Ideologically he now aligned himself with the political abolitionists who saw the Constitution as a proslavery document and political action under it against slavery as both moral and necessary. His impressive career as a newspaper editor and journalist (*North Star, 1847–1851; Frederick Douglass' Paper*, 1851–1860; *Douglass' Monthly*, 1860–1863; and the *New National Era*, 1870–1873) enhanced his knowledge and influence. It also enhanced his fame and skill as an orator. Throughout the remainder of his life, he derived much of his income from an often demanding series of lectures on a diverse range of subjects—from abolitionism to the World's Columbian Exposition of 1893. Much of his rhetorical energy went to his deep-seated reform commitment, which encompassed woman's rights, temperance, peace, and the abolition of capital punishment. Moreover, as the preeminent black Republican after the Civil War, he gave increasing attention to the demands of political speech making for the party and its candidates. Still, a tangible freedom for blacks and the alleviation of race prejudice remained his primary concerns.

In a lifetime filled with many great oratorical moments, Douglass responded to the momentous decade of the 1850s and the coming of the Civil War with many of his best efforts. As his abolitionist and reform oratory relied upon the moral suasionist, perfectionist, millennial, and optimistic threads of nineteenth-century American culture, so did his political oratory. In fact, the 1850s witnessed his emergence as a more versatile and well-rounded lecturer who spoke to issues of broad humane, social, and cultural, as well as political and historical, concern.

In 1852 during an Independence Day celebration at Rochester's Corinthian Hall, Douglass asked, "What, to the American slave, is your 4th of July?" In the course of analyzing the cruel paradox of black chattel slavery in a land of freedom, he resorted to "scorching irony": "a fiery stream of biting ridicule, blasting reproach, withering sarcasm, and stern rebuke." For the slave, he retorted, the Fourth of July signified "the gross injustice and cruelty to which he is the constant victim." Such rhetoric both grew out of and contributed to the heightening sectional tensions deriving principally from the slavery controversy. By speaking boldly and clearly on behalf of abolition and equality, Douglass helped to pave the way for black freedom.

A deep-seated belief in human equality earmarked Douglass's rhetoric. "The Claims of the Negro Ethnologically Considered"—first delivered in Hudson, Ohio, July 12, 1854, and subsequently many times in various forms—was a scholarly and trenchant lecture. Foreshadowing W. E. B. Du Bois's famous early twentieth-century dictum that "the problem of the twentieth century is the problem of the color line," Douglass similarly observed that "the relation subsisting between the white and black people of this country is the vital question of the age." Blasting the unconscionable racism of the Negro's ethnological detractors, he countered with a well-reasoned and cogent exposition of the common brotherhood, unity, and equality of all humanity. Alleviating ignorance and race prejudice, he argued, demanded that moral vision and justice inform scholarly inquiry; in such a battle, neutrality was impossible. After this lecture, his first delivered from a completely written text, he might speak from a written text, but he would often extemporaneously revise his remarks, peppering them with relevant and pointed observations.

As an activist and social reformer, Douglass was committed to social change. In a now-famous "Dred Scott Decision" speech on the need for struggle as basic to social change, he argued in 1857 that "those who profess to favor freedom, and yet deprecate agitation, are men who want crops without plowing up the ground." This forceful articulation of his philosophy of reform likewise warned that "power concedes nothing without a demand. It never did and it never will." Over the years, that speech—and those words in particular—has provided intellectual and emotional inspiration for innumerable activists, especially many of those involved in the modern civil rights and black power insurgencies.

Because his speeches might last for two hours, Douglass stayed active, current, and fiery so as to engage most fully his audiences. When a pivotal event transpired, his public demanded his reaction, and he seldom disappointed, particularly prior to 1865. With emancipation, Reconstruction, redemption, and his transition to Republican party functionary, as well as middle-class race leader, however, at times his postwar speeches lacked the fervor and excitement of his prewar and wartime ones. Similarly, his leadership met and generally weathered growing challenges. Except for his stirring yet ineffective efforts to convince Republicans to maintain their commitment to deal fairly with blacks, much of his postwar political oratory was traditional Bloody Shirt and stump rhetoric. Earlier, though, at the height of his oratorical prowess, he was not firmly committed to a political party, and his orations were often awesome.

He excoriated the Supreme Court's 1857 *Dred Scott* decision at New York City, May 11, as inhumane and execrable. This "hell-black" and "demoniacal" decision, which legally undermined the citizenship status of blacks, he contended, would eventually give way to justice and righteousness. The underside of his optimism revealed his use of the jeremiad as he prodded the nation's conscience. If the infamous decision were not reversed and slavery and race hatred persisted, then "the lightning, whirlwind, and earthquake may come."

Douglass, like so many others of his time, saw the Civil War as the inevitable punishment for the sin of slavery. The war provided him with irrefutable proof of the horror and intransigence of slave power. He was a major voice urging President Lincoln to make the war an abolition struggle, to recruit black troops and treat them fairly, and to begin the process of national regeneration by supporting black male suffrage and equality in general. Most of his wartime speeches dealt with the imperative of a just and moral vision, both to guide the Union effort and to ensure a lasting victory and peace. He upbraided Lincoln for his cautious and dilatory approach to black freedom. "Our chief danger," he maintained, "lies in the absence of all moral feeling in the utterances of our rulers." The "mission of the war," however, demanded an ethical as well as "abolition peace."

Between 1865 and his death in 1895, Douglass continued to speak out force-fully for the oppressed—notably blacks and women—and for a more humane and representative country. While he remained the most widely acknowledged spokesman for his people, he did encounter opposition. The declining commit-ment of the post-Reconstruction Republican party to blacks—especially the freed people—led many to question Douglass's position that for blacks the Republicans were the deck of the ship and all other parties the sea. While painfully aware of the party's shortcomings—he once labeled himself an "uneasy Republican"—he could not bring himself to switch his support to either the rabidly racist Democrats or an uncertain third-party insurgency.

Similarly, the widespread black criticism of his opposition to the exoduster movement—a migration of blacks from Tennessee, Texas, Mississippi, and Louisiana to Kansas during the spring of 1879—clearly showed that his rhetoric did not always convince. Woefully underestimating the oppression southern blacks endured, he remarked that those awful conditions were "exceptional and transient." While several years later he modified his view and supported black migration out of southern areas where whites customarily abused and killed blacks, his speech on the exodusters plainly revealed that earlier he had mis-understood and misconstrued their plight.

More representative of his late nineteenth-century rhetoric, however, was his persuasive analysis "Why Is the Negro Lynched?" He rejected the racist cant that allegedly showed that the increasing number of lynchings of black men by white mobs derived from a variety of causes, including innate black criminality. He also demonstrated that the alleged rationale for these lynchings—black male attacks on white women—was demonstrably false. Those in power, he charged, manipulated this cruel yet powerful hoax as a means to degrade further black people and to ensure their disfranchisement and racial separation. The ultimate dilemma, he stressed, was whether the United States could live up to its basic ideals. "It is not a Negro problem, but in every sense a great national problem." He concluded that "it involves the question, whether after all our boasted civ-ilization, our Declaration of Independence, our matchless Constitution, our sub-lime Christianity, our wise statesmanship, we as a people, possess virtue enough to solve this problem in accordance with wisdom and justice, and to the advantage of both races."

INFORMATION SOURCES

Research Collections and Collected Speeches

Researching Douglass's rhetoric requires consulting two major collections. First, the definitive edition of *The Frederick Douglass Papers* is being edited by John W. Blas-singame at Yale University. The initial series, three volumes of which have appeared, include speeches, debates, and interviews. Second, the Library of Congress collection of Douglass Papers (available on microfilm) has texts and some drafts of most of his major speeches, as well as a diary, letters, various writings, and personal papers.

Douglass, Frederick. *The Frederick Douglass Papers*. Edited by John W.   *FDP*
    Blassingame. New Haven: Yale University Press, 1979-.
————. *The Frederick Douglass Papers*. Library of Congress Collection.   *FDPLC*
    Washington, D.C.: Library of Congress, 1976.
————. *The Life and Writings of Federick Douglass*, Edited by Philip S.   *LWFD*
    Foner. 5 vols. New York: International Publishers, 1950–1971.

Selected Critical Studies

Blassingame, John. "Introduction to Series One." In *The Frederick Douglass Papers*.
    Edited by John Blassingame et al. Series 1, vol. 1. New Haven: Yale University
    Press, 1979.
Cooke, J. W. "Freedom in the Thoughts of Frederick Douglass: 1845–1860." *Negro
    History Bulletin* 32 (1969): 6–10.
Dick, Robert C. *Black Protest: Issues and Tactics*. Westport, Conn.: Greenwood Press,
    1974.
Hale, Frank W. "A Critical Analysis of the Speaking of Frederick Douglass." Master's
    thesis, University of Nebraska, 1951.
————. "Frederick Douglass: Antislavery Crusader and Lecturer." *Journal of Human
    Relations* 14 (1966): 100–11.
Ladner, Cornelius A. "A Critical Analysis of Four Anti-Slavery Speeches of Frederick
    Douglass." Master's thesis, State University of Iowa, 1947.

Selected Biographies

Foner, Philip S. *Frederick Douglass*. New York: International Publishers, 1964.
Huggins, Nathan I. *Slave and Citizen: The Life of Frederick Douglass*. Boston: Little,
    Brown, 1980.
Martin, Waldo E., Jr. *The Mind of Frederick Douglass*. Chapel Hill: University of North
    Carolina Press, 1984.
Quarles, Benjamin. *Frederick Douglass*. Washington, D.C.: Associated Publishers, 1948.

CHRONOLOGY OF MAJOR SPEECHES

See "Research Collections and Collected Speeches" for source codes.

"Farewell to the British People," London, England, March 30, 1847; *FDP*, series 1, vol. 1, pp. 19–52; *LWFD*, 1:206–33; *FDPLC*, Reel 13.

"What to the Slave Is the Fourth of July," Rochester, New York, July 5, 1852; *FDP*, series 1, vol. 2, pp. 359–88; *LWFD*, 2:181–204.

"The Claims of the Negro Ethnologically Considered," Hudson, Ohio, July 12, 1854; *FDP*, series 1, vol. 2, pp. 497–525; *FDPLC*, reel 14; *LWFD*, 2:289–309.

"The Dred Scott Decision," New York, May 11, 1857; *FDP*, series 1, vol. 1, pp. 163–83; *FDPLC*, reel 14; *LWFD*, 2:407–24.

"West India Emancipation," Canandaigua, New York, August 4, 1857; *FDP*, series 1, vol. 2, pp. 183–208; *FDPLC*, reel 14; *LWFD*, 2:426–39.

"The Mission of the War," New York, February 13, 1864; *FDPLC*, reel 14; *LWFD*, 3:386–403.

"The Negro Exodus from the Gulf States," Saratoga Springs, New York, September 12, 1879; *FDPLC*, reel 15; *LWFD*, 4:324–42.

"Why is the Negro Lynched?" Baltimore, Maryland, January 9, 1894; *FDPLC*, reel 17; *LWFD*, 4:491–523.

JONATHAN EDWARDS
(1703–1758), eighteenth-century preacher

BERNARD L. BROCK

Jonathan Edwards was born on October 5, 1703, the only son and the fifth of eleven children of Esther Stoddard and Timothy Edwards. As a minister's son and the grandson of the aristocratic, revivalist Solomon Stoddard, Jonathan's early education, conducted by his father, mother, and older sisters, emphasized Greek, Latin, and the Bible. His early interest in religion was evident in his praying five times a day and discussing religious issues with friends in a secluded hut. Edwards's keen mind and power of observation were demonstrated by ages eleven and twelve when he wrote the essays "Of Insects" and "Of the Rainbow." His understanding of spiders and nature could only have resulted from patient and intense observation coupled with sound deductions.

Jonathan's formal education began at thirteen upon entering Yale College. At Yale he read Locke and Newton and reflected these authors' ideas in his writing "Notes on the Mind" and "Notes on Natural Science." Edwards extended Locke's concept that "knowledge is the perception of the agreement or disagreement of two ideas" and established his own definition of truth: "TRUTH is *The perception of the relations there are between ideas. Falsehood is the supposition of relations between ideas that are inconsistent with those ideas themselves; not their disagreement with things without.* All truth is in the mind, and only there." Edwards easily might have had a successful career in science. In September 1720, Jonathan graduated but remained at Yale to study the ministry.

In August 1722, Edwards accepted his first call as minister for the Scotch Presbyterian church in New York. He returned to Yale College for his Master of Arts degree in 1723 and soon became a tutor. His next move was to a colleague pastorate with his grandfather, Solomon Stoddard, at Northampton, Massachusetts, in 1727. On July 28, he married Sarah Pierrepont, and on February 22, 1729, Solomon Stoddard died. Jonathan Edwards preached the funeral sermon and assumed his grandfather's ministry. From the Northampton pulpit, the most prominent church outside Boston, Edwards launched his preaching career.

JONATHAN EDWARDS AS REVIVAL PREACHER

Jonathan Edwards's life was dedicated to bringing an increasingly secular people back to pure Calvinism through his preaching and writing. This dream, which at times seemed within his grasp, would never be realized.

The first challenge to Edwards's preaching ability was an invitation from the New England clergy to present a public lecture at the First Church in Boston on July 8, 1731. Attention was focused on Edwards not only because he was Stoddard's heir and a leading Yale graduate but also because he might allow religious differences to divide communities again. The halfway covenant, which extended church membership and baptism to those who provided convincing evidence of conversion, was the church's compromise with the traditional Calvinist concept of only allowing the elect of God who had undergone a personal conversion experience into the church's inner circles. Stoddard, however, had liberalized this compromise and had required only a profession of faith and repentance for sins. Maintaining this position, Stoddard successfully led the Connecticut Valley churches away from the control of Cotton and Increase Mather in Boston. The Boston clergy now wondered whether Edwards would follow Stoddard's liberal tradition and how formidable an opponent he would be. Edwards preached "God Glorified in Man's Dependence." His speaking and language styles were plain, but the well-reasoned, conservative message—"that the creature is nothing, and that God is all"—was what the clergy wanted to hear though they did not see its full implications. Edwards passed the test, and his sermon was published.

Jonathan Edwards's approach to preaching carefully combined the modern scientific thinking of John Locke and Sir Isaac Newton with Calvinist philosophy. His early writing had reflected his reading of Locke's *Essay Concerning Human Understanding*. Edwards continued to adhere to Locke's ideas throughout his entire career. In August 1733, Edwards delivered and later published a sermon that set forth his philosophy: "A Divine and Supernatural Light, Immediately Imparted to the Soul by the Spirit of God, Shown to Be Both a Scriptural, and Rational Doctrine." Edwards believed that perception of reality was central to man's experience and that spiritual enlightenment occurred through the senses. Locke argued that men acquire the materials of reason and knowledge solely from experience, and for Edwards, God spoke to man through the experiences of his senses. He set forth his simple doctrine in a short sermon. This simple approach, however, became powerful in 1734–1735 as Edwards led a religious awakening.

Northampton had been an uneasy community when Edwards replaced Stoddard; however, under his preaching, feuds and disputes were put aside, and people were filled with the power of religious emotion. In six months there were more than 300 conversions, and about 100 people were admitted to the church. At the close of the awakening, Edwards, in *A Faithful Narrative of the Surprising Work of God in the Conversion of Many Hundred Souls in Northampton, and the Neighboring Towns and Villages*, provided an account of both his actions and the events. This document, consisting of an introductory statement, a description of the process of conversion, and two detailed case studies, became a handbook for revivalism. Much of the document's rhetorical power came from vivid descriptions of the religious experiences of Abigail Hutchinson and Phebe Bartlet, an adult and a child, respectively. These two cases were clear applications of Locke's concept that words stand for sense experience, so language can effectively be used to communicate experience and gain knowledge. Edwards described Abigail's terror: "Her great terror, she said, was, that she had sinned against God: her distress grew more and more for three days; until she saw 'nothing but God's wrath.' " He also described her comfort: "She had several days together a sweet sense of the excellency and loveliness of Christ in his meekness.'' Edwards's reputation for preaching grew, so he was able to publish four of his revival sermons under the title *Justification of Faith Alone*. This book was so well received that it had three printings. Edwards realized, however, that the revival had its dangers. Hysteria had increased in the community to the point that a prominent merchant committed suicide. This atmosphere spread as others said they too heard voices telling them to cut their throats. This suicide and the hysteria were factors in the revival's subsiding.

The revival inspired by Edwards in 1734–1735 was just a precursor of the Great Awakening in 1740–1741 that erupted in the wave of George Whitefield as he traveled throughout New England. Unlike Edwards, who was known for his plain delivery, Whitefield was a spirited, emotional revivalist. On July 8, 1741, in Enfield, Edwards preached what was his most popular sermon, ''Sinners in the Hands of an Angry God.'' The response was tremendous; women fainted, and men cried out and wept. Edwards's message that an all-powerful God controlled people who were completely at his mercy was quite clear: ''The God that holds you over the pit of hell, much as one holds a spider, or some loathsome insect, over the fire, abhors you, and is dreadfully provoked; his wrath towards you burns like fire; he looks upon you as worthy of nothing else, but to be cast into the fire.'' The sermon depicts a dreadful state for man, but it also presents hope for salvation through Christ: ''And now you have an extraordinary opportunity, a day wherein Christ has thrown the door of mercy wide open, and stands in calling and crying with a loud voice to poor sinners.'' Edwards's sermon conformed with the awakening message of the times. His message focused more on application than philosophy, his language was unusually strong and vivid, and his structure was uncharacteristically simple. People were taking religion into their lives, and Edwards saw his dream as partially realized.

Again, the religious revival had its price for Edwards. Thomas Clap, a religious conservative and rector of Yale, opposed the Great Awakening partially because he thought Whitefield wanted to expel long-standing New England clergymen in favor of young Methodists from England. Although Edwards denied association with Whitefield's plan, a personal feud developed between Edwards and Clap. As a result, Edwards ceased attending Yale commencements in favor of those at the College of New Jersey, which eventually became Princeton. In September 1741, at his last Yale commencement, Edwards defended his role in the Great Awakening against attacks from Charles Chauncy in ''The Distinguishing Marks of a Work of the Spirit of God.'' In this sermon Edwards identified the five distinguishing marks of a divine work. He argued that the awakening was God inspired though there had been some excesses.

Resistance to the revival had grown so that when Whitefield returned to Boston for a second visit, his reception was cool. However, Edwards's philosophy that religious experience arose from the senses forced him to believe that the religious stirring was basically good, so he continued to defend the Great Awakening. In 1742, he expanded his earlier sermon by adding his wife's religious experience in *Some Thoughts Concerning the Present Revival of Religion in New England*. He presented Sarah Edwards's experience in much the same way he had described two earlier conversions. Although he realized the awakening was no longer popular, Edwards had continued to carry his thinking further. Apparently he wanted to understand the precise nature of religious experience. He reworked some earlier sermons and in 1746 published *A Treatise Concerning Religious Affections*. His purpose was to distinguish between emotions or physical reactions of the glands and actual religious experiences: "Trials, above all other things, have a tendency to distinguish true religion and false, and to cause the difference between them evidently to appear." Edwards employed a metaphor: as gold is purified by firing, so pure religion is strengthened through persecutions. "Love to Christ" and "Joy in Christ" operate in the true Christian to bring about the affections of beauty and amiableness. On the other hand, the body brings forth passions and fluids that "are only effects or concomitants of the affections." Edwards's defense of the Great Awakening went largely unnoticed; attention had shifted to other concerns. This dedication to truth was characteristic of Jonathan Edwards's life. But in distinguishing between true and false religious experience, Edwards argued that some people had not been truly converted, yet they were admitted to the church.

The peak of the awakening and of Edwards's preaching passed because people were now more interested in solving the daily problems of their lives. Furthermore, a series of events led Edwards into actions that undermined his position in the church. In March 1744, Edwards spoke out against and even provided the names of youths who were reading a "bad book"—a midwife's handbook. Northampton was in an uproar because some of the best families were involved. Also, Edwards's work on *Religious Affections* convinced him that the halfway covenant had led to practices that were inconsistent with true religious feelings, so he returned to the strict Calvinist practice of making a public confession of Christian faith and providing proof of a conversion experience as a requirement of church membership. When Edwards abandoned the more liberal Solomon Stoddard tradition, most of his congregation actively opposed him on this issue. Further, Colonel John Stoddard, Edwards's uncle and protector in Boston, died, leaving him more vulnerable to attack. Finally, in June 1748, Edwards delivered the funeral sermon "Account of the Life of the Late Reverend Mr. David Brainerd." Brainerd, a highly emotional, yet sincere, Yale student, was expelled by Rector Thomas Clap. He was stricken with tuberculosis and died in the Edwards's household while being nursed by Jerusha, Edwards's daughter and David's fiancée. Edwards's love for both his daughter and David led him into eloquent praise for his future son-in-law. Edwards realized these events were making his position untenable and his dream unattainable, but he refused to compromise.

In 1749, the confrontation between Edwards and his church could no longer be avoided. The requirement of a public confession of a conversion experience had blocked new members for four years because Edwards insisted on it and church members would not permit it. He stated this position in *An Humble Inquiry into the Rules of the Word of God Concerning the Qualification Requisite to a Compleat Standing and Full Communion* and in April offered his resignation, demanding that his opponents read his statement and accept his argument or reject it and him. His congregation refused to read his argument, and by June 1750 they were able to find a council of ministers who by a five-to-four vote dismissed Jonathan Edwards from the Northampton church.

In July 1750, Jonathan Edwards preached his "Farewell Sermon" in Northampton. He spoke directly to the issues at hand in his usual restrained and well-reasoned manner. He reviewed his time with them and said farewell until they meet "each other before the great tribunal at the day of judgment." However, it was not farewell because Edwards had no other position, and it was years before the church found a willing replacement. For about a year, he continued to preach in Northampton until he was offered and accepted a dual position as minister in Stockbridge and missionary to the Indians.

Jonathan Edwards was now out of the spotlight, and he could devote time to writing. As a result, this was the most peaceful and productive period in his life. In 1754 he published *A Careful and Strict Enquiry into the modern Prevailing Notions of That Freedom of Will, Which is Supposed to Be Essential to Moral Agency, Virtue and Vice, Reward and Punishment, Praise and Blame*. Edwards argued the position he had always accepted that it was impossible for man to have a free will since God's rule was complete. In 1755 he commenced work on two documents, *The Nature of True Virtue* and *Concerning the End for which God created the World*. These works, coupled with *Freedom of Will*, represent Edwards's most original thinking. Edwards's speaking and writing pose one answer for man: God is all powerful, and man's identity is God.

In 1757, Edwards was offered the presidency of the college in Princeton. He accepted it, bringing to an end this quiet, productive period in his life. On March 22, 1758, after receiving an inoculation against smallpox, Jonathan Edwards died.

Jonathan Edwards was a paradoxical speaker. His content and his form were traditional, but his use of language was radical. Edwards's message was that the truth of religion was contained in the Bible, that man was a sinner who was completely dependent on God, and that God is sovereign and supreme. His sermons were complex and highly organized. His thesis was carefully stated, developed, and applied following the tradition in early American preaching. Edwards's proofs were quite rational, employing authority, usually the Bible, and experience. His form was typically deductive, but individual arguments were frequently inductive. Jonathan Edwards's style was plain, as was his delivery. He used short words and phrases that could easily be understood by his audience. His images and metaphors were usually based on the Bible. His effectiveness lay in the traditional, logical structure of his argument and, paradoxically, the Lockean and Newtonian experiential language of his message.

Edwards lost in his effort to lead America back to pure Calvinism, but he has been acknowledged as one of America's truly outstanding thinkers for his development of a rhetorical system based on Locke's and Newton's writings. Ironically, Edwards's scientific approach to language based on Locke and Newton was more responsible for his significant place in history than was the Calvinist philosophy he preached his entire life.

INFORMATION SOURCES

Research Collections and Collected Speeches

Researchers of Jonathan Edwards's rhetoric have a wealth of material available. Most of his manuscripts are at the Library of Yale University, New Haven, Connecticut, and the Andover-Harvard Theological Seminary, Cambridge, Massachusetts; his personal books are at the Princeton University Library; background material is available at Forbes Library, Northampton, Massachusetts; and a variety of materials are held at the Library of Congress and other northeastern libraries. Two guides are available to researchers: *Jonathan Edwards: A Reference Guide*, edited by M. X. Lesser (Boston: G. K. Hall & Co., 1981), and *Jonathan Edwards: Bibliographical Synopses*, edited by Nancy Manspeaker (New York: Edwin Mellon Press, 1981).

Edwards, Jonathan. *Puritan Sage: Collected Writings of Jonathan Edwards.*   PS
    Edited by Vergilus Ferm. New York: Library Publishers, 1953.
————. *The Works of Jonathan Edwards.* General editor Perry Miller,
    succeeded in 1963 by John E. Smith. New Haven: Yale University
    Press. This edition includes scholarly introductions to the individual
    volumes as secondary sources.
Freedom of the Will. Edited with Introduction by Paul Ramsay, 1957.   FW
Religious Affections. Edited with Introduction by John E. Smith, 1959.   RA
Original Sin. Edited with Introduction by Clyde A. Holbrook, 1970.   OS
The Great Awakening. Edited with Introduction by C. C. Goen, 1972.   GA
Apocalyptic Writings. Edited with Introductions by Stephen J. Stein, 1977.   AW
Scientific and Philosophical Writings. Edited with Introduction by Wallace   SPW
    E. Anderson, 1980.
The Life of David Brainerd. Edited with Introduction by Norman Petitt,   LDB
    1985.
————. *The Works of President Edwards.* 4 vols. Edited by Samuel Austin.   WPE
    Worcester, 1847; New York, 1947.

Selected Critical Studies

Angoff, Charles, ed. *Jonathan Edwards: His Life and Influence.* Leverton Lecture Series. Rutherford, N.J.: Fairleigh Dickinson University Press, 1975.

Baumgartner, Paul R. "Jonathan Edwards: The Theory behind His Use of Figurative Language." *Publications of the Modern Language Association* 78 (1963): 321–25.

Collins, Edward M., Jr. "The Rhetoric of Sensation Challenges the Rhetoric of the

Intellect." In *Preaching in American History*. Edited by DeWitt Holland. New York: Abingdon Press, 1969.

Conrad, Leslie, Jr. "Jonathan Edwards' Pattern for Preaching." *Church Management* 33 (1957): 45–47.

Davison, Edward H. "From Locke to Edwards." *Journal of the History of Ideas* 24 (July-September 1963): 355–72.

Evans, W. Glyn. "Jonathan Edwards—Puritan Paradox." *Bibliotheca Sacra* 124 (January 1967): 51–65.

Hitchcock, Orville. "Jonathan Edwards." In *History and Criticism of American Public Address*. Edited by William Norwood Brigance. New York: Russell & Russell, 1960.

Miller, Perry. *Errand into the Wilderness*. Cambridge: Harvard University Press, 1956.

———. *Jonathan Edwards*. Amherst: University of Massachusetts Press, 1981.

Scheick, William J. *Critical Essays on Jonathan Edwards*. Boston: G. K. Hall & Co., 1980.

Selected Biographies

Dwight, Sereno Edwards, ed. *Life of President Edwards*. 10 vols. New York: S. Converse, 1829.

Parkes, Henry Bamford. *Jonathan Edwards: The Fiery Puritan*. New York: Minton, Balch & Company, 1930.

Winslow, Ola Elizabeth. *Jonathan Edwards*. New York: Macmillan, 1940.

CHRONOLOGY OF MAJOR SPEECHES AND WORKS

See "Research Collections and Collected Speeches" for source codes.

"God Glorified in the Work of Redemption, By the Greatness of Man's Dependence upon Him, in the Whole of it," Boston, July 8, 1731; *PS*, pp. 144–56; *WPE*, 4:169–78.

"Divine and Supernatural Light, Immediately Imparted to the Soul by the Spirit of God, Shown to Be Both a Scriptural, and Rational Doctrine," Northampton, Massachusetts, August 1733; *PS*, pp. 157–63; *WPE*, 4:438–50.

"Faithful Narrative of the Surprising Work of God in the Conversion of Many Hundred Souls in Northampton, and the Neighbouring Towns and Villages of New-Hampshire in New-England," Northampton, Massachusetts, November 6, 1736; *GA*, pp. 99–211; *PS*, pp. 164–218; *WPE*, 3:231–72.

"Justification by Faith Alone in Discourses on Various Important Subjects, Nearly Concerning the Great Affair of the Soul's Eternal Salvation," Northampton, Massachusetts, 1734; *PS*, pp. 219–65; *WPE*, 4:64–132.

"Sinners in the Hands of an Angry God," Enfield, Massachusetts, July 8, 1741; *PS*, 365–78; *WPE*, 4:313–21.

"The Distinguishing Marks of a Work of the Spirit of God," New Haven, New Jersey, September 10, 1741; *GA*, pp. 215–88; *WPE*, 1:519–62.

"Some Thoughts Concerning the Present Revival of Religion in New-England," New Haven, Connecticut, 1742; *GA*, pp. 289–530; *PS*, pp. 379–414; *WPE*, 3:277–425.

"Stoddard's Funeral," Boston, June 26, 1748; *WPE*, 3:604–14.

"Life of Brainerd an Account of the Life of the Late Reverend Mr. David Brainerd, Minister of the Gospel, Missionary to the Indians, from the Honorable Society in Scotland, for the Propagation of Christian Knowledge, and Pastor of a Church of Christian Indians in New-Jersey," Northampton, Massachusetts, October 9, 1747; *LDB*, pp. 543–54; *WPE*, 3:624–39.

"Farewell Sermon," Northampton, Massachusetts, June 22, 1750; *PS*, pp. 466–79; *WPE*, 1:59–82.

RALPH WALDO EMERSON
(1803–1882), essayist, philosopher, poet

MARK R. WINCHELL

Emerson is to American literature what Gordon S. Wood claims Jefferson is to American politics: "a symbol, a touchstone, of what we as people are, someone invented, manipulated, turned into something revealing about ourselves." Although Ralph Waldo Emerson was one of the towering figures of the high culture of his time, his thought has exerted its most lasting influence on middlebrow apostles of optimism and self-reliance in a line that can be traced from Mary Baker Eddy through Norman Vincent Peale to Robert Schuller. As Harold Bloom has noted, Emerson "founded the actual American religion, which is Protestant without being Christian." Highbrow writers of our time may peer more deeply into the dark nights of the soul than did Emerson; but when they are being most pessimistic, ironic, and tough-minded, it is the spirit of Emerson against which they are likely to be rebelling. In the words of Cleanth Brooks, R. W. B. Lewis, and Robert Penn Warren, "Emerson is, somehow, the *indispensable* figure in American literary history. . . . The themes he sounded most frequently will always be found close to the center of any fair account of the continuity and development of American literature."

It was not, however, as a writer that Emerson was best known during his life, nor was it with his pen that he made his living. During the golden age of the lyceum in the 1840s and 1850s, he delivered more speeches than any other American of his time. After the interruption of the Civil War, he returned to the circuit and continued lecturing well into the 1870s. Although the lyceum was in existence prior to his participation, it is George Willis Cooke's opinion that Emerson "shaped its character, and made it an efficient instrument of popular instruction. . . . He gave it a literary, moral, and reformatory character, and shaped its destiny." Moreover, the essays for which Emerson is most famous, "The American Scholar," and most infamous, "The Divinity School Address," were originally given as lectures, albeit not on the lyceum circuit. Through his role as rhetorician, Emerson helped determine the course of public speaking in his own time and the character of American literature for all time.

EMERSON AS ORATORICAL SEER

There was little in the first three decades of his life to suggest the future prominence Emerson would attain. After the death of his father when the boy was eight, Emerson was raised in genteel poverty by his mother, Ruth Ripley Emerson, and his strong-willed aunt, Mary Moody Emerson. In 1821 he graduated from Harvard, thirtieth in a class of fifty-nine, and subsequently followed the example of his father and grandfather by pursuing theological studies. He began preaching in 1826 and was ordained to the Unitarian ministry at the Second Church of Boston on March 11, 1829. In September of that year, he married Ellen Tucker, a wealthy heiress afflicted with consumption. Ellen died on February 8, 1831, and a year and a half later, on October 28, 1832, Emerson resigned his clerical post. His religious views had become increasingly heterodox, even by Unitarian standards, and the legacy from Ellen's will made it financially possible for him to leave the ministry. After nearly a year of travel in Europe, where he met such literary giants as Wordsworth, Coleridge, and Carlyle, Emerson moved to Concord, Massachusetts, and began his career as a public lecturer.

The problem facing commentators on Emerson's oratory, from contemporaneous newspaper writers to such present-day scholars as Frederick J. Antczak, is to account for the man's immediate popularity and continuing influence. Conventional criteria for judging rhetorical success are of little help. If, for example, we ask how many converts Emerson won to transcendentalism, we must judge him less effective than even the most moderately successful radio preacher of our own time. Nor was he exactly a prepossessing presence on the lecture platform. Writing in the *Cleveland Plain Dealer* of January 26, 1859, one reporter observed: "We had quite as lief see a perpendicular coffin behind a lecture desk as Mr. Emerson. The one would amuse us as much as the other."

The tales of Emerson's awkwardness on the podium are legendary. According to Edward Wagenknecht, Emerson would typically shuffle the pages of his speech and rummage through his pockets, "as if he expected to find something there; he lost his place, omitted passages, and skipped inadvertently. Once he is supposed to have stopped in the middle of a sentence, searched vainly among his papers and then left the platform. . . . His delivery was, generally speaking, monotonous; he rocked his body and took a hasty backward step after reading a striking passage. His endings were always abrupt, and he left the platform without giving the audience a chance to applaud."

Neither a soul winner nor a rabble-rouser, Emerson was not even adept at communicating the substance of his thought in an entirely coherent manner. He was essentially an inspired phrasemaker with an unsure sense of such larger rhetorical units as the paragraph and the essay. According to Otis Aggert, a Chicago reporter summed up the matter well when he wrote, "Emerson says some of the most original as well as some of the most unintelligible things of any man in the United States." That, despite all these handicaps, Emerson could have been such a seminal figure in the history of American oratory forces us to seek some other standard by which to measure his rhetoric. Antczak notes that one such standard was suggested by a washerwoman who, upon being asked if she understood Mr. Emerson, replied: "Not a word, but I like to go and see him stand up there and look as though he thought everyone was as good as he was."

Emerson's success as an orator lay not in the brilliance of his thought or in the grace of his delivery but in the persona he managed to project. His was preeminently an ethical appeal. But the *ethos* he conveyed was not that of a religious guru or even a secular leader of men. He was rather the representative democratic man, whose spiritual enlightenment was no special gnostic gift but a paradigm of what all people could and ought to achieve. Emerson wanted his audience to listen not to him as a dogmatist but to the promptings of their own souls. As Roberta K. Ray has pointed out, Emerson believed that "this should be the function of the preacher, orator, or teacher—not to give men truth but to provoke them to seeking it on their own."

It was this impulse that made Emerson the first and perhaps greatest example of what Antczak has called the "democratic educator," the orator who represents himself in such a way that the audience can find their better selves reflected in him. The orator in his virtues "would seem representatively like them; but in the discipline his thought had given him, he would seem somehow more so." By emulating the orator, "the democratic auditor could become more like himself—literally find himself in the popularizer's mind." We can see Emerson using this approach throughout his long oratorical career but never to more memorable effect than in "The American Scholar" and "The Divinity School Address."

In the century and a half that has elapsed since Emerson addressed the Phi Beta Kappa chapter of Harvard College on August 31, 1837, that occasion has been duly mythologized in the annals of American oratory. The actual circumstances surrounding the address, however, were far from auspicious. Emerson was called upon to speak only after the first choice of the selection committee, a noncontroversial clergyman named Jonathan Mayhew Wainwright, bowed out. Today we recall that Oliver Wendell Holmes, Sr., declared Emerson's address to have been "our intellectual Declaration of Independence" and that he described the young men who heard it as leaving the hall "as if a prophet had been proclaiming to them 'Thus saith the Lord.' " What we are likely to forget is that Holmes was not in the audience that day and that his praise appeared in a biography published nearly fifty years later, two years after Emerson's death. Like Lincoln's Gettysburg Address, Emerson's "The American Scholar" was a remarkable speech whose true significance was not apparent until years after its delivery.

There was nothing unusual about the ostensible topic of Emerson's address. For years, cultural nationalists had called for the creation of an indigenous American literature. What Emerson did was to elevate the issue to a metaphysical level by discussing it in terms of his own hybrid American philosophy, transcendentalism. Because transcendentalism held that each man is connected to the divine oversoul, spiritual introspection was a surer path to enlightenment than was the study of past (and largely foreign) cultures. Specifically, Emerson said that "a nation of men will for the first time exist because each believes himself inspired by the Divine Soul which also inspires all men."

That Emerson believed this to be true of the poet has long been recognized, and the significance of his address for the development of American literature has been justifiably celebrated. But it is no less true that Emerson saw the orator as also a representative spokesman for that which inspires all men, and in "The American Scholar" he gave his most forthright explanation of the orator's function in a democratic society:

The orator distrusts at first the fitness of his frank confessions, his want of knowledge of the persons he addresses, until he finds that he is the complement of his hearers;—that they drink his words because he fulfills for them their own nature; the deeper he dives into his privatest secretest presentiment, to his wonder he finds this is the most acceptable, most public, and most universally true. The people delight in it; the better part of every man feels, This is my music; this is myself.

Like all of the infinitely more vulgar exponents of self-help and positive thinking, Emerson enjoyed the rhetorical advantage of praising his audience. People are generally not averse to being told that they are potential geniuses and are likely to think well of the person who tells them they are. Because Emerson presented himself as an example of what his listeners could become, he could speak with supreme self-confidence without seeming unduly egotistical. The persona he projected may have been an actual "I," but it was also a potential "we." This representative democratic *ethos* allowed Emerson to make highly dogmatic statements about the nature of reality with no appeal to logic, evidence, or authority. His strongest selling points were his own obvious sincerity and the desire of his listeners to believe what he said.

Read in the light of Emerson's theology, "The American Scholar" reveals a rather obvious internal logic. If there is something of God in every man and something of every man in God, then veneration of the self becomes a kind of religious duty. The fact that "The American Scholar" created less of a stir than did Emerson's July 15, 1838, address to the graduating class of the Harvard Divinity School may suggest that the audience for the former assumed Emerson's references to the divine spirit of man to be so much lofty metaphor. For those who heard him speak at Harvard's Divinity Hall, there could be no mistaking that Emerson meant to be taken literally.

If "The American Scholar" was initially greeted with lukewarm praise, the response to "The Divinity School Address" was positively apoplectic. Brooks, Lewis, and Warren relate that "Nathan Hale, Jr., wanted to kick all the ministers he could find for inviting Emerson to talk in the first place; another gentleman enjoined all New Englanders 'to abhor and abominate R. W. Emerson as a sort of mad dog.' " Although Emerson was speaking primarily to the graduating divinity students—it was they who had invited him—his audience also included the divinity faculty and other older clerics. While the essentially guileless Emerson may not have intended to exacerbate or even play to the generation gap in his audience, that was one of the effects of his address. Among his critics, none were more savage than the Unitarians. According to Brooks, Lewis, and Warren, the Unitarians were outraged to find Emerson denouncing their liberalism as insufficiently radical rather than patting them on the back for having supplanted the hidebound Puritans.

If the scholar is "*Man Thinking*," then the truly religious person might be defined as "*Man Praying*." It is not, however, to an awesome and omnipotent

God that he prays but rather to the God within. That this can lead to a kind of moral and spiritual solipsism bothered Emerson not at all. Some might worry that replacing objective standards of morality with the supremacy of the individual conscience would open the door to all sorts of evil, but not Emerson. For him evil scarcely seemed to exist. It was not his rejection of original sin, however, that infuriated his Unitarian critics. It was his belief that the source of good lay in the spirit, not the intellect. Perry Miller accurately described Emerson's transcendentalism as a "religious radicalism in revolt against a rational conservatism."

By conceiving of God as both an omnipresent spirit and an omnipotent person, orthodox Christianity has always tried to maintain a precarious balance between divine transcendence and divine immanence. To simplify greatly, the bridge between God the transcendent Father and God the Immanent Holy Ghost is provided by God the Incarnate Son—Jesus, the Word made flesh. Unitarianism streamlined the Holy Trinity by worshipping God the Father, demoting Jesus to the status of a great but nondivine prophet, and ignoring the Holy Ghost altogether. Emerson took a substantially different approach by defining God as the transcendent oversoul, which is something like the Holy Ghost; by denying that there is the sort of divine person traditional theists have in mind when they speak of God the Father; and by joining the Unitarians in applying Occam's razor to the divinity of Jesus. Thus, in direct comparison to both Unitarianism and orthodox Christianity, Emerson's philosophy could be more properly called immanentism than transcendentalism.

In no ultimate objective sense did Emerson believe that Jesus was any more the son of God than is any other man. Rather, Jesus's greatness lay in his being the person to realize most fully that innate divinity he shared with all other men. To worship Jesus as a unique manifestation of the divine is to turn an inspiration into an idol. Because of its idolatry of Jesus, traditional Christianity has succumbed to two serious pitfalls: exclusiveness of doctrine and insensitivity to continuing revelation. When Catholics burned heretics, Puritans hanged witches, and Unitarians excoriated transcendentalists, it was not just the ostensible victims who suffered. The victimizers, and indeed all people, were denied the insights and wisdom the heterodox might provide. Dogmatism always restricts the content of belief. It also makes a past revelation the sole object of worship.

Emerson's philosophy was vague, cloudy, and impressionistic. Even if his audiences thought him a good man and found his ingenuous flattery of them personally congenial, he was ill equipped to respond to attempts at logical refutation. Knowing this to be the case, he simply ignored counterarguments. As Edwin Percy Whipple observed, Emerson "went on, year after year, in affirming certain spiritual facts which had been revealed to him when the soul was on the heights of spiritual contemplation; and if he differed from other minds, he thought it ridiculous to attempt to convert them to his individual insights and experiences by *arguments* against their individual insights and experiences." Having thus excluded *logos* as a possible source of appeal, Emerson was forced to rely on his peculiar sort of *ethos* and a *pathos* that was essentially aesthetic.

Emerson was such a consummate master of language that what he said sounded as if it ought to be true. The loftiness of his rhetoric was so ideally suited to the loftiness of this thought that those who delighted in the former were moved to accept the latter. The felicitous phrase, of which Emerson was the undisputed master, carried with it a kind of aesthetic authority that sanctified the thought being expressed. In short, the perspicacity of Emerson's rhetoric was so manifest that those who were unwilling to subject his thoughts to logical analysis felt as if they were listening to a prophet in whom truth and beauty were joined in perfect harmony.

The vividness of Emerson's language is evident in his frequent use of metonymy. In "The American Scholar," for example, he illustrated the dehumanizing effects of the division of labor by saying: "The priest becomes a form; the attorney a statute book; the mechanic a machine; the sailor a rope of the ship." The quality of diminution is further emphasized by the lack of conjunctions between clauses. Later in this speech, he used these same techniques in suggesting that each person incarnates the principal literary ages within his individual life span: "The boy is a Greek; the youth, romantic; the adult, reflective." Here the ellipses, emphasized by the insertion of commas in the printed text, add a note of ambiguity. If only the verb is being omitted, then *romantic* and *reflective* function as adjectives. However, if the omission of the indefinite article is also indicated, these terms are nouns. By reminding us that *romantic* and *reflective* can function as both nouns and adjectives, this syntactical ambiguity emphasizes the metonymic character of language—the interchangeability of things and their attributes.

Emerson was also adept at the artful use of repetition. In describing the mental alchemy by which the scholar transforms brute fact into poetic insight, he said: "It came into him life; it went out from him truth. It came to him short-lived actions; it went out from him immortal thoughts. It came to him business; it went from him poetry." By thus employing repetition at the beginning and toward the end of his clauses, Emerson gives to an essentially evanescent process the aura of regularity and order.

The complementary use of anaphora and epistrophe has a somewhat different effect in a passage from "The Divinity School Address":

The spirit only can teach. Not any profane man, not any sensual, not any liar, not any slave can teach, but only he can give who has; he only can create, who is. The man on whom the soul descends, through whom the soul speaks, alone can teach. Courage, piety, love, wisdom, can teach; and every man can open his door to these angels, and they shall bring him the gift of tongues. But the man who aims to speak as books enable, as synods use, as the fashion guides, and as interest commands, babbles. Let him hush.

The incremental pairing of *not* and *teach* emphasizes what it is that the non-spiritual man is incapable of doing. Moreover, the climactic use of *teach* at the

end of successive clauses calls attention that much more forcefully to the unexpected appearance of *babbles* at the end of the penultimate sentence of the
paragraph. *Let him hush* is fittingly anticlimactic.

One could fill volumes analyzing the grace and power of Emerson's language.
These few examples, however, should indicate that the force of his rhetoric far
exceeded the rigor of his thought. For this reason, Emerson could inspire listeners
to adopt widely divergent positions while feeling themselves faithful to his
example, if not his doctrine. In the years since his death, Emerson's influence
on American culture has been so diffuse that his work has become a kind of
philosophical Rorschach test in which nearly everyone can find his or her own
values reflected. Far from resenting this legacy, Emerson no doubt would have
seen it as a vindication of his singularly dogmatic antidogmatism. Not only did
he regard a foolish consistency as the hobgoblin of little minds, but he surely
would have agreed with his disciple Walt Whitman that by contradicting himself
he embraced multitudes.

INFORMATION SOURCES

The majority of Emerson's papers are held in the Houghton Library, Harvard University. For additional bibliographical information, see Joel Myerson, *Ralph Waldo Emerson: A Descriptive Bibliography* (Pittsburgh: University of Pittsburgh Press, 1982).

Collected Speeches

Emerson, Ralph Waldo. *The Collected Works of Ralph Waldo Emerson.*   CW
     Edited by Robert E. Spiller and Alfred R. Ferguson. Vol. 1: *Nature,*
     Addresses, and Lectures. Cambridge: Harvard University Press,
     1971.
————. *The Early Lectures of Ralph Waldo Emerson.* Edited by Stephen   EL
     E. Whicher, Robert E. Spiller, and Wallace E. Williams. 3 vols.
     Cambridge: Harvard University Press, 1959, 1964, 1972.
————. *Representative Men.* Edited with notes and an Introduction by Philo   RM
     Melvyn Buck, Jr. New York: Macmillan, 1906.
————. *Young Emerson Speaks: Unpublished Discourses on Many Subjects.*   YES
     Edited by Arthur Cushman McGiffert, Jr. Boston: Houghton Mifflin,
     1938.

Selected Critical Studies

Antczak, Frederick J. *Thought and Character: The Rhetoric of Democratic Education.*
     Ames: Iowa State University Press, 1985.
Aggert, Otis. "The Public Speaking of Ralph Waldo Emerson." Master's Thesis, Uni-
     versity of Illinois, 1947.
Bloom, Harold. "Mr. America." Review of *Ralph Waldo Emerson: Days of Encounter*
     by John McAleer. *New York Review of Books,* November 22, 1984, pp. 19–24.

Brooks, Cleanth, R. W. B. Lewis, and Robert Penn Warren. "Ralph Waldo Emerson."
In *American Literature: The Makers and the Making*. Vol. 1. New York: Saint
Martin's, 1973.

Buell, Laurence J. "Reading Emerson for the Structures: The Coherence of the Essays."
Quarterly Journal of Speech 58 (1972): 58–69.

Ray, Roberta K. "The Role of the Orator in the Philosophy of Ralph Waldo Emerson."
Speech Monographs 41 (1974): 215–25.

Sloan, John H. " 'The Miraculous Uplifting': Emerson's Relationship with His Audience." *Quarterly Journal of Speech* 52 (1966): 10–15.

Wagenknecht, Edward. *Ralph Waldo Emerson: Portrait of a Balanced Soul*. New York:
Oxford University Press, 1974.

Whipple, Edwin Percy. "Some Recollections of Ralph Waldo Emerson." In *Ralph Waldo
Emerson: A Profile*. Edited by Carl Bode. New York: Hill and Wang, 1968.

Wichelns, Herbert A. "Ralph Waldo Emerson." In *A History and Criticism of American
Public Address*. Edited by William Norwood Brigance. Vol. 2. New York:
McGraw-Hill, 1943.

Yannella, Donald. *Ralph Waldo Emerson*. Boston: Twayne, 1982.

Selected Biographies

Cooke, George Willis. *Ralph Waldo Emerson: His Life, Writings, and Philosophy*. Boston: James R. Osgood, 1882.

McAleer, John. *Ralph Waldo Emerson: Days of Encounter*. Boston: Little, Brown, 1984.

Porte, Joel. *Representative Man: Ralph Waldo Emerson in His Time*. New York: Oxford
University Press, 1979.

Rusk, Ralph. *The Life of Ralph Waldo Emerson*. New York: Scribner's, 1949.

CHRONOLOGY OF MAJOR SPEECHES

See "Collected Speeches" for source codes.

"The American Scholar," Phi Beta Kappa Society Oration, Harvard College, Cambridge,
Massachusetts, August 31, 1837; *CW*, pp. 49–70.

"Biography," lecture series, January-March 1835; *EL*, pp. 93–204.

"Divinity School Address," Harvard College, Cambridge, Massachusetts, July 15, 1838;
CW, pp. 71–94.

"Representative Men," lecture series, December 1845, January 1846; *RM*.

EDWARD EVERETT
(1794–1865), scholar, politician, ceremonial orator

_____ RONALD F. REID

Edward Everett presents a host of paradoxes to scholars. Well known in his own time, he is scarcely remembered today. His voluminous manuscript collection is consulted frequently by historians but rarely for studying Everett himself. He made marks in several fields but could not settle on a single career that might have ensured his fame. He made a mark in politics and lusted for public office, but he found political controversy distasteful. He had no aptitude for the stump speaking that developed during his lifetime or for the rough and tumble of legislative debate, but when he is remembered, it is for his oratory, especially lecturing and ceremonial speaking.

EDWARD EVERETT: CHANGING CAREERS, CONSISTENT ORATORY

Another paradox is that much of Everett's oratory celebrated the American Revolution, but as he confessed in an unpublished autobiography, his maternal grandparents were Loyalists. Dismayed at the absence of a strong central government after independence, they became Federalist to the core, and having an unusually strong influence on their grandson because of his father's early death, they embued him with a strong love of the American union.

His love of the Union, which eventually reached religious proportions, was reinforced by being reared in the Federalist environs of Boston. There he received a traditional classical education, which included studying under the first Boylston Professor of Rhetoric and Oratory, John Quincy Adams, and his successor, Joseph McKean. After graduating from Harvard as valedictorian in 1811, he earned an M.A. (1813) and was ordained as minister of the fashionable Brattle Square Church. More attracted to biblical scholarship than pastoral chores, he was one of the first Americans to imbibe the higher criticism that was beginning to be imported from Germany. Soon he was dreaming of studying at the fountainhead of knowledge.

In 1815 Harvard appointed Everett to the newly created professorship of Greek language and literature and gave him time to study at Göttingen. Everett reveled in an environment more like a twentieth-century university than the small provincial college he had known. After becoming the first American to receive a Ph.D. (1817), he spent two more years traveling in Europe. These experiences gave him unusual scholarly credentials and a huge inventory of historical information that he would use in his later speaking, especially for drawing contrasts between the New and Old Worlds. Most useful would be Europe's history of unrelenting warfare and poverty, which Everett attributed to its lack of a strong central government. Thus his love of Union was strengthened even as he developed Germanic attitudes toward higher education.

The mixture of Germanism and Americanism was manifested after his return to Harvard in 1819. While his faculty colleagues confined themselves to the classroom, Everett imitated German professors. He gave public lectures on ancient civilizations even before the lyceum movement began. He edited the *North American Review*, turning the fledgling quarterly into a financial success and introducing German scholarship to Americans. Using the *Review* as his forum, the patriot defended American literature after it was deprecated by a British quarterly in the so-called literary war. Although his patriotism was popular, Everett's pioneering efforts to Germanize higher education were anything but appreciated on campus. Complaining that Harvard wanted a grammatical drillmaster, not a scholar, the preacher-turned-professor began looking for still another career.

In 1824, he was elected to Congress, his success being due in large part to his first ceremonial oration, delivered on August 26, 1824. It was a Phi Beta Kappa oration, which ordinarily would not have attracted much public attention, but this was not an ordinary occasion. The Revolutionary hero, Lafayette, was touring the country, with thousands cheering his every move, and Lafayette was one of the hundreds who heard Everett's highly publicized oration.

Speaking on "The Circumstances Favorable to the Progress of Literature in America," the hero of the literary war began by refuting the notion that good literature depends on royal patronage. No, he declared; the first circumstance favorable to American letters is democracy, which furnishes "the motives to intellectual effort." The second circumstance "is the extension of one government, one language, and, substantially, one character, over so vast a space as the United States of America." The third is the rapid growth of the country. Everett developed his points with historical analogies, showing that America was superior even to the Roman Republic and the Greek democracies. In a highly emotional peroration, he turned to the guest of honor: "Welcome, friend of our fathers, to our shores! . . . Enjoy a triumph such as never conqueror nor monarch enjoyed."

Although the occasion precluded his mentioning his candidacy, the speech functioned as a campaign address by enhancing his *ethos* as a true patriot. The thrill of victory, however, was soon tempered by the rapid political changes that occurred during his ten years in Congress (1825–1835). Jacksonians routed Everett's former professor from the White House. They introduced a style of political campaigning to which Everett could not adapt. Even more disconcerting were two threats to Everett's beloved Union, the birth of Garrisonian abolitionism and Calhoun's doctrine of nullification.

Although he joined the newly formed Whig party, Everett deplored controversy too much to become a major legislative leader. Only once, in opposing Jackson's infamous Indian policy, did he lead the minority. Yet Everett's popularity grew at home, largely because of his reputation as a ceremonial orator. He spoke frequently at Fourth of July celebrations, commemorated historical events such as the landing of the Pilgrims, and eulogized departed patriots such as John Adams.

Everett's well-prepared orations contained a wealth of historical information that was presented clearly and vividly, but they were not just historical essays. They were filled with patriotic themes, the most fundamental being a secularized version of the old Puritan millennarianism: America is a chosen nation. Tracing the history of liberty in a Fourth of July oration in 1828, he presupposed that history is divinely planned. After relating the destruction of liberty in Europe, he declared that God arranged for the discovery of America "to prepare the theatre for those events by which a new dispensation of liberty was to be communicated to man." Under God's guiding hand, oppressive laws drove Europeans to the colonies, the Revolution freed the colonies from English tyranny, and then Americans fulfilled the "final design of Providence" by becoming a nation.

Secure in the knowledge that America is chosen, Everett repeated another theme: America has a divine mission. In another Fourth of July oration (1826), he alluded to the recent revolutions in Latin America and declared that "when we consider that it is our example which has aroused the spirit of independence . . . we learn the importance of the post which Providence has assigned to us in the world." America's mission was to be a model of freedom for the rest of the world to imitate.

Such themes were common in Everett's day, but he articulated them with uncommon rhetorical skill. His delivery was smooth and polished. His style, although overly ornate by today's standards, was clear, vivid, and appropriate for his time. He adapted to each specific rhetorical situation, making references to local citizens in Revolutionary battles and displaying physical objects used by some listener's forefather.

If Everett's oratory seems chauvinistic, it was chauvinism with two practical purposes. First, Everett saw historical rhetoric as a unifying social force. In a ceremonial speech given in Worcester in 1833, he said that "it is the natural tendency of celebrating the fourth of July, to strengthen the sentiment of attachment of the Union." Remembering "those who bled in the sacred cause," he continued, tells us "not to permit our feuds and dissensions to destroy the value of that birthright which they purchased with their precious lives." A second purpose was more personal: it furthered Everett's political career.

In 1835, Everett was elected governor. Alarmed by abolitionism, he said in his first message (January 1836) that people should "abstain from a discussion" of slavery because it might "prove the rock on which the Union will split." During his four one-year terms, Everett downplayed controversy, but growing Democratic strength caused his narrow defeat in 1839. Whigs won the presidency the next year, and Everett was appointed minister to Britain (1841–1845). Then a Whig defeat brought him back to America to assume the presidency of Harvard, but his return to education was marred by his distaste of administrative chores and the students' habit of behaving like students. He resigned in 1849, hoping that he would be returned to London now that a Whig again sat in the White House, but Taylor ignored Everett's hints. It was not until the last few months of Fillmore's presidency that Everett returned to politics and then only to serve the remainder of the late Daniel Webster's term as secretary of state. Everett's career was floundering. He continued giving ceremonial speeches but found it difficult because, as he confided to a friend, patriotism was being overwhelmed by abolitionism.

Other antiabolitionists shared Everett's concern. A coalition of Democrats and Whigs in the state legislature elected him to the Senate in 1852 as a counter to the abolitionist Charles Sumner. Everett, however, lacked the stamina to remain. Disheartened by the Kansas-Nebraska Act, which he predicted would destroy the Union, he resigned in 1854 and returned to Massachusetts to brood.

He could not brood indefinitely; and with the lecture platform having become a major cultural institution, he turned his avocation of speech making into a vocation. Everett delivered a lecture "The Character of Washington" on the legendary hero's birthday, February 22, 1856, and repeated it three times in rapid succession. These presentations, he confided to his diary, were "successful beyond any thing I ever delivered," and he soon envisioned great possibilities. The Ladies Mount Vernon Association had been formed recently to purchase Washington's estate and turn it into a national memorial; and the orator who had long believed that remembrance of America's glorious past would build national unity offered his services. Beginning with its fifth delivery (in Richmond, Virginia), the speech was used to raise funds for the Ladies. By April 1860, when he gave it for the 137th time, he had raised approximately $80,000. He raised another $10,000 with a series of essays about his European travels entitled "Mount Vernon Papers."

The text of the speech varied, partly because the meticulous scholar liked to tinker with it and partly because he continued his old practice of including material of local interest as he went from place to place. The general outline, however, was the same. He began with a long chronologically organized biography. Then he discussed Washington's personal qualities and contrasted him with other so-called greats, such as Alexander and Napoleon. His emotional peroration was what he privately called his "union sentiments," an appeal for unity: "But to us citizens of America, it belongs above all others to show respect to the memory of Washington, by the practical deference which we pay to those sober maxims of public policy which he has left us,—a last testament of affection in his Farewell Address. Of all the exhortations which it contains, I scarce need say to you that none are so emphatically uttered, none so anxiously repeated, as those which enjoin the preservation of the Union of these States."

Although "Washington" was his most significant oratorical effort in the immediate prewar years, it was not the only one. "The Uses of Astronomy," a lecture delivered eight times, stressed the practical uses of knowledge. One on charities, delivered fifteen times, raised money for various causes. One on Franklin's boyhood, given thirty times, celebrated another Revolutionary hero.

Notwithstanding Everett's rhetorical strategy of calling up the past to save the Union, the country was on the verge of disunion by 1860. In a last-ditch effort,

Everett ran for the vice-presidency on the Constitutional Union party ticket, but election results soon had him brooding again.

Northern Constitutional Unionists and other antiabolitionists took different roads during the war. Some followed the *Boston Courier* in its pro-southern sympathies. Others opposed Lincoln while they supported the war as long as the objective was to save the Union, not to abolish slavery. Still others gravitated to the Republican camp. Despite his original scorn of Lincoln, Everett chose the last alternative; and many former critics, as well as friends, credited him with carrying the bulk of his old constituency with him. Charles Francis Adams, Jr., went so far as to attribute Lincoln's 1864 electoral victory in Massachusetts to Everett's "manly course."

Adams might have overestimated Everett's influence, but there is no doubt that Everett was active and that his rhetorical appeals were well adapted to his old constituency. Early in the war, he developed what he called a lecture on "The Causes and Conduct of the Civil War," but many of the sixty occasions on which it was delivered were more like rallies than a typical lecture hall, and the content was argumentative. In the first part, he traced the history of southern sectionalism in conspiratorial terms. The plot originated with Calhoun, and conspirators used various "pretexts" to mislead the southern people into secession. Slavery, to which he only alluded, was not the cause of the war; the cause was the untamed ambition of conspirators. In the second part of the lecture, Everett advanced legalistic reasons to show the unconstitutionality of secession and argued that if secession were permitted, it would establish a precedent for future divisions that would eventually turn America into another Europe.

Given his oratorical reputation and his influence among moderates, it was natural for Everett to be selected as the main orator at the dedication of the Gettysburg cemetery. His speech has since been overshadowed, but it was important in its own day, appearing on the front pages of most metropolitan newspapers either in full or in substantial excerpts.

The Gettysburg address was like Everett's earlier ceremonial orations in that it contained historical information and used history as a plea for unity; but it was different in that the history was more recent and the plea much more explicit. The first half of the speech was a detailed account of the battle, perhaps the best that had been reported up to that time. In the second half, he reiterated his legalistic arguments against secession and repeated his warning that permitting secession would lead to the same horrors that now faced disunited Europe. He also included what he privately considered his most important argument, a refutation of a common antiwar assertion that the bitterness of the war would leave the nation divided psychologically. Again resorting to history, Everett recounted a host of civil conflicts that had been followed by national unity.

Everett's last major speech was given three weeks before the election of 1864 in favor of Lincoln's reelection. Ironically, it was the first time the seventy-year-old man had ever given a stump speech and it not only received considerable newspaper coverage but also was distributed widely as a pamphlet. Not surprisingly, some observers claimed that he had abandoned his old conservatism. Perhaps the claim has some merit, but Everett followed a consistent course. His wartime oratory, like his prewar speaking, was designed to save his beloved Union.

INFORMATION SOURCES

Research Collections and Collected Speeches

The Everett Manuscripts is the second largest manuscript collection in the Massachusetts Historical Society, Boston. Everett's habit of selling speech manuscripts for charity left few in the collection; but his meticulous habit of keeping a diary, filing incoming correspondence, and maintaining a letterbook makes the collection unusually valuable.

Excepting sermons, texts of which are available in the manuscript collection, almost all speeches are readily accessible in published form. Congressional speeches are in the *Register of Debates* or *Congressional Globe*, and a few were published as pamphlets, as were some of his ceremonial orations. A list of pamphlets, as well as nonoratorical writings is readily available in vol. 164, s.v. "Everett, Edward," *National Union Catalog, Pre-1965 Imprints* (London: Mansell, 1971).

Everett, Edward. *Orations and Speeches on Various Occasions*. 7th ed. 4   OSVO
    vols. Boston: Little, Brown, 1868. Comprehensive collection of ceremonial orations and lectures. Partisan speaking is omitted except for wartime oratory. Collection began as one volume in 1836, grew to two by 1850, three by 1859, and four by 1868. The twelfth and last edition appeared 1890–1895. Also available from University Microfilms, American Culture series, reel 409.3.

Selected Critical Studies

Petersen, Svend. *The Gettysburg Addresses: The Story of Two Orations*. New York: F. Ungar, 1973.
Reid, Ronald F. "Edward Everett, Rhetorician of Nationalism, 1824–1855." *Quarterly Journal of Speech* 42 (1956): 273–82.
———. "Edward Everett's 'The Character of Washington.' " *Southern Speech Journal* 22 (1957): 144–56.
———. "Newspaper Response to the Gettysburg Addresses." *Quarterly Journal of Speech* 53 (1967): 50–60.
Stripp, Fred. "The *Other* Gettysburg Address." *Civil War History* 1 (1954), 161–73. Unacknowledged revised republication in *Western Speech* 32 (1968): 19–26.

Biography

Frothingham, Paul Revere. *Edward Everett: Orator and Statesman*. Boston: Houghton Mifflin, 1925.

CHRONOLOGY OF MAJOR SPEECHES

See "Research Collections and Collected Speeches" for source code.

Phi Beta Kappa oration: "The Circumstances Favorable to the Progress of Literature in America," Harvard College, Cambridge, Massachusetts, August 26, 1824, *OSVO*, 1: 9–44.

Fourth of July orations: 1826, Cambridge, Massachusetts, *OSVO*, 1: 103–30; Charlestown, Massachusetts, 1828, *OSVO*, 1: 150–72; Worcester, Massachusetts, 1833, *OSVO*, 1: 377–401; New York, 1861, *OSVO*, 4: 345–406.

Eulogy of Adams and Jefferson, Charlestown, Massachusetts, August 1, 1826; *OSVO*, 1: 131–49.

"Battle of Lexington," Lexington, Massachusetts, April 20, 1835; *OSVO*, 1: 526–60.

Governor's message, *Boston Weekly Messenger*, January 21, 1836.

Inaugural address as president of Harvard University, Cambridge, Massachusetts, April 30, 1846; *OSVO*, 2: 493–518.

"The Character of Washington," 137 times beginning in Boston, February 22, 1856; *OSVO*, 4: 3–51.

"Uses of Astronomy," 8 times beginning in Albany, New York, August 28, 1856; *OSVO*, 3: 422–65.

"Charitable Institutions and Charity," 15 times beginning in Boston, December 22, 1857; *OSVO*, 3: 568–602.

"Franklin the Boston Boy," 30 times beginning in Boston, January 19, 1859; *OSVO*, 4: 108–29.

"Causes and Conduct of the Civil War," 60 times beginning in Boston, October 16, 1861; *OSVO*, 4: 464–89.

Gettysburg address, Gettysburg, Pennsylvania, November 19, 1863, *OSVO*, 4: 622–59.

"The Duty of Supporting the Government," Boston, October 19, 1864; *OSVO*, 4: 698–726.

CHARLES GRANDISON FINNEY
(1792–1875), evangelist and educator

CHARLES J. GRIFFIN

Charles Grandison Finney was one of nineteenth-century America's most influential and innovative religious orators. Born in Warren, Connecticut, Finney grew up in the comparative wilderness of western New York. He was an able student and taught in the common schools where he had been educated before returning to Connecticut to continue his own studies at the Warren Academy. After a period during which he alternated between teaching and attending school at Warren, Finney returned to New York in his mid-twenties. There he arranged to study law in the small town of Adams, not far from the family home on the shores of Lake Ontario.

Finney's commanding physical presence and great personal charm soon established him as a leader among the young people of Adams. A talented musician and public speaker, he played an active role in the local Presbyterian church, though by his own admission he was at the time "almost as ignorant of religion as a heathen." But frequent talks with his minister and his own professional study of Mosaic law soon led Finney to take a serious interest in the Bible. By the summer of 1821, his third in Adams, Finney had grown convinced of the truth of Christ's gospel. This intellectual assent to Christianity spurred Finney onward until, in October 1821, he experienced a powerful conversion. Almost immediately, he embarked upon a preaching career that was to last some fifty years and was to establish him as one of the pivotal figures in American revivalism.

Finney's significance to American religious oratory flows from two related sources: his own remarkable talents as a revivalist and his great desire to teach others the principles on which his success rested. The former allowed him to move tens of thousands through his preaching, the latter to pioneer techniques of mass evangelism that touched millions more.

FINNEY AS REVIVALIST

After his conversion, Finney wasted no time in taking up his life's work. "I had the impression," he later recalled, "that God wanted me to preach the Gospel and that I must begin immediately." So pressing was this call that Finney abandoned his law practice on the moment, telling one startled client that he had "a retainer from the Lord Jesus Christ to plead his case and cannot plead yours." Finney began to speak on an informal basis in Adams and surrounding villages while taking up the study of theology with his pastor, the Reverend George Gale. By the time of his ordination by the Oneida Presbytery on July 1, 1824, Finney had already preached extensively in the Jefferson County area of western New York. Already his dynamic and somewhat unorthodox preaching style, though frowned upon by Gale among others, had begun to earn Finney a reputation in the region. Having received no formal seminary education, Finney planned to avoid cities and cultivated areas and to preach in schoolhouses and barns on the frontier. But in time he began to accept invitations to preach in larger towns such as Utica, Troy, and Auburn, where his efforts to promote revivals enjoyed remarkable success. During these visits, Finney honed his speaking skills while developing a concept of preaching suited to the rhetorical demands of revivalism.

Finney's endeavors were not universally applauded. The so-called new measures that he and others pioneered were as controversial within conservative Protestant theological circles as they were popular with the public at large. New England conservatives accused Finney of compromising the sovereignty of God and the dignity of the pulpit. Many who had no personal knowledge of Finney succumbed to rumors that he was wild and reckless in his preaching methods. Under the leadership of Boston's Lyman Beecher, conservatives called a meeting with Finney at New Lebanon, Massachusetts, in 1827. Beecher hoped to thwart the spread of Finney's popularity by confirming the latter's faults as publicly as possible. But since most of the charges brought against him proved groundless, the conference probably did more to dispel eastern misconceptions about Finney than anything else. By the end of the decade, Finney had been welcomed in both Philadelphia and New York City.

The event that firmly established Finney as the nation's foremost revivalist occurred in the bustling market town of Rochester, New York, on the Erie Canal. There, in the winter of 1830–1831, Finney orchestrated a spectacular city-wide revival that caught the attention of the entire country. Estimates as to the number of converts gained by the city's churches ranged from the hundreds into the thousands. Finney took special pride in his success among the business and professional classes of Rochester. Former critics, such as Lyman Beecher, were stunned by Finney's accomplishment. Declaring Rochester's reclamation to be the greatest event of its kind in history, Beecher, who had once set out to squelch "Finneyism," was soon inviting his former rival to evangelize Boston itself. At the behest of philanthropists Lewis and Arthur Tappan, Finney suspended his itinerant labors in 1832 in order to occupy the pulpit of the Second Free Presbyterian Church of New York City, located in the former Chatham Street Theatre. Later that year, Finney contracted cholera, nearly died, and required several months to regain his strength. During his recuperation, events took place that encouraged him, when recovered, to preach a series of lectures on revivals of religion.

Commencing on a Friday evening in December 1834, Finney delivered a course of twenty-two weekly lectures on the subject he knew best. Speaking in the crisp, extemporaneous manner to which he was accustomed, he ranged freely about the subject of revivals, choosing the following week's topic only after consulting a transcript of his previous lecture in order to discover "the next question that would naturally need discussion." Each of the one- to two-hour presentations addressed a different aspect of the means and ends of revivalism. Among the subjects Finney discussed were the origins of revivals; the place of prayer in revivals; the proper roles of clergy and laity in promoting and sustaining revivals; how to spread the work of the revival; and the nature of effective revival preaching. Collected for publication, Finney's revival lectures sold a remarkable 12,000 copies in just three months. The continued popularity of several later editions reflected Finney's widespread popularity, as well as the usefulness of his advice. Indeed, one reason for the enduring appeal of the lectures was that Finney provided in them a virtual blueprint for effective evangelism.

Soon after completing his lecture series, Finney accepted an offer to serve as professor of theology at tiny Oberlin College in Ohio. Oberlin had recently been founded by a group of dissident students from Cincinnati's Lane Seminary, led by a Finney convert, Theodore Dwight Weld. For several years, Finney divided his time between Oberlin and his preaching duties in New York. But at length, he increasingly devoted himself to his teaching interests. In 1851, he was named president of Oberlin College, a post he held until 1866. Finney continued to make occasional preaching tours, including two successful ventures to Great Britain in 1849–1850 and again in 1859–1860. But his greatest public triumphs as an evangelist, the Rochester revival and the New York revival lectures, were already recorded. He died at Oberlin in 1875 at the age of eighty-three.

Finney's preaching style and the concept of preaching effectiveness that evolved out of it were greatly influenced by his legal training and his personal theology of conversion. From the former he derived the ability to transform a moment's inspiration into an organized, compelling presentation. Rejecting the common practice of writing out sermons to read verbatim, Finney preferred to address his audiences extemporaneously, often pacing the aisles in the manner of a lawyer before a jury. He customarily wore a dark business suit in place of clerical garb. On occasion, Finney would clutch a terse outline, or "skeleton" as he called it, but more often these aids were composed only after he spoke in order to help him reconstruct a particularly effective sermon. Normally Finney relied on spiritual inspiration and his grasp of local affairs in planning his sermons. He typically spent a long period in intense, private prayer before confronting his audience. Then, speaking with an almost hypnotic fervor, Finney would lay out his case carefully, insisting on a personal verdict from each listener in the house.

Finney's theology of conversion also made a distinct contribution to his concept of effective preaching, beginning with his rejection of the strict Calvinist doctrine of man's total depravity and the passive regeneration of God's elect. According to this orthodox view, individual men and women were powerless to contribute to their own salvation. Conversion was a miraculous event that could not be encouraged by any human action. Since it followed from this view that revivals also were divine interventions in human affairs, many conservatives held that attempts to promote or sustain revivals were futile and possibly blasphemous. Finney could not accept the idea that men and women are helpless in the matter of their own souls. He refused to believe that salvation was beyond the grasp of any man, woman, or child who sincerely repented and took up the Cross.

God's command to obey, he argued, presumed a human ability to obey. Men and women must be active partners with God in the conversion process. Thus Finney held that revivals, which created an emotionally charged atmosphere in which the potential for personal action was heightened, were essential tools for evangelism. He believed it sinful for ministers to stand by passively when means existed to promote and organize these essential tools for doing God's work.

As for effective preaching, Finney deplored the dry expositions of doctrine to which most churchgoers were subjected week after week. Even Gale, his friend and teacher, "seemed to take for granted that all his hearers were theologians, and therefore that he might assume all the great and fundamental doctrines of the Gospels." At first, Finney had been "perplexed rather than edified" by this kind of preaching, but he soon realized that it resulted naturally from the view that the lost were beyond hope and the redeemed needed only instruction in God's Word, not motivation to accept it. Out of this realization, Finney fashioned an approach to preaching that, in its emphasis on securing personal action from listeners, reflected his own view that "all ministers should be revival ministers and all preaching should be revival preaching." Much of Finney's preaching doctrine was set down in two lectures, "A Wise Minister Will Be Successful" and "How to Preach the Gospel."

Wisdom in preaching, Finney maintained, embraced both the content and the presentation of pulpit address. With respect to the former, Finney called upon ministers to preach directly to the consciences of their auditors. He found no virtue in ministers' preaching about humanity when the real challenge was to reach each man and woman individually with the gospel. Too many ministers, afraid of offending their parishioners or convinced that preaching played no great part in God's plan of salvation, hid themselves behind abstruse doctrinal sermons. Still others dispensed soothing nostrums designed to relieve the guilt and anxiety of sinners. Finney argued that a minister's duty lay not in comforting poor, "doomed" sinners but in blasting them from their refuges. The goal of effective preaching lay not in comforting people but in making them repent and obey God's Word. Wise preaching always led sinners to feel their guilt, not to escape it. Ministers should never give sinners the impression that they are pitiable creatures, rejected for want of some action on God's part, Finney counseled. In Christ, God had freely offered salvation to all who would accept.

Preaching of the bold, uncompromising sort that Finney advocated required a minister to be intimately familiar with his audience. "How can he know to bring forth things old and new, and adapt truth to their case . . . unless he knows where they hide themselves?" Audience analysis thus played an important role in the inventional process of good preaching, Finney believed. It also assisted him in organizing his sermons effectively so that the proper portion of God's Word could be applied to his audience at just the right moment. Taking his own advice, Finney often canvassed a town before he preached there, familiarizing himself with local issues and with the names of prominent and worldly residents.

On occasion, these citizens found themselves called out by name and publicly urged to repent during the course of a Finney meeting.

Finney pioneered other techniques as well, including the use of prolonged meetings—a series of revival meetings lasting several days or more—in order to impress and motivate revival audiences. He was often associated with the so-called anxious seat, a device that in fact he employed sparingly. The anxious seat was a bench located in the front of the meeting house to which sinners convinced of their need for help were urged to repair for special ministrations.

Finney believed that good preaching should be unpretentious and conversational. He advised ministers to draw on day-to-day experiences for illustrations to use in sermons. He urged the liberal use of repetition, a rhetorical device many ministers avoided for fear that it made their sermons seem simplistic. But such men, Finney believed, preached without regard for the basic rules of the human mind. Often the most intelligent listeners were so preoccupied with worldly matters that they lacked the patience to endure a complex sermon. These very men and women might be most affected by preaching that was pointed, concrete, and simple.

In its delivery, good preaching followed Finney's definition of eloquence as "that gushing, impressive, and persuasive oratory, that naturally flows from an educated man whose soul is on fire with his subject, and who is free to pour out his heart to a waiting and earnest people." The directness required of good preaching and the sheer amount of it entailed in an extended revival rendered the written sermon impractical and undesirable. While ministers must put prayer and careful thought into their sermons, Finney believed that they must become as skilled as lawyers in anticipating and defeating the objections of their opponents. No one accused lawyers of being careless speakers, he argued, nor should any decry the art of extemporaneous preaching.

Aware that some condemned his concept of preaching as overly dramatic, Finney responded that the dignity of the pulpit lay in saving souls, not in giving dignified sermons. The bishop of London, ran one of his favorite anecdotes, had once inquired of the great actor Garrick why it was that actors, who portrayed imaginary problems, should be able to move an audience, while ministers, who dealt with life and death matters, could scarcely get an audience to pay attention to them. Garrick is said to have replied that "it is because we represent fiction as a reality and you represent reality as a fiction." Critics might disparage Finney's methods, "but let them remember," he countered, "that while they are thus turning away and decrying the art of the actor, and attempting to 'support the dignity of the pulpit,' the theaters can be thronged every night."

Finney's legal background and his theology of conversion thus led him to proclaim the importance of effective preaching in the struggle to convert the world. The wise minister knows how to bring God's Word effectively to bear upon his audience and realizes that the purpose of preaching is to make people act. Ministers must learn to adapt to their audiences; make good use of means such as public prayer and the anxious seat to impress sinners of their guilt; and employ a style that is simple and a manner of presentation that is extemporaneous. Turning aside charges that his brand of preaching was undignified, Finney pointed out that it worked, something his critics could never dispute. In the end, many ministers who had been skeptical of Finney's methods were converted to his concept of effective preaching.

Charles Grandison Finney pioneered the transition from rural to urban evangelism and from Calvinism's bleak doctrine of predetermination to the contemporary view of conversion as an act, at least in part, of individual conscience and will. Though not the first to emphasize the role of the individual in the conversion process, Finney's systematic effort to develop a rhetoric appropriate to this position marked an important milestone in American religious oratory. His revival lectures represent an important contribution to nineteenth-century revivalism and to the evolution of modern preaching methods. Moreover, the democratic atmosphere of Finney's revivals, which cut across denominational, class, and sexual lines, made them ideal historical models for nascent reform movements in the mid-nineteenth century. His principles of preaching, designed to move audiences to commitment and action, suited the needs of many reformers. Some, like Theodore Dwight Weld, began their careers in the revival movement before taking up other reform causes. Others learned by observing the techniques of Finney and fellow revivalists. Thus, while the ideological debt owed by such reform causes as temperance and antislavery to revivalism has long been acknowledged, it should be noted that revivalists, and Finney in particular, left a rich rhetorical heritage to American social movements in general. Finney's reputation as the Father of Modern Revivalism carries with it a sense of his legacy to both secular and religious public address in the United States.

INFORMATION SOURCES

Research Collections and Collected Speeches

The letters and papers of Charles Grandison Finney have been collected by the Oberlin College Library, Oberlin, Ohio, and microfilmed under the direction of Robert S. Fletcher (nine reels). The Finney papers contain correspondence between the evangelist and his associates, letters from converts, invitations to preach, sermon outlines, and a draft manuscript of the 1868 revision of Finney's revival lectures. Another valuable source of insight into Finney's oratorical career is his autobiography, published posthumously in 1876. First appearing weekly in the *New York Evangelist*, Finney's revival lectures were published in a single volume in 1835. William G. McGloughlin's scholarly edition of the lectures provides useful background and detail on this important work.

Finney, Charles G. *Lectures on Revivals of Religion.* Edited by William G.   *LRR*
    McGloughlin. Cambridge: Belknap Press of Harvard University
    Press, 1960.
———. *Lectures to Professing Christians.* Oberlin: E. J. Goodrich, 1878.

————. *Sermons on Gospel Themes*. New York: E. J. Goodrich/Dodd
    Mead, 1876.

————. *Sermons on Important Subjects*. New York: John Taylor, 1836.   *SIS*

Selected Critical Studies

Quimby, Rollin. "Charles Grandison Finney: Herald of Modern Revivalism." *Speech
    Monographs* 20 (1953): 293–99.

Selected Biographies

Finney, Charles G. *Memoirs*. New York: A. S. Barnes, 1876.
Wright, George F. *Charles Grandison Finney*. Boston: Houghton Mifflin, 1891.

CHRONOLOGY OF MAJOR SPEECHES

See "Research Collections and Collected Speeches" for source codes. The exact dates
on which the speeches were delivered are not known.

"A Wise Minister Will Be Successful," New York, 1835; *LRR*, pp. 174–93.

"How to Preach the Gospel," New York, 1835; *LRR*, pp. 194–222.

"Sinners Bound to Change Their Own Hearts," New York, 1836; *SIS*, pp. 3–42.

"God Cannot Please Sinners," New York, 1836; *SIS*, pp. 165–85.

BENJAMIN FRANKLIN
(1706–1790), printer and founding father

Benjamin Franklin remains a mysterious curiosity. Was he a humanitarian or an opportunist, a scientist or a dabbler, a member of the literati or a hack, an investor or an exploiter, a patriot or a spy, a genius or a sham, a gentleman or a rogue, a rhetorician or a sophist? A keen intellect driven by insatiable curiosity stimulated Franklin's many interests and abilities. He was tradesman, public servant, politician, philosopher-scientist, philanthropist-civic leader. Throughout life, he was proud to be identified as a printer. This trade led to his involvement in related fields—publisher, journalist, diarist, pamphleteer, propagandist. As a public servant, he is remembered as the first postmaster-general of the United States.

With only two years of formal education, Franklin became an apprentice printer at the age of twelve in his brother's shop and an anonymous author at the age of sixteen. At twenty-four, he became the owner and publisher of the *Pennsylvania Gazette*. As a result of his competence, shrewdness, and personality, the business grew. He married, started a family, and created a lucrative publication, *Poor Richard's Almanack*, in 1733 at the age of twenty-seven. Although his attempt to launch a magazine failed in 1741, he was an adroit businessman, as well as a successful husband and father. In fact, he was able to retire at the early age of forty-two in order to pursue his many avocations.

FRANKLIN AS CONGENIAL PERSUADER

Franklin's *Autobiography* describes how he attempted to teach himself rhetoric and dialectic. He read "my father's books of dispute about religion," then "put my arguments in writing" in order to gain some grasp of argumentation. He obtained an English grammar, which included "two little sketches of the arts of rhetoric and logic" that introduced him to the Socratic method. For further enlightenment, he obtained a copy of Xenophon's *Memorable Things of Socrates* and consequently "dropt my abrupt contradiction and positive argumentation, and put on the humble inquirer and doubter." After a few years, he abandoned the use of such inflexible words as "certainly, undoubtedly" in favor of such terms as "it appears to me," "I imagine," "if I am not mistaken." Thus, his persuasive discourse deliberately evolved from a studied confrontational approach, to an art of inquiry that drew the respondent into concessions, and finally to a rhetorical demeanor of "modest diffidence."

In 1727, Franklin formed the Junto, "a club of mutual improvement" that met weekly. The rules required "that every member, in his turn, should produce one or more queries on any point of Morals, Politics, or Natural Philosophy, to be discuss'd by the company; and once in three months produce and read an essay of his own writing." Thus, Franklin established an arena for practicing the arts of oral discourse. In 1730, he published *On Conversation* in which he warned against "talking overmuch," "raillery," and other problems. His *On Ill-Natured Speaking* (1733) and *Rules for Making Oneself a Disagreeable Companion* (1750) reinforced these warnings. One of the thirteen "virtues" that he advocated, "Silence," admonished readers to "avoid trifling conversation." In London, he joined the Honest Whigs, a debate-discussion club that replaced the Junto during his absence from Philadelphia.

Several primary items offer examples of Franklin's discourse. First, his *Examination* provides the text of the first American ever to testify before the British House of Commons, February 13, 1766. Second, "Causes of the American Discontents before 1768" is an essay that was delivered originally as a speech and published in the *London Chronicle* in January 1768. Third, "Rules by Which a Great Empire May Be Reduced to a Small One" is a 1773 satirical treatment of British colonial policy. Finally, Franklin's concluding speech to the Constitutional Convention on September 17, 1787, probably defused tension and set the proper tone for the ultimate approval of a most significant document.

Franklin's *Examination* survives as one of the twelve most widely published pamphlets on the American question to appear in the colonies between 1765 and 1776. It offered many people in Britain and Europe the first opportunity to grasp the intensity of the issues simmering in the American colonies. It enhanced Franklin's name internationally at a time when his effectiveness was being questioned by opponents, and it solidified his credibility as the key speaker for American interests. The *Examination* includes 174 questions and answers developed over the course of several hours before the British House of Commons. Franklin ostensibly served as a witness in opposition to the Stamp Act; but potent adversaries, such as George Grenville and Charles Townshend, dominated the number, length, frequency, and order of the questions. Consequently his success was even more remarkable.

For the most part, Franklin's answers were polite, firm, direct, and usually brief. "In my opinion, there's not gold and silver enough in the Colonies to pay the stamp duty for one year." What about a "moderate" duty? "No, never, unless compelled by force of arms." However, even if military troops were sent to America, "They cannot force a man to take stamps who chooses to do without them." Then, quite prophetically, "They will not find a rebellion; they may indeed make one." Intermittently, characteristic "modest diffidence" surfaced: "It is hard to answer questions of what people at such a distance will think"; "That is a question I cannot answer"; "That is a deep question"; and many reactions were preceded by "I suppose," "I believe," "In my opinion," "I think." His responses sometimes had the pungent ring of *Poor Richard*: "They would manufacture more, and plough less." Out of 174 answers, 60 totaled 10 words or fewer, with only 14 totaling 100 words or more. He delivered only two lengthy replies—one of 658 words and another of 454 words. Both were valuable contributions. Franklin's early preparation and disciplined skill in dialectic contributed to his effectiveness.

"Causes of the American Discontents before 1768," according to Verner

Crane, is "perhaps the most famous contribution by Franklin, after the *Examination*, to the propaganda of the American Revolution." The essay evolved from Franklin's oral presentation "to a large gathering that included some members of Parliament" and, as William Willcox notes, "the statement was well received, and he was urged to write it out and publish it." This evolutionary process from oral discourse to written publication, often under a variety of pseudonyms, was the rhetorical route taken by many of Franklin's published pieces. As a foremost member of the guild, Franklin was granted considerable freedom and choice space by his fellow printers in Britain. He used these outlets to identify issues, to clarify colonial positions, to correct English errors, and to appeal to the readers' sense of fairness.

In his *Causes*, Franklin remained a loyalist while challenging sharply the actions and authority of "a H[ouse] of C[ommons], in which there is not a single member of our chusing." He charged that George Grenville attempted "to raise money on America by Stamps," then compounded this error with another proposal "in the same Session . . . whereby it was to be made lawful for military Officers in the Colonies to quarter their soldiers in private houses" in an effort "to awe the people into a compliance" with the Stamp Act. He warned "*that money is not to be raised on English subjects without their consent* [italics in original." He recommended that the colonists give these tax collectors "as little trouble as possible, by not consuming the British manufactures on which they are to levy the duties. Let us agree to consume no more of their expensive gewgaws. Let us live frugally, and let us industriously manufacture what we can for ourselves" and work in "the service of our gracious Sovereign . . . in the old *constitutional* manner [italics in original]."

"Rules By Which a Great Empire May Be Reduced to a Small One" is a delightful satire on British colonial policy.

Let the Parliaments flount their Claims, reject their Petitions, refuse even to suffer the reading of them, and treat the Petitioners with the utmost Contempt. Nothing can have a better Effect . . . for though many can forgive Injuries, *none ever forgave Contempt*. . . . To make your taxes more odious, and more likely to procure Resistance, send . . . the most *indescreet, ill-bred* and *insolent* [collectors] you can find. . . . Thus shall the Trade of your Colonists suffer more from their Friends in Time of Peace, than it did from their Enemies in War. . . . Threaten to carry all the Offenders three thousand Miles to be hang'd, drawn and quartered. *O! this will work admirably* [italics in original].

Although the "Rules" gave these points a special sting and wide notoriety, Willcox declares, "Satire is a poor instrument of persuasion, for the open-minded are likely to be entertained . . . and the close-minded to be angered."

Now eighty-one and in poor health, Franklin prepared a manuscript of his final speech to the Constitutional Convention, September 17, 1787, which was delivered by his friend, James Wilson, and recorded in Madison's *Journal*. It combines a deft balance of grandfatherly advice and "modest diffidence" sufficient to stimulate audience acceptance:

I confess that there are several parts of this constitution which I do not at present approve, but I am not sure I shall never approve them: For having lived long, I have experienced many instances of being obliged . . . to change opinions even on important subjects, which I once thought right, but found to be otherwise. It is therefore that the older I grow, the more apt I am to doubt my own judgment, and to pay more respect to the judgment of others. . . . I doubt too whether any other Convention we can obtain may be able to make a better Constitution. . . . Thus I consent, Sir, to this Constitution because I expect no better, and because I am not sure, that it is not the best. . . . I cannot help expressing a wish that every member of the Convention who may still have objections to it, would with me, on this occasion doubt a little of his own infallibility—and to make manifest our unanimity, put his name to this instrument.

Why is Franklin usually omitted in a list of notable American speakers? First, as a successful propagandist, he persuaded posterity that he was not worthy: "I was but a bad speaker, never eloquent, subject to much hesitation in my choice of words, hardly correct in language, and yet I generally carried my points." Critics are too prone to grasp the first part of the quotation and ignore the concluding phrase. Was this more of Franklin's "modest diffidence"? His reputation was secure in his many fields of endeavor; he desired no acclaim as an effective speaker.

He devoted primary effort to those small-group and interpersonal skills during a period when they were less appreciated. While he spoke seldom in the Assembly of Pennsylvania during the 1750s, he "worked rather behind the scenes, shaping opinions, harmonizing differences." He was "informing, explaining, consulting, disputing, in a continual hurry from morning to night" in dealing with members of Parliament. His nature, according to Carl Van Doren, was "to be thoughtful, witty, benevolent, cheerful, and homely." Carl Becker calls him a "master of discussion"; Max Farrand says that he was "an excellent listener"; Franklin notes that he was "always ready and willing to receive and follow good advice"—stellar attributes for any era.

He did not deliver long speeches to a generation that sometimes confused lengthy oratory with eloquence. Several enduring classics of eighteenth-century parliamentary discourse consumed four and five hours, ending only at the break of day. But Franklin's brief, simple, direct style lacked protracted adornment. Jefferson observes that he never heard Washington or Franklin "speak ten minutes at a time, nor to any but the main point which was to decide the question." Van Doren applauds Franklin's "summing up in incomparable and irresistible statements." While such abilities may have saved the Constitutional Convention, they have not enhanced Franklin's reputation as a speaker.

He was not given to emotional display in speech making. Farrand concludes that Franklin's "ability to take a detached, impersonal, dispassionate point of view" was "a leading intellectual quality." A public speaker has a difficult time maintaining such consistent neutrality. Some writers have depicted Franklin as taciturn and reticent, aloof from the final outcome. He probably conditioned himself, as early as the Junto debates, to remain stoically silent as long as possible in order to reach a more objective conclusion.

He was both a student and a practitioner of dialectic—a form of discourse rarely analyzed by critics. His *Examination* and reports of less formal oral exchanges attest to considerable prowess in this genre. Yet Franklin's dialectical accomplishments remain relatively unacknowledged.

He is classified as a writer, not a speaker. Of course he was both. In fact, some of his writings, like those of other notables, initially were speeches.

His humor and brevity could have been perceived as flippant. Franklin's contemporaries were captivated by his charm in executing a well-told story. Funny one-line maxims with the sting of truth account for the popularity of *Poor Richard*. As a journalist, he delighted in producing spoofs, such as *An Edict by the King of Prussia*; sexually related items during a prudish age, such as *Advice to a Young Man on the Choice of a Mistress* and *The Speech of Polly Baker*; or semiserious pieces, such as the *Dialogue between Franklin and the Gout*. But the world has never been tolerant of mixing much humor with politics. According to Becker, "Franklin was not entrusted with the task of writing the Declaration of Independence for fear he might conceal a joke in the middle of it."

A poignant challenge to Franklin's elevated image evolves from the pen of Ronald F. Reid in *The American Revolution and the Rhetoric of History*. In declaring that "the less praiseworthy aspects of Franklin's life are handled very gingerly" by biographers, Reid suggests a concerted cover-up of the subject's tainted credibility. Franklin's son, William, was illegitimate; Franklin and Deborah had a common-law marriage; Deborah apparently was never legally divorced from her first husband; Franklin engaged in suspicious land speculation; and questions remain concerning his financial accounts while in France during the Revolution. Reid justifiably declares that the Revolutionists have been portrayed as "near-perfect, larger-than-life demigods" with "a high degree of ethos, thereby giving them considerable suasory power." Such distortions need correction. Certainly Franklin was a mere mortal who, as a printer, probably manipulated his own favorable press on occasion.

But as matters are being placed in perspective, the negative side of an equation should not be allowed to smother its positive elements. After all, the subject cannot be held accountable for the omissions of his biographers. Not a secretive person by nature, Franklin's shortcomings were on exhibit during an era less inclined to confess human frailty. While his son technically was illegitimate, Franklin apparently was an unusually loving father who provided every means of support and attention. Franklin accepted the full legal responsibility imposed by common law, granted his wife full power of attorney over his affairs during his absences, and nurtured an obviously successful marriage that ended after forty-four years only upon Deborah's death in 1774. There is no evidence that Franklin benefited illegally from any land deals. Moreover, despite the almost constant snooping and carping of his adversaries, particularly Arthur Lee and John Adams, nothing surfaced to indicate that Franklin was a war profiteer. He provided considerable sums from his personal resources over several decades to abate colonial fiscal crises and never was compensated fully at the agreed stipend for his foreign service. While certainly not a demigod, Franklin's reaction to adversity often exceeded the ethical level of behavior typical of his and subsequent generations.

Admittedly never an orator, Franklin was the spokesperson for America on the international scene for at least a quarter of a century. Despite any credibility encumbrances, he applied impressive oral and written skills in helping to forge a favorable beginning for the new republic. None of the American triumvirate of the period—Washington, Jefferson, Franklin—was a consummate orator, but this is not to dilute their effectiveness as oral communicators. Franklin's quiet, sensitive, interpersonal diplomacy remains a significant contribution to the emerging nation.

INFORMATION SOURCES

Research Collections and Collected Discourses

The American Philosophical Society, Philadelphia, houses the principal Franklin manuscript collection. Franklin's incomplete *Autobiography*, in reality a memoir, offers excellent detail on his early life.

Pamphlets and the American Revolution: Rhetoric, Politics, Literature, and   AM
    the Popular Press. Edited by G. Jack Gravlee and James R. Irvine.
    Delmar, N.Y.: Scholars' Facsimiles and Reprints, 1976.
The Papers of Benjamin Franklin. Edited by Leonard W. Labaree and   BF
    William B. Willcox. New Haven: Yale University Press, 1959f.
The Records of the Federal Convention of 1787. Edited by Max Farrand.   FC
    New Haven: Yale University Press, 1966.

Selected Critical Studies

Andrews, James R. "From Penn to Franklin: Rhetoric in Colonial Pennsylvania." In *A History of Public Speaking in Pennsylvania*. Edited by DeWitte Holland and Robert Oliver. *Pennsylvania Speech Annual*, special edition, 27 (1971): 5–20.
———. "The Rhetoric of a Lobbyist: Benjamin Franklin in England, 1765–1775." *Central States Speech Journal* 18 (1967): 261–67.
Gravlee, G. Jack, and James R. Irvine. "Franklin Reexamined: A Rejection of Parliamentary Manipulation." *Southern Speech Communication Journal* 48 (1983): 167–81.
Lewis, Sandra. "Franklin's Advice to Speakers." *Today's Speech* 7 (1959): 18–21.
Reid, Ronald F. *The American Revolution and the Rhetoric of History*. Falls Church, Va.: Speech Communication Association, 1978.

Selected Biographies

Becker, Carl L. "Benjamin Franklin." In *Dictionary of American Biography*. Vol. 4. Edited by Allen Johnson and Dumas Malone. New York: Charles Scribner's Sons, 1931.

Crane, Verner W., ed. *Benjamin Franklin's Letters to the Press, 1758–1775*. Chapel Hill: University of North Carolina Press, 1950.

Franklin, Benjamin. *The Autobiography of Benjamin Franklin*. Edited by Leonard W. Labaree, Ralph L. Ketchum, Helen C. Boatfield, and Helene H. Fineman. New Haven: Yale University Press, 1964.

Van Doren, Carl. *Benjamin Franklin*. New York: Viking Press, 1938.

CHRONOLOGY OF MAJOR SPEECHES

See "Research Collections and Collected Discourses" for source codes.

"Examination before the House of Commons," London, February 13, 1766; AM, n.p.; BF, 23: 124–62.

"Causes of the American Discontents before 1768," *London Chronicle*, January 7, 1768; BF, 15: 3–13.

"Rules by Which a Great Empire May Be Reduced to a Small One," *Public Advertiser*, London, September 11, 1773; BF, 20: 389–99.

"Final Speech of the Constitutional Convention," Philadelphia, September 17, 1787; FC, 2: 641–47.

WILLIAM LLOYD GARRISON
(1805–1879), abolitionist

LLOYD E. ROHLER

William Lloyd Garrison personified the abolitionist agitation to end slavery in the United States. His persistence in the struggle in spite of an indifferent public, financial hardship, and personal abuse places him in the first rank of American reformers. His early life gave little indication of the later achievement. Born into a demoralized family, he grew up a poor but pious youth who apprenticed several trades before finding his vocation as a printer. His education consisted of reading the exchange papers and the few books that fell into his hands in the newspaper office where he worked. His vague desire to be involved in the growing reform movement of the time drew him to a partnership with Benjamin Lundy and the co-ownership of a struggling Baltimore paper, the *Genius of Universal Emancipation*. Writing for this paper, Garrison first displayed his talent for invective and found himself jailed for libeling a leading citizen of the community. After his release from jail, Garrison returned to Boston to lecture about his experience and soon attracted a small but devoted band of reformers who agreed to support his plan to found an abolitionist newspaper. On January 1, 1831, the first issue of the *Liberator* appeared with Garrison's widely quoted declaration of principles. Shortly after its founding, Nat Turner's rebellion occurred in Virginia, and the alarmed local authorities blamed the incident on "seditious" materials circulated by abolitionists and named Garrison and the *Liberator* as prime instigators. Overnight, his enemies made him notorious and gained the small journal national recognition.

English abolitionists eager to support agitation in the United States soon began to channel funds to Garrison and even invited him to tour Great Britain. His successful lecture tour gained additional recognition for him and his paper, but increasing notoriety did not mean public acceptance. On one occasion he was dragged through the streets of Boston with a rope around his neck and jailed by the mayor for his own safety. His meetings were mobbed; he was heckled and egged. Still he persisted. His growing devotion to Christian perfectionism led him to declare himself a nonresistant—a Christian anarchist. In doing so he elevated moral example above political action and refused to vote or engage in any political activity. These views led to a split within the abolitionist ranks as many former colleagues worked for the Liberty party and, later, the Free Soil party. Eventually he decided that the Constitution was a pact with the devil and proclaimed the urgency of "No Union with slaveholders." He advocated that the free states separate themselves from the slave states and even welcomed the secession of the South when it came. The terrible ferocity of the Civil War softened his bellicose attitude, and he endorsed Lincoln for reelection in 1864. When the war ended with the ratification of the Thirteenth Amendment, he closed the *Liberator* certain that his work was ended. He lived to 1879, serene in the comfort of his family until illness ended his life.

GARRISON'S ANTISLAVERY AGITATION

Garrison's agitational activities centered on the *Liberator*, which served the dual role of a highly personal newspaper and a public bulletin board. A typical issue contained an editorial statement or a speech text by Garrison, a report of the activities of one of the many affiliated organizations, letters from friends recounting the latest news of their work for the cause, reprints of articles drawn from the southern press illustrating the degradation of the slaves or violently attacking the abolitionists, perhaps a column or two giving publicity to allied reform movements such as communitarianism or dietary reform, and, always, appeals for money. Weekly for thirty-four years Garrison managed to issue the paper with the help of his devoted followers. It became the Bible of the move- ment—the source not only for information on the latest developments in the crusade but also for inspiration and encouragement. Garrison's writings and speeches blended together in the *Liberator*'s pages to be recycled again and again in the repetition of the major themes and arguments of his persuasion. A speech given extemporaneously would be written out and printed in the journal; speech manuscripts would be revised before printing; information published in the form of editorials, reports, or passing comments would become the substance of further speeches. Garrison understood the power of repeating a few simple ideas and capturing them in slogans. From the first issue to the last, the *Liberator* focused on the need for immediate emancipation, the humanity of the slaves, the right and even duty of the free states to agitate for an end to slavery, and the shared responsibility for slavery by those who failed to sever social, eco- nomic, and political ties with the slaveholders.

Garrison valued direct contact with an audience. The *Liberator* noted and preserved almost a thousand speeches that he made during his long career. Not all the speeches were memorable; most consisted of the repetition of familiar arguments and examples. The major speeches were classics of the jeremiad tradition designed to demonstrate how far Americans had fallen into sin and error. His sacred text was always the Declaration of Independence and its pro- clamation of the inalienable rights of all to life, liberty, and the pursuit of happiness. The style was Hebraic, echoing the denunciations of the prophets of old as Garrison insistently proclaimed that slavery is evil and there must be no compromise with anyone or anything supporting it. Garrison saw the establish- ment of his day compromised by a willingness to avert its eyes from the evil of slavery and do business with the devil. The attitude of the churches particularly galled him, and he accused them of the rankest hyprocrisy for sanctifying the foulest evil imaginable. He also denounced the political establishment for giving respectability and even legal sanction to slavery. He roundly denounced the Constitution as a pact with the devil and on several occasions publicly burned copies of the document. When southerners threatened to secede from the Union, he welcomed the idea and even proposed that the free states do it first.

Garrison gave his first major speech on abolition at the Park Street Church in

Boston on July 4, 1829, shortly before leaving for Baltimore to join Benjamin Lundy in publishing the *Genius of Universal Emancipation*. Although he was only twenty-four at the time of the speech, the major themes of his later agitation are all present save one: in this speech Garrison spoke for gradual, not immediate, emancipation. In this first effort, too, can be seen Garrison's characteristic style. He referred to slavery as a "gangrene preying upon our vitals" and an "earthquake rumbling under our feet." His use of emotional language was relatively mild in this speech; later his habitual use of invective and abuse made his name odious to respectable people. This early effort in the jeremiad contained the requisite passage showing the failure of Americans to live up to their ideals, but it was restrained compared to the power he achieved in such abundance in later Fourth of July speeches.

Eighteen months later in the opening issue of the *Liberator*, Garrison apologized for merely advocating gradual emancipation in his Park Street address and asked pardon for uttering a "sentiment so full of timidity, injustice, and absurdity." In the intervening time, his reading of the debates in the British Parliament over emancipation and his stint in jail had convinced him that immediate emancipation was the only answer to the evil of slavery. In a ringing statement he proclaimed boldly his tactics for agitating the issue: "I *will be* harsh as truth, and uncompromising as justice. On this subject, I do not wish to think, or speak, or write with moderation." The *Liberator* with Garrison at its helm was prepared to do battle with the devil and his allies and to give no quarter. Garrison predicted in that first issue that "posterity will bear testimony that I was right."

Garrison's curious mixture of pugnacity and Christian piety faced its greatest test over the issue of violence, especially violent resistance by the slaves themselves. Garrison's editorial on Nat Turner's rebellion revealed his ambiguous attitude and the conflicting emotions he felt. On the one hand, he seemed to welcome the revolt as a harbinger. He called it "the first step of the earthquake, . . . the first flash of lightning" and expressed little sympathy for the "first drops of blood . . . and the first wailings of bereavement." He further denounced "ye patriotic hypocrites . . . ye fustian declaimers for liberty" for condemning the insurrectionists and forgetting their legitimate grievances. But in the midst of this panegyric to violence and bloodshed, he stopped short as if suddenly remembering his Christian pacifism and proclaimed, "We are horror struck at the late tidings," and he used the occasion to remind slaveholders that "we have warned of the danger of their unrighteous conduct." He concluded that only "IMMEDIATE EMANCIPATION can alone save her [this guilty land] from the vengeance of Heaven."

This issue troubled Garrison throughout his career. The slaveholders held the abolitionists and Garrison in particular responsible for any disturbance among the slaves. When political tensions increased between North and South, politicians seeking compromise claimed that fanatics on both sides of the issue had inflamed the controversy and made compromise impossible. Garrison always retorted that the "slaves need no incentives at our hands" to resist their captivity and argued that only by accepting the abolitionist position and freeing the slaves could a large-scale slave revolt be prevented.

Garrison's powerful invective and harsh language became especially pronounced in his annual Fourth of July jeremiads where he profaned the traditional celebration of liberty to show the hypocrisy of keeping over 2 million persons in slavery. His address on July 4, 1838, is perhaps the first jeremiad he delivered. He began by observing that "this is the time-honored, wine-honored, toast-drinking, powder-wasting, tyrant-killing Fourth of July—consecrated, for the last sixty years, to bombast, to falsehood, to impudence, to hypocrisy. It is the great carnival of republican despotism, and of Christian impiety, famous the world over. Since we held it last year, we have kept securely in their chains, the stock of two millions, three hundred thousand slaves we then had on hand in spite of every effort of fanaticism to emancipate them." He admitted "I use strong language and will make no apology for it because 'no man true to his nature can speak but in the language of . . . righteous denunciation.' " He demanded "the immediate emancipation of all who are pining in slavery on American soil" and asserted the "perfect equality" of the slaves "with ourselves as a part of the human race and their inalienable right to liberty and the pursuit of happiness." On this issue he proclaimed his resolution "to link my destiny with that of the slave, to plead his cause, to rebuke his oppressors and to AGITATE THE LAND." Like the Puritan preachers of old, he warned his audience that "it is useless, it is dreadful, it is impious for this nation longer to contend with the Almighty. All his attributes are against us, and on the side of the oppressed. Is it not a fearful thing to fall into the hands of the living God? . . . Woe to this bloody land! it is all full of lies and robbery." This speech represented Garrison's characteristic pose of a prophet who foresees a terrible fate for those who fail to heed his warnings. A deeply religious man who quoted incessantly from the Bible, Garrison habitually framed all questions in religious terms. The format of the jeremiad, in which the preacher shows the congregation how far they have fallen into sin and warns of the consequences of continuing in their present condition, perfectly suited Garrison's temperament.

Perhaps the most mature statement of his principles as an abolitionist appeared in Garrison's Broadway Tabernacle address in 1854. In this lengthy attempt to defend his position against criticism from other abolitionists and from outsiders, Garrison based his case on three propositions: the American dream of life, liberty, and the pursuit of happiness is promised to all men; Americans hypocritically preach liberty for all but deny it to the slaves; and abolitionism is the "law of God" who will give the land no rest until his law is obeyed. Although the speech was developed by Garrison's usual technique of disjunctive enthymemes leading either to total good or total evil and contained its share of loaded language, it was a more restrained and reasoned defense of his position than the typical jeremiad.

The language of Garrison's speeches gained him notoriety. His critics within the abolitionist movement claimed that his intemperate language so offended the sensibilities of the public that he lost more converts than he made. Garrison was sensitive to this issue and on more than one occasion defended his conduct by claiming to imitate the example of Christ who "when he had to do with people of like manners called them simply by their proper names—such as, an adulterous and perverse generation, a brood of vipers, hypocrites, children of the devil." He turned the argument back upon his critics saying that when he called a slaveowner a thief because he stole human beings, the critics called him abusive. When he called a man who picked his pocket a thief, all the people said, "Right! right! so he is" and the court sent the thief to prison. What "wonderful consistency!" he cried.

For a man with such a ferocious reputation, Garrison surprised audiences with his mild manner. Most accounts describe his speaking as mild and even dull. One observer described his manner as "calm and gentleman like." He himself apologized for his ability, saying, "What the speaker lacks, the cause will supply." He certainly never equaled the platform manner of Frederick Douglass or Wendell Phillips in graceful expression or passionate delivery.

Garrison's reputation is far from settled; it rises or falls with each new interpretation of the legacy of the abolitionists. To some extent, his name evokes a set response from the critic, which reveals more about his or her own assumptions than about Garrison himself. To critics who minimize conflict and stress consensus, Garrison is a nuisance—always saying the wrong thing at the wrong time and alienating potential supporters. To those who view conflict as necessary to change an essentially static and conservative social order, Garrison is the necessary gadfly whose stinging criticism and personal attacks goad the society toward change. A just estimate requires stating the obvious: Garrison was not the abolitionist movement or even the leader of the largest faction in the movement. The movement itself was faction ridden, locally and at times regionally oriented, and composed of many people with competing and conflicting ideas about means and ends. Garrison's insistence on doctrinal purity and his refusal to sanction political activity left him isolated and contributed to his reputation as a crank and a fanatic. Certainly others, notably the Tappans and Theodore Weld, achieved far more than he did in converting the undecided to the cause. Garrison's limitations as a persuader are clear. A fair estimate also requires acknowledging his equally impressive achievements. Garrison was one of the most effective agitators for reform in the nineteenth century. He saw the necessity for an uncompromising position based on moral principles. He utilized all the means of persuasion at his disposal to force a reluctant society to confront the evil of slavery. His uncompromising and unyielding fervor finally awoke the conscience of a nation. He was hated by many whites, especially in the South, and equally loved by the free blacks and escaped slaves. His faith in progress and in Christian perfectionism was the source of both his greatness and his limitations.

INFORMATION SOURCES

Research Collections and Collected Speeches

The Boston Public Library has William Lloyd Garrison's papers and those of many of his colleagues in the abolitionist crusade. Most research libraries have a complete file of the *Liberator* on microfilm, which is a public record of Garrison's speeches, editorials, and activities. Harvard University Press has published *The Letters of William Lloyd Garrison* in six volumes.

American Forum: Speeches on Historic Issues, 1788–1900. Edited by Ernest   AF
    J. Wrage and Barnet Baskersville. Seattle: University of Washington
    Press, 1960.

Documents of Upheaval: Selections from William Lloyd Garrison's The   DOC
    Liberator, 1831–1865. Edited by Truman Nelson. New York: Hill
    and Wang, 1966.

Forerunners of Black Power: The Rhetoric of Abolition. Edited by Ernest   FBP
    G. Bormann. Englewood Cliffs, N.J.: Prentice-Hall, 1971.

Garrison, Wendell Phillips, and Frances Jackson Garrison. *William Lloyd*   WLG
    Garrison, 1805–1879: The Story of His Life Told by His Children.
    4 vols. New York, 1885–1889.

Liberator, 1831–1865.   LIB

William Lloyd Garrison. Edited by George M. Fredrickson. Englewood   FR
    Cliffs, N.J.: Prentice-Hall, 1968.

Selected Critical Studies

Barnes, Gilbert H. *The Anti-Slavery Impulse, 1830–1844*. Gloucester, Mass.: Peter Smith,
    1957.

Bormann, Ernest G. *The Force of Fantasy: Restoring the American Dream*. Carbondale:
    Southern Illinois University Press, 1985.

Dillon, Merton L. "The Abolitionists: A Decade of Historiography, 1959–1969." *Journal
    of Southern History* 25 (1969): 500–22.

Duberman, Martin. *The Antislavery Vanguard: New Essays on the Abolitionists*. Prince-
    ton: Princeton University Press, 1965.

Dumond, Dwight L. *Antislavery: The Crusade for Freedom in America*. Ann Arbor:
    University of Michigan Press, 1961.

Filler, Louis. *The Crusade against Slavery*. New York: Harper & Row, 1960.

Kraditor, Aileen S. *Means and Ends in American Abolitionism: Garrison and His Critics
    on Strategy and Tactics, 1834–1850*. New York: Random House, 1969.

Stewart, James B. "The Aims and Impact of Garrisonian Abolitionism, 1840–1860."
    Civil War History 15 (1969): 197–209.

Walters, Ronald G. *The Antislavery Appeal: American Abolitionism after 1830*. Baltimore:
    The Johns Hopkins University Press, 1976.

Woodward, C. Vann. "The Antislavery Myth." *American Scholar* 31 (1962): 312–18.
Wyatt-Brown, Betram. "William Lloyd Garrison and Antislavery Unity: A Reappraisal."
    Civil War History 13 (1967): 5–24.

Selected Biographies

Garrison, Wendell Phillips, and Frances Jackson Garrison. *William Lloyd Garrison, 1805–
    1879: The Story of His Life Told by His Children.* 4 vols. New York, 1885–1889.
Merril, Walter M. *Against Wind and Tide: A Biography of Wm. Lloyd Garrison.* Cam-
    bridge: Harvard University Press, 1963.
Nye, Russel B. *William Lloyd Garrison and the Humanitarian Reformers.* Boston: Little,
    Brown, 1955.
Thomas, John L. *The Liberator: William Lloyd Garrison.* Boston: Little, Brown, 1963.

CHRONOLOGY OF MAJOR SPEECHES

Fourth of July address at Park Street Church, Boston, July 4, 1829; *FR*, pp. 11–21.

"Declaration of Principles," *LIB*, January 1, 1831; *FR*, 22–23; *WLG*, 1: 224–25.

Editorial on Nat Turner's rebellion; *LIB*, January 7, 1832; *DOC*, pp. 41–44; *FR*, pp. 24–26.

Fourth of July address, Marlboro Chapel, Massachusetts, July 4, 1838; *FBP*, pp. 96–104.

Broadway Tabernacle address, New York, February 14, 1854; *AF*, pp. 169–79.

JOSHUA REED GIDDINGS
(1795–1863), congressional antislavery agitator

HAL W. BOCHIN

First elected to Congress as a Whig from Ohio's Western Reserve in 1838, Joshua R. Giddings spent the next twenty years attempting to mobilize his congressional allies and public opinion against slavery. He verbally assaulted the "slave conspiracy" on three fronts. On the House floor, he was the constant agitator, seldom winning a vote but always reminding his colleagues of the economic and political power of the South. He spoke out against the gag rule, the role of the United States in the war with Mexico, the compromise measures of 1850, and the *Dred Scott* decision. On the stump he campaigned tirelessly for whatever party and candidates he thought best able to handle the slavery question. When he found himself unable to convince a majority of the Whigs to accept his antislavery views, he joined the Free Soil party. When they seemed unwilling to confront slavery everywhere, Giddings played a major role in the formation of the Republican party. Finally, at the close of his congressional career, forced from office by ill health and for holding opinions too radical for even his new party, Giddings took his antislavery message to the lyceum circuit, where he earned top dollar speaking to large, appreciative audiences. Throughout his political career, Joshua Giddings used public address to force the United States to face and destroy the moral evil of slavery.

GIDDINGS AS ANTISLAVERY AGITATOR

Soon after his arrival in Washington, D.C., Giddings met and quickly fell under the influence of John Quincy Adams, former president and now a Whig congressman from Massachusetts. He enthusiastically joined Adams's crusade against the gag rule, which, adopted in 1836, required that all petitions to the House dealing with any aspect of slavery be automatically tabled without discussion, printing, or response of any kind.

Unable to speak against slavery directly, Giddings determined to bring up slavery issues collaterally where other matters constituted the main subject of discussion. The first successful example of this strategy occurred in the lengthy speech Giddings delivered on February 9, 1841, against further appropriations for the Seminole War in Florida. Giddings argued that the only reason the war was being fought against the Seminole Indians was that they had offered refuge to escaped slaves whom their owners wanted returned. To southerners in the House, Giddings suggested that such use of federal troops violated the constitutional doctrine that the federal government had no power over slavery in the several states. To northerners, he compared the $40 million cost of the war to what a similar amount for internal improvements would accomplish. In answering Giddings, southern representatives angrily defended slavery and failed to notice that issues concerning slavery were indeed being debated on the House floor. Giddings's strategy had proved successful.

When the *Creole*, a U.S. slave-trading ship, was taken over by the slaves on board and forced to land in Nassau, British law declared the slaves to be free. Their American owners, however, denied British jurisdiction and demanded that the Negroes be returned to them or that they receive reparation. When the secretary of state instructed the U.S. minister in London to seek such compensation, Giddings offered, on March 21, 1842, a series of resolutions that affirmed the right of slaves to rebel against their masters once out of the jurisdiction of a slave state. The resolutions were defeated, and Giddings was censured on the grounds that he had tried to create "excitement, dissatisfaction, and division" among the people. Through parliamentary maneuvering, Giddings was not allowed to defend himself, and the motion of censure passed 125 to 69. Giddings immediately resigned his seat and left for home to seek reelection. By a majority of 7,469 to 393, he defeated a Democratic opponent and returned to Washington an antislavery hero. On June 3, 1842, he spoke to a packed House about the *Creole* affair, repeating the arguments for which he had been censured previously. Henceforth the House could not prevent antislavery sentiments from being spoken by threatening expulsion from the body.

Still unsatisfied with the formal restrictions the gag rule placed on House debate, Giddings continued to speak for its removal. On February 13, 1844, he concluded an hour-long presentation with the words: "he who refuses to discuss this subject [slavery], and he who refuses to repeal acts of Congress, will be held responsible to the country, to posterity, and to God, for the crimes committed under the protection of these laws." The House reenacted the gag rule by a single vote, but it was clearly on its way to oblivion, and Giddings and Adams congratulated each other on their success. Giddings's biggest battle in the House lay just ahead.

On May 11 and May 12, 1846, by votes of 174 to 14 in the House and 40 to 2 in the Senate, Congress granted President James K. Polk's request for permission to enroll 50,000 volunteers in a war begun "by the act of the Republic of Mexico." The few Whigs who had defied their party caucus and voted against the war were subject to a shower of abuse, and Giddings feared that unless he could rally his friends, he would stand nearly alone. He opened his campaign against the Mexican War on May 12, 1846, with the speech he later considered to be the most important he ever made. He denounced the war as an act of "invasion and conquest" and claimed it was being waged on behalf of slavery.

Recognizing that much of the persuasiveness of Polk's war message rested on his claim that Mexico had "shed American blood upon the American soil," Giddings used examples and expert testimony to show that the territory east of the Rio Grande, where the hostilities began, had always been controlled by Mexico. To inspire his allies, he ridiculed Polk's arguments and boldly announced that he would not vote for men and supplies to fight an unholy war. He would lend the war effort "no support whatever."

Although most members of the Whig party never adopted his position on supplies, Giddings's speech did as much as he could reasonably expect. His arguments on the boundary question became commonplace in Whig criticism of the war, and a number of Whig congressmen were inspired to denounce the war in spite of their party's official position.

On July 14, 1846, Giddings renewed his attack on the war and suggested that northern Whigs and Democrats should unite against their southern brethren for economic reasons. Giddings pointed to the fact that, with both newly installed senators from Texas voting for it, the Senate had recently passed a low tariff bill by a single vote. Clearly southern interests were overriding those of the North, and Giddings offered a controversial view of what such a "revolution" meant. The Union, he claimed, had "ceased. It no longer protects our interests, our rights, or our honor." Contrary to the wording of the Constitution, men who had six months earlier been citizens of a foreign country, Texas, were now voting members of Congress, supporting the South against the North. Giddings claimed that since this had occurred without the direct consent of the people, each state was now free to associate with others belonging to the Union or to refuse political connection with them.

Such ideas proved too radical for most of Giddings's supporters, and the Whig papers in his district failed to print the speech. Giddings left Washington to tour New England and rally antiwar forces there. On the stump in Bangor, Augusta, and Portland, Maine, he claimed that the war was being waged for the purpose of extending the "empire of slavery" and for delivering the "best rights of the North" to the South. Cheering audiences greeted Giddings, and he gained a host of new friends for the antiwar movement.

December 15, 1846, found Giddings again on the House floor denouncing the war, this time in response to President Polk's State of the Union message. Polk had claimed that critics of the war were giving "aid and comfort to the enemy." Giddings responded by reexamining the origins and objectives of the war. Citing the actions of Edmund Burke and Charles Fox in Parliament during the American Revolution, Giddings hoped to show his Whig colleagues that political success and popular approval could be attained while voting to withhold funds for a war in which one's own country was involved.

Again on February 13, 1847, Giddings described the war as being fought "to extend the cause of slavery." With all the moral righteousness at his command, Giddings proclaimed that the slavery question allowed no compromise: "Slavery and freedom are antagonisms. They must necessarily be at war with each other." Slavery was a moral issue that transcended traditional political parties, and Giddings rejoined that, for the first time in his life, northern men of both political parties were standing shoulder to shoulder in the cause of human rights. Although the federal government could do nothing about slavery where it already existed, Giddings offered a rationale for its prohibition in the territories. He found it "in the power to prevent assault and battery, outrage, and crime. The law which prevents one man from beating and scourging another is a total prohibition of slavery."

For Giddings, compromise on the slavery issue was impossible. Moral men could never allow slavery to be established in the territories. Even the destruction of the Union would not be too high a price to keep them free. For the moment, Giddings would not interfere with slavery where it already existed, but the federal government had a right to control the territories. By making slavery an affront to God and man, however, Giddings justified those who were willing to extinguish it wherever it existed. The war, which brought the territorial issue to the front, would end in 1848, but the ideas Giddings presented in his speeches against the war would persist until slavery was abolished.

Giddings had always been a maverick in the Whig party, but as the war drew to a close, he found himself even more out of step with the majority of his party. First, they wanted to place Robert Winthrop, a prowar Whig, in the Speaker's chair. Second, they favored Zachary Taylor, the war's leading general, for the presidency in 1848. Giddings could not support either of these men. He voted against Winthrop and on February 28, 1848, took the House floor to denounce Taylor for not refusing to serve in the war and to claim that Taylor's hands were "dripping with human gore." Giddings found that traditional political goals of the Whigs were being subverted to support Taylor: "The most ultra supporters of free trade and the most determined adherents of a protective tariff are to unite in support. Each knows that he or his allies must find themselves deceived after the election. But each is hoping it will not be himself." Giddings joined the Free Soil party in support of Martin Van Buren for the presidency; but in spite of the strong opposition Giddings raised in northern Ohio, Taylor carried the election.

As a Free Soil member of the House, Giddings continued his agitation against slavery whenever possible. He rejected Clay's compromise proposals in 1850, believing that they favored the South. On August 12, 1850, he attacked that portion of the compromise in which the federal government assumed the $10 million Texan debt. To the threat that Texas might secede from the Union unless the bill were passed, Giddings responded: "It may alarm gentlemen here; but I do not think you can find in northern Ohio an equal number of nervous old women or love-sick girls, who could be moved by it." Giddings would not consent to the passage of any law that taxed the people of Ohio to pay the debts of Texas, but the Texas bill passed by a small majority, and the House eventually ratified all the compromise measures.

In one of his sharpest attacks against slavery in a long career of speaking on the subject, Giddings addressed the House on May 16, 1854, to speak against the Kansas-Nebraska Act. "To vote for the repeal of the Missouri compromise is to vote for the abolition of freedom," he argued. Citing specific examples of cruelty to slaves, he warned that such activities would be commonplace in Nebraska if slavery were allowed. "Will Northern men vote for such a proposition?" he wondered. "Will they bathe their hands in the blood of innocents; participate in crimes that smell to Heaven, and call for vengeance on this guilty hand?" Giddings correctly predicted bloodshed would result from the bill's passage, but the House again refused his advice.

The *Dred Scott* decision, which invalidated every law prohibiting the spread of slavery into the territories, called for strong action, and Giddings was among the first to demand open defiance. On February 26, 1858, in spite of a sore throat that caused many to be unable to hear him, Giddings attacked "this atrocious decision." Giddings called on his colleagues to act with religious character to enact laws for the progress and "moral elevation" of the entire human race. Refusal to act would make the House guilty of any crimes committed against Negroes in newly formed slave areas.

In 1858, Giddings, suffering from ill health and still considered a radical by many in the new Republican party, failed to get renominated to Congress. Needing a source of income as well as a new platform for his antislavery views, he joined the lyceum circuit. Lecturing on the "Trial of John Quincy Adams" and "The Higher Law," he found he could net two hundred dollars a week, bettering the amounts paid to Horace Greeley and Henry Thoreau. The public platform also allowed Giddings to discuss the public questions of the day, whatever the announced topic.

Giddings's finest hour may have come at the 1860 Republican National Convention. When his plea to add the sentiments of the Declaration of Independence to the party platform (as had been done in 1856) was denied, Giddings stormed from the convention. A motion to reconsider was passed, and Giddings returned to the floor to receive a thunderous ovation. With Abraham Lincoln's election to the presidency, Giddings, an old messmate of the president in 1848–1849, was appointed consul general to Canada, where he served until his death in 1863.

Giddings's tremendous success in the House as an agitator but failure as a persuader may have been the result of the intense language he used. Those who supported Giddings were stimulated by his sarcasm and ridicule, his use of exaggeration, and his uncompromising tone. He reenforced their values and beliefs. Those who opposed him, however, would never be reconciled. To Giddings they were "doughfaces" whose "hands are dripping with human gore." Such opponents were more likely to reject the picture of themselves as immoral and to remain unmoved by appeals based on fear than they were motivated to change. Especially on slavery issues, Giddings allowed no room for compromise. One had to agree with him totally or not at all.

Giddings had great success as a stump speaker. He knew how to handle an audience. This description on October 4, 1884, from the editor of the *Cleveland Plain Dealer*, a paper always unfriendly to Giddings, shows his unique platform manner:

He commenced the humble, anxious inquirer after truth; said he loved everybody; was open to reproof, correction and conviction. If he, in his innocence stated anything wrong, he hoped to be corrected and desired his auditors to ask him any question they pleased. Thus adorned with the robe of sanctity he commenced his speech. He would make statements and then call upon his audience to know if he was not right. If none answered, of course silence was presumed to give consent, and in this way he went on swimming by for a while.

In his many campaigns for reelection, in speaking to antiwar rallies, and on the lyceum circuit, Giddings was usually well received, even by hostile audiences.

Never completely trusted by abolitionists who abhorred his decision to work within the constitutional system, Giddings nevertheless served their cause as a politician and as a propagandist. Giddings attempted to convert the political parties with which he was associated, the House of Representatives, and the country at large to the cause of antislavery. Through his speeches in the House and on the stump, he courageously forced his generation to face the foremost moral and political questions of the day.

INFORMATION SOURCES

Research Collections and Collected Speeches

The Joshua R. Giddings Papers at the Ohio Historical Society, Columbus, offer family letters and correspondence from a large number of political sources. The society also contains a scrapbook of newspaper clippings and two partial diaries. The Joshua R. Giddings–George W. Julian Papers at the Library of Congress contain a number of letters written by Giddings to his family that were collected by Julian (his son-in-law) for a biography. Other significant letters can be found in the George W. Julian Collection, Indiana State Library, Indianapolis, Indiana, and in the Joshua R. Giddings–Milton Sutliffe Papers, Western Reserve Historical Society, Cleveland. All of Giddings's speeches in the House can be found in the U.S. Congressional Globe or in its Appendix on the date they were given. Many were reprinted in the *Ashtabula Sentinel* and other northern Ohio newspapers.

Congressional Globe.	*CG*
Congressional Globe Appendix.	*CGA*
Giddings, Joshua R. *Speeches in Congress.* 1853; rpt., New York: Negro Universities Press, 1968.	*SIC*

Selected Critical Studies

Bormann, Ernest G., ed. *Forerunners of Black Power.* Englewood Cliffs, N.J.: Prentice-Hall, 1971.
Gamble, Douglas A. "Joshua Giddings and the Ohio Abolitionists: A Study in Radical Politics." *Ohio History* 88 (1979): 37–56.
Long, Byron R. "Joshua Giddings, A Champion of Political Freedom." *Ohio Archaeological and Historical Quarterly* 28 (1919): 1–47.
Ludlum, Robert P. "Joshua R. Giddings, Radical." *Mississippi Valley Historical Review* 23 (1936): 49–60.
Pease, Jane H., and William H. Pease. *Bound with Them in Chains.* Westport, Conn.: Greenwood Press, 1972.

Savage, Sherman W. "The Origins of the Giddings Resolutions." *Ohio Archaeological and Historical Quarterly* 48 (1938): 20–39.

Selected Biographies

Julian, George W. *The Life of Joshua R. Giddings*. Chicago: A. C. McClurg, 1892.
Stewart, James B. *Joshua R. Giddings and the Tactics of Radical Politics*. Cleveland: Press of Case Western Reserve University, 1970.

CHRONOLOGY OF MAJOR SPEECHES

See "Research Collections and Collected Speeches" for source codes.

Speech on the Florida War, Washington, D.C., February 9, 1841; *CGA*, 9 (1841): 346–52; *SIC*, pp. 1–20.

Speech on the reduction of the army, Washington, D.C., June 3, 1842; *CG*, 11 (1842): 575–76; *SIC*, pp. 21–31.

Speech on the rights of the states concerning slavery, Washington, D.C., February 13, 1844; *CGA*, 13 (1844): 652–56; *SIC*, pp. 52–72.

Speech on the Mexican War, Washington D.C., May 12, 1846; *CGA*, 15 (1846): 641–45; *SIC*, pp. 177–201.

Speech on the Mexican War, Washington, D.C., July 14, 1846; *CGA* 15 (1846): 826–29; *SIC*, pp. 250–64.

Speech on the president's annual message, Washington, D.C., December 15, 1846; *CG*, 16 (1846): 34–36; *CGA*, 16 (1846): 47–52; *SIC*, pp. 265–88.

Speech on the Wilmot Proviso, Washington, D.C., February 13, 1847; *CGA*, 16 (1847): 237–46; *SIC*, pp. 202–20.

Speech on the Mexican War, Washington, D.C., February 28, 1848; *CG*, 17 (1848): 393–95; *CGA*, 17 (1848): 380–83; *SIC*, pp. 319–32 (misdated in text).

Speech on New Mexico, Washington, D.C., August 12, 1850; *CG*, 19 (1850): 1561–63; *CGA*, 19 (1850): 1124–28; *SIC*, pp. 403–19.

Speech on the moral responsibility of statesmen, Washington, D.C., May 16, 1854; *CGA*, 23 (1854): 986–89.

Speech on the *Dred Scott* decision, Washington, D.C., February 26, 1858; *CG*, 27 (1858): 894–98; *CGA*, 27 (1858): 65–68.

HENRY GRADY
(1850–1889), southern statesman

FERALD J. BRYAN

Georgia's Henry Woodfin Grady's short life was marked by oratory of such wide regional influence that his "New South" speech of 1886 became synonymous with the economic success of the post-Reconstruction South of the 1880s and 1890s. He spent most of his life devoted to the study and practice of oratory. As a freshman at the University of Georgia, he joined the Phi Kappa Forensic Society and in his senior year was unanimously selected as this prestigious organization's commencement speaker.

Leaving his family's home and his undergraduate career in Athens, Georgia, Grady traveled to the University of Virginia to further his dream of becoming a political leader who would end the economic turmoil of Reconstruction. In Charlottesville, Grady studied graduate courses in history, literature, and rhetoric. When denied the position of commencement orator for the Washington Literary Society in 1869, he left the university and returned to Georgia convinced that his potential as a future southern leader was at an end.

The young Grady turned to journalism, and after working at numerous newspapers in north Georgia as staff writer and editor, he became managing editor of the *Atlanta Constitution* in 1876. Since the *Constitution* was the largest and most influential newspaper in the South, Grady's editorials calling for a sectional reconciliation with the North for economic reasons attracted the attention of important business leaders on Wall Street. Beginning in 1886, Grady delivered a series of ceremonial orations to northern and southern audiences depicting a rich vision of an economically vibrant South. After the "New South" speech was presented to the New England Society of New York City, Grady acquired a national reputation as the key spokesman for economic and social harmony between the North and South. Grady's speeches in the late 1880s represented a powerful persuasive effort to lead an entire region of the country toward a brighter future.

GRADY AS SOUTHERN ORATOR

Henry Grady was one of the most famous ceremonial speakers of his era. Although his speeches were often politically motivated, Grady never held an elected office. The speeches he delivered in the 1880s were either banquet addresses or keynote presentations on special occasions such as fairs and graduation ceremonies. Although American ceremonial oratory during the nineteenth century most often developed traditional patriotic themes, Grady used these special occasions to assert a futuristic vision of how the South could transform itself into an important economic partner with the industrial North. Usually speaking extemporaneously from limited notes, Grady constructed his vision using imagery and vivid metaphors that contrasted the desolate post–Civil War agrarian South with the new energy of mechanized production.

The South of the 1880s was still dependent on King Cotton as the key cash crop. Lacking capital and labor, the post-Reconstruction southerner looked to traditional democratic leaders for economic assistance. These politicians, however, typically called for a return to principles of the Old South. Former Confederate General John B. Gordon, for example, urged a Georgia audience in 1886 to "hold to the characteristics of our old civilization." Speeches like these tended to discourage northern interest in possible investment throughout the South. Reports of the legal disenfranchisement of former slaves and of violence at the polls when southern blacks did attempt to vote were carried extensively in major northern newspapers. In an effort to counter these images in the minds of northern leaders, Grady delivered three of his best and most influential speeches.

The New South oration, delivered December 21, 1886, was his greatest effort before a northern audience. A model of the persuasive power of an after-dinner speech, this single presentation before the New England Society of New York City made Grady a regional hero and a national celebrity. Although other newspaper editors in the South had used the "New South" phrase before, Grady's unique presentation made him famous after national newspapers such as the *New York Tribune* reprinted the text of his speech in full. The Georgian not only won over Wall Street with his charm and a warm sense of humor, but he also overcame the chilling presence of General William T. Sherman with whom he shared the dais. Grady eloquently argued that through the horror of Civil War, the cavalier and soldier of the Old South had been replaced by a "loyal American citizen." He maintained that this New South, now "enamored with her new work," should be viewed as a new "soul stirring with the breath of a new life." Grady used this personification of the defeated South symbolically to reunite the region with the North. In order to explain the "sum of works" in which southerners had been engaged since the end of the Civil War, Grady argued that "we have planted the schoolhouse on the hilltop and made it free to black and white. We have sowed towns and cities in place of theories, and put business above politics." The harvests of results from the newly transformed South was even now prepared to "challenge spinners in Massachusetts and iron-makers from Pennsylvania" in Grady's vision. While the Old South rested its future on slavery and agriculture, Grady emphasized that the New South presented a "perfect democracy," with "a hundred farms for every plantation, fifty homes for every palace—and a diversified industry" that could meet the "complex need of a new complex age." In his conclusion, Grady pleaded with the "northern conquerors" to forget the "prejudice of War" and stand as an "eloquent witness in [their] white peace and prosperity to the indissoluble union of American States and the imperishable brotherhood of the American people."

On Thanksgiving Day 1887, Grady addressed the Augusta Exposition in Augusta, Georgia, on the announced theme "The Solid South." After humorously slicing the "Republican turkey" with a few jokes, Grady stressed that the South confronted two dangers: the threat of a "permanent sectional alignment" on the national level and the specter of a "divided political system" within the region. Since the South was declining in population, Grady feared that the political influence of the region would also deteriorate to the point where it would remain in a "perpetual minority" to the North. It would be much worse, however, in Grady's perspective, if the South were to have its "white vote divided into factions, and each faction bidding for the negro," who held "the balance of power." In order to confront these political problems and to fulfill its regional destiny, the South had "to maintain the political as well as the social integrity of her white race, and to appeal to the world for justice." He contended that finding the path to true justice for the South required an accurate appraisal of race relations in the region. Specifically, Grady used *tu quoque* argumentation (from the Latin meaning "you also") to assert that northern elections were essentially no different from their southern counterparts. The editor admitted that some violence had occurred during the recent elections, but he asserted that the incidents in the South did not keep Negro voters away from the polls and that southern elections were "less brutal and more honest" than those in West Virginia or Chicago. Since "the Lord God Almighty decreed" the separateness of the races, Grady explained to his Augusta audience that "the people of the North will not be committed to a violent policy." In contrast to the fear of federal troops, Grady argued that through "industrial growth the South is daily making new friends. Every dollar of northern money invested in the South gives us a new friend in that sector." With the steady rising tide of northern investment in the South, he concluded that these economic ties would soon "solve the southern problem."

Less than two years after his "New South" speech, Grady presented his most detailed vision for the future of the region to a large audience at the Dallas, Texas, State Fair. In this lengthy address of October 26, 1888, the editor considered "The South and Her Problems." Pledging to avoid political issues in his oration, he asserted that the future of the South was clouded by the presence of "two separate races" nearly equal in numbers in the region. The problem was that these former slaves represented "a vast mass of ignorant or purchasable votes." In order to ensure the continued supremacy of the white race, Grady urged his fellow southerners to resist the efforts of northern Republicans to take charge of the "colored vote." With these divisional efforts under control, the "southern pioneer would replace the soldier" and take his place in the struggle for new commercial markets around the world. Grady concluded his Dallas speech by arguing that the South must abandon one-crop farming by diversifying its agricultural and industrial output. Although Grady intended "The South and Her Problems" address to reach a national audience, the texts of this speech, sent to national newspapers before he left his home in Atlanta, were ignored except by southern papers. The impact of Grady's Dallas oration was to strengthen his personal standing in his home region, but his national following had been diminished by the racial and political barbs in his message.

Once Grady established the framework for reviving the South's economic future, he was forced to use his rhetorical skills to bolster the morale of Southern farmers. With cotton prices at an all-time low in the summer of 1889, Grady feared the growing appeal of the populist movement and the possible splintering of the Democratic vote throughout the South. In a commencement speech to the literary societies of the University of Virginia on June 25, 1889, he agreed that the federal government too tightly controlled the "arteries of trade" and that the "money power" flourished while the southern farmer starved. The answer to this oppression, Grady argued, was a new emphasis on the benefits of science and the restoration of a sense of personal pride and regional unity. On the subject of a separate political movement by southern farmers, Grady spoke in July 1889 to a rural audience in Elberton, Georgia on the proper status of "The Farmer and the Cities." In this address, he acknowledged that large numbers of south-erners were rapidly migrating from rural areas to the big cities. He saw this migration as a "great calamity" because a "rural birthright" had been bartered away for the "feverish and uncertain life of the City." Grady recognized that the oppressive weight of mortgage and interest payments on farmers created an intolerable situation, but he pleaded with his Elberton audience to place blame squarely at the feet of the Republican party. If southern farmers would only stay loyal to the Democratic party, Grady proclaimed, "The great masses will rise in their might, and breaking down the defenses of the oligarchs, will hurl them from power and restore the republic to the old moorings from which it had been swept by the storm."

After completing his series of speeches to southern farmers, Grady felt con-fident that the Democratic party in the South would withstand any assaults from the young Farmer's Alliance. Grady's metaphors, however, demonstrated that he took this stormy competition seriously. Although several state and national candidates were elected in 1888 under the Farmer's Alliance banner in Georgia, Grady's rhetorical efforts during this election were influential in maintaining the unity of Georgia's Democratic party. The editor's speeches continued to show former slaves in a very inferior light, but his position was that any political infighting among white southerners along economic battle lines would result in a Republican victory and the continuation of economic policies that would hurt southern whites and blacks combined.

On December 3, 1889, Henry Cabot Lodge, the key Republican leader in the U.S. Senate, introduced a force bill calling for federal protection of voting rights in the southern states. Grady had long feared this action, and he accepted an invitation to deliver a series of speeches in Boston, Massachusetts, in an effort to sway northern public opinion against this use of troops. On December 12, he addressed the annual meeting of the Boston Merchant's Association on the theme of southern race relations. After emphasizing that he stood firmly behind every word uttered in the "New South" speech a few years ago, Grady observed that his sentiments on economic development were now "universally approved in the South." But in the midst of this new industrialization drive, Grady argued that perceptions of poor race relations presented the biggest hurdle slowing southern progress. To correct this problem, the Georgian suggested that continued extensive northern investment in the South would offer the best solution since the investors would pay special attention to their new enterprises.

Grady spoke to another Boston group, the Bay State Club, on December 13, 1889. On this occasion, President Grover Cleveland was a member of the audience. Even with a bad cold, the editor vigorously outlined the economic struggle that was taking place throughout the nation. On one side, the "consolidation of power and the convention of capital" were overwhelming the forces "of local sovereignty and the dwarfing of the individual citizen." In the midst of this economic warfare, Grady concluded that southerners would retain their "charm and strength" and would never sacrifice their traditions, independence, and regional pride. Henry Grady returned to Atlanta on December 16 but was so ill that he had to be assisted from the train. During his return trip from Boston, Grady's cold developed into pneumonia, and his condition worsened as Christmas approached. On December 23, 1889, Grady died. He was thirty-nine.

Grady's short speaking career was especially influential on three fronts. First, the vivid metaphors of Grady's speeches provided a powerful sense of direction for the typical white southerners' economic future from the mid–1880s onward. Second, Grady reassured northern audiences that the South had learned its lesson from the Civil War and was now free from any racial conflict that might hinder economic development. Finally, Grady's plea for political unity helped blunt the development of the populist movement in Georgia at a crucial time in its history. In the "New South" speech, Grady began the restructuring of wealthy northern audiences' perceptions of southerners. He used metaphors indicating that the South had been reborn to reassure New York investors that the lazy cavalier image of the southerner had been forever transformed by the war. Grady bluntly explained the Negro's status in the South, but he used vague metaphors to describe the future social standing of these former slaves. Grady concluded the speech with an emotional appeal to accept the newly reborn South as a good financial investment for northerners and to worry less about the status of the Negro.

The imagery he used in his Dallas speech provides the most complete articulation of Grady's vision for racial relations in the South. In this lengthy oration, Grady's metaphors most clearly reveal his thinking about the financial future for southern white males. Instead of offering a new view on race relations, he reassured his white audience that they would be able to take their place as world merchants while the inherently inferior blacks would remain laborers on the farms. Throughout southern society, the editor maintained, it was essential for whites and blacks to progress along separate paths. He envisioned these paths as being "made equal—but separate" in areas such as schools, churches, and accommodations. As the public wealth grew, southern states would provide separate but equal education and transportation facilities to both races even though blacks paid a very small share of state taxes. In Grady's vision, the white soldier-farmer would assume a special role in the industrialized world as a close partner with northern financiers. Without a trace of regional bitterness to hold them back, Grady demonstrated how the symbolic blood and courage of the white southern farmer-soldier was especially well suited to cooperate with his northern brothers to become merchants to the whole world.

In his University of Virginia and Elberton speeches, Grady used emotional appeals to the values of partnership and friendship in his argument that farmers and science-inspired industry had common interests and goals. If southern farmers somehow felt separated from the economic growth being forged by science, then Grady attached blame metaphorically to a Republican-inspired plot to centralize government for the benefit of a select few. He ultimately urged southern farmers, who had traditionally allied themselves to the Democratic party, to stick with their party, for eventually science and mechanization would unite in the new industrial order. Any effort on the part of farmers to join a movement to fight governmental centralization without the Democratic party, Grady finally warned, would only allow the Negro to join ranks with the Republicans and make the economic situation worse.

Among the political and ceremonial orators of his time, Henry W. Grady was uniquely influential. Through a few short years of oratory, he led a devastated region of the country away from economic confusion and toward sectional unity. Although the eloquent editor believed he could speak on behalf of his entire native region, it was clear that Grady's speeches provided a vision of newness only for selected audiences. He achieved many of his goals almost singlehandedly, but after Grady's premature death, devoted disciples carried on his mission of leading the South into an industrial union with the North.

Grady reached a considerable audience by speaking to as many large indoor and outdoor gatherings on ceremonial occasions as the train travel of the times would permit. He became a national celebrity and a regional hero that southern town squares still immortalize. Grady's great promise as a southern orator was cut short, but his timely ceremonial addresses live on as models of the genre, and his rhetoric seems especially prophetic in this era of rapid sunbelt industrialization.

INFORMATION SOURCES

Research Collection and Collected Speeches

Researchers of Grady's oratory can rely on the resources of the Special Collections Department of the Woodruff Library at Emory University, Atlanta, Georgia. This library in Grady's home city contains the few private papers the editor left behind at his death. Researchers concerned with Grady's rhetoric will find the following sources useful: reprints of the "New South" speech, news clippings related to his speech making, and a private diary recording the trip to Dallas, Texas, in 1888 to deliver "The South and Her Problems." In addition, the Emory Library maintains valuable secondary materials, Raymond Nixon's biography, *Henry W. Grady: Spokesman of the New South*, and a complete microfilm collection of the *Atlanta Constitution* for the period Grady served as managing editor.

American Speeches. Edited by Wayland Maxfield Parrish and Marie Hoch-   AS
    muth. New York: Longmans, Green and Co., 1954.
The Complete Orations and Speeches of Henry W. Grady. Edited by Edwin   COS
    DuBois Shurter. Norwood, Mass.: Norwood Press, 1910.
Life of Henry W. Grady Including His Writings and Speeches. Edited by   LHG
    Joel Chandler Harris. New York: Cassell Publishing, 1890.
The New South: Writings and Speeches of Henry Grady. Edited by Mills   NSW
    Lane. Savannah, Ga.: Beehive Press, 1971.
The New South and Other Addresses. Edited by Edna Henry Lee Turpin.   NSO
    New York: Charles E. Merrill, 1904.
A Treasury of the World's Great Speeches. Edited by Houston Peterson.   TWG
    New York: Simon and Schuster, 1965.

Selected Critical Studies

Bauer, Marvin G. "Henry W. Grady." In *A History and Criticism of American Public Address*. Edited by William Norwood Brigance. New York: McGraw-Hill, 1943.
Braden, Waldo W. "Southern Oratory Reconsidered: A Search for an Image." *Southern Speech Communication Journal* 29 (1964): 303–15.
Campbell, J. Louis. "In Search of the New South." *Southern Speech Communication Journal* 47 (1982): 361–88.
Clark, E. Culpepper. "Henry Grady's New South: A Rebuttal from Charleston." *Southern Speech Communication Journal* 41 (1976): 346–58.
Gaston, Paul M. *The New South Creed: A Study in Mythmaking*. Baton Rouge: Louisiana State University Press, 1970.
Lindsay, Charles F. "Henry Woodfin Grady, Orator." *Quarterly Journal of Speech Education* 6 (1920): 27–42.
Metheny, David L. "The New South: Grady's Use of Hegelian Dialectic." *Southern Speech Communication Journal* 31 (1965): 34–41.
Mixon, Harold D. "Henry W. Grady as a Persuasive Strategist." In *Oratory in the New South*. Edited by Waldo W. Braden. Baton Rouge: Louisiana State University Press, 1979.

Selected Biographies

Bauer, Marvin G. "Henry W. Grady: Spokesman of the New South." Ph.D. dissertation, University of Wisconsin, 1937.
Nixon, Raymond B. *Henry W. Grady: Spokesman for the New South*. New York: Alfred A. Knopf, 1943.
Terrell, Russell Franklin. *A Study of the Early Journalistic Writings of Henry W. Grady*. Nashville: George Peabody College For Teachers, 1927.

CHRONOLOGY OF MAJOR SPEECHES

See "Research Collections and Collected Speeches" for source codes.

"The New South," New York, December 21, 1886; *AS*, pp. 450–60 (this text is authoritative and includes audience applause); *COS*, pp. 7–22; *LHG*, pp. 83–93; *NSW*, pp. 14–41; *NSO*, pp. 23–43; *TWG*, pp. 628–33.

"The Solid South," Augusta, Georgia, November 24, 1887; *COS*, pp. 65–97; *LHG*, pp. 121–41; *NSW*, pp. 42–63.

"The South and Her Problems," Dallas, Texas, October 26, 1888; *COS*, pp. 23–64; *LHG*, pp. 94–120; *NSW*, pp. 14–41; *NSO*, pp. 43–91. (Note that several sources incorrectly cite the date of the speech as 1887.)

"Against Centralization," commencement address to the Literary Societies of the University of Virginia, Charlottesville, Virginia, June 25, 1889; *COS*, pp. 134–57; *LHG*, pp. 142–57.

"The Farmer and the Cities," Elberton, Georgia, July 25, 1889; *COS*, pp. 158–91; *LHG*, pp. 158–79; *NSW*, pp. 64–86.

"The Race Problem in the South," speech before the Boston Merchant's Association, Boston, December 12, 1889; *COS*, pp. 192–220; *LHG*, pp. 184–98; *NSW*, pp. 87–105; *NSO*, pp. 92–123.

Bay State Club address, Boston, December 13, 1889; *COS*, pp. 221–33; *LHG*, pp. 199–207; *NSO*, pp. 124–36.

ALEXANDER HAMILTON
(1757–1804), founding father and first treasury secretary

EDWARD L. SCHAPSMEIER

Alexander Hamilton was born in the British West Indies and emigrated to the colony of New York in 1773. He attended King's College (now Columbia University) and while a student became a fervent convert to the patriot cause. He gave high-level declamations at public rallies and wrote well-reasoned propaganda tracts in defending the rights of the thirteen colonies against the supposedly unwarranted exercise of arbitrary power by the Parliament in London in violation of the British Constitution. Nevertheless, because of his strong belief in law and order, Hamilton was not above chastising a rampaging mob for violating the civil liberties of Tories.

The teen-age Hamilton quit college at the onset of the Revolutionary War to organize and command a volunteer company of soldiers. In 1777, General George Washington appointed Hamilton to be his aide-de-camp with the rank of lieutenant colonel. His valor on the battlefield, as well as his demonstrated ability as General Washington's de facto chief of staff, earned him a deserved reputation as one of the memorable young heroes of the American Revolution.

After leaving the Continental Army, Hamilton studied law and soon became a leading member of the bar in New York City. He quickly won renown for his expertise in jurisprudence and display of exceptional forensic talent. He was not afraid to defend Loyalists against illegal actions taken against them by wrathful Americans seeking vengeful retribution. In 1782 Hamilton was selected by the New York legislature as a representative to the Continental Congress. From his wartime experience, he was aware of the shortcomings of this body and now witnessed firsthand the gross inadequacies of the Articles of Confederation. Some states simply ignored the requisition of revenues imposed by the Congress. The fledgling nation was sorely in debt, dissatisfied Revolutionary War veterans were near the point of rebellion, there was no national regulation of trade or interstate commerce, and the nation's monetary policy was in a total shambles.

Hamilton was elected to the New York State Assembly in 1786. He frequently rose to engage in debate, at times rendering learned disquisitions on the need for his state to support the sovereign power of Congress to levy taxes. When Hamilton was designated to be one of New York's delegates at the commercial convention at Annapolis, Maryland, in 1786, he utilized his position to push through a resolution calling for a meeting of all the states at Philadelphia the following year to consider needed revisions of the Articles of Confederation.

HAMILTON AS POLITICAL PHILOSOPHER AND POLEMICIST

Alexander Hamilton was one of the select group of fifty-five delegates who assembled at Independence Hall in Philadelphia on May 25, 1787. Hamilton, who was well read in the literature of natural law philosophy and excelled as a master in the literary and oral art of expression, won everlasting fame not only as one of the framers of the U.S. Constitution but as the founding father most responsible for its ultimate ratification. While not recorded as being a highly vocal participant in the day-to-day deliberations at the Constitutional Convention, Hamilton made a singularly important contribution on June 18 when he delivered an impressive five-hour address. It was the longest single speech given by any delegate. His learned discourse was a calculated attempt to make an intellectual imprint on the minds of his august audience in order to influence the direction of their thinking.

In this significant speech, which contained the essence of his political thought (and remained a subject of enduring controversy during his lifetime), Hamilton laid out the bold outlines for a strong national government. He seized an opportune moment to speak after William Paterson of New Jersey presented a set of resolutions to amend the existing articles. This was done to counter the Virginia plan submitted previously by Edmund Randolph. The Virginia plan proposed altering the currently existing confederation by dramatically transforming it into a new federal union with two legislative houses and a chief executive. In his extended verbal presentation, Hamilton took an audacious and unexpected stance by challenging the efficacy of both the New Jersey and Virginia plans as suitable frames of government for uniting the thirteen states into a truly sovereign nation-state.

Upon commencing his scholarly disquisition, noted for its informed array of historical facts, methodical logic, and reliance on rational argument (rather than on fervid flights of flamboyant oratory), Hamilton forthrightly asserted to the delegates on June 18, 1787:

My situation is disagreeable, but it would be criminal not to come forward on a question of such magnitude. I have well considered the subject, and am convinced that no amendment of the confederation can answer the purpose of a good government, so long as state sovereignties do, in any shape, exist; and I have great doubts whether a national government on the Virginia plan can be made effectual.

The delegates listened with rapt attention, despite the hot and humid conditions in the small hall, while Hamilton appealed to their reason, not emotions. He declared: "I shall now show, that both plans are materially defective." Hamilton then contended that successful nationhood was possible only if the proposed constitution contained the following theoretical constructs:

1. A good government ought to be constant, and ought to contain an active principle.
2. Utility and necessity.
3. An habitual sense of obligation.
4. Force.
5. Influence.

What Hamilton desired was not a continuation of a weak confederacy or even a loose federation of states but a unified nation with a strong central government that would "preserve the peace and happiness of the community as a whole." What abstract paradigm was he to offer as a substitute for the plans he considered to be flawed? None. Instead Hamilton drew on the practical historical experience of their former mother country. He maintained:

I believe the British government forms the best model the world ever produced, and such has been its progress in the minds of the many, that this truth generally gains ground. This government has for its object public strength and individual security. It is said with us to be unattainable. If it was once formed it would maintain itself.

To achieve what he deemed to be the necessary checks on the impetuosity of the uneducated masses, Hamilton proposed that although the people at large (he supported a broad suffrage) should vote directly for members of the House of Representatives (corresponding to the British House of Commons), in contrast the Senate (resembling a House of Lords) and the presidency (tantamount to an elective monarchy) would be selected by electors chosen by the voting citizenry to hold office "during good behavior"—meaning for life. He also suggested the establishment of a supreme judicial body of twelve judges who would hold office for life.

No one in the convention rose to challenge the postulates Hamilton laid down. Later in his career it would be claimed by James Madison, who was present and took notes (and also by Thomas Jefferson as leader of the political opposition), that the New Yorker was at heart a cryptomonarchist who wanted to subvert the Republic and stifle democracy. This was not accurate. While Hamilton favored a republican form of government, he did fear possible mobocracy and presciently foresaw trouble over states' rights with its potential threat of dissolving the union via secession. His intellectual tour de force was aimed primarily at polarizing the debate between his ultranationalism and the determined exponents of state supremacy so that the Virginia plan would appear to be the wiser option among the two extremes. The eventual Connecticut compromise, which gave states equal representation in the Senate but based the makeup of the House on population, cleared the way for replacing the impotent confederation with a more robust federal union.

On June 26 Hamilton again rose to join the debate. He reminded his fellow delegates: "We are now to decide forever the fate of Republican Government. If we do not give to that form due stability and wisdom, it will be disgraced and lost to mankind forever." Exhorting his colleagues to avoid constructing a weak central government that would be overly subject to the immediate whims of the electorate, he vowed: "I am as zealous an advocate for liberty as any man, and would cheerfully become a martyr to it. But real liberty is neither found in despotism or the extremes of democracy, but in moderate governments." He dreaded the irrational and impulsive acts of direct (or participatory) democracy as evidenced by the unwise disposition of the ancient Greeks to embrace tyrants when the masses were swayed by the impassioned pleas of popular demagogues.

In his last major speech to the convention on June 29, Hamilton was fully aware of the diversity of opinions and lack of a clear consensus. He earnestly implored:

This is a critical moment of American liberty—We are still too weak to exist without union. It is a miracle that we have met—they seldom occur.

We must devise a system on the spot—It ought to be strong and nervous [that is, energetic], *hoping* that the good sense and principally the necessity of our affairs will reconcile the people to it.

Hamilton was the only member of the New York delegation to sign the embossed copy of the U.S. Constitution. Those still hesitant to endorse the final document took careful note of Hamilton's final words when he approached the table to affix his signature to the finished product of months of heated disputation. He commented candidly that "no man's ideas were more remote from this plan than his own were known to be; but it is possible to deliberate between anarchy and convulsion on the one side, and the chance of good to be expected from the plan on the other."

Once the Constitutional Convention adjourned, Hamilton threw all of his effort into the fight for ratification. He authored the major portion of *The Federalist* (1787–1788) and did everything in his power to publicize the virtues of the Constitution. It was vital that the Empire State ratify it. When New York's state convention convened at Poughkeepsie on June 17, 1788, with Governor George Clinton presiding, the Anti-Federalists (who opposed ratification) were in total control, with a majority of twenty-five. To stave off a quick and sure defeat, Hamilton, in repeated solo performances, ingeniously utilized every oratorical artifice at his command to sway the delegates and force them to give thorough consideration to all aspects of the Constitution. The *New York Journal* of July 4, 1788, likened Hamilton's stellar performance, at what amounted to an enlightened filibuster, to that of a "political porcupine, armed at all points and brandish[ing] a shaft to every opposer: a shaft powerful enough to repel and keen to wound."

Sometimes speaking in tempestuous tones and at other times presenting a temperate lecture couched in terms of didactic reasoning, Hamilton repeatedly took the floor to defend the Constitution against its many detractors. On June 25, Hamilton edified his hostile audience by informing them:

There are two objects to forming systems of government—safety for the people, and energy in the administration. When these objects are united, the certain tendency of the system will be to the public welfare. . . . Good constitutions are formed upon a comparison of the liberty of the individual with the strength of government: If the tone of either be too high, the other will be weakened too much.

Hamilton's effective oratory, whether part of a telling dialogue or in sharp rebuttal, educated the assembled body and prevented it from voting prematurely for rejection. His trenchant speech making persuaded opponents while effectively stalling the proceedings until news came indicating Virginia's favorable action. Even then Hamilton thwarted a provisional approval with another brilliant speech convincing the bellicose convention not to attach debilitating conditions. After five weeks, on July 27, the unencumbered document was ratified by a thirty-to-twenty-seven vote. His persuasive orations, both as a skilled floor debater and an extremely erudite expounder of the principles of federalism, was the most important factor in gaining the ultimate victory.

The rest of Hamilton's public career was devoted to making the Constitution a viable document for governing a growing nation. President George Washington appointed Hamilton the first secretary of the treasury (a post he held from 1789 to 1795). His luminous season as a resplendent orator was at an end; his reputation thereafter was that of a creative architect of a dynamic fiscal system. In so doing, he interpreted the Constitution broadly and invested it with implied powers. The "colossus of the federalists" (an apt appellation given him by Thomas Jefferson) subsequently became noted for his impressive series of economic reports: *Public Credit* (1790), *Manufactures* (1790), and *Establishment of a Mint* (1791).

Alexander Hamilton died at the age of forty-seven on July 12, 1804, after being mortally wounded while involved in a duel with Aaron Burr. His splendid career was cut short, but his lasting influence on U.S. history still continues. While Hamilton's early years were especially highlighted by his elocutionary brilliance, his overall intellectual dexterity, ability as a publicist, and administrative genius testified to his greatness as a premier statesman. Hamilton's literary legacy, whether the spoken word or the product of his prolific pen, constitutes a monumental body of rhetoric that extols the service rendered to his country by this titan among the founding fathers.

INFORMATION SOURCES

Research Collections and Collected Speeches

The major archival repositories for Hamilton's speeches are the Library of Congress and the National Archives.

Hamilton, Alexander. *The Law Practice of Alexander Hamilton: Documents*   LPAH
    and Commentary. Edited by Julius Goebel, Jr. 2 vols. New York:
    Columbia University Press, 1964, 1969.
————. *The Papers of Alexander Hamilton*. Edited by Harold C. Syrett.   PAH
    26 vols. New York: Columbia University Press, 1961–1969.

Selected Critical Studies

Adair, Douglass, and Marvin Harvey. "Was Alexander Hamilton a Christian Statesman?"
    William and Mary Quarterly 12 (1955): 308–29.

Caldwell, Lynton K. *The Administrative Theories of Hamilton and Jefferson: Their Contributions to Thoughts on Public Administration.* Chicago: University of Chicago Press, 1944.

Crosby, Richard Wheeler. "Alexander Hamilton's Political Principles: Natural Rights, Democracy, and the Good Regime." Ph.D. dissertation, Cornell University, 1970.

Dietze, Gottfried. "Hamilton's Federalist—Treatise for Free Government." *Cornell Law Quarterly* 36 (1957): 501–18.

Govan, Thomas P. "The Rich, the Well-born, and Alexander Hamilton." *Mississippi Valley Historical Review* 36 (1950): 675–80.

Lycan, Gilbert L. *Alexander Hamilton and American Foreign Policy: Design for Greatness.* Norman: University of Oklahoma Press, 1970.

Miller, John C. *Alexander Hamilton and the Growth of the Nation.* New York: Harper & Row, 1964.

Schapsmeier, Edward L., and Frederick H. Schapsmeier. "The Hamilton-Jefferson Confrontation: Origins of the American Political System." *Social Science* 46 (1971): 139–47.

Stourzh, Gerald. *Alexander Hamilton and the Idea of a Republican Government.* Stanford: Stanford University Press, 1970.

White, Leonard D. *The Federalists: A Study in Administrative History.* New York: Free Press, 1948.

Selected Biographies

Hendrickson, Robert A. *The Rise and Fall of Alexander Hamilton.* New York: Van Nostrand Reinhold Company, 1981.

McDonald, Forrest. *Alexander Hamilton, A Biography.* New York: W. W. Norton and Company, 1979.

Miller, John C. *Alexander Hamilton, A Portrait in Paradox.* New York: Harper, 1959.

Mitchell, Broadus. *Alexander Hamilton.* 2 vols. New York: Macmillan, 1957 and 1962.

CHRONOLOGY OF MAJOR SPEECHES

See "Research Collections and Collected Speeches" for source codes.

Speeches in the Constitutional Convention on a plan of government, Philadelphia, June 18, 26, 29, 1787; *PAH*, 4: 178–211, 218–19, 220–21.

Remarks in the Constitutional Convention on the manner of ratifying the Constitution, Philadelphia, September 10, 1787; *PAH*, 4: 246–47.

Speech in New York ratifying convention enumerating the requirements for an effective government, Poughkeepsie, New York, June 25, 1788; *PAH*, 5: 80–90.

Speech in New York ratifying convention on the constitutional system of checks and balances, Poughkeepsie, New York, June 27, 1788; *PAH*, 5: 94–112.

ROBERT HAYNE
(1791–1839), eloquent spokesman for the South

LLOYD E. ROHLER

Historians do not always deal kindly with individuals who support the losing side in major controversies. Such is the fate of Robert Young Hayne, senator and governor of South Carolina during the nullification controversy that foreshadowed the coming of the Civil War. One American historian, Henry W. Elson, dismissed him with the phrase that he "would scarcely be known except that he drew from the greatest orator his best speech." Surely this is unfair to a man elected to the state legislature at the age of twenty-three, elevated to Speaker at age twenty-seven, state attorney general at age twenty-eight, U.S. senator at age thirty-two, reelected without opposition for a second term, and governor at forty-one.

Born into a distinguished South Carolina family, Robert Hayne absorbed at an early age an abiding passion for politics and a devotion to public service. As a young man, he so distinguished himself in the local debating society that he was selected to deliver the Fourth of July oration before the city notables of Charleston. He read law in the office of Langdon Cheeves, a public-spirited man whose later career included election in 1814 as Speaker of the U.S. House of Representatives. Soon after Hayne had been admitted to the bar, Cheeves's partner died, and the young lawyer became a partner in the most successful and prestigious legal firm in Charleston. His subsequent marriage to Francis Pinckney, whose father was a delegate to both the Continental Congress and the Constitutional Convention, furthered his political prospects and contributed to his rapid rise to prominence. In the Senate, he allied himself with John C. Calhoun and ably defended the interests of his state and section in lower tariffs. As chairman of the Naval Affairs Committee, he introduced a bill to establish a naval academy. His role in the debate over the Foote resolution brought him nationwide fame. Subsequently he left the Senate to become governor, providing South Carolina leadership during the nullification confrontation with President Andrew Jackson. Following resolution of the controversy, he devoted his remaining years to building a railroad, the Louisville, Cincinnati, and Charleston, to link the West and the South. While engaged in this endeavor, he suddenly took ill and died at the age of forty-eight. Upon his death, it was said of him, "At an early age he was borne into public life on a flood tide of popular favor and retained it without ebb or abatement to the hour of his death."

HAYNE AS SPOKESMAN FOR HIS REGION

Although a lawyer by profession with an extensive legal practice, Robert Hayne's name is not associated with any major forensic speech. As a leading political figure in this state, he gave many epideictic speeches, but with the exception of his Inaugural Address as governor of South Carolina, none is particularly memorable. As an active member of the Senate, much of his speaking and writing concerned the necessary business of the day. For example, his important and useful work as chairman of the Naval Affairs Committee yielded no great speeches on the foreign or military policy of the United States or any far-reaching pronouncements on future strategy. Most of his speeches are difficult to locate; even the justly famous debate with Webster is known more by reputation than reading. Yet when an issue of national importance seized the attention of the Senate, Hayne achieved eloquence in his deliberative speaking.

Four speeches in this genre stand out from all the others for thought and expression and deserve to be remembered: his speech opposing the tariff of 1824; his speech opposing the Panama mission of 1826; the debate with Webster on the Foote resolution; and his speech opposing the Pension Act of 1830. These speeches demonstrated that his early reading of Hugh Blair taught him the importance of reason and argument as the basis for persuasion. All these speeches were rigorously constructed from premises abundantly supported with facts and documentation. He placed such great emphasis on evidence that he customarily brought the relevant materials to the floor of the Senate with him and read directly from them.

All of these speeches were in opposition to the developing industrial economy represented by Clay's American system. Although these speeches defended the self-interest of his constituents, Hayne did not depend merely on arguments of expediency. In all four speeches, Hayne derived his premises from the principles of economic liberalism taught by Adam Smith and David Ricardo: free trade and minimal government regulation of the affairs of free men. With the exception of his defense of slavery, which offends contemporary moral sensibilities, Hayne's position was consistently libertarian and reflected a strong Jeffersonian influence.

Never an original or profound thinker, Hayne early in his career fell under the influence of John C. Calhoun who presided over the Senate during his second term. His close friend Senator Thomas Hart Benton of Missouri believed that Hayne acted as a foil for Calhoun during his vice-presidential years and claimed that Calhoun coached Hayne during the recess of the famous debate with Webster. That they acted in tandem cannot be denied. During the confrontation with Jackson over nullification, Hayne resigned from the Senate to become governor of South Carolina, and Calhoun, who had resigned the vice-presidency, promptly took Hayne's place in the Senate.

For both men, the tariff became the major focus for sectional differences over economic policy and the role that the federal government should play in the national life. The immediate background for the controversy is easy to sketch. During the economic disruption of the Napoleonic Wars, New England and the mid-Atlantic states expanded their new industries to capture a larger share of the American market. The peace that followed burst the bubble of hasty expansion as industry on the Continent returned to full-time production for export and promptly sought to recover lost markets. A tariff to prohibit foreign-manufactured goods from entering the United States and destroying the infant industries became the political program of the manufacturing states. While such a policy undoubtedly benefited northern manufacturing interests, it imposed higher costs for manufactured goods on the South and West without producing a visible economic benefit. This conflict over economic interests became a political struggle regarding the role of the federal government in economic affairs as Henry Clay and Daniel Webster pushed the American system of high tariffs and public works to promote the growth of a strong industrial nation. Hayne and Calhoun led the opposition to this vision by proclaiming the virtues of free trade.

Hayne's speech on the tariff of 1824 is a good example of his use of reasoning and argumentation in legislative debate. He began by examining the claimed justification for the measure that it was designed to raise revenue and by rigorous argument concluded that "its true character and . . . probable effects" will be to prohibit "the importation of all foreign goods . . . which we are capable of making at home." He next considered the "visionary theories and false doctrines" that formed the basis for this policy and identified the assumption basic to all of them: "government is capable of regulating industry better than individuals." Using *reductio ad absurdum*, he deduced from this assumption a basis for universal tyranny over all private decisions and magnified the danger of this depotism by historical example and contemporary analogy to China. Having disposed of the principle underlying a protective tariff, he turned to an examination of the economic conditions of the day and asked, What are the "causes . . . of our calamities?" He argued that the United States benefited from its neutral position in the Napoleonic Wars to expand its manufacturing beyond prudent limits. Now that peace has been restored, American manufacturing interests were no longer competitive with their continental rivals. He granted that the United States was in an economic depression but insisted that the tales of "great distress and acute suffering are exaggerated." His solution to the economic crisis was to restore trade in primary products such as agriculture and timber in which the United States possessed a comparative advantage. After developing the classic topics of the free trade argument, he concluded with an organic metaphor borrowed from Washington:

Everything, indeed, great or good is matured by slow degrees. That which attains a speedy maturity is of small value and is destined to a brief existence. It is the order of Providence that powers gradually developed shall alone attain permanency and perfection. Thus must it be with our national institutions and national character itself. . . . On this very question before us, "the Father of his country" (in his legacy to his children) marks out the true American policy in language which ought to sink deep into our hearts: "Our policy (he instructs us) should hold an equal and impartial hand, neither seeking nor granting exclusive favors or preferences; consulting the natural course of things; diffusing, by gentle means, the stream of commerce but forcing nothing."

Hayne opposed the tariff not only because of the unequal economic burden it imposed on his constituents but because it represented a dangerous centralizing tendency on the part of the national government. He returned to this theme in his speech opposing the Pension Act of 1830, which eased the eligibility requirements for qualifying for a pension for service in the Revolutionary War. After making the obligatory professions of gratitude to the soldiers of the Revolution—"I will yield, sir, to no gentleman here, in a deep and abiding sense of gratitude for Revolutionary Service"—Hayne scathingly denounced the "squandering away" of the "public treasure" among the "mere sunshine and holiday soldiers, the hangers on of the camp, men of straw, substitutes who never enlisted until after the preliminaries of peace were signed." To support this claim, he reminded his colleagues that when the Pension Act of 1818 became effective, over 30,000 men applied, "a number greater than that of General Washington's army at any period of the war." Hayne's judicious mix of argument and outraged indignation served as preliminary to his major contention: "I consider this bill as a branch of a great system calculated and intended to create and perpetuate a permanent charge upon the treasury. . . . It is an important link in the chain by which the American system party hope to bind the people now and forever to the payment of the enormous duties deemed necessary for the protection of domestic manufactures." He claimed that this is a "fixed and settled policy" of the Whigs and denounced "the astonishing spectacle" of "a free popular Government" constantly spending money "merely for the sake" of spending it. He next surveyed all the proposals for public spending and found the pension scheme to be "by far the most specious, the most ingeniously contrived and the best calculated for the accomplishment of the object." He recognized that the bill provided "popular topics which will carry away the feelings of the people and reconcile them to a . . . permanent charge upon the treasury . . . and furnish a plausible excuse for keeping the system of high duties."

As important as his philosophical objections to the Whig program stood a more practical objection: "This country is divided into two great parts, the paying and receiving states, or as they have some times been called, 'Plantation States' and 'the Tariff States.' " He claimed that the "present system operates as to lay the taxes chiefly on one portion of the country and to expend them on another; and while it is in the interest of the former to diminish the expenditures and to lessen the taxes, it is manifestly the policy of the latter to increase both." To support his claim, he turned to the records of the pension system and found that "of the twenty millions paid to pensioners, about fifteen millions have gone North and only five millions have been expended in the South and West." He concluded: "When [the pension system] degenerates into a mere scheme for the distribution of the public money, we have a right to complain of the gross inequality of [it]. I will not say that it is the object of this bill to make a distribution of the public revenue . . . on unjust and unequal principles, but I will say that this will unquestionably be its effect."

As a politician defending the interests of his state and region, Hayne spoke of slavery in ways that offend sensibilities. But he rarely spoke on the issue directly, and when he did, he did not engage in racist diatribes. Perhaps the most extensive commentary on slavery occurred in the debate over President

Adams's proposal to send a U.S. delegation to the Pan American Congress meeting in Panama in 1826. Senator Hayne opposed the mission partially because the agenda of the conference included a discussion of slavery and the slave trade. On that occasion, he expressed not only his own opinion of the institution of slavery but also warned the federal government of the consequences of acting on the issue:

On the slave question, my opinion is this: I consider our rights in that species of property as not even open to discussion, either here or elsewhere. . . . Let me solemnly declare, once and for all, that the Southern States never will permit, and never can permit, any interference, whatever, in their domestic concerns, and that the very day on which the unhallowed attempt shall be made by the authorities of the Federal Government, we will consider ourselves as driven from the Union.

The Pan American Congress speech is notable also as an example of Hayne's skillful tactics in legislative debate. Although the original issue is long dead, the lively style of the speech still sustains interest. He used the occasion of the speech to needle his Whig opponents about the American system and to belittle President Adams's vision of inter-American unity. He concluded with a typical flourish invoking the name of Washington and his Farewell Address: "We are about to violate the maxim of the Father of his Country which enjoins upon us the most sacred duties 'to cultivate peace and honest friendship with all nations, entangling alliances with none' . . . . Shall we abandon this high and honorable ground to engage in a crusade, the end of which no human being can foresee? . . . If this extraordinary mission must be sanctioned, I will wash my hands of it."

The debate with Webster that brought Hayne national recognition in 1830 began over a minor resolution introduced by Senator Foote of Connecticut instructing the Committee on Public Lands to study the "expediency" of limiting their sales. This suggestion roused the ire of Senator Thomas Hart Benton of Missouri who perceived it as a sinister plot by the eastern states to hinder the growth of the West. Hayne, who saw an opportunity to gain the political favor of the western states, rose to support Benton and in passing defended the constitutional view held by Calhoun and his supporters by asserting that there was "no evil more to be deprecated than the consolidation of [the national] government." Daniel Webster, who had been arguing a case before the Supreme Court, drifted into the Senate in time to hear this remark and the next day attacked Hayne and his South Carolina allies in an offensive and insulting speech. Stung by Webster's remarks, Hayne rose to the challenge and on January 21 spoke for about an hour before stopping so that Webster could keep a legal appointment. He resumed the following Monday, speaking for two and one-half hours more.

From the opening lines that mock Webster for his failure to answer Senator Benton's attack, to his peroration quoting Edmund Burke, Hayne demonstrated the inconsistencies in Webster's position and skillfully defended his own and

Calhoun's view of the limited constitutional powers of the national government. The first part of the speech is a point-by-point refutation of Webster's previous speech on the resolution; the second part of the speech is a strong affirmation of the compact theory of the federal Union. Throughout the speech, Hayne used wit and invective to poke fun at Webster's position. Hayne was particularly effective in demonstrating the hypocrisy and inconsistency of New England's position on the nature of the Union by reading extracts from the Hartford Convention. He held Webster up to ridicule by reading from his speeches in previous congressional debates on the questions of the tariff and public lands to demonstrate that Webster had completely changed his position on both issues. He further demonstrated that the New England states opposed appropriations for internal improvements in the West until 1825 when, as part of the "corrupt bargain" to win the presidency for John Quincy Adams, the New England states gave support to Clay's American system.

Hayne's speech brought from Webster his equally eloquent reply with the famous peroration that generations of school children learned to declaim by heart. The debate created great excitement not only in the capital but throughout the rest of the country. Both speeches were widely reprinted and commented on. Hayne found himself transformed into a celebrated figure with a national reputation as an accomplished orator. His own state and section widely hailed him as an effective spokesman for their grievances.

All contemporary accounts describe Robert Young Hayne as a charming man of easy manners and affable disposition. His evident sincerity, charm, and enthusiasm completely captivated audiences and predisposed them to accept his arguments. Always totally committed to his position, Hayne's confidence generated a passionate enthusiasm that swayed audiences. His well-modulated voice and clear though rapid enunciation made him a graceful and persuasive speaker whose surface charm concealed a brilliant mind and a burning ambition to gain fame through public service.

To assess Hayne's accomplishment, the contemporary critic must uncover the fundamental question that unites all the major speeches of his career: what is the nature of the American political system? Issues such as the tariff, the public lands, and the Pan American Congress served as mere counters in a larger dispute over the fundamental question of the nature of the U.S. Constitution. This contest involved two competing visions of the American polity. Hayne and Calhoun spoke for the vision of a limited federal government that acted as a caretaker over an essentially agrarian society. It had limited powers and limited tasks and devoted its energies to clearly defined spheres while respecting the sovereignty of the several states. In contrast, Webster and Clay shared a vision of a developing industrial and commercial power led by a national government that energized the several sections into a dynamic social order. The one vision derived from the past; the other represented the future. Hayne chose the losing side, but this should not blind us to the power of his arguments or the brilliance of his expression.

It was Hayne's fate to be out of step with the major forces of his time. In the Senate he devoted his talent and energy to defending a way of life that was passing and futilely struggled against the industrial capitalism that would soon sweep it away. When he left politics and tried to share his vision of a great railway link between the West and the South, he found that his dreams were far in advance of the economic resources available. He died at the meridian of his life, having achieved high office at an early age. His brief career foreshadowed the even greater promise of his maturity.

INFORMATION SOURCES

Research Collections and Collected Speeches

Few of Robert Y. Hayne's personal papers survive, and they are scattered among the libraries of Clemson University, Clemson, South Carolina; Duke University, Durham, North Carolina; and the University of South Carolina, Columbus.

Famous American Statesmen and Orators. 6 vols. Edited by Alexander K. McClure and Byron Andrews. New York: F. F. Lovell Publishing Company, 1902.   FAS

Great Debates in American History. 14 vols. Edited by Marion Mills Miller. New York: Current Literature Publishing Company, 1913.   GDA

Modern Eloquence. 15 vols. Edited by Thomas B. Reed. Philadelphia: John D. Morris Company, 1901–1903.   ME

Register of Debates in Congress. Edited by Gales and Seaton. Washington, D.C., 1824–1830.   RDC

Orations of American Orators. 2 vols. Edited by Timothy Dwight. New York: Colonial Press, 1900.   OAO

Selected Critical Studies

Adams, John Quincy. *Memoirs of John Quincy Adams.* Edited by Charles Francis Adams. New York: AMS Press, 1970.

Benton, Thomas Hart. *Thirty Years' View.* New York: Appleton, 1856.

Hayne, Paul H. *Lives of Robert Young Hayne and Hugh Swinton Legare.* Charleston, S.C., 1878.

Houston, David Franklin. *A Critical Study of Nullification in South Carolina.* Gloucester, Mass.: Peter Smith, 1968.

Jervey, Theodore. *Robert Y. Hayne and His Times.* New York: Macmillan, 1909.

Langley, Harold D. "Robert Y. Hayne and the Navy." *South Carolina Historical Magazine* 82 (1981): 311–30.

CHRONOLOGY OF MAJOR SPEECHES

See "Research Collections and Collected Speeches" for source codes.

Speech in the Senate opposing the Tariff Act of 1824, Washington, D.C., April 30, 1824; *RDC*, 1824, pp. 618–51.

Speech in Senate opposing Panama mission, Washington, D.C., March 14, 1826; *RDC*, 1826, pp. 152–75.

Debate in Senate with Webster on the Foote resolution, Washington, D.C., January 20–30, 1830; *RDC*, 1830, pp. 4–24, 35–41, 43–50; *OAO* 2: 97–145; extracts in *GDA*, 4: 38–46; *ME*, 12: 1170–77.

Speech in Senate opposing the Pension Act of 1830, Washington, D.C., April 29, 1830; *RDC*, 1830, pp. 396–403.

PATRICK HENRY
(1736–1799), orator of liberty and republicanism

DAVID A. MCCANTS

Patrick Henry excelled as an orator at the bar and in the assembly. Throughout his career as attorney and legislator, outstanding oratory was the chief basis for his growing influence and continual renown. The application of this remarkable gift to democratic Revolutionary interests in Virginia in the contest with Great Britain was of such heroic proportions that Henry earned a secure place among American patriots.

Admitted to the bar in 1760, Henry established himself quickly as a lawyer in his native Hanover and adjacent counties. He made his initial reputation as an orator in a courtroom when, in one of the proceedings of the Parsons' Cause (1763), he turned a legal controversy into a political grievance. From 1765 to 1774, Henry addressed larger forums: the House of Burgesses and the General Court. During this period, he positioned himself as the head of the democratic and liberal leadership of the colony, beginning with his role in the Stamp Act debate (1765). In the fevered days of 1774 to 1776, Henry, who was among the earliest to realize that a break with Great Britain was inevitable, fomented revolution with speeches to the continental congresses, the Virginia convention (March 23, 1775), and military volunteers.

During most of the period from 1776 until his death in 1799, Henry continued to play a leading role in Virginia politics. He served five terms as governor (1776–1779, 1784–1786). From 1780 to 1784 he served in the Virginia Assembly, usually espousing progressive legislation. Out of fear of antirepublican or centralizing tendencies, he marshaled his oratorical skill to oppose the Constitution strenuously in the Virginia ratifying convention (June 2–25, 1788) and for the next three years led the fight for amendments (Bill of Rights). In his later years Henry continued to enhance his reputation as an attorney. Admitted to the U.S. District Court in 1791, he established himself as a civil rights lawyer of national distinction with the British Debts case (1791–1793).

Henry began retirement in 1794 and declined numerous overtures for high-ranking appointments and elective office. When he viewed his nation at risk again, however, an infirm Henry stood for election to the Virginia Assembly in 1799 and just a few weeks before his death eloquently campaigned against Virginia's attempt to nullify acts of the federal government, deeming the threat of civil war a greater threat to liberty than the abominable Alien and Sedition Acts.

HENRY'S MAJOR ADDRESSES

Henry's first remarkable oratorical achievement occurred in the Parsons' Cause. Anticipating a short tobacco crop, the Virginia House of Burgesses in 1758 passed the Second Two-Penny Act. The act authorized that debts due in tobacco could be paid in cash at the rate of two pennies per pound. One group, the clergy, pressed their grievances against the act. The Reverend James Maury's case was one of five clerical suits to recover damages. When Patrick Henry entered the case, the king had ruled that the Two-Penny Act was invalid *ab initio* (1759), and the Hanover County court had upheld the plaintiff's entitlement to damages on November 5, 1763. The purpose of the December 1 hearing was to fix the amount of damages.

Acceptance of the defense role in a seemingly settled proceeding by the popular, rising, young Piedmont attorney infused the case with new excitement. In the hearing, plaintiff's counsel, Peter Lyons, argued for the difference between what Maury had been paid and what he would have received at the fair market price of tobacco. Henry ignored the legal issue; instead, he challenged the constitutionality of the king's annulment of the Two-Penny Act. Arguing from the compact theory of government, Henry claimed that the disallowance was an instance of royal misrule. The king's action, he said, considered neither the appropriateness of the Two-Penny Act for relieving the colony's economic distress nor the propriety with which the act had been promulgated through the legislative system.

Besides challenging the king's authority, Henry challenged the authority of the clergy. Just as the king had denied his duty to the people, so the clergy, by refusing to accept the two-penny law, had corrupted the function of an established church and clergy in society: the enforcement of obedience to civil sanctions and the observance of duties of imperfect obligation. The clergy, like the king, were enemies of the people and deserved punishment instead of protection and damages, Henry concluded. Through parallel arguments drawn from the nature of mutual obligations of king and subjects and clergy and people, Henry made a compelling case for social relations based on the principles of consent and the common good and transferred popular animosities toward the king to the clergy, and vice-versa, by revealing the contempt of each for these laws of nature. Upon conclusion of the pleas, the jury awarded, in less than five minutes, damages of one penny.

Henry's Parsons' Cause speech, in its espousal of the compact theory of government, may be viewed as a rehearsal for his defense of constitutional rights in the momentous Stamp Act debate, May 29–31, 1765. The adoption of the Stamp Act Resolves was the first declaration of resistance by a legislature; moreover, it was the action of an influential colony. Governor Francis Bernard of Massachusetts called the publishing of the Virginia Resolves "an alarm bell to the disaffected." Henry, a newcomer to the House of Burgesses, played a large role in this vigorously contended, narrowly determined debate. He was a fomenter of the debate, author of the resolves, co-strategist of the parliamentary moves with George Johnston, and chief advocate on the assembly floor. Henry likely entered the debate at several points, perhaps speaking to each resolution in turn and perhaps speaking during more than one of the three readings. Although the accounts of the debate are too scanty to reconstruct the arguments Henry advanced, the testimony of multiple observers supports the view that Henry shared responsibility for the violence, heat, and bloodiness of the debate. With directness, firmness, and cogency, Henry's resolves asserted exclusive power of the assembly to tax, condemned Parliament's usurpation of the power as an act of enmity, and affirmed the colonists' right to disobey. Even if all of Henry's resolutions were not introduced and even if Henry did not argue orally as explicitly as he did in the resolutions, it is certain that he attacked the authority of the Parliament and the king and, at least implicitly, advocated resistance in a manner that was viewed as seditious, if not treasonous.

Henry delivered the speech for which he is best remembered on the fourth day of the Virginia Convention, March 23, 1775. The three resolutions he proposed put the colony in a posture of defense by raising and training a militia. The proposal turned the delegates' attention from a philosophical discussion of imperial relations to a consideration of the urgency of colonial grievances, which he termed an issue of freedom or slavery. The report of the speech, as assembled by William Wirt primarily from the recollections of St. George Tucker, suggests that the speech is a model oration. In its careful integration on the speaker's analysis of subject and audience, the speech, organized by the problem-solution plan, is a paradigm of oratorical structure. The problem, as Henry saw it, was the audience's psychological state: the wish not to confront the problem. Indeed, Henry's proposals, despite the proximity of the outbreak of hostilities, took many by surprise. Only after he had awakened the audience to their psychological inertia did he attempt to persuade of an imminent military danger and then to propose his solution—arms. Anticipating a counterargument about the inequality of American and British military might, he argued that the colonies would be victorious in the armed conflict with England to satisfy the delegates' psychological need to know that acceptance of the ultimate risk to which he was calling them would be rewarded.

As well as being a paradigm of oratorical structure, the speech is a paradigm of oratorical strategy. The speaker amplified his arguments in such a manner that the audience drew deeply upon their psychological selves to supply conclusions for arguments well before Henry stated them, conclusions based on strongly motivating beliefs such as the desire to be physically safe, politically free, and true to conscience. Another recurring strategy is appeal to religious-political texts and creeds. Henry's speech played superbly upon emotional attachment to the Scriptures. The speech is a profusion of biblical paraphrases, allusions, and religious metaphors, many of which help to develop arguments characteristic of civil piety oratory: for example, America is the new promised land; the impending war is a holy crusade to ensure that divinely ordained political liberty shall prevail. The speech, in addition to being a model of oratorical structure and strategy, is a model of persuasion by character. By the end of the speech, Henry emerged as a prophet of the American democratic experience, saintly in his compulsion to face the truth and fervent in his judgment of the righteousness of the colonial cause, and a patriot in the tradition of heroic individuals (''I know not what course others may take, but as for me give me liberty, or give me death''), the consummate prophet-patriot of secular salvation in the American Revolution.

For twenty-three days, June 2–25, 1788, Patrick Henry led a laborious fight to defeat ratification of the U.S. Constitution in the Virginia convention. Henry, whose speeches constitute one-fifth of the stenographic report of the debate, argued against the Constitution on eighteen of twenty-three days, speaking frequently and lengthily. The delegates listened to him with unflagging interest, and to him belongs the credit for the Federalists' slim victory (eighty-eight to seventy-nine). While the Federalists stressed, with good effect, the inefficiency of government under the Articles of Confederation, Henry offered a weak defense of the status quo. Demonstrated failures of government under the articles precluded an effective defense-of-the-status-quo case. Usually Henry argued from the position that the proposed government created an evil worse than any inefficiency of the present government, a position that provided him a strong base from which to operate. Henry believed that the centralization of government as provided for in the Constitution would lead to the loss of personal liberty. The relinquishment of states' rights, he reasoned, would create such a powerful and remote government that the loss of personal liberty was inevitable. Since the proposed Constitution did substitute a federal for a confederated system, Henry could represent the proposal as a major change, and since the proposed government was admittedly an original form of government, he could forecast fearsome uncertainties. Although he proved to be a formidable opponent, Henry, by forensic standards, presented a flawed performance. He relied greatly on emotional appeals and unsupported assertions; he frequently rambled and repeated himself. In one of his most important speeches, delivered on June 5, he analyzed the Constitution provision by provision, word by word. The strategy was to overwhelm by the accumulation of defects. In this case, the effectiveness of the strategy was diminished by strained interpretations of the language of the Constitution and the intent of the framers, logical contradictions, and a scattershot-type attack that indiscriminately mixed weak and strong arguments. Throughout this speech and the debate, however, Henry strategically focused attention upon his principal contention: the loss of liberty. As always, Henry was the orator of liberty and republicanism.

At issue in the British debts case was the liability of Virginia citizens for prewar debts to British merchants. In 1777, the Virginia Assembly, for the purpose of filling the state's war treasury, authorized the fulfillment of debts to British subjects by payments to the state treasury in Virginia currency. And like other states that adopted laws of sequestration, Virginia solidified its posture with a 1782 law preventing recovery of the debts in the state's courts. Such laws were in conflict with the Treaty of Paris (1783), which denied all legal impediments to the collection of debts in sterling money. So British creditors, upon the creation of the federal judicial system in 1789, began entering suits. *Jones v. Walker*, later called *Ware v. Hylton*, was the first of hundreds of such suits to be tried. A formidable array of legal talent represented the plaintiff and the defendant, but attention focused on Patrick Henry, the renowned orator and political figure with a long reputation as champion of debtor interests, patriotic causes, and the confiscatory legislation.

Henry's three-day argument for the defense, which he began on November 25, 1791, is a remarkable combination of emotionalism and legal reasoning. From ancient legal theory by Grotius and Vattel, Henry argued that a state has the right to confiscate debts owed an enemy, including debts of private citizens, as well as property. He countered the argument that the ancient principle was inapplicable because of the absence of precedent in Europe with the argument that Virginia, because it had never adopted the European custom, was unbound by European practice. He countered the argument that the Treaty of Paris recognized citizens' liability for debts with the argument that a treaty cannot require that debts be paid twice and, further, that British violations of the treaty rendered it null and void. Within and between the legal arguments, Henry wove appeals based on national animosities over British tyranny, unjust pursuit of a war against the rights of humanity, and anticipated incivilities to which the states would have been subjected by a victorious England. The law was not clearly on the side of the defense in this case. However, by thorough preparation through diligent research and acute analysis, and by splendid presentation, Henry won a decision that debts that had been paid to the state treasury were legally fulfilled. Although this decision, upheld by the circuit court in 1793, was reversed in 1796 by the U.S. Supreme Court, opinion of Henry's expert legal proficiency endured.

Henry's contemporaries praised his oratory. George Mason judged him "by far the most powerful speaker" he ever heard; Jefferson termed his eloquence sublime and estimated that he was "the greatest orator that ever lived"; easterners, such as John Adams and Silas Deane who observed Henry in national forums, held him in similar esteem. Henry overpowered his listeners. They described themselves as being enchanted and made bereft of their senses. Stenographer David Robertson, who recorded the Virginia ratifying convention debate and the proceedings of the British debts case, found himself listening instead of recording Henry's most eloquent moments. Opposing counsel were also enraptured by Henry. Colonel Edward Carrington, upon conclusion of the "Liberty or Death" speech, exclaimed, "Let me be buried at this spot." A member of the audience at the Virginia ratifying convention said that he believed that his wrists were fettered and the gallery was a dungeon when Henry described the people enslaved by a federal executive in command of an armed force. The great influence to which Henry's contemporaries testified derived from three major sources: he aroused powerful motivations inherent in popular sentiments, he disarmed with his boldness, and he wed delivery and language to communicate the sense of cause that animated his leadership.

Henry understood the powerful motivations inherent in popular sentiments, and when he aroused them, audiences united in support of his appeals. Certainly this was true when he articulated the elements of feeling and belief that gave rise to the revolution. In the Parsons' Cause, he tapped religious, economic, and political discontent. The Anglican clergy, much reputed for incompetence and immorality, were held in low esteem throughout the colony; Hanover County was a center of religious dissent; and Henry, an unsuccessful farmer and merchant, knew the economic hardship of the Piedmont's small planters. In the Stamp Act controversy, as in the Parsons' Cause, Henry espoused the independency of the assembly, a view subscribed to by the entire Virginia political leadership and represented repeatedly by feisty burgesses.

Besides articulating deep-seated, popular sentiments, Henry commanded attention by the boldness of his oratory, which according to Edmund Randolph, could rob danger of terror. In the Parsons' Causes Henry moved the clergy from mockery to alarm and despair by his attack on them; while cries of treason greeted his attack on the king, the people bore him on their shoulders around the courtyard. Fully aware of the danger to him and to the assembly in advocating disobedience to the Stamp Act law, Henry proceeded to be magnificently defiant. Though greeted again with cries of treason, Henry's optimism about "a united sentiment and sound patriotism" prevailed among the people in Virginia and beyond. The speech at St. John's Church, in which he ridiculed the idea of peace where there is no peace and challenged the audience with his personal commitment to liberty, was equally bold and inspiring.

John Randolph considered Henry a Shakespeare and Garrick combined. This critique suggests another major source of Henry's excellence: expression in language and delivery of the intense sense of cause he felt. Henry's leadership was built on a strong identification with the populace. In the assembly, he represented the Piedmont planter class whose economic circumstances, style of life, and tensions with the aristocratic Tidewater leadership he thoroughly appreciated. He subscribed to the principle of imperial relations that was widely shared by the Virginia leadership in the advancing controversy with Great Britain. Early in his public career, he established himself as a disciple of the laws of nature: for example, rule by consent, the common good, the rights of suffrage, and the rule of justice for individuals and nations. Henry's deep convictions sparked in him a candor and courage that he expressed in words, tones, and gestures that were inextricably part of his argument and influence. He spoke simply and directly in an oral style. He was often unpolished and repetitious; he was often moving and poetic. He made ideas concrete by images he drew from the Bible or common experience, especially images that embodied righteousness and force. The images, in concert with first person speech, rhetorical questions, and linguistic absolutes, brought speaker and audience heart to heart to challenge fears, affirm aspirations, and animate decisions. Henry exercised complete control over a clear, powerful, and flexible voice to communicate a range of attitudes and feelings. He could be polite, humble, shy, humorous, and sarcastic in quick succession. He was characteristically awkward—a gentleman's modesty—in the beginning of his speeches; he remained collected and dignified when animated and maintained self-control even in moments of high oratorical excitement, as when, for example, in the "Liberty or Death" speech he brought the condemnation of God upon Great Britain with the zeal of a crusader or uttered his dramatic personal pledge to die for liberty. Henry used his voice and body with the skill of an actor. On more than one occasion, he dramatized his speech, heightening the impact of his message with complete bodily expressiveness. The final sentence of the "Liberty or Death" speech was one such instance. From a submissive posture and countenance, Henry straightened, struggled to burst bonds, and, while his voice swelled to say "give me liberty," wrenched his upended hands apart, revealing a letter opener that he raised aloft and then aimed at his heart as he exclaimed "or give me death."

Patrick Henry enjoyed a lengthy career as a premier orator, applauded by lay and peer reviewers for excellence in deliberative and legal speaking. He won renown at the bar for representing criminal and civil cases and in legislative assemblies of Virginia and the nation for patriotism, progressivism, and statesmanship. In both forums, masterful exercise of the art of public address was the continual foundation for his reputation. Henry rallied support for his views by linking them to powerful human motivations at work in his audiences, by presenting himself as unreservedly committed to acting in conformity with those views, and by articulating the wisdom of the principles from which he derived his positions on political and judicial issues and the urgency for their application in the situation at hand.

INFORMATION SOURCES

Research Collections and Collected Speeches

Henry materials are located in the Patrick Henry Papers, Library of Congress, and in the William Wirt Papers, Maryland Historical Society, Baltimore.

American Forum: Speeches on Historical Issues, 1788–1900. Edited by   *AF*
Ernest J. Wrage and Barnet Baskerville. New York: Harper &
Brothers, 1960.

Carrington, Paul, to William Wirt, October 3, 1815. Patrick Henry Pa-   *PHP*
pers, Library of Congress.

Henry, William Wirt. *Patrick Henry: Life, Correspondence and*   *PHLCS*
Speeches. 3 vols. New York: Scribner's, 1891.

Jefferson, Thomas, to William Wirt, August 4, [1805]; August 14, 1814;   *WWP PMHB*
May 12, 1815; William Wirt Papers, Maryland Historical Society,
Baltimore. The letters were published in "Jefferson's Recollec-
tions of Patrick Henry," *Pennsylvania Magazine of History and
Biography* 34 (1910): 385–418.

"Journal of a French Traveller in the Colonies, 1765, I." *American*   *AHR*
Historical Review 26 (1921): 726–47.

Memoirs of a Huguenot Family: Translated and Compiled from the Orig-   *MHF*
*inal Autobiography of the Rev. James Fontaine, and Other Family
Manuscripts*. Edited and translated by Ann Maury. New York,
1853.

The Debates in the Several State Conventions, on the Adoption of the   DSSC
    Federal Constitution. Edited by Jonathan Elliot. 2d ed. 5 vols.
    Philadelphia: J. B. Lippincott Company, 1901.
Wirt, William. *Sketches of the Life and Character of Patrick Henry.*   SLCPH
    Rev. ed. Ithaca, New York: Mack, Andrus & Company, 1848.

Selected Critical Studies

Einhorn, Lois J. "Basic Assumptions in the Virginia Ratification Debates: Patrick Henry
    vs. James Madison on the Nature of Man and Reason." *Southern Speech Com-
    munication Journal* 46 (1981): 327–40.
Hample, Judy. "The Textual and Cultural Authenticity of Patrick Henry's 'Liberty or
    Death' Speech." *Quarterly Journal of Speech* 63 (1977): 298–310.
McCants, David A. "The Authenticity of James Maury's Account of Patrick Henry's
    Speech in the Parsons' Cause." *Southern Speech Communication Journal* 42
    (1976): 20–34.
———. "The Authenticity of William Wirt's Version of Patrick Henry's 'Liberty or
    Death' Speech." *Virginia Magazine of History and Biography* 87 (1979): 387–
    402.
———. "McCants on Hample." *Quarterly Journal of Speech* 65 (1979), 80–86.
———. "Hample on McCants." *Quarterly Journal of Speech* 65 (1979): 86–92.
———. "The Role of Patrick Henry in the Stamp Act Debate." *Southern Speech Com-
    munication Journal* 46 (1981): 205–27.
Mallory, Louis A. "Patrick Henry." In *A History and Criticism of American Public
    Address.* Vol. 2. Edited by William Norwood Brigance, New York: McGraw-
    Hill, 1943.

Selected Biographies

Beeman, Richard R. *Patrick Henry: A Biography.* New York: McGraw-Hill, 1974.
Henry, William Wirt. *Patrick Henry: Life, Correspondence and Speeches.* 3 vols. New
    York: Scribner's, 1891.
Meade, Robert Douthat. *Patrick Henry.* 2 vols. Philadelphia and New York: J. B.
    Lippincott Company, 1957–1969.
Wirt, William. *Sketches of the Life and Character of Patrick Henry.* Rev. ed. Ithaca,
    N.Y.: Mack, Andrus & Company, 1848. (Originally published in 1817, Wirt's
    biography of Henry was issued in many editions in the nineteenth century.)

CHRONOLOGY OF MAJOR SPEECHES

    See "Research Collections and Collected Speeches" for source codes.

Parsons' Cause speech, Hanover County Courthouse, Virginia, December 1, 1763; *MHF*,
pp. 418–24. The only account of Patrick Henry's speech in the Parsons' Cause was
written by the plaintiff, the Reverend James Maury, in a letter to the Reverend John
Camm, December 12, 1763.

Stamp Act speech, Williamsburg, Virginia, May 29, 1765. Although there is no text or reliable account of the Caesar-Brutus speech, presumably delivered during the debate on the fifth resolution, pertinent details are contained in *AHR*, pp. 745–46; *PHP*; *SLCPH*, pp. 48–55; *WWP*; *PMHB*, pp. 386–408.

Liberty or Death speech, Richmond, Virginia, March 23, 1775; *SLCPH*, pp. 88–95; *PHLCS*, 1 :261–66. The text of this speech is inextant. Wirt presents a "speech report" as provided by his sources.

Virginia ratifying convention speech, Richmond, Virginia, June 5, 1788; *PHLCS*, 3:434–58; *AF*, pp. 7–22; *DSSC*, 3:43–64.

British debts case speech, Federal District Court, Richmond, Virginia, November 25–28, 1791; *PHLCS*, 3:601–48.

ROBERT GREEN INGERSOLL
(1833–1899), lawyer, politician, social critic of religious doctrine

_____ HERMANN G. STELZNER

In the late nineteenth century, Robert G. Ingersoll's three interrelated interests brought him to the attention of a variety of publics. He practiced general law, but it was as a corporate and trial lawyer that he earned a reputation and high fees. Neither a scholar of the law nor a legal philosopher, his talents were practical. He organized assistants to prepare cases and to manage routine day-to-day courtroom procedures. His contribution was made before judges and juries where his sense of the drama and his ability through language and delivery to capitalize on courtroom tensions led audiences to identify with his clients. Ingersoll defined law, especially its practice, as drama; he was an actor whose photographic mind absorbed scripts and whose platform skills reduced their complexities to simplicities. The *Munn* case (1876) established him as a criminal lawyer; the *Star Route* case (1882–1883), the *Davis* will case (1891), and the *Russell* will case (1899) enhanced his reputation. Only one volume of *The Collected Works of Robert Green Ingersoll* contains legal addresses.

Ingersoll, a staunch Republican, flirted with electoral politics. He was attorney general of Illinois (1867–1869) and ran an aborted campaign for the governorship in 1868. In the years following, he developed a regional reputation for waving the bloody shirt at Democrats as the party of slavery and treason and enmity toward civil liberties. In the presidential campaign of 1868, he supported U. S. Grant, and his vigorous stump oratory portrayed the Republican party as virtue personified. It also gained him a national audience. By 1876 his reputation was secure, and he supported James G. Blaine as Republican party standard-bearer. On June 15, 1876, he placed Blaine's name in nomination and delivered one of the most remembered nomination speeches in American political history, the "plumed knight" speech. Blaine lost the nomination to Rutherford B. Hayes of Ohio, but Ingersoll's political stock soared, and for almost a decade the "Centennial Spread Eagle" of the Republican party was counted upon to proclaim its virtues in rousing philippics.

It was as a commemorative speaker and social critic, especially of organized religion, that Ingersoll, an agnostic, achieved notoriety. He lectured in every state of the Union except two, North Carolina and Mississippi, and for a time he was among the most popular speakers in James Redpath's Lyceum Bureau. How Ingersoll came to his agnosticism is best left to a full-fledged biographical study, but his position was a partial reaction to his father, a Congregational minister, and his experience in the Civil War. Finally, he was influenced by Darwin and science, especially biology, as resources for an explanation of the human condition.

THE ETHOS AND LANGUAGE OF A SOCIAL CRITIC

Reporters' descriptions of scenes illustrate the interaction among Ingersoll, his message, time, place, and audience. Lengthy excerpts capture moments in situ. The first is a *Chicago Tribune* reporter's description of Ingersoll's nomination of Blaine, the "plumed knight" speech, in Cincinnati, Ohio, on June 15, 1876:

> Possessed of a fine figure, a face of winning cordial frankness, Ingersoll had half won his audience before he spoke a word. It is the attestation of every man that heard him, that so brilliant a master stroke was never uttered before a political Convention. Its effect was indescribable. The coolest-headed in the hall were stirred to the wildest expression. . . . The matchless method and manner of the man can never be imagined from the report in type.

A *New York Herald* reporter described the setting on October 30, 1880, in Brooklyn, New York, where Ingersoll spoke for James A. Garfield, the Republican nominee for president:

> The Rev. Henry Ward Beecher and Colonel Robert G. Ingersoll spoke from the same platform last night, and the great preacher introduced the great orator and free thinker to the grandest political audience that was ever assembled in Brooklyn. The reverend gentleman presided over the Republican mass meeting held in the Academy of Music. When he introduced Ingersoll he did it with a warmth and earnestness of compliment that brought six thousand lookers-on to their feet to applaud. . . . The orator spoke in his best vein and his audience was responsive to the wonderful magical spell of his eloquence. And when his last glowing utterance had lost its echo in the wild storm of applause that rewarded him at the close, Mr. Beecher again stepped forward and, as if to emphasize the earnestness of his previous compliments, proposed a vote of thanks to the distinguished speaker. The vote was a roar of affirmation. . . .

The third example is from Butte, Montana. Ingersoll represented clients who contested a will (*Davis* will case) that disposed of millions of dollars. A divided jury led to an out-of-court settlement, and Ingersoll's fee was not paid until long after his death. On September 5, 1891, a reporter for the *Anaconda Standard* filed this account:

> The matchless eloquence of Ingersoll! Where will one look for the like of it? What other living man has the faculty of blending wit and humor, pathos and fact and logic with such exquisite grace, or with such impressive force? Senator Sanders this morning begged the jury to be aware of the oratory of Ingersoll as it transcended that of Greece. Sanders was not far amiss. In fierce and terrible invective Ingersoll is not to be compared to Demosthenes. But in no other respect is Demosthenes his superior. To a modern audience, at least Demosthenes on [*sic*] the Crown would seem a pretty poor sort of affair by the side of Ingersoll on the Davis will. It was a great effort, and its chief greatness lay in its extreme simplicity.

The reporter noted Ingersoll's adaptation to the jury. He "stepped up to the jurors as near as he could get and kept slowly walking up and down before them. At times he would single out a single juryman, stop in front of him, gaze steadily into his face and direct his remarks for a minute or two to that one man alone." His ability to change his mood helped to maintain the jury's attention. The reporter judged that "if the jury could have retired immediately upon the conclusion of Ingersoll's argument, there is little doubt as to what the verdict would have been." The audience, too, responded to Ingersoll's rhetorical efforts.

Individuals noted specific talents and often ranked him using comparison. Henry Ward Beecher saw him as a "man who—and I say it not flatteringly—is the most brilliant speaker of the English tongue of all men on this side of the globe." Commenting on his speech nominating Blaine in 1876, Cameron Rogers said: "He was, in the seasoned opinion of men who had sat in Congress for thirty years and more, the ranking orator of all those that they had heard, Clay, Webster, Everett, Calhoun and the rest."

Mark Twain referred to his toast at a banquet for Grant in Chicago as the "supremest combination of English words that was ever put together since the world began." Later he wrote, "My Dear Ingersoll: If you have a perfect copy of your peerless Chicago speech to spare, please let me have it. I have imperfect copies, but no others. I'm to read the speech to a young girl's club here, Saturday—but that is not the main thing. I want a perfect copy for my private scrapbook."

The size of audiences that heard his political and religious lectures is still another index of his standing. Newspaper accounts regularly mention numbers from 5,000 to 50,000. The fact that Ingersoll liked newspapermen—he was good copy—may have inflated the figures somewhat. The attendance of women at political meetings in numbers large enough to note was significant. A reporter said that "they came by the hundreds, and the speaker looked down from his perch upon thousands of fair upturned faces." The number who attended his lectures was large despite the standard admission fee of one dollar. Ingersoll's 60 percent cut from an evening's income regularly reached $1,500. The largest amount he received was for a single lecture in Chicago in 1892, when his share of the receipts was $3,500. His critics also contributed to his audiences, and Ingersoll was appreciative of them because they were his advanced agents. The *San Francisco Daily Evening Post* observed, "The surest way in the world to fill a house for Colonel Ingersoll is for some blatant ass to go mouthing around about 'Pope Bob' and 'blasfeming infidel.' " In Brooklyn, New York, the YMCA distributed 20,000 circulars to churches warning the parishioners not to attend an Ingersoll lecture on a Sabbath evening. The lecture was sold out. Ingersoll's compensation was widely reported by the orthodox who envied his income. A ditty expressed the frustration: "Though Colonel Robert Ingersoll/Is guilty of some follies,/He made his queer ideas pay,/And that's his Ingersollace."

A final measure of audiences' interest in him is the production of lectures. He had standard series, of course, but each year he added one or two to his arsenal. His first antitheological lecture, "Progress," was delivered in Pekin, Illinois, in 1860. A long, rambling exercise in definition, Ingersoll illustrated the numerous ways theology restrained social and political development of persons and institutions. His tone and energy were reserved in marked contrast to his later mature efforts. In 1899, the year of his death, ''The Devil'' and ''What Is Religion'' were completed. Between 1860 and 1899, he wrote forty-seven lectures and discussions; the latter first appeared in print journals.

Audiences attending his political messages expected to hear partisanship grounded in principle and supported by appeals to science, reason, experience, liberty, humanity, freedom, and their synonyms. Not a teacher, though he did teach in Illinois and Tennessee, but a popularizer, he understood that a message was in bondage to an audience. As a lawyer, he knew the importance to a case of argument and evidence. He also knew how to transcend the bellicose and to ground analyses in detailed, precise, and convincing historical precedents. His speech at Indianapolis, Indiana, in 1868 in support of Grant's candidacy for the presidency was a model for an argument based on the American political tradition in which he did not deny charges raised by Democrats but reversed them and used them against his opponents. The schema followed the structure of Lincoln's Cooper Union address and was often used by Ingersoll. If the reversal provided a tone of attack, it also prepared for a move to new ground, transcending, if necessary, the protagonist-antagonist confrontation.

In the Indianapolis speech, Ingersoll refuted two specific accusations, the first that under Lincoln, Republicans used the suspension of habeas corpus as a political means of imprisoning Democrats. He did not deny the charge but used a historical parallel between the Revolutionary War and the Civil War as the logical justification for the policy:

I lay this down as a proposition, that we had a right to do any thing to preserve this government that our fathers had a right to do to found it. If they had a right to put Tories in jail, to suspend the writ of *habeas corpus* . . . in order to found this government, we had a right to put rebels and Democrats in jail . . . in order to preserve the government they thus formed.

The second accusation, that of arming, freeing, and enfranchising Negroes, Ingersoll also acknowledged, but he showed that Negroes had participated in the Revolution, that freedoms were extended to them in many of the states, and that there were documents authorizing freedom to Negro troops after the war. Ingersoll agreed Republicans ''freed Negroes'' and ''allowed them to vote'' and also ''made them citizens.'' He concluded briskly: ''What are you Democrats going to do about it?''

If Ingersoll displayed keen analysis and logical development, he also entertained by use of ridicule and invective. For example in Chicago, October 10, 1876, he denounced Samuel J. Tilden, Democratic candidate for the presidency, via a coarse *ad hominem* argument:

I am opposed to him, first, because he is an old bachelor. In a country like ours, depending for its prosperity and glory upon an increase of the population, to elect an old bachelor is a suicidal policy. Any man that will live in this country for sixty years, surrounded by beautiful women with rosy lips and dimpled cheeks, in every dimple lurking a Cupid, with pearly teeth and sparkling eyes—any man that will push them all aside and be satisfied with the embraces of the Democratic party, does not even know the value of time.

Repetition intensified attacks upon groups. In September 1876, before Civil War veterans in Indianapolis, he attacked the Democratic party. The partisan audience cared little that his accusations were not true. Its emotions were raised to an intense pitch, and they appreciated the performance:

I am opposed to the Democratic party, and I will tell you why. Every State that seceded from the United States was a Democratic State. Every ordinance of secession that was drawn was drawn by a democrat. Every man that endeavored to tear the old flag from the heaven that it enriches was a Democrat. Every enemy this great Republic has had for twenty years has been a Democrat. Every man that shot Union soldiers was a Democrat. Every man that denied to the Union prisoners even the worm-eaten crust of famine, and when some poor, emaciated Union patriot, driven to insanity by famine, saw in an insane dream the face of his mother, and she beckoned him and he followed, hoping to press her lips once again against his fevered face, and when he stepped one step beyond the dead line, the wretch that put the bullet through his loving, throbbing heart was and is a Democrat.

In "Some Mistakes of Moses" (1879) he attacked an education based on the assertion that the Bible is the inspired word of God. The young men at Andover Academy, Massachusetts, he charged, were being "taught to repeat a creed and despise reason." A rapier-like satirical exposition amplified the proposition:

They have, in Massachusetts, at a place called Andover, a kind of minister factory, where each professor takes an oath once in five years—that time being considered the life of an oath—that he has not, during the last five years, and will not, during the next five years, intellectually advance. There is probably no oath that they could easier keep. Probably, since the foundation stone of that institution was laid there has not been a single case of perjury. The old creed is still taught. They still insist that God is infinitely wise, powerful and good, and that all men are totally depraved. They insist that the best man God ever made, deserved to be damned the moment he was finished. Andover puts its brand upon every minister it turns out, the same as Sheffield and Birmingham brand their wares, and all who see the brand know exactly what the minister believes, the books he has read, the arguments he relies on, and just what he intellectually is. They know just what he can be depended on to preach, and that he will continue to shrink and shrivel, and grow solemnly stupid day by day until he reaches the Andover of the grave and becomes truly orthodox forever.

Ingersoll often employed sharp, nervous rhetorical questions to test the clarity of an opponent's position and to strengthen his conclusion. A typical example appeared in a discussion with the Reverend Henry M. Field: "Did God hear the prayers of the slaves? Did he hear the prayers of imprisoned philosophers and patriots? Did he hear the prayers of martyrs, or did he allow fiends, calling themselves his followers to pile the faggots round the forms of glorious men? Did he allow the flames to devour the flesh of those whose hearts were his? Why should any man depend on the goodness of a God who created countless millions, knowing that they would suffer eternal grief?''

In 1867, Ingersoll, in his capacity as attorney general of Illinois, addressed a meeting of blacks in Galesburg, Illinois. The speech, ''An Address to the Colored People,'' is notable because it rose above party politics and its tone was not condescending. It represented Ingersoll the educator at his best as he clarified the concept of human freedom, the role of dedicated men in making it a reality, and its potential for future enlargement. Slavery was a dimension of the human condition that ''has in a thousand forms existed in all ages, and among all people. It is as old as theft and robbery.'' The American experience paralleled the historical experience until the United States became ''grand enough to say, 'Slavery shall be eradicated from the soil of the Republic.' '' The policy sustained Ingersoll's faith in progress, but he respected the actions of agitators: ''If the Black people want a patron saint, let them take the brave old John Brown.'' He acknowledged that both parties supported the Fugitive Slave Law and that conditions, not altruism, produced the Emancipation Proclamation. ''I hate to think that all'' the inhumanity ''was done under the Constitution of the United States, under the flag of my country, under the wings of the eagle.'' The magnitude of the injustices against blacks made him wonder about the future, which depended upon education, mutual help, and freedom for all. ''I feel like asking your forgiveness for the wrongs that my race has inflicted upon yours. If, in the future, the wheel of fortune should take a turn, and you should in any country have white men in your power, I pray that you will not execute the villainy we have taught you.''

Ingersoll's clear arguments were supported by an energetic style. He was brief, direct, and economical. The tension between his argument and style and the ambiguity and obscurity of his opponents created a polarity between him and them. When theme and occasion required a high style, he created poetically appropriate passages, as well as extended purple patches. An example of the latter was his ''Vision of War,'' which was embedded in an address to Civil War veterans, September 20, 1876; a soliloquy, it stands independent of the text. A flight of sentimental fancy sustained by the iambic stress of the prose, the soliloquy provided the rationale for the strong alliance between the Grand Old Party and the Grand Army of the Republic. It reawakened the memories of the veterans: ''The heroes are dead. . . . In the midst of battle, in the roar of conflict, they found the serenity of death. I have one sentiment for soldiers living and dead: cheers for the living, tears for the dead.'' An example of the former is his apostrophe to ''Liberty,'' which concludes ''The Liberty of Man, Woman, and Child'':

Oh Liberty, float not forever in the far horizon—remain not forever in the dream of the enthusiast, the philanthropist and poet, but come and make thy home among the children of men!

I know not what discoveries, what inventions, what thoughts may leap from the brain of the world. I know not what garments of glory may be woven by the years to come. I cannot dream of the victories to be won upon the fields of thought; but I do know, that coming from the infinite sea of the future, there will never touch this "bank and shoal of time" a richer gift, a rarer blessing than liberty for man, for woman, and for child.

His arguments were addressed directly to his hearers, and his style, whether sublime or vulgar, had the quality of colloquy. The qualities of his style, constant variety, simplicity of structure, concrete diction, and unvarying lucidity fused matter and manner. His lectures arrested attention.

For two decades after Ingersoll's death, examples of his prose appeared in school textbooks. Most of the examples illustrated tropes and figures, centering on his style, including his careful preparation of lectures. Political and literary figures who were influenced by him include Albert J. Beveridge, William E. Borah, Clarence Darrow, Eugene Debs, Robert La Follette, and Sinclair Lewis.

There is no question that Ingersoll's private and public character attracted support. He had a sense of duty, responsibility, and stewardship, and he worked best when he worked alone. Although he spoke for the Republican party and its office seekers, he did not work with either toward programmatic objectives. A staunch nonjoiner with supreme self-confidence, he turned away as easily as he accepted. In 1880 he told a political audience in Brooklyn, New York: "No party has a mortgage on me. I am the sole proprietor of myself." Neither friend nor foe questioned the depth of his sincerity. To both friend and foe he became Matchless Bob, Handsome Bob, or Royal Bob.

If he did not have a great intellect, he was a quick study. A photographic mind assembled bits and pieces of literature, law, and life into a thick commonplace book of illustrations. He first learned about religion from his father and the standard Calvinistic classics, and he maintained a lifelong interest in theology. His formal schooling was not systematic, but there is ample evidence of an eclectic curiosity about literature, philosophy, and science. He read Paine, Voltaire, Humboldt, Spencer, Jackel, and Darwin, "one of the greatest men who ever touched this globe." Robert Burns and Shakespeare provided him insights into the human condition with which the narrow Calvinist world of his youth could not compare. From Burns he learned joy: "Burns you know is a little valley, not very wide, but full of sunshine." "From Shakespeare he got a vision of man's glory: "The sacred books of all the world are worthless dross and common stones, compared with Shakespeare's glittering gold and gleaming gems." He supported the arts, especially drama and music, and often frequented the theaters. Actors, musicians, artists, and writers were welcome guests in his home.

In 1862 Ingersoll married Eva Parker, a distant cousin of Theodore Parker and herself a religious skeptic. Their two daughters were raised in a climate of free thought and did not attend public schools. On Sunday evenings, the Ingersolls entertained lavishly, and the good life enlarged the lives of all who attended. Ingersoll's personal charm and interpersonal skills impressed visitors from all walks of life. In such settings, as well as from the platform, he expressed his opposition to vivisection, his support for decent hours and wages for labor, penal reform, equal rights for Negroes, birth control, and revision of procedures for divorce. However, he joined no groups committed to reforms.

Ingersoll and his brother, Ebon, practiced law together in Peoria, Illinois, and Washington, D.C. Ebon's death in 1879 touched him deeply and his "Tribute to Ebon C. Ingersoll," delivered to a large gathering of distinguished persons, was moving and touching. Antithesis is central to its development: "While yet in love with life and raptured with the world, he passed to silence and pathetic dust." His brother "in every storm of life was oak and rock; but in the sunshine he was vine and flower." He was a "worshipper of liberty, a friend of the oppressed." Often he had quoted these words: "For justice all place and temple, and all season, summer."

In his career, Ingersoll delivered many tributes, and the best of them became familiar through inclusion in collections of declamations. One of the best known was his tender words of comfort spoken "At a Child's Grave." It, too, employed antithesis for its balance and proportion: "Every cradle asks us 'Whence?' and every coffin 'Whither?' The poor barbarian, weeping above his dead, can answer these questions just as well as the robed priest of the most authentic creed. The tearful ignorance of the one, is as consoling as the learned and unmeaning words of the other." Drawing from "our religion," he concluded with a crisp line: "Help for the living—Hope for the dead."

Standing almost six feet tall and weighing over two hundred pounds, his presence was felt. When lecturing, he controlled the scene. At the appointed moment, he appeared without props, often without an introducer, and often without notes or manuscript. He faced the audience and settled it with a gesture for silence. His voice carried well, and he spoke rapidly yet clearly and forcefully. He made few gestures or larger physical movements. His introductions were brief; he announced his proposition quickly. His showmanship fused his logic and language. And the audiences, prepared for effective oratory, would shortly surrender to his matter and manner.

Robert Green Ingersoll is a secure figure in nineteenth-century social history. He made no original contributions to the philosophy of free thought, but his lectures and essays contributed to the movement to secularize America. To free people from the dogma of the past and substitute for it a belief in the reality of material nature and of human intelligence was his central objective. As "Darwin's Bulldog," he proceeded with force, vigor, wit, and courage. His eloquence and rhetorical magic invited audiences to consider and respond.

INFORMATION SOURCES

Research Collections and Collected Speeches

The New York Public Library, the British Museum, London, the Library of Congress, and the Illinois State Historical Society, Springfield, Illinois, contain collections of Ingersoll papers. The Dresden edition of *The Works of Robert G. Ingersoll* was the authorized publisher of Ingersoll.

Stein, Gordon. *Robert G. Ingersoll: A Checklist*. Kent, Ohio: Kent State University Press, 1969.
The Field-Ingersoll Discussion. New York: C. P. Farrell, 1895.
The Letters of Robert G. Ingersoll. Edited by Eva Ingersoll Wakefield. New York: Philosophical Library, 1951.
The Works of Robert G. Ingersoll. Edited by Dresden, and C. P. Farrell.   *WRGI* 12 vols. New York: Dresden Publishing Co., 1907.

Selected Critical Studies

Anderson, David D. *Robert Ingersoll*. New York: Twayne Publishers, 1972.
Braden, Clark. *Ingersoll Unmasked: A Scathing and Fearless Exposé of His Life and Real Character*. New York: Clark Braden, 1901.
Crocker, Lionel. "Robert Green Ingersoll's Influence on American Oratory." *The Quarterly Journal of Speech* 24 (1938): 299–312.
Lampert, Rev. Louis. *Notes on Ingersoll*. Buffalo, N.Y.: Catholic Publication Co., 1884.
McClure, J. B., ed. *Mistakes of Ingersoll and His Answers Complete*. Chicago: Rhodes and McClure, 1882.
Parrish, Wayland Maxfield. "The Style of Robert G. Ingersoll." In *Studies in Speech and Drama*. Edited by Herbert A. Wichelns. New York: Russell and Russell, 1968.
———, and Huston Alfred Dwight. "Robert G. Ingersoll." In *History and Criticism of American Public Address*. Vol. 1. Edited by William Norwood Brigance. New York: McGraw-Hill, 1943.

Selected Biographies

Baker I. Newton. *An Intimate View of Robert G. Ingersoll*. New York: C. P. Farrell, 1920.
Cramer, C. H. *Royal Bob*. Indianapolis: Bobbs-Merrill, 1952.
Rogers, Cameron. *Colonel Bob Ingersoll*. New York: Doubleday, Page & Co., 1927.
Smith, Edward G. *The Life and Reminiscences of Robert Green Ingersoll*. New York: National Weekly Publishing Co., 1904.

CHRONOLOGY OF MAJOR SPEECHES

See "Research Collections and Collected Speeches" for source codes.

"Progress," Pekin, Illinois, 1860; *WRGI*, 4: 423–52.

"An Address to the Colored People," Galesburg, Illinois, 1867, *WRGI*, 9:5–17.

Speech nominating Blaine, Cincinnati, Ohio, June 15, 1876; *WRGI*, 9:55–60.

Indianapolis Speech, Indianapolis, Indiana, September 20, 1876, *WRGI*, 9: 157–223.

Speech denouncing Samuel Tilden, Chicago, October 20, 1876; *WRGI*, 9:191–223.

"The Liberty of Man, Woman, and Child," n.p., 1877; *WRGI*, 1: 329–98.

"Some Mistakes of Moses," n.p., 1879; *WRGI*, 2: 13–25.

"Tribute to Ebon C. Ingersoll," Washington, D.C., May 31, 1879; *WRGI*, 12: 389–91.

Speech in support of Garfield's candidacy for the presidency, Brooklyn, New York, October 30, 1880; *WRGI*, 9: 347–403.

"At a Child's Grave," Washington, D.C., January 8, 1882; *WRGI*, 12: 399–400.

Address to the jury in the *Davis* will case, Butte, Montana, September 5, 1891; *WRGI*, 10:535–85.

"What Is Religion?" n.p., June 2, 1899; *WRGI*, 4: 429–96.

ANDREW JACKSON
(1767–1845), seventh president of the United States

THOMAS M. LESSL

Andrew Jackson is better known as a man of action than as a man of words; he is known better for his indomitable spirit and the wooden determination of his leadership than for his grace of speech. Jackson is also well known for the novelty of his presidency and for the formative role he played in the evolution of American democracy. Jackson's oratory is an expression of this notable political personality and of the new democratic worldview he championed.

The Jacksonian style of leadership, as it was manifested in his oratory, left a permanent mark on the U.S. presidency. Jackson's predecessors in the White House possessed an ethos colored by the lingering aura of European aristocracy. The Jacksonian ethos brought the latent militancy and frontier values of the new American Republic to the forefront of politics. As much as any other historical personage of his age, Jackson, who was both pioneer and warrior, embodied these two prominent characteristics of nineteenth-century America.

The phenomenal popularity that Jackson enjoyed during the last thirty years of his life defies any commonsense equation we might wish to posit between oratorical skill and political success. Indeed Jackson cannot be discounted as an orator, but the light of his oratorical skill is often lost to our distant vision in the lustrous brilliance that emanates from the more cultivated oratory of such notable contemporaries as Thomas Hart Benton, John C. Calhoun, Henry Clay, and Daniel Webster. While these contemporaries were champions of eloquence, Jackson alone obtained the mantle of the presidency. The remarkable persona out of which Jackson's oratory arose segregates him from others as a notable rhetorical figure of the early nineteenth century. Examining the Jacksonian ethos, we peer into a mirror reflecting the emergent nationalism and the awakening democratic consciousness of the early American Republic.

JACKSON'S PUBLIC CHARACTER

Immersed as a young boy in the internecine carnage of the American Revolution, Jackson bore throughout his life the insignia of frontier hardship and war. Jackson's birth in the Waxhaw settlement of South Carolina followed only two days after the collapse and death of the immigrant father after whom he was named. By the time Jackson reached the age of fourteen, the remaining members of his family had died, each directly or indirectly at the hands of the British invaders. Jackson himself, who at the age of thirteen found himself a British prisoner of war, nearly perished from a saber blow delivered to his head after he refused to black the boots of one of his captors. Jackson possessed a temperament that even at an early age preferred the brutal cut of an enemy's sword to subservience of any kind. Although he never cared for books and was in fact notoriously unlearned, he seems to have instinctively regarded what meager literacy he did possess as an instrument for moving men to action. At the age of eleven, Jackson took it upon himself to compose and deliver before his classmates a rousing proclamation urging his South Carolinian neighbors to maintain their perseverance in the bitter war against Britain. Jackson also boasted of his selection as a young boy to read publicly the Declaration of Independence when it first arrived in the Waxhaw settlement. Following the war, Jackson led a carefree life until 1784, when he decided to read law at Salsbury, North Carolina. Having been admitted to the bar three years later, he accepted an appointment as public prosecutor in the western region of North Carolina, now Tennessee, and eventually moved on to the frontier settlement at Nashville, which became his home for the greater duration of his life.

Jackson quickly connected himself with the political establishment of the new state, becoming a delegate to the Tennessee constitutional convention in 1796, a federal representative during the same year, and a U.S. senator shortly after. Jackson spent less than two years in federal politics before being elected president. His most enduring political post during this period of his life was a six-year term as judge of the state superior court. Both politically and privately, Jackson manifested the complexity of his personality. He was known in the face of competition or battle to be uncompromising, vituperative, and a fearless man of iron determination, yet he could also be self-possessed, chivalrous, even magnanimous. While Jackson made enemies of numerous rival politicians, at times these same opponents could not help expressing adulation for him. Daniel Webster, who like many other representatives of the eastern political establishment feared the rise of this rough-hewn westerner, expressed surprise with Jackson, whom he found to be "grave, mild and reserved," even "presidential." Although never losing his appeal for the common electorate as a rugged man of the wilderness, Jackson exhibited a native rhetorical sense that enabled him to coexist with the eastern establishment.

The earliest accounts of Jackson's public character show divided opinions concerning his qualifications as a speaker. Thomas Jefferson was unimpressed by the young Andrew Jackson's speaking performance as a senator from Tennessee during 1797–1798. Jefferson once observed that in his efforts to express himself, Jackson often was strangled by an inability to control his passions. This impression seems to have caused Jefferson to turn aside Jackson's bid for a governorship in the newly acquired Louisiana Territory and later to scoff at his candidacy for the presidency. In the same period, however, others describe Jackson as a notable communicator who spoke slowly and fluently with notable conviction. Numerous and disparate observers of Jackson's oratory have independently commented on the remarkable directness of Jackson's speech making. Although reviled as an illiterate, this backwoods "hickory pole" always managed to have a point to make in public discussion and to make his point memorable to those who heard it. The younger Jackson was known to become excited occasionally, speaking during these moments with a noticeable north Irish accent and all the while awkwardly piercing the air with a long, bony forefinger. Observers, however, note that the older Jackson's self-control increased as his anger mounted, allowing him to articulate coolly his political reprisals.

The Jackson that was called to Richmond in 1807 as a witness at the trial of Aaron Burr was certainly not the tongue-tied senator whom Jefferson had encountered in previous years. Frustrated by his conviction of Burr's innocence and persuaded that the drawn-out trial was merely a red herring conceived of by the Jefferson administration to distract attention from its own weak response to British aggression, Jackson announced in Richmond newspapers that he would address the public on the steps of the state house. Although no complete text of this speech has been preserved, fragments surviving in the accounts of listeners show it to be representative of Jackson's native temperament. So pointed and personal was the enmity in this speech that many expected at least two of those it attacked to demand satisfaction of Jackson in the manner customary to that age—dueling with weapons. This speech not only drew the attention of political observers but also foreshadowed the rhetorical reputation the general would later earn as a military leader.

Undoubtedly Jackson regarded oratory as but a subdued version of warfare. The combativeness of Jackson's personality is evident in the plain pioneer images of this extemporaneous attack on the Jefferson administration. Of the attempt to convict Burr of treason, Jackson said, "This persecution was hatched in Kentucky. The chicken died and they are trying to bring it to life here." The general spoke of Jefferson as one who having been kicked downstairs by the British now gets "revenge by standing out in the middle of the street and making faces at him!" The simplicity of Jackson's speaking style betrayed him as a man not deeply devoted to book learning, yet he spoke with unmistakable conviction. Thomas Ritchie, a newspaperman from Richmond, said that Jackson's speech reminded him of an ax felling a giant tree. The homely metaphors that Jackson used to assail his opponents were always part of his private speech but disappeared from his public discourse after his ascendancy to the White House. When speaking privately of the dangerous precedent set by South Carolina's doctrine of nullification, Jackson said, "If this thing goes on, our country will be like a bag of meal with both ends open. Pick it up in the middle or endwise and it will run out. I must tie the bag and save the country." In his presidential address from Washington on December 10, 1832, responding to South Carolina's derogation of federal law, Jackson dropped the familiar expressions from his speech, voicing his opinion of nullification in plain but forceful terms: "If South Carolina considers the revenue laws unconstitutional, and has a right to prevent their execution in the port of Charleston, there would be a clear constitutional objection to their collection in every other port, and no revenue could be collected any where; for imposts must be equal." Though colorful and often rural images were more natural to Jackson than to modern presidents such as Franklin Roosevelt or Ronald Reagan, who seem to have strategically used common imagery in their oratory, we never find such expressions preserved in Jackson's formal speeches as president. Although this could be attributed largely to the oratorical fashions of his day, in part it may also have been due to the special rhetorical burden put on Jackson to counteract the barbarian image laid upon him by his political opponents.

The two most notable of Jackson's ceremonial speeches are his Second Inaugural Address of March 4, 1833, and his Farewell Address given March 4, 1837. The first Inaugural Address, given when Jackson was weighed down by illness and grief over the death of his wife, disappointed admirers, who expected a forceful exhibition of frontier bombast but instead heard the thin voice of a broken old man uttering not the manifesto of a new era but the well-worn platitudes of administrations gone by. While the first Inaugural Address, with its surprising assertion of states' rights, suggested the pen of Jackson's vice-president, John C. Calhoun, the Second Inaugural showed Jackson's more consistent emphasis on the preservation and integrity of the Union. Also of note in the Second Inaugural is Jackson's depiction of himself and the presidential office as the voice of the people. Taking advantage of his heroic stature and overwhelming election victory over Henry Clay, Jackson opened with a depiction of the executive role as mandated by the "will of the American people, expressed through their unsolicited suffrages." Jackson's Farewell Address, like George Washington's, warned against party divisions that "excite the South against the North and the North against the South," designs to "sever the Union," and "the assumption of a power not given by the Constitution." Jackson added to these warnings his own admonitions against the centralization of wealth in a national bank and the proliferation of paper currency. In this speech, Jackson spoke sagaciously as one of "advanced age and failing health," who must soon "pass beyond the reach of human events." Despite its somber forebodings, Jackson's farewell was a triumphant celebration of his years in office. Of all his speeches, Jackson's annual messages best represent his Jeffersonian conceptions of democratic government and constitutional authority. The most notable of these is his first, which proclaimed his declaration of war against the remnants of aristocracy lingering in American government such as the bank, tenured public offices, and legislative elections of presidents.

The combative speaking style that Jackson invoked on occasion would at other times be complemented by a more diplomatic approach suggestive of the general's inherent political shrewdness. During his forays with South Carolina over the nullification issue, Jackson privately swore to hang the first man he caught engaged in a treasonous act. But in the public response made from Washington on December 10, 1832, Jackson adopted a paternal tone and pleaded: "Fellow citizens of my native state!—let me not only admonish you as the first magistrate of our common country, not to incur the penalty of its laws, but to use the influence that a father would over his children whom he saw rushing to certain ruin." Although Jackson was enraged against the nullificationists and was prepared to spill blood to enforce federal law, his wisdom as a political strategist caused him to adopt a conciliatory tone in this speech. At other times Jackson would let the full explosive force of his well-known temper fall upon his listeners as if the words were so many carefully placed artillery placements. While members of the political establishment that Jackson's administration supplanted would often shudder at the thought of this incendiary backwoodsman occupying the White House, the common electorate, which had expanded greatly into the western frontier during the early nineteenth century, lionized the old general for these traits.

Although he used ghostwriters during his presidency, Jackson insisted that the raw ideas he turned over to the more literate members of his kitchen cabinet were not substantially distorted in the process of composition. Jackson had a habit of writing stray ideas on bits of paper and then having his staff organize them into a whole for his congressional messages. The chief rhetorical power behind the president was Amos Kendall, a gifted polemicist who seems to have had an important hand in most of Jackson's public discourse. Other members of the Jackson cabinet also commonly participated in the composition process. Jackson would carefully pour over speeches, rejecting outright several drafts. Even the famous toast "Our Federal Union! It Must and Shall be Preserved," which became a national antinullification slogan after its utterance, devastated John C. Calhoun at a Jefferson day banquet, was deliberated upon by Jackson for days and submitted to the review of several of his staff, including Martin Van Buren, Thomas Benton, Amos Kendall, Isaac Hill, and William Lewis. The version finally selected was Jackson's own.

Jackson is well known for his exercise of the veto. The messages that accompanied these vetoes are among the most memorable expressions of Jacksonian democracy. Unlike his predecessors, Jackson found it possible to oppose policies that were both strongly supported in Congress and had general public support. He was able to do this on the strength of his own widespread popularity together with the careful diplomacy of his addresses. Jackson would override the usual political process by going directly to the people and in this way sweep away congressional opposition by creating a public confederation of support behind him. Jackson's habit of addressing his veto messages to Congress but intending them for the public became a recurrent strategy of presidents after him.

The most illustrious example of this rhetorical tactic can be found in Jackson's speech of July 10, 1832, which accompanied his veto of a bill to recharter the Bank of the United States. Although Jackson had garnered some popular support for his position on the bank in his first annual message, his sentiments on this issue were not widely shared by Congress or even by his own cabinet. Jackson's political enemies, led by Henry Clay, thought that forcing a decision on the bank would put Jackson in a dilemma: Jackson would either back down and lose face or stand firm in his opposition to the bank and lose popular support. Jackson responded with a carefully written but uncompromising veto message, the result of a three-day marathon of writing and rewriting coordinated by Jackson but carried out, as usual, by various members of his cabinet. Jackson's bank veto message was formulated first by Kendall and then thoroughly revised by a number of other Jackson men but chiefly by Roger Taney, who would later be Jackson's appointee as chief justice to the Supreme Court. The result of this process was a forceful speech articulating an image of government free of laws that "undertake to add to these natural and just advantages artificial distinctions, to grant titles, gratuities and exclusive privileges, to make the rich richer, and the potent more powerful." The Jeffersonian influence can be seen in the maxim: "There are no necessary evils in government. Its evil arises only in its abuses. If it would confine itself to equal protection, and as heaven does its rains, shower its favors alike on the high and low, the rich and the poor; it would be an unqualified blessing."

Although the veto message was attacked by opponents and some Jacksonians as an effort to stir up a class war, it became, by virtue of its appeal to the have-nots, a powerful campaign document in Jackson's hands. Instead of bringing on the political demise of Andrew Jackson, the speech was taken to heart by the voting public. More than this, the veto message showed the progenitive part Jackson played in formulating an enduring American concept of government as the guardian of equality.

The popular image by which Jackson's political career prospered is often difficult to discern in his presidential speeches, which are somewhat less warlike than the popular image and, at times, the real temperament of the man would suggest. Instead of a warrior, we often find in Jackson's oratory a gentle diplomacy, an even-handed and magnanimous temperament showing Jackson's ability to adapt to the presidential office and its concomitant exigencies. Jackson as an orator seems to have been at his best when he spoke informally. In the later years of his presidency, it is reported that during one such impromptu address presented at Bunker Hill, John Quincy Adams, one of Jackson's staunchest political rivals, was moved to tears. Posterity has preserved only fragments of these addresses. The legendary image of Old Hickory, an *ethos* that Jackson used to make his presidential tenure most effective, was formed in great part by such rhetoric. Through his image and his speaking, Jackson created a new formula for presidential leadership. We might rightly regard Jackson's political career as the first built by means of what has come to be known as image politics, but, unlike many rhetorical constructions that would follow, the Jacksonian ethos was no mere phantasm of American hubris. The real Andrew Jackson seems to have been very much like the Jackson of legend. He was the first of several presidents to rise to power by means of a charismatic image and a keen understanding of the common people.

INFORMATION SOURCES

Research Collections and Collected Speeches

Although many of the private papers of Andrew Jackson are scattered among small collections and libraries, a great number of these can be found in the Jackson Papers in the Library of Congress and in a collection housed by the Tennessee Historical Society, Nashville. J. S. Bassett's *Correspondence of Andrew Jackson* contains most of these papers.

The Statesmanship of Andrew Jackson as Told in his Writings and Speeches.   SAJ
    Edited by Francis Newton Thorpe. New York: Tandy-Thomas Co.,
    1909.

Orations from Homer to William McKinley. Edited by Mayo W. Hazeltine.   OHWM
    25 vols. New York: P. F. Collier and Son, 1902.

The World's Famous Orations. Edited by William Jennings Bryan. 10 vols.   WFO
    New York: Funk and Wagnalls Company, 1906.

Selected Biographies

Bassett, John Spenser. *The Life of Andrew Jackson.* 2 vols. New York: Archon Books,
    1911.

Buell, Augustus. *History of Andrew Jackson: Pioneer, Patriot, Soldier, Politician, Pres-
    ident.* 2 vols. New York: Charles Scribner's Sons, 1904.

Davis, Burke. *Old Hickory: A Life of Andrew Jackson.* New York: The Dial Press, 1977.

Parton, James. *Life of Andrew Jackson in Three Volumes.* 3 vols. New York: Mason
    Brothers, 1861.

CHRONOLOGY OF MAJOR SPEECHES

See "Research Collections and Collected Speeches" for source codes.

First Annual Message, Washington, D.C., December 8, 1829; *SAJ*, pp. 35–65.

Bank of the United States veto, Washington, D.C., July 10, 1832; *SAJ*, pp. 154–76.

Antinullification proclamation, Washington, D.C., December 10, 1832; *SAJ*, pp. 232–56.

Message on the South Carolina Ordinance and Proclamation of Governor Hamilton, Washington, D.C., January 16, 1833; *SAJ*, pp. 200–31.

Second Inaugural Address, Washington, D.C., March 4, 1833; *OHWM*, pp. 3711–15; *WFO*, pp. 204–09; *SAJ*, pp. 257–60.

Farewell Address, Washington, D.C., March 4, 1837; *OHWM*, pp. 3715–27; *WFO*, pp. 209–17; *SAJ*, pp. 493–515.

THOMAS JEFFERSON
(1743–1826), third president of the United States

Probably the most intelligent and philosophical of all U.S. presidents, Thomas Jefferson must be counted at the same time as one of the least effective public speakers to hold the nation's highest office. He was a reluctant orator, well aware of his rhetorical deficiencies. He avoided lengthy addresses before plenary legislatures or public rallies, usually confining his comments to a few sentences. Beyond the expression of brief remarks, his voice would strain and falter, growing less audible by the minute.

Jefferson's mediocre abilities as a public speaker derived not from a lack of exposure to fine oratory. He himself witnessed and commented admiringly upon the dramatic speeches delivered by leaders of the Cherokee and Mingo Indian tribes; their strong voices and animated flourishes impressed him deeply, though he lacked fluency in their languages. His instructors at William and Mary College, moreover, exposed him to classic oratory both by their example and through assigned readings in the famous orations from antiquity to the eighteenth century. Jefferson was especially drawn to Demosthenes, Livy, Sallust, and Tacitus of old and Lord Chatham, Eugene Aram, Carnot, and the Indian Chief Logan from his own time. Further, his legal training taught him by example how inelegant the English language could be in the hands of attorneys. He wisely eschewed the "tautologies, redundancies, and circumlocutions" (as he once complained) common to legal writing, preferring close logic and pithy expression. Finally, Jefferson's approach to public speaking was molded by his considerable experience as a diplomat (he was diplomatic commissioner of Congress in Europe, U.S. diplomat minister to France, and first U.S. secretary of state) and as a politician (he served as a member of the Virginia legislature and of that state's delegation to Congress, as governor of Virginia, as vice-president under John Adams, and as president of the United States from 1801 to 1809). In these capacities—especially in the early, formative experiences in legislative bodies—his work was done primarily in committees: small group settings where his logic and clarity of thought, along with his impressive physical presence, had a strong effect. It was in these low-key, informal circumstances where Jefferson matured into a highly respected advocate—not before large crowds where a premium was placed on rousing rhetoric. His was a style of dispassionate reason and cool logic, not the fiery oratory of a Patrick Henry. He valued, above all, sober reasoning and solid argumentation; outdoor eloquence he left to others.

JEFFERSON AS RELUCTANT ORATOR

Despite his voluminous and distinguished corpus of written work, including the Declaration of Independence, Jefferson's collection of public addresses is modest. The texts of as few as twelve speeches qualify for admission to the most recent anthology of Jefferson's lasting contributions, some quite brief and others (such as his annual messages to Congress) read on his behalf by legislative clerks. As one would expect from a man of his undisputed genius, however, among these dozen stand remarks of enduring value. The first of the collection is known as his "Response to the Citizens of Albemarle," delivered on February 12, 1790. Jefferson lived in the county of Albemarle, Virginia, most of his life. In these brief words to his constituents, offered a few months after his return from a five-year absence in Europe and on the eve of assuming his duties as secretary of state, Jefferson thanked the people of Albemarle for their support for his political and diplomatic career. He referred to their affection as "the source of my purest happiness" and, with an endearing humbleness, spoke of his own "feeble and obscure exertions in their service." As in most of his other speeches, he celebrated the joys of the American experiment in democracy. "It rests now with ourselves alone to enjoy in peace and concord the blessings of self-government, so long denied to mankind," he said, "to show by example the sufficiency of human reason for the care of human affairs and that the will of the majority, the Natural law of every society, is the only sure guardian of the rights of man."

Over a decade later, on March 4, 1801, President Jefferson gave his first Inaugural Address, generally considered his most masterful speech. It was the first presidential inaugural in Washington, and the event attracted a crowd in the Senate chamber. Reportedly Jefferson's voice—within a few minutes husky and inarticulate—barely carried to the first rows in the chamber; all but a few of the spectators remained unaware of what the new president had said until they read the newspaper accounts. (The full text was printed in the *National Intelligencer* newspaper in Washington.) Though the delivery may have been characteristically muted, the text was strong and classic Jefferson: thoughtful, precise, elegant in style, and admired widely by those who read it. His purpose was to heal a nation still struggling for identity and plagued by bitter political disputes between merchant and farmer, rich and poor, northerner and southerner, federalist and republican. Jefferson observed that "every difference of opinion is not a difference of principle" and declared in a spirit of conciliation, "We are all republicans; we are all federalists." His words meant to be a soothing balm, he further urged, "Let us restore to social intercourse that harmony and affection without which liberty and even life itself are but dreary things." He went so far as to offer an olive branch to the monarchical Federalists, whom he privately despised. "If there be any among us who would wish to dissolve this Union or to change its republican form," he said, "let them stand undisturbed as monuments of the safety with which error of opinion may be tolerated where reason is left free to combat it." His idealism shone brightly in a passage, often quoted, about the purposes of government. He advocated "a wise and frugal government, which shall restrain men from injuring one another, which shall leave them otherwise free to regulate their own pursuits of industry and improvement, and shall not take from the mouth of labor the bread it has earned." That his professed beliefs in minority rights and freedom of the individual were denied by his own practice of slavery remained an uncomfortable contradiction in an otherwise brilliant exposition.

Although his first Inaugural Address was a success, in content if not in oration, Jefferson declined to appear before the Congress to present his first and subsequent annual messages, though he did deliver his second Inaugural Address. This practice was embraced by his successors until Woodrow Wilson in 1913. Jefferson explained to the Congress in a letter that his absence was for the "convenience of the Legislature": members would not have to spend their time preparing a formal reply (as was the custom) but could move directly to committee considerations of his proposals. Beneath this explanation, however, one suspects other reasons for his decision. The president was keenly aware that his proficiencies in oral advocacy left something to be desired; further, he knew that, unlike his conciliatory first Inaugural, his first message dealt with specific budgetary and policy issues sure to provoke sharp outcries from Federalist opponents. He believed it better to be away when the fireworks began. His proposals to repeal internal taxes and to reform the judiciary (and therefore weaken the hold of the Federalist party over the courts) did indeed lead to an immediate donnybrook in the Congress that the president presciently avoided.

Among his other statements to Congress, his Second Inaugural and his third, sixth, and eighth messages are often viewed as the most important, though all pale in contrast to the First Inaugural. A quorum of neither the Senate nor the House bothered even to attend the Second Inaugural—a discourse on taxes, Indians, and (a favorite theme for most presidents) the unfairness of the press. Perhaps salons had concluded that Jefferson was a man to be read in the *National Intelligencer*, not listened to in a crowded Senate chamber with poor acoustics. As he had done four years earlier, Jefferson again spoke in a voice so low that few could hear his words—none of which was as lofty and lasting as those in his First Inaugural.

While the president's second message to Congress appeared to some as a thin wafer without much substance (a "lullaby," said Alexander Hamilton, for it ignored the growing French threat in Louisiana), the third, delivered on October 1803, was vintage Jefferson: a low-keyed marshaling of evidence in support of the treaty to purchase Louisiana, replete with facts and figures as if a committee report. The treaty was approved in the Senate by a margin larger than anticipated: twenty-four to seven votes. His fourth and fifth messages fluctuated between benign neglect and truculence toward various machinations in Europe; with the sixth, delivered in December 1806, he spelled out more directly steps he had taken to protect the United States from foreign threats and domestic insurrections, namely, the designs of Aaron Burr, whom he never mentioned by name though he made clear that the government intended to suppress "the criminal attempts of private individuals to decide for their country the question of peace or war." The Burr conspiracy was the subject of a special message Jefferson sent to Congress in January of 1807. Though successful in its attempt to calm legislators alarmed by this threat and impressive in its description of measures that had been taken to stop Burr, historians have criticized Jefferson's message for its prejudgment of the "principal actor" as guilty "beyond question" before all the evidence was presented and consequently making a martyr out of Burr. Another special message a month later on the need for more gunboats addressed in a practical manner the dangers of war from abroad (Jefferson's subsequent seventh message to Congress was sharply anti-British); and the president's eighth, farewell message in November 1808 spoke eloquently—if morosely—of his continuing concern for the safety of the nation from "powerful enemies" abroad who had "overspread the ocean with danger."

Though Jefferson may have prejudged Burr, in another of his more notable addresses, "To Elias Shipman and Others, A Committee of the Merchants of New Haven" in July 1801, the president went to great lengths to avoid the prejudgment of an appointment to the position of collector in the district of New Haven. Jefferson dismissed complaints that the man was seventy-seven years old, urging his distractors to remember that Benjamin Franklin had not been young either and to let the new collector be "tried without being prejudged." This address also contains a moving, persuasive argument defending Jefferson's right to remove late appointees made by the Federalists who held no loyalty to the new president, especially since the Federalist party had kept others out of appointive office for so long; henceforth, however, Jefferson hoped that "the only questions concerning a candidate shall be, is he honest? Is he capable? Is he faithful to the Constitution?" The speech exhibits a fine display of the rhetorical question; indeed, the key section contains seventeen sentences, ten of which are rhetorical questions.

The list of Jefferson's dozen noteworthy speeches is completed with two brief statements, one to the Danbury Baptist Association of Connecticut in 1802 and a final appearance in 1809 before his constituents of Albemarle County at the end of his remarkable career. The Danbury statement, though short, remains celebrated as a reflection of the president's staunch secularism. His observation that a "wall of separation" had been properly established between church and state was widely viewed by minority religious groups as a defense of their right to exist without interference from federal or local governments. For the Danbury Baptists and others, Jefferson stood as a shining champion of religious freedom. In his last address, Jefferson, graceful and gracious in retirement, told his Albemarle neighbors and friends that he was happy to exchange "the pomp, the turmoil, the bustle and splendor of office" for the "tranquil and irresponsible occupations of private life." Here was a man honored to have served but happy to be home.

Worthy of separate comment are Jefferson's Indian addresses, twenty-six speeches he made as president to Indian audiences. The purpose of these speeches was to try to build better relations with, in Jefferson's phrase, the "aboriginal inhabitants." Though the Indians were inclined to use a rich, florid style of public speaking, Jefferson stuck to his own belief in simple, clear statements free of metaphor and ceremony. The speeches are serious but friendly. To today's audience, though, they seem acutely condescending, as the Great White Father of the federal government tutored his "children" on how to behave properly. ("You and all red men are my children" said Jefferson in a meeting with one tribe on December 30, 1806.) As with the black man so with the red man, Jefferson's cherished principles of liberty and equality were preached more than they were practiced.

In sum, Thomas Jefferson—one of the greatest presidents despite his failure to carry democracy to some minorities—has to be judged as one of the more lackluster public speakers. At least this must be the verdict if the yardstick is ability to stir and persuade a large audience. His voice was too soft and unreliable to raise the rafters or even provoke rapt attention in the third row. This measure, though, is only one index of speaking ability. If instead one were to select such criteria as skill in small group settings, lasting value of the text, or acumen in adapting the message to the audience (as displayed in the Danbury speech), then Jefferson moves closer to the front of the class. Though no Woodrow Wilson in forensic skill, Jefferson's brilliance as a writer, his charm and intelligence in small groups, and his admirable integrity as a public official make him nonetheless an American orator whose timeless texts and effectiveness over a long career cannot be dismissed.

INFORMATION SOURCES

Research Collections and Collected Speeches

Jefferson's few speeches have been gathered in various collections. The several biographies on Jefferson also contain references to his speeches, as do the newspapers of Jefferson's era (especially the *National Intelligencer*) and some of his letters.

The Papers of Thomas Jefferson. 16 vols. Princeton, N.J.: Princeton University Press, 1961. — *PTJ*

Thomas Jefferson. Edited by Merrill D. Peterson. New York: Library of America, 1984. — *TJ*

The Writings of Thomas Jefferson. Washington, D.C.: Thomas Jefferson Memorial Association, 1905. — *WTJ*

Selected Critical Studies

Berman, Eleanor Davidson, and E. C. McClintock, Jr. "Thomas Jefferson and Rhetoric." *Quarterly Journal of Speech* 33 (1947): 1–8.
Hendrix, J. A. "Presidential Addresses to Congress: Woodrow Wilson and the Jeffersonian Tradition." *Southern Speech Journal* 31 (1966): 285–94.
Hillbruner, Anthony. "Word and Deed: Jefferson's Addresses to the Indians." *Speech Monographs* 30 (1963): 328–34.
Young, James Sterling. *The Washington Community: 1800–1828*. New York: Columbia University Press, 1966.

Selected Biographies

Bowers, Claude. *Jefferson in Power*. Boston: Houghton Mifflin, 1936.

Brodie, Fawn. *Thomas Jefferson: An Intimate History*. New York: Norton, 1974.

Chinard, Gilbert. *Thomas Jefferson: The Apostle of Americanism*. Boston: Little, Brown, 1929.

Malone, Dumas. *Jefferson the President*. 2 vols. Boston: Little, Brown, 1970, 1974.

————. *The Sage of Monticello*. Boston: Little, Brown, 1981.

Randall, Henry S. *The Life of Thomas Jefferson*. New York: Derby and Jackson, 1858.

Russell, Phillips. *Jefferson: Champion of the Free Mind*. New York: Dodd, Mead, 1956.

CHRONOLOGY OF MAJOR SPEECHES

See "Research Collections and Collected Speeches" for source codes.

"Response to the Citizens of Albemarle," Albemarle County, Virginia, February 12, 1790; *TJ*, p. 491; *PTJ*, pp. 178–79.

First Inaugural Address, Washington, D.C., March 4, 1801; *TJ*, pp. 492–96; *WTJ*, 3: 317–24.

"Address to Elias Shipman and Others. A Committee of the Merchants of New Haven," New Haven, Connecticut, July 12, 1801; *TJ*, pp. 497–500; *WTJ*, 10: 268–73.

First Annual Message, Washington, D.C., December 8, 1801; *TJ*, pp. 501–09; *WTJ*, 3: 327–40.

"Address to Messrs. Nehemiah Dodge and Others, A Committee of the Danbury Baptist Association," Danbury, Connecticut, January 1, 1802; *TJ*, p. 510; *WTJ*, 16: 281–82.

Third Annual Message, Washington, D.C., October 17, 1803; *TJ*, pp. 511–17; *WTJ*, 3: 351–60.

Second Inaugural Address, Washington, D.C., March 4, 1805; *TJ*, pp. 518–23; *WTJ*, 3: 375–83.

Sixth Annual Message, Washington, D.C., December 2, 1806; *TJ*, pp. 524–531; *WTJ*, 3: 414–26.

Special message on the Burr conspiracy, Washington, D.C., January 22, 1807; *TJ*, pp. 532–38; *WTJ*, 3: 427–37.

Special message on gunboats, Washington, D.C., February 10, 1807; *TJ*, pp. 539–42; *WTJ*, 3: 439–43.

Eighth Annual Message, Washington, D.C., November 8, 1808; *TJ*, pp. 543–49; *WTJ*, 3: 475–86.

"Remarks to the Inhabitants of Albemarle County, Virginia," April 3, 1809; *TJ*, p. 550; *WTJ*, 12: 269–70.

LUCIUS Q. C. LAMAR
(1825–1893), lawyer, politician, jurist

_____ WILLIAM LASSER

In the constantly changing career of Lucius Quintus Cincinnatus Lamar, perhaps the only constant was his tremendous skill at oratory. Born into a wealthy slaveholding family in Georgia in 1825, Lamar first came to prominence as a firebreathing advocate of states' rights and defender of southern interests, qualities that led to his election to Congress from his adopted state of Mississippi in 1857. Lamar's first stint in Congress enhanced his reputation as an uncompromising radical, and, after the election of Lincoln to the presidency in 1860, he resigned his congressional seat and returned to Mississippi. He had a distinguished career during the Civil War as a soldier and diplomat, though his service was interrupted by attacks of apoplexy. Lamar suffered personally and professionally from the South's defeat. At the end of the war, his personal prospects were bleak; he was disenfranchised and disqualified from public office; he felt disgraced and discredited in the eyes of his fellow citizens; and, as one of their leaders, he felt personally responsible for their defeat and sufferings.

Lamar's fortunes soon took an upward swing, however. In 1872 he was once again elected to the House, and he successfully petitioned Congress to have his disqualification removed. He immediately captured the attention and admiration of the national public with a moving eulogy of Charles Sumner, the Massachusetts abolitionist leader. He played an active role in the negotiations that led to the Compromise of 1877 (which ended Reconstruction) and was elected to the Senate in 1876, where his oratorical skills were especially well displayed and where his national reputation continued to increase. He was named secretary of the interior by President Grover Cleveland in 1885 and was appointed as an associate justice of the U.S. Supreme Court in 1887. He served on the Court until his death in 1893 at the age of sixty-seven.

LUCIUS Q.C. LAMAR, ORATOR AS POLITICIAN

Any discussion of Lucius Q. C. Lamar's life and oratory must begin with his eulogy of Charles Sumner in April 1874. Sumner, perhaps more than any other man, represented the forces that had defeated the South and that had subjugated the region under the harsh rule of military reconstruction. Sumner had been a leader in the abolitionist movement, a founder of the Republican party, and a leading force among the Radical Republicans during Reconstruction. So hated had Sumner been among southerners that, after an antislavery speech in 1856, he had been attacked and nearly killed by Congressman Preston Brooks (D-South Carolina).

Lamar had been looking for an opportunity to make a peace overture to the North since his return to Congress in December 1873. Like many other southern conservatives, Lamar had accepted the outcome of the war and the destruction of slavery, but he desperately wanted an end to federal interference in southern affairs. The way to accomplish this result, he was convinced, was to educate the North about the true sentiments of the southern people. His biographer, Wirt Armistead Cate, quotes him as saying shortly before his election to Congress, "The two sections are estranged simply because each is ignorant of the inner mind of the other, and it is the policy of the party in power to keep up and exaggerate the mutual misunderstanding."

Before he could convince the northerners that the South was reconciled to its defeat and wished to leave the past behind it, however, he had to get their attention. What better way to do so than for an acknowledged southern radical to rise in the Senate for the purposes of eulogizing the man who was a virtual symbol of the sectional antagonism. Those in his audience who were not totally baffled by Lamar's decision to speak of Sumner probably expected at most a perfunctory, formal address, but Lamar delivered a stirring appeal to friendship and harmony between the sections.

The speech is brief and eloquent. Its success stems from its simplicity and its honesty. Lamar did not merely speak well of the dead out of respect for convention; instead, he found in Sumner a quality that all people, northerners and southerners, could admire. That quality, Lamar said, was the "peculiar and strongly marked traits of his character which gave the coloring to the whole tenor of his singularly dramatic public career," traits that, Lamar admitted, "made him for a long period to a large portion of his countrymen the object of as deep and passionate a hostility as to another he was one of enthusiastic admiration."

Lamar set the tone of the Sumner eulogy at the beginning. "Strange as, looking back upon the past, the assertion may seem," he told a packed House chamber, "to-day Mississippi regrets the death of Charles Sumner, and sincerely unites in paying honors to his memory." Lamar's bold statement of this incongruous theme made it clear from the start that this was to be no ordinary address. In one sentence, Lamar made it apparent that a new age had dawned for relations between the two sections. If Mississippi could regret the death of Sumner, he seemed to be implying, it was time for the North and the South to reconsider their attitudes toward their former enemies.

The qualities that made Sumner a great man—and that made his death a source of sorrow even to the South—were precisely those qualities that had always made great men; they were neither northern virtues nor southern virtues but human virtues. Sumner possessed an "all-controlling love of freedom," a "moral sensibility keenly intense and vivid," a "conscientiousness which would never permit him to swerve by the breadth of a hair from what he pictured to himself as the path of duty." Combined in Sumner were "the characteristics which have in all ages given to religion her martyrs, and to patriotism her self-sacrificing heroes."

To such a man, Lamar said, slavery was "a wrong which no logic could justify." Lamar, of course, did not agree with Sumner's views on slavery, for, to Sumner, "It mattered not how humble" the slave was or "that he might be contented with his lot"; or that slavery gave the slave "more physical comfort" and "mental and moral elevation" than in his previous state; or that the "fathers of the republic" found slavery "too complicated to be broken up without danger to society itself." But just as Lamar could admire Sumner's disagreement over slavery, so also could Sumner condemn slavery without condemning the slave-holder: "here let me do this great man the justice which, amid the excitement of the struggle between the sections—now past—I may have been disposed to deny him," Lamar said. "In this fiery zeal, and this earnest warfare against the wrong, as he viewed it, there entered no enduring personal animosity toward the men whose lot it was to be born to the system which he denounced." Lamar's willingness to deal with the slavery question—his refusal to gloss over the issue— helped give the speech its honest and straightforward quality. His treatment of the conflict over slavery as a mere difference of opinion, now settled, helped set the tone of reconciliation and forgiveness that marks the whole speech.

Both northerners and southerners could learn from Sumner's "spirit of mag-naminity," expressed in gracious gestures toward the South in his last years. Sumner proposed amnesty for the leaders of the South, for example, and called for a congressional resolution forbidding the members of the U.S. Army from wearing battle decorations earned in the war against their fellow citizens. Lamar would go even further, however. Just as he dealt forthrightly with the question of slavery, so he would deal the same way with the question of battle decorations. Instead of putting their medals away, "both sections should gather up the glories won by each section; not envious, but proud of each other, and regard them as a common heritage of American valor." The soldiers' bravery, like Sumner's moral convictions, should become the common property of all Americans.

Lamar's eulogy of Sumner was not an abstract appeal to general principles but a deeply personal statement concerning Lamar and Sumner that reached out to all other Americans who wanted to look toward the future instead of the past. "Charles Sumner, in life, believed that all occasion for strife and distrust between the North and the South had passed away, and that there no longer remained any cause for continued estrangement between those two sections of the country. Are there not many of us who believe the same thing? Is not that the common sentiment—or if it not, ought it not to be—of the great mass of people, North and South?" Northerners and southerners, Lamar concluded, were one people, with common feelings, attitudes, and heritage, a link perhaps symbolized by the bond between Lamar in life and Sumner in death: "Shall we not now at last endeavor to grow toward each other once more in heart, as we are already indissolubly linked to each other in fortunes?" If Sumner could speak from the grave, Lamar declared, he would say, "My countrymen! *know* one another, and you will *love* one another."

The Sumner speech caused an immediate sensation and catapulted Lamar to national prominence. "My God, what a speech," said Congressman Lymon Tremaine. "It will ring through the country." The speech was widely circulated and reprinted and drew praise across the country, though some southern papers responded negatively. "It was a bold, brave, eloquent appeal to the old fraternal feelings between the Northern and Southern people," wrote the *Richmond Enquirer*. "How quickly L.Q.C. Lamar has become famous—famous above all American orators and statesmen!" said the *Memphis Appeal*. More important, the speech was seen as a major catalyst for reconciliation between the two sections. Said the *Springfield* (Massachusetts) *Republican*: "When such a Southerner of Southerners as Mr. Lamar, of Mississippi, stands up . . . to pronounce a generous and tender eulogy upon Charles Sumner . . . it must begin to dawn upon even the most inveterate rebel haters in Congress, and the press, that the war is indeed over, and that universal amnesty is in order." The speech was "an evidence of the real restoration of the Union in the South," observed the *Boston Globe*, and would "certainly attract much attention in Europe."

Lamar's address set in motion the events that would lead, within three years, to the end of Reconstruction and to the removal of federal troops from the South. Lamar's speech on Sumner had a profound impact on both his own career and on the shape of sectional relations in the postwar era. He immediately became a leader in the House of Representatives and played a major role in exposing election irregularities in Louisiana, a scandal with connections to the Grant White House. Lamar used the Louisiana controversy to make a plea for an end to federal occupation of the South. "The Southern people . . . fully recognize the fact that every claim to the right of secession from this Union is extinguished," he conceded. "They believe that the institution of slavery, with all its incidents and affinities, is dead." But, he reminded the North, the people of the South had "borne unprecedented indignities, wrongs, oppressions, and tortures," and should be treated with compassion and respect.

The Democratic party, buoyed by the scandal, swept to a dramatic and overwhelming victory in the 1874 midterm elections and gained control of the House for the first time since 1857. Between December 1874 and March 1875, while Republicans maintained a lame-duck majority, Lamar worked to defeat the force bill, which would have strengthened the president's hand in dealing with the southern states, and the civil rights bill. The force bill came up for consideration in the House only seven days before the end of the congressional session, and Democrats pulled out every delaying tactic in their bag of parliamentary tricks. Lamar convinced Speaker James Blaine to work for the defeat of the bill, and Blaine suggested to Lamar that the Democrats request a reading of the minutes of the preceding day, including the names of every representative on every roll call vote. To do so would have taken hours, and in the end consideration of the force bill was postponed. By the time the measure reached the Senate, it was too late, and the bill was killed.

The democratic ascendancy in the House allowed Lamar to take his place among the leadership of that body. He removed himself from the race for Speaker (fearing, he told a friend, that his close association with the secessionist movement would be a problem for his party) and was unanimously elected chairman of the Democratic caucus. Lamar's most important service in the House was his participation on the commission that investigated the election of 1876 and produced the Compromise of 1877, ending northern occupation of the South.

Lamar made numerous speeches during his four years in the House. In the main, they reflect the major themes of his Sumner eulogy. Over and over, Lamar stressed the necessity for home rule in the South, the need for understanding and compassion between the two sections, and the willingness of the South to accept its defeat and the consequent demise of slavery. Frequently Lamar used the technique of reporting his own hopes and aspirations as if they were already true. In his first speech to the Democratic caucus, for example, he declared, "Apprehension and distrust of one part of the nation that the portion of the Southern people who were arrayed against the authority of the Federal Government in the late war would be an element of disturbance to the American Union, has mainly disappeared. In its place was "a more fraternal feeling, which regards us of the Southern States as fellow-citizens of the same great nation." At the end of a speech on the centennial of American independence, Lamar declared somewhat incongruously that "the alienation hitherto existing between the two sections of the Union" no longer existed, since "if each of the two sections could be brought to see and understand the inward feeling and inspiration of the other the real fact would be developed that at no period since the inauguration of Mr. Jefferson have the entire body of the American people been animated by such a universal and common sentiment in favor of harmony and fraternal union"—this after the bitterly contested election of 1876.

Lamar went on to give many speeches in the Senate. Among the most important were a speech on the silver question in 1878 and a speech on the alleged causes for the exodus of southern Negroes to the North. Throughout his congressional career, as Donald Streeter argues, Lamar continued to draw on the three major themes: "that the war was completely and unalterably over; that through understanding of each other's problems the North and South would reunite in fraternalism; and that the welfare of the South was dependent on the progress and prosperity of the nation." By continual repetition of these themes, Lamar built up his own reputation as a thoughtful, level-headed moderate. He made repeated references to his own speech on Sumner, thus drawing upon that reputation and turning it to rhetorical advantage. Once he had established his own reputation, he frequently strengthened his speeches through the use of ethical proof, pointing out to his audiences, for example, his personal concern with the problems of the South or his reluctance to enter into contentious debate.

The rhetorical qualities that marked Lamar's later speeches are also evident in the speeches he gave as a young man, before the Civil War; Lamar earned his reputation as a great orator long before his famous eulogy of Sumner. In fact, it was speech making that first opened the doors of the national political arena for Lamar. In 1851, at the age of twenty-six, Lamar (then a professor at the University of Mississippi) was asked on short notice to debate Senator H. S.

Foote on behalf of Jefferson Davis, Foote's opponent for the Senate (Davis's activities in the campaign were limited by poor health). The subject of the debate was to be the Compromise of 1850.

On the face of things, the experienced Senator Foote seemed to enjoy a great advantage over the young Lamar. The latter, as his son-in-law and biographer Edward Mayes wrote, "had had no practice in polemical discussions, and was without experience in practical politics." What Lamar did have, and would have at his advantage whenever he would rise to speak, were, according to Robert Oliver, the natural abilities of a gifted speaker: "a keenly analytical mind and an ability to state complex matters in appealingly simple terms." To make up for his lack of preparation time, Lamar had the benefit of being (as he would discover then and later) extraordinarily good at preparing quickly for a public address. Years later, Lamar reported, "I am the most habitual extemporaneous speaker that I have known. Whenever I get the opportunity I prepare my argument with great labor and thought . . . but my friends all tell me that my offhand speeches are by far more vivid than my prepared efforts." Often, as on the occasion of the debate at Oxford, Lamar drew upon his vast store of knowledge to prepare hastily a few notes and then embellish the speech as he went along. Later in his life, especially after 1873, Lamar seems to have devoted much more time and energy to preparing and memorizing his orations.

An exact transcript of Lamar's remarks in the debate with Foote is unavailable; all that is left are Lamar's notes for a brief part of his statement. Even from these few notes, however, Lamar's brilliance in debate shines through. He began by engaging the sympathy of his audience by presenting himself as an oratorical David against Foote's Goliath. "He [Lamar said of himself] felt keenly his own incompetency to encounter one who was so greatly his own superior in age, position, abilities, and experience," one who "is demolishing every one who meets him on the stump." Moreover, Foote could draw upon his senatorial experience and inside information: "he will tell you of his expectations, founded upon reports picked up during his pilgrimages to the North or gathered from his numerous correspondents, of whom the speaker [Lamar] never heard and of whom you know he has many, whose disclosures he publishes or keeps to himself, as shall best serve his purposes." Lamar, by contrast, could boast of no particular advantages. Still, forced as he was to appear on behalf of his state and his section (as he put it), he "did not consider himself at liberty to consult of his own reputation or interests." He would do the best he could.

The best that he could do was to cut the older man to pieces. The part of the speech that survives is an intensely personal attack on Foote in which Lamar skillfully identified his opponent with the North and with everything that was wrong with the Compromise of 1850. Lamar, conscripted as it were in defense of his homeland, cast Foote as the enemy of both Mississippi and the South. Foote had "Northern allies"; his "particular friends" were northern supporters of the Compromise like Clay, Cass, and Webster; he "has turned a somersault into the enemy camp, and now attempts to speak to his old friends in the delusion that he has taken the whole force prisoners of war." Foote's support of the Compromise of 1850 was more than bad policy; it was a repudiation of the express desires of the Mississippi legislature and a betrayal of Foote's own prior beliefs. "Even the Union men of this State shall be convinced that Mr. Foote is not the man whose leadership even they acknowledge . . . for the plain reason that his being a Union man to-day is no guaranty that he will not be a fire eater to-morrow, what he advises and promises to-day he will repudiate to-morrow, whom he hails as friends he will count as enemies to-morrow, whom he attacks as enemies to-day he will colleague with to-morrow."

It is ironic, in view of this first great speech, that Lamar's rise to greatness came about precisely because he changed his mind and, from being a fire-eating secessionist, became a staunch supporter of the Union. His apparent inconsistency, Lamar explained in the mid–1870s, was an illusion. "I am consistent in *purpose* and *principles*," he wrote to a friend, "though I have changed my relative position as to men and measures. This is true patriotism and statesmanship in my opinion. Consistency in your *end* and *aim*; variety, change, and adaptability in the use of your means." Whatever the validity of this argument as applied to Lamar's career, it is certainly valid as an explanation of the power and success of his oratory.

INFORMATION SOURCES

Collected Speeches

Edward Mayes. *Lucius Q.C. Lamar: His Life, Times, and Speeches, 1825–*   LQCL
    1893. Nashville, Tenn.: Publishing House of the Methodist Episcopal
    Church, South, 1896.

Selected Critical Studies

Dickey, Dallas C. "Lamar's Eulogy on Sumner: A Letter of Explanation." *Southern Speech Journal* 20 (1955): 316–22.
Streeter, Donald C. "The Major Public Addresses of Lucius Q. C. Lamar during the Period 1874 to 1890."*Speech Monographs* 16 (1949): 114–24.

Selected Biographies

Cate, Wirt Armistead. *Lucius Q. C. Lamar: Secession and Reunion*. Chapel Hill: University of North Carolina Press, 1935.
Oliver, Robert T. *History of Public Speaking in America*. Boston: Allyn and Bacon, 1965.
Paul, Arnold M. "Lucius Q. C. Lamar." In *The Justices of the United States Supreme Court 1789–1969: Their Lives and Major Opinions*. 4 vols. Edited by Fred L. Israel and Leon Friedman. New York: Chelsea House Publishers, 1969.

CHRONOLOGY OF MAJOR SPEECHES

See "Research Collections and Collected Speeches" for source codes.

Debate with Senator H. S. Foote, Oxford, Mississippi, November 1851; *LQCL*, pp. 51–54 (abstract).

Eulogy of Charles Sumner, Washington, D.C., April 28, 1874; *LQCL*, pp. 184–87.

Speech on the Louisiana contested election, Washington, D.C., June 8, 1874; *LQCL*, pp. 659–69.

Speech to the Democratic caucus, U.S. House of Representatives, Washington, D.C., December 4, 1875; *LQCL*, pp. 265–68.

Centennial celebration of American independence, U.S. House of Representatives, Washington, D.C., January 25, 1876; *LQCL*, pp. 670–74.

"On Paying Government Bonds in Silver," U.S. Senate, Washington, D.C., January 24, 1878; *LQCL*, pp. 701–18.

"Exodus of Negroes," U.S. Senate, Washington, D.C, June 14, 1880; *LQCL*, pp. 723–38.

ABRAHAM LINCOLN
(1809–1865), sixteenth president of the United States

WALDO W. BRADEN

In their estimates of American presidents, historians usually place Abraham Lincoln first on their lists. They commend the martyred leader for how he coped with the difficult and tragic years of the Civil War and provided leadership to the Union cause. Through his words and actions, he is the embodiment of the American experience and personifies what popular government means to persons everywhere who cherish freedom.

Born in a log cabin near Hodginville, Kentucky, February 12, 1809, Lincoln lived in that state until the age of seven, moved with his family in 1816 to southern Indiana (what is now Spencer County) and later to southeastern Illinois (1830). He was largely self-educated in blab schools for what "did not amount to one year." When he "came of age," he confessed that he "did not know much"; the "little advance" that he made he said "he picked up from time to time under the pressure of necessity." In 1830 Lincoln settled in New Salem, Illinois, where he worked at various jobs—doing day labor, tending a store and the post office, serving as a captain in the Black Hawk War, surveying, and representing the district in the state legislature for four terms. Here he learned his first lessons in politics and stump speaking. He also did further reading and study of grammar. From borrowed books he gained sufficient knowledge of Illinois law to be admitted to the bar (1836). In 1837 he resettled in Springfield, where he became a successful trial attorney practicing in the several counties of Eighth Circuit, as well as before the Supreme Court of Illinois. While he was in the Illinois legislature (1834–1841), he was recognized as a leader of the Illinois Whigs and was influential in moving the capital to Springfield from Vandalia. He served one term in the U.S. House of Representatives (1847–1849).

The speaking career of Lincoln falls into three phases. The first covers his early speaking through his two years in Washington. The second (1854–1860) was occupied primarily with political speaking in three state campaigns (1854, 1856, 1858) and his prepresidential campaigning (1859–1860). The third (1861–1865) embraced his presidential years.

LINCOLN, PRESIDENTIAL PERSUADER

The contemporaries of Lincoln never thought of him as an orator in the traditional sense, never associated with his speaking the word *eloquence*, and never put him in the same class as Daniel Webster, Edward Everett, and Charles Sumner. They were in agreement about his effectiveness as a stump speaker, a storyteller, a debater, and a courtroom pleader. Close observers often spoke of his sincerity and his great concern about making what he said understood by the plain people. Reporter Horace White of the *Chicago Tribune* wrote about Lincoln: "The successful speaker was he who could make himself best understood by the common people and in turn best understand them.'' The nearest that Lincoln ever came to recording his rhetorical goals is in his eulogy of Henry Clay, his beau ideal. Lincoln observed that Clay's speeches did not consist of

many fine specimens of eloquence . . . but rather of that deeply earnest and impassioned tone, and manner, which can proceed only from great sincerity and a thorough conviction, in the speaker of the justice and importance of his cause. This it is, that truly touches the chords of human sympathy; and those who heard Mr. Clay, never failed to be moved by it, or ever afterwards, forgot the impression. All his efforts were made for practical effect. He never spoke merely to be heard.

During the period from 1830 through 1849, the first phase of his rhetorical career, Lincoln mastered the art of political speaking in the give and take of several state campaigns. Following his return from Congress in 1849, for five years he abandoned politics and concentrated on his law practice. But in 1854, according to his own admission, ''the repeal of the Missouri Compromise aroused him as he had never been before.'' The issue brought out of Lincoln the mature political persuader.

For six crucial years, a record exists of at least 175 speeches that Lincoln delivered, most in central Illinois, and after 1858 his horizon included appearances in Iowa, Indiana, Ohio, Kansas, and Wisconsin, as well as New York City and in New England in February and March 1860. Previously a prominent Whig, Lincoln in 1856 became a leader in the young Republican party and helped to nurture it into a viable force in Illinois.

In contrast to his later reluctance to speak, these were years when Lincoln eagerly sought audiences and was always available to address rallies, no matter how rough the travel or primitive the accommodations. Becoming a one-issue man, he concentrated on his opposition to the spread of slavery in the territories and made Senator Stephen A. Douglas his principal target. Twice (1854, 1858) he failed to gain his primary objective, a seat in the U.S. Senate.

The high points in Lincoln's political speaking are five: (1) the Peoria speech, October 16, 1854; (2) the Bloomington speech (''the lost speech''), May 29, 1856; (3) the ''House Divided'' speech, Springfield, June 16, 1858; (4) the joint debates with Stephen A. Douglas in 1858; (5) and the Cooper Union Address, New York City, February 27, 1860.

Paul Angle, a lifelong student of Lincoln, pointed to the 1854 Peoria speech as Lincoln's first great speech. It is important because it presented for the first time Lincoln's constructive case against the spread of slavery. In this longest of his political speeches, Lincoln included the essence of what he would argue constantly for six years and culminate at Cooper Union in 1860.

By no means an accident or routine stump speech, it showed Lincoln's mastery of historical details, his comprehension of the vital issues, and his skill in argumentative analysis. To build his case against the spread of slavery in the territories, he traced the controversy from colonial times and suggested a trend toward extinction of the peculiar institution. Albert J. Beveridge, the biographer, wrote that "for weeks Lincoln had spent toilsome hours in the State Library, searching trustworthy histories, analyzing the Census, mastering the facts, reviewing the literature of the subject." He further refined his thinking through ghosting editorials for Whig newspapers. Twelve days before he had tried his ideas in a speech in Springfield, but only a newspaper report of the first effort survived. The anti-Nebraska supporters, including the first Illinois Republicans, wanted a campaign document on which to build the party. Lincoln gave it to them at Peoria. Today it is not exciting reading, but in 1854 it was most timely as a Republican pamphlet.

The Bloomington speech of 1856 (often referred to as "the lost speech") has been heralded as one of Lincoln's most emotional and moving. Forgetting his usual reserve, Lincoln, speaking extemporaneously, stirred the delegates to the anti-Nebraska Convention "to an uproar, applauding and cheering and stamping." William Herndon called it "the grand effort of this life . . . full of fire and energy and force." Admirers and reporters, says Benjamin Thomas, "listened transfixed"; consequently they dropped their pens and pencils and failed to take notes. The problem today with this speech is that no one knows what Lincoln said. Afterward, he made no attempt, as he did in other such cases, to reconstruct what he had said. Republican strategists perhaps thought that as a campaign document, the speech would have been disruptive among some elements of the new party. This convention sounded the death knell of the old Whig party and the beginnings of the Republican party in Illinois.

The "House Divided" speech of 1858 to the state Republican convention after he had been nominated to run against Douglas was Lincoln's most inflammatory and quoted statement prior to his election. This controversial, misinterpreted, and misunderstood political pronouncement became the focal point of Douglas in opposing Lincoln for the Senate and for the presidency. Southerners found it threatening and cause for talk of secession and war. Its strategy and content were shrewdly conceived. There can be no doubt that Lincoln weighed thoughtfully the possible implications of what he put into his manuscript. According to his personal secretaries, John Nicolay and John Hay, Lincoln "was at it off and on about one month. If a good idea struck him . . . he penciled it down on a small slip of paper and put it in his hat where he carried quite all of his plunder." Nicolay and Hay report that "every word of it was written, every sentence had been tested. . . . It was not an ordinary oration." Behind closed doors he read an early version to his partner and later to a dozen or so of his friends, including Jessie K. Dubois, James C. Conkling, and James H. Matheny. In spite of their counsel to the contrary, Lincoln remained determined to present it as he had written it.

The emphasis that they objected to and the passage most often quoted is found in the introduction:

A house divided against itself cannot stand.
I believe this government cannot endure, permanently half slave and half free.

I do not expect the Union to be dissolved—I do not expect the house to fall—but I do expect it will cease to be divided.

It will become all one thing, or all the other.

Either the opponents of slavery, will arrest the further spread of it, and place it where the public mind shall rest in the belief that it is in course of ultimate extinction; or its advocates will push it forward, till it shall become alike lawful in all the States, old as well as new—North as well as South.

According to Horace White, Lincoln read the speech from manuscript, "The only one I ever heard him deliver that way." "After the convention adjourned," White continues, "he [Lincoln] handed me his manuscript and asked me to read the proof of it at the office of the *Illinois State Journal* where it had already been put in type." Lincoln also stopped by the newspaper office to look "over the revised proofs." White recalls that Lincoln stressed that "he had taken a great deal of pains with his speech and that he wanted it to go before the people just as he had prepared it." Lincoln's eagerness to preserve a verbatim copy of the house divided pronouncement suggests that he was confident about his position and was aware of the firm line drawn between himself and Douglas. At many later occasions, Lincoln read to audiences from the printed version to leave no doubt what he had said—and still believed.

The debates with Douglas in their 1858 senatorial campaign became Lincoln's most publicized political speaking; they were not his best, but they were his most dramatic. Because he faced Douglas, a recognized national Democratic leader, Lincoln received coverage throughout the country, and his ideas were much quoted by Republican speakers. The canvass lasted from July through October with the two adversaries constantly on the stump. Lincoln delivered sixty-three speeches, covering 4,350 miles in thirty-nine of the hundred Illinois counties. Douglas exceeded his rival in numbers of appearances and miles traveled. Lincoln had originally planned to follow along after Douglas and to speak in the same towns where the senator had appeared. After a few weeks, the two agreed to share the same platforms in the seven remaining congressional districts where they had not appeared. (They had already spoken at Chicago and Springfield.) The speaking arrangements provided an opening speech of an hour, followed by an hour and a half speech by the opponent, and a concluding rebuttal by the first. They met at Ottawa (August 21), Freeport (August 27), Jonesboro (September 15), Charleston (September 18), Galesburg (October 7), Quincy (October 13), and Alton (October 15). The speeches were stenographically reported and published in full in Illinois newspapers and widely discussed throughout the country. They revealed little new ground and became tedious as the two men attempted to gain advantage. They opened the way to Lincoln's nomination in 1860 and demonstrated what Douglas meant when he said of Lincoln: "He is the strong man of his party—full of wit, facts, dates—and the best stump speaker, with his droll ways and dry jokes in the West."

When he spoke at Cooper Union in New York City on February 27, 1860,

Lincoln reached the climax of what he had been striving for for six years. It was at the moment that Lincoln brought to fruition what he was arguing in the Midwest. Aware of his chances at the Republican nomination, Lincoln saw in the invitation an opportunity to gain the respect of an important eastern audience.

But before going east, he spent weeks in the state library perusing *Elliot's Debates* and the *Congressional Globe* to marshal concrete evidence that indeed a majority of the founding fathers had expected the demise of slavery. Herndon reported, "It was constructed with view of accuracy of statement, simplicity of language, and unit of thought. . . . No former effort in the line of speech-making had cost Lincoln so much time and thought."

Many of the 1,500 listeners were curious about how the westerner, famous as a stump speaker and for droll humor, would match up against the dapper Douglas and the popular Seward. Lincoln developed his address in three parts. The first was a refutation of Douglas. Taking a statement of his rival—"Our fathers when they framed the Government under which we live, understood this question [slavery in the territories] just as well, and even better than we do now"—Lincoln, turning the tables on Douglas, demonstrated through a detailed analysis of their votes that a majority of the fathers favored the "prohibition of slavery" in the territories. The second part, "words of kindly admonition and protest," refuted the southern "charges." The concluding section ("a few words . . . to Republicans") was admonition to hold fast to their moral stand. In a striking passage, Lincoln reasserted his view on the wrongness of slavery:

If slavery is right, all words, acts, laws, and constitutions against it, are themselves wrong, and should be silenced, and swept away. If it is right, we cannot justly object to its nationality—its universality; if it is wrong, they cannot justly insist upon its extension—its enlargement. All they ask, we could readily grant, if we thought slavery right; all we ask, they could as readily grant, if they thought it wrong. Their thinking it right, and our thinking it wrong, is the precise fact upon which depends the whole controversy. Thinking it right, as they do, they are not to blame for desiring its full recognition, as being right; but, thinking it wrong, as we do, can we yield to them? Can we cast our votes with their view, and against our own? In view of our moral, social, and political responsibilities, can we do this?

A comparison of Lincoln's speaking before and after 1860 suggests that the Illinois stump speaker was not the same man who served as the wartime president. The prepresidential Lincoln sought audiences, was cooperative, energetic, and indefatigable, and made the best of rough stumping. It is true that he used much of the same material over and over, adapting it to a variety of situations, and spoke extemporaneously and sometimes impromptu. He showed no qualms about facing hostile opponents or reporters and enjoyed vigorous head-on confrontations. This was the Lincoln that Douglas declared to be the "best stump-speaker in the West."

After his nomination for the presidency, Lincoln altered his rhetorical strategy, became cautious about what he said, never again campaigned, and seldom advanced doctrinal points in a speech. Consistent with the customary practice of presidential candidates, he let surrogates speak for him in 1860 and refused to discuss personally the platform or to amplify what he had said on current issues. Repeatedly Lincoln reaffirmed his determination to remain silent. In a letter to Samuel Galloway on June 19, 1860, Lincoln wrote, "But, in my present position, when, by the lessons of the past, and the united voice of all discreet friends, I am neither [to] write or speak a word for the public." When urged to respond at a Republican rally at Springfield on August 8, 1860, he told the home folks that he had come "with no intention of making a speech. It has been my purpose, since I have been placed in my present position [the nomination], to make no speeches." In the words of J. G. Randall, he was enunciating "a continuance of the policy of silence, a prudent caution to avoid misrepresentation, a wish to make no mistake before taking further bearings, and a deferment of difficult public questions for appropriate and mature treatment in the coming inaugural."

Throughout his years in Washington, Lincoln continued his "prudent caution," generally limiting his public speeches to short, often impromptu remarks necessitated by the immediate occasions. As president, he delivered fewer than one hundred responses that may be called speeches, many fewer than two minutes in length; eighty of these were at the White House, in his office, a reception room, or from a window or balcony. Lincoln soon realized that his rhetoric must reflect the aura of his high office. As chief executive he soon learned that he no longer was speaking for himself or his party but for his administration and the nation as a whole. Such responsibility weighed heavily upon him and influenced his rhetorical choices. What he previously might have said casually to friends at Edwardsville or Peoria in the midst of the give and take of a stump speech became inappropriate and unwise, for the slightest slip or impropriety became grist for snide reporters and hostile editors who delighted in writing sensational stories and biting editorials.

Nevertheless Lincoln's reputation for eloquence rests upon the three formal presidential addresses: the First Inaugural (1861), the Gettysburg Address (1863), and the Second Inaugural (1865). These classics, well spaced throughout his tenure, were comparatively short, ranging from 267 to 3,700 words, thoughtfully and meticulously prepared, and delivered with manuscript in hand. Lincoln took pride in each of these ceremonial addresses.

In his First Inaugural (1861), in preparation over a month and carefully reviewed by trusted advisers Orville Browning and William Seward, Lincoln sought to answer questions that had impatiently been pressed upon him since his nomination. With little emotion and using a legalistic approach that seemed cold to some, Lincoln the lawyer responded to the impending crisis with tolerance and conciliation. Remaining true to his prepresidential pledges, he reaffirmed that he would abide strictly by the Constitution and the Republican platform, carry out the obligation of his oath of office, not disturb domestic institutions (slavery) within the states, and not force "obnoxious strangers among the people" in rebellion. He reasoned, "There needs to be no bloodshed or violence unless it be forced upon the national authority.'' But Lincoln showed no reticence about calling secession ''insurrectionary or revolutionary'' and about his determination to protect federal property. ''In your hands, my dissatisfied fellow-countrymen, not in mine, is the momentous issue of civil war. The government will not assail you. You can have no conflict without being yourselves the aggressors. You have no oath registered in heaven to destroy the government, while I shall have the most solemn one to 'preserve, protect, and defend' it.'' Thus he shut the door on compromise and shifted the onus of aggression to the seceders. With a wait-and-see attitude, the reluctant Lincoln begged for patience, expressing what J. B. Randall calls ''sentiment and affection.'' Some interpreted his mood as conciliatory and some indecisive, but southerners, well along in their plans to secede and to move against federal properties, denounced it as a declaration of war. Some saw it as a play for time to mobilize.

The Gettysburg Address was delivered November 19, 1863, at the dedication of the national cemetery. The invitation to the president to attend was an after-thought of the committee, many of whom were not confident that Lincoln could speak fittingly at a grave and solemn occasion. The committee invited Edward Everett, thought to be one of the most eloquent men of the time, to make the main presentation. This assignment to a secondary role caused Lincoln neither sensitivity nor rancor. Following Everett, who devoted two hours to his oration, spacious in its strivings to achieve a grandeur fitting the emotion of the scene, Lincoln humbly expressed his ''few appropriate remarks'' in two minutes or ten sentences of 267 words. Gilbert Highet called it ''a skillfully contrived speech'' that described the occasion, dedicated the place, and urged the living to preserve the Union. Another way to look at the organization is to notice the movement from birth (''a new nation conceived in Liberty''), death (''a final resting place''), and finally rebirth (''a new birth of freedom'').

Easy to memorize and recite, the address possesses what Elton Trueblood thought was a ''magnificent simplicity.'' The cadence of the King James version of the Bible and the stylistic devices of repetition, antithesis, and parallelism give a poetic quality, causing Carl Sandburg to call it ''the Great American Poem.'' In a rhetorical shift of focus, characteristic of Lincoln's rhetoric, the president minimized his own role and the formalities of the day: ''The world will little note, nor long remember what we say here, but can never forget what they [the brave men] did here.'' Sober and meditative in mood and word, Lincoln expressed contriteness, selflessness, and good taste—without oratorical flourish or pomposity. It was his way of giving full respect to ''these honored dead'' and to the freedom ideal. In 1863 in the midst of the Civil War, he, of course, was eager to make common ties more evident and more binding. Fully aware that the long, terrible war had weakened historical patriotic resolves, he wanted to dispel gloom and hopelessness and restore the enthusiasms of ''the fore-fathers.'' Rhetorically he sought words to lift and inspire, to exceed standard Fourth of July oratory or polished declamation like that of Edward Everett. What marks Lincoln as a superior speaker was that he had captured in ten sentences what Orton H. Carmichael has called "the comprehensive and perfect grasping of great ideas . . . in language that is condensed, crystalline and perfectly simple." In uttering these revered sentiments, he identified with the founding fathers, Patrick Henry, Thomas Jefferson, Daniel Webster, and his mentor Henry Clay. Furthermore he became consubstantial with freedom lovers throughout time.

Of the Second Inaugural, Carl Sandburg wrote, "Seldom had a President been so short-spoken about the issues of so grave an hour." In opening, the reelected president reflected humbleness, almost embarrassment about taking time for a second inaugural address, which was one of the shortest inaugurals (700 words) up until that time. He did not choose to wave the bloody shirt or brag about military successes, suggesting only that the "progress of our arms . . . [is] reasonably satisfactory and satisfactory to all." At a moment when total victory was at hand, Lincoln "ventured" "no predictions" about the future. The Second Inaugural, sometimes called "Lincoln's Sermon on the Mount," gave evidence of Lincoln's knowledge of and respect for the Bible, which he read regularly. It has fourteen references to the deity, three mentions of prayer, and four paraphrases of Scripture. In the heart of the address he said:

Each looked for an easier triumph, and as a result less fundamental and astounding. Both read the same bible and pray to the same God, and each invokes His aid against the other. It may seem strange that any men should dare to ask a just God's assistance in wringing their bread from the sweat of other men's faces, but let us judge not, that we be not judged. The prayers of both could not be answered.

Unlike his First inaugural, which offered a policy statement, the second Inaugural was philosophical and even theological in its message. Lincoln suggested that by the war, God was punishing the American people, both North and South, for the "offenses" of slavery. His theology of agony became explicit in the following passage:

The Almighty has His own purposes. "Woe unto the world because of offences! for it must needs be that offences come, but woe to that man by whom the offence cometh!" If we shall suppose that American slavery is one of those offences which, in the providence of God, must needs come, but which, having continued through His appointed time, He now wills to remove, and that He gives to both North and South, this terrible war, as the woe due to those by whom the offence came, shall we discern therein any departure from those divine attributes which the believers in a living God always ascribe to Him? Fondly do we hope, fervently do we pray, that this mighty scourge of war may speedily pass away. Yet, if God wills that it continue until all the wealth piled by the bondsman's two hundred and fifty years of unrequited toil shall be sunk, and until every drop of blood drawn with the lash shall be paid by another drawn with the sword, as was said three thousand years ago, so still it must be said, "the judgments of the Lord are true and righteous altogether."

The final paragraph, showing Lincoln's compassion and humanity, is the most famous passage of the speech: "With malice toward none; with charity for all;

with firmness in the right, as God gives us to see the right, let us strive on to finish the work we are in; to bind up the nation's wounds; to care for him who shall have borne the battle, and for his widow, and his orphan, to do all which may achieve and cherish a just, and a lasting peace, among ourselves and with all nations." Here he demonstrated his gift at finding simple language to express his profound thoughts. Lincoln said that he expected this utterance "to wear well, as perhaps better than anything" that he had "produced."

The orators of Lincoln's day, many of whom became almost folk heroes of their communities, attracted admirers by their elocutionary perfection: classical allusions, sweeping metaphors, rich, rotund voices, and grandiloquent manner. Not so with Lincoln; he did not strive to emulate these oratorical greats. He presented himself as a common man, as honest Abe Lincoln, as a friendly down-to-earth lawyer and friend with genuine sympathies for the common folk from whom he had come. He often talked about his simple beginnings and his humbleness. And winning the presidency did not make much difference in his rhetorical strategy. Once in Washington, he became more reserved and formal, and wearing his glasses, he read his important speeches. As early as 1842 he explained his basic appeals:

When the conduct of men is designed to be influenced, *persuasion*, kind, unassuming persuasion, should ever be adopted. It is an old and a true maxim, that a "drop of honey catches more flies than a gallon of gall." So with men. If you would win a man to your cause, *first* convince him that you are his sincere friend. Therein is a drop of honey that catches his heart, which, say what he will, is the great high road to his reason, and which, when once gained, you will find but little trouble in convincing his judgment of the justice of your cause, if indeed that cause really be a just one.

By training and physical endowment, Lincoln was limited in what he could achieve on the platform. His voice was described as thin, high pitched, shrill, "not musical," and even "disagreeable." Herndon remembered Lincoln's voice as "shrill-squeaking-piping, unpleasant. . . . As Mr. Lincoln proceeded further along with his oration . . . he gently and gradually warmed up—his . . . voice became harmonious, melodious-musical." Reporting the Cooper Union Address, the *New York Herald* (February 28, 1860) declared Lincoln's voice to be "sharp and powerful at times" with "a frequent tendency to dwindle into a shrill and unpleasant sound. His enunciation [was] slow and emphatic." But important to Lincoln, he could be heard at "the remotest edge of the vast assemblage." In contrast to the deep-voiced Douglas, who was bothered with hoarseness, Lincoln could speak day after day without strain or fatigue. At the end of a long canvass, he seemed as vigorous as ever. Horace White, who heard Lincoln many times, declared that he had an "accent and pronunciation peculiar" to his native state of Kentucky.

Lincoln found his forte in naturalness and simplicity—cogent argument, plain language, pithy, often amusing illustrations, and an unassuming delivery and composure. Cartoonists and journalists caricatured and lampooned him for rusticity and awkwardness, but his opponents found him a formidable adversary.

Perhaps the element of Lincoln's makeup that received the most comment was his gangling body of about 6 feet 4 inches with a weight of 180 pounds. In describing him, observers said that he was "not muscular," "wiry," "raw boned," "tall," "gaunt," "awkward," "ill proportioned," and "ungainly," and "ugly." John G. Nicolay, his private secretary, listed his characteristics as "a thin, but sinewy neck, rather long; long arms; large hands; chest thin and narrow as compared with his great height; legs of more than proportionate length and large feet." Probably his leanness was accentuated because his coat sleeves and pants were usually too short, and a stovepipe hat made him tower over his companions such as the Little Giant who was a foot shorter. Undoubtedly his height, slenderness, and clothing made Lincoln seem awkward, angular, and eccentric.

Youthful Carl Schurz who heard Lincoln during his debate with Douglas in 1858 pictured Lincoln at the hustings:

On his head he wore a somewhat battered "stovepipe" hat. His neck emerged, long and sinewy, from a white collar turned down over a thin black necktie. His lank ungainly body was clad in a rusty black dress coat with sleeves that should have been longer; but his arms appeared so long that the sleeves of a "store" coat could hardly be expected to cover them all the way down to the wrists. His black trousers, too, permitted a very full view of his large feet. On his left arm he carried a gray woolen shawl, which evidently served him for an overcoat in chilly weather. His left hand held a cotton umbrella . . . and also a black satchel that bore the marks of long and hard use.

At the Illinois hustings, Lincoln made his image a vital element in his campaign strategy. The "poor, lean lank face," the squeaky voice, the ill-fitting clothing, the shawl, and the battered carpetbag contributed to the Lincoln appeal and trustworthiness. The common folk regarded Honest Old Abe as a fellow traveler who identified with them and understood their problems. Therein was the drop of honey that won them to his cause. Lincoln relied heavily on that element of persuasion that the ancient rhetoricians called *ethos*; he demonstrated that he was a man of common sense, good moral character, and goodwill. The presidential Lincoln, reserved and dignified, under the burden of "the mighty scourge of war," found eloquent but familiar words and high thoughts to express his formal speeches, messages, and letters. What he produced, particularly at the Gettysburg and the Second Inaugural, surpassed all other presidential rhetoric and is recognized among the best addresses in the English language.

INFORMATION SOURCES

Research Collections and Collected Speeches

Lincolniana has enlisted many collectors, researchers, hobbyists, and writers in the search for every scrap of information about the Illinoisan. The Library of Congress has the largest holdings of Lincoln material. Fortunate for Lincoln scholars and researchers, the Lincoln letters and manuscripts have been published in the *Complete Works*, edited by Roy Basler. In addition, the Library of Congress also has the William H. Herndon Papers, which contain a large collection of recollections, the principal source of information about Lincoln's early life. For a selection of these, see Emanuel Hertz, *The Hidden Lincoln* (New York: Viking, 1938). In addition, Lincoln materials are found at the Illinois State Historical Library, Springfield; the Chicago Historical Society; Brown University, Providence, Rhode Island; Huntington Library, San Marino, California; Lincoln Memorial University, Harrogate, Tennessee; and the Louis A. Warren Lincoln Library and Museum, Fort Wayne, Indiana (publisher of *Lincoln Lore*, a monthly leaflet which has appeared since 1929).

American Public Address, 1740–1952. Edited by A. Craig Baird. New York: *APA*
McGraw-Hill, 1956.
Collected Works of Abraham Lincoln. Edited by Roy P. Basler. 14 vols.   *CW*
New Brunswick, N.J.: Rutgers, 1953.
Created Equal? The Complete Lincoln-Douglas Debates of 1858. Edited by   *CE*
Paul M. Angle. Chicago: University of Chicago Press, 1958.

Selected Critical Studies

Berry, Mildred F. "Abraham Lincoln: His Development in the Skills of the Platform."
In *A History and Criticism of American Public Address*. Edited by William Norwood Brigance. Vol. 2. New York: McGraw-Hill, 1943.
Leff, Michael, and G. P. Mohrmann. "Lincoln at Cooper Union, A Rhetorical Analysis of Text." *Quarterly Journal of Speech* 60 (1974): 346–58.
Nichols, Marie Hochmuth. "Lincoln's First Inaugural Address." In *Antislavery and Disunion, 1851–1861*. Edited by J. Jeffery Auer. New York: Harper & Row, 1963.

Selected Biographies

Herndon, William H., and Jesse W. Weik. *Herndon's Life of Lincoln*. Cleveland: World, 1942.
Neely, Mark E., Jr. *The Abraham Lincoln Encyclopedia*. New York: McGraw-Hill, 1982.
Nicolay, John G., and John Hay. *Abraham Lincoln: A History*. 10 vols. New York: Century, 1904.
Oates, Stephen B. *Abraham Lincoln: The Man behind the Myth*. New York: Harper, 1984.
Randall, J. G. *Lincoln: The President*. 3 vols. New York: Dodd, Mead, 1952.
Thomas, Benjamin P. *Abraham Lincoln*. New York: Knopf, 1952.

CHRONOLOGY OF MAJOR SPEECHES

See "Research Collections and Collected Speeches" for source codes.

Speech at Peoria, Illinois, October 16, 1854; *CW*, 2: 247–83.

"A House Divided," Springfield, Illinois, June 16, 1858; *CW*, 2: 461–69

Lincoln-Douglas debates of 1858; *CW*, 3: 1–325; CE.

Cooper Union address, New York, February 27, 1860; *CW*, 3: 522–50.

First Inaugural Address, Washington, D.C., March 4, 1861; *CW*, 4: 249–71; *APA*, pp. 107–14.

Gettysburg Address, Gettysburg, Pennsylvania, November 19, 1863; *CW*, 7: 17–23; *ABA*, p. 115.

Second Inaugural Address, Washington, D.C., March 4, 1865; *CW*, 8: 332–333; *APA*, pp. 116–17.

JAMES RUSSELL LOWELL
(1819–1891), man of letters and diplomat

THOMAS WORTHAM

James Russell Lowell won many honors and titles. Statesman, diplomat, scholar, poet, man of letters, and "a Lowell," he measured large in his contemporaries' eyes. Nor has the century since his death greatly diminished his significant place in the history of American culture. But the title of orator would have appeared to him a dubious distinction, even though much of his contemporary reputation depended on his decided ability as a public speaker, especially following his appointment in 1880 as U.S. minister to the Court of St. James. If later generations sometimes failed to see why their fathers ranked Lowell higher than his merits and acts (and, indeed, his own self-estimation) could justify, it was undoubtedly owing to the loss of his human presence, the immediacy of that "felicity of public and private speech," which his friend George William Curtis found one of his greatest and most appealing intellectual and artistic gifts.

LOWELL AS ORATOR ON POLITICS AND LITERATURE

Lowell always insisted on his dislike of public speaking, but this professed antipathy did little to discourage the scores of requests from committees in the United States and Great Britain, and more often than not he accepted their invitations and fulfilled his duties with grace and charm. His fatherly brag from London in 1882 to his daughter at home in Massachusetts was no great exaggeration: "As for me I continue to be the greatest orator in England (next to Mr. Gladstone) and might speak almost every day in the week if I were fool enough." Nor is that evident delight before the fact of his success either immodest or undeserved. Poor, shy, retiring Henry James was appalled at the strain Lowell's public appearances placed on the older man, and with good cause. Few events, at least of a literary nature, that occurred during Lowell's tenure in London failed to include a few words by the Honorable Mr. Lowell. Sometimes these were informal remarks made after dinner; other times, they were formal orations and public addresses.

Lowell's remarkable success as a public speaker during his diplomatic years should have come as no surprise. The two professions to which he was heir—those of law and the church—depended largely on skill in public speaking. For seven generations, Lowells had addressed their communities from the pulpit or before the bar. Lowell himself took a degree in law upon his graduation from Harvard in 1838, but he quickly found legal practice uncongenial to his temperament. He was lacking in those simple organizational skills that both law and business require, or, perhaps more accurately, he was too quickly bored by the tedium of any systematic conduct of action. Perhaps had his age and circle been one of more profound belief, he would have followed in his father's footsteps and entered the ministry. His passion for justice and veracious conduct was unmistakable, and his oratorial skills would have satisfied the most demanding of congregations; but in matters of dogma, he was at best a freethinker. Not until his Harvard appointment in 1855 as Smith Professor of Modern Languages did Lowell have what his practical neighbors in Cambridge would call a regular profession. Until that time he had made his way (greatly softened by the generosity and common roof of his father) by the pen, either editorially in behalf of certain reform causes of the day, especially the antislavery movement, or poetically in service of the Muse.

It was his resounding success as a lecturer on "The English Poets" before the Lowell Institute in Boston in 1855 that convinced the powers at Harvard to name him Longfellow's successor as Smith Professor. Lowell's practical training as an advocate for unpopular causes and his skill in the poet's craft provided him with remarkable resources for public and academic discourse. The lecture room—which often was the library study at Elmwood, his stately house in Cambridge to which he invited small classes of Harvard students—proved a convenient place to consider, both in theory and practice, the power of the spoken word to entertain and instruct. Barrett Wendell, himself later a distinguished Harvard professor, recalled Lowell's "conversational" style in the classroom: "Now and again some word or some passage would suggest to him a line of thought—sometimes very earnest, sometimes paradoxically comical—that it never would have suggested to any one else; and he would lean back in his chair, and talk away across country till he felt like stopping; or he would thrust his hands into the pockets of his rather shabby sack-coat, and pace the end of the room with his heavy laced boots, and look at nothing in particular, and discourse of things in general."

But a far greater oratorical success than that in the classroom was his performances after dinner during that period in Great Britain when he represented the United States. Here Lowell was in his imagined element, on equal footing with the men of letters and the statesmen, along with their ladies, who constituted intelligent society in London, a far cry from those green undergraduates who attended his words with awe and amusement at home. "Consummate tact and singular felicity, he spoke with a charm that seemed to disclose a new art of oratory," wrote George William Curtis who witnessed Lowell's after-dinner successes on many occasions. Lowell always "seemed to have the fitting word for every occasion, and to speak it with memorable distinction." Or as the august *London Times* remembered on the occasion of Lowell's centenary in 1919: "He delighted his hearers and often converted them, for he was really a great improviser; he nearly always conveyed the impression that he was not going to make a speech, but really had something to say."

Lowell would have been delighted at the praise, for it was an affirmation of his intentions. He once revealed—after dinner, of course—his formula for a successful speech: "I have my own theory as to what after-dinner speaking should be. I think it should be in the first place short; I think it should be light; and I think it should be both extemporaneous and contemporaneous. I think it should have the meaning of the moment in it, and nothing more.'' The formula worked like a charm. George Washington Smalley, European correspondent for the *New York Tribune*, recalled: "His speaking was like that of no other. Who else was there who could be amusing and instructive in the same breath, who could talk in parables, make the keenest wit do the work of sense and reason, and when he was called upon for a homily, make a story serve instead?'' Something of an actor-manque, Lowell was helped by a cultivated and naturally appealing voice, "deep and full, with vibrating tones''; "he understood,'' said Smalley, "how to take and sustain a note and not let it go.'' He avoided excessive gestures and the oratorial climaxes so much in vogue, but then he avoided most other things of common currency.

With the fatigue of years and routine, Lowell eventually grew weary at being called on to speak for his supper. He complained to his daughter: "The fact is I have talked so often after dinner that beside not knowing what to say, I can't remember what I may have said and am afraid of plagiarizing from my former self.'' Or to another: "There was a time when, after thinking over a subject rapidly, I could speak my ten minutes upon it unprompted by notes, with assurance that the right word would sometimes come at the right time. Now I must write down beforehand what I have to say and a speech loses half its effectiveness if it hobbles along with the staff of manuscript.'' His recall to the United States in 1885 when his party lost its control of the government brought to an end this ministerial duty that he had done so remarkably well and in the estimations of those whose opinions matter on such questions did much to repair friendly feelings between Great Britain and its former colony in North America.

Far better known to the general public than his informal remarks after dinner were Lowell's public addresses, though he was never so comfortable behind the dais as he was at the dinner table. As the spokesman for America, for the literature and culture of the New World, and as an accomplished poet and critic, Lowell was in constant demand at unveilings and memorial celebrations of those ideas and literary figures the two nations shared. His "Address on Unveiling the Bust of Fielding'' at Taunton in 1883, his speech made at Westminster Abbey in 1885 when a bust of Coleridge was dedicated, his address as president of the Wordsworth Society in 1884, some very learned and thoughtful "Notes'' he read on Don Quixote at the Workingmen's College in London in 1880, and, at home again in Massachusetts, his address on "Books and Libraries'' in 1885: these literary orations are masterful examples of popular criticism and effective public address. Lowell well understood that the first element of oratorial success "is undoubtedly the power of entertaining. If a man have anything to tell, the world cannot be expected to listen to him unless he have perfected himself in the best way of telling it.''

But it was on public issues that Lowell's oratorical skills were chiefly valued by his times. Most famous of his political addresses was the inaugural speech on assuming the presidency of the Birmingham and Midland Institute in October 1884, for which he selected as his topic democracy. Ferris Greenslet, one of

Lowell's early biographers, compared Lowell's address to that which his fellow American, Henry Ward Beecher, had given in Liverpool during the Civil War on the Union. Unlike the flamboyant and popular preacher, Lowell attempted no great "flights of oratory, no passionate periods; rather he presented the eternal ideals of democracy with a lucidity, a suggestiveness, and a secure conviction that gave his utterances the accent of finality." Lowell's defense of that form of government, which was then still largely identified with the American experiment, was befitting his office as U.S. ambassador to Great Britain. Wise and temperate, he avoided the empty phrases and uncritical encomiums of Fourth of July celebrations; still, neither his words nor his reputation left his auditors in any doubt as to the strenuousness of his Americanism. Frequently the speaker was self-effacing, and never did he avoid noting the pitfalls of a government owing its existence to universal suffrage. It was indeed the very reasonableness and restraint of his remarks, the simple modesty of his pretensions, that were most moving in his words in behalf of the democratic movement. His faith assured his audience that the particular was typical, the common universal. If, indeed, the democratic system had not already proved itself so largely successful in the United States, would its opponents in the Old World be so vexed as they were by "fears of its proving contagious."

Just as effective and, in its matter, as important as the Birmingham address was Lowell's speech several years later before the Reform Club of New York on "The Place of the Independent in Politics." Again, his proposals were on the surface modest, his manner easy and considered. But on this occasion his audience was American and largely sympathetic with his own views and prejudices. His criticisms were generally more pointed, and any defense of the American system's weaknesses was for the most part eschewed. And where the "Democracy" address was largely argued in general terms, his concern in this was with the practical workings of an imperfect government in an imperfect world. Here he called for action and participation, and for a generation of mugwumps and party radicals, Lowell's words and example were a measure of both the meaning and spirit of their political careers and thoughts.

Probably his political addresses read better than they were first heard, and it is clear Lowell wished them reread. But there can be no question that Lowell's personal manner and literary talent—along with his passionate belief that politics was too important a matter to leave to the politicians—helped redeem the arena of the political man in the eyes of the educated and refined in America during this age of the bosses and the "great unwashed."

They were sorry times—the "Age of the Great Mistake," Henry James afterward named it. What made the years most unbearable to men of Lowell's age and intellectual position was the memory of those foolish, forlorn dreams of a better, even perfect society, which was supposed to have had emerged following the bloodletting of the Civil War. Unlike the war against slavery, which could be waged with heroic valor, reformers of the 1870s increasingly had to work through committees and associations. Many gentlemen found themselves in the position of preferring no longer to participate in the government of an America Lowell called in a moment of despair "a Land of Broken Promises." But he did not retreat. His strict notion of patriotic duty, along with an inherited sense of individual rectitude and moral performance, led him to the public platform either as poet or orator.

It was the plain oratorical style of Demosthenes that Lowell respected in the political arena. The enormous danger of popular oratory was, for Lowell, the fact that "few men have any great amount of gathered wisdom, still fewer of extemporary, while there are unhappily many who have a large stock of accumulated phrases, and hold their parts of speech subject to immediate draft." This was in no way a uniquely nineteenth-century problem, but nineteenth-century man did become increasingly aware of its consequences. Typically, Ralph Waldo Emerson put it best: "The corruption of man is followed by the corruption of language." And if Emerson's meaning should be misunderstood, Parson Wilbur, Lowell's fictitious editor, interpreted it in practical terms in one of his "learned" commentaries to *The Biglow Papers* when he observed that "there are few assemblages for speech-making which do not deserve the title of *Parliamentum Indoctorum* [Congress of the Unlearned.]." This wise New Englander's explanation for this remarkable phenomenon is noteworthy for both its humorous originality and its important distinctions: "The two faculties of speech and of speech-making are wholly diverse in their natures. By the first we make ourselves intelligible, by the last unintelligible, to our fellows. It has not seldom occurred to me that Babel was the first Congress, the earliest mill erected for the manufacture of gabble."

Lowell knew that the aims of oration are practical and affective, that its object is not truth but persuasion, and that an orator was to be judged not so much by his printed discourses as by the memory of the effect he has produced. But too often that effect was won by the cheap appeal to prejudice and emotion, and this Lowell deplored. Democracy's greatest enemy was the demagogue, that individual "exceptionally adroit in using popular prejudice and bigotry to his purpose, exceptionally unscrupulous in appealing to those baser motives that turn a meeting of citizens into a mob of barbarians." Modern newspapers and magazines exacerbated the problem in their desire for sensation and crisis, forcing the writer "to strive for startling effects"; all that had been lost was "the simplicity of antique passion, the homeliness of antique pathos."

What Lowell in his comments on oratory reiterated was the necessity of wide knowledge and general culture; after these, balance and sanity, grace and wit naturally would follow. Edmund Burke, for instance, was in Lowell's opinion rescued from the usual doom of orators because of "his learning, his experience, his sagacity"; he could "distil political wisdom out of history because he had a profound consciousness of the soul that underlies and outlives events, and of the national character that gives them meaning and coherence." In addition, Burke possessed what Samuel Johnson had happily called a "generosity of 'communication.' "

Charles Fox and Burke in England, Fisher Ames and Daniel Webster in the United States: these were chief among the orators to whom Lowell was most attracted. But above them all was Abraham Lincoln, Lowell's "true democrat," whose genius was in assuming that a democracy can think. Never appealing to the vulgar sentiments, Lincoln put himself on a level with his audience, "not by going down to them, but only by taking it for granted that they had brains and would come up to a common ground of reason." This sympathy with those he addressed, that "certain tone of familiar dignity," was characteristic of all great orators, a quality not of style but of character:

There must be something essentially noble in an elective ruler who can descend to the level of confidential ease without forfeiting respect, something very manly in one who can break through the etiquette of his conventional rank and trust himself to the reason and intelligence of those who have elected him. No higher compliment was ever paid to a nation than the simple confidence, the fireside plainness, with which Mr. Lincoln always addresses himself to the reason of the American people.

Regarding Lincoln's oratorical style, Lowell's words are as valid today as they were in 1864 when they first appeared, and they are the confession by a lesser man of those ideals of character and art to which he most aspired: "In the earnest simplicity and unaffected Americanism of his own character" Lincoln possesses the

one art of oratory worth all the rest. He forgets himself so entirely in his object as to give his *I* the sympathetic and persuasive effect of *We* with the great body of his countrymen. Homely, dispassionate, showing all the rough-edged process of his thought as it goes along, yet arriving at his conclusions with an honest kind of every-day logic, he is so eminently our representative man, that, when he speaks, it seems as if the people were listening to their own thinking aloud. The dignity of his thought owes nothing to any ceremonial garb of words, but to the manly movement that comes of settled purpose and an energy of reason that knows not what rhetoric means. He has always addressed the intelligence of men, never their prejudice, their passion, or their ignorance.

INFORMATION SOURCES

Research Collections and Collected Speeches

Researchers of Lowell's rhetoric must rely on the printed texts of his addresses. Most of his public speeches and odes were collected by his friend and literary executor Charles Eliot Norton. Many of Lowell's Harvard lectures, along with newspaper accounts of other lectures and speeches, are preserved in the Lowell Collection in the Houghton Library, Harvard University, Cambridge, Massachusetts.

The Complete Writings of James Russell Lowell. Cambridge Edition. Edited   *CW*
    by Charles Eliot Norton. 16 vols. Boston: Houghton Mifflin, 1904.
Lectures on the English Poets. Cleveland: Rowfant Club, 1897.   *EP*

Selected Critical Studies

Curtis, George William. "James Russell Lowell." In *Orations and Addresses*. Edited
    by Charles Eliot Norton. 3 vols. New York: Harper & Brothers, 1894.
Mims, Edwin. "Lowell as a Citizen." *South Atlantic Quarterly* 1 (1902): 27–40.
Smalley, George W. "Mr. Lowell in England." *Harper's Monthly* 92 (1896): 788–801.
Tyson, Raymond W. "The Public Speaking of James Russell Lowell in England."
    Southern Speech Journal 28 (1962): 59–65.
Woodberry, George E. "Lowell's Addresses." In *Literary Memoirs of the Nineteenth
    Century*. New York: Harcourt, Brace, 1921.
Workman, Arvin LeRoy. "A Rhetorical Analysis of Selected Public Speeches of James
    Russell Lowell." Ph.D. dissertation, Michigan State University, 1965.

Selected Biographies

Duberman, Martin. *James Russell Lowell*. Boston: Houghton Mifflin, 1966.
Scudder, Horace Elisha. *James Russell Lowell: A Biography*. 2 vols. Boston: Houghton
    Mifflin, 1901.

CHRONOLOGY OF MAJOR SPEECHES AND PUBLIC POEMS

See "Research Collections and Collected Speeches" for source codes.

"The Lowell Lectures: The English Poets," Boston, 1855; *EP*.

"Democracy" inaugural address on assuming the presidency of the Birmingham and Midland Institute, Birmingham, England, October 6, 1884; *CW*, 7: 3–37.

"Books and Libraries," address at the opening of the Free Public Library, Chelsea, Massachusetts, December 22, 1885; *CW*, 7: 95–118.

"Harvard Anniversary," address delivered in Sanders Theatre, Cambridge, Massachusetts, on the two hundred fiftieth anniversary of the foundation of Harvard University, November 8, 1886; *CW*, 7: 167–215.

"The Place of the Independent in Politics," address delivered before the Reform Club of New York, Steinway Hall, New York, April 13, 1888; *CW*, 7: 233–68.

JAMES MADISON, JR.
(1751–1836), fourth president of the United States

_____ STEPHEN A. SMITH

Although James Madison served sixteen years in such powerful and highly visible national offices as secretary of state (1801–1809) and president (1809–1817), neither his revered reputation as a statesman nor his record as an important and persuasive communicator were earned in that capacity. In fact, Madison rated rather poorly as a platform orator in the traditional executive public speaking situation, but his temperament, training and tactical mastery of reasoned debate made him one of the more effective communicators in the history of American deliberative assemblies.

Madison was also elected to the Virginia House of Delegates/Constitutional Convention of 1776, to the Virginia Council of State (1778–1779), to the Continental Congress (1780–1783, 1787), again to the Virginia House of Delegates (1784–1786, 1799–1800), to the Annapolis Convention of 1786, to the Constitutional Convention of 1787, to the Virginia ratifying convention of 1788, to the U.S. Congress (1789–1797), and to the Virginia Constitutional Convention of 1829. In these forums, he made his major contributions to public policy and achieved his most lasting accomplishments as an orator.

Madison's place in history would have been earlier secured and no less important had he never held executive office. Because of the controversial Embargo Act, which marked his tenure as secretary of state and the inconclusive War of 1812 conducted during his presidency, historians such as Henry Adams called him dull and weak; however, Albert Gallatin thought him the most effective legislator in the history of Congress, and Thomas Jefferson, his confidant and collaborator, once referred to him as the greatest man in the world. His crucial roles in the Constitutional Convention of 1787 and the Virginia ratifying convention of 1788 earned him the appellation Father of the Constitution, and his leadership in the First Congress to produce the Bill of Rights did more to enhance his image in history and to secure contemporary freedoms than did any of his accomplishments as president.

JAMES MADISON AS ADVOCATE IN ASSEMBLIES

Madison was well prepared by his classical education to understand and advocate the political philosophy that marked his public career. He studied at Montpelier under the tutelage of Reverend Thomas Martin, a recent graduate of the College of New Jersey and the local Anglican rector, who was influential in Madison's decision to attend Princeton rather than the College of William and Mary in Williamsburg.

Arriving at Princeton during the summer of 1769, Madison quickly passed the freshman examinations. He was an early member of the American Whig Society, a patriotic literary and debating club, and with William Bradford, Samuel Stanhope Smith, John Henry, Henry Lee, John Blair Smith, Hugh Henry

Brackenridge, Gunning Bedford, Caleb Wallace, Philip Freneau, and other students destined for prominence in the early Republic, he participated in informal debates and discussions of political philosophy and the nature of governments. The intellectual spirit of the Scottish enlightenment permeated the Princeton curriculum, and Madison followed the standard course of study, which included rhetoric, logic, moral philosophy, mathematics, Greek, and Latin.

Finishing the bachelor's degree in two and one-half years, he continued another six months to study Hebrew and law with John Witherspoon, president of the College of New Jersey (Princeton). Witherspoon's teaching had a considerable influence on Madison's public career as a speaker and as a statesman. Besides requiring considerable reading in Hutcheson, Kames, Ferguson, Harrington, Locke, Montesquieu, Grotius, Pufendorf, and Vattel, Witherspoon demanded logical thinking and effective speaking. His students studied Watt's *Logick*, declaimed the works of Demosthenes and Cicero from the stage, and orally defended their senior theses syllogistically and forensically. Nevertheless, although Madison was persuasive in conversation and legislative debates through the force of his reasoned arguments, he never became a forceful platform speaker. His principal biographer, Irving Brant, suggested that Madison's weak voice and consequent diffidence inhibited his participation in the graduation declamations and his speaking in subsequent public situations until after his election to the Continental Congress. Whatever the reason for his reluctance regarding oratory, Madison always seemed to have followed Witherspoon's dictum: ''Ne'er do ye speak unless ye ha' something to say, and when ye are done, be sure and leave off.''

Madison considered careers in law and ministry, but he chose public service and was elected to the Orange County Committee on Safety in 1775. In 1776, at the age of twenty-five, he was elected to the Virginia House of Delegates, which framed the state's first constitution and Declaration of Rights. Madison did not participate actively in the debates, but he prevailed upon Patrick Henry to introduce and advocate his amendment to strengthen the religious freedom provision in George Mason's draft for a declaration of rights. Although only partially successful, having lost his attempt to prohibit state support for the Anglican church, Madison was pleased with what he did accomplish. Reflecting on his role as a delegate in his 1832 ''Autobiographical Notes,'' he wrote:

Being young & in the midst of distinguished and experienced members of the Convention he did not enter into its debates; tho' he occasionally suggested amendments, the most material of which was a change of the terms in which freedom of conscience was expressed in the proposed Declaration of Rights. This important and meritorious instrument was drawn by Geo. Mason, who had inadvertently adopted the word *toleration* on that subject. The change suggested and accepted substituted a phraseology which declared the freedom of conscience to be a *natural* and absolute right.

Despite his success in the convention, Madison was less successful in the 1777 campaign for the House of Delegates, his only electoral defeat and one that he attributed to his refusal to ply the voters of Orange with liquor. He was, however, elected by the house to the Council of State, serving during 1778–1779 under Governors Henry and Jefferson, and to the Continental Congress, serving from 1780 to 1783. Entering Congress at twenty-nine and being the youngest member, Madison did not speak during debates for six months, and his tenure there was personally frustrating and generally uneventful. Among his more notable legislative defeats was a proposal to establish a congressional library to aid the Congress in its research and debates. He worked with Jefferson to prepare a list of 307 titles covering all aspects of political philosophy, international law, concepts of government, and the published works on America, but Congress rejected the appropriation as being too expensive.

Madison returned to Virginia to resume his study of law, but in 1784 he was again elected to the House of Delegates where he began forging his reputation as a skillful debater and a philosopher of freedom. In 1784 he spoke persuasively to delay Patrick Henry's bill for taxation to support the Anglican church; in 1785 he anonymously authored the Memorial and Remonstrance against Religious Assessments, published by George Mason and credited with ending that campaign in Virginia; and in 1786 he secured enactment of the Virginia Statute for Religious Freedom, drafted and unsuccessfully proposed by Jefferson in 1779.

Madison served as a delegate to the Annapolis Convention of 1786 and was instrumental in organizing the states to call for and send delegates to the Federal Convention at Philadelphia in 1787. In addition to recording the most complete notes of the convention debates, Madison was the leading philosopher in that assembly. He spoke 161 times during those debates, and he proposed 31 of the 84 provisions found in the final draft of the Constitution. Perhaps his speech of June 6, 1787, on the nature of republican government is most representative of his learning and his influence in the convention. Gaillard Hunt, an early Madison biographer, drew on contemporaneous sources to reconstruct a description of his speaking style during the debates:

When he rose to speak he usually carried his hat in his hand, as though he had not intended to make a set speech. His thin voice was hardly audible when he began and often sank so that it failed to reach the reporter's desk. He gesticulated but little, and as he warmed with his argument his body swayed to and fro with a see-saw motion. . . . He usually carried notes of his speech, written on slips of paper in a microscopic hand, and they were a complete skeleton of his argument. He used simple and direct language without any ornamentation, and he engaged in no verbal flights. He spoke only for the purposes of explaining, defending, and convincing, and seemed indifferent to applause.

Delegate William Pierce of Georgia, commenting on Madison's role in the convention debates, wrote:

He blends together the profound politician with the scholar. In the management of every great question he evidently took the lead in the Convention, and tho' he cannot be called an Orator, he is a most agreeable, eloquent, and convincing Speaker. From a spirit of industry and application which he possesses in a most eminent degree, he always comes forward the best informed Man on any point in debate.

Madison's reasoning on behalf of the proposed Constitution was further developed as he joined with Alexander Hamilton and John Jay to write the Federalist essays, but the speech for which he is best known came during his service as a delegate to the Virginia ratifying convention. In response to Patrick Henry's vociferous attack on the perceived dangers of the proposed Constitution, Madison rose on June 6, 1788, and countered Henry on each objection. Defending both the document and his own style of debate, Madison said, "We ought not to address our arguments to the feelings and passions, but to those understandings and judgements which were selected by the people of this country to decide this great question by a calm and rational investigation. I hope that gentlemen, in displaying their abilities on this occasion, instead of giving opinions and making assertions, will condescend to prove and demonstrate, by a fair and regular discussion." Madison's reasoned eloquence prevailed over Henry's opposition, and Virginia ratified the Constitution, eighty-nine to seventy-nine.

Patrick Henry successfully blocked Madison's election to the first U.S. Senate; however, Madison was elected to the House in 1789 after a spirited but friendly campaign against James Monroe. On his way to take his seat, Madison stopped at Mount Vernon (becoming the first presidential ghostwriter) to provide Washington with a draft of an inaugural speech, much of which appeared in Washington's message delivered at Federal Hall in New York. Madison served in Congress until his voluntary retirement in 1797, after a successful tenure in which he secured passage of the Bill of Rights, encouraged foreign and domestic commerce, argued for friendly relations with France, and provided leadership for the emerging Republican party. At Jefferson's urging in 1791, Madison had prevailed on his former Princeton classmate, Philip Freneau, to begin publication of the *National Gazette*, and Madison's frequent essays in that journal expressed his own philosophy of government while also developing the parameters of his party's positions on public issues.

Madison returned to Virginia, and in 1798 he was once again elected to the House of Delegates at a propitious time. Working secretly with Vice-President Jefferson, he secured passage of the Virginia Resolution against the Alien and Sedition Acts, authored the assembly's "Address to the People" in 1799, and prevailed upon his friend George Nicholas to introduce the Kentucky Resolution in that state. Upon Jefferson's elevation to the presidency in 1801, he quickly named Madison to the foremost cabinet post, secretary of state, and Madison served a difficult eight years in that position, working to promote U.S. shipping interests while minimizing problems with Great Britain as a result of the Embargo Act.

Madison was the obvious choice to succeed Jefferson as president, and he easily defeated Charles Cotesworth Pinckney, 122 to 47, in the 1808 electoral college. His first Inaugural Address, delivered on March 4, 1809, was not noteworthy for delivery, and even the content has received varying assessments. Henry Adams, the historian most critical of Madison's career in all respects, disparaged the language, style, delivery, and content of the speech. He contended that few in the audience could hear Madison and suggested that Madison might not have wanted to be understood. Margaret Bayard Smith, a friend of the Madisons, wrote that Madison trembled and was inaudible during the first part of his speech, and Merrill Peterson thought the speech rather "commonplace." The text of Madison's speech, however, offers evidence to refute those who discount its eloquence or importance. He supported domestic commerce, both agricultural and industrial. He reaffirmed the wisdom of his commitment to personal liberties, extolled the policy preference for freedom of conscience, religion, and press, and supported "the diffusion of knowledge as the best aliment to true liberty." Madison reminded the nation "that without standing armies their liberty can never be in danger, nor with large ones safe." He defended the country's neutrality in foreign wars, saying, "It has been the true glory of the United States to cultivate peace by observing justice," and he reiterated his policy "to prefer in all cases amicable discussion and reasonable accommodation of differences to a decision of them by an appeal to arms." As essential and eloquent as these words were, they were equally ironic in view of subsequent events leading to war with Great Britain. In fact, Madison's Second Inaugural, delivered on March 4, 1813, was devoted exclusively to explaining the antecedents and justifying the conduct of "Mr. Madison's War."

Madison retired to Montpelier in 1817, was active in the Agricultural Society of Albemarle and the American Colonization Society, carried on an active correspondence regarding historical events, and succeeded Jefferson as rector of the University of Virginia in 1826. In 1829, he served as a delegate to the Virginia Constitutional Convention, being the only surviving member of those who adopted the first constitution in 1776 and this time joining with a group that included James Monroe, John Marshall, Philip Barbour, John Randolph, William Giles, and John Tyler to draft another. On December 2, 1829, Madison addressed the convention in his last public speech. When he rose to speak, the other delegates rushed to be close enough to hear, and Madison again offered his insightful thoughts on the nature of governments and the human spirit, specifically the relations between majorities and minorities in a democratic republic. In his remarks and memoranda on suffrage, he acknowledged the inherent problems in a slaveholding society, a theme that would occupy his attention for the rest of his life and that of the nation for the next three decades. In 1830, he wrote a rebuttal to Robert Hayne in the *North American Review*, and in 1834, in a document that was not made public until after his death on June 28, 1836, he wrote the short and sublime "Advice to My Country," pleading and exhorting for preservation of the Union.

Throughout Madison's public life, he was thoughtful and deliberate, always supporting his arguments with rational proofs and sound logic. Although he was acknowledged as foremost among the founders in his philosophical grounding and intellectual defense of democracy in a republican government, his reputation as an outstanding orator suffered by comparison with the style of many of his contemporaries. He lacked the volume, flair, and style of Patrick Henry, and Jefferson was far superior in reducing complex arguments to memorable epigrams. Nonetheless, he bested Henry in the most important debate of their careers, and he secured passage of the Virginia Statute for Religious Freedom where Jefferson had failed. John Marshall, a political foe who heard him often, observed that if eloquence were defined as the art of persuasion through reasoned argument, then Madison was the most eloquent speaker he had ever heard. For that reason, for his contribution to the architecture of the Constitution, and for securing passage of the Bill of Rights, Madison should be included among the nation's great speakers. His victories through persuasion provided subsequent generations with models of reason and opportunities for democratic debate of public issues.

INFORMATION SOURCES

Research Collections and Collected Speeches

The largest single collection of Madison's papers and correspondence, approximately 11,000 items, is in the Manuscript Division, Library of Congress. Additional official materials, related to his service in the Continental Congress, the U.S. House of Representatives, and as secretary of state, are held in the National Archives. Additional Madison manuscripts are located in approximately 250 public and private collections, most notably those of the Virginia State Library, Richmond, and the University of Virginia Library, Charlottesville, which also maintains a comprehensive index to Madison materials in other collections.

The Writings of James Madison. Edited by Gaillard Hunt. 9 vols. New York: WJM
    G. P. Putnam's Sons, 1900–1910.

The Papers of James Madison. Edited by William T. Hutchinson et al. 15   PJM
    vols. to date. Chicago and Charlottesville: University of Chicago
    Press and University Press of Virginia, 1962-.

Selected Critical Studies

Haselow, Adelaide. "A Rhetorical Study of James Madison." Master's thesis, Kent State
    University, 1950.

Moore, Wilbur E. "Analysis and Criticism of Madison as a Debater in the Virginia
    Federal Constitutional Convention." Master's thesis, University of Iowa, 1932.

———. "James Madison, the Speaker." *Quarterly Journal of Speech* 31 (1945): 155–
    62.

Selected Biographies

Brant, Irving. *James Madison.* 6 vols. Indianapolis: Bobbs-Merrill, 1941–1961.

Hunt, Gaillard. *The Life of James Madison.* New York: Doubleday, Page & Co., 1902.

Ketcham, Ralph. *James Madison: A Biography*. New York: Macmillan, 1971.
Peterson, Merrill D. *James Madison: A Biography in His Own Words*. New York: Newsweek Books, 1974.
Rutland, Robert A. *James Madison and the Search for Nationhood*. Washington, D.C.: Library of Congress, 1981.

CHRONOLOGY OF MAJOR SPEECHES

See "Research Collections and Collected Speeches" for source codes.

"On Republican Governments," Philadelphia, June 6, 1787; *WJM*, 3: 102–05.

"Necessity for the Constitution," Richmond, Virginia, June 6, 1788; *WJM*, 5: 123–37.

"Amendments to the Constitution," New York, June 8, 1789; *WJM*, 5: 370–95.

First Inaugural Address, Washington, D.C., March 4, 1809; *WJM*, 8: 47–50.

Second Inaugural Address, Washington, D.C., March 4, 1813; *WJM*, 8: 235–39.

"Governments and Interests," Richmond, Virginia, December 2, 1829; *WJM*, 9: 358–64.

GEORGE MASON
(1725–1792), Revolutionary and antifederalist

JAMES JASINSKI

Although George Mason had a tremendous effect on the course of events in early America, he managed to avoid the historical spotlight, and his place in American history is not widely recognized. Part of the reason scholars have neglected Mason is that much of his public service was at the local level. Since record keeping at that level was incomplete, few of Mason's speeches have survived. Mason's service to the local community was considerable. In the late 1740s and throughout the 1750s, he served as a justice of the peace for Fairfax County, Virginia, a vestryman of Truro parish, and, along with neighbor George Washington, was a trustee for the town of Alexandria, Virginia. Involvement in local affairs helped shape Mason's commitment to the principle that republican government requires an active and involved citizenry.

Through correspondence with such central figures as Washington and Richard Henry Lee, Mason helped establish the nonimportation, or boycott, movement of 1769–1770. Mason's first wife, the former Ann Eilbeck, died in 1773, and his grief, along with chronic poor health, caused him to withdraw from even local affairs. Yet the magnitude of events would not permit him to rest. As a member of a Fairfax County committee in 1774, Mason was principal author of the Fairfax Resolves, which proved to be a catalyst for establishing the Continental Congress. When the royal colonial government of Virginia collapsed in 1775, he accepted a call to represent Fairfax County in the Virginia conventions that acted as a provisional government. As a member of the fifth convention meeting in May and June 1776, he authored the original draft of Virginia's Declaration of Rights, a landmark document in republican political theory. During this same convention, Mason and Jefferson contributed substantially to the development of the Virginia Constitution. Mason continued to serve in the newly created Virginia House of Delegates from 1777 to 1781, helping to ensure the political stability that would make military victory possible. Despite this already distinguished career of public service, it was the constitutional period of 1787–1788 that thrust Mason into the national spotlight.

GEORGE MASON AS ANTIFEDERAL SPOKESMAN

Before recounting Mason's oratorical efforts as an antifederal spokesman, it is useful to uncover the antecedents of his rhetoric contained in a short address made to the Fairfax militia in April 1775. (Inadequate records make it impossible to give an exact date of the speech; Mason's editor, Robert Rutland, puts it between April 17 and 26.) His speech, "Remarks on Annual Elections for the Fairfax Independent Company," outlined principles that appeared in the Declaration of Rights and also served as the foundation for Mason's arguments in defense of antifederalism. Mason began by declaring, "No institution can long be preserved, but by frequent recurrence to those maxims on which it was formed.'' A republican society, Mason insisted, could survive only as long as the basic maxims or principles existed in the public's memory. The ''frequent recurrence'' to these principles, Mason seemed to imply, would necessitate the practice of rhetoric in public life, since rhetoric is a critical means of renewing the beliefs and values of society.

In ''Remarks,'' Mason identified several specific maxims as the guiding principles of republicanism. It is important to recognize these maxims since they would constitute the substance of Mason's rhetorical arguments. First, he maintained: ''We came equals into this world, and equals shall we go out of it. All men are by nature equally free and independent.'' Given this state of equality, he concluded that ''the most effectual means that human wisdom hath ever been able to devise'' for resolving political questions ''is frequent appealing to the body of the people, to those constituent members from whom authority originated, for their approbation or dissent.'' Mason invoked this maxim as a warrant for his argument supporting the annual election of militia officers. Mason recognized that there existed a counterargument, which maintained that longer tenure in office allowed officers to acquire ''a superior degree of military knowledge.'' While this kind of technical knowledge is valuable, it was no substitute for the public's need for ''an inexhaustible fund of experienced officers.'' Additionally, Mason developed what rhetorical theorist Chaim Perelman refers to as an ''argument of direction'' in claiming that long tenure for officers established ''a precedent which may prove fatal.'' Mason concluded: ''In all our associations; in all our agreements let us never lose sight of this fundamental maxim: that all power was originally lodged in, and consequently derived from, the people. We should wear it as a breastplate, and buckle it on as our armour.'' The stylistic flourish signals how important popular sovereignty was for Mason.

Mason wore this armour to the Philadelphia convention in May 1787. His orations at the convention reveal that his commitment to popular sovereignty functioned as the principle that warranted his arguments. In his remarks of July 6, 1787, ''A Clarification on the Prohibition against Money Bills from the Senate,'' for example, he urged the delegates to restrict the Senate's power over expenditures. ''Should the [Senate] . . . have the power of giving away the people's money they might soon forget the source from which they received it.'' This would mean that ''we might soon have an aristocracy.'' Although the Senate was important for national stability, it was also removed from the realm of public debate. This removal, Mason argued, restricted the Senate's ability to reflect popular sentiment and thus warranted limiting the Senate's role in fiscal affairs. He believed this was a critical subject in the convention's deliberations; in addition to the July 6 speech, he addressed this topic at least four more times in remarks delivered on August 8, 9, 13, and 15, 1787.

A second example of Mason's commitment to popular sovereignty occurs in remarks delivered on July 26, ''A Reexamination of the Selection and Tenure of the Chief Executive.'' Returning to a theme he emphasized in the 1775 ''Remarks'' to the Fairfax militia, Mason argued for the mandatory rotation of the chief executive. He contended that "the great officers of State, and particularly the Executive, should at fixed periods return to that mass from which they were at first taken, in order that they may feel and respect th[e] rights and interests" of the people. Mason's personal experience in public life led him to distrust professional politicians. Good intentions alone would not, he felt, keep legislators responsive to the people. This could be accomplished only through an institutional prescription requiring that officials step down at regular intervals and return to private life. Mason also revealed his commitment to popular sovereignty in his remarks of August 7, "In Opposition to Restraints upon the Right to Vote." In early America, it was a maxim that those with a stake in society were the only people entitled to the franchise. Typically the stake required property ownership, but Mason maintained this was unfair to those disenfranchised. His rhetorical task in the convention was to extend the idea of having a stake in, or permanent attachment to, society beyond the limitations of property qualifications. Mason accomplished this extension by advancing the franchise criterion that a person "give evidence of a common interest with the community." He reasoned analogically: parents have a strong attachment to or interest in their children although the children are not the parents' property; in similar fashion a citizen can have a strong bond with the community although the citizen is devoid of property. The final outcome in convention did not reflect the franchise extension as completely as Mason wanted, but he helped establish the principle that all who have a commitment to a republican society should be enfranchised.

Mason's speeches and remarks in the convention during May, June, and July were forceful, but he always remained open to reconciliation with opposing points of view. Toward the end of August, however, Mason's conciliatory temperament evaporated. He believed that the document emerging in the convention departed from true republican principles. It was not a republican constitution in the manner of Virginia's. In his remarks of August 29, "Southern Interests Would Be in Jeopardy If a Majority in Congress Regulated Trade," Mason revealed his growing disaffection. He implied that the commercial power given to Congress required southern states to "deliver themselves bound hand in foot to the Eastern states." The full scope of Mason's opposition is reflected in the often-quoted threat he made on August 31: "[I would] sooner chop off [my] right hand than put it to the Constitution as it now stands." From the end of August until the conclusion of the convention in mid-September, Mason, fellow Virginian Edmund Randolph, and Elbridge Gerry of Massachusetts worked feverishly to alter the direction of the convention. On September 12, Mason defended the necessity of prefacing the Constitution with a bill of rights and, on September 15, the desirability of holding a second convention to consider the changes and modifications proposed in the state ratifying conventions. The delegates rejected both proposals. Mason declined to sign the final product of the convention and left Philadelphia staunchly opposed to the proposed constitution.

Mason did not participate vigorously in the pamphlet and newspaper essay debate that followed the submission of the proposed Constitution to the states; the one exception was a brief list of objections originally composed for private circulation—Washington received a copy of the objections in early October, for example—published without Mason's permission and then widely reprinted. When the Virginia ratifying convention convened at Richmond in June 1788, however, Mason was ready to defend his antifederal principles and opposition to the Constitution. He articulated many of his central themes in two early addresses to the convention: "Taxing Power of Congress May Annihilate Us," delivered on June 4, and "Supporters of the Constitution Use Weak Arguments and Avoid the Question of Previous Amendments," delivered on June 11.

One theme Mason developed was the nature of representation secured by the Constitution. Mason maintained that the Constitution provided an insufficient number of representatives to satisfy the requirements of the American people. Representation was inadequate, Mason argued, because representatives under the Constitution could not "be acquainted with the situation" of the people since there was no mandatory rotation and the number of representatives provided would require large electoral districts. Mason captured this idea with the constant refrain that under the proposed Constitution, representatives would lack "fellow-feeling" with the people. It was direct knowledge of popular conditions rather than the "technical" knowledge possessed by so-called professional politicians that Mason found to be essential for republican representatives. Based on the principle that representatives, at minimum, must have "fellow-feeling" with the people, Mason introduced an antifederal version of the Revolutionary cry: no taxation without representation. He asserted, "The great object we wish to secure [is] that our people should be taxed by those who have a fellow-feeling for them."

In this argument, Mason creatively applied the Revolutionary maxim to the constitutional debate: taxation was improper if not established by truly republican representation. He built on this initial indictment by claiming that if representation was inadequate, then restrictions on the power granted to the national government were required. "No power ought to be given," Mason insisted, "but such as are absolutely necessary." Federalists argued that increasing the power of the central government would secure American prestige and thus result in the further protection of liberty. Mason responded: "Let us secure that liberty—that happiness first, and we shall then be respectable." In other words, he urged Americans to build their international reputation on the basis of real liberty rather than protecting liberty by becoming an international power.

Federalists also offered a pragmatic argument in favor of the Constitution: the new national government would consolidate the Revolutionary state debt and remove that burden from individual states. For Mason, this argument was nothing more than a legerdemain. He asked: "Will this system enable us to pay our debts and lessen our difficulties?" His sardonic response indicated how illegitimate the federalist claim was: "Perhaps the new government possesses some secret, some powerful means of turning everything to gold." Unless the federalists had solved the alchemists' dilemma, Mason insisted, the money to pay the debt would have to come from somewhere and that somewhere would be the individual states. His strategy in the convention, then, was to elaborate the "real" republican principles (such as the nature of representation) that the federalists failed to grasp, as well as to refute federalist arguments in support of the Constitution.

Despite the forceful oratory of Mason and fellow antifederalist Patrick Henry, Virginia became the tenth state to ratify the Constitution. The convention voted to adopt it eighty-nine to seventy-nine on June 25, 1788. Although Mason was defeated in his oratorical efforts at Philadelphia and Richmond, his career as an orator was not wholly unsuccessful. Although his oratory did not have the stylistic touch of Henry's, Mason developed significant arguments with enduring historical power. Perhaps his greatest accomplishment in Philadelphia was his argument to extend the franchise beyond property qualifications. His most creative argument was his application of the Revolutionary doctrine of taxation and representation to the political exigence faced by antifederalists. As many contemporary historians have noted, our understanding of history is sometimes distorted when the victors write history. Although the antifederalist movement was defeated in 1788, the principles they defended in their oratory have endured. In the antebellum South, Mason's attachment to local institutions was used to claim states' rights and thereby to defend slavery. Ironically Mason abhorred slavery though he kept slaves at Gunston Hall. As historians and political theorists recognize, however, antifederalism cannot be seen only in terms of one negative development it spawned—the prejudice and narrowmindedness commonly associated with the Old South. This analysis of Mason's oratory indicates some of the important themes of antifederalism that remain germane for contemporary political and rhetorical theory. Mason's insistence on the necessity of a popularly based form of republicanism did not aim simply to keep power in the hands of local politicians, as critics of antifederalism, then and now, charge. Rather, Mason was articulating a particular view of republicanism. His vision of popular participation as an essential element in a republican society and his belief, expressed in the Virginia Declaration of Rights, that the true republican principles are "justice, moderation, temperance, frugality, and virtue" are still pertinent. Public debate must be fostered and protected at every level of society and not restricted to a domain of great men if Mason's vision of republicanism is to be achieved. That vision of republicanism remains as important today as it was in 1786.

INFORMATION SOURCES

Research Collections and Collected Works

Researchers of Mason's political oratory and rhetoric can rely on the resources of the George Mason archive located in the refurbished ancestral home of Gunston Hall, Lorton,

Virginia. The archive houses the Mason family papers, which include the personal papers of George Mason. Additionally, the archive maintains valuable secondary sources, such as genealogical records and newspaper reproductions, which may be of use to students of Mason's rhetoric.

The Papers of George Mason. Edited by Robert A. Rutland. 3 vols. Chapel   PGM
      Hill: University of North Carolina Press, 1970.
Rowland, Kate Mason. *The Life and Correspondence of George Mason*. 2   LCGM
      vols. 1892; rpt., New York: Russell and Russell, 1964.

Selected Biographies

Hill, Helen, *George Mason: Constitutionalist*. Gloucester, Mass.: Peter Smith, 1966.
Rutland, Robert A. *George Mason: Reluctant Statesman*. Williamsburg, Va.: Colonial Williamsburg, 1961.

CHRONOLOGY OF MAJOR SPEECHES

See "Research Collections and Collected Speeches" for source codes.

"Remarks on Annual Elections for the Fairfax Independent Company," Fairfax County, Virginia, April 1775; *PGM*, 1: 229–32; *LCGM*, 1: 430–33.

"A Clarification on the Prohibition against Money Bills from the Senate," Philadelphia, July 6, 1787; *PGM*, 3: 921.

"A Reexamination of the Selection and Tenure of the Chief Executive," Philadelphia, July 26, 1787; *PGM*, 3: 931–32.

"In Opposition to Restraints upon the Right to Vote," Philadelphia, August 7, 1787; *PGM*, 3: 949–50.

"Southern Interests Would Be in Jeopardy If a Majority in Congress Regulated Trade," Philadelphia, August 29, 1787; *PGM*, 3: 972–73.

"Opposition to Constitution," Philadelphia, August 31, 1787; *PGM*, 3: 973–74.

"A Bill of Rights Should Preface the Constitution," Philadelphia, September 12, 1787; *PGM*, 3: 981.

"Another Federal Convention Is Necessary," Philadelphia, September 15, 1787; *PGM*, 3: 990–91.

"Taxing Power of Congress May Annihilate Us," Richmond, Virginia, June 4, 1788; *PGM*, 3: 1050–54.

"Supporters of the Constitution Use Weak Arguments and Avoid the Question of Previous Amendments," Richmond, Virginia, June 11, 1788; *PGM*, 3: 1059–68.

DWIGHT L. MOODY
(1837–1899), evangelist, humanitarian, educator

——————— RONALD E. SHIELDS, JANIS CAVES MCCAULEY, and JO BOLIN SHIELDS

A major figure in the history of American evangelism, Dwight Lyman Moody, although never ordained as a minister, transformed the revival tradition during the second half of the nineteenth century. Whereas his famous predecessor, Charles Finney, kindled revival first in the local church and then in the community, Moody took revival from the church to the realm of the hippodrome, arena, and large assembly hall, thereby bringing the gospel to nonbelievers. Evangelism was not new; however, Moody's systematized plans for urban revival created a sensation. In fact, on four separate occasions, he built temporary assembly halls in order to accommodate the crowds.

Moody possessed the business skills necessary for the efficient organization of mammoth urban revival meetings. Born on a small farm in East Northfield, Massachusetts, and reared as a Unitarian, Moody moved to Boston in 1854, where he was converted to Protestant evangelicalism. Then moving to Chicago in 1856, he became a successful shoe and boot salesman. After dedicating his life to Christian service in 1861, Moody worked with the local Young Men's Christian Association. There he learned of the organization's success in establishing city-wide services, organizing Bible study groups, distributing tracts, holding street evangelistic meetings, and caring for the needs of the poor. It was from this background that Moody emerged to present his evangelistic message to the urban populace enmeshed in the complex milieu of rapid social change, economic depression, and the social ills attendant to an industrialized society.

In his sermons, Moody avoided the rigid language of denominationalism; instead, his revival campaigns brought together those from all denominations under the banner of the simple gospel message. He fervently believed that sectarian doctrines served only to divide the Christian community. However, toward the end of his career, Moody embraced the doctrine of the premillennial Second Coming of Christ. Throughout his career, he stressed in his sermons the authority of the Scripture as the Word of God while deploring the encroaching evils of Darwinism and higher biblical criticism.

Within his meetings, Moody altered Finney's traditional use of the anxious seat in which sinners were counseled in front of the congregation. Continuing the practice of an open invitation at the end of each sermon, Moody instructed his ushers to direct those who came forward to inquiry rooms so that they could be counseled in a private setting. His revival themes and practices are still used in most urban revivals.

Although preaching that social ills could be eliminated only through the personal salvation of souls, Moody nonetheless worked through such agencies as the YMCA and temperance groups to minister to the physical needs of the deprived. Toward the end of his life, Moody believed that Christian education would serve to train future generations of evangelists. Conscious of his failure to reach the poor during his urban revivals, Moody hoped that graduates of

Christian schools would reach those sinners neglected during his campaigns. Thus he established the Bible Institute of Chicago in 1889, now known as the Moody Bible Institute, and two private academies in Northfield, Massachusetts: Northfield Seminary for Girls (1879) and Mount Hermon School for Boys (1891).

MOODY AS PULPIT ORATOR

Moody's sermons number around 400. Not collected in a standard edition, they are printed piecemeal in scores of works, many of which are out of print. Since the evangelist used most of them at least twenty times during his speaking career, it is difficult to establish authoritative textual versions of all but those few speeches that Moody himself eventually prepared for publication as devotional works. The sermons were taken down in a variety of versions by a variety of stenographers, who complained that Moody's rapid rate of delivery made their task difficult, if not impossible. When Moody preached one sermon twice in the same day to divided audiences, he varied it considerably, usually making the second effort more earnest and compressed than the first. All of these factors account for the tentative nature of any chronology of Moody's sermons.

"Heaven," the most often anthologized of Moody's sermons, was first preached at an "all-day meeting" of six hours' duration in Sunderland, England, on September 10, 1873, and repeated dozens of times in slightly altered versions over the next ten years in such cities as London and Manchester in England and Chicago, Philadelphia, New York, and Cleveland in the United States. Moody abandoned the customary mystical approach to the familiar topic of Last Things, preferring to handle divine mysteries in a direct, concrete fashion. In its commonsense approach to the reality of an afterlife and the prospects of eternal bliss for those who have been divinely redeemed, the sermon exemplified the way in which Moody's business training carried over into his career as a public speaker. All parts of "Heaven" were aimed at the one most important order of business: salvation for lost sinners by the grace of God. All adjuncts were submerged in this one theme. The tone of the work was sober and direct, at one with its purpose: to show people how to secure in this life a bargain that would benefit them for eternity. Moody's sermons, like his view of the Christian life, were practical, manly, and genial but intense. In a straightforward, businesslike manner, he talked sense to his listeners as he drove home his bargain.

In the opening phase of "Heaven," Moody established a conversational tone by directly addressing his audience: "If I were going to talk to you tonight about America, . . . '' Throughout the sermon, he continued to address the hearers directly with the familiar *you* and in the phrase "my friends" and to incorporate such conversational transitions as, "Why, my friends," and "Then, you know." He strengthened his relationship with the audience as his comrades by the use of topical allusions, tailored to each group, which underscored the speaker's bond of shared experiences with his audience. In the New York version of the speech, for example, he alluded to politicians Rutherford B. Hayes, Wheeler,

Samuel Tilden, and Hendricks and to a "great rich farmer in this State who gave his check for ten thousand dollars to the Christian Commission." Similarly, in Manchester, England, Moody drew the audience into the inner circle of his friends by sharing with them a conversation that he had had with one of the dignitaries who sat on the platform with him, the famed evangelist Henry Moorhouse: "Mr. Moorhouse was telling me . . . ."

"Heaven" was also typical of Moody's sermons in its incorporation of graphic illustrations and anecdotes drawn principally from the speaker's own experiences as an evangelist: "I remember how some of us were unable to find accommodation at the Great North-Western Hotel, in Liverpool"; "I once went out to California, hoping that God would give me a few souls on the Pacific Coast." These illustrations were so well applied as to become capital hits, never missing the mark Moody intended. In "Heaven," Moody employed sequences of questions and answers, as well as rhetorical questions, to achieve drama. He used a high degree of coordination in his sentence style. Of the 134 sentences in "Heaven," 38 were compound, most of them created by the coordinating conjunction *and*, which appeared 70 times in the Chicago version of the speech. As in most of his other speeches, Moody incorporated in "Heaven" a few minor ungrammatical colloquialisms, among them the misuse of *was* for *were* in a subjunctive mood construction—"If . . . I . . . was here." In another sentence, he used an adjective in a context that called for an adverb and created an illogical construction by incorporating a *what* clause: "God keeps His books altogether different from what they keep the church books." By contrast, the ending of "Heaven" might be considered one of Moody's purple passages, exemplary in its balanced clauses, graphic metaphors, and alliteration: "Give me the Christian whose heart is above the world, whose sails are filled with the gales of grace, and who, by the power of the Holy Spirit, sweeps through the stormy waters of life right up to the port of heaven."

On the night following his preaching of "Heaven," Moody usually delivered a sermon entitled "Hell," first presented December 14, 1874, in Manchester, England and repeated in the Philadelphia and New York campaigns of 1875–1876. The piece was unusual among his works, for he rarely referred to hell, preferring to dwell on the difficulties encountered by sinners in the present world as contrasted to the pleasures of Christianity that he had denied himself. Said one New York observer of Moody's audiences, "They go away from the Hippodrome brightened and sweetened." In this respect, Moody differed from Finney and other well-known revivalists who employed graphic, frightening depictions of the tortures to be endured by the damned. For the most part, Moody avoided the stimulation of such purely subjective sensations as fear. His aim was to convey the calm, quiet blessedness of the better world. Even his invitations to sinners included no frantic or passionate appeals. He fostered self-restraint, genuineness, and quiet devotion. Horatius Bonar, a Scottish Presbyterian minister and hymn writer, described the atmosphere of Moody's gatherings as one of "exceeding calmness at all times." He remarked, "I have not seen or heard any impropriety or extravagance. I have heard sound doctrine, sober, though sometimes fervent and tearful speech. . . . I have not witnessed anything sensational or repulsive." Rather than arousing fear, Moody often created scenes of pathos for his audiences.

According to an observer in New York, Moody's description of the deathbed of an unrepentant sinner in "Hell" evoked an emotional response: "A thrill of horror passed through the vast assemblage and tears rolled down many a furrowed cheek." Similarly, in London on March 14, 1875, after Moody used the illustration of a poor child's drowning in an attempt to procure driftwood from the river for his mother, "a most striking scene of weeping such as that hall had never seen before" ensued. In its organization, "Hell" was also typical of Moody's other sermons. It did not exemplify tight, logical developing argumentation. Based on the general subject of hell, it began with the citation of a scriptural passage, Luke 16:25, and proceeded to incorporate many other passages on the same general subject. Interwoven with illustrations and anecdotes were allusions to Caine, Judas, Satan, Eve, and Noah. Such a loose, associational structure produced tireless repetition of the simple theme: the human need for salvation by faith. In "Hell," in particular, Moody used the rhetorical device of repetition to good advantage, threading throughout the sermon the phrase, "Son, remember," from the passage with which he had begun his speech and varying in tone each reiteration just enough to prevent monotony.

Moody's contemporary critics suggested that by the 1876 New York campaign, the evangelist had tightened the organization of his sermons, making them pithier, more systematic, and much more powerful than they had been just a few months earlier in Brooklyn. In addition, he had slowed his rate of delivery from approximately 220 words per minute to approximately 180 during the same brief period. "Hell" offers many examples of Moody's use of vivid metaphoric language and drama: "Memory is God's officer, and when he shall touch these secret springs and say, 'Son, daughter, remember'—then tramp, tramp, tramp will come before us, in a long procession, all the sins we have ever committed." Moody's point of view was always one of positive assertion; he was not a philosophical disputant. He dealt with concrete facts and events, not theory. He did not address the opposition or attempt to refute the tenets of atheism or skepticism. Nor did he engage in theological debate concerning the fine points of eschatology. To have done so would have alienated his audience. He conveyed an air of absolute certainty concerning the truth of his simple gospel message. His fresh, direct approach in large part accounted for the degree to which his teachings were admired and accepted. "Hell" closes quietly with a rhetorical question, two imperative statements, and a sincere application of the message: "You can be saved if you will."

Another sermon greatly coveted by Moody's audiences wherever he went was "The Prophet Daniel," also first preached in Manchester in December 1874. Based on the first six chapters of the book of Daniel, it traced Daniel's career through the reigns of Nebuchadnezzar, Belshazzar, and Darius. Moody's major theme was that Daniel, a man loved by God, had mastered the art of saying no. In thus depicting Daniel, Moody satirized modern man's easy yielding to external pressures, pointing his remarks at the young men in his audience. The sermon was one of Moody's finest in its dramatic enactment and embellishment of biblical accounts. One Philadelphia reporter commented, "It is simply the Bible made alive!" Moody constructed "Daniel" to utilize his storytelling ability, filling it with invented dialogue and such extrabiblical characters as "modern professors of religion." Being powerfully realistic to Moody himself, the biblical story came alive for his audiences as well, for he made them part and parcel of it. He concluded the message with an account of Daniel's friends who refused to bow to idols and were cast into the fiery furnace, Shadrach, Meshach, and Abednego, to illustrate that "you can never do any real harm to a man who is one of God's obedient children." Moody closed the sermon with a call to action: "If we only had a few such Christians . . . I believe there would be ten thousand conversions in the next twenty-four hours."

Another Bible portrait, that of Zaccheus, was among Moody's most effective sermons. First delivered in London's Agricultural Hall on March 10, 1875, to an audience estimated at 20,000, it exemplified Moody's masterful blending of anecdote, illustration, scriptural allusion, dramatic enactment, pathos, and persuasion, as well as his sense of humor. Moody's purpose in "Zaccheus" was to convince his audience of the instant nature of true religious conversion. Quipped Moody, to his audience's great enjoyment, "Zaccheus was converted between the branches and the ground." Also to their delight, he created an extrabiblical meeting of Zaccheus with Bartimeus, who had recently had his sight restored. Then he called upon his audience to make restitution, in the manner of Zaccheus, to those they had wronged: "Then Christ will come into your home as he did into the home of Zaccheus. He not only blessed Zaccheus himself, but Zaccheus's wife, Mrs. Zaccheus, and all the little Zaccheuses too." In "Zaccheus" as in other sermons, Moody coupled humor with pathos to the intensification of both. According to one observer in London, "As the interest heightened and story after story was told, many could be seen wiping the tears openly, apparently unconscious of what they were doing." After his story of a "young man who was converted on his mother's grave," Moody appealed to his audience to turn to Jesus then and there.

The effect of these sermons and, indeed, of Moody's oratory in general, was described in one account as "a great smashing up of souls." Some sources estimated that the tangible result of Moody's preaching was around 1 million permanent conversions. Moody actually strove to prevent the working up of religious frenzy. If he felt the audience being swept away by emotion during the congregational singing that preceded his message, for example, he changed the song between stanzas or led in prayer. A source from Philadelphia reported, "Converts who would jump . . . into the pulpit, etc., had a plain speaking to." Moody was described by some as a general who firmly managed his audience, insisting that they seat themselves in the front of the hall, manipulating them in a "kindly but businesslike" manner. During the services, thousands of people sat "impressively still" for two hours or longer. They seemed to share Moody's sense of purpose and his desire for the spiritual awakening of the unconverted among them. Theirs was a participative, group aim, earnest and profound in nature. Moody fostered a spirit of prayer and a consciousness of God's presence among them. A Dubliner wrote, "A wave of prayer is continually going up to the throne from the Lord's people." Every part of the service contributed to the individual's sense of his own involvement in the meeting. Thirty minutes of prayer, congregational singing, and solos by baritone Ira Sankey established an informal, warm atmosphere. Moody would not tolerate long, tedious prayers. Once in a question-and-answer session he suggested that a person engaged in a lengthy, vague prayer should be cut short by the ringing of a bell. Wrote one Brooklyn reporter, "He opens a meeting as though his audience were the stock-holders of a bank to whom he was about to make a report. He has the air of a businessman to whom time is extremely valuable."

Although he was always master of his audience, Moody was not by technical standards a masterful speaker. He was said, for example, to stammer badly early in his career, but he worked to attain clear, distinct enunciation as he matured. His voice was not melodious or great in range, but it could be clearly heard and easily understood. His Massachusetts regionalisms included clipped pronunci-ations of certain words and the elision of internal syllables. Thus Moody pro-nounced *Daniel* as "Dan'l" and *Samuel* as "Sam'l." Among Moody's strengths as a speaker were his vigor and stamina. Addressing up to thirty-four meetings in a single week, he was adept at conserving his energy. His sturdy, wholesome appearance and his equable temperament were assets to his delivery as well. At the height of his career Moody was capable of establishing rapport with all social groups. Having the equivalent of a fifth-grade education, he nonetheless drew most of his audience from the ranks of the middle and upper classes (and this to his chagrin, for he desired to reach the poor and unchurched instead). The few gestures that he used were restrained. His plain language and homely sen-tences underscored the simplicity of his gospel message. His delivery was, like the tone of his sermons, a reflection of his own deep, earnest faith. In short, Moody's natural manner, sense of conviction, and compassionate tone more than compensated for his lack of eloquence.

Dwight L. Moody's major contribution to American religious life was the shaping of a fully systematized pattern of urban revivalism. By using such promotional techniques of the efficient businessman as detailed advance planning, trained personal workers, and an extensive budget, he attempted to eliminate social ills, restore national confidence, smooth denominational and theological schisms, and bring sinners to a personal affirmation of faith in a loving God.

Although lacking formal education, Moody constructed sermons that incor-porated poignant narrative and homely illustrations designed to establish rapport and elicit a strong response from the audience. His carefully orchestrated services included the popular hymns and simple gospel songs of Ira Sankey. Although the eternal results of these campaigns cannot be measured, Moody's external innovations in the design of revival services and his promotion of premillennial doctrine as a catalyst for world evangelism shaped the future efforts of such revivalists as Billy Sunday and, in our own time, Billy Graham.

INFORMATION SOURCES

Research Collections and Collected Speeches

The institutions closest to Moody in his lifetime serve as the major repositories for primary documents describing his rhetoric as an evangelist and educator. The Historical Collection and Archives of the Moody Bible Institute Library, Chicago, is the largest and most important body of primary materials. It includes newspaper clippings, letters and papers of the Moody family and several of their associates, and documents describing the history of the institute. Mount Hermon School, Northfield, Massachusetts, holds a significant smaller collection in the Moody Museum located at the rear of the Moody birthplace. Of interest to oratorical researchers are the following: Moody's study Bible; family letters and photographs; professional correspondence; sermon notes by D. L. Moody, Henry Ward Beecher, and Henry Drummond; and collected clippings and cartoons concerning Moody's various campaigns. Also the Mount Hermon Library contains file boxes of printed and manuscript documents tracing the history of Moody's schools in Northfield.

Goodspeed, Edgar Johnson. *A Full History of the Wonderful Career of*   *AFH*
    Moody and Sankey in Great Britain and America. 1876; rpt., New
    York: AMS Press, 1973.
Moody, Dwight L. *Dwight L. Moody. Great Pulpit Masters.*Vol. 1. New   *GPM*
    York: Fleming H. Revell Company, 1949.
————. *The Gospel Awakening: Sermons and Addresses.* Chicago: Fleming   *TGA*
    H. Revell Company, 1877.
————. *Thou Fool! And Eleven Other Sermons Never Before Published.*   *TFA*
    New York: Christian Herald, 1911.
————. *Moody His Words, Work, and Workers.* Edited by D. W. Daniels.   *MHW*
    New York: Nelson and Phillips, 1877.

Selected Critical Studies

Huber, Robert B. "Dwight L. Moody." In *A History and Criticism of American Public
    Address.* Edited by Marie Kathryn Hochmuth. New York: Longmans, Green,
    1955.
————. "Dwight L. Moody: Master of Audience Psychology." *Southern Speech Journal*
    17 (1952): 265–71.
Quimby, Rollin W. "How D. L. Moody Held Attention." *Quarterly Journal of Speech*
    43 (1957): 278–83.
————. "The Western Campaigns of Dwight L. Moody." *Western Speech* 18 (1954):
    83–90.
Shields, Jo Bolin. "Jonathan Edwards and Dwight L. Moody: New Awakenings." Paper

presented at the Fall Conference on Rhetoric and Public Address, Clarksville, Tennessee, 1981.

Weisberger, Bernard A. "Evangelists to the Machine Age." *American Heritage* 6 (1955): 20–23, 100–101.

Selected Biographies

Bradford, Gamaliel. *D. L. Moody: A Worker in Souls*. New York: George H. Doran, 1927.

Curtis, Richard K. *They Called Him Mr. Moody*. Garden City, N.Y.: Doubleday, 1962.

Daniels, W. H. *D. L. Moody and His Work*. Hartford, Conn.: American Publishing, 1875.

Findlay, James F. *Dwight L. Moody: American Evangelist 1837–1899*. Chicago: University of Chicago Press, 1969.

Fry, August F. "D. L. Moody: the Formative Years, 1856–1873." B.D. thesis, Chicago Theological Seminary, 1955.

Moody, Paul D. *My Father: An Intimate Portrait of Dwight Moody*. Boston: Little, Brown, 1938.

Moody, William R. *D. L. Moody*. New York: Macmillan, 1930.

Muser, Joe. *Moody!* With Bill Rodgers, Moody Bible Institute in association with Quadrus Media Ministry, 1986.

Pollock, John C. *Moody: A Biographical Portrait of the Pacesetter in Modern Mass Evangelism*. New York: Macmillan, 1963.

CHRONOLOGY OF MAJOR SPEECHES

See "Research Collections and Collected Speeches" for source codes.

"Heaven," Sunderland, England, September 10, 1873; *TGA*, pp. 264–73; *GPM*, pp. 207–20.

"The Prophet Daniel," Manchester, England, December 1874; *MHW*, pp. 65–90; *TGA*, pp. 576–88.

"Hell," Manchester, England, December 1874; *MHW*, pp. 457–66.

"Zaccheus," London, England, March 10, 1875; *MHW*, pp. 247–49.

"The Blood," New York, February 7, 1876; *AFH*, pp. 479–503; *TGA*, pp. 247–63; *GPM*, pp. 125–52.

"Thou Fool!" Boston, February 25, 1897; *TFA*, pp. 11–30.

JAMES OTIS
(1725–1783), colonial leader and lawyer

———————————————————————————— MICHAEL RICCARDS

Long after the American War of Independence, John Adams wrote to Thomas Jefferson, "What do we mean by the Revolution? The war? That was no part of the Revolution. It was only an effect and consequence of it. The Revolution was in the minds of the people, and this was effected, from 1760 to 1775, in the course of fifteen years before a drop of blood was drawn at Lexington." During most of that seminal period, one of the major patriot leaders was James Otis, a Boston lawyer, who helped crystallize opposition to British taxation policies. From 1760 to 1770, Otis achieved a popular prominence in the colonies that was probably matched only by Patrick Henry.

Otis's role in the patriot movement though, is more complicated than Henry's, and his active participation ceased before the Revolution began in earnest. Some of his greatest speeches have come down to posterity in fragments; his major political works remain neglected; his biographers are often confused by his changes of mind and sentiment. Part of the problem in identifying his lasting contribution is that Otis exhibited symptoms of mental imbalance that curtailed his political activities and took away from the genuine brilliance of his intellect. Yet his supporters and detractors agree that he was a superb orator and a persistent and dedicated organizer.

OTIS AS PATRIOT AND PLEADER

As a young man, Otis was a fine scholar who wrote on Latin and Greek prosody and published a volume on the first topic and circulated a manuscript on the second. He worked for his father as a commercial agent and lawyer and was made advocate general of the Vice-Admiralty Court in Boston. Otis tried to persuade the royal authorities to appoint his father chief justice of the superior court, but that office went instead to Thomas Hutchinson. Otis's enemies later argued that his opposition to the Crown's policies in general, and to Hutchinson in particular, was due to this slight. They quoted Otis as having threatened that if his father were denied the justice position, he would "set the province in a flame, tho' he perished in the attempt." Otis denied the accuracy of the quotation, but when Hutchinson took office, he resigned the advocate general post.

Otis claimed that the real issue he was protesting was the decision of the British ministry to crack down on violations of the dormant Molasses Act of 1733. In order to tighten up on lax enforcement of the act, the royal governor, Francis Bernard, pressed for the use of peremptory search warrants, called writs of assistance. These general writs, which had been rarely used in the British New World, granted to customs officials the right to search for contraband items without the permission of the owner. The superior court in Massachusetts was not convinced of the legality of these writs in the colony, and the previous chief justice, Stephen Sewall, had expressed great doubts about their use. Thus the appointment to the court of Thomas Hutchinson, Otis's prime enemy, took on important political as well as personal overtones.

Boston merchants protested the proposed harsh enforcement of these writs, and they decided to retain the younger Otis and a colleague, Oxenbridge Thacher, to oppose the law and challenge in court the issuing of such instruments. Before the superior court, headed now by Chief Justice Hutchinson, Otis gave a four-hour speech that would make his reputation as an orator and early leader of the patriot cause. For posterity, his fame is linked to his opposition to the writs of assistance, and to his contemporaries, his contribution was to lay very early the philosophical basis for the Revolution.

Beginning his speech, Otis reminded his audience that he had just resigned a Crown position because he doubted the constitutionality of some of the laws he was being asked to enforce. The admiralty court had been instructed to examine the legality of the writs, and now, he concluded ironically, he was appearing before the superior court to give his findings. Otis observed in passing that he did not intend to accept a fee for his services on behalf of the merchants, for he was speaking instead for the rights of man, adding "I will to my dying day oppose with all the powers and faculties God had given me, all such instruments of slavery on the one hand, and villainy on the other, as this writ of assistance is."

Otis then went on to attack the British navigation acts, characterizing them as "narrow, contracted, selfish," and he warned against the general writs. He recalled the instance of a customs official who was arrested for cursing and who then used the writ to harass the constable and judge involved in his case. Most important, Otis cited Coke and Vattel, early constitutional authorities, that any act contrary to the unwritten British constitution was invalid. Otis laid before his audience, and consequently the literate colonial community, the position that Parliament had the right to make law but that it had to do so with reason and fairness.

He argued that there exists natural law against which positive man-made laws were to be measured. Referring to arbitrary edicts, Otis warned, "I oppose that kind of power, the exercise of which in former periods of English history cost one king of England his head and another his throne." Concluding his address, he insisted, "As to Acts of Parliament, an Act against the Constitution is void: an Act against natural Equity is void: and if an Act of Parliament should be made, in the very words of this Petition, it would be void." In a broad sense, Otis's appeal was based on rather old Western political notions: natural rights, the baronical provisions of the Magna Carta, and an unwritten British constitution of accumulated liberties. His view of law and Parliament reflected the more limited legislative politics that had occurred before the Glorious Revolution and not the realities of his own time. By the middle of the eighteenth century, most British constitutional authorities had recognized the supremacy of the Parliament and its right to change the basic framework of liberties and rights.

Many years later, John Adams still could recall with deep admiration the effect of this rhetorical display in the writs case. He found Otis a "flame of fire" and recorded how he used effectively classical allusions, scholarly research, a broad survey of historical events and dates, legal authorities, and a "torrent of impetuous eloquence" to make his case. "American independence was then and there born," he concluded. "Every man of a crowded audience appeared to me to go away, as I did, ready to take arms against writs of assistance."

One of Otis's most recent biographers, John R. Galvin, has described his appearance in this period as that of "a provincial farmer, with a roundish face set on a short, thick neck and powerful shoulders." He had bright eyes, an easy smile, but a way that hinted at a barely controlled tension. His impulsive mind seemed at times to range impatiently, "punctuating his brilliant talk with occasional incoherences."

What also made Otis confusing, if not mysterious, to his counterparts was his apparent vacillation on basic political controversies. Surely few others can claim to have articulated more eloquently the philosophical basis for revolution as Otis did. Unlike Patrick Henry, he was no frontier Demosthenes; Otis's public oratory rested on a broad range of knowledge and historical erudition. Yet when the crisis against Crown policy grew the most intense, Otis insisted on reaffirming his loyalty to the Crown, his pride in being part of the British empire, and his personal devotion to order, harmony, and tradition. He even is supposed to have approached Hutchinson and apologized for his public agitation and personal criticism of the chief justice. To Otis's critics, then and now, such behavior is seen as erratic and clear evidence of his mental instability and personal problem in dealing with authority figures.

After the writs of assistance case, the superior court postponed the decision until advice was received from London. Overnight Otis became a major figure known to merchants and tradesmen alike and an increasingly visible figure of political resistance whose works were published in London as well. One of his adversaries, Peter Oliver, claimed that Otis helped to turn the lower house of the Massachusetts legislature into a "Bedlam." Later in November, when the high court reconvened in Boston, Hutchinson produced proof that the writs were used in England and thus, in his opinion, were appropriate legal instruments in the colonies as well.

This new session gave Otis another opportunity to restate his philosophical objections to the writs and, more important, to the ways in which political power was being exercised in the colony and in Britain. Otis ventured forth with the view that even if Parliament approved of these writs, it mattered little. The writs were contrary to the British constitution and to the old Massachusetts Bay charter. Defiantly he argued, "Let a warrant come from where it will improperly, it is to be refused and the higher the power operating it, the more dangerous." The London precedent, however, proved to be the deciding factor in the case, and the court upheld the use of the writs in the colony. Ironically, few of the controversial writs were ever issued after the controversy, and in 1766, the English attorney general ruled that there was no legal basis for the colonial authorities to issue the writs since they lacked the authority of the English exchequer court that handled such instruments in Great Britain.

In the general court (the legislature of Massachusetts), Otis continued his opposition to Governor Bernard's rule. On a seemingly minor issue, Otis challenged the spending of public money without prior approval of the popularly elected house. In a much criticized speech, Otis again attacked the arbitrary use of power and remarked, "It would be of little consequence to the people whether they were a subject to George or Lewis, the King of Great Britain or the French King, if both were arbitrary as both would be if both could levy taxes without Parliament." The use of the British monarch's name in such a disrespectful way brought forth cries of treason, and the governor refused to accept any resolutions with such an affront to the king's dignity. The house relented, but Otis's reputation as a daring opposition leader advanced in the controversy.

His longer response was a vigorous fifty-three-page pamphlet, *Vindication of the Conduct of the House of Representatives of the Province of Massachusetts Bay*. Otis explained his "George or Lewis" remark by insisting that all men are equal and subject to the law. Once again, though, he pledged his personal loyalty to the monarch, and to the great British constitution, but he warned, "Kings were (and plantation governors should be) made for the good of the people, and not the people for them." Borrowing from the writings of John Locke, Otis emphasized the limits of executive power and went on to affirm the right of the colonial legislatures to make themselves heard in defense of the people's liberties.

By early 1763, Otis's critics were publicly charging that he was mad, citing as evidence his stuttering and ungovernable passions when he got excited. But to many Bostonians, those attacks only proved Otis's conviction as an uncompromising advocate of their rights against an increasingly unsympathetic Crown ministry. When Parliament passed the Sugar and Stamp acts, American rancor increased, but Otis stressed at first reconciliation and patience instead. In his essay *The Rights of the British Colonies Asserted and Proved*, Otis reaffirmed his vision of an empire with American representation. Yet in opposing the provisions of the Stamp Act, Otis was to formulate a slogan that was to breed a revolution: no taxation without representation. His popular position seemed clear. Then he published a confusing pamphlet, *Vindication of the British Colonies*, in which he admitted the right of Parliament to tax Americans, although he questioned the fairness. Later he was to conclude that the colonies had legal but not actual membership in the British legislative body.

Thus, in the difficult period of 1764–1765, Otis both emphasized reconciliation and the glories of being part of the empire and yet was also identified with stirring appeals and systematic essays on American rights and liberties. To his enemies, his contradictions were compelling proof of an unstable personality, made all the more volatile by the unsettling events of British colonial policy and family opposition to Bernard and Hutchinson. Meanwhile, in Virginia, the issues were becoming more clear-cut as Patrick Henry offered in the house of burgesses a series of strongly worded resolutions that sharply challenged royal authority.

Otis at first was somewhat shocked at Henry's audacity, even calling it "high treason." Soon, though, Otis changed his stance and argued that Americans were not represented in Parliament and therefore could not be taxed by that body. In place of the old imperial system, he advocated a loose union, one that recognized American colonial legislatures as the proper bodies for self-government.

The Stamp Act, with its provisions that affected the workings of the professional and commercial classes, helped mobilize the more conservative sectors of society against British policies. Otis's response was to call for meetings of committees throughout the colonies to formulate a common petition to the king, asking him to repeal the act. The result of his effort was the Stamp Act Congress, meeting in New York; Otis was chosen one of the delegates from Massachusetts. At that time he was probably the best known of the major figures at the congress, and one delegate commented that he was "the boldest and best speaker" at the meeting. Yet once again it appears that Otis felt uncomfortable with some of the more radical overtones of the final resolutions—despite the fact that he had partially laid the groundwork for those sentiments and had even provided much of the vocabulary they came to use.

Working closely with Otis at this time, John Adams observed, "His passions blaze—he is liable to great inequities of temper—sometimes in despondency, sometimes in a rage." Otis, however, continued his organization of the opposition forces and spoke out forcibly against Crown taxation policies. Then, under pressure from British mercantile interests and after a brilliant speech by William Pitt the Elder, the ministry of George Grenville ended, and the Stamp Act was repealed. The colonists regarded the remarkable about-face as a vindication of their rights, and Otis as a major figure in the repeal battle earned some of the honors. But the victory proved short-lived. The chancellor of the exchequer, Charles Townshend, proposed a series of tax levies on paper, lead, glass, and tea entering the American colonies. The American response was predictable.

Otis continued his personal attack on Governor Bernard and on Hutchinson, focusing again on the writs of assistance and other issues. Hutchinson wrote that "the language he uses in the House of Representatives is extravagant to an immediate degree and he meets with no check." Some of Otis's opponents had tried to attack him from another angle, charging that he really was a Tory supporter of the Crown parading as a patriot leader. However, Otis's popularity was due not just to his oratory and essays but also to his years of quiet organizing and committee meetings. One admirer, James Putnam, concluded that Otis was "the most able, manly, and commanding of his age at the bar." Those sorts of sentiments were more numerous than the diametrically opposed judgments of people such as Peter Oliver, who found Otis "rash, unguarded, foul-mouth, and openly spiteful."

Otis's reaction to the Stamp Act had exhibited once again his considerable ambivalence. He led the opposition forces, denouncing with tears in his eyes that "a wicked and unfeeling Minister has caused a People, the most loyal and affectionate that ever a King was blessed with, to groan under the most unsupportable Oppression. But I think, Sir, that he now stands upon the Brink of inevitable Destruction; and trust that soon—very soon, he will feel the full weight of his injured Sovereign's righteous Indignation." Yet, he also warned on another occasion that it was "the duty of all humbly and silently to acquiesce in all the decisions of the supreme legislature." When public agitation focused on the Townshend Acts, Otis headed up a town meeting to oppose any violent demonstrations of protest. His advice was, "We ought to behave like men, and use the proper and legal measures to obtain redress." Working with Samuel Adams, who had little ambivalence, Otis pushed for a colonial-wide committee of correspondence that would present the American case to major British leaders. In the general court, Otis again, though, turned his animus on Hutchinson and stopped his election to the council by interrupting the proceedings and asking if anyone knew if Hutchinson was indeed a "pensioner." That hated term from a Crown patronage appointee linked Hutchinson with the despised taxation policies of the ministry. As his colleagues voted, Otis moved around the chamber repeating over and over again "pensioner or no pensioner," obviously attempting to intimidate the representatives. A bitter Hutchinson recorded that Otis acted "like an enraged Demon."

Despite his genuine pleas for moderation, Otis, like many other colonists, was deeply affected by the news of June 18, 1768, that British troops were being sent to Boston to deal with the mounting opposition to royal authority. When Bernard dutifully demanded that the house repudiate its circular letter against the Townshend Acts, Otis responded with a two-hour speech that bitterly attacked the king's ministers but not the monarch. Bernard called the address "the most violent, insolent, abusive, treasonable declamation that perhaps was ever delivered." Otis characterized the ministers as boys who played with titles and badges and who were venal and corrupt. He even went on to call the House of Commons, which he had once respected "a parcel of button-makers, pin-makers, horse jockey gamesters, pensioners, pimps, and whoremasters."

While Otis proved to be hardworking and committed to the patriot cause, he seemed to have grown increasingly weary and may have been experiencing some slippage in his ability to deal with his personal imbalances. Yet he continued to show flashes of eloquence that alternated with some eccentric outbursts. On one occasion, he interrupted a speech in support of the Crown with the effective outburst, "Oh, Mr. Speaker, the liberty of this country is gone forever! And I'll go after it."

Then in September 1769, Otis was involved in an altercation with one of his bitterest critics and was severely caned. Although he recovered, he began to drink heavily, lamented his mortality, and appeared to behave more erratically. John Adams recorded that he was "not in his perfect mind" and noted that Otis "loses himself . . . rambles . . . talks so much," and engages in extensive profanity. Otis's public role was over. He played no further part in the coming revolution and was killed by lightning in 1783.

Despite his excesses and contradictions, Otis seemed a superb and eloquent spokesman. His prominence was due to his intellectual command of the philosophical underpinnings of the controversies. In a region given to classical learning, he established his credibility even further by his clear mastery of that tradition. When he spoke to his colleagues and fellow colonists, he used not the language of revolution as much as the revered vocabulary of ancient rights, English liberties, and constitutions and charters of limited powers.

Surely Otis's idiosyncrasies hurt him in some quarters, but he spent enough years working with the patriot leadership in Boston and enough hours pleading the causes of workmen and merchants to establish himself as a sincere advocate of the cause. As an orator, Otis was a master of invective, of quick cutting and telling criticism, of broad historical allusion. His detractors and admirers agreed on one judgment: that Otis was a brilliant and explosive speaker in an age that appreciated both qualities. To some extent, his effectiveness was also grounded in his ability to articulate the raw urgings on self-government emerging in the colonies. At times, though, this profoundly conservative man, this genuine admirer of royal authority, seemed frightened by the implications of his own declarations.

Still, to the winners, who invariably write the early history of their times, Otis was a prime influence in laying out the political contours of the debate that led to a revolution. An admiring John Adams wrote in old age, "I have never known a man whose love of his country was more ardent or sincere; never one who suffered so much; never one, whose services for any ten years of his life were so important and essential to the cause of his country, as those of Mr. Otis from 1760 to 1770."

INFORMATION SOURCES

Research Collections and Collected Speeches

The main collections of Otis's papers are housed in the Massachusetts Historical Society, Boston, and the Butler Library, Columbia University, New York. His major published works can be found in Charles F. Mullett, ed., "Some Political Writings of James Otis," *University of Missouri Studies* 4, no. 4 (July and October 1929).

Quincy, Samuel M. *Reports of Cases Argued and Adjudged in the Superior*   SQ
    Court . . . 128. Edited by Josiah Quincy, Jr. Boston: Little, Brown,
    1865.
Tudor, William. *The Life of James Otis of Massachusetts.* 1823; rpt., New   WT
    York: DaCapo Press, 1970.
Works of John Adams. Edited by Charles F. Adams. 1856; rpt., Freeport: JA
    Books for Libraries, 1969. Vol. 2.

Selected Critical Studies

Banninga, Jerald L. "James Otis on the Writs of Assistance: A Textual Investigation."
    Speech Monographs 27 (1960): 351–52.

Benson, James A. "James Otis and the 'Writs of Assistance' Speech in Fact and Fiction." *Southern Speech Journal* 34 (1969): 256–62.

Shipton, Clifford Kenyon. "James Otis and the Writs of Assistance." *Proceedings of the Bostonian Society* (1961): 17–25.

Weatherly, Michael. "Propaganda and the Rhetoric of the American Revolution." *Southern Speech Journal* 36 (1971): 352–63.

Selected Biographies

Adams, John. *Diary and Autobiography of John Adams*. Edited by L. H. Butterfield. Cambridge: Harvard University Press, 1961.

Galvin, John R. *Three Men of Boston*. New York: Thomas Y. Crowell, 1976.

Marson, Philip. *Yankee Voices*. New York: Schenkman, 1967.

Shaw, Peter. *American Patriots and the Rituals of Revolution*. Cambridge: Harvard University Press, 1981.

Waters, John J. *The Otis Family in Provincial and Revolutionary Massachusetts*. Chapel Hill: University of North Carolina Press, 1968.

CHRONOLOGY OF MAJOR SPEECHES

See "Research Collections and Collected Speeches" for Source codes.

"The Writs of Assistance," Boston, February 10, 1761; *JA*, pp. 522–55.

"Remarks in Baker v. Mattocks," Boston, April 1763; *SQ*, pp. 89 passim.

"Remarks in Bannister v. Henderson," Boston, March 1765; *SQ*, pp. 119 passim.

"Memorial of Boston on the Stamp Act," Boston, December 20, 1765; *SQ*, pp. 201 passim.

"Address at Cambridge," Cambridge, Massachusetts, May or June 1769; extracts in *WT*, pp. 354–56.

THEODORE PARKER
(1810–1860), Unitarian clergyman

DANIEL ROSS CHANDLER

As a student, Theodore Parker was inquisitive and independent. One summer day during 1830, he walked from the family farm in Lexington, Massachusetts, to Harvard College, where he passed the entrance examinations and enrolled as a nonresident student. Although financial limitations prohibited him from paying the tuition, he continued his studies and was awarded an honorary master's degree in 1840. When twenty-year-old Theodore ventured toward Boston to accept an assignment as a public school teacher in 1831, he discovered this "Athens of America" pervaded with theological controversy between New England Congregationalists and rational Unitarians. Remaining in Boston until 1832, Parker moved to Watertown, planning to establish a private school. In Watertown, he was influenced by Convers Francis, a Unitarian minister, and Sunday school teacher Lydia D. Cabot, whom he married in 1837.

The young scholar entered the Divinity School in Cambridge during 1834 and graduated in 1836. Although he received no regular instruction in composition and declamation during his early education, Parker was an impassioned speaker who evoked considerable applause. "He was," Octavius Frothingham reported, "the best debater, though not the best writer, in the Hall; always speaking vigorously, and to the point, with an independence of thought, an enthusiasm of manner, and a freshness, that gave promise of greater pulpit power than he at first displayed." His seminary sermons were scholastic and uninteresting, and his preaching in the village church was disappointing and uninspired. Following his graduation, Parker spent several weeks serving at Barnstable on Cape Cod and preached at Waltham, Concord, and Leominster before accepting a ministerial settlement at West Roxbury, where he was ordained on June 21, 1837.

PARKER AS TRANSCENDENTALIST

Parker's West Roxbury ministry was reflected through his written compositions and his sermonic discourse. He began translating Wilhelm M. L. DeWette's *Beitrage zur Einleitung in das Alte Testament*, which Robert Albrecht described subsequently as "a significant achievement showing immense erudition." Parker entered the growing transcendentalist dispute with a pamphlet written under the pseudonym Levi Blodgett, contending that an intuitive religious impulse within an individual makes external evidences such as miracles unnecessary. An increasing preference for a rational approach toward universal religion and a scientifically critical orientation attracted him. On July 15, 1836, he was profoundly impressed and enormously inspired by hearing Ralph Waldo Emerson's address delivered before the graduating seniors at Harvard Divinity School. Returning to West Roxbury with his spirit shaken, he resolved to write several sermons, describing Emerson's sermon in a letter to George Ellis as the "noblest of all his performances." "I shall give no abstract," he wrote in his journal, "so beautiful, so just, so true, and terribly sublime, was his picture of the faults of the Church in its present position.''

Controversy ensued when Parker presented an ordination sermon for Charles C. Shackford at Hawes Place Church in South Boston on May 19, 1841. Among the most significant sermons in American intellectual history, Parker's address was entitled "The Transient and Permanent in Christianity." He described "absolute religion" as "always the same thing, in each century and every land." Christianity, he contended convincingly, is not "a system of doctrines, but rather a method of attaining oneness with God." Absolute religion is comprehended immediately through an individual's intuition; religious and moral truth is "perceived intuitively, and by instinct, as it were, though our theology be imperfect and miserable." The preacher described the transient as "the thought, the folly, the uncertain wisdom, the theological notions, the impiety of man" and the permanent as absolute, pure morality and religion, love of man and God unhindered and unimpeded. Significantly Parker separated Jesus's teachings from Jesus's authority when he questioned why "the great truths of Christianity rest on the personal authority of Jesus, more than the axioms of geometry rest on the personal authority of Euclid, or Archimedes." Had Jesus never lived or been human, Christianity would endure; Christianity remains "not because its record was written by infallible pens" or "lived out by an infallible teacher" but because Christianity is true. Distinguishing between historical referents and experiential reality, Parker maintained that persons are saved not by the historic Jesus but through the Christ created within human hearts. Parker stressed that "the Christ that is born within us, is always the same thing to each soul that feels it." Jesus exerted no efforts to preserve his teachings, establish an institution, or ordain a priesthood. Indeed, since the fourth century, Christianity had remained outside the ecclesiastical establishment. Parker envisioned a universal humanistic religion rooted within mankind's spiritual nature.

Although the themes Parker developed were also presented in Emerson's historic Divinity School Address and in George Ripley's ordination sermon for Orestes Brownson in 1834, Parker's speech provoked antagonism not from the immediate but from the extended audience. Writing in 1864, Parker biographer John Weiss reported that the occasion passed without excitement; the clergyman who gave the ordination prayer acknowledged Parker's heresy and petitioned that Shackford possess a living faith; one person arose and departed during the sermon without suggesting the motivation; and several clergymen expressed satisfaction tempered with reservations. This sermon seemed destined for what Weiss described as "that limbo of imperfect sympathies whither so many of Mr. Parker's productions had gone before." Albrecht mentioned that an orthodox minister demanded Parker's arrest, and several Unitarian ministers denounced the controversial clergyman. In an autobiographical account, Parker indicated: "I printed the sermon, but no bookseller in Boston would put his name to the title-page—Unitarian ministers had been busy with their advice. The Swedenborgian printers volunteered the protection of their name; the little pamphlet was thus published, sold, and vehemently denounced.''

Two months later, Parker declined an invitation to present a lecture series the following winter in Boston but reconsidered and presented several speeches, which were published in spring 1842 as *A Discourse of Matters Pertaining to Religion*. In this series, Parker described Christianity as the highest evolutionary assent toward human experiential contact with divinity. He proposed a systematic theology interpreting the immanence of God within nature and mankind, developed scientifically and confirmed historically. In January 1843, several members affiliated with the Boston ministerial association gathered and pressured Parker for his resignation. His refusal to withdraw and limit his intellectual freedom accelerated refusals from his ministerial colleagues to exchange pulpits.

In December 1844, as a member of the ministerial association, Parker presented a Thursday lecture at the First Church entitled "The Relation of Jesus to his Age and the Ages." He described Jesus as the greatest person and proudest achievement of the human race. In his own age, Jesus was cursed, rejected, and persecuted in God's name by the sectarians; although his character and teachings remain unchanged, Jesus is worshipped as God. "That God has yet greater men in store," Parker declared, "I doubt not; to say this is not to detract from the majestic character of Christ, but to affirm the omnipotence of God. When they come, the old contest will be renewed,—the living prophet stoned, the dead one worshipped." Soon the administration was altered, and the lectureship was discontinued. Almost a month after Parker presented this lecture, the ministers pondered his expulsion.

The controversy continued, and on January 22, 1845, several Bostonians gathered and concurred that Theodore Parker "shall have a chance to be heard in Boston." On February 16, 1845, a congregation gathered in the Melodeon Theatre. In November 1845, the Twenty-eighth Congregational Society was established by the growing congregation; and during December, Parker was invited to become the first permanent minister. During his installation on January 4, 1846, Parker preached his inaugural sermon, "The Idea of a Christian Church." He identified the congregation's purpose as establishing a Christian church, which he described as "a body of men and women united together in a common desire of religious excellence" and with a common regard for Jesus of Nazareth as "the noblest example of morality and religion." The Christian church should teach the members "to hold the same relation to God that Christ held; to be one with Him; incarnations of God, as much and as far as Jesus was one with God, and an incarnation thereof—a manifestation of God in the flesh." Jesus was described as "the manliest of men, the most divine because the most human"; Jesus was "humane as a woman" and "brave as man's most daring thought." Parker admonished the audience: "If a church were to waste less time in building its palaces of theological speculation . . . erecting air-castles and fighting to defend those palaces of straw, it would surely have more time to use in the practical good works of the day." He contended that the church that sufficed for the fifth and fifteenth centuries was insufficient; what served at Rome, Oxford, or Berlin was inadequate for contemporary Boston.

Through his sermons and lectures, Parker reached a growing audience that outgrew the Melodeon. In the final sermon, Parker delivered in that theater on November 14, 1852, he insisted: "I do not believe that the Old Testament was God's first word, nor the New Testament his last. . . . I do not believe the miraculous origin of the Hebrew Church, or the Buddhist Church, or the Christian Church; nor the miraculous character of Jesus. I take not the Bible for my master, nor yet the church; nor even Jesus of Nazareth for my master." While Roman Catholics claimed the church and Protestants cherished the sacred Scriptures as ultimate authority in theological speculation, Parker emphasized an immediate intuition available to individuals.

Having exceeded the accommodations provided in the Melodeon, the growing congregation convened in the spacious Music Hall, which provided seating for approximately 3,000 persons. With a fundamental membership numbering 500 and with 700 names appearing on the register, the society became the largest, and perhaps the most distinguished, in Boston. Weiss reported that during Parker's illness, no Boston group "wielded so great a practical and charitable power as the Fraternity of the Music Hall." The powerful preacher spoke with a manuscript, read his sermons slowly and earnestly, and presented a brilliant message that remains relevant. "The most impressive thing in all Boston on those famous Sundays," Weiss remembered, "was the moral sincerity of the preacher's voice, as it deepened from common-sense to religious emotion, or sparkled into indignation that was not for sale, or softened into sympathy and human pleasure at the Beautiful and the Good." Parker's hour-long excursions exploring literature, government, history, and science were incorporated into a simple service containing prayer and hymns. When Parker preached his initial sermon, "Of the Position and Duty of a Minister," on November 21, 1852, he stated that a minister's essential responsibility is "not to communicate a mysterious salvation from an imaginary devil in another world; but in this life, to help men get a real salvation from want, from ignorance, folly, impiety, immorality, oppression, and every form of sin."

Moving into the Music Hall, Parker secured a national platform, exerted an international influence, and became one of the country's greatest preachers. Before the world, he stood as a prophet, the inaugurator of a contemporary religious reformation. Estranged from the ecclesiastical establishment, he described himself as "an outcast and the companion of outcasts." Reflecting on his extensive lecturing, Parker said: "I sign myself Theodore Parker of everywhere, and no place in particular. I live in taverns, move in railroad cars, and have my being in the Music Hall and other places of public speaking." Parker remained a professional public speaker who possessed an uncompromised intellectual freedom.

As sectional conflicts deepened and civil war commenced, Parker armed himself and composed his sermons with a pistol upon his desk and a drawn sword within reach. His speeches smelled of gunpowder. During these turbulent times, two firearms hung in Parker's study; his grandfather, John Parker, had carried one rifle when he had marched into the Battle of Lexington on April 19, 1775, and Captain Parker captured the other rifle during that historic battle. In 1845, Parker wrote *A Letter to the People of the United States Touching the Matter of Slavery*. In 1850 he delivered in Faneuil Hall his speeches denouncing Daniel Webster's March 7 speech and the Fugitive Slave Law; in 1852 he delivered a critical eulogy evaluating Webster's career a week after the Massachusetts statesman's death. When he was indicted in 1854 for a disturbance arising from returning an escaped slave and the charges were dropped, he published his 221-page defense. Through William H. Herndon, Parker indirectly influenced Abraham Lincoln, who perhaps derived from the Boston preacher the enduring phrase, "government of the people, by the people, for the people."

After Parker died in Florence, Italy, on May 10, 1860, a magnificent memorial meeting was conducted in Boston's Music Hall on June 17, 1860. His congregation returned to the Melodeon in 1863, moved eventually into fraternity quarters located on Washington Street, constructed the Parker Memorial Meetinghouse in 1873, and subsequently dissolved with a dwindling congregation in 1889.

Hearing Parker preach was a powerful experience partly because he espoused a different philosophy without employing conventional rhetorical techniques. The popular Boston preacher who reached a continuously growing, international audience illustrated what William Ellery Channing described as a free mind that "jealously guards its intellectual rights and powers, which calls no man master, which does not content itself with a passive or hereditary faith, which opens itself to light whencesoever it may come." Henry Steele Commager emphasized that Parker "had no tricks of oratory" but gave his audiences "the hard, gritty truth, and learning too." Commager wrote: "He relied on the spoken, not the written word. . . . What he wrote for the pulpit or the platform was not designed primarily for publication." Frothingham stated that he had "no rhetorical gifts" and was "no juggler with speech"; his addresses contained "no ambitious flight of rhetoric" and were never "an attempt to carry the heart in opposition to the judgment." According to Commager, he was not aesthetically attractive: "He stood there on the platform, simple, unaffected, a stocky, ungainly figure in black broadcloth, a little awkward but never ill at ease, his great Socrates-like head almost bald, his features plain, yet with a certain beauty, and when he folded his hands in prayer you could see that they had guided a plow." However, the speaker balanced the ethical, intellectual, and emotional appeals skillfully. Fred Bratton concluded that the secret of Parker's preaching was not intellection but passion, not erudition but prophetic genius; but Bratton recognized that "emotional fervor would have been shallow without his deep learning, mental poise, and rationality." Weiss reported that Parker's preaching was an "attempt to emancipate the common mind from the vices of traditional belief" and that his speeches reflect a rare comprehension of the general intelligence communicated through a style designed to inspire his hearers with simple religion, charity, and good works. Parker was an independent, self-reliant prophet, pandering to no prescribed dogmas and doctrines.

For a generation prominent Harvard divinity professors and countless Unitarian clergymen had renounced the traditional theological beliefs about the Trinity, vicarious atonement, human depravity, and Jesus's divinity. These religious thinkers contended that such historic affirmations were unsupported by the sacred Scriptures. Parker realized the conclusions drawn by contemporary German biblical scholars revealed the Scriptures as a fallible human document flawed with internally inconsistent and illogical statements rather than divinely revealed and supernaturally disclosed truth. Parker described the Scriptures as standing between humanity and God, and he professed that nothing should violate an individual's intellect or conscience. He raised the persistent, provocative question concerning the essential source that provides spiritual knowledge and religious authority; presented a transcendental emphasis on an individual's intuitive awareness; and contended that a person can experience the sacred immediately without the sacraments and the Scriptures.

Parker secured an enduring reputation as a significant thinker, orator, and prophetic social activist. In *Transcendentalism in New England*, Frothingham identified him as the "preacher" who proclaimed the transcendentalist philosophy. Emerson considered Parker "an excellent scholar, in frank and affectionate communication with the best minds of his day, yet the tribune of the people, and the stout reformer to urge and defend every cause of humanity with and for the humblest of mankind." During the crucial decade preceding his untimely death, Parker spoke between eighty and one hundred times annually in every northern state east of the Mississippi River and reached from 60,000 to 100,000 persons. Albrecht concluded that Parker challenged his countrymen to fulfill their highest idealism and perform a required righteousness; indeed, to appreciate Parker's outstanding achievement, one must comprehend what Albrecht called "the central political, social, and religious conflicts of the critical period of his century during which the nation bled to find its shape and direction." Commager concluded that as a speaker, Parker constituted the "conscience of his generation" and that "the history of America was the history of the actualization of his ideas." The genius whom Parrington described as "the greatest scholar of his generation of New England ministers" and "the embodiment and epitome of the New England Renaissance" successfully combined and effectively championed the idealistic theism within Unitarianism, the transcendentalist emphasis on divine immanence, and a persistent passion that required social righteousness. Believing absolute or natural religion to constitute a genuine, universal reality, Parker contended that "the religion I preach will be the religion of enlightened men for the next thousand years." John Dirks recognized that Parker was among the earliest scholars who accepted the emerging historical-literary research methodologies as scientific disciplines; the perceptive vanguard who understood the sacred Scriptures as a human and historical document; and the courageous pioneers who realize that a revitalized Christianity required rejecting biblical infallibility. Parker, like Emerson, encouraged spiritual enlightenment when he spread transcendentalism during extensive speaking tours, and like Beecher, he became a forerunner of the Social Gospel movement when he recommended the progressive application of religious principles in solving perplexing contemporary problems. Popularizing German higher criticism in American theological scholarship, he provided an intellectual credibility for the liberal religious movement in the twentieth-century United States.

From Parker's ministry stemmed an enduring tradition sustained by spiritual giants nurturing a relevant religion. Almost a century after Parker's generation, Harry Emerson Fosdick enunciated Parker's essential contentions when Fosdick became the founding minister serving the Riverside Church in New York City. Preston Bradley, the founding minister of the Peoples Church of Chicago, regarded Parker as a spiritual hero and inspiring influence. And John Haynes Holmes, whose ministry transformed the traditional Church of the Messiah into a nondenominational Community Church of New York, described the Boston preacher as among the most brilliant scholars, prophetic leaders, significant reformers, and greatest preachers. Testimony from these distinguished twentieth-century pulpit giants confirms the inscription on Parker's monument above his grave in Florence, Italy, as "The Great American Preacher."

INFORMATION SOURCES

Research Collections and Collected Speeches

The essential resource for conducting scholarly research examining Parker remains the Boston Public Library, which possesses all Parker's works published as pamphlets and books, an inventory of Parker's sermons deposited at the Andover-Harvard Theological Library, and a book listing the times and places Parker spoke and indicating the sermons that are numbered within the collection. Most printed sources are available at the Massachusetts Historical Society, Boston, and Andover-Harvard Theological Library, Cambridge, Massachusetts. Parker-Sumner correspondence is located at Harvard University; Parker-Herndon correspondence is preserved at the University of Iowa Library, Iowa City; and miscellaneous manuscripts are maintained at the Library of Congress. The final volume of Parker's journal was given by John Haynes Holmes to Donald Szantho Harrington and is located at the Community Church of New York. A helpful biography is contained in volume 15 of the centenary edition.

Parker, Theodore. *The Collected Works of Theodore Parker*. Edited by   CWTP
Frances P. Cobbe. 14 vols. London: Tubner and Company, 1863–1874.
———. *The Critical and Miscellaneous Writings of Theodore Parker*. Bos-   CMW
ton: James Munroe and Company; London: John Green, 1843.
———. *The Idea of a Christian Church*. Boston: B. H. Greene, 1846.   ICC

———. *The Relation of Jesus to His Age and to the Ages.* Boston: C. C.   *RJAA*
    Little and J. Brown, 1844, 1845.
———. *The Works of Theodore Parker.* 15 vols. Boston: American Uni-   *WTP*
    tarian Association, 1907–1913.
———. *Two Sermons Preached before the Twenty-eighth Congregational*   *TS*
    Society of Boston. Boston: Benjamin B. Mussey and Company, 1853.
———. *West Roxbury Sermons.* Boston: American Unitarian Association,   *WRS*
    1902.
———. *Views of Religion.* Introduction by J. F. Clarke. Boston: American   *VR*
    Unitarian Association, 1888.
Three Prophets of Religious Liberalism: Channing, Emerson, Parker. Edited   *TPRL*
    by Conrad Wright. Boston: Beacon Press, 1961.

Selected Critical Studies

Bratton, Fred Gladstone. *The Legacy of the Liberal Spirit.* New York: Charles Scribner's
    Sons, 1943.
Chandler, Daniel Ross. "Octavius Brooks Frothingham." *Religious Humanism* 19 (1985):
    102–10, 154–65.
Dirks, John Edward. *The Critical Theology of Theodore Parker.* New York: Columbia
    University Press, 1948.
Frothingham, Octavius Brooks. *Recollections and Impressions, 1822–1890.* New York:
    G. P. Putnam's Sons, 1891.
———. *Transcendentalism in New England.* New York: G. P. Putnam's Sons, 1876.
Harrington, Donald Szantho. "Theodore Parker, Crusader." In *The Rhetorical Tradition.*
    Edited by Daniel Ross Chandler. Dubuque, Iowa: Kendall/Hunt Publishing Com-
    pany, 1978.
Hutchison, William R. *The Modernist Impulse in American Protestantism.* Cambridge:
    Harvard University Press, 1976.
———. *The Transcendentalist Ministers.* New Haven: Yale University Press, 1959.
Holmes, John Haynes. *The Social Message of Theodore Parker.* Boston: Unitarian Fel-
    lowship for Social Justice, 1913.
McCall, Roy C. "Theodore Parker." In *A History and Criticism of American Public
    Address.* Edited by William Norwood Brigance. New York: Russell and Russell,
    1960.
Martin, John H. "Theodore Parker." PhD. diss., University of Chicago, 1953.
Parrington, Vernon Louis. *The Romantic Revolution in America.* New York: Harcourt,
    Brace and Company, 1939.
Persons, Stowe. *Free Religion: An American Faith.* New Haven: Yale University Press,
    1947.
Rein, Irving Jacob. "The New England Transcendentalists: Rhetoric of Paradox." Ph.D.
    diss., University of Pittsburgh, 1966.
Wright, Conrad, ed. *A Stream of Light.* Boston: Unitarian Universalist Association, 1975.
———. *The Liberal Christians.* Boston: Beacon Press, 1970.

Selected Biographies

Albrecht, Robert C. *Theodore Parker.* New York: Twayne Publishers, 1971.
Chadwick, John White. *Theodore Parker: Preacher and Reformer.* Boston and New
    York: Houghton Mifflin and Company, 1900.

Clarke, J. F. *A Look at the Life of Theodore Parker*. Boston: Walker, Wise and Company, 1860.

Commager, Henry Steele. *Theodore Parker*. Boston: Beacon Press, 1947.

Frothingham, Octavius Brooks. *Theodore Parker*. Boston: James R. Osgood and Company, 1874.

Weiss, John. *Life and Correspondence of Theodore Parker*. 2 vols. New York: D. Appleton and Company, 1864.

CHRONOLOGY OF MAJOR SPEECHES

See "Research Collections and Collected Speeches" for source codes.

"The Transient and Permanent in Christianity," Hawes Place Church, Boston, May 19, 1841; *CMW*, pp. 136–69; *TPRL*, pp. 113–49.

"The Relation of Jesus to His Age and to the Ages," First Unitarian Church, Boston, December 26, 1844; *RJAA*, pp. 1–18; *VR*, pp. 256–72.

"The Idea of a Christian Church," Twenty-eighth Congregational Society, Boston, January 4, 1846; *ICC*, pp. 3–36.

"Some Account of My Ministry," Boston, November 14, 1852; *TS*, p. 14.

"Of the Position and Duty of a Minister," Twenty-eighth Congregational Society, Boston, November 21, 1852; *TS*, pp. 35–59.

WENDELL PHILLIPS
(1811–1884), abolitionist, social and political reformer

JOHN LOUIS LUCAITES

Wendell Phillips, "the golden trumpet of abolition," was born to a prominent and wealthy aristocratic family on Boston's Beacon Hill in 1811. As a student at Harvard College (1827–1831), he distinguished himself as the class orator and was selected to deliver the commencement address; his topic was "Parliamentary Reform and the British Aristocracy." He graduated from Harvard Law School in 1834 and began a relatively brief and unsuccessful law practice in Lowell, Massachusetts, the following year. The same year he met Anne Terry Greene, an active member of the Boston Female Anti-Slavery Society, whom he would marry in 1837 and who introduced him to William Lloyd Garrison, the radical abolitionist and editor of the *Liberator*.

Phillips first spoke out in support of abolition at a Massachusetts Anti-Slavery Society Meeting in March 1837 in "The Right of Petition," served as an introduction to his more famous, "The Murder of Lovejoy," delivered eight months later at Boston's Faneuil Hall. By 1838 he had abandoned his law practice and devoted his full time and energy to the antislavery cause, advocating a multitude of radical positions, such as disunion and popular resistance, and publicly attacking all who rejected the call for abolition. Phillips was not simply an abolitionist, however. Throughout his life he spoke out in favor of a multitude of social and political reforms.

Following the Civil War he committed himself most fully to securing universal male suffrage and then workmen's rights. Additionally, he was a lifelong supporter of the woman's movement and frequently delivered addresses to national woman's rights conventions, though he did not always support the call for female suffrage. Phillips was also an extremely popular speaker on the growing lyceum circuit, reputedly commanding a $250 platform fee for the delivery of lectures such as "The Lost Arts," and encomia to such historical figures as Kossuth, Crispus Attucks, Toussaint L'Ouverture, and Daniel O'Connell. He delivered his last major address, "The Scholar in a Republic," in 1881 at the centennial anniversary of Phi Beta Kappa of Harvard College, thus effectively ending his career as an orator at the same place that it had begun fifty years earlier as a commencement speaker.

WENDELL PHILLIPS AS POLITICAL AGITATOR

Wendell Phillips was a political agitator, not a politician. Although he was in the public eye for over forty years, he never once held public office, and although he advocated particular causes, he aligned himself with a specific political party only once and very late in his life. Nevertheless, between 1837 and 1881, he addressed virtually every key social and political issue of his time in thousands of speeches to audiences throughout the nation. What linked all of those speeches together was his motive to agitate, to stir up his audience, to lead them to question their most deeply held values and behaviors, and to dare them to change in ways that would increase public order and liberty. Phillips heralded the importance of agitation to a democratic society throughout his life, but he perhaps gave his most eloquent statement of it in "The Scholar in a Republic":

The freer a nation becomes, the more utterly democratic in its form, the more need of this outside agitation. Parties and sects laden with the burden of securing their own success cannot afford to risk new ideas. "Predominant opinions," Disraeli said, "are the opinions of a class that is vanishing." The agitator must stand outside of organizations, with no bread to earn, no candidate to elect, nor party to save, no object but truth,—to tear a question open and riddle it with light. *In all modern constitutional governments, agitation is the only peaceful method of progress.* (Emphasis added.)

As a political agitator, Wendell Phillips is most closely identified with the movement for the abolition of slavery. In 1835, he was at work at his desk when he was disturbed by the shouts of an angry and riotous mob dragging William Lloyd Garrison down the street on the end of a rope. Garrison managed to escape unharmed, but the scene was indelibly imprinted in Phillips's mind, and descriptions of it served as a standard narrative for the relationship between civil disorder and violations of civil liberty to which he would return over and over again throughout his career as a reformer. The following year, Congress passed a procedural gag rule designed to eliminate discussion of antislavery petitions and thus effectively undermined any opportunity that the abolitionists might have had to introduce legislation. On March 28, 1837, Phillips spoke out in public for the first time, condemning this action as inimical to the free and open discussions necessary to an orderly and democratic society in "The Right of Petition," a speech addressed to the Massachusetts Anti-Slavery Society. In that speech he noted:

We render to those who ask us why we are contending against Southern slavery, *that it may not result in Northern slavery*; because time has shown that it sends out its poisonous branches over all our fair land, and corrupts the very air we breathe. Our fate is bound up with that of the South, so that they cannot be corrupt and we sound; they cannot fall, and we stand. Disunion is coming *unless* we discuss this subject; for the spirit of freedom and the spirit of slavery are contending here for the mastery. They cannot live together.

Phillips had yet officially to declare himself an abolitionist, and the clear focus of this speech was a defense of the right of petition, not an attack on slavery, but his linkage of the two issues provided the rhetorical and ideological frame for most of the arguments that he would make over the next thirty years.

That frame was developed and elaborated when Phillips next spoke in public on December 8, 1837, in his most famous speech, "The Murder of Lovejoy." Elijah Lovejoy was the editor of an abolitionist newspaper in Alton, Illinois. On three occasions, angry antiabolitionist mobs destroyed his press and threatened his life. On the fourth such occasion, Lovejoy defended himself against the mob and was killed in the ensuing riot. When news of Lovejoy's death reached Boston, the abolitionist forces chose to meet in Faneuil Hall to praise their new-found martyr and to condemn the lawless mob that had murdered him. Over 5,000 people packed the hall. Following several speeches in support of resolutions condemning the events that took place in Alton, James T. Austin, the attorney general of Massachusetts, stood forward and praised the "orderly mob" in an analogy that compared them with America's Revolutionary founding fathers. When the crowd seemed to be swayed by Austin's words, Phillips worked his way to the podium and began to speak. When he was finished, the hall echoed with applause, and the resolutions previously introduced quickly passed.

"The Murder of Lovejoy" was a significant speech, not only because it represented one of the most dramatic moments in the emerging abolitionist cause, with Phillips pointing to the "pictured lips" of James Otis, John Hancock, and Samuel Adams hanging on the walls of Faneuil Hall rebuking Austin as a "recreant American," or because it helped to secure the link between the issues of slavery and free speech, but also because it vividly portrayed the strategies that would dominate Phillips's agitational discourse in the ensuing years. Two such strategies are worthy of note. First, perhaps forced by the terms of Austin's argument, Phillips disputed the comparison between the "drunken murderers of Lovejoy" and "those patriot fathers who threw the tea overboard" by reversing the terms of the analogy in a carefully constructed narrative of the events as they unfolded in Alton according to which the mob was characterized as tyrannical and Lovejoy as the victim of "illegal exactions." Throughout his career as a speaker and agitator, whatever the cause, Phillips would utilize the narrative reconstruction of historical events as a way of breathing life into key ideological concepts, such as liberty, public order, and the like, as well as to polarize his opponents in opposition to these principles.

Second, and again perhaps forced by the exigency of this particular situation, Phillips developed his argument for linking the issues of abolition and the freedom of speech through the biographical description of Lovejoy's motives and actions, characterizing him as a great American hero—in this case, an ordinary individual willing to act, indeed to sacrifice his life, in the combined interests of civil liberty and order. The use of biography as argument became a standard ploy in many of Phillips's speeches. Whether he praised ordinary individuals moved to action in the face of crisis, such as Lovejoy, or excoriated those he opposed, usually statesmen such as Daniel Webster in "Public Opinion," "Surrender of Sims," and "Idols," he always encouraged his audience to understand his biographical sketches as cases that demonstrated or contributed to a larger argument.

Following his maiden speech in Faneuil Hall, Phillips's commitment to abolition became total, and he quickly emerged as one of its leading spokespersons. Although he delivered hundreds of speeches in support of the abolition of slavery between 1838 and 1861, his commitment to this cause was always instrumental, predicated as a means for securing a free, stable, and open society. Three of his speeches in particular characterize the temper and tone of his agitation during these years. Following the Compromise of 1850, Phillips mounted a vicious crusade against Daniel Webster whose March 7 address helped to secure its passage and in so doing strengthened the constitutionality of slavery. Webster responded in kind, attacking Phillips and his fellow abolitionists as idealistic and ineffectual. In 1852 Phillips responded to these charges in his ''Public Opinion'' address to the Massachusetts Anti-Slavery Society. Much of that speech consisted of ad hominem attacks against Webster, but the underlying purpose of the speech was to identify the power of public opinion and to explain the necessity of moral suasion in a democratic society. Phillips further developed these arguments the following year in ''Philosophy of the Abolition Movement.'' Throughout the 1840s, the radical Garrisonians who demanded immediate ab- olition came under attack from moderate abolitionists as being fanatics. When the moderate Free Soil party demonstrated popular support in the late 1840s and early 1850s, such charges could no longer be safely ignored, and Phillips re- sponded at great length by detailing the abolitionist philosophy of agitation and justifying it in terms of its effectiveness, arguing that in the mere twenty years since its inception, it had entrenched the issue of slavery in the public con- sciousness. Taken together, these two speeches contain virtually every one of the key arguments that dominated Phillips's abolitionist discourse for almost thirty years.

The one key topic not dealt with fully in these two speeches was his call for disunion. Ever since his speech on the right of petition, Phillips had argued in public that a union half-slave and half-free could not succeed. Unlike Lincoln, however, who maintained that the first duty of the government was to preserve the Union, Phillips maintained that the first duty of government was justice; and in this case, he argued, severing the Union connecting the North and the South was the only viable peaceful means of eliminating the injustices perpetrated by the ''Slave Power.'' Such a position was extremely unpopular, especially in the industrialized North, where an economic reliance on southern commerce was beginning to develop. Nevertheless, on January 20, 1861, in Boston's Music Hall, he delivered his most explicit and seering condemnation of the union before a largely hostile and threatening audience. The title of his speech was ''Disu- nion,'' and like most of the rest of Phillips's abolitionist rhetoric, his arguments were incendiary. He maintained that the Union was an experiment that had failed, that its only remaining function was to fortify and protect the ''Slave Power,'' and that the elimination of such fortifications and protections would signal the natural demise of slavery. ''Disunion,'' he concluded, ''is abolition.'' It is, of course, unlikely that this speech gained many adherents to Phillips's cause, but given his belief that agitation was necessary to the maintenance of a free and open society, it might have been enough for him that it functioned as an articulate opposition to the advocates of unionism, forcing them to provide more careful justifications for their position. Ironically enough, when the Civil War broke out, Phillips recognized the opportunity to crush the ''Slave Power'' once and for all and shifted his allegiance to the preservation of the Union in "Under the Flag," a masterful speech in which he convincingly denied that he was changing his position, arguing that the real question at issue was still one of opinions: "it is Civilization against Barbarism: it is Freedom against Slavery. The cannon shot against Fort Sumter was the yell of pirates against the DEC-LARATION OF INDEPENDENCE, the war-cry of the North is the echo of that sublime pledge."

Following the Civil War, Phillips dedicated his efforts to achieving universal male suffrage, a cause that often found him in conflict with the advocates of female suffrage. Phillips had been a lifelong supporter of the woman's movement and as late as 1861 had advocated suffrage for women. By 1866, however, he came to the realization that female suffrage was far too radical a policy to be practical at that time, and he feared that its inclusion in any proposed consti-tutional amendment would place at grave risk its chances for adoption. It was thus that he polarized himself from the forces of the woman's movement when he addressed the topic "Woman's Rights and Woman's Duties" by arguing that women possessed a "moral influence" that far exceeded the power of the ballot, implying that it was far more important that they develop an understanding of their "duty" to this "unrecognized influence" than that they demand entrance to the voting booth.

When the Fifteenth Amendment was adopted in 1869, the American Anti-Slavery Society was dissolved. Phillips was not at a loss for a cause, however, and he quickly dedicated himself to the tasks of social and political reform that he imagined were necessary to the reconstruction of a nation caught in the throes of an industrial revolution. He spoke out frequently and forcefully in favor of temperance and the need for public education reform, but his cause célèbre during these years was labor reform. As early as 1865, he had recognized the potential danger produced by the tension between the interests of capital and labor, and he advocated the eight-hour workday as a means "to make the labourer more comfortable, and a more worthy citizen." When the eight-hour movement failed to make headway, Phillips urged the forces of labor to enter the political arena and to demonstrate their power and influence through their franchise. In 1870 he made a feeble attempt to run for governor in Massachusetts as the nominee of the Labor Reform and Temperance parties, his only foray into electoral politics. When this effort failed, he once again took on the role of agitator and abandoned all caution by declaring war against the "great money power" in "The Foundation of the Labor Movement," a speech in which he urged land reform, the equalization of property, and radically progressive taxation.

Phillips's popularity as a speaker was not limited to his speeches on the dominant political issues of the age. He was also in great demand as a lyceum speaker, a lecturer, and a eulogist. Perhaps his most popular lecture was "The Lost Arts," originally presented in 1838 but subsequently delivered over a thousand times and said to have earned him in excess of $250,000 over the course of his lifetime. The speech was simple and direct, indicating that the inventions of modern science, such as the making of glass, were little more than the rediscovery of the lost arts of ancient civilizations. Phillips rarely spoke in public without exploiting the opportunities for agitation. In "The Lost Arts" he encouraged his audiences to understand that this rediscovery was necessary only because knowledge, which was the "human property," had been controlled in the past by an aristocracy that feared its popular dissemination. The deliberative implications of this were clear to Phillips's nineteenth-century audiences: to ensure that history does not repeat itself, we must ensure that learning and knowledge remain in the custody of the many and never again become the privileged domain of the few. In a like fashion, Phillips would exploit his opportunities to deliver lectures on various historical figures. In the most popular of these encomia, he would regale his audiences with the bravery of such individuals as Crispus Attucks, Toussaint L'Ouverture, John Brown, and Daniel O'Connell, always careful to turn his hero's biography into an argument appropriate to the occasion—justification of agitation in a democracy, the propriety of popular resistance under certain circumstances, and so on.

Phillips's final major public presentation, "The Scholar in a Republic," was delivered to his alma mater in 1881. When Phillips excoriated the privileged classes that controlled learning and knowledge in "The Lost Arts," he might just as easily have substituted "scholars and academics" for the aristocracy. In "The Scholar in a Republic," he did just that, attacking the debilitating and limiting prejudices that scholars brought to their work. For example, he disputed their definition of education as "book learning"; he ridiculed their treatment of "history" as the facts culled from journals written by "milksops and fribbles," arguing instead that the study of history should be an attempt to assess the character and motives of the men and societies of the past as a standard against which to judge the present and the future; and he held in disdain their "chronic distrust of the people." Phillips had long been a critic of those who sequestered themselves in the ivory towers of the academy and refused to integrate their scholarship with social and political action. On one occasion he was asked how it was that there was so much learning at Cambridge. He responded, "Because nobody carries any away." Ever the critic and agitator, here, in his final opportunity to address America's best and brightest, he crystallized that critique in a call for action that prescribed the proper behavior for a scholar in a republic:

I urge on college-bred men, that as a class they fail in republican duty when they allow others to lead in the agitation of the great social questions which stir and educate the age. . . . To be as good as our fathers we must be better. They silenced their fears and subdued their prejudices, inaugurating free speech and equality with no precedent on the file. . . . Let us rise to their level. Crush appetite, and prohibit temptation if it rots great cities. Intrench labor in sufficient bulwarks against that wealth which, without the tenfold strength of modern incorporation, wrecked the Grecian and Roman States; and with a sterner effort still, summon women into civil life as reinforcement to our laboring ranks in the effort to make our civilization a success.

Nineteenth-century America was an era of social and political reform. Americans were confronted with movements for the abolition of slavery, woman's suffrage, labor reform, land reform, temperance, prison reform, education reform, and others. Wendell Phillips was unique among nineteenth-century reformers in that his name was linked with virtually every one of these movements. The typical nineteenth-century reformer was committed to a specific cause; Phillips was committed to the idea of reform itself as a means of producing social and political growth and of securing civil liberty and order. It was to these ends that he operated outside the constraints of political office and government as a political agitator, a role he considered as necessary to the maintenance of a democratic society as a commitment to the sovereignty of the people. The chief weapon in his arsenal for reform was oratory; he delivered thousands of speeches in a career that spanned nearly fifty years. Frequently those speeches were incendiary and abusive; just as often they were revolutionary, demanding radical social and political changes; but always they were designed to affect public opinion through moral suasion. In the end, our verdict of Wendell Phillips's contribution to the progress of American society must be judged not in terms of his successes or failures with respect to any particular cause or movement but in terms of his legacy as a reformer committed to the progressive and emancipatory growth of the nation. In that domain he was without peer in the nineteenth century.

INFORMATION SOURCES

Research Collections and Collected Speeches

Those interested in studying the full range of Wendell Phillips's public discourse should check the pages of William Lloyd Garrison's *Liberator*, Boston, 1837–1865, and the official paper of the American Anti-Slavery Society, the *National Anti-Slavery Standard*, New York City, 1841–1870, both of which contain many of his speeches, as well as numerous editorials that he wrote. Some speeches delivered subsequent to the dissolution of the American Anti-Slavery Society in 1870 can be found in the *National Standard*, New York City, 1870–1872. The most available texts of Phillips's speeches are contained in the two volumes of *Speeches, Lectures and Letters* published originally in the nineteenth century, but there are some problems of accuracy here (see Yeager, pp. 353–56). Collections of Phillips's papers can be found in the Antislavery Collection of the Boston Public Library and in the Harvard University Archives.

Phillips, Wendell. *Speeches, Lectures, and Letters*. 1st ser. 1884; rpt., New   SLLFS
        York: Negro Universities Press, 1968.
———. *Speeches, Lectures, and Letters*. 2d ser. 1891; rpt., New York: SLLSS
        Arno Press and New York Times, 1969.

Wendell Phillips on Civil Rights and Freedom. Edited by Louis Filler.   **WPCRF**
    Lanham, Mo: University Press of America, 1982.
Martyn, Carols. *Wendell Phillips: The Agitator.* 1890; rpt., New York: **WPTA**
    Negro Universities Press, 1969.

Selected Critical Studies

Barnard, Raymond H. "The Freedom Speech of Wendell Phillips." *Quarterly Journal of Speech* 25 (1939): 596–611.
Bartlett, Irving H. "Wendell Phillips and the Eloquence of Abuse." *American Quarterly* 11 (1959): 509–20.
Doyle, J. H. "The Style of Wendell Phillips." *Quarterly Journal of Speech* 2 (1916): 331–39.
Fletcher, Winona. "Knight-Errant or Screaming Eagle? E. L. Godkin's Criticism of Wendell Phillips." *Southern Speech Journal* 29 (1964): 214–23.
Marcus, Robert D. "Wendell Phillips and American Institutions." *Journal of American History* 56 (1969): 39–56.
Yeager, William Hayes. "Wendell Phillips." In *A History and Criticism of American Public Address.* Edited by William Norwood Brigance. New York: McGraw-Hill, 1943.

Selected Biographies

Austin, George Lowell. *Wendell Phillips.* Boston: Lee and Shepard, 1888.
Bartlett, Irving. *Wendell Phillips: Brahmin Radical.* Boston: Beacon Press, 1961.
Hofstadter, Richard. "Wendell Phillips: The Patrician as Agitator." In *The American Political Tradition and The Men Who Made It.* New York: Alfred Knopf, 1948.
Sears, Lorenzo. *Wendell Phillips: Orator and Agitator.* 1909. New York: Benjamin Blom, 1967.
Sherwin, Oscar. *Prophet of Liberty: The Life and Times of Wendell Phillips.* New York: Bookman Associates, 1958.
Stewart, James Brewer. *Wendell Phillips: Liberty's Hero.* Louisiana State University Press, 1986.

CHRONOLOGY OF MAJOR SPEECHES

See "Research Collections and Collected Speeches" for source codes.

"The Right of Petition," Lynn, Massachusetts, March 28, 1837; *SLLSS*, pp. 1–6; *WPCRF*, pp. 23–27.

"The Murder of Lovejoy," Boston, December 8, 1837; *SLLFS*, pp. 1–10; *WPCRF*, pp. 1–9.

"The Lost Arts," 1838; *SLLSS*, pp. 365–83; *WPTA*, pp. 533–47.

"Kossuth," Boston, December 27, 1851; *SLLSS*, pp. 40–68.

"Public Opinion," Boston, January 28, 1852; *SLLFS*, pp. 35–54.

"Surrender of Sims," Boston, January 30, 1852; *SLLFS*, pp. 55–70.

"Philosophy of the Abolition Movement," Boston, January 27, 1853; *SLLFS*, pp. 98–153; *WPCRF*, pp. 28–71.

"Crispus Attucks," Boston, March 5, 1858; *SLLSS*, pp. 69–76; *WPCRF*, pp. 72–79.

"Idols," Boston, October 4, 1859; *SLLFS*, pp. 242–62; *WPCRF*, pp. 95–113.

"[John Brown at] Harper's Ferry," Brooklyn, New York, November 1, 1859; SLLFS, pp. 263–88; *WPCRF*, pp. 95–113.

"Disunion," Boston, January 20, 1861; *SLLFS*, pp. 343–370; *WPCRF*, pp. 114–36.

"Under the Flag," Boston, Massachusetts, April 21, 1861; *SLLFS*, pp. 396–414.

"Suffrage for Woman," Cooper Institute, New York, May 10, 1861; *SLLSS*, pp. 110–27.

"Toussaint L'Ouverture," New York and Boston, December 1861; *SLLFS*, pp. 486–94; *WPCRF*, pp. 163–84.

"The Eight-Hour Movement," Boston, November 2, 1865; *SLLSS*, pp. 139–44; *WPCRF*, pp 192–97.

"Woman's Rights and Woman's Duties," New York, May 10, 1866, *SLLSS*, pp. 128–38.

"The Foundation of the Labor Movement," Boston, October 31, 1871; *SLLSS*, pp. 152–67; *WPCRF*, pp. 197–207.

"Daniel O'Connell," Boston, May 28, 1879; *SLLSS*, pp. 459–72.

"The Scholar in a Republic," Cambridge, Massachusetts, June 30, 1881; *SLLSS*, pp. 330–64; *WPTA*, pp. 570–94.

JOHN RANDOLPH
(1773–1833), U.S. congressman and senator

———————————————————————————————— DAVID HENRY

John Randolph of Roanoke, Virginia, recognized early the importance oratory would have in his life. Circumstance was partly responsible. In the relatively secluded environs in which he was reared, entertainment was limited to the minister's performance on Sunday and the public meetings at which prominent political leaders held forth. And since the predominantly Presbyterian church-goers preferred calmness in the pulpit, political orators who exhibited zeal and conviction found eager audiences. Randolph's desire to be such an orator, he once recalled, could be traced to his mother, who had "expressed a wish to me, that I might one day or other be as great a speaker as Jerman Baker or Edmund Randolph. That gave the bent to my disposition." That disposition put Randolph on a path that would lead to a public career of more than three decades in the House of Representatives (1799–1813, 1815–1825), the U.S. Senate (1825–1827), and as minister to Russia (1830–1831).

Throughout his political life, Randolph used his oratorical skill primarily to oppose change. During the Virginia convention, called in 1829 to consider alterations of the state constitution, for example, Randolph established at the outset of his speech the principles he contended should guide the body's delib-erations: "The grievance must first be clearly specified, and fully proved; it must be vital, or rather, deadly in its effect; its magnitude must be such as will justify prudent and reasonable men in taking the always delicate, often dangerous step, of making innovations in their fundamental law; and the remedy proposed must be reasonable and adequate to the end in view." Though articulated succinctly at this relatively late stage of his life, these precepts consistently undergirded Randolph's rhetoric of opposition.

RANDOLPH AND THE RHETORIC OF OPPOSITION

Randolph's resistance to change emerged from his upbringing, education, and commitment to a conservative political philosophy. Born into the gentry class descended from a traditional Anglo-Virginia alliance, Randolph's allegiance was to his station and his sense of history rather than to the democratic impulse that was fast defining the new nation. As he observed, "I am an aristocrat; I love liberty, I hate equality." His family's status permitted him access to Princeton, Columbia, and the College of William and Mary, but two years at Columbia constituted his most extensive contact with formal education. Although he also read law under the direction of his uncle, Edmund Randolph, who was Wash-ington's attorney general, Randolph's learning derived primarily from intensive independent reading.

Robert Dawidoff, a biographer who focused on Randolph's education, divides the readings into stages. At the formative level, Randolph read widely, but most significant for his oratorical career were two tracks of study. One consisted in imaginative works, especially those of Shakespeare and Milton, which instilled in Randolph a flair for the dramatic that would characterize his public speaking. The Augustan satirists, particularly Pope and Swift, provided in the other track the substantive worldview that informed Randolph's dramatic performances. The Augustans' warning of the corruption and disorder that would inevitably follow a shift in power away from the traditional aristocracy and their advocacy of a class-conscious society headed by a noble elite appealed to Randolph. That their eighteenth-century British ideas were badly out of place in nineteenth-century America did little to diminish that appeal. Once Randolph entered public life via his election to Congress in 1799, the requirements of his career dictated subsequent readings. Edmund Burke's writings became a frequent touchstone and yielded a rationale for Randolph's innate conservatism, as both men emphasized tradition, inheritance, and continuity as political principles. He found as well in Burke's works an authoritative confirmation for his oppositionist tendencies, and Randolph's readily apparent admiration for the man he termed the "illustrious statesman" ultimately led to his identification as an "American Burke."

In advocating his conservative philosophy, almost exclusively in deliberative forums and predominantly in the House of Representatives, Randolph employed distinctive rhetorical techniques. Key dimensions of his oratory included his affinity for extemporaneous speaking, curious habits of arrangement, a memorable manner of delivery, and an argumentative method dependent equally on wit and reason. Nathan Sargent, who observed Randolph and his contemporaries during debate, marvelled at their capacity for recall, which negated the need for manuscripts. "There were giants in those days," he noted; "their weapons were drawn impromptu from the armory of a well-supplied brain,—not wrapped up in paper and carried in a pocket." Randolph was no exception. Following a clash with proponents of a second war with Great Britain in the winter of 1811–1812, for instance, he wrote to his nephew, "Speaking, as I always do, from the impulse of the moment, the *verba ardentia* cannot be recalled. The glowing picture fades—the happy epithet, the concise and forcible expression is lost, never again to be retrieved." Lest the picture fade completely, however, Randolph developed a habit of correcting reporters' notes of his speeches before they were published, and he would then send the corrected versions to correspondents for newspapers in other regions of the country.

Although the absence of a script allowed Randolph to roam freely in the course of debate, the organization of his thoughts often suffered. Nathan Sargent commented that Randolph's speeches "rambled everywhere" as he threw "his shafts right and left, hitting promiscuously those around him as well as those absent; nothing was too grave or too sacred, nothing too trivial, to be brought into his speeches." To follow "the thread of his discourse," Sargent concluded, "would be to attempt to follow the thread of the spider in its already-formed web. It was not one thread, but a thousand."

Despite confusing and disjointed arrangement, Randolph retained his audience's attention because of his delivery. His penchant for the dramatic, nurtured by his early appreciation of imaginative literary works, led him to approach each speech almost as a theatrical performance. But it was his voice listeners could not ignore. Although he took the stage with a bearing and authority that anticipated powerful, resonant sounds, he spoke in high-pitched tones akin to an operatic soprano. The product of a 1792 illness, which, as one biographer put it, left "him without the palpable signs of manhood," Randolph's frequently shrill voice was alternately an asset in advancing his case or a bane when exploited by his opponents who substituted ridicule of his manner for refutation of his ideas. Randolph responded to the latter by adopting an argumentative method that blended his talent for wit and narrative into a unique form of reasoning. While his detractors criticized Randolph for his tendency to stray into tangential territory, they often misconstrued his disparate discourse as logically flawed. Joseph Glover Baldwin, perhaps Randolph's most formidable biographer, offered a different perspective. Randolph's "statements were so clear, so simplified, and so vivid," wrote Baldwin, "that they saved him much of the laborious process of argumentation. Much that looked like declamation was only illustration, another form of argument." And his wit gave force to the illustrations. His humor, aptly described by Sargent as a "fine-tempered rapier of sarcasm," frequently contrasted sharply with his opponents' more heavy-handed ad hominem attacks. His clash with Rhode Island's Tristam Burgess on the floor of the House of Representatives is exemplary. Burgess opened the dispute with a bludgeoning tomahawk. After he called Randolph a monster, he gave thanks that "monsters cannot perpetuate their species," a none-too-subtle reference to the effects of Randolph's illness. Randolph countered with the rapier. "Mr. Speaker," he observed, "the gentleman makes a boast of his virility: he boasts of that in which the goat is his equal, and the jackass his superior."

A survey of selected speeches from 1799 to 1829 reveals that these distinctive oratorical characteristics evolved over the course of Randolph's political career. He was not, for example, caustic or contentious when he shared the platform with Patrick Henry during his initial campaign for Congress. Despite Henry's earlier opposition to a strong central government, he advocated acceptance of centralization in 1799 as preferable to the absence of a constitution. Although he rejected Henry's viewpoint, Randolph was gracious and respectful in his opposition. He praised Henry as "the high priest from whom I have received the little wisdom my poor abilities were able to carry away from the droppings of the political sanctuary." What "the inspired statesman" had taught Randolph, however, was "to be jealous of power, to watch its encroachments, and to sound the alarm on the movement of usurpation." Randolph saw no option but to reject federal control, for acceptance of the proposal amounted merely to a "change of our masters—New England for Old England." Both Henry and Randolph won their campaigns, the former to the state legislature and the latter to the House of Representatives, but where Henry's illustrious career was near its end, Randolph's was just beginning.

Randolph initially aligned himself in Congress with the Jeffersonians and determined to work within the power structure to achieve change. By 1805, though, he found his views becoming increasingly contrary to his colleagues', particularly when the legislative proclivity for compromise was at issue. The debate over the Yazoo claims illustrates. Shortly after a corrupt state legislature in Georgia sold parcels of the Yazoo lands to speculators in 1795, an irate citizenry replaced the corrupt lawmakers with new legislators, who immediately repudiated the land sales. The land companies sought compensation from the federal government. Proponents of a compromise that would provide partial reimbursement, including Madison and Jefferson, argued that the act of 1795 constituted a contract between the state and the grantees. Randolph rooted his objection in principle. The proponents' premise, he maintained, "is nothing less than begging, or rather a flagrant robbery, of the question. We deny that any contract has been, or could be made under such circumstances—that fraud is a basis on which a contract can be created." Because supporters of the compromise hinged their case on the expertise of a respected Supreme Court justice and a popular U.S. senator, both since deceased, Randolph had to handle carefully the issue of their authority. He did so by balancing wit with appropriate deference to their status. "Private character, always dear, always to be respected," he observed, "seems almost canonized by the grave. When men go hence, their evil deeds should follow them, and, for me might sleep oblivious in the tomb. But if the mouldering ashes of the dead are to be raked up, let it not be for the furtherance of injustice." The senator in question had, in fact, benefited from the land sales and "were he here now, would disdain to deny it. With all his faults, he was a man of some noble qualities."

A year later, Randolph's break with the Jeffersonians was complete, and he began in earnest what Henry Adams labeled his "career of public opposition." In contention was Jefferson's proposal to purchase West Florida from Spain, a plan that materialized on the floor of the House as the Gregg resolution. Randolph claimed that his speech against the resolution was the only one he ever prepared carefully in advance, and the structure of the text supports his claim. In contrast to his usual habit of moving from one topic to another with no apparent concern for the interrelationships of ideas, Randolph explicated at the outset his central objection: this was "a war resolution in the guise of peace." He then proceeded to treat serially three incrementally linked themes: the new nation's dubious ability to contend with Great Britain for the land in dispute, the policy such a contest would yield, and the implications of that policy for the manner in which "we can . . . re-act upon, annoy our adversary." These questions were too serious, he concluded, to entrust to the wisdom of a president who had defied congressional will in the past. "You give him money to buy Florida," said Randolph, "and he purchases Louisiana. You may furnish the means; the application of those means rests with him."

Suspicion of his adversaries' motives also permeated Randolph's arguments against war with Great Britain in 1811. Though advocates of a declaration of war cited British offenses at sea as the source of America's grievance, Randolph countered that territorial expansion formed their true cause. "Agrarian cupidity," he exclaimed, "not maritime right urges this war. Ever since the report of the Committee on Foreign Relations came into the House, we have heard but one word—like the whip-poor-will, but one eternal monotonous tone—Canada! Canada! Canada!" He urged consideration of a war's consequences. "Who will profit by it?" he asked. "Speculators; a few lucky merchants who draw prizes in the lottery; commissaries and contractors. Who must suffer by it? The people. It is their blood, their taxes, that must flow to support it." His concern for the people notwithstanding, Randolph retained his allegiance to the English elitism his education had produced. Thus, he framed his appeal as analogous to that of British aristocrats who had opposed war with the colonies. Just as "Chatham and Burke, and the whole band of his patriots, prayed for her defeat in 1776," he argued, "so must some of the truest friends of their country deprecate the success of our arms." That success was unlikely also deserved contemplation, he charged, for the government born of the Constitution "was not calculated to wage offensive foreign war; it was instituted for the common defense and general welfare; and whosoever should embark it in a war of offense, would put it to a test which it is by no means calculated to endure." That nation would take up arms, Randolph warned, "at the risk of the Constitution." His colleagues accepted the risk, and the people registered their opinion of Randolph's perspective by turning him out of office in the next election.

In 1815, he returned to Congress, where the threat to the Constitution resurfaced as a stock issue in Randolph's opposition to proposed policies in the House and, later, the Senate. In 1816, for instance, the House debated passage of the enabling legislation that would give force to a commercial treaty Madison had signed with Britain the previous year. Randolph contended that the issue was not whether Congress should support the treaty but whether Madison should have negotiated and signed it without congressional consultation and approval. The president's actions, he said, amounted to moving "the Constitution from its orbit." The Constitution's proper orbit underlay his objections to the bill on internal improvements in 1824, in what Henry Adams called Randolph's "most important speech." Though treaty making fell within the "original design" of the federal government as a regulator of foreign trade, Randolph acknowledged, that design did not imply the right to regulate interstate commerce. He averred that the Constitution created "a system of two distinct governments—the one general in its nature, the other internal." To consolidate them, Randolph continued, would be "a mockery—a greater mockery than it was to talk to these colonies of their virtual representation in the British Parliament." He turned for authority to Madison's report to the Virginia legislature, not least for its precision in expression and content. Only a gross misinterpretation of language could deny either constitutional intent or Madison's analysis, a point Randolph illustrated by dramatic exaggeration. "Since the days of that unfortunate man of the German coast," he began, "whose name was originally Fyerstein, Anglicised to Firestone, but got, by translation, from that to Flint and from Flint to Pierre-a-Fusil, and from Pierre-a-Fusil to Peter Gun—never was greater violence done to the English language than by the construction that . . . we have the right to construct the way on which [commerce] is to be carried.''

Wit served Randolph well until he moved beyond humor to invective, in which case he at least once invited more than mere verbal retaliation. As a member of the Senate in 1826, Randolph took exception to a proposal by Secretary of State Henry Clay and John Quincy Adams that the United States send commissioners to a convention of new Latin American republics. He assailed the plan to participate in the "Panama Congress" as an action taken without Congress's sanction and proceeded to cast aspersions on the character of its advocates. He termed the plan a pact between "Blifil and Black George," though "I shall not say which is Blifil and which Black George. I do not draw my pictures in such a way as to render it necessary to write under them, 'this is a man, this is a horse.' '' Though supporters of U.S. participation maintained that they were only reacting to written requests from Latin countries, Randolph implied that the documents had originated in Clay's office when he retorted that, in reading them, the "first thing that struck me was how wonderfully these Spaniards must have improved in English in their short residence in the U.S." Randolph's invective left Clay with no choice, Nathan Sargent wrote, but to challenge the senator to a duel. They met on the field of honor on April 8. Both men fired twice, Randolph's coat the lone casualty.

Randolph left the Senate the following year, but just as it had during his congressional career, the question of the relationship between the individual and the government occupied his thought and discourse as an elder statesman in American politics. In one of his last major addresses, Randolph shared his concerns with participants in the Virginia State Convention of 1829. In so doing, the conservative philosophy that had guided his public career of opposition crystallized. "Among the strange notions which have been broached since I have been on the political theatre," he said, "there is one which has lately seized the minds of men: that all things must be done for them by the Government, and that they do nothing for themselves. The Government is not only to attend to the great concerns which are its province, it is to step in and ease individuals of their natural and moral obligations." Randolph predictably objected to such a conception of government and therefore stood, fittingly, in opposition to proposed changes in the state charter.

INFORMATION SOURCES

Research Collections and Collected Speeches

The University of Virginia's Alderman Library, Charlottesville, is the central reference center for the study of Randolph's oratorical and political career. The library houses the Randolph Papers, as well as many of the papers and manuscripts of his associates and family. Relevant collections are also found at locations throughout the country, including the Virginia State Library, Richmond; Duke University, Durham, North Carolina; Yale University, New Haven, Connecticut; the State Library of North Carolina, Raleigh; and the Henry E. Huntington Library, San Marino, California. William Ewart Stokes, Jr., and Francis L. Berkeley, Jr., have done researchers a significant service with their compilation *The Papers of Randolph of Roanoke: A Preliminary Checklist of His Surviving Texts in Manuscript and in Print* (Charlottesville: University of Virginia Library, 1951).

American Orations. Edited by Alexander Johnston. New York: G. P. Putnam's Sons, 1896. 2 vols. — *AO*

Annals of Congress. Debates and Proceedings in the Congress of the United States, 1789–1824. Washington, D.C.: Gales and Seaton, 1853. — *AC*

Garland, Hugh A. *The Life of John Randolph of Roanoke*. New York: D. Appleton & Company, 1857. 2 vols. — *LJRR*

Kirk, Russell. *John Randolph of Roanoke: A Study in American Politics, with Selected Speeches and Letters*. Chicago: Henry Regnery Company, 1964. — *JRR*

Niles' Weekly Register. Edited by H. Niles. Baltimore: Franklin Press, 1816. — *NWR*

Proceedings and Debates of the Virginia State Convention of 1829–30. Richmond, 1830. — *PD*

Register of Debates in Congress, 1824–37. Washington, D.C.: Gales and Seaton, 1825–1837. — *RDC*

Selected Critical Studies

Corts, Paul R. "Randolph vs. Clay: A Duel of Words and Bullets." *Filson Club History Quarterly* 43 (1969): 151–57.

Hatzenbuehler, Ronald L., and Robert L. Ivie. *Congress Declares War: Rhetoric, Leadership, and Partisanship in the Early Republic*. Kent, Ohio: Kent State University Press, 1983.

Henry, David. "John Randolph vs. the War Hawks: A Weaverian Analysis of Argumentation in the War of 1812 Debates." Paper presented at the annual meeting of the Speech Communication Association, Houston, Texas, December 1975.

Johnston, Alexander. "John Randolph." In *American Orations*. Edited by Alexander Johnston and James A. Woodburn. New York: G. P. Putnam's Sons, 1896.

Sargent, Nathan. "John Randolph." In *Public Men and Events*. Philadelphia: J. B. Lippincott & Co., 1875.

Weaver, Richard. "Two Types of American Individualism." In *Life without Prejudice and Other Essays*. Chicago: Henry Regnery Company, 1965.

Winn, Larry J. "The War Hawks' Call to Arms: Appeals for a Second War with Great Britain." *Southern Speech Communication Journal* 37 (1972): 402–12.

Selected Biographies

Adams, Henry. *John Randolph*. Boston: Houghton, Mifflin and Company, 1884.

Bruce, William Cabell. *John Randolph of Roanoke, 1773–1833*. 1927; rpt., New York: Octagon Books, 1970. 2 vols.

Dawidoff, Robert. *The Education of John Randolph*. New York: W. W. Norton & Company, 1979.

Dudley, Theodorick B., ed. *Letters of John Randolph*. Philadelphia: Carey, Lea, and Blanchard, 1834.

Garland, Hugh A. *The Life of John Randolph of Roanoke*. 11th ed. 2 vols. New York: D. Appleton & Company, 1857.

Kirk, Russell. *John Randolph of Roanoke: A Study in American Politics, with Selected Speeches and Letters*. Chicago: Henry Regnery Company, 1964.

CHRONOLOGY OF MAJOR SPEECHES

See "Research Collections and Collected Speeches" for source codes.

Election campaign address on the Virginia Assembly, Charlotte, Virginia, March 1799; *LJRR*, 1: 133–41.

"Debate on the Yazoo Claims," U.S. House of Representatives, Washington, D.C., February 1, 1805; *JRR*, pp. 257–66.

"On Gregg's Resolution," U.S. House of Representatives, Washington, D.C., March 5, 1806; *JRR*, pp. 266–91.

"Against War with England," U.S. House of Representatives, Washington, D.C., December 10, 1811; *AC*, 12th Cong., 1st sess., pp. 441–55; *AO*, 1: pt. 1, pp 164–79; *JRR*, pp. 291–310; *NWR*, 1: 315–21.

Speech on treaty-making power, U.S. House of Representatives, Washington, D.C., January 10, 1816; *AC*, 14th Cong., 2d sess. pp. 579–91; *JRR*, pp. 310–25.

Address on internal improvements, U.S. House of Representatives, Washington, D.C.: January 30, 1824; *AC*, 18th Cong., 2d sess., pp. 1296–1311; *JRR*, pp. 337–57.

Address on the Panama Congress (speech on executive powers), U.S. Senate, Washington, D.C., March 30, 1826; *RDC*, 19th Cong., 2d sess., pp. 389–406; *JRR*, pp. 357–84.

On king numbers, speech at the Virginia State Convention, Richmond, Virginia, December 30, 1829; *PD*, pp. 312–21; *JRR*, pp. 437–57.

RED JACKET
(1758?–1830), council spokesman for the Seneca Indians

HARRY W. ROBIE

Red Jacket was the last prominent member of his tribe to use the indigenous rhetorical strategies of the Iroquois council spokesmen. Employing formulas that for centuries had been a part of the Iroquois oratorical tradition, he consistently opposed land sales, war against the colonists and new nation and imposition of white culture upon his people. By the 1820s, according to the future historian Henry Manley, his reputation as a speaker "resembled that of Clarence Darrow a hundred years later." A generation after his death, Frank Moore thought Red Jacket important enough to include three of his speeches in *American Eloquence*, and the Indian spokesman had become the subject of extensive treatments by Thomas L. McKenney, B. B. Thatcher, William L. Stone, and DeWitt Clinton. Roberta Briggs Sutton's *Speech Index* still includes more citations under his name than for any other native American speaker.

Red Jacket's birth name was Otetiani, "Always ready." He was born into the wolf clan of the Seneca tribe, one of the five members of the Iroquois Confederacy. He grew up around the shores of Cayuga Lake, near present-day Geneva, New York, during a period when many traditional values of his tribe were being called into question for the first time. As a young adult, he shared the bitter defeat his tribe suffered as British allies during the Revolution, and he later saw the loss of most of the Seneca territory during American expansion in the first decades of the nineteenth century. Unable to become a sachem in the Iroquois Confederacy because his family was not *hoyaney* (of a noble lineage), he nevertheless rose to become his tribe's most prominent spokesman. In speeches delivered over a forty-year period, he endeavored to protect the Seneca way of life from the onslaught of white civilization. In doing so, he became one of the first to call into question some of the basic *topoi* of the new nation.

It was through public address, and for no other reason, that Red Jacket achieved his reputation among both Indians and whites. As a young adult, he was renamed Sagoyewatha ("He keeps them awake") by the members of his tribe. His speeches formed the major content of two of the first books published in western New York. His speaking was well enough known to the rest of the nation that prominent visitors to western New York, such as Lafayette, made a visit to Red Jacket an obligatory part of their itineraries. Once, when asked by a white about his career as a warrior, Red Jacket is reported to have dodged the question. "I am an orator," he was reported as saying. "I was born an orator."

RED JACKET AS A COUNCIL SPOKESMAN WITHIN THE IROQUOIAN CONTEXT

As a speaker, Red Jacket was continuing a rhetorical tradition that predated white contact. The Iroquois Confederacy to which his tribe belonged also included the Cayugas, Onondagas, Oneidas, Mohawks, and (after the Revolution) the Tuscaroras. They conceived of themselves as members of a metaphorical family, which inhabited a longhouse coextensive with the league itself. They had developed an indigenous conference procedure based on reciprocal obligations among family members and on the speaking skills of male spokesmen (who, however, were selected for that function by females since Iroquois society was matrilineal). Their league provided enough strength that the Iroquois could maintain their independence through two centuries of white pressure and extend their influence during colonial times from Illinois to the Carolinas.

Councils, held on all levels of Iroquois society, provided the cohesion that enabled the confederacy to operate so effectively. To outsiders, however, the most characteristic features of Iroquois speech practice were not the councils but the speeches delivered by the spokesmen, such as Red Jacket, who articulated their views. Over three centuries, Iroquois spokesmen maintained a continuous speaking tradition, which was sophisticated in matters of content and presentation. With respect to inventive processes, they made use of ethical appeals created by their positions as the voices of a united confederacy, and they used kinship terms that presupposed an imagined or adoptive relationship with the other party. They made use of pathetic appeals directed toward pride, blood and tribal relationships, fear, greed, and fair-mindedness. Their logical reasoning frequently involved turning the tables by taking the arguments advanced by the other party and turning them against them. Reliance was also made on historical precedent, and major arguments were further buttressed by gifts, such as the presentation of wampum, which validated the claims being presented.

In matters of organization, spokesmen seemed to vary little from a five-part structure: (1) invocation of the Great Spirit and statement of purpose, (2) description of the journey to council, (3) historical narration, (4) presentation of major claims, and (5) appeals to kinship ties. Although the words of the spokesmen are preserved largely in translation, and we thus have difficulty making comments about verbal style, the speakers appeared to make extensive use of metaphor, even if the nature of their languages did not force them to do so. And in place of lying, which was culturally proscribed, the spokesmen made heavy use of irony. In matters of delivery, spokesmen were much more stylized than they were in ordinary discourse. Their eye contact was direct, for this was a means of guaranteeing truth saying. Their vocalization was artificial and declamatory, their gesture and movement frequently pantomimic, so much so that aristocratic French observers compared their performances favorably with what was then appearing on the Parisian stage. This delivery took place within a circular council ring, which allowed speakers free and varied movement. Spokesmen were permitted limited flexibility in style and delivery, but in their content they were expected to follow the dictates of the councils for which they spoke.

As a boy, Red Jacket may have been inspired to become a spokesman when he attended a council on the Shenandoah River and heard Logan, an Iroquois speaker now best known through his letter to Lord Dunsmore, a colonial governor of Virginia. Certainly Red Jacket would have seen many other models at the numerous councils held at his village. Later he served as a runner for his tribe and delivered messages to other villages. For a limited time, he was also a warrior, though his rivals frequently called his bravery into question, and one of them, the Mohawk chief Joseph Brant, branded him with the derisive name "cow killer." During the Revolution, when his tribe fought with the British, Red Jacket's village moved to the protection of the guns at Fort Niagara. It was there that a British officer presented him with a red coat. Later he was presented with a similar garment by the American interpreter Jasper Parrish. The budding speaker began to favor this article of clothing in his public appearances, and this led to the nickname by which he is most familiarly known. Completing his speaking costume was a tomahawk and the large silver medallion, now in the Buffalo Historical Society, that had been given to him personally by George Washington.

There are no likenesses from Red Jacket's early years, though a number of portraits were made in the last decade of his life. They indicate a man who, except for his dark and penetrating eyes, was probably rather average in appearance. Auditors were more impressed by Red Jacket's command of gesture and vocal variety. In public, Red Jacket always spoke in the mellifluous Seneca language, though he also knew English. Trusted translators, such as Horatio Jones and Jasper Parrish, worked with him over a period of years and provided audiences with accurate translations. The translators were carefully prepped by Red Jacket before the actual speech occasions. They admitted, however, that much of the beauty in the originals was necessarily lost. It is good that Red Jacket had a hand in the translations of his speeches because none of his oratory still exists in the Seneca language.

Red Jacket was illiterate and therefore found it necessary to cultivate his powers of memory. Wampum strings and belts were traditional mnemonic aids for Iroquois spokesmen, but within his lifetime, they were coming into disuse because of their prohibitive expense, and Red Jacket may have needed to resort to other memory aids. One observer reported that he saw Red Jacket rehearsing an address by throwing sticks on the ground and picking them up in a particular order. Whatever techniques he used, the facts remain that he was possessed of a phenomenal memory that served him in good stead when he had to remember the details of important transactions. In a celebrated exchange with New York's Governor Daniel Tompkins, Red Jacket objected to the white interpretation of a treaty signed years before. "You have forgotten," responded the governor, "we have it written down on paper." "The paper then tells a lie—I have it written here," Red Jacket replied, placing his hand on his brow. "You Yankees are born with a feather between your fingers, but your paper does not speak the truth. The Indian keeps his knowledge here—this is the book the Great Spirit gave them; it does not lie." When the treaty in question was brought out, Red Jacket's memory proved to be correct.

Because western New York was still a frontier and because Red Jacket was unable to make records himself, even the English translations of his speeches exist in a relatively fragmentary form. Nothing remains of Red Jacket's first major address, delivered before a largely Indian audience on the banks of the Detroit River in 1786, though one white auditor deemed it "a masterpiece of oratory." The first record of a speech by Red Jacket exists in a fragmentary paraphrase from a council at Tioga, New York, in 1790. The second fragment comes from Buffalo Creek in the spring of 1791. It was at Buffalo Creek, the major Seneca reserve after the Revolution, that Red Jacket and his family settled. Two complete speeches and other remarks are preserved from a 1792 council at Philadelphia. Other government sources record two speeches delivered in Washington, D.C., in 1801 and his council speech at the upper rapids of the Sandusky River in 1816. More extensive federal reports were probably destroyed in the British attack on Washington during the War of 1812.

White admirers in western New York published two books that preserve some of Red Jacket's rhetorical efforts. The first of these, *Native Eloquence*, was published in 1811 in Canandaigua, New York, by the area's first printer, J. D. Bemis. The book contains four of Red Jacket's speeches, as well as one by Farmer Brother, another spokesman who had moved to the Buffalo Creek reserve.

The first of Red Jacket's efforts in *Native Eloquence*, the 1805 reply to Reverend Cram, is probably a typical example of the spokesman's antimissionary oratory. In the speech he argued that the Great Spirit had made each people a religion appropriate to their condition, that the proximity of white civilization could only corrupt native Americans, and that if whites wished to convert others, they should do less preaching and live better lives. Red Jacket then concluded with an interesting offer. "Brother," he said, "we are told that you have been preaching to the white people in this place. These people are our neighbors. We are acquainted with them. We will wait a little while, and see what effect your preaching has upon them. If we find it does them good, makes them honest, and less disposed to cheat Indians; we will then consider again of what you have said." Actually Red Jacket expected little improvement in his white neighbors. As he later remarked to another missionary, "If you white men murdered the Son of the Great Spirit, we Indians had nothing to do with it, and it is none of our affair. If he had come among us, we would not have killed him; we would have treated him well; and the white people who killed him ought to be damned for doing it. You must make amends for that crime yourselves."

The other speeches in *Native Eloquence* offer equally interesting examples of Red Jacket's argumentative skills. The book's second speech, an 1811 response to Reverend Alexander, claimed that "forms of worship are indifferent to the Great Spirit—it is the offering of a sincere heart that pleases him," and asserted Indians already worshipped him in this manner. The third speech, also delivered in 1811, was a reply to a Mr. Richardson, who had attempted to buy some of the tribal lands at Buffalo Creek. In his response, Red Jacket made use of a favorite argument, the hypocrisy of the whites, and like so many of his ancestors, he played one group of whites against another, in this case the Americans against the British who controlled the Canadian territory on the other side of Lake Erie.

"At the treaties held for the purchase of our lands," he asserted, "the white men with sweet voices and smiling faces told us they loved us, and that they would not cheat us, but that the king's children on the other side of the lake would cheat us. When we go on the other side of the lake the king's children tell us your people will cheat us, but with sweet voices and smiling faces assure us of their love and that they will not cheat us. These things puzzle our heads," he concluded, "and we believe that the Indians must take care of themselves, and not trust either in your people or in the king's children." *Native Eloquence* ends with a speech given when the Senecas remanded an Indian fugitive to white authorities in 1802. In it Red Jacket compared native American and white conceptions of justice in a review of Indian rights under the laws of the new nation. However, he did not convince the judge that an Indian accused of murdering a white man should be tried under Indian law instead of the laws of New York.

The second volume to contain speeches of Red Jacket, and the first book to be published in Buffalo, was entitled *Public Speeches* and was issued to record the Seneca position with respect to the War of 1812. In it two speeches of Red Jacket bracket a speech by Erastus Granger, a representative of the federal government. Together they give a flavor of what a complete council meeting must have been like. In particular, they show the government agent Granger adapting his speech style to many of the Iroquoian rhetorical patterns. In addition to the speech texts contained in these two books, there are a number of fragments and paraphrases preserved by Red Jacket's biographers, particularly Stone. Of particular note are fragments from Red Jacket's speech at the murder trial of Tommy Jemmy, in 1821, and his own defense when Christian elements at Buffalo Creek reserve tried to depose him from office in 1827. In sum, the remaining examples of Red Jacket's oratory prove that he was the product of a sophisticated and effective speaking tradition and that he correctly analyzed many of the problems minorities would face in the years ahead as they struggled against being submerged in mainstream American culture.

A complicated personality, Red Jacket often signed the land treaties he had earlier attacked. In his later years, his activities were punctuated by bouts of drunkenness. Gradually he lost influence to the missionaries at the same time that the tribe's pagan elements were flocking to the teachings of Handsome Lake, his rival from the Allegheny reservation. On his death, he was given a Christian burial by his second wife, who had converted some years before. Shortly after, the Buffalo Creek reserve itself was sold to the whites. The Seneca Indians have fought to retain the rest of their western New York lands, however, and in doing so they have utilized many of the arguments enunciated by Red Jacket. They have also continued to use councils in their political and religious life. In those councils, traces still remain of the rhetoric first developed by the Iroquois in the centuries before the European colonization of North America.

INFORMATION SOURCES

Research Collections and Collected Speeches

Much material on Red Jacket and the Iroquois can be found in the New York State Library, Albany; the University of Rochester library; the library of the Buffalo Historical Society; and the Seneca-Iroquois Museum, Salamanca, New York.

Aboriginal American Oratory. Edited by Louis Thomas Jones. Los Angeles: *AAO*
   Southwest Museum, 1965.

American Eloquence. Edited by Frank Moore. 2 vols. New York: D. Ap-   *AE*
   pelton and Company, 1857.

Native Eloquence, Being Public Speeches Delivered by Two Distinguished   *NE*
   Chiefs of the Seneca Tribe of Indians. Canandaigua, N.Y.: J. D.
   Bemis, 1811.

Public Speeches Delivered at the Village of Buffalo Respecting the Part the   *PS*
   Six Nations Would Take in the Present War against Great Britain.
   1812, rpt., *Publications of the Buffalo Historical Society.* Vol. 4.
   Buffalo: Peter Paul Book Company, 1896.

Stone, William L. *Life and Times of Sa-Go-Ye-Wat-Ha, or Red Jacket.*   *LT*
   Albany: J. Munsell, 1866.

The World's Great Speeches. Edited by Lewis Copeland. 2d rev. ed. New   *WGS*
   York: Dover Publications, 1958.

Selected Critical Studies

Reynolds, Wynn R. "A Study of the Persuasive Speaking Techniques of the Iroquois
   Indians: 1678–1776." Ph.D., diss., Columbia University, 1957.

Robie, Harry W. "Red Jacket's Reply to Reverend Cram: A Contribution to the An-
   thropology of Communication." Ph.D., diss., Michigan State University, 1972.

Selected Biographies

Hubbard, J. Niles. *An Account of Sa-go-ye-wat-ha or Red Jacket and His People.* Albany:
   John Munsell's Sons, 1886.

Parker, Arthur C. *Red Jacket, Last of the Seneca.* New York: McGraw-Hill, 1952.

Thatcher, B. B. *Indian Biography.* Vol 2. New York: Harper & Brothers, 1837.

CHRONOLOGY OF MAJOR SPEECHES

See "Research Collections and Collected Speeches" for source codes. Speeches at Philadelphia council, Philadelphia, March and April 1792; *LT*, pp. 164–93.

Condolence speech on General Israel Chapin, Canandaigua, New York, April 1729; *LT* pp. 235–36.

Speeches at Washington council, Washington D.C., 1801; *LT*, pp. 255–63.

Courthouse statement, Canandaigua, New York, August 3, 1802; *NE* pp. 18–24.

Reply to Reverend Cram, Buffalo Creek, New York, summer 1805; *LT*, pp. 272–81; *NE* pp. 5–12; *WGS*, pp. 222–26.

Reply to Reverend Alexander, Buffalo Creek, New York, May 1811; *NE*, pp. 12–14.

Reply to Mr. Richardson, Buffalo Creek, New York, May 1811; *NE*, pp. 14–18.

Speeches at Buffalo council, Buffalo, New York, July 6, 8, 1812; *PS*, pp. 5–6, 18–28.

Speech at Sandusky council, upper rapids of the Sandusky, Ohio, November 1816; *LT*, pp. 352–59.

Speech at Buffalo council, Buffalo, New York, summer 1819 (?); *LT*, pp. 363–76.

ELIZABETH CADY STANTON
(1815–1902), first U.S. feminist

KARLYN KOHRS CAMPBELL

Elizabeth Cady Stanton was one of the great speakers and writers of the nineteenth century, but her rhetorical prowess has gone unrecognized for several reasons. First, she espoused positions that were radical for her time, and some of them, such as anticlericalism, have remained controversial. As a result, the more conservative Susan B. Anthony has been used to typify women's struggle for civil rights and enfranchisement. Moreover, because she worked for causes that have not been popular with white male academics who have dominated pedagogy, publishing, and canon formation, texts of her speeches have not been included in standard anthologies, and no collection of her speeches exists. In addition rhetorical scholars have failed to recognize the excellence of women speakers because they have not been exposed to their speeches and because public speaking has traditionally been seen as the exclusive domain of males. Yet Elizabeth Cady Stanton launched what became the social movement for woman's rights, including woman suffrage, and she was the movement's chief philosopher and publicist.

Because her parents were landed gentry and her father a judge, Elizabeth Cady had opportunities available to few other women of her time. She was the only girl to graduate from the Johnstown, New York, high school, and, although barred from higher education by her sex, for two years she attended Emma Willard's Troy Female Seminary, a finishing school with a somewhat enlarged curriculum. A clergyman neighbor tutored her in Greek, and by her own report, she read some law in her father's office. For the most part, however, she was self-educated, and she was a voracious reader throughout her life.

Because she fulfilled traditional expectations for women of her time, she was a more effective woman's rights advocate. In 1840 she married Henry Brewster Stanton, and they were the parents of seven children. Despite family responsibilities, which were particularly onerous because her husband was often absent on business for months at a time, she became an active reformer. In addition to being the moving force behind the first woman's rights convention at Seneca Falls, New York, in 1848, she was a founder and president of the New York Woman's Temperance Society (1851–1853), a founder and president of the American Equal Rights Association (1867–1869), a founder and president of the National Woman Suffrage Association (1869–1890), and president of the merged National American Woman Suffrage Association (1890–1892). In 1866 she became the first woman to run for the U.S. Congress (Eighth District, New York), taking advantage of the paradoxical situation in which women were prohibited from voting but not from running for office. For eight months of the year between 1869 and 1882 she lectured, usually twice a day, on the lyceum circuit.

Although Mary Wollstonecraft in England and Margaret Fuller, Judith Sargent Murray, and Angelina and Sarah Grimké in the United States had recognized and articulated women's disadvantages, Cady Stanton launched what became the woman's rights movement. She was one of five women who called the first woman's rights convention at Seneca Falls, New York, in 1848, and it was she who refashioned the Declaration of Independence into a Declaration of Sentiments stating women's specific grievances. The resolutions adopted at Seneca Falls, including a controversial demand for woman suffrage, were reaffirmed at later conventions and led to organized agitation to change state laws regarding women and to pass a federal woman suffrage amendment. Thus, more than any other one person, she was the founder of the early feminist movement.

STANTON AS PUBLIC ADVOCATE AND PHILOSOPHER

Many others made significant contributions to the cause of woman's rights and woman suffrage, but Cady Stanton merits special recognition for several reasons. The first is that she was the movement's chief public advocate during her life. From 1848 until her death in 1902, Cady Stanton's voice and pen were dedicated to woman's rights. Her output was prodigious. In addition to countless newspaper articles and letters to the editor, she made numerous speeches, many of which were published in newspapers and as tracts. With Susan B. Anthony as publisher, she and Parker Pillsbury edited *The Revolution* (1868–1870); with Susan B. Anthony and Matilda Joslyn Gage, she compiled and edited the first three volumes of the *History of Woman Suffrage* (1881, 1886); she authored an autobiography (1898); and she was the editor and chief author of the two volumes of *The Woman's Bible* (1895, 1898).

In addition to launching a social movement and functioning as its chief public advocate, Cady Stanton was the movement's philosopher, and the philosophy she developed is what is now called feminism. Although early woman's rights and woman suffrage advocates never used that term, the label is an apt description for several reasons. First, even as she worked for temperance and the abolition of slavery, she argued that woman's rights were fundamental. For example, in her opening address to the New York Woman's Temperance Society in 1853, she explained: "We have been obliged to preach woman's rights, because men, instead of listening to what we had to say on temperance, have questioned the right of a woman to speak on any subject. . . . Let it be clearly understood, then, that we are a woman's rights Society; that we believe it is a woman's duty to speak whenever she feels the impression to do so." Second, she saw all reforms as inevitably tied to civil rights for women. For example, in the speech just cited, she made an impassioned plea for consistency between emotional appeals based on women's plight and political action for their rights:

Shall these classes of sufferers [drunkards' wives, children, widows, and orphans] be introduced but as themes for rhetorical flourish, as pathetic touches of the speaker's eloquence; shall we passively shed tears over their condition, or by giving them rights bravely open to them the doors of escape from a wretched and degraded life? . . . If in showing her wrongs, we prove the right of all womankind to the elective franchise; to a fair representation in the government; to the right in criminal cases to be tried by peers of her own choosing, shall it be said that we transcend the bounds of our subject?

Third, despite the severe economic, social, and political disabilities under which women labored, Cady Stanton believed in women's abilities to bring about change. At Seneca Falls, she asserted that "woman herself must do this work," calling attention to the rhetorical power of women speaking for their own rights and to women's deeper understanding of their problems. In 1860, speaking to the American Anti-Slavery Society, she said: "A privileged class can never conceive the feelings of those who are born to contempt, to inferiority, to degradation. Herein is woman more fully identified with the slave than man can possibly be, for she can take the subjective view." She then proceeded to illustrate her claim with a uniquely woman-centered appeal for the abolition of slavery: "Are not nearly two millions of native-born American women at this very hour, doomed to the foulest slavery that angels ever wept to witness? Are they not doubly damned as immortal beasts of burden in the field, and sad mothers of a most accursed race? Are not they raised for the express purpose of lust? . . . And this is the condition of woman in republican, Christian America, and you dare not look me in the face and tell me that, for blessings such as these, my heart should go out in thankfulness."

Cady Stanton espoused a feminist philosophy because, unlike most other early woman's rights advocates, she believed men and women had identical natures and that differences between them reflected socialization. As a result, her arguments were grounded in natural rights philosophy, a perspective that inevitably led to an enlarged conception of woman's rights. Her philosophical position was apparent when, in speaking to the New York legislature in 1860, she said: "If, then, the nature of a being decides its rights, every individual comes into the world with rights that are not transferable." In 1867, speaking to the American Equal Rights Association, she made the link between natural rights and civil rights: "To discuss this question of suffrage for women and negroes [sic], as women and negroes, and not as citizens of a republic, implies that there are some reasons for demanding this right for these classes that do not apply to 'white males' . . . as if they were anomalous beings, outside all human laws and necessities." Sometimes she used the linkage sarcastically to raise her hearers' consciousness, as in 1860 when she said to white male New York legislators: "We may safely trust the shrewd selfishness of the white man, and consent to life under the same broad code where he has so comfortably ensconced himself."

Her role as movement philosopher was enhanced by the fact that, from the outset, she recognized the fundamental arguments that had to be attacked if women were to attain full citizenship. Her speech at Seneca Falls was a detailed refutation of the three major justifications used by opponents to limit woman's sphere: the biological argument that, in effect, anatomy is destiny; the theological argument that God ordained woman's limited and subservient place; and the sociological view that woman is one element in a family unit publicly represented by the husband. Her early insistence on the goal of female enfranchisement reflected her inclusive, holistic view of the struggle. She shocked the New York Woman's Temperance Society in 1852 by advocating liberalized laws to permit women to divorce husbands who were perpetual drunkards, and as early as 1853, she was writing to Susan B. Anthony that "this whole question of woman's rights turns on the pivot of the marriage relation." She took the position that marriage was a contract like any other, not a religious sacrament, a view reflected in her speeches advocating liberalized divorce laws. She recognized that the church, the clergy, and theology were major obstacles to woman's rights, and she spoke and wrote in support of that view throughout her life. Such views were highly controversial, and her final major work, *The Woman's Bible*, was repudiated by the National American Woman Suffrage Association (NAWSA), despite the impassioned pleas of her revered friend and coworker, Susan B. Anthony. She is often described as speaking for the radical wing of the movement, and she described herself as a radical in public as early as 1852. Late in life she wrote in her diary what other suffragists would not have disputed: "I tell her [Susan B. Anthony] that I get more radical as I grow older, while she seems to grow more conservative."

Cady Stanton was such an effective public advocate for woman's rights because she grounded her appeals in basic cultural values—natural rights philosophy and the principles underlying the American Revolution. This highly consistent philosophical position made her less vulnerable to attack and strengthened the refutation she made of opponents' arguments. Despite the unchanging character of her basic premises, she was skilled in adapting to diverse audiences.

For example, in addressing the joint Judiciary Committees of the New York legislature in 1854, she organized her speech to consider woman as citizen, as wife, as widow, and as mother, a topical structure that allowed her to combine appeals for the natural rights women claimed as citizens with appeals to the chivalry of her male audience to protect women in their traditional roles. Because she was addressing lawyers on legal issues, she drew her evidence from legal sources: constitutions, statutes, and legal authorities. Because she was appealing to male chivalry, she told moving stories of the plight of widows and mothers under current laws. To these were added religious appeals based on the Golden Rule and an invidious comparison of the attitudes of southern planters toward their slaves and of males toward females. Although her appeals were rejected in 1854, in 1860 the legislature passed laws alleviating most of the conditions she had deplored in 1854.

Like others who spoke and wrote frequently to many different audiences, Cady Stanton repeated arguments and themes. For example, there were echoes of speeches given earlier that year in her first speech of the 1867 Kansas referendum campaign, delivered in Lawrence. However, her speech was crafted for this time and place. Her introduction reflected her adaptive skills and hinted at the meaning of Kansas for reformers of her time, particularly those who had worked in the movement to abolish slavery. She began her speech this way: "How shall I find fitting words to express all I would say as I stand for the first time before an audience in Kansas? As the pious Catholic on entering his cathedral kneels and with holy water makes the sign of the cross upon his brow before lifting his eyes to the Holy of Holies, so would I reverently treat this soil as the vestabule [*sic*] to our Temple of Liberty, the opening vista to the future grandeur of the new republic." She invited Kansas voters to play a historic role:

Fresh from the corrupting influences of Kings and Courts, it was a great thing for our Fathers to get the idea of equality on paper. . . . but it is a greater thing for you today to make it a fact in the government of a mighty state. . . . If you realize what you propose, to you will belong the honor of solving the national problem that has so long perplexed our political leaders, for as in war freedom was the key note in victory, so now is universal suffrage the key note of reconstruction.

She was a particularly effective advocate because she understood the rhetorical problems—the barriers to persuasive success—that confronted the movement. For example, speaking to the national convention of the National Woman Suffrage Association in 1870, she said:

Knowing that we hold the Gibraltar rock of reason on this question, they resort to ridicule and petty objections. Compelled to follow our assailants, wherever they go, and fight them with their own weapons; when cornered with wit and sarcasm, some cry out, you have no logic on your platform, forgetting that we have no use for logic until they give us logicians at whom to hurl it, and if, for the pure love of it, we now and then rehearse the logic that is like a,b,c, to all of us, others cry out—the same old speeches we have heard these twenty years.

As her statement implies, Cady Stanton understood that she and other woman's rights advocates had to use a variety of rhetorical strategies, and this she did. The chief resources in her rhetorical arsenal were tightly reasoned deductive arguments based on legal evidence and authority, skillful use of analogy, metaphor, and vivid depiction, and humor.

No brief quotation could illustrate adequately Cady Stanton's argumentative prowess. Her speeches to the New York legislature in 1854 and 1860 and to U.S. congressional committees in 1890 are masterworks of discursive proof. Some examples from her speeches give a flavor of her skill in argument. For instance, she frequently used natural rights principles to pose a dilemma for her male audiences: "If the sexes are alike in their mental structure, then there is no reason why women should not have a voice in making the laws which govern her. But if they are not alike, most certain woman must make laws for herself; for who else can understand her wants and needs?" She could make her refutation clear and vivid. For example, in April 1894, in an essay entitled "Women Do

Not Wish to Vote,'' she wrote: "We do not fence the cornfields because we think the cattle will not eat the corn, but because we know they will. And the word 'male' in the Constitution [Fourteenth Amendment], is a standing admission that men know women would vote if the barriers were down, no matter what they say to the contrary.''

As the last quotation illustrates, her speeches were replete with metaphors, analogies, and descriptions, the rhetorical means by which ideas are embodied and made vivid and by which audience members are enabled to move from the known and familiar to the unknown and unfamiliar. Her 1854 speech to the Judiciary Committees of the New York legislature concluded with a metaphor designed to refute the argument that she and other woman's rights advocates did not speak for all women: "Who are they that we do not now represent? But a small class of fashionable butterflies who, through the short summer days, seek the sunshine and the flowers; but the cool breezes of autumn and the hoary frosts of winter will soon chase all these away; then, they too will need and seek protection, and through other lips demand, in their turn, justice and equity at your hands.''

Cady Stanton made detailed comparisons between the legal positions of slaves and women. In her 1860 speech to the New York legislature, she said:

How many of you have ever read the laws concerning them [women] that now disgrace your statute books? In cruelty and tyranny, they are not surpassed by any slaveholding code in the Southern States. . . . The negro [*sic*] has no name. He is Cuffy Douglas or Cuffy Brooks, just whose Cuffy he may chance to be. The woman has no name. She is Mrs. Richard Roe or Mrs. John Doe, just whose Mrs. she may chance to be. Cuffy has no right to his earnings; he cannot buy or sell, or lay up anything he can call his own. Mrs. Roe has no right to her earnings.

She went on to recount other legal similarities in regard to child custody, legal recognition, and physical restraint and chastisement, effectively exploiting audience revulsion regarding the conditions of slaves.

Humor, frequently satirical, regularly appeared in her speeches. In an 1867 speech to the New York legislature urging that women be allowed to vote for delegates to the state constitutional convention, she recalled that women had voted in New Jersey between 1776 and 1807 and then asked: "Did the children, fully armed and equipped for the battle of life, spring Minerva-like, from the brains of their fathers? Were the laws of nature suspended? Did the sexes change places? Was everything turned upside down? No, life went on as smoothly in New Jersey as in any other State in the Union.'' Later in the same speech, she drew an ironic contrast: "Does the North consider its women a part of the family to be represented by the 'white male citizen,' so views the South her negroes [*sic*]. And thus viewing them, the South has never taxed her slaves; but our chivalry never fails to send its tax gatherers to the poorest widow that holds a homestead.'' Finally, she told a story to support her view that suffrage should be universal and without qualification: "In the old days of the Colonies when the property qualification was £5—that being just the price of a jackass—Benjamin Franklin facetiously asked, 'If a man must own a donkey in order to vote, who does the voting, the man or the donkey?' "

Many causes Cady Stanton espoused were successful in her lifetime as a broad array of woman's rights were passed by many state legislatures. Full woman suffrage came only after her death; other goals she fought for have yet to be achieved. A statement she made before the U.S. Senate Committee on Woman Suffrage in 1888 provides a context for viewing her achievements and those of the early feminist movement. She said: "[William Edward Hartpole] Lecky, the historian, has well said the success of a movement depends much less on the force of its arguments, or upon the ability of its advocates, than the predisposition of society to receive it." Despite what she described as "the merciless storm of ridicule and persecution, . . . [being] ostracized in social life, scandalized by enemies, denounced by the pulpit, scarified and caricatured by the press," she spoke where few or no women had spoken before, and she was honored in her life time as one of the greatest women the United States had produced.

Such an estimate is confirmed rhetorically. She produced one of the masterpieces of rhetorical literature, "The Solitude of Self," the speech she made to committees of the U.S. House and Senate and to the convention of the NAWSA in 1892. The address is a manifesto for humanistic feminism and lyric expression of the experience of human life. It remains an enduring rationale for the civil rights of individuals based on the U.S. republican tradition, the Protestant concept of the priesthood of believers, and the American credo of individualism and self-reliance.

Not only was Cady Stanton a speaker who dominated the American scene for over half a century, she was a leader of a great social movement. Her speeches addressed issues of continuing concern, her arguments were grounded in cherished cultural values, and her skills with metaphor, analogy, and humor brought her ideas vividly before our eyes.

INFORMATION SOURCES

Research Collections and Collected Speeches

Those who wish to study Elizabeth Cady Stanton's rhetoric must rely on two major sources, the Elizabeth Cady Stanton Papers, Library of Congress, available on microfilm (ECSP, reels 1–5), and the History of Women collection (HOW), available on microfiche, incorporating materials from many special collections and most issues of the journals that were the major outlets for woman's rights advocates, such as the *Lily*, the *Una*, the *Revolution*, the *Woman's Journal*, and the *Woman's Tribune*.

Elizabeth Cady Stanton As Revealed in Her Letters, Diary, and Reminis-   LDR
    cences. 2 vols. Edited by Theodore Stanton and Harriot Stanton
    Blatch. New York: Harper & Brothers, 1922.
Elizabeth Cady Stanton, Susan B. Anthony: Correspondence, Writings,   ECSSBA
    Speeches. Edited by Ellen Carol DuBois. New York: Schocken,
    1981.
History of Woman Suffrage. 3 vols. 1848–1884. Edited by Elizabeth Cady   HWS
    Stanton, Susan B. Anthony, and Matilda Joslyn Gage. New York:
    Fowler & Wells, 1881; Rochester: Susan B. Anthony, 1886.
Outspoken Women: Speeches by American Women Reformers, 1635–1935.   OW
    Edited by Judith Anderson. Dubuque, Iowa: Kendall/Hunt, 1984.
Stanton, Elizabeth Cady. *Eighty Years and More: Reminiscences 1815–*
    1897. Introduction by Gail Parker. 1898; rpt., New York: Schocken,
    1971.
Stanton, Elizabeth Cady, and the Revising Committee. *The Woman's Bible.*
    2 vols. 1895, 1898; rpt., European Publishing ed. Seattle: Coalition
    Task Force on Women and Religion, 1974.
We Shall Be Heard: Women Speakers in America, 1828-Present. Edited by   WSBH
    Patricia Scileppi Kennedy and Gloria Hartmann O'Shields. Dubuque,
    Iowa: Kendall/Hunt, 1983.

Selected Critical Studies

Campbell, Karlyn Kohrs. "Stanton's 'The Solitude of Self': A Rationale for Feminism."
    Quarterly Journal of Speech 66 (1980): 304–12.
Caroli, Betty Boyd. "Women Speak Out for Reform." In *The Rhetoric of Protest and*
    Reform, 1878–1898. Edited by Paul Boase. Athens: Ohio University Press, 1980.
Goodman, James E. "The Origins of the 'Civil War' in the Reform Community: Elizabeth
    Cady Stanton on Woman's Rights and Reconstruction." *Critical Matrix: Princeton*
    Working Papers in Women's Studies 1, no. 2 (1985): 1–29.
McCurdy, Frances. "Women Speak Out in Protest." In *The Rhetoric of Protest and*
    Reform, 1878–1898. Edited by Paul Boase. Athens: Ohio University Press, 1980.
O'Connor, Lillian. *Pioneer Women Orators: Rhetoric in the Ante-Bellum Reform Move-*
    ment. New York: Columbia University Press, 1954.
Yoakum, Doris G. "Woman's Introduction to the American Platform." In *History and*
    Criticism of American Public Address. Vol. 1. Edited by William Norwood Brig-
    ance. New York: Russell & Russell, 1960.

Selected Biographies

Banner, Lois. *Elizabeth Cady Stanton: A Radical for Women's Rights.* Boston: Little,
    Brown, 1980.
Bullard, Laura Curtis. "Elizabeth Cady Stanton." In *Our Famous Women.* Edited by
    Elizabeth Stuart Phelps et al. Hartford, Conn.: Hartford Publishing, 1888.
Griffith, Elisabeth. *In Her Own Right: The Life of Elizabeth Cady Stanton.* New York:
    Oxford, 1984.

Lutz, Alma. *Created Equal: A Biography of Elizabeth Cady Stanton.* New York: John Day, 1940.

CHRONOLOGY OF MAJOR SPEECHES

See "Research Collections and Collected Speeches" for source codes.

Address delivered at Seneca Falls and Rochester, New York, July 19, August 2, 1848; *HOW*; holograph *ECSP*, reel 2.

Address to the New York State Temperance Convention, Rochester, New York, April 20–21, 1852; *HWS*, 1: 481–83.

Address to the First Annual Meeting of the Woman's State Temperance Society, Rochester, New York, June 1–2, 1853; *HWS*, 1: 494–497.

Address to the New York legislature, adopted by the State Woman's Rights Convention, Albany, New York, February 14–15, 1854; *HOW; ECSP*, reel 5; *HWS*, 1: 595–605.

Address to the New York legislature, Albany, New York, February 18, 1860, as published May 11, 1860, *ECSP*, reel 5; excerpted *HWS*, 1: 679–85.

Speech on the anniversary of the American Anti-Slavery Society, New York, May 18, 1860; *Liberator*, May 18, 1860, p. 78; excerpted *ECSSBA*, pp. 78–85.

Speech on marriage and divorce at the Tenth National Woman's Rights Convention, New York, May 12, 1860; *Proceedings of the Woman's Rights Convention*, May 12, 1860.

Address on the divorce bill before the Judiciary Committee of the New York Senate, Albany, New York, February 8, 1861; *ECSP*, reels 2, 4.

Address to the New York legislature on universal suffrage, Albany, New York, January 23, 1867; *HOW; ECSP*, reels 3, 5; excerpted *HWS*, 2: 271–82, reprinted *OW*, pp. 164–68.

Speech to the American Equal Rights Association convention, New York, May 9, 1867; *Proceedings of the American Equal Rights Association*, May 9, 10, 1867 (New York: Robert J. Johnston, 1867); excerpted *HWS*, 2: 185–90.

First speech of the 1867 Kansas referendum campaign, n.d. Lawrence, Kansas, Kansas State Historical Society, Topeka.

"President's Address to the National Woman Suffrage Association Convention, 10 May 1870." *Revolution* 5 (19 May 1870): 305–7; excerpted *HWS*, 2: 348–55.

Address before the House Judiciary Committee, Washington, D.C., January 10, 1872; *ECSP*, reel 5; excerpted *HWS*, 2: 506–13.

Address of welcome to the International Council of Women, Washington, D.C., March 25, 1888; *Report of the International Council of Women* (Washington, D.C.: Rufus H. Darby, 1888); holograph, *ECSP*, reel 4; *Woman's Tribune*, March 27, 1888, p. 5; *Woman's Journal*, March 31, 1888, pp. 103, 106.

Speech to the U.S. Senate Special Committee on Woman Suffrage, Washington, D.C., February 8, 1890; to the House Judiciary Committee, February 12, 1890. *HOW; Woman's Tribune*, February 15, 1890, pp. 50–53; *ECSP*, reels 4, 5.

"Change Is the Law of Progress," address at the National American Woman Suffrage

Convention, Washington, D.C., February 18, 1890; *Woman's Tribune*, February 22, 1890, pp. 58–61; holograph, *ECSP*, reel 4; excerpted *HWS*, 4: 164–66.

"The Solitude of Self," Washington, D.C., address to the House Judiciary Committee and the National American Woman Suffrage Association convention, January 18, and to the Senate Committee on Woman Suffrage, January 20, 1892; *HOW; The Woman's Journal*, January 23, 1893, pp. 1, 32; *ECSP*, reels 4, 5; *HWS*, 4: 189–91; *WSBH*, pp. 66–74.

ALEXANDER H. STEPHENS

(1812–1883), representative, senator, and governor in Georgia, U.S.
congressman, and vice-president of the Confederacy

_____ CALVIN MCLEOD LOGUE

In his farewell speech from the House of Representatives in Augusta, Georgia, on July 2, 1859, Stephens called the period during which he served as an elected official a time of great fury. Stephens served in the Georgia House of Representatives from 1836 to 1840 and the state senate from 1841 to 1842. He was elected to the U.S. House of Representatives (1843–1859) and was returned to Congress (1874–1882). He was elected governor of Georgia in 1882 and died in office in 1883. Between 1841 and 1883, Stephens participated in many of the nation's most significant decision-making debates. He advocated the annexation of Texas, the Kansas-Nebraska Act, and the Compromise of 1850. He spoke against the concept of nullification, the Mexican War, the Wilmot Proviso, and the secession of southern states from the Union.

Because of his reputation of being sickly, reinforced by his weak physical appearance, audiences did not expect Stephens to be an impressive public advocate. When they initially saw this Georgian, they assumed him to be too feeble to withstand the rigors of a campaign or to defend a cause forcefully. Stephens's contemporaries described him as being pale, fair, slight, ungainly, and physically emaciated. One writer noted Stephens's "cadaverous face." He spoke in a voice characterized as squeaky, shrill, and inclining to the falsetto, that of a youth.

Despite his physical infirmities, Stephens was a formidable advocate. His frail physical appearance contrasted with his mental decisiveness, verbal facility, and general preparation for speaking to produce an electric impact on audiences. Paradoxically Stephens's sickly constitution gave him an advantage with listeners. Although unendowed with impressive physical and vocal attributes, he delivered ideas and arguments impressively. Witnesses recalled how Stephens was able to develop an argument coherently. They mentioned also the remarkable distinctness of his enunciation and how his rhetoric ranged from being rapid, vehement, and of the highest passion to one of collected and calm deliberation. A reporter for the _Savannah Daily News and Herald_, on August 28, 1866, described how Stephens was able to transfigure an image of physical frailty and vocal impotency into a forceful rhetorical performance: "His voice, when he commences to speak, is shrill and unlike that of any other man's voice we ever heard. As he progresses it increases in volume, and in the talent of the orator the audience seem to lose sight of the oddity of his appearance." After listening to an address Stephens delivered before the House of Representatives, Abraham Lincoln called it the "best speech of an hour's length" he had heard.

SPOKESMAN FOR STATES' RIGHTS WITHIN THE UNION

One of Stephens's most consuming concerns during the period in which he served in public office was what authority the general government should have compared with the powers of state governments. Stephens advocated that the southern states continue in the Union to meet their needs best. His public arguments, private entries in his diary, newspaper coverage of the period, and other materials reveal his motivation for expressing the minority view that southern states should remain part of the Union. One also learns the nature of Stephens's persuasive justifications for staying in the Union and for other causes.

Stephens believed the Constitution was the ultimate authority of democracy in the United States. Even the rights of states were limited to those granted to them by the Constitution. When justifying his decisions in a speech before the House of Representatives on January 25, 1845, on the question of the annexation of Texas, Stephens said he would not "claim one construction of the constitution one day, when it favors my interests, and oppose the same . . . the next day." Stephens talked of truth being "fixed, inflexible, immutable, and eternal," but only as prescribed by constitutional law and not primarily from the composition of the Union. Stephens defined the Constitution as "unbending in time, circumstances, and interests," but in practice he was not reluctant to interpret law in order to fit a situation as he perceived it. For example, Stephens maintained that the U.S. House of Representatives had ultimate authority over elections, but the states were to decide the "times, places, and manner" of choosing representatives, allowing white southerners to restrict participation by blacks in political decisions in southern states. Stephens judged control of suffrage by the states to be of utmost importance as a means of racial and political control in the South. In his speech on the admission of Minnesota and alien suffrage in Congress, on May 11, 1858, Stephens insisted that "there is nothing in the doctrine of state rights that I would . . . fight for harder" than the "right of suffrage in my State." Stephens was able to embellish the argument for southern self-government with historical details drawn from House of Representatives debates. In his speech on the Missouri Compromise in the House on December 14, 1854, Stephens emphasized the widening division between sections by isolating the federal system as "your" government. He legitimized his claim for the satisfaction of southern states' needs by contrasting how numerous northern interests had been fulfilled: "the South has never asked any thing from your government. . . . Who is it that is constantly appealing here for legislative aid . . . ? Who ask for fishing bounties . . . protection to navigation . . . ? Why, it is the industrial interests of the North. We of the South . . . sometimes grumble and complain but . . . all that we ask of you is, keep your hands out of our pockets . . . and we do not get even that."

Being a strict follower of the Constitution, as he interpreted it, influenced Stephens's stands on a number of issues. In his speech on the bill to admit Kansas as a state under the Topeka Constitution in the House of Representatives on June 28, 1856, Stephens argued that the Constitution did not attribute the "blessings of liberty" to blacks, justifying in his own mind and speeches the subservient status required of blacks. He insisted that the general government had "no power" to legislate on questions of slavery because that was a "domestic institution.'' Speaking on the territorial bill in Congress on August 7, 1848, Stephens defended the rationale that the "constitution recognizes slavery" unless it was prohibited by laws of individual states. Stephens refracted that premise into the following arguments, in his speech on the Missouri Compromise, December 14, 1854, in the House of Representatives. He stated that it is impossible to "raise" blacks to the "level" of whites; white southerners provide for blacks' "reception," shelter, clothing, food, happiness, and work; blacks under slavery in the South, because of "Christian philanthropy," were more productive than "free labor." Using biblical examples in his address on admitting Kansas as a state, Stephens equated the southern treatment of blacks with deeds of the good Samaritan and northern interests with that of the "free-soil Levite" who would abandon blacks to "starve." He extended his case for states' rights to justify the expansion of slavery into the territories and in newly admitted states. Ironically, in his June 28, 1856 speech on Kansas, Stephens defended slavery as a form of free choice. He insisted that the general government and state governments "leave the question" of whether slaves would be brought to Kansas to settlers who would "be affected by it," meaning potential white owners of blacks, thereby ignoring the plight of blacks in the racist arrangement. Usually speaking without benefit of manuscript, Stephens was able to embellish his argument for state control with vivid details. In a speech on Nebraska and Kansas in the House of Representatives, on February 17, 1854, for example, he stated: "Citizens who go to the frontier, penetrate the wilderness, cut down the forests, till the soil . . . do not lose . . . their capacity for self-government."

Spokesmen disagreed on the nature and extent of the distribution of powers between the general and state governments. What distinguished Stephens from many of his southern colleagues was what he referred to in his Maryland Institute address on February 23, 1852, as his "ardent" and outspoken "attachment" to the Union. A recurring theme in Stephens's legislative discourse was his call for unity among representatives from the states. He viewed "patriotism" as a form of self-government. For example, in the Maryland Institute address, Stephens argued that patriotism "is the same everywhere . . . on the most sterile soil of the East as . . . upon the fairest plains of the South." He intended no oratorical hyperbole when he argued that southerners depended on the Union for "prosperity, happiness, and safety."

Throughout his tenure in the House of Representatives, Stephens stood as a protector of the Union. He counseled listeners at the Maryland Institute that the Union was a "political organization." For this arena of diverse representation and ideas to endure, citizens would have to be willing to weigh a variety of views in a constructive manner. In his speech on the annexation of Texas in Congress on January 25, 1845, Stephens warned that the "agitation" of the issue might threaten the existence of the Union. In 1852 and 1854, he counseled compromise and Union. He urged southerners and northerners to "stand by the constitution." He admonished northerners to end their "crusade against the South." In his speech on Kansas in 1856, Stephens contended that the choice before the country was nationalism or sectionalism. The Union, he advised, could "only be preserved by conforming" to its laws, and not "by force." In 1854, when congressmen were debating the future of Nebraska and Kansas, Stephens argued that "patriotism" should "trample . . . over faction," legislation over force, as was accomplished, he reminded, when he and others reached a compromise in 1850. In 1856, when addressing Kansas's status in the Union, Stephens opposed persons he believed to be "engaged in . . . unholy work of attempting to get up civil war in the country."

By 1860, Stephens was portraying the movement in the South to secede from the Union as evil. He argued that secession would leave southern states politically impotent. He believed that the South's political and economic interests would be far more secure in the Union than without. He trusted established institutions of decision making. Stephens argued that southern states should fight for their rights within the general government under the protection of the Constitution. In 1860, Stephens traveled throughout the state attempting to persuade Georgians to remain in the Union. With Robert Toombs and supporters arguing for secession, Stephens, speaking by special invitation to the Georgia legislature on November 14, 1860, insisted that Georgia could best salvage its interests in the halls of Congress. More than governmental guarantees, however, Stephens warned that success depended primarily on effective leadership by individual representatives. Whereas Howell Cobb of Georgia argued that the general government had failed, Stephens placed the blame on the poor judgment of particular "public men."

Stephens was generally optimistic about the future for southerners living under Union government. In 1852, in the Maryland Institute address, he expressed "confident hope" for the general government. In 1859, in a farewell speech in Augusta, Stephens asserted that in the fields of trade and commerce, he and colleagues had left the nation "in better condition than" they had "found it." Bolstered by the occasion of his retirement and his accomplishments for state and country, Stephens overstated: "All those great sectional questions which so furiously . . . agitated the public mind . . . have been amicably . . . adjusted."

As the momentum in Georgia for secession accelerated, Stephens hoped to persuade elected officials to reconsider what he believed to be a tragic decision. He reproved legislators for considering whether Georgia would leave the Union, arguing that a choice so vital was beyond the authority of the legislature. Stephens insisted, in a speech against secession before the Georgia legislature on November 14, 1860, that only citizens meeting in a special convention should decide whether to "sever our federal relations. . . . Wait to hear from the cross-roads and groceries." Stephens warned that Georgians held different views concerning the relative merits of secession and that those judgements should be heard and weighed. Recalling the many legislative entanglements in which he and colleagues had participated over the years, often with results that he desired, Stephens explained, "Resistance don't mean secession." Stephens was also motivated by a belief that he stated on June 16, 1846, when debating the Mexican

War in the House of Representatives, that wars were "great national calamities" and should never be "rushed into blindly or rashly."

There were occasions when Stephens recognized the seeds of destruction of the Union. In his arguments one finds justification for secession—for example, when principle becomes more important than form of government. From an early period, Stephens defended the states' right to secede. In 1855 in Augusta, Georgia, while announcing his candidacy for reelection to Congress, Stephens addressed the issue of whether Kansas territory would be admitted to the Union with slavery. He insisted that the South could not "surrender" this issue and remain consistent with "her safety and honor." He chose home interests over Union: "As much as I am devoted to the Union, whenever it puts . . . the South and her institutions under the ban of its proscription, I shall be its enemy." By 1859, Stephens was phrasing the choice faced by citizens between general and state governments less in arguments of constitutionality and more in expressions of personal feelings and loyalties. In his speech on the admission of Oregon on February 12, 1859, in the House of Representatives, Stephens reduced the stasis of the debate to home versus assailant: "when aggression comes . . . I shall be for resistance, open, bold, and defiant. I know of no allegiance superior to that due the hearthstones of the homestead." Although highlighted in his speeches in the early 1860s, Stephens's sectional loyalty was not new. As early as 1845, when debating the annexation of Texas, Stephens identified with his region. This is a "sectional question," he judged, "a Southern question" that could "give us political weight." He continued with a loyalty oath to the South, a vocabulary behind which most southern advocates entrenched in defense of their causes. In this argument, Stephens shifted the emphasis away from political themes to the sacredness of birthright: "My feelings of attachment are most ardent toward . . . the South. . . . There sleep the ashes of my sires and grandsires; there are my hopes and prospects." In 1859 in the speech on the admission of Oregon, Stephens identified his ultimate allegiance to family and friends, referring to himself "as a Southern man." By 1860, the optimism for prosperity by the South under Union that Stephens had exaggerated just one month earlier, on the occasion of his retirement, had turned to despair. He told the Augusta, Georgia, audience on September 1, 1860, that he regretted that "all the questions . . . thought to be settled . . . have been opened up afresh. . . . The signs of the times . . . portend evils of the gravest magnitude." "Keep your powder dry but wait for an act of aggression."

Why, to the moment of secession by Georgia, did Stephens urge his colleagues and citizens to remain in the Union? An extension of his belief in the Constitution was Stephens's faith in legislative debate within the Union as the appropriate forum in which to make decisions and certainly the best available arena in which to defend the South's interests. Unlike many other southern officials, Stephens also believed that the Union functioned effectively in that it allowed congressmen to represent the interests of their constituencies. This belief in the general government as an effective instrument for protecting the rights and interests of states and citizens grew out of Stephens's personal experience as an elected official. Having served in the House of Representatives and having participated in critical debates and in the making of vital decisions over a long period on issues of war, peace, territorial expansion, economics, nature of government, and slavery, he believed that the parliamentary system worked well. Stephens demonstrated through historical example how competent representatives could influence political choices. In a speech against secession before the Georgia legislature in 1860, he explained how, in 1832, while he was in college, elected officials from South Carolina talked of nullification or seceding from the Union because of the question of tariffs. Stephens explained that this highly controversial issue was dealt with adequately through "reason and argument."

Adapting these lessons from history to the new threat to the Union in 1860, Stephens advised that legislative debates could be productive only when representatives studied issues carefully and when they persuaded in an informed and reasonable manner. A congressman, he admonished in his speech on the Missouri Compromise in 1854, should not reflect "solely" what one's "constituents wish." In the Augusta speech in 1855, he added: "It is easy to join the shouts of the multitude, but it is hard to say to a multitude that they are wrong." With the militant persuasion of Toombs and followers dominating debate, Stephens rebutted that "insolence" in political discussion, "when indulged, not unfrequently overdoes itself by its own extravagance." In his speech on the Missouri Compromise in 1854, he advised that elected officials should determine "whether any measure presented . . . is right." "I would rather be *defeated* in a good cause," he argued in his Augusta speech, "than to *triumph* in a bad one." Concerned about the highly emotional and exaggerated claims of Robert Toombs and others calling for separation from the Union, Stephens asked for calm, deliberate, and reliable discussions of issues and solutions. In Stephens's judgment, there was no reason why judicious deliberation by competent people could not solve problems confronting the citizenry in the late 1850s and early 1860s, as it had done in the past. In a speech in 1861 before the secession convention of Georgia on the evils of secession, Stephens reminded Georgians that the South had prospered within a Union that provided channels through which their interests had been defended and protected, including the slave trade, return of fugitives, and extension of slavery. He asked: "Can either of you to-day name one governmental act of wrong, deliberately and purposely done by the government of Washington, of which the South has a right to complain? . . . For you to attempt to overthrow such a government as this . . . is the height of madness, folly, and wickedness, to which I can lend neither my sanction nor my vote."

INFORMATION SOURCES

Research Collections and Collected Speeches

Stephens's papers are found in a variety of manuscript collections, including Alexander Hamilton Stephens Letters, 1858–1882, Historical Society of Pennsylvania, Philadelphia;

Alexander Hamilton Stephens Papers, 1784–1886, Library of Congress, Manuscript Division; and Alexander Hamilton Stephens Papers, 1822–1911, Duke University Library, Durham, North Carolina.

Alexander H. Stephens, in Public And Private with Letters and Speeches   AHSPP
    before, during, and since the War. Edited by Henry Cleveland.
    Philadelphia: National Publishing Co., 1866.
Atlanta Constitution.   AC
Library of Oratory, Ancient and Modern; 15 vols. Edited by Chauncey M.   LIB
    Depew. New York: A. L. Fowle, 1902; vol. 8.
Savannah Daily Herald.   SDH
Southern Federal Union.   SFU

Selected Critical Studies

Beck, Nemias B. "Alexander H. Stephens, Orator." Ph.D. dissertation, University of Wisconsin, 1938.

Brumgardt, John R. "Alexander H. Stephens and the State Convention Movement in Georgia: A Reappraisal." *Georgia Historical Quarterly* 59 (1975): 38–49.

Franklin, John Hope. "The Southern Expansionists of 1846." *Journal of Southern History* 25 (1959): 323–38.

Hubell, John T. "Three Georgia Unionists and the Compromise of 1850." *Georgia Historical Quarterly* 51 (1967): 307–23.

Johnston, Richard Malcolm, and William Hand Browne. *Life of Alexander H. Stephens.* Philadelphia: J. B. Lippincott and Co., 1878; rpt., Freeport: Books for Libraries Press, 1971.

Lampton, Joan E. "The Kansas-Nebraska Act Reconsidered: An Analysis of Men, Methods, and Motives." Ph.D. dissertation, Illinois State University, 1979.

Pendleton, Louis. *Alexander H. Stephens.* Philadelphia: George W. Jacobs & Company, 1907.

Rabun, James W. "Alexander H. Stephens, 1812–1861." Ph.D. dissertation, University of Chicago, 1949.

Reid, Jasper Bradley, Jr. " 'The Mephistopheles of Southern Politics': A Critical Analysis of Some of the Political Thought of Alexander Hamilton Stephens." Ph.D. dissertation, University of Michigan, 1966.

Richardson, E. Ramsay. *Little Aleck: A Life of Alexander H. Stephens: The Fighting Vice-President of the Confederacy.* Indianapolis: Bobbs-Merrill, 1932.

Schott, Thomas Edwin. "Alexander H. Stephens: Antebellum Statesman." Ph.D. dissertation, Louisiana State University, 1978.

Von-Abele, Rudolph R. "Alexander H. Stephens, A Biography." Ph.D. dissertation, Columbia University, 1947.

CHRONOLOGY OF MAJOR SPEECHES

See "Research Collections and Collected Speeches" for source codes.

Speech on annexation of Texas, U.S. House of Representatives, Washington, D.C., January 25, 1845; *AHSPP*, pp. 280–302.

Speech on the Mexican War, U.S. House of Representatives, Washington, D.C., June 16, 1846; *AHSPP*, pp. 302–20.

Speech on the Territorial Bill, United States House of Representatives, Washington D.C., August 7, 1848; *AHSPP*, pp. 334–52.

Address at Emory College, Oxford, Georgia, July 21, 1852; *AHSPP* pp. 364–76.

Maryland Institute Address, Baltimore, Maryland, February 23, 1852; *AHSPP*, pp. 352–64

Speech on Nebraska and Kansas, United States House of Representatives, Washington, D.C., February 17, 1854; *AHSPP*, pp. 394–415.

Speech on Missouri Compromise, U.S. House of Representatives, Washington, D.C., December 14, 1854; *AHSPP*, pp. 416–32.

Slavery debate, U.S. House of Representatives, Washington, D.C., January 17, 1856; *AHSPP*, pp. 489–15.

Speech on admitting Kansas under Topeka Constitution, U.S. House of Representatives, Washington, D.C., June 28, 1856; *AHSPP*, pp. 531–60.

Speech on admission of Minnesota and alien suffrage, U.S. House of Representatives, Washington, D.C., May 11, 1858; *AHSPP*, pp. 580–91.

Speech on the admission of Oregon, United States House of Representatives, Washington, D.C., February 12, 1859; *AHSPP*, pp. 621–37.

Farewell speech, Augusta, Georgia, July 2, 1859; *ASHPP*, pp. 637–51.

Speech against secession to Georgia Legislature, Milledgeville, Georgia, November 14, 1860; *AHSPP*, pp. 694–13.

On the Evils of Secession, Secession Convention of Georgia, Milledgeville, Georgia, January 18 [?], 1861; LIB, pp. 363–68.

Cornerstone speech, Savannah, Georgia, March 21, 1861; *SFU*, April 2, 1861; *AHSPP*, pp. 717–29.

Speech to Virginia secession convention, Richmond, Virginia, April 23, 1861; *AHSPP*, pp. 729–45.

Speech at Crawfordville, Georgia, November 1, 1862; *AHSPP*, pp. 749–61.

Address before General Assembly of Georgia, Milledgeville, Georgia, February 22, 1866; *SDH*, February 26, 1866; *AHSPP*, 804–18.

On the civil rights bill, U.S. House of Representatives, Washington, D.C., January 5, 1874; *AC*, January 14, 1874.

LUCY STONE
(1818–1893), suffragist and reformer

——————————————————————————————— BETH M. WAGGENSPACK

Lucy Stone's fame today often rests on a single fact: that she refused to take her husband's name. Yet this symbolic act was only one of the many victories she helped to win for women.

Stone came to the conviction early in life that women's rights were severely limited in a male-dominated society. She was told as a child that men were divinely ordained to subjugate women; this caused her to study Greek and Hebrew in order to translate the Bible for herself. This intellectual determination was a constant quality throughout her life.

With her family unwilling to support her education, Stone began at sixteen to teach district school. For the next nine years, she alternated between periods of teaching and periods of study. When she saved enough money from teaching, she would attend school, returning to teach when funds ran out. During this period she became involved in controversy through the antislavery movement. Her convictions about her destiny to speak against injustice were born.

Stone finally earned enough money to start college study at Oberlin College in 1843. There she was looked upon as a dangerous radical due to her outspoken advocacy of women's rights, abolition, and temperance. But Oberlin allowed her mind and spirit to chase her goals, and in 1847 she was the first Massachusetts woman to earn an A.B. degree.

Stone's public speaking career began immediately upon graduation when she gave her first women's rights speech at her brother's church in Gardner, Massachusetts. In 1848, she began her career as a lecturer for the Anti-Slavery Society. Stone headed the call for the first National Woman's Rights Convention at Worcester, Massachusetts in 1850, and she was active in arranging for and participating in later conventions. Stone traveled extensively, lecturing on suffrage in Canada as well as the United States.

Following her marriage on May 1, 1855, to Henry Brown Blackwell, the two of them kept up many joint protests of the legal disabilities of women. Stone was a member of the American Equal Rights Association (AERA) Executive Committee (1866); president of the New Jersey Woman Suffrage Association (1868); and founder of the Massachusetts Woman Suffrage Association (1870). When the split occurred in the AERA, Stone helped to form the American Woman Suffrage Association in 1869, which concentrated on gaining suffrage victories state by state. Stone also helped create and edit the *Woman's Journal* in 1870, which existed for forty-seven years and was the only long-continuing woman's suffrage paper published in the United States.

LUCY STONE AS SUFFRAGE SPEAKER

While at Oberlin, Stone helped organize the first debating society ever formed among college women. Although enrolled in a rhetoric class, she had no opportunity to practice, for women were banned from public speaking. The debating society, formed by Stone and Antoinette Brown, met secretly to practice rhetorical and elocutionary skills. These skills were put to use as her career as a lecturer for the Anti-Slavery Society began. However, she had trouble with the society early on, for although she pleaded eloquently for Negro rights, she could not resist including arguments for women as well. Abolitionists, fearing Stone was hurting the cause, worked out a compromise: Stone would speak on abolition on weekends and women's rights during the rest of the week.

The issues concerning the early women's rights movement were contained in Stone's three stock lectures on women: one was on their social and industrial disabilities; the second on political and legal handicaps; and the third on religious and moral discrimination. Initially Stone did not charge admission to these lectures, but she usually passed a hat and collected enough money to pay for the hall and her lodging. Later, she charged a minimal fee, around 12½ cents, which kept out the hecklers. It also allowed her to put aside $7,000 in three years.

One of the more memorable speeches of Stone's career was presented at the National Woman's Rights convention in Cincinnati on October 17, 1855. Responding to a previous speaker who claimed the woman's movement was composed of a few disappointed women, she replied that she had always been a disappointed woman. In employment, in education, in marriage, in everything else, Stone claimed, "disappointment is the lot of woman." She declared that it was her life's purpose to deepen this disappointment in all women until they would bow down to it no more.

The 1863 Women's National Loyal League Convention afforded Stone the chance to call on Congress to pass a constitutional amendment abolishing slavery by creating a nationwide petition. Her speech, which linked Negro and women's rights, argued that if the rights of one person were disregarded, then everyone failed in loyalty to the country. Others at the convention opposed the combination of these two issues, but Stone insisted that the government could derive its just powers only from the consent of all of the governed.

Stone and Blackwell played an important role in the 1867 Kansas campaign for women's suffrage, traversing the state and lecturing daily for nearly three months. Stone wrote that she was speaking in fine form, and a telegram by a prominent local organizer said, "With the help of God and Lucy Stone, we shall carry Kansas! The world moves!" Despite this optimism, the measure failed, but Stone continued her lectures in other states facing similar referendums.

The split that occurred in the women's movement in 1869 because of the divergent styles and temperaments of its major forces (including Elizabeth Cady Stanton, Susan B. Anthony, Lucy Stone, and Henry Ward Beecher) created two national suffrage associations: the National Woman Suffrage Association (Stanton and Anthony) and the American Woman Suffrage Association (Stone and Beecher). The American welcomed males; the National did not. The American was run by a variety of delegates; the National was run by a small group of leaders. The American worked chiefly for state and municipal suffrage and limited itself to that topic; the National was concerned with many issues, including the passage of a federal suffrage amendment.

Stone's address at the first annual convention of the AWSA in Cleveland in 1870 noted progress in various states. Her optimism said that by keeping the question of woman's right to the ballot clear and unmixed with other issues, then growing public sympathy would lead to success. By spreading outward from a small base, each small victory would bring women closer to enfranchisement.

The Concord Convention of 1875 was held about a month after the Centennial Tea Party in Boston; that celebration had no women in seats of honor, no official role, no memorial—yet women had to pay their share in increased taxes to pay for it. Stone's speech at the convention centered on the theme of taxation without representation and argued that the present situation had not changed for women. While avoiding a call for open rebellion, she did say that she would not pay taxes unless she had a voice in how they were to be spent.

In one of the final speeches of her life, Stone addressed the Senate committee on Woman Suffrage, February 20, 1892, along with Elizabeth Cady Stanton, Susan B. Anthony, and Isabella Beecher Hooker. Her speech resounded with her recurring theme that women had been handicapped, cheapened, and violated without the vote. The fundamental principle of government, according to Stone, was simple justice and fair play—that those who obey the laws should make them. As long as women were shut out and kept helpless, the principle was held in disrespect.

Throughout her life, Stone drew the themes for her speeches and writings from the basic principles of justice and equality. Despite frequent bouts of ill health, she displayed unflagging optimism in the face of numerous defeats and was as dedicated to her family as to her convictions. Her earnest persuasiveness served as a beacon for the unconvinced.

Lucy Stone was the opposite of the popular conception of what a woman's rights advocate was. Typically her critics pictured her as a large woman with a bellowing voice, swearing, and puffing on a cigar. Instead her demure, ladylike manner and actual appearance denied this caricature. Stone was short, nicely proportioned, gentle, kindly, sympathetic, and sweetvoiced. She loved children, was a devoted wife and mother, and had great empathy for the oppressed.

Stone was a highly effective speaker, possessing personal magnetism, rugged honesty, and a fearlessness that aided her oratorical style. As a lecturer for the Anti-Slavery Society, Stone frequently faced hostile, violent audiences. Yet published reports say that her manner and soft, musical voice stilled even the rowdiest audience. Stone did not write many of her speeches down and often spoke without notes, letting her convictions guide what she said. Her ideals were not particularly original, and she had little sense of humor. The hallmark of her speaking style was that she grasped the importance to cultivate her audience's goodwill. Rather than attacking the opposition, she praised what allegiance was shown. For instance, she did not often attack man as an oppressor but instead praised those who were helping women, or she would admit that blame lay on both sides. Elizabeth Cady Stanton described Stone as young, magnetic, eloquent, and having a soul filled with new ideas. She also claimed Stone was the first speaker to stir the nation on wrongs done to women.

It was characteristic of Lucy Stone that she downplayed her role in history. In 1876, when Elizabeth Cady Stanton began collecting material for the *History of Woman Suffrage*, Stone responded to the request for materials by saying, "I have never kept a diary or any record of my work, so am unable to furnish you with required dates." Her daughter's biography reports that Stone was modest and unassuming, having no thirst for fame. Stone preserved no record of her early work and saved no press clippings. When asked to furnish particulars of her life for books on famous women, she always refused.

What was the rhetorical effect of Lucy Stone on the United States? The ratification of the Nineteenth Amendment in 1920 stands as one monument to her tireless crusades. Her rhetoric was marked by a sense of hope for the world; she argued that the influence of liberated women would sweep away all corruption. Stone's refusal to accept the legal dictates of the marriage contract have continuing repercussions; women who keep their birth names after marriage are still occasionally referred to as Lucy Stoners. Lucy Stone was the first woman— and for years the only one—who made woman's rights her chief topic. It was Stone who represented that cause to the public, and that was why she earned the name "Morning Star of the Woman's Rights Movement."

INFORMATION SOURCES

Research Collections and Collected Speeches

Much of the manuscript material on Lucy Stone is available in several locations, so researchers may face difficulty in conducting inquiry. Added to that is the fact that Stone did not keep notes on many of her activities. The *History of Woman Suffrage* was published during the movement's split, and while this authoritative document is widely used by historians, Lucy Stone's achievements are virtually ignored.

Four major collections containing Stone's general correspondence, articles, some speech notes, and other miscellaneous materials are available. The Blackwell Family Papers (1830–1950) are housed in the Library of Congress Manuscript Division; these are the papers of Lucy Stone, Henry Blackwell, Alice Stone Blackwell, and others. This material is also available on microfilm. A second group of Blackwell Family Papers (1784–1944) exists at the Arthur and Elizabeth Schlesinger Library on the History of Women in America, at Radcliffe College, Cambridge, Massachusetts. Also at the Schlesinger Library are a series of Lucy Stone's papers (1850–1893). The Boston Public Library also has a collection of Lucy Stone Papers (1848–1893).

Three other collections contain useful material on Lucy Stone. The National American Woman Suffrage Association's records, housed in the Sophia Smith Collection, Women's History Archives, Smith College, Northampton, Massachusetts, contain records, reports, programs, and proceedings. A small updated collection of Lucy Stone's papers are found at the Dorchester, Massachusetts, Historical Society. Finally, the Amelia Bloomer Papers, which contain correspondence and clippings of some of Stone's speeches, are at the Council Bluffs, Iowa, Free Public Library.

Finally, researchers may consider the *Woman's Journal*, published in Boston by the National American Woman Suffrage Association, as a near diary of Lucy Stone's public life. Available on microfilm, it documents her efforts on behalf of suffrage and woman's industrial, educational, legal, and political equality.

Harper, Ida. *The Life and Work of Susan B. Anthony*. Vol. 1. Indianapolis: *SBA*
     Bowen-Merrill Company, 1898.
History of Woman Suffrage. 6 vols. Edited by Elizabeth Cady Stanton et   *HWS*
     al. Rochester, N.Y.: Susan B. Anthony, 1889.
Congress of Women. Chicago: World's Congress of Representative Women,   *CW*
     1893.

Selected Biographies

Blackwell, Alice Stone. *Lucy Stone, Pioneer of Woman's Rights*. Boston: Little, Brown, 1930.
Hays, Eleanor Rice. *Morning Star: A Biography of Lucy Stone, 1818–1893*. New York: Octagon Books, 1978.
Wheeler, Leslie, ed. *Loving Warriors: Selected Letters of Lucy Stone and Henry B. Blackwell, 1853–1893*. New York: Dial Press, 1981.

CHRONOLOGY OF MAJOR SPEECHES

See "Research Collections and Collected Speeches" for source codes.

Debate on the elevation of women, at the Second Worcester, Massachusetts, Convention, October 1851; *HWS*, 1: 233.

Address at the Woman's Rights Convention, Syracuse, New York, September 8, 1852; *SBA*, 1: 73–74.

Address at the Woman's Rights Convention, New York, September 6 (?) 1853; *HWS*, 1: 163.

Debate at the Fourth National Convention, Cleveland, Ohio, October 1853; *HWS*, 1: 163.

"I Have Been a Disappointed Woman," National Woman's Rights Convention, Cincinnati, Ohio, October 17, 1855; *HWS*, 1: 165–67.

President's address at the Seventh National Woman's Rights Convention, New York, November 25, 1856; *HWS*, 1: 632–33.

Address on women and religion, Seventh National Woman's Rights Convention, New York, November 26 (?), 1856; *HWS*, 1: 650–52.

Closing remarks at the Seventh National Woman's Rights Convention, New York, November 26, 1856; *HWS*, 1: 665–66.

Debate at the Women's National Loyal League Convention, New York, May 14, 1863; *HWS*, 2: 64–65.

Concluding remarks at the Women's National Loyal League Convention, New York, May 14, 1863; *HWS*, 2: 78.

Debate at the Third Annual Meeting of the American Equal Rights Association, New York, May 1869; *HWS*, 2: 383–84.

Annual report of the chairman, First Annual Meeting of American Woman Suffrage Association, Cleveland, Ohio, November 22 (?) 1870; *HWS*, 2: 803–04.

Address to the Semi-Annual Meeting of the American Woman Suffrage Association, New York, May 10, 1871; *HWS*, 2: 811.

Speech to the Concord Convention of the Massachusetts Suffrage Association, Concord, Massachusetts, May 20 (?) 1875; *HWS*, 3: 271.

Closing address at the Annual Meeting of the American Woman Suffrage Association, Chicago, November 20, 1884; *HWS*, 4: 415–16.

Address to the Senate Committee on Women Suffrage, Washington, D.C., February 20, 1892; *HWS*, 4: 191–93.

"The Progress of Fifty Years," Chicago, 1893; *CW*, pp. 58–61.

CHARLES SUMNER
(1811–1874), U.S. senator

RONALD K. BURKE

Charles Sumner did not realize the personal satisfaction to be derived from effective public discourse until he reached the age of thirty-four. After that he took every opportunity to speak in favor of many reforms, including world peace, prison reform, and, most important, the abolition of slavery. Educated at the Boston Public Latin School, he associated with young men who in later years would become outspoken reformers. These intimates were the crusader, author, and Unitarian clergyman James Freeman Clarke, Congressman Robert Winthrop, and the Boston Brahmin-turned-abolitionist Wendell Phillips. Sumner attended Harvard College (class of 1830) and while there showed great aptitude for history, literature, and forensics. In the classroom of Harvard professor Edward T. Channing, he learned that every speech should have exordium, narration, partition, proof, refutation, and peroration. He studied at Harvard Law School (1831–1833) and became the friend and student of the eminent professor Joseph Story. At the completion of his studies, Sumner was asked to remain as an instructor, but he chose to practice law. Before settling in to the routine of law, he visited Washington, D.C., to attend sessions of the Supreme Court upon which his friend Story was sitting. For weeks he enjoyed the company of Chief Justice John Marshall and others. He listened to Daniel Webster and Francis Scott Key argue before the Court. And in the Senate he listened to the compelling oratory of Henry Clay.

At twenty-six Sumner borrowed money and took a three-year sojourn in Europe, making friends with many influential Europeans. In every country Sumner visited, he was a conscientious student and thorough observer. After his return to Boston, he was seen frequently in the company of the intelligentsia. He participated in social reform activities in Boston for a number of years before he entered the U.S. Senate. There he became one of the prominent advocates of the complete abolition of American slavery. He reached the pinnacle of his senatorial career when he was appointed chairperson of the Committee on Foreign Relations. His close personal relationships with many leaders in England, France, and Germany and his effective rhetorical skills aided him in transacting successfully many sensitive negotiations while in this position. The speeches Sumner delivered during the time he participated in reform activities in Boston and during his tenure in the Senate reflect the thoughts of a militant crusader for human rights around which a firestorm of controversy raged.

CHARLES SUMNER AS DEFENDER OF HUMAN RIGHTS

The oratorical career of Charles Sumner can be divided into two periods: his speaking career as a lawyer-activist in Boston and his speaking career in the U.S. Senate.

In 1845 Boston city officials chose Sumner to deliver the Fourth of July oration.

Traditionally, the address lauded the valor demonstrated by Revolutionary patriots, but Sumner addressed his remarks not to war but to peace. In the introduction he announced his theme: "What is the true grandeur of nations?" Then he proceeded to assail the military in the audience with an openly frank style of oratory that soon became familiar to Sumner's listeners. He told the Independence Day assembly "to declare independence of the bestial, to abandon practices found on this part of our nature, and in every way beat down that brutal spirit which is the Genius of War." Balancing a phrase for its rhetorical impact, he asked: "Can there be in our age any peace that is not honorable, any war that is not dishonorable?" A witness remarked that the military and naval personnel in attendance were visibly disturbed, and several auditors restrained themselves from walking out on Sumner, who spoke for two hours. Publicity from the oration catapulted Sumner into the public arena, where he received national recognition. The speech drew the attention of theologian and social reformer Theodore Parker and political activist John A. Andrew, both celebrated advocates of reform. Sumner realized now his ability to excite and sway large audiences. From this time forward, Sumner thrilled numerous crowds with his public discourses.

Characteristic of his unswerving championship of human rights, Sumner cancelled a speaking engagement at the New Bedford lyceum when he learned blacks were denied membership. Employing the personal letter as a rhetorical form, he wrote to the committee of the lyceum: "In lecturing before a Lyceum which has introduced the prejudice of color among its laws, and thus formerly reversed an injunction of highest morals and politics, I might seem to sanction what is most alien to my soul, and join in disobedience to that command which teaches that the children of earth are all one blood. I cannot do this." Shortly after the New Bedford Lyceum Committee reacted by rescinding the discriminating rule. Sumner agreed then to lecture.

A familiar figure now on the speaking circuit, Sumner assumed his rightful place among notable abolitionists of Boston. At a public meeting in Faneuil Hall in Boston on November 4, 1845, Sumner railed against the admission of Texas as a slave state in "The Wrong of Slavery." On the platform with Sumner were his former schoolmate Wendell Phillips, the abolitionist Henry Brewster Stanton, and firebrand editor of the *Liberator* William Lloyd Garrison. Sumner informed his audience about the evils of annexation, his main concern being that it would expand the slave trade further. "In this," he recommended, "we should have no part or lot in it." Appealing to the auditors' humanity and compassion, he said: "Let us wash our hands of this great guilt. As we read its horrors, may each of us be able to exclaim, with conscience void of offence, 'Thou canst not say I did it.' " The rhetorical strategy of antislavery activists was to select Faneuil Hall for meetings because of its history of being a forum for Revolutionary oratory. Meeting in this cradle of liberty could not have been more suitable for their purposes. Other topics Sumner addressed during the Boston years were "Slavery and the Mexican War," "White Slavery," and "Equality before the Law,'' the last protesting the separate public school system in Boston. These were disheartening times for antislavery activists, but Sumner's continued presence, oratorical skills, enthusiasm, and popularity gave them new hope.

Sumner continued his oratorical career in the Senate where he presented his credentials at the opening of the Eighty-second Congress on December 1, 1851, and took the oath of office. Nine days later he delivered his first speech in the Senate, "Welcome to Kossuth.'' This ceremonial oration welcomed the Hungarian patriot and revolutionary Lajos Kossuth who visited the United States seeking funds and moral support. Deeply sympathetic to this guardian of freedom, Sumner said: "He deserves it [welcome to the United States] as the early constant, and incorruptible champion of the Liberal Cause in Hungary. He deserves it by the great principles of democracy which he caused to be recognized—representation of the people without distinction of rank or birth, and *Equality before the law.*'' A dedicated believer in freedom for all, Sumner took delight in giving a welcoming speech honoring this freedom fighter.

Sumner's next speech of consequence concerned the Fugitive Slave Act, "Freedom National, Slavery Sectional,'' given August 26, 1852. This oration represented the first in a series of extended and contentious speeches on slavery he presented in the Senate. The supporters of the slave-catching act proposed an amendment to pay the expenses accumulated while performing matters pertaining to the bill. Sumner rose and proposed an amendment to the amendment: "that no such allowance shall be authorized for any expense incurred in executing the Act of September 15, 1850, for the surrender of fugitives from service or labor; which said Act is hereby repealed.'' Sumner viewed the enactment of this legislation as an attempt to legitimize the notion of slavery as national and freedom as sectional. Therefore he undertook to demonstrate the unconstitutionality and repugnant character of this bill in a speech that lasted three and three-quarters hours. He argued by reversing the phrase of the law's supporters and insisting that slavery was sectional and freedom national. Alluding to legal and historical documents for logical proof, Sumner reminded his colleagues that the preamble to the Constitution proclaimed liberty foremost. He declared: "Thus, according to undeniable words, the Constitution was ordained, not to establish, secure or sanction Slavery,—not to promote the special interests of Slaveholders,—not to make Slavery national, in any way, form, or manner,— but to 'establish justice,' 'promote the greater welfare,' and 'secure the blessings of liberty.' Here, surely, Liberty is national.''

Continuing his argument Sumner asserted that slaves represented persons, not property. He recalled that Roger Sherman, delegate to the Continental Congress, had opposed the notion of human property. Sherman stated that the Constitution does not look upon these persons as "species of property'' but speaks of them as persons. Sumner concluded by stating the framers of the Constitution favored freedom and not slavery. He thereby affirmed the idea that freedom was national and slavery sectional.

Acclaimed for its importance to the abolition movement, publishers were ordered to print the oration in a large pamphlet edition numbering several hundred thousand. Additionally, it was translated into German. Daniel Webster reportedly watched from the gallery for one hour as Sumner spoke. The extended oration and divisive debate with southern senators served to exacerbate matters. Four votes were cast in favor of Sumner's motion. Despite this defeat of Sumner's motion, "Freedom National, Slavery Sectional" restored the confidence of Massachusetts constituents, who had been waiting for their senator to speak out against slavery.

Sumner maintained a relentless attack on proslavery forces, especially with his famous oration "The Crime against Kansas" in 1856. Two days before he delivered the speech, he wrote to fellow reformer Theodore Parker: "I shall pronounce the most thorough phillipic ever uttered in a legislative body." Mainly because of its results, it is the speech for which Sumner is best remembered because it caused some members of Congress to reveal their darker side. In the address, he complained bitterly of the Kansas-Nebraska bill, which threatened to extend slavery into the territories. "Urged as a bill of peace," he said, "it was a swindle to the whole country." Referring to the senators who "Had raised themselves to eminence on this floor by the championship of human wrongs," he compared Senator Andrew P. Butler of South Carolina with Don Quixote, who paid his vows to a mistress who "though polluted in the sights of the world, is chaste in his sights, I mean the harlot, Slavery." Senator Stephen A. Douglas of Illinois was compared to Sancho Panza. Going after Butler again, he said: "He is the uncompromising, unblushing representative on this floor of a flagrant sectionalism now domineering over the republic." He spoke for three hours against the slavocrats, concluded for the day, and then resumed the following day for two hours.

Two days later, an enraged relative of Senator Butler, Congressman Preston Brooks of South Carolina, approached Sumner, who looked up from his desk on the Senate floor and heard Brooks say: "I have read your speech twice over carefully; it is a libel on South Carolina, and Mr. Butler who is a relative of mine." With that said, he commenced to beat Sumner on the head with a walking stick. Sumner fell bleeding and unconscious to the floor. From the North came outcries of universal indignation and expressions of sympathy for its victim. In reacting to the attack Frederick Douglass, the illustrious black emancipator, wrote: "No one act did more to rouse the North to a comprehension of the infernal and barbarous spirit of slavery and its determination to 'rule or ruin' than the cowardly and brutal assault." In the meantime, while Sumner recuperated, he had been reelected to the Senate.

Having endured great suffering on behalf of the antislavery cause, Sumner returned to the Senate eager to continue his verbal battle with proslavery advocates. He found the southern leaders taking more aggressive ground than ever before and decided to give a speech indicting slavery in all its evil. On June 4, 1860, he presented a four-hour-long diatribe, "The Barbarism of Slavery." The essence of the discourse can be summed up in this way: "All of the social, moral, political, and economical implications of the 'peculiar institution' of slavery are categorically horrendous.'' Reaction to the speech—positive and negative—came in from all quarters. Reminiscent of the beating Sumner received was a threat of violence to him at his lodgings from a southern slaveholder who "had called for an explanation of the speech, and to hold its author responsible." Thereafter friends of Sumner arranged for him to have protection until the fear of assault abated.

Favorable response to "The Barbarism of Slavery" appeared in newspapers as far away as London. From upstate New York the philanthropist and abolitionist Gerrit Smith wrote to Sumner: "For, though the 'Crime Against Kansas' *was* the speech of your life, this *is* the speech of your life. This eclipses that. It is far more instructive, and will be far more useful, and it is not at all inferior to the other in vigor or rhetoric." In addition to letters from whites, blacks wrote to Sumner. He heard from Robert Morris, a black lawyer in Boston who had worked with him on the separate school issue. Morris thanked Sumner in behalf of the young blacks of Boston. John S. Rock, a black lawyer who was admitted to the bar of the Supreme Court on motion of Sumner, wrote: "Your immortal speech has sent a thrill of joy to all lovers of Freedom everywhere, and especially so to the down-trodden." The strength of Sumner's oratory lay in the fact that he remained consistent in his ideology. He said what he believed regardless of how it would be received.

Sumner's speeches reflect his early classical training; they are replete with quotations and classical allusions. His addresses, in addition, have been compared with ancient and modern classics. *The Missouri Democrat* opined that in oratorical ability, Sumner "was no unworthy successor to Adams, Webster, and Everett." The *New York Evening Post* said, "The Crime against Kansas" speech contained "clear statement, close and well-put reasoning, piquant personality and satire, freighted with a wealth of learned and apposite illustrations." Although he disagreed, in kind, with the Massachusetts lawmaker, Senator John B. Weller of California said one of Sumner's speeches "has been handsomely embellished with poetry, both Latin and English, so full of classical allusion and rhetorical flourishes, as to make it much more palatable." Sumner's intense dedication to antislavery did not overshadow his other duties. He exemplified the conscientious legislator. His effective persuasive skills in dealing with complex details of foreign policy, money and finance, the tariff, and postal regulations commanded respect from his peers.

Because his speech topics were invariably controversial, this imposing 6 foot, 2 inch figure of a man weighing 185 pounds used gestures reflecting strength and vigor rather than eloquence. His subject matter was close to his heart, and he took excessive care preparing a speech by working on a manuscript months at a time. Most of his discourses were memorized thoroughly. This meticulous attention to manuscripts caused abolitionist Cassius Clay to observe that one of Sumner's speeches "smells too much of the lamp." One of his black admirers, Archibald H. Grimké, remarked that Sumner's oratory was the "eloquence of industry rather than the eloquence of inspiration." Although he received criticism for lacking original thought, blacks appreciated fully Sumner's efforts in behalf of the antislavery cause. For example, close friend and fellow activist Frederick Douglass said of Sumner: "He was not only the most clearsighted, brave and uncompromising friend of my race who had ever stood upon the floor of the Senate, but was to me a loved, honored, and precious personal friend—a man possessing the exalted and matured intellect of a statesman, with the pure and artless heart of a child."

Sumner devoted a lifetime defending freedom and equality for the oppressed through his oratory. In his early career in Boston, he associated with the well-known cadre of reformers and spoke out against racism. In his later career in the Senate, his rhetorical strategy involved being certain that nothing about the evils in slavery went unscathed. He did that by extended orations containing bitter invective. Not overlooking the persuasive power of the pen, he used the personal letter to battle discrimination. Also he offered moral support to other defenders of human rights. In praise of Charles Sumner, the eminent publisher George P. Putnam of New York said he wished to join with others in admiring "the man who thus stands up in the front ranks of the battle for Freedom and Humanity."

INFORMATION SOURCES

Research Collections and Collected Speeches

There are several biographies of Sumner written by his contemporaries, which are mostly eulogistic. The most helpful biography with a sense of proportion is Edward L. Pierce's four-volume *Memoir and Letters of Charles Sumner* (Boston: Robert Bros., 1877). An excellent book on Sumner is David Donald, *Charles Sumner and the Coming of the Civil War* (New York: Knopf, 1960).

Charles Sumner: His Complete Works. Edited by George Frisbie Hoar.   CSCW
    Statesman ed. Boston: Lee and Shepard, 1900.
Douglass, Frederick. *Life and Times of Frederick Douglass.* 1892; rpt.,   LTFD
    London: Collier-MacMillan Ltd., 1962.

Selected Critical Studies

Dickey, Dallas D. "Lamar's Eulogy on Sumner: A Letter of Explanation." *Southern Speech Communication Journal* 20 (1955): 316–22.
Ek, Richard A. "Charles Sumner's Address at Cooper Union." *Southern Speech Communication Journal* 32 (1967): 169–79.
Pagel, Elaine, and Carl Dallinger. "Charles Sumner." In *A History and Criticism of American Public Address.* Edited by William Norwood Brigance. New York: McGraw-Hill, 1943.
Stocker, Glen. "Charles Sumner's Rhetoric of Insult." *Southern Speech Communication Journal* 38 (1975): 223–34.

Selected Biographies

Haynes, George H. *Charles Sumner*. Philadelphia: George W. Jacobs and Co., 1909.
Schurz, Carl. *Charles Sumner: An Essay*. Urbana: University of Illinois Press, 1951.
Storey, Moorfield. *Charles Sumner*. Boston: Houghton Mifflin, 1900.

CHRONOLOGY OF MAJOR SPEECHES

See "Research Collections and Collected Speeches" for source codes.

Independence Day oration, Boston, July 4, 1845; *CSCW*, 1: 5–132.

"The Wrong of Slavery," Boston, November 4, 1845; *CSCW*, 1: 151–59.

"Welcome to Kossuth," U.S. Senate, Washington, D.C., December 10, 1851; *CSCW*, 3: 173–79.

"Freedom National, Slavery Sectional," U.S. Senate, Washington, D.C., August 26, 1852; *CSCW*, 3: 264–366.

"The Crime against Kansas," U.S. Senate, Washington, D.C., May 19–20, 1856; *CSCW*, 5: 137–256.

"The Barbarism of Slavery," U.S. Senate, Washington, D.C., June 4, 1860; *CSCW*, 6: 119–237.

THOMAS DEWITT TALMAGE
(1832–1902), orthodox spokesman of the Gilded Age

JOHN W. MONSMA

Reverend Thomas DeWitt Talmage spoke to more parishioners and to larger lecture audiences during the last part of the nineteenth century than any other clergyman. He held important pastorates in Syracuse, 1859–1862, Philadelphia, 1862–1869, Brooklyn, 1869–1894, and Washington, D.C., 1895–1899. He lectured extensively on the Chautauqua and lyceum circuits. He made several speaking and lecture tours of Europe and one around the world. Wherever he spoke, he found enthusiastic audiences, composed largely of the readers of his weekly syndicated sermons (published in 3,500 newspapers of 30,000 circulation) or of the nearly thirty-six volumes of authorized sermon anthologies and miscellaneous writings.

The public knew Talmage not only as a minister and lecturer but as the developer of a new form of church architecture, as the builder of three impressive and unique tabernacles, as the creator of an unusual homiletic style, and as a prolific writer. Critics attacked his delivery. An ecclesiastical trial rigorously examined his ethics and actions; Robert G. Ingersoll engaged him in a lengthy public debate; and tabernacle finances posed a problem for all careful observers. Nevertheless, when he died, writers eulogized him as the equal of Henry Ward Beecher or Charles Spurgeon and the ablest expounder of biblical truths in Protestantism.

TALMAGE AS PREACHER AND LECTURER

Throughout his life, Talmage preached scriptural concepts as he read them, without question. By inflexibly aligning himself with old-time theology, he never compromised with liberals or with the higher critics, as did his colleague, Henry Ward Beecher.

Although Talmage spoke to all classes of people, his sermons and lectures appealed basically to unsophisticated middle- and lower-class listeners. With colorful phrasing, he described scenes they had never viewed, quoted books they had never read, and told stories they had never heard. He emphasized his points with dramatic delivery. Talmage's topics had interest because he considered human problems; his supporting materials held attention because he took them from daily experience.

The adaptation of Scripture to the needs of humanity instead of theological exegesis, the stress upon the blessings of atonement, and a consistent attempt to make Christian faith a happy, hopeful experience characterize Talmage's sermons. The application of these concepts to his subject material, estimated at over 4,000 different themes in Brooklyn alone, attracted international attention. His sermons ranged from a condemnation of big city morals to a prediction of future greatness for America, from a review of a trip abroad to a plea for grain for Russia, and from an attack on Robert G. Ingersoll to a description of heavenly joys for Christians. Talmage once told a group of students at Drew Theological Seminary that ministers should recognize the people before them as struggling, dying sinners, sympathize with their problems, and present appropriate helpful sermons. Pastors should "tear out" theology wherever it hindered understanding and apply their ideas directly to the minds of listeners.

The sermon "Vicarious Suffering" exemplifies how easily Talmage strayed from strict doctrinal exegesis to practical application. Instead of presenting the usual explanation of Christ's death, he spent most of the sermon describing voluntary sacrifices of humans for each other: fathers toiling to provide necessities for their families, mothers tending sick children during the night, soldiers dying to protect their country, and doctors risking their lives to help the diseased.

The desire to assist and to save others became a concept for other homilies. In "The Three Greatest Things to Do," Talmage described a young merchant near bankruptcy, a woman unable to find employment, and an underprivileged child. Most people will never become famous as political leaders or inventors, he told the audience, but they can easily accomplish the three most important things in life: help a man, help a woman, help a child. Some topics encouraged and inspired listeners. "Garrison Duty," one of Talmage's favorite homilies, stressed the value of everyday work. All work is essential. Prominent people can exist only because unknowns perform their tasks faithfully, he said, citing as examples merchants who needed clerks, railroad presidents who needed section men, and captains who needed crews. Talmage wanted to make Christianity a happy religion. His last syndicated sermon, "David's Harp" (February 1902) is typical. Using Psalm 33:2 as a text—"Sing unto him with . . . an instrument of ten strings"—he noted that David wrote songs of praise even when in trouble. Suggesting a blessing for each string of an imaginary harp—food, eyesight, hearing, sleep, movement, illumined nights, reason, friends, the gospel, and anticipation of heaven—Talmage urged his parishioners to play all the strings of their harps, to concentrate on the good things of life.

During the Brooklyn years, Talmage delivered a popular weekly Friday night lecture, usually a talk on politics, an important person, or a significant event. Talmage's intense political interest often stimulated him to demand reform. He ridiculed one candidate as "this hero of fisticuffs," described the U.S. Senate of 1881 as the "poorest yet," and labeled the 1886 Chinese immigration policy as "un-American" and "God-defying." Lectures about important people were generally laudatory or eulogistic. When Pius IX died, Talmage declared that denominations did not save people, only the personal relationship with Christ, regardless of whether a person kneels in St. Peter's Cathedral or a log cabin. Sometimes Talmage moralized or discussed a theme: a protest against the indiscriminate sale of firearms or a warning that communism could destroy the church. Most of all, Talmage liked to talk about his favorite subject, the present glories and future greatness of the United States.

Talmage demonstrated less diversity in selecting secular topics for his professional lectures. At first he restricted himself mostly to versions of the five original

Philadelphia speeches: "Grumbler and Company," "The New Life of the Nation," "Our New Home," "Big Blunders," and "The Bright Side of Things," gradually adding lectures about his trips: "Up and Down the Holy Land," "Russia and the Czar," "Journey around the World"; and social welfare talks; "The School for Scandal" and "Bright and Happy Homes." Requests for speeches on special topics arrived frequently, and occasionally Talmage obliged. Generally, however, Talmage preferred to use his stock lectures for professional engagements. He developed his speech "Russia and the Czar" as a rebuttal to Russian critics in America, a rebuttal that included erroneous assertions. "Big Blunders" consisted of humorous attacks on five human errors: trying to master too many occupations, indulgence in bad humor, excessive amusement, forming wrong domestic relations, and the spirit of reckless enterprise.

Convinced that too many sermons "reeked of the study," Talmage sought his speech materials from human experience. He once spent several nights visiting tenderloin districts and police courts before writing a series of homilies on crime and vice. He took daily walks, recording in his ever-present notebook the observations of housewives, laborers, and children. The notebook became a constant source of ideas and illustrations. Entries include an important event—eleven people dying on Mount Blanc; an observed incident—a boy scolding his mother; an anecdote—the dying words of a railroad conductor; a quotation—"'Twon't matter about our bein' bootblacks. There we shall join, not somehow or other, but straight through the gate"; and an undocumented statistic—30 percent of actresses are dope addicts. Occasionally Talmage inserted potential sermon titles: "Up the Stairs, or Diary of a Redeemed Soul"—a homily on dying; quotable epigrams—"Conscience is the epidermis of the mouth"; or random thoughts— "My creed: the loving Lord. To hail Him, love Him, and obey Him is all that is required. To that creed I write all work. T. DW. T."

Talmage supplemented observation and conversation with considerable reading. Each morning he scanned fifty major newspapers. Sometimes he wrote to experts for specific data, such as crop statistics for use in a Thanksgiving sermon; more often he referred to the numerous literary and historical books in his library.

Talmage planned his speech outlines while walking; he returned to his study for the final composition. Despite his contempt for those who read their speeches, Talmage never depended on sudden inspiration. He consequently dictated sermons and lectures, at speeds up to 150 words per minute. He paced the study floor, sometimes stopping to seize a book and search for an appropriate idea. When the quotation was located, he cut it from the book, handed it to the secretary, and placed the mutilated volume aside. "I never want to refer to the quotation again," he told those who expressed surprise at his mangled library.

The composing process took two to three days. The finished draft always included extra material so that Talmage could adapt ideas to his specific audience. He concluded his preparation by reading the manuscript twice to memorize key ideas, although he generally improvised part of the delivered address. During the Philadelphia pastorate, he stopped taking manuscripts with him, relying entirely on his memory and a few notes pinned into his Bible or lecture book. His prodigious memory failed only once. After reading the text, he could not recall a sermon. He vainly reread the scripture and then resignedly told a surprised Tabernacle congregation, "Brethren, let us now close with a hymn." He remarked afterward that many sermons would be considerably improved if begun with the same statement.

Talmage considered embellishment essential for retaining audience attention and frequently employed illustrations, metaphors, personifications, hyperboles, and similes. Talmage profusely used illustrative material from his experience and reading. "Garrison Duty," one of his favorite sermons, contained thirty-one illustrations; the "Russia and the Czar" lecture had thirty. These illustrations, coupled with figures of speech, epigrams, and a vast amount of descriptive detail, gave his phrasing the verbosity the critics attacked.

Talmage often used long sentences for detailed descriptions, reserving shorter sentences for contrast. He used rhetorical questions and reiterations as the primary means of emphasis. In "Garrison Duty," he asked fourteen rhetorical questions and restated his thesis verbatim eight times; the fourth sermon against Ingersoll contained twenty-six questions, four verbatim restatements, and numerous approximate restatements. This constant stress and reiteration gave his speeches a sense of immediacy and prevented wordiness from obliterating the message.

Talmage used laugh-provoking anecdotes and comments to stress points and add variety to the subject material. When opponents complained, calling it the language of the street, he defended his choice of words, claiming that ideas and concepts taken from human experience could be explained better in a forceful, familiar language than obsolete clerical vocabulary.

Talmage used the Bible extensively as proof, although he preferred to employ passages for emotional rather than logical verification. Talmage applied a similar rationale to the selection of nonbiblical proof, convinced that appeals to human emotions were more effective than appeals to human reason. Talmage used ethical proof in an indirect manner. He did not use his reputation as a persuasive device but represented himself as a typical messenger of God. He seldom questioned evidence that seemed reasonable to his point of view and stubbornly retained his original viewpoints despite contrary data. His implicit faith in common men, his overriding optimism, and his continual stress on the good aspects of life prevented him from ever achieving a satisfactory critical attitude toward potential proof.

Talmage employed a simple topical organization for his speeches. He usually began with a one- or two-paragraph introduction, stated his thesis, proved it inductively, and ended with a one-paragraph conclusion. He used no particular strategy in the arrangement of his main points. The thesis generally emerged as he made a transition to a new point or summarized in the conclusion. Talmage held his sermons to an average of 4,000 words and adopted the practice of using audience attention as a criterion for length of his secular lectures. He liked to begin lectures with a reference to his audience and accomplished the same results for sermons by reading the scriptural text and vividly describing a problem or situation relevant to the specific audience.

Talmage's delivery attracted as much interest as his ornamental style and exciting topics; he became famous for a variety of energetic gestures and movements and an ability to address crowds of 20,000 people. Talmage was not handsome, but his physical size commanded attention. He dressed casually, preferring business clothes to clerical attire. He advocated using a natural, conversational vocal pattern and once told an audience of seminarians to avoid developing a "pulpit tone." Evidence indicates that Talmage was not a silver-tongued orator; his voice lacked distinction, although he spoke in a resonant, conversational manner. His voice had considerable power and carried well, even in large auditoriums. Talmage's numerous platform movements and gestures generated much attention. Despite awkwardness and lack of coordination, Talmage conveyed his ideas so forcefully and so dramatically that some called him a David Garrick. He liked to act out parts of his speeches and once described a young man who had gone to Coney Island, met evil companions, and returned home drunk. Talmage lurched around the platform, imitated the broken gibberish, and fell to the floor. Then he stood up and philosophized about drinking. Talmage boldly created a new school of pulpit oratory that combined dramatic forcefulness with the spirituality of his profession. By not reading from a manuscript or speaking from behind a rostrum, he communicated directly with his listeners; by using physical movement and a powerful voice, he added excitement to his speeches.

Talmage enjoyed unprecedented popularity while he lived. Consistently large lecture audiences attest to the acceptability of his secular speeches. He spoke to more parishioners than any other clerical contemporary, including Beecher. He developed the Brooklyn Tabernacle into one of the largest Protestant churches in the world. Yet the tabernacle congregation disintegrated when he resigned, and followers forgot him soon after he died.

Talmage's colorful phrasing and histrionic delivery made him an idol of the Gilded Age, but the superficial content of his speeches prevented him from having a permanent effect. He stimulated people to remain orthodox while he lived but failed to influence theology significantly; he generated a buoyant optimism that reality quickly undermined. His influence ended when he died. Today he is relatively unknown.

INFORMATION SOURCES

Research Collections and Collected Speeches

The Thomas DeWitt Talmage Manuscript Collection is located in the Library of Congress. Thirty-four boxes contain uncataloged hand-written speech drafts, notebooks, assorted personal writings, letters, and pictures. Newspapers, especially the *Brooklyn Daily*

Eagle, are helpful for obtaining transcripts of sermons, lectures, and information about important Talmage events.

American Forum: Speeches on Historic Issues: 1788–1900. Edited by Ernest   *AF*
    J. Wrage and Barnet Baskerville. New York: Harper & Brothers,
    1960.
Talmage, T. DeWitt. *The Brooklyn Tabernacle, A Collection of 104 Sermons*   *BT*
    Preached by T. DeWitt Talmage, D.D. New York: Funk & Wagnalls,
    1884.
————. *The Earth Girdled.* Philadelphia: Shepp Publishing Co., 1896.   *EG*
————. *500 Selected Sermons.* Grand Rapids: Baker Book House, 1956   *SS*
————. *Gathered Gems.* New York: J. S. Ogilvie Publishing Co., 1889.   *GG*
————. *The Masque Torn Off.* Chicago: J. Fairbanks & Co., 1878.   *MT*
————. *Sermons.* New York: Funk & Wagnalls, 1886.   *S*
————. *T. DeWitt Talmage: His Life and Work.* Edited by Louis Banks.   *TDT*
    New York: Christian Herald, 1902.

Selected Critical Studies

Monsma, John W. *Thomas DeWitt Talmage: Orthodox Spokesman of the Gilded Age.*
    Bloomington: Indiana University, 1966.

Selected Biographies

Northrop, Henry, et al. *Life and Teachings of Rev. T. DeWitt Talmage, D.D.* New York:
    D. E. Howell, 1902.
Rusk, John. *The Authentic Life of T. DeWitt Talmage.* New York: L. G. Stahl, 1902.
Talmage, T. DeWitt. *T. DeWitt Talmage As I Knew Him.* New York: E. P. Dutton,
    1912.

CHRONOLOGY OF MAJOR SPEECHES

See "Research Collections and Collected Speeches" for source codes.

Talmage's speeches and lectures often followed no special chronological sequence. Dates and places are provided if known.

"Big Blunders," Philadelphia, c. 1862–1869; *EG*, pp. 182–98.

"Bright Side of Things," Philadelphia, c. 1862–1869; *EG*, pp. 113–34.

Series of sermons delivered against Robert G. Ingersoll, Brooklyn Tabernacle, Brooklyn, New York, January 15-February 26, 1882; *BT*, pp. 93–120; *SS*, 4: 23–112; *AF*, pp. 289–300.

"Garrison Duty," October 22, 1982; *BT*, pp. 234–36, *SS*; 11: 273–85.

"Russia and the Czar," c. 1893; copy given to writer by Maude Talmage.

"David's Harp," February 3, 1902; *TDT*, pp. 489–97.

"Three Greatest Things to Do," n.d.; *SS*, 3: 85–97.

"Vicarious Suffering," n.d.; *SS*, 5: 145–57.

ROBERT A. TOOMBS
(1810–1885), defender of constitutional and southern rights

DALE G. LEATHERS

Robert A. Toombs is recognized by those who have studied his persuasion carefully as one of the most gifted and brilliant orators of the pre–Civil War period. His brilliance as an orator has been obscured in part by the fact that he has been so closely associated in the popular mind with a series of lost causes.

Toombs was a southerner from the time of his birth, July 2, 1810, in Washington, Georgia, until his death on July 15, 1885, in the same place. In 1824 Toombs entered the University of Georgia. He left in a few months after being threatened with dismissal for playing cards. He then enrolled in Union College, Schenectady, New York, where he obtained his A.B. degree in 1828. After studying law in 1829 for one year at the University of Virginia, Toombs was admitted to the bar as a practicing attorney in Elbert County, Georgia, on March 18, 1830. Biographer Pleasant Stovall noted that Toombs and other prominent lawyers of the day "made the circuit with their saddle-bags." Toombs soon became recognized for the brilliance of his legal arguments. He would "plunge immediately into his fierce and impassioned oratory, and pour his torrent of wit, eloquence, logic, and satire upon judge and jury."

Toombs was elected to the general assembly of Georgia in October 1838 five years after he joined the conservative Whig Party. In 1844 he was elected to the U.S. House of Representatives and in 1851 was elected for the first of his two terms in the U.S. Senate; he actually began serving his first Senate term in 1854.

When Toombs became convinced in 1861 that the Union could not be preserved, he resigned from the Senate and on February 27, 1861, was appointed secretary of state of the Confederate States of America by Jefferson Davis. In less than six months, Toombs resigned that office to become a brigadier general in the Confederate army. His undistinguished war record did not contribute to his stature in the eyes of historians.

At the end of the Civil War, Toombs went into exile through an escape route that took him to Paris via Havana, Cuba. When Toombs returned from European exile, an interview with President Andrew Johnson assured him that he would not be arrested. Nonetheless he became increasingly bitter and disillusioned as he viewed the exploitation of the South during Reconstruction. Since Toombs neither applied for amnesty nor took the oath of allegiance after the Civil War, he lived out his last years and died as a man without a country.

ROBERT TOOMBS AS SENATORIAL SPOKESMAN DURING THE 1850s

Robert Toombs was recognized by his contemporaries and his three biographers as an unusually skilled practitioner of three types of oratory: courtroom pleadings before juries, stump speaking, and political addresses delivered in the U.S. Congress. Toombs's great oratorical skill in the courtroom accounted in large part for the fact that he became probably the most prominent attorney of his time in Georgia and accumulated considerable wealth. He may have been at his best, however, before a large crowd at open-air political rallies in the 1840s and 1850s. Since he had few peers when it came to giving extemporaneous speeches on complex issues, his most caustic critics were wary of challenging him to debate on the political hustings; Robert Toombs, the political stump speaker, was rarely challenged, and the question of whether he was ever vanquished on the stump is still open to debate.

Although Toombs displayed remarkable oratorical skills in the courtroom and on the stump, his oratorical efforts in the U.S. Congress have received the most attention. This is true for at least two reasons. First, detailed records of his speeches in Congress are available. There is, however, reason to doubt the textual accuracy and completeness of Toombs's speeches recorded in the *Congressional Globe* before 1850. Students of his stump speaking and legal oratory must rely on fragmentary descriptions by his biographers. Second, his impact on the nation and the great issues that precipitated extended debate in the 1850s was manifested largely through his speeches in the U.S. Senate.

When Toombs moved from the House of Representatives to the Senate in 1854, the giants of the Senate, such as Calhoun, Webster, and Clay, were gone either as a result of death or electoral defeat. Thompson notes in *Robert Toombs of Georgia* that the historic Senate chamber was "a small semicircular room topped by a low half-domed ceiling" and "open fires lent an atmosphere of conviviality and comfort to the surroundings." This was an age when senators wore long frock coats, sported bushy chin whiskers, frequently had a big chew of tobacco in their mouths, and liked to lounge and relax with their feet up on their desks.

But although the physical atmosphere in the early 1850s in the Senate was convivial, the passions that motivated and the issues that divided the occupants of the chamber were among the strongest and most significant in the history of the United States. In this atmosphere in the short period of seven years, Robert A. Toombs became recognized as one of the most important senators of his era. Until the fateful day in 1861 when Toombs decided that secession was unavoidable, he attained and retained his prominence among his peers in the Senate by his remarkable ability to defend the U.S. Constitution at the same time that he championed the rights of the southern states and the South's most unpopular institution, slavery.

Toombs gave no fewer than eighteen major speeches while he served in the U.S. Congress. Most of his speeches, and certainly his most impassioned oratory, focused on three great issues of the time: the acquisition of new territories, slavery, and secession. The issues were, of course, interrelated and inseparable. The dominant issue whenever a new territory was to be admitted to statehood was how the issue of slavery was to be handled; ultimately, the failure to resolve that issue resulted in the secession of the southern states.

Contrary to popular opinion, Robert Toombs, who began addressing the territorial question in 1846, was neither "a wild Georgian" nor a "fire eater" during most of his time in Congress. He was, instead, a national spokesman who transcended narrow regional interests in his attempts to preserve the Union by defending the principles on which the U.S. Constitution is based. In his first speech on the Oregon question, January 12, 1846, Toombs took pains to cultivate the image of a national spokesman for the entire Union, for he "had no reproaches to cast, no complaints to make, anywhere. . . . We were all embarked in the same ship, and we ought all to make common cause when it was threatened with danger. We were watched in every traverse of our course by a sleepless and a powerful adversary." In his subsequent speech, "Admission of California," February 27, 1850, he developed persuasive themes on the question of acquiring new territories that would reappear in subsequent speeches on the subject. He argued that the right to hold slaves as property was a basic right given by the Constitution and that "those who claim the power in Congress to exclude slavery from the territories rely rather on authority than principle to support it." In one of his most moving statements on the subject, Toombs steadfastly maintained:

We have the right to call on you to give your blood to maintain these thousands and all the rest of the slaves of the South in bondage. "It is so nominated in the bond." Yet with these obligations resting upon you, we are told by you that slave property is out of the protection of the Government. Gentlemen, deceive not yourselves, you cannot deceive others. This is a pro-slavery government. Slavery is stamped upon its heart—The Constitution.

Toombs's argument was difficult to rebut for he was in fact using the most sacred instrument developed by his nation, the Constitution, to defend a sectional institution, at the same time maintaining that he was motivated by and spoke for the national interest.

In his Senate speech on January 24, 1860, "Invasion of the States," Toombs repeated and refined arguments on the acquisition of territories that appear in many other speeches on the subject. He argued that the right to own slaves as property was a property right protected by the Constitution, that opponents were lying when they asserted that fathers of the Constitution were antislavery, that northern senators violated their oath of office when they openly opposed the institution of slavery in the new territories, and that southerners were being treated as second-class citizens. Sharpening his attack on northern Republican senators who opposed slavery, Toombs said, "No sir: they mock at constitutional obligations, jeer at oaths. They have lost their shame with their virtue, and no longer feel humiliated at the commission of these great crimes."

Slavery was the issue Toombs addressed most often and with greatest passion. In July 1853, he gave a speech on slavery in the United States to the

Few and Gamma societies of Emory College. This speech was the most detailed defense of slavery ever given by a southerner. On January 24, 1856, Toombs delivered basically the same speech at the Tremont Temple in Boston. Since he spoke in the heart of abolitionism, friend and foe alike recognized the courage that was characteristic of his public career. Toombs's thesis was straightforward: "In glancing over the civilized world, the eye rests upon not a single spot where all classes of society are so well content with their social system, or have greater reason to be so, than in the slave-holding states of the American Union."

Toombs was, of course, a racist. Unlike many of his more cautious contemporaries, however, he seemed eager to claim that blacks were inferior to whites in all fundamental respects and then try to support that sweeping claim. In this noted speech, Toombs declared that the behavior of Negroes, where they had been emancipated, had been disastrous. He made the telling point that northerners also considered the Negro to be inferior since they had granted this race neither the vote nor citizenship in spite of their bitter attacks on the institution of slavery in the South. The thrust of Toombs's speech on slavery is summed up in his peroration:

Such is our social system and such our condition under it. Its political wisdom is vindicated in its effects on society, its morality by the practices of the Patriarchs and the teachings of the Apostles; we submit it to the judgment of the civilized world with the firm conviction that the adoption of no other system under our circumstances would have exhibited the individual man (bond or free) in a higher development, or society in a happier civilization.

In his speeches in the late 1850s, Toombs began to imply that secession might be inevitable. It was not until January 7, 1861, in his farewell speech to the Senate, that he addressed this subject explicitly and in detail. This is the speech generally recognized as his best, as one of the finest speeches on the pre–Civil War era, and it is arguably one of the most outstanding political speeches ever given in the United States.

Toombs structured this speech around five basic demands of the southern states that needed to be met if secession was to be avoided; in effect Toombs was enunciating what he perceived to be the southern bill of rights. He demanded what he viewed as the South's constitutional rights to have slaves protected as property, that slaves be surrendered by other states when they fled across state lines, and that those who aided or abetted insurrection by support of the antislavery cause be punished by new federal legislation. In his concluding summary, Toombs emphasized that "all these charges I have proven by the record; and I put them before the civilized world, and demand the judgment of today, or tomorrow, or distant ages, and of Heaven itself upon the justice of these causes."

From a rhetorical perspective, a number of features of Toombs's oratory made it distinctive. First, his arguments for the Union and southern rights, which were carefully grounded in constitutional principle, were recognized for both their resilience to refutation and as the sincere expression of a man committed to the preservation of the Union. Second, his impressive management skills were reflected in his attempt to link his supporters with an almost limitless array of desirable personal qualities while associating his opponents with the most base of motivations and personal qualities. Third, his remarkable sense of humor was used too infrequently to build credibility by disarming opponents and too frequently to mount bitter personal attacks on opponents that featured sarcasm and hyperbole.

Toombs's arguments grounded in constitutional principle were carefully crafted for the most part and not easily attacked. However, Joseph Hemmer claimed that Toombs was sometimes inconsistent in his application of the Constitution to the invention process. He used the constitutional argument when it suited his purposes but was quick to disregard the principles of equality enunciated by Jefferson even as he used the Constitution to condemn northern violations of southern rights.

Toombs also specialized in the use of emotionally loaded terms calculated to project an image of heroism for his supporters and villainy for his opponents. Larry Lowe noted that Toombs focused "primarily upon the association of his cause with that which is virtuous, noble, and desirable; while associating the opposition's cause with that which is non-virtuous, ignoble, and undesirable."

Toombs's extraordinary sense of humor could have been used more effectively to build his credibility and win converts to his point of view. When one of his early opponents for the U.S. House cast doubt on his attendance record, Toombs wryly observed that in view of his opponent's intellect, his opponent, if elected, would serve his constituents best by a poor attendance record. He also delighted in questioning the ability of his opponents to comprehend complex points; he once dismissed the befuddled state of mind of a senator from Oregon as understandable since he had "just come in out of the woods." Biographer Phillips noted that Toombs's favorite character in literature was Falstaff. Toombs was fond of quoting Falstaff's request to Prince Henry, "Rob me the exchequer." When Toombs did so, Falstaff's request was invariably made by one of Toombs's opponents. On at least one occasion, Toombs used a remarkable throwaway line in a Senate speech. Referring sarcastically to the "roar of indignation" from northerners who denounced the southern system, Toombs said in an aside to members of the Senate that the "roar" was "as yet inaudible." If his humor had been used with greater moderation, it could have been a great asset to him.

Too frequently, however, Toombs used his humor to eviscerate an opponent rather than to charm or disarm. Exaggeration became a bothersome hallmark of his public style. His propensity for exaggeration was evident in 1860 when Toombs was asked whether he thought his friend, Senator Stephen Douglas of Illinois, was a great man. Replied Toombs, "There has been but one greater, and he, the Apostle Paul." More often than not, the unfortunate opponents, whom Toombs used as scapegoats, became "perfidious liars" and "traitors."

Characteristically, Toombs, in his "Invasion of the States" speech, described the behavior of his Republican opponents as "plain, open, shameless, and profligate perfidy."

As it became increasingly apparent that Toombs's attempt to preserve the Union would fail, he became less tactful and more irresponsible in his attacks on the scapegoats who were his opponents. As early as February 23, 1854, in his Senate speech on Kansas and Nebraska, Toombs dismissed his opponents as "men who have stood in moral complicity with treason, arson, and murder." In his last years in the Senate, Toombs's propensity for ad hominem argument resulted in ill-chosen remarks that seemed to exceed the bounds of fair play and good taste. For example, in his May 7, 1861, Senate speech on secession, Toombs said of Abraham Lincoln that "Lincoln denounced that bill. He places the stamp of his condemnation upon a measure intended to promote the peace and security of confederate States. He is, therefore, an enemy of the human race . . . [and he] deserves the execration of all mankind."

In many respects, Toombs was a great orator. Although he lacked tact and moderation, the power, detail, and force of his arguments are undeniable. He used his remarkable oratorical skills over a considerable period of time in a sincere attempt to preserve the Union. When secession came, he was a vigorous supporter of that cause. In fact, his true stature as a great orator has probably not been recognized because his association in the popular mind with a number of lost causes has relegated him to an almost secondary role as a historical figure.

The none-too-complimentary assessment of historians may be attributed to a number of factors. Unlike a number of other southern politicians, he attempted to defend slavery as a positive good rather than a necessary evil. Second, he refused to take an oath of allegiance for the U.S. government after the Civil War. Finally, his bitter disillusionment at southern treatment during Reconstruction, when combined with an increasingly serious drinking problem, led him to make incendiary and perhaps irresponsible statements during his later years. From a historical perspective, the "unreconstructed rebel" may have been a living legend whose accomplishments never quite matched his promise. From a rhetorical perspective, Toombs was an orator with remarkable skills and a demonstrated record of persuasive performance that was matched by few of his peers—many of whom have ironically achieved much greater posthumous fame in the annals of American public address.

INFORMATION SOURCES

Research Collections and Collected Speeches

Researchers of Toombs's oratory will find the primary sources concentrated in the Georgia Room of the University of Georgia Library, Athens, Georgia. Since Toombs attended the University of Georgia and was later a long-time and devoted member of its board of trustees, the university has made a special effort to collect important research materials on Toombs. Students of Toombs's persuasion will find the following sources particularly useful: copies of all of his major speeches in the House of Representatives and in the U.S. Senate are contained in relevant issues of *The Congressional Globe*; a number of his post–Civil War speeches along with regional and national reaction to them are contained in the state's major newspaper, the *Atlanta Constitution*; multiple volumes of *The Correspondence of Robert Toombs, Alexander H. Stephens, and Howell Cobb*, as well as a collection of Toombs's letters to his wife, are also available in the Georgia Room. The references here include the three major biographies written about Toombs, as well as a Ph.D. dissertation and master's thesis that focus directly on his oratory. Additionally researchers may wish to visit the Toombs family home and museum in nearby Washington, Georgia, and discuss him with his great-grandson, Bolling DuBose, and his family, who live in Athens, Georgia.

American Forum: Speeches on Historic Issues, 1788–1900. Edited by Ernest J. Wrage and Barnet Baskerville. New York: Harper and Brothers, 1960.	*AF*
Atlanta Constitution, July 23, 1868.	*AC*
Congressional Globe. January 1846-January 1861.	*CG*
Hemmer, Joseph J., Jr. "A Rhetorical Analysis of the Political Oratory of Robert Toombs." Master's thesis, Bradley University, 1962.	*RAPO*
Lowe, Larry V. "A Rhetorical Analysis of Robert A. Toombs of Georgia." Ph.D. dissertation, Michigan State University, 1965.	*RART*
The Correspondence of Robert Toombs, Alexander H. Stephens, and Howell Cobb. Edited by Ulrich Bonnell Phillips. Vol. 2. 1911; rpt., DaCapo Press, New York, 1970.	*CRT*

Selected Biographies

Phillips, Ulrich Bonnell. *The Life of Robert Toombs*. New York: Burt Franklin, 1913.
Stovall, Pleasant A. *Robert Toombs*. New York: Cassell Publishing Company, 1892.
Thompson, William Y. *Robert Toombs of Georgia*. Baton Rouge: Louisiana State University Press, 1966.

CHRONOLOGY OF MAJOR SPEECHES

See "Research Collections and Collected Speeches" for source codes.

"Oregon Question," U.S. House of Representatives, Washington, D.C., January 12, 1846; *CG*, pp. 185–86; *RART*, pp. 285–92.

"Admission of California," U.S. House of Representatives, Washington, D.C., February 27, 1850; *CG*, pp. 196–201; *RAPO*, pp. 126–42.

"Slavery in the United States: Its Consistency with Republican Institutions, and Its Effect upon the Slave and Society," delivered before the Few and Phi Gamma Societies of Emory College, Oxford, Georgia, July 1853; *AF*, pp. 158–68.

"Kansas and Nebraska," U.S. Senate, Washington, D.C., February 23, 1854; *CG*, pp. 346–51.

Speech on president's Kansas message, U.S. Senate, Washington, D.C., February 28, 1856; *CG*, pp. 115–18; *RART*, pp. 325–37.

"Invasion of the States," U.S. Senate, Washington, D.C., January 24, 1860; *CG*, pp. 88–93; *RART*, pp. 338–59.

"Property in Territories," U.S. Senate, Washington, D.C., May 21, 1860; *CG*, pp. 338–45.

Speech on secession, farewell to the Senate, U.S. Senate, Washington, D.C., January 7, 1861; *CG*, pp. 267–71; *RAPO*, pp. 155–75.

Selected Critical Studies

Hemmer, Joseph, Jr., "Robert A. Toombs Speaks for the South." *Southern Speech Journal* 28 (1963): 251–59.

SOJOURNER TRUTH
(c. 1797–1883), antislavery and women's rights lecturer

Sojourner Truth gained prominence as a respected and powerful reform speaker in the period surrounding the Civil War. Yet the first forty years of her life contained virtually every barrier imaginable to oratorical success. Born a slave in New York State, Isabella, as she was called, spoke only Dutch, the language of her master, until the age of ten. Although she eventually learned English, she never learned to read or write and had no formal education.

When New York emancipated its slaves in 1827, Sojourner Truth made her way to New York City, where she worked as a domestic. While always highly religious, her decision to become a "sojourner" for God was sudden. In 1843, she had a religious vision in which she was told to take a new name—that of Sojourner—and to begin traveling and sharing God's message. Her last name was revealed to her when she "told the Lord I wanted another name, 'cause everybody else had two names; and the Lord gave me *Truth* because I was to declare the truth to the people."

Sojourner Truth spent her first winter in Northampton, Massachusetts, on a communal farm founded by George Benson, the brother-in-law of the renowned abolitionist William Lloyd Garrison. At the community, she met Garrison and other leaders in the abolitionist cause, including Frederick Douglass, the first escaped slave to lecture for the antislavery cause, and Olive Gilbert, who later wrote Sojourner's life story and had it published as a source of income for her. She gained her first formal speaking experiences on lecture tours with the Northampton abolitionists.

The close association between the abolition and women's rights movements—many abolitionists understood that white women were little better off than slaves—brought Sojourner in contact with the women's rights leaders of the day, including Frances Gage, Lucy Stone, and Lucretia Mott. She began to speak out on both issues, seeing the abolition of slavery and women's rights as part of a larger sense of justice. Although these are the two issues for which she most often is remembered, Sojourner also spoke out on temperance and capital punishment. During the Civil War, she helped care for wounded soldiers and urged that freed black men be allowed to fight in the Union army. Her last cause—and her only unsuccessful one—was a petition campaign urging Congress to give land in the West to freed slaves.

SOJOURNER TRUTH AS A REFORM LECTURER

Sojourner Truth spoke at camp meetings, revivals, roadside meetings, and in town squares as well as at more formal meetings and conventions in twenty-one states and the District of Columbia between 1843 and 1878. Unique in her ability to speak as one doubly oppressed by race and sex, she was known across the country for her simple yet unforgettable brand of oratory. Although the majority of Sojourner's speeches went unrecorded or are known only partially from newspaper accounts, similar substantive and stylistic features characterize the speeches that do remain. Sojourner consistently argued from basic principles of equality and fairness, which she believed were not only commonsensical but supported by Christian doctrine as well. In her speech to the Women's Rights convention in Akron, Ohio, in 1851, Sojourner refuted previous speakers who maintained that women should not vote because they were helpless and less intelligent than men. On the issue of intellect, she argued that even if she had less intelligence, she should be allowed to exercise what she had. On women's helplessness, she pointed out that although she was a woman, she never had been treated as helpless. In both instances, Sojourner made the point that the basic issue of human rights was in danger of being lost in discussion over peripheral issues.

Two years later, at the women's rights convention in New York City, Sojourner Truth made similar appeals to basic human rights: women were not asking for "half of a kingdom" but merely for the rights that were their natural due. She brought the debate back to the core issues involved and refused to be distracted by extraneous arguments. At yet another women's rights convention in 1867, she made the same point with equal simplicity: "Men have got their rights, and women has not got their rights. That is the trouble." She felt no need to elaborate or explain her ideas; she simply allowed the underlying principles to speak for themselves. Whether the issue was women's rights or the abolition of slavery, Sojourner's basic approach was the same: she cut through the surface issues being addressed and insisted that her audiences focus on the universal principles of human rights involved.

Sojourner Truth used two rhetorical techniques to support her notions about human rights. First, she made extensive use of metaphors, similes, and analogies. Her speeches were filled with comparisons of various sorts, which functioned to relate the issues under debate to everyday experiences. In her 1851 address, Sojourner used a metaphor of measures to argue for rights in spite of differences in intellect: "If my cup won't hold a pint, and yourn holds a quart, wouldn't ye be mean not to let me have my little half-measure full?" A similar cooking metaphor was woven throughout her 1867 speech to argue for continued agitation: "I am keeping the thing going while things are stirring; because if we wait till it is still, it will take a great while to get it going again." She mixed two other metaphors in the same speech to convey the tension men experienced when confronted with giving up some of their control: "I know that it is hard for one who has held the reins for so long to give up; it cuts like a knife. It will feel all better when it closes up again." Sojourner's comparisons were persuasive because they enabled her to take abstract discussions and make them understandable in terms of commonsense principles and everyday experiences.

Sojourner Truth also used biblical allusions extensively to provide support for her arguments. Although she could not read the Bible, others had read it to her, and she memorized much of it. At the Akron convention, she refuted the idea that women not be allowed to vote because Christ was a man by asking, "Where did your Christ come from? From God and a woman! Man had nothing to do with Him.'' Among her better-known passages is her reference to Eve with which she ended this speech: ''If the first woman God ever made was strong enough to turn the world upside down all alone, these women together ought to be able to turn it back, and get it right side up again!'' And in her speech celebrating the anniversary of the Emancipation Proclamation, she told how she had found Jesus and discovered that she was able to ''love everybody and the white people too.'' By mentioning this experience, she hoped the whites in her audience would reciprocate by supporting her petition to resettle blacks in the West. Sojourner then appealed to Christian Scripture and sentiments to reinforce the logic of her arguments. Like her argumentative style generally, her use of biblical references was literal and straightforward; she did not complicate issues by excessive interpretation.

Sojourner Truth's logical arguments were bolstered by a combination of ethos and pathos. First, as a black woman and a former slave, she was a highly credible speaker who personally had experienced the conditions about which she spoke. She frequently reminded her audiences of her past, thus prompting strong emotional responses to them. In her Akron speech, she dismissed arguments about women needing special protections and privileges by contrasting the treatment she received as a slave woman with that accorded white women: ''I could work as much and eat as much as a man—when I could get it—and bear the lash as well! And ain't I a woman?'' Her 1853 speech opened with a reference designed to establish common ground with her audience as a native New Yorker, but she did not let them forget that she had not always been eligible for citizenship: ''I am a citizen of the state of New York; I was born in it, and I was a slave in the state of New York, and now I am a good citizen of this state.'' Similarly, her speech at the meeting of the American Equal Rights Association opened with a reference to her slave background: ''I came from another field—the country of the slave.'' Her address commemorating the Emancipation Proclamation contained the most lengthy references to her life as a slave, undoubtedly because of the centrality of the issue of slavery to the occasion. Sojourner Truth used her slave background, then, to convince her audiences—intellectually and emotionally—of the need for both blacks and women to be free from the yoke of slavery.

The effectiveness of Sojourner's argumentation was especially noteworthy given the constraints that governed the act of public speaking in her day. She embodied two groups—blacks and women—believed incapable of the intellect needed for public expression. Thus her mere presence on a public platform called into question basic beliefs of the society and typically generated considerable hostility. In each of her speeches, Sojourner had to dissipate the anger of her audiences, incensed that she would think she had something of value to say, and then motivate them to listen to her message. She handled this situation by assuming a maternalistic stance toward her audiences, which consisted of simultaneously scolding and praising them. Inherent in scolding is a kind of superior wisdom; the one doing the scolding has seen more of life and has a right to make such judgments. Such a superior attitude is allowable, however, and even expected in the mother-child relationship and is softened by the sense of caring that accompanies it. While Sojourner, in all likelihood, did not use this mothering strategy deliberately, her age, range of life experiences, and physical presence certainly enhanced it. She opened two of her speeches with "Well, Children," and at one point commented, "I call you children, you are somebody's children, and I am old enough to be mother of all that is here." At the 1853 convention, also known as the mob convention because of the unruly audience, her scolding was especially harsh: "Sons and daughters ought to behave themselves before their mothers, but they do not. . . . If they'd been brought up proper, they'd have known better than hissing like snakes and geese."

Sojourner Truth's audiences put up with her scolding, however, because she also showed them that she understood their discomfort, not only about granting rights to blacks and women but about her own disregard of public speaking norms. At the 1853 convention, she acknowledged the crowd's anger by mentioning how unusual it was for someone like her to be speaking: "I know that it feels a kind o' hissin' and ticklin' like to see a colored woman get up and tell you about things." Other indications that she identified with what men were experiencing are found throughout her speeches in statements such as, "I know it is hard for men to give up entirely" and "I know that it is hard for one who has held the reins for so long to give up." In addition, she pointed out what men already had accomplished—emancipation of slaves and rights for black men—and also praised their willingness at least to listen to a discussion of the issues with remarks such as, "I'm glad to see so many together." Sojourner's maternalistic posture, then, allowed her to assume the superior stance necessary for a public speaker but in a way that made it more palatable to her audiences.

Sojourner Truth's almost magical effects on audiences stemmed from a simple and straightforward argumentative style that still has appeal today: powerful emotional and ethical appeals and a maternalistic posture that allowed her to handle the hostility of audiences toward a black woman speaker. She campaigned vigorously for the social causes of her day, living up to her self-appointed task of keeping "the thing stirring, now that the ice is cracked."

INFORMATION SOURCES

Research Collections and Collected Speeches

Black Women in Nineteenth-Century American Life: Their Words, Their Thoughts, Their Feelings. Edited by Bert James Loewenberg and Ruth Bogin. University Park: Pennsylvania State University Press, 1976.   BWAL

Black Women in White America: A Documentary History. Edited by Gerda Lerner. New York: Pantheon Books, 1972.   BWWA

Stanton, Elizabeth Cady, Susan B. Anthony, and Matilda Joslyn Gage.   *HWS*
        History of Woman Suffrage. 6 vols. 1882; rpt. New York: Arno and
        the New York Times, 1969.
Truth, Sojourner. *Narrative of Sojourner Truth*. 1878; rpt., New York: Arno   *NST*
        Press, 1968.
The Voice of Black America: Major Speeches by Negroes in the United   *VBA*
        States, 1797–1971. Edited by Phillip S. Foner. New York: Simon
        and Schuster, 1972.
Voices from Women's Liberation. Edited by Leslie Tanner. New York: New   *VWL*
        American Library, 1970.

Selected Critical Studies

Graves, Zena Orphelia. "Sojourner Truth: A Study in Personality and Culture." Master's
        thesis, Fisk University 1943.
Lebedun, Jean. "Harriet Beecher Stowe's Interest in Sojourner Truth, Black Feminist."
        American Literature 46 (1974): 359–63.
Montgomery, Janey Weinhold. *A Comparative Analysis of the Rhetoric of Two Negro
        Women Orators—Sojourner Truth and Frances E. Watkins Harper*. Hays: Kansas
        State College, 1968.
Wagner, Gerard A. "Sojourner Truth: God's Appointed Apostle of Reform." *Southern
        Speech Journal* 28 (1962): 123–26.

Selected Biographies

Bernard, Jacqueline. *Journey toward Freedom: The Story of Sojourner Truth*. New York:
        W. W. Norton, 1967.
Brawley, Benjamin. *A Social History of the American Negro*. New York: Macmillan,
        1921.
———. *Negro Builders and Heroes*. Chapel Hill: University of North Carolina Press,
        1937.
Brown, Hallie Q. *Homespun Heroines and Other Women of Distinction*. Freeport, N.Y.:
        Books for Libraries Press, 1971.
Chittenden, Elizabeth F. "Glorious Old Mother: Sojourner Truth." *Black Collegian*
        (May-June 1978): 14, 16, 82.
Faust, Arthur Huff. *Sojourner Truth: God's Faithful Pilgrim*. New York: Russell &
        Russell, 1971.
Pauli, Hertha. *Her Name Was Sojourner Truth*. New York: Avon, 1962.
Redding, Saunders. *The Lonesome Road: The Story of the Negro's Part in America*.
        Garden City: N.Y. Doubleday, 1958.
Shafer, Elizabeth. "Sojourner Truth." *American History Illustrated*, 8 (1974): 34–39.

CHRONOLOGY OF MAJOR SPEECHES

See "Research Collections and Collected Speeches" for source codes.

Address to the Women's Rights Convention, Akron, Ohio, May 29, 1851; *BWAL*,
pp. 235–36; *HWS*, 115–17; *NST*, pp. 133–35; *VBA*, pp. 100–01; *VWL*, pp. 60–62.

Address to the Fourth National Woman's Rights Convention, New York, September 7, 1853; *BWWA*, pp. 566–68; *HWS*, 2: 657–58.

Address to the First Annual Meeting of the American Equal Rights Association, New York, May 9, 1867; *BWAL*, pp. 238–39; *BWWA*, pp. 568–71; *VBA*, pp. 345–47.

Address at the commemoration of the eighth anniversary of Negro freedom in the United States, Boston, January 1, 1871; *BWAL*, pp. 240–42; *NST*, pp. 213–16.

MARK TWAIN
(1835–1910), novelist and humorist

_____ RICHARD J. CALHOUN

No other man of letters was more popular as a public speaker in his own time or has been regarded as more relevant in our times than one of America's greatest writers of fiction, Mark Twain. Yet he is rarely considered a major orator, expert rhetorician, or even an important public speaker worthy of serious consideration in the history of American oratory. Mark Twain was visibly a public phenomenon but less recognized as a craftsman in fiction or in oratory. He was late in receiving credit for his craft of fiction and has yet to receive just notice for his rhetorical skills.

The public personality, Mark Twain, was created in 1863 when Sam Clemens was becoming a celebrity as a humorous lecturer and journalist in the West. His creator, Samuel Langhorne Clemens, was born in Florida, Missouri, on November 30, 1835, and grew up from the age of four near the banks of the Mississippi River in Hannibal, Missouri, at a time of excitement from the activity of flatboats and steamboats but also a period of violence, with occasional river-front brawls and the injustice of the slave trade carried on in the town market.

His formal education ended in 1848 on the death of his father, and his education thereafter was limited to work as an apprentice journalist for his brother Orion at the exact moment when the tall tales of the Southwest were being published in the newspapers. From 1857 to 1861 he served as an apprentice and then pilot on the Mississippi River, an experience that convinced him later that he had met every character type. He escaped from his one minor brush with the Civil War by journeying with his brother Orion to Nevada, where he failed as a silver miner but succeeded as a journalist, first in Virginia City, then in San Francisco. Out West he encountered the new breed of professional humorists, represented by Artemus Ward, the ruler of the lecture platform, and Bret Harte, the master of the humorous tale. The notice brought by the publication of his "Celebrated Jumping Frog" story and his success as a lecturer on his experiences as a reporter in the Sandwich Islands inaugurated a career as lecturer begun as the acknowledged successor to Artemus Ward. When he published his newspaper reports on his voyage on the Quaker City to the Holy Land and an account of his travels to Nevada, he had two books, *Innocents Abroad* (1869) and *Roughing It* (1872), and he had begun a literary career. His marriage to Olivia Langdon and into eastern respectability located him permanently in the East, in New York and Connecticut, and encouraged efforts to quit the lyceum circuit. Neither Twain nor his audience could ever permit a complete break with public appearances, however. He discovered the subject that was to make him a major American writer on a trip back to Hannibal and to the Mississippi River to gather material for a series of articles on the old steamboating days on the river for the *Atlantic Monthly*. His literary masterpieces are *Tom Sawyer* (1876), *Life on the Mississippi* (1883), and *The Adventures of Huckleberry Finn* (1885), all utilizing a pastoral and yet often disturbing view of the subject matter of Hannibal.

MARK TWAIN, THE STAGE PERSONA

There can be little doubt as to the popularity of the public persona Mark Twain. His contemporaries flocked by the thousands to hear a consummate actor-storyteller performing on the lecture platform. What obscured the craft was that for Samuel Langhorne Clemens to write and to lecture, he needed a public persona, Mark Twain, a vernacular perspective and democratic counter to the genteel position on matters of social, political, or literary pretensions. He had learned out West the reverse of Quintilian's dictums on style. His intention was, above all, to be entertaining, and the best style for that was not the high but the vernacular. But there was more to it than that. He saved truly vernacular diction for his anecdotes. His appeal stemmed from the character of the speaker he established, if not exactly of high moral character, one capable of vernacular common sense and apparently unconsciously humorous perspectives that the factual accounts might miss, whether on the Sandwich Islands, the Holy Land, or, much later and more satirically, U.S. imperialism in the Philippines. By then he had seemingly lost the distinction between his two personalities, Samuel L. Clemens and Mark Twain.

From contemporary testimony, we know that what his audience experienced transcended the printed page of his talks. Without exception, those who heard him contended that without the presence of the platform persona, the effect of the written words could not be imagined. In our time, we have had an approximation of how suited persona was to text through the well-researched performances of Hal Holbrook in his "Mark Twain Tonight." Twain's authorized biographer, Albert Bigelow Paine, said of his platform and dinner speaker appearances: "Not to have heard Mark Twain is to have missed much of the value of the utterance. He had immeasurable magneticism and charm. . . . No one could resist him—probably nobody ever tried to do so."

The sheer number and the variety of his speeches should speak to Mark Twain's importance as a public speaker. The most recent collection has 195 speeches over a period of forty-five years (1864–1909). The humorous lecture was his bread and butter, but there were talks on travel, lectures on social and political foibles, speeches for causes, whether for the Chinese, Negroes, or women, even proposals, and his polemics, especially against imperialism. The last of these he usually saved for letters to newspapers or privately published pamphlets, although he effectively aired his feelings in introducing young Winston Churchill, fresh from the Boer War, December 12, 1900:

Yes, as a missionary I have sung this song of praise and still sing it; and yet I think that England sinned in getting into a war in South Africa which she could have avoided without loss of credit or dignity—just as I think we have sinned in crowding ourselves into a war in the Philippines on the same terms.

Mark Twain began and ended his career on stage. Before he began professionally in San Francisco, he had a taste of his abilities when he was called on to make an impromptu speech at a printer's banquet in Keokuk. He began embarrassed and stammering but ended in a minor triumph of impromptu wit and humor. In Nevada he made two or three memorable toasts and responses at public banquets, enough to win flattering accounts in the local newspapers. He spoke briefly before the territorial legislature in Carson City and commented: "I guess that is a pretty good result for an incipient oratorical slouch like me, isn't it?"

His professional debut began in San Francisco on October 2, 1865, with a lecture on the Sandwich Islands, which he had covered in letters to the *Alta Californian*. He needed money to publish his letters in book form, and he rented the largest hall in town at half-price. He was aware of his potential and knew that he had observed as a reporter the major lecturers to come to Nevada and California. As a journalist, he also knew the value of advertising and self-promotion. He called on all his newspaper friends for notices and allusions and set the tone for his appearance with handbills and a large advertisement. He told of what would transpire—"a lecture on the Sandwich Islands, with mention of the American Missionaries, etc. and the absurd Customs and Characteristics of the Natives"—and what would not be seen—"a Den of Ferocious Wild Beasts," "Magnificent Fire Works." He concluded with an imaginative flourish that, with variations, would be his trademark: "The trouble begins at 8 o'clock." San Francisco had never seen such preparation before. The house was filled, and the evening was a success.

An eyewitness account quoted by Fred Lorch confirmed that Mark Twain had studied the manner of Artemus Ward and other professional humorists carefully: the cultivated casualness of manner, the deadpan simulated unawareness that anything funny had been said, and the matter of timing required to drop a studied remark with the appearance of not knowing it. But there was something new: an art of making everything seem natural and of winning rapport with his audience. Here was an original:

His slow deliberate drawl, the anxious and perturbed expression of his visage, the apparently painful effort with which he framed his sentences, and above all, the surprise that spread over his face when the audience roared with delight or rapturously applauded the finer passages of his word-painting, were unlike anything of the kind they had ever known. All this was original; it was Mark Twain.

Mark Twain had perhaps instinctively, with his marvelous feel for an audience, practiced his own vernacular perspective version of the Ciceronian dictum that an orator should conciliate an audience. All was not yet perfect. He learned in a second appearance in San Francisco on October 2 that audiences expected humor but also instruction. He got his balance wrong on this occasion but did not repeat his error, although regretting that humor alone in a lecture was not enough. His second slight fumble was a harder one for him to correct, especially when he went East: how to be funny and critical from a vernacular perspective without having what he said judged as bad taste. He made only one further major miscalculation, much later, on the occasion of his Whittier birthday speech in Boston on December 17, 1877. No one took that harder than his friend William Dean Howells, who made Twain suffer agonies over a miscalculation that Bostonians could appreciate vernacular humor at the expense of their brahmins—Emerson, Longfellow, Holmes, Whittier. Twain toned down the vernacular diction in his lectures after this but eventually decided that the fault lay not in him but in his audience. He also depended on others whose ears were more sensitive to what might offend those who expected not the vernacular perspective but the genteel tradition—friends like Howells or his own family.

He toured the West with the Sandwich Islands lecture and carefully moved East, stopping first for trial runs back home at Hannibal and Keokuk, where he drew a larger crowd than Emerson had just a few months before. His first appearance in the East was as the successor to Artemus Ward at Cooper Union on May 6, 1867. The news was good: audiences in the East were as susceptible to the charm of Mark Twain as those in the West had been. His only problem was a need for new material, which his sailing on the Quaker City to the Holy Land and along the Mediterranean supplied, first for his newspaper reports to the *Alta Californian*, then for chapters for a book and for new lectures, first back on familiar ground in the mining towns of California and in San Francisco. Encouraged by the response to an "innocents abroad" New World approach to the storied wonders of Venice, he prepared a new lecture, "The American Vandal Abroad," a look at both the Old World wonders and New World tourists who flock to see them, for his 1868–1869 tour, which he began in Cleveland on November 17. He was able to report to his family, "I captured them, if I do say it myself." He also captured the notice of a man, James Redpath, who was opening a bureau that was to dominate the lyceum circuit for a number of years. The first issue of his new magazine, the *Lyceum*, published in August 1869, listed Mark Twain as "celebrated."

Mark Twain's marriage to Olivia Langdon on February 2, 1870, kept him off the circuit for one year, but he was back the following season. By 1872 the name Mark Twain was known from coast to coast, and he tried his luck in the land of the British author who had stirred his interest in the possibilities of narrative on the lecture platform, Charles Dickens. He proved to his satisfaction that the humorous American lecture could be as successful in Liverpool and in London as in New York City, San Francisco, or Cleveland. He decided not to tour regularly as a lecturer but to give, as Dickens had, readings from some of his best tales: "The Golden Arm," "Baker's Blue Jay Yarn," "The Notorious Jumping Frog of Calaveras County" and "Grandfather's Old Ram." His success at such places as Philadelphia, Boston, and the U.S. Military Academy during the next few years led to a tour in 1884–1885 sharing the platform with another reader, the new literary sensation from Louisiana, George Washington Cable. They began on November 5, 1884, in New Haven, Connecticut, and traveled into Michigan, Ohio, and Pennsylvania, and on through Illinois, Missouri, Iowa,

Minnesota, and Wisconsin, then north into Canada, back through New York and the eastern seaboard, to a final joint lecture in Washington, D.C., on the last day in February 1885. Twain was good, but so was Cable. The total impression on audiences of two such contrasting personalities but effective readers was powerful. Bothered by minor inconveniences during winter travel and the unexpected competition from Cable, and finding himself a literary name with the publication of *Huckleberry Finn*, Mark Twain decided not to tour again and did not until his world tour of 1895–1896. He remained a highly successful and much-sought-after introducer and after-dinner speaker.

If his tour with Cable was one of the most remarkable in lyceum performances of the 1880s, Mark Twain's tour around the world was a personal act of courage and one of the mammoth undertakings in American lecturing of this period: 110 lectures, 85 days aboard ship. He began in Cleveland on July 14, 1885, worked his way west through Michigan, Minnesota, Montana, Washington and Oregon to Vancouver, British Columbia, where he sailed for Australia. He then lectured in Australia, New Zealand, India, Ceylon, the island of Mauritius, and South Africa, concluding there one year and one day later and sailing for England on July 15, 1896. It was a celebrated act of personal courage because he did it to pay off his debts rather than to escape them through bankruptcy; he was sixty years of age and had not been in the best of health.

It was a smashing success. Everything that worked in the United States succeeded abroad. His foreign audiences were especially surprised by the distinctiveness of his diction and the clarity of his slow drawl. His act of entering the stage and then for moments just staring at his audience in silence drew applause. He was perceived as a very funny man but as much more than a humorist, a man sincerely aware of human suffering. It was the effect that Mark Twain now wanted to create. He established himself as truly an international figure. At every stop he was besieged as a celebrity by reporters who recorded his comments as significant international news.

Mark Twain was a pragmatist in what to use before an audience, a realist as an author of fiction, and a perfectionist, as all other good writers are, in finding the right word. By the time he turned to writing his autobiography, he knew that no one had learned the art of giving a humorous lecture better or could recount the history of the lyceum movement under Redpath in the 1860s and 1870s more tellingly. He could identify the house fillers and the house emptiers of this period and explain the difference. His knowledge was not from the textbook but from experience. Successful lyceum lecturing was a difficult rhetorical art and a matter of presenting one's self to an audience. A speech must be memorized but give the appearance of spontaneity and extemporaneousness. What works goes, but it must be rehearsed before it is tried out, and then tried "on the dog" in small towns before risking important places like the Music Hall in Boston. Nothing was more important than the introduction of the speaker. He quickly learned the disadvantages of the artificial formal introduction in vogue at the time and substituted a practiced deception for as long as he could get away with it, pretending to be merely the introducer, praising the speaker extravagantly, and then revealing himself as the subject of the praise: "I am the man! I was obliged to excuse the chairman from introducing me, because he never compliments anybody and I knew I could do just as well."

In his essay entitled "How to Tell a Story," Mark Twain made it clear that knowing how to tell a story was the secret to success in fiction. In humorous lecturing, how to use an anecdote was the secret. In his "Sandwich Island" lecture he told of the ability of the natives to will their own dying, concluding: "They are an odd sort of people, too. They can die wherever they want to. That is a fact. They don't mind dying any more than a jilted Frenchman does." Since so many of his early lectures featured travel, a highlight of his lectures was vivid description, for which his reviewers praised him. In this lecture he graphically described a volcano as a sublime but terrible beast on the loose, "tearing up forests in its awful fiery path, swallowing up huts, destroying all vegetation, rioting through shady dells and sinuous canyons." He could skillfully use a melodramatic touch, as in his offer to demonstrate cannibalism to his audience if he could get the aid of a volunteer. He had learned his lesson well that his audience wanted to leave with a sense of having learned something. The Sandwich Islands offered the escape of a pastoral setting "where things tend to repose and peace, and to emancipation from the labor, and turmoil and weariness and anxiety of life." His lecture "The American Vandal Abroad" was a double-edged satire of hyperbole on the wonders of the Old World and the vulgarity of the American tourists as the new Vandals, but even for these "a store of softly-tinted images will remain in their memories—and float through their reveries and dreams for many and many a year to come."

What speeches reveal Mark Twain at his best? A personal favorite was "The Babies," given on November 13, 1879, for the thirteenth reunion banquet for the Army of Tennessee with Generals Grant, Sherman, Sheridan, Pope and others present. Before those who had faced "the death storm at Donelson and Vicksburg," he made the unlikely contention that it "was high time for a toastmaster to recognize the importance of the babies" reminding his august company in military language how "when that little fellow arrived at family headquarters you had to hand in your resignation. He took entire command, You became his lackey—his mere body servant. . . . He treated you with every sort of insolence and disrespect, and the bravest of you didn't dare to say a word." He was pleased that "it fetched" the usual taciturn General Grant when he concluded with an image of "the future illustrious commander in chief of the American armies . . . trying to find some way to get his own big toe into his mouth—an achievement which, meaning no disrespect, the illustrious guest of this evening turned his whole attention to some fifty-six years ago."

The actor Hal Holbrook has dramatized the relevance of Mark Twain to Vietnam by quoting from his polemic pieces against imperialism in the Far East, most of which, such as "To the Person Sitting in Darkness" and "The Czar's Soliloquy," were not given but published in the *North American Review*. Another fine actor, Dan O'Herlihy, in a television dramatization a decade ago read powerfully from Mark Twain's speech for the Lord Mayor's Dinner in Liverpool, given in 1907 following the award of his honorary degree at Oxford. Twain was proud and yet humble about his award and reminded of an incident in Charles Dana's *Two Years before the Mast* telling of the comeuppance received by a "frivolous little self-important captain of a coasting sloop" on hailing every vessel that came into the harbor:

One day a majestic Indiaman came plowing by, with course on course of canvas towering in the sky, her decks and yards swarming with sailors; with macaws and monkeys and all manner of strange and romantic creatures populating her rigging; and thereto her freightage of precious spices lading the breeze with gracious and mysterious odors of the Orient. Of course, the little coaster captain hopped into the shrouds and squealed out a hail: "Ship Ahoy!" What ship is that, and whence and whither? In a deep and thunderous bass came the answer back through a speaking trumpet: "The Begum of Bengal, a hundred and twenty-three days out from Canton—Homeward Bound! What ship is that." The little Captain's vanity was all crushed out of him, and most humbly he squeaked back: "Only the Mary Ann—Fourteen hours out from Boston, Bound for Kittery Pint with—nothing to speak of!" The eloquent word "only" expressed the deeps of his stricken humbleness.

He turned the audience's attention back to his own feeling of being proud and humble:

And what is my own case? During perhaps one hour in the twenty-four—not more than that—I stop and reflect. Then I am humble, then I am properly meek, and for that little time I am "only the Mary Ann," fourteen hours out, and cargoed vegetables and tinware.

Mark Twain always spoke of lecturing as his alternate career. It was more accurately parallel to his books and his journalism. He once remarked that his ability to talk was superior to his ability to put thoughts down on paper. Recent criticism reveals that it was his ability to simulate talk that permitted his greatest successes in what he put down on paper. What Mark Twain said became important to the entire country and to a large part of the world. Howells referred to him as the "Lincoln of our literature." Hal Holbrook is quoted by Louis Budd as having said that Mark Twain is what our national character is "ideally supposed to be but rarely is—independent, skeptical, rational, humorous, plagued by demons but coping." This is Mark Twain.

INFORMATION SOURCES

Research Collections and Collected Speeches

Not surprisingly Mark Twain has been a favorite of American collectors, and there are several important collections. The most outstanding is at the University of California at Berkeley, and it is from that collection that most of the posthumously published items have come. There are other valuable collections of Twainiana in the Berg collection, New York Public Library; the Huntington Library, San Marino, California; Princeton University Library, Princeton, New Jersey; and the University of Virginia, Charlottesville.

Mark Twain Speaking. Edited by Paul Fautout. Iowa City: University of   MTS
    Iowa Press, 1976.
Mark Twain's Speeches. Edited by Albert Bigelow Paine. New York: Harper   MTSS
    and Brothers, 1923.

Selected Critical Studies

Budd, Louis J. *Our Mark Twain: The Making of His Public Personality*. Philadelphia: University of Pennsylvania Press, 1984.
Fautout, Paul. *Mark Twain on the Lecture Tour*. Bloomington: University of Indiana Press, 1969.
Lorch, Fred W. *The Trouble Begins at Eight*. Ames: Iowa State University Press, 1966.

Selected Biographies

Emerson, Everett. *The Authentic Mark Twain: A Literary Biography of Samuel L. Clemens*. Philadelphia: University of Pennsylvania Press, 1984.
Kaplan, Justin. *Mr. Clemens and Mark Twain: A Biography*. New York: Simon & Schuster, 1966.

CHRONOLOGY OF MAJOR SPEECHES

See "Research Collections and Collected Speeches" for source codes.

"Sandwich Islands," Maguire's Opera House, San Francisco, October 2, 1865; *MTS*, pp. 4–15.

"The American Vandal Abroad," lyceum season, November 17, 1868, March 3, 1869; *MTS*, pp. 27–36.

"The Babies, As They Comfort Us in Our Sorrows, Let Us Not Forget Them in Our Festivities," thirteenth reunion banquet, Army of the Tennessee, Chicago, November 13, 1879; *MTS*, pp. 131–3.

"Introducing Winston S. Churchill," New York, December 12, 1900; *MTS*, pp. 367–69.

"Our Guest," Lord Mayor's Banquet for Mark Twain, Liverpool, July 10, 1907; *MTS*, pp. 577–84.

BOOKER T. WASHINGTON
(1856–1915), black educator and leader

————————————————————————— JAMES S. OLSON

To a generation of American history students in the 1960s and 1970s, Booker T. Washington was a foil for liberal critics bent on using the past to correct, in their own minds, the legacy of slavery and racism. For them, Booker T. Washington was the quintessential "Uncle Tom," a black leader committed to permanent second-class status for his people. They usually compared him with W. E. B. Du Bois, a founding father of the NAACP and lifelong advocate of black civil rights. Countless college students wrote papers extolling Du Bois as a freedom fighter and blasting Washington as a reactionary. That is ironical. Born a slave in the antebellum South and liberated by the Civil War, Washington became the president of Tuskegee Institute, dined at the White House with President Theodore Roosevelt, and eventually became the most prominent black leader in the country. But because of his famous "Atlanta Compromise" speech of 1895, many of his contemporaries, as well as modern civil rights activists, came to view him as an obstacle to black equality.

Washington's life began on April 5, 1856, on the James Burroughs plantation near present-day Roanoke, Virginia. His mother was a cook on the plantation, and his father, whom Washington never knew, was a white man from a neighboring plantation. His mother called him Booker, but he did not take a surname until years later when, in school, a teacher asked him his last name, and he quickly answered Washington, after the first president of the United States. His mother gave him the middle name of Taliaferro, after a prominent white family in Rocky Mount, Virginia.

After the Civil War, his mother moved the family to Malden, West Virginia. Just nine years old, Booker went to work in the local salt mines. He was enterprising and desperate for a way out, and in 1871 he became a houseboy to the owner of the mines, Lewis Ruffin. Ruffin's wife helped Washington and convinced him in 1872 to enter the Hampton Institute, a new school for blacks, in Virginia. Founded by General Samuel C. Armstrong, Hampton emphasized technical and vocational education, as well as etiquette and good manners for its black students. Washington worked as a janitor to pay his room, board, and tuition, formed an abiding friendship with Armstrong, and graduated in 1875.

At Hampton, Washington excelled on the debating team and spent long hours studying speech with his favorite teacher, Nathalie Lord. She taught him diction, breathing, delivery, emphasis, timing, and articulation, and Washington never missed a session of the weekly Saturday evening meetings of the debating societies. He also helped organize after-supper Clubs, where current events could be discussed and debated.

After graduating from Hampton, Washington taught school in Malden for three years and then attended the Wayland Seminary, a Baptist school, in Washington, D.C. At Wayland, Washington became even more committed to the value of practical, vocational education and the questionable value of purely academic studies. In 1879 Washington returned to the Hampton Institute as a teacher. That lasted for just two years when Washington moved to Tuskegee, Alabama, where the state legislature had appropriated money for a normal school to train black teachers. Twice widowed, Washington soon married Margaret Murray, a principal at Tuskegee, and together they built Tuskegee into a respectable school for young black men and women.

WASHINGTON AS A NATIONAL LEADER

Washington came to prominence during the birth of the New South. After 1877, when the last of the northern troops left the occupied South, political power returned to the planter elite that had dominated the region before the Civil War. But even while that restoration of power was occurring, a new generation of businessmen, urban professionals, and journalists—located primarily in such major cities as Atlanta, New Orleans, Richmond, and Mobile—were calling on the South to abandon the shackles of the past. They were convinced that before the Civil War, the South had locked itself into an elitist, preindustrial caste structure that left it out of the main currents of modernization. The legacy of ruralism, racism, and reactionism had to be laid to rest. The southern economy had to be diversified, racial relations enlightened, and politics opened. This New South would rise from the rubble of slavery, plantation commerce, and total war. As part of that campaign, the *Atlanta Constitution* helped sponsor the Cotton States and International Exposition in Atlanta on September 15, 1895. It was a regional fair where the virtues of industrialization, racial harmony, democracy, and controlled change could be promoted. Since Booker T. Washington was the president of the Tuskegee Institute, he was the most prominent black leader in the South and the most likely candidate to address the question of race relations in the New South.

By that time, his reputation as an orator was firmly established. His debating experience at Hampton had given him firm grounding in the principles of speech and argument, and the faculty selected him to speak at the 1875 commencement. After coming to Tuskegee, Washington spoke widely throughout the North to white audiences trying to drum up financial support from philanthropic groups. His addresses were always impressive, not simply because of his speaking style, which was animated and fluid, but because he had a clear philosophical theme behind his remarks and because he was always acutely aware of his audience. In 1884, the National Education Association invited Washington to address its annual convention in Madison, Wisconsin. Delivered on July 16, 1884, that speech became a trademark of his educational and racial philosophy:

Any movement for the elevation of the Southern Negro, in order to be successful, must have to a certain extent the cooperation of the southern whites. They control government and own the property—whatever benefits the black man benefits the white man. The proper education of all the whites will benefit the Negro as much as the education of the Negro will benefit the whites. . . .

Brains, property, and character for the Negro will settle the question of civil rights. . . . Good teachers and plenty of money to pay them will be more potent in settling the race question than many civil rights bills and investigating committees. . . . Let there be in the community a Negro who by virtue of his superior knowledge of the chemistry of the soils, his acquaintance with the most improved tools and best breeds of stock, can raise fifty bushels of corn to the acre while his white neighbor only raises thirty, and the white man will come to the black man to learn. Further, they will sit down in the same train, in the same coach and on the same seat to talk about it.

Booker T. Washington walked a precarious tightrope in the South by trying to upgrade the status of black people even while the jim crow system was falling into place all around him. Separate but equal schools, residential covenants, white primaries, poll taxes, literacy tests, grandfather clauses, and a host of other legal restrictions were tightening the social noose around black people, just as Washington was trying to bring them into the twentieth century. But to do it he needed money, and the address to the National Education Association was only one of hundreds he gave in the 1880s, 1890s, and early 1900s. Back in the 1860s and 1870s, the Freedmen's Bureau had built schools for blacks throughout the South, but when Reconstruction ended, federal troops withdrew from the South, and white Democrats returned to power. Without federal funding, Washington had to look elsewhere for the money to finance Tuskegee in particular and black colleges in general. The money could not come from black people; they lacked the resources. It would have to come from white philanthropists. Washington knew that he could not afford to alienate sympathetic whites with the rhetoric of social and political activism. He had to rely on the resources of enlightened northern and southern whites willing to accept the notion of educated blacks. He could expect no assistance from bitter southern racists, but he did expect the exponents of the New South to be prepared to assist young black students. So instead of civil rights and politics, Washington concentrated on economics and education.

But the speech before the National Education Association was only a preliminary. It was the address before the Cotton States and International Exposition on September 18, 1895, that rocketed him to national attention. In that address Washington eloquently appealed to southern whites to understand the needs of his people, to put aside their fears and work with them in building the New South:

One-third of the population of the South is of the Negro race. . . . Our greatest danger is that, in the great gap between slavery and freedom, we may overlook the fact that the masses of us are to live by the production of our hands, and fail to keep in mind that we shall prosper in proportion as we learn to dignify and glorify common labor and put brains and skill into the common occupations of life. . . . It is at the bottom of life we must begin and not at the top. Nor should we permit our grievances to overshadow our opportunities.

To those of the white race . . . we shall stand by you with a devotion no foreigner can approach, ready to lay down our lives, if need be, in defense of yours; interlacing our industrial, commercial, civil, and religious life with yours in a way that shall make the interests of both races one. In all things that are purely social we can be as separate as the fingers, yet one as the hand in all things essential to mutual progress.

The wisest among my race understand that agitation of questions of social equality is the extremest folly, and that progress in the enjoyment of all the privileges that will come to us must be the result of severe and constant struggle. No race that has anything to contribute to the markets of the world is long in any degree ostracized. . . . The opportunity to earn a dollar in a factory just now is worth infinitely more than the opportunity to spend a dollar in an opera house.

The Atlanta compromise reverberated throughout the United States, especially in the South. It provided something for everyone. To bigoted southern whites, Washington offered the reassurance that social separation would continue and that it was not necessarily a bad situation, at least in the short run. To white southern liberals, Washington promised a black people committed to hard work, progress, and economic advancement. To black people, Washington promised opportunity, achievement, and an improvement in their standard of living. In the long run, he offered them equality by virtue of his conviction that civil rights would inevitably come in the wake of economic achievement.

After the speech, Washington found himself the toast of white people but the object of severe criticism from black intellectuals. His most severe critic was W. E. B. Du Bois, who said Washington should not spend his time demeaning blacks with second-class status. Du Bois instead insisted on a different course of action for black people. Du Bois would become a popular figure to civil rights activists in the 1960s and 1970s because he spent a lifetime demanding equality for black people. But his background was dramatically different from that of Booker T. Washington, as was his constituency. Born to a middle-class black family in Massachusetts, Du Bois received a Ph.D. from Harvard University and taught at Atlanta University. His constituency was, in his own words, the "talented tenth" of the black community—lawyers, teachers, physicians, nurses, dentists, and businessmen who enjoyed a measure of economic security and yearned for civil equality. Du Bois urged black youth to secure good professional educations and black adults to demand the right to vote, hold public office, and attend theaters, restaurants, and public transportation on an equal footing with whites. That he was making these demands before World War I, and seemed so ahead of his time, endeared Du Bois to a later generation of civil rights activists anxious to identify historical role models.

Booker T. Washington was addressing a different black constituency. While Du Bois was dealing with relatively small numbers of middle-class blacks living in the North, Washington was preoccupied with the plight of millions of southern blacks only recently liberated from bondage. Poorly educated, living on the edge of economic existence, vulnerable to white racism, and without political power, southern blacks were in a trap unknown to middle-class northern blacks. Washington was worried about his people—the sharecroppers, tenant farmers, migrant laborers, maids, laundresses, and stevedores of the South. For Washington to have carried the Du Bois message to southern blacks would have been disastrous, triggering a white backlash and more repression. In Washington's mind, social equality was a luxury that would have to be postponed until economic security had been realized. Instead of demanding civil rights, southern blacks would have to invest their energies in acquiring job skills. From technical expertise would automatically flow social acceptance. It was a message Washington delivered a thousand times from lecterns across the United States.

Washington's social conservatism was more political than ideological. It was a necessary accommodation to existing circumstances in the South rather than any conviction about the permanent status of black people. Privately Washington hoped for nothing less than the complete redemption of his people—political, economic, and social equality. But Washington also knew that transformation of the southern social structure was an evolutionary, not revolutionary, process. He was quite sympathetic with Du Bois's goals for northern blacks, to the point of contributing money privately, but he also knew that southern blacks were not prepared for civil liberation because of their own economic desperation and the flagrantly racist attitudes of most southern whites. Later generations of black and white activists who accused Washington of reactionary Uncle Tomism did not understand him, his personal convictions, or his political wisdom.

Some of the critics who turned their wrath on Booker T. Washington, however, had strong arguments against his efforts at Tuskegee Institute. Tuskegee was not an institution of higher learning, at least not in the sense of other colleges in the midst of late nineteenth-century educational reform. While the classics were giving way to empirical sciences, Tuskegee was emphasizing vocational and technical training. That was how Washington wanted it. In one of the last speeches of his life, which he delivered to the National Negro Business League in Boston on August 19, 1915, Washington said:

Why, don't you know the Greeks have come over here to this country and have taken the shoe-shining trade from the colored man? Just think of it—the black boy studying Greek and the Greek boy is blacking shoes . . . there is no hope for us as a race except we learn to apply our education in a practical manner to the resources of our country and to the common activity of the life of the community in which we live. . . . An ounce of application is worth a ton of abstraction.

Washington trained sharecroppers to become independent farmers just as the modernization of agriculture was making small farms obsolete. While Tuskegee trained young black men in craftsmen skills and home manufacturing, mass production rendered those skills inefficient and marginal. Blacks who chose to remain in the South, despite a Tuskegee education, were not necessarily prepared for economic success and independence, but they did not languish in the slave quarters, unable to read or write or improve their lot in life. The graduates of Tuskegee Institute were literate and confident about their prospects, even if Booker T. Washington's educational philosophy had its limitations.

In the years after the "Atlanta Compromise" speech, Washington became a national figure and one of the most popular speakers in the country. Invitations for speeches were so frequent that he had the luxury of choosing the most important ones. He tailored his remarks to his audience. When speaking before a group of southern whites, Washington always was gracious and courteous, always supportive of southern values, always insisting that blacks had much to learn and a long way to go before they could ever think of equality. Before groups of northern blacks, Washington praised them for their success and urged them on to more accomplishment and achievement. Among southern whites, Washington always demanded hard work, literacy, and social skills. He spoke with animation and force, his gesticular language in perfect coordination with his words. Observers often commented on his ability to achieve a sense of intimacy with every audience, regardless of its size.

But while traveling across the country, Washington remained completely dedicated to building Tuskegee. In 1900, he wrote his autobiography, *Up from Slavery*, and it became a runaway best-seller. Philanthropists such as George Peabody, John Slater, Andrew Carnegie, and John D. Rockefeller read the book and became generous supporters of Tuskegee. Although Washington continued to encounter criticism from some northern black intellectuals, he had a canny instinct for public relations. In December 1898 he invited President William McKinley to visit Tuskegee, and his campaign to launch an endowment fund for Tuskegee at Madison Square Garden that year read like a who's who of New York society. In 1901 President Theodore Roosevelt invited Washington to dine at the White House, where they discussed patronage appointments and politics in the South. Conservative Democrats in the region thought both Roosevelt and Washington had stepped beyond the boundaries of propriety, but Washington's reputation survived the controversy.

Booker T. Washington died on November 13, 1915, more than twenty years after the "Atlanta Compromise" speech. During those two decades, he continued his drive for black technical education, economic progress, and social conservatism. He occasionally spoke out against lynchings and voting discrimination, but Washington was true to the political philosophy he had accepted early in his life. Progress for southern blacks would come on the economic ladder, not on any stairway of political and social agitation. If history did not understand him, it was only because of the seduction of activism in the 1960s and 1970s. Booker T. Washington was as great a black leader as the United States has ever produced.

INFORMATION SOURCES

Research Collections and Collected Speeches

Scholars interested in the life of Booker T. Washington must rely on the extensive collection of his personal papers at the Library of Congress. The most extensive collection of the writings and speeches of Booker T. Washington have been edited by Louis R.

Harlan and published by the University of Illinois Press. Finally, the library and archives of the Tuskegee Institute, Tuskegee, Alabama, contain a wealth of primary source material dealing with the life of Booker T. Washington.

The Booker T. Washington Papers. Vols. 1–2. Edited by Louis R. Harlan.   BTWP
    Urbana: University of Illinois Press, 1972.
The Booker T. Washington Papers. Vols. 3–11: 1889–1912. Edited by Louis
        R. Harlan. Urbana: University of Illinois Press, 1974–1981.
Booker T. Washington. Edited by E. L. Thornbrough. Englewood Cliffs,   BTW
    N.J.: Prentice-Hall, 1969.
Selected Speeches of Booker T. Washington. Edited by Edward Davidson.   SSBTW
    Garden City, N.Y.: Doubleday, 1932.

Selected Critical Studies

Heath, Robert L. "A Time for Silence: Booker T. Washington." *Quarterly Journal of Speech* 64 (October 1978): 385–99.
King, Andrew A. "Booker T. Washington and the Myth of Heroic Materialism." *Quarterly Journal of Speech* 60 (October 1974): 323–27.
Wallace, Karl R. "Booker T. Washington." In *A History and Criticism of American Public Address.* Edited by William Norwood Brigance. New York: McGraw-Hill, 1943.

Selected Biographies

Harlan, Louis R. *Booker T. Washington: The Making of a Black Leader, 1856–1901.* New York: Oxford University Press, 1972.
————. *Booker T. Washington: The Wizard of Tuskegee.* New York: Oxford University Press, 1983.
Spencer, Samuel R., Jr. *Booker T. Washington and the Negro's Place in American Life.* Boston: Little, Brown, 1955.

CHRONOLOGY OF MAJOR SPEECHES

See "Research Collections and Collected Speeches" for source codes.

Speech before the Alabama State Teachers' Association, Selma, Alabama, April 4, 1882; *BTWP*, 1: 191–95.

Speech before the National Education Association, Madison, Wisconsin, July 16, 1884; *BTWP*, 1: 255–62.

Speech before the Unitarian National Conference, Saratoga Springs, New York, September 21, 1886; *BTWP*, 1: 308–13.

Speech before the Cotton States Exposition, Atlanta, Georgia, September 18, 1895; *BTW*, pp. 33–36.

Speech before the Southern Industrial Convention, Huntsville, Alabama, October 13, 1899; *BTW*, pp. 46–47.

Speech before the National Negro Business League, Boston, August 19, 1915, *SSBTW*, pp. 262–64, 167.

GEORGE WASHINGTON
(1732–1799), first president of the United States

George Washington was not an orator in the classic mold. Primarily a man of action rather than a man of words, he had a meager formal education, possessed neither a quick nor inventive mind, and was usually reserved even in private conversation. A member of the Virginia House of Burgesses for sixteen years, a delegate to both the First and Second Continental Congress, and president of the Constitutional Convention, he did not stand out in any of these deliberative bodies as a debater or as a maker of policy. He contributed little to the political thought of the American Revolution or to the intellectual disputes over ratification of the Constitution. Always diffident about his abilities as a speaker, he lacked the verbal pyrotechnics that made Fisher Ames a brilliant stylist, the appetite for controversy that made Alexander Hamilton a masterful polemicist, the Ciceronian delivery that made Patrick Henry an irresistible exhorter.

Yet Washington was more a man of words than is generally recognized. From the time of his entrance into the public arena at the age of twenty to his death forty-seven years later, he produced a steady stream of letters, reports, memoranda, addresses, messages, and speeches designed to express his views and to persuade other people to them. Like most other eighteenth-century gentlemen, he was acutely aware of his public persona, and he took care to write and speak so as to create a favorable view of his motives, character, and achievements. Although most of his speeches were ceremonial in nature, he faced a number of critical rhetorical situations as commander in chief of the American army during the Revolution and as first president of the United States. His speeches in response to those situations marked pivotal moments in the history of the new nation, contributed to his image as the embodiment of republican virtue, and created precedents for presidential discourse that endure to this day.

WASHINGTON AS A MILITARY AND PRESIDENTIAL SPEAKER

Like most other successful commanders, Washington required considerable rhetorical sensitivity in addition to a knowledge of military strategy and tactics. Throughout the Revolutionary War, he faced the problems of persuading Congress and the states to provide adequate men and materiel, of recruiting new enlistments and convincing soldiers already in the army to reenlist, of communicating orders clearly and precisely, of maintaining discipline and morale, of keeping civilian authorities informed about military operations, of sustaining a positive attitude toward the war and the army among the general population, and, after the entry of France in 1778, of carrying out a delicate correspondence with America's first foreign ally. He even proposed at one stage that the Continental Congress provide him a portable press and a printer so he could keep up with "the multiplicity of writing and other business" that occupied so much of his time.

Although Washington's burdensome wartime correspondence was not matched by equally extensive oratorical responsibilities, his first act as commander in chief was to present a speech to the Continental Congress accepting his appointment. Taking only about two minutes to deliver, it proved to be of more lasting importance than any of the delegates in the Pennsylvania State House on June 16, 1775, could have imagined. Expressing his personal sentiments at the same time that he adhered to the stylistic and thematic commonplaces of office-taking as practiced in the eighteenth century, Washington thanked Congress for the "high honor" of his appointment, pledged to exert "every power" for the cause of liberty, and declared that he did not think himself equal to the "momentous duty" awaiting him. Then came the master stroke. "As to pay," he said, "no pecuniary consideration" could tempt him to accept "this arduous employment." He desired only that Congress meet his expenses, of which he would keep "an exact account." As it turned out, Washington's expenses during the war ran to just about what he would have received had he drawn his salary of $500 a month. But the symbolic value of his speech—and particularly of his declaration not to profit monetarily from his command—was incalculable. In addition to demonstrating the rectitude of his intentions in leading what George III had branded a treasonous war against the mother country, it forged the first link in his reputation as a disinterested patriot who placed the good of his country above personal reward.

Almost immediately upon being appointed commander in chief, Washington became the living symbol of the Revolution. As he rode from Philadelphia to Boston to take charge of the army, he was greeted and feted by local dignitaries in town after town along his entire route. Could he have peered into the future, he would have seen that such ceremonies were to become part of his travels for the rest of his life. Often the festivities included addresses of tribute from civic or religious organizations. Whenever possible, advance copies of these addresses were given to one of Washington's aides or secretaries, so Washington could present a brief, formal speech in response. Over the years he delivered scores of such speeches, but none would be more noteworthy than that which he presented to the New York legislature on June 26, 1775, as he made his way north to the troops in Boston. The legislature had concluded its address to Washington by stating its "fullest assurance that whenever this important contest shall be decided, . . . you will cheerfully resign the important deposit committed into your hands and resume the character of our worthiest citizen." Washington's response, as was customary in such speeches, echoed the sentiments of the legislature. "When we assumed the soldier," he said, "we did not lay aside the citizen; and we shall most sincerely rejoice with you in that happy hour when the establishment of American liberty, upon the most firm and solid foundations, shall enable us to return to our private stations in the bosom of a free, peaceful, and happy country." Here, prompted by the New York legislature, was the first expression of Washington's promise to resign his commission when the military conflict was over. No other words of his were quoted more frequently during the war, and he underlined their significance by repeating the same pledge on other occasions.

Washington's most famous wartime speech was his address to the potentially mutinous officers at Newburgh, New York. Unpaid, restless, and angry over Congress's repeated failure to fulfill its obligations to the men who had risked everything for American independence, many of Washington's officers were sympathetic to claims that the army should take matters into its own hands. They were encouraged by schemers within Congress and by March 1783 had come, in Washington's view, to "a tremendous precipice." Knowing full well the justice of the officers' complaints but committed to the supremacy of civil authority, he scorned all overtures that he lead the army against Congress. On March 15, he addressed the discontented officers in the new meeting hall of the army's winter camp at Newburgh. Appealing to their sense of duty and honor, he urged them to avoid any measures that would "tarnish the reputation of an army which is celebrated through all Europe for its fortitude and patriotism." Rather than open "the flood gates of civil discord, and deluge our rising empire in blood," the officers should follow "the calm light of reason" and trust Congress to do all it could to render the officers "complete justice" for their "faithful and meritorious services."

Then came one of the great pieces of theater in American oratory. Having completed his prepared text—which probably took about seventeen minutes to deliver—Washington started to read to the officers a letter he had received from a member of Congress. Unable to decipher the small handwriting, he reached into his pocket for the pair of spectacles he had recently acquired. "Gentlemen, you must pardon me," he said. "I have grown gray in your service and now find myself growing blind." Only his closest associates knew Washington had come to need glasses. His statement brought tears to the eyes of many in the hall and reunited them behind the man who had led them for so long. After reading the congressman's letter, he left the meeting—implying thereby that the issue was settled—and rode back to headquarters. The officers voted a motion of thanks to Washington, and whatever threat of mutiny existed before the meeting disappeared in the wake of his speech. It seemed, Jefferson wrote, as if Washington had singlehandedly "prevented this revolution from being closed, as most others have been, by a subversion of that liberty it was intended to establish."

Washington's Newburgh speech was the stuff of which legends are made. Yet few of his deeds earned greater applause than his appearance before the Continental Congress on December 23, 1783, in Annapolis, Maryland, to resign his commission. To a people steeped in the history of ancient republics whose freedom had been usurped by military leaders, Washington's fulfillment of the pledge he had made eight years earlier confirmed his stature as a modern Cincinnatus. Romanticized in John Trumbull's painting *The Resignation of General*

Washington, the scene in the Maryland State House was one of high drama, and Washington played it like a master. With appropriate humility, he attributed America's victory to the valor of his soldiers, the interposition of providence, and the support of his countrymen. Because of their efforts, he could now "resign with satisfaction" the trust he had "accepted with diffidence." His hands shaking with emotion, he paused twice in his brief speech to recover his voice. "Having now finished the work assigned me," he concluded, "I retire from the great theatre of action; and bidding an affectionate farewell to this august body under whose orders I have so long acted, I here offer my commission and take my leave of all the enjoyments of public life." Then, displaying the same kind of dramatic gesture he had employed when drawing out his spectacles at Newburgh, he reached into the breast of his uniform coat, withdrew his commission, and, stepping forward, handed it to Thomas Mifflin, president of Congress. The simple eloquence of his speech, punctuated by the physical surrender of his commission, drew tears from members of Congress, as well as from many of the spectators who filled the galleries and crowded along the walls.

If Washington's resignation secured his fame on both sides of the Atlantic, it created a potential problem as well. Having characterized his Annapolis speech as the "last solemn act of my official career," he would have to protect himself against charges of duplicity should circumstances ever compel him to reenter public life. It should not be surprising, then, that he came out of retirement to become America's first president with great reluctance and only after friends convinced him that the Constitution could not succeed without him at the helm. Nor should it be surprising that he began his Inaugural Address—his first official public speech since his resignation—by justifying his decision to assume political office as a matter of duty to his country. As in his 1775 speech accepting the position of commander in chief, he stressed "the difficulty of the trust" to which he had been called, talked of his "incapacity" for the "weighty and untried cares" before him, and declined to receive any remuneration other than his expenses. Staying with familiar themes, Washington tendered his homage to the "Almighty Being who rules over the Universe" and disparaged any "party animosities" that might disturb the operation of the new government. Knowing that many Americans remained suspicious that the Constitution endangered the liberty of ordinary citizens, he offered a carefully worded endorsement of amending it to settle "the degree of inquietude" caused by the lack of a bill of rights.

Designed to get the new government off to a smooth start, Washington's First Inaugural succeeded so brilliantly that today we forget how unsettled the situation was when he took office on April 30, 1789. Two states—Rhode Island and North Carolina—had yet to ratify the Constitution. Many antifederalists in the other eleven states were far from reconciled to it, and some still hoped to call a second constitutional convention to rectify the handiwork of the first. While there is no doubt that Washington's presence at the head of the government was the most important factor reconciling the doubtful to it, his First Inaugural Address is a neglected masterpiece that deserves to be ranked with the First Inaugurals of

Jefferson, Lincoln, and Franklin Roosevelt for its impact on the course of American history.

While Washington's First Inaugural established a prototype followed by all subsequent presidents, his Second Inaugural did not. In that speech of 135 words, by far the briefest of presidential inaugurals, Washington perfunctorily acknowledged his reelection and signified his commitment to the oath of office he was about to take. Although the unusual nature of his Second Inaugural has puzzled many scholars, it is explained when we understand that he wanted a simple ceremony without the great pomp and extravagance of his first inauguration. In Washington's view, the political situation of March 1793 did not require more than a few brief comments before being sworn into office for a second term, while that of April 1789 had demanded a major speech to help develop confidence in the new government. The prototype for second inaugurals was not established until Thomas Jefferson's speech of March 4, 1805.

Typically circumspect in his public statements and exceedingly respectful of the prerogatives of Congress, Washington did not campaign for legislation as do modern presidents. His only major presidential speeches, apart from his inaugural addresses, were his eight annual messages to Congress. Modeled on the British monarch's speech from the throne at the beginning of each new session of Parliament and on its American analogue, the governor's speech to the colonial assembly, Washington's messages derived also from the constitutional provision that the president "shall from time to time give to the Congress information of the state of the Union, and recommend to their consideration such measures as he shall judge necessary and expedient." Although presidents from Jefferson through Taft would send their messages to Congress in writing, Washington delivered his in person.

The most controversial was that of November 19, 1794, in which Washington attacked the Democratic Societies for their role in fomenting the insurrection in western Pennsylvania against the excise tax on whiskey. By doing so, he appeared to align himself with the Federalists in their party battles with the Democratic-Republicans. James Madison thought it was perhaps Washington's greatest political error. The most adroit of Washington's messages was that of December 8, 1795. Delivered during the prolonged agitation over the Jay Treaty and at a time when Washington was under fierce attack in the Democratic-Republican newspapers, it rose above the strife by focusing attention on America's abundant blessings. In contrast to his sharply worded message of the previous year, Washington avoided all mention of internal discord and portrayed the country as exhibiting "a spectacle of national happiness never surpassed if ever before equalled." By acting as if there were no cause for contention, he helped restore a measure of public harmony at a critical point in the life of the young Republic.

Although often treated as a speech, Washington's greatest public paper, his Farewell Address, was never delivered orally. Released to the public through *Claypoole's American Daily Advertiser* of September 19, 1796, it was quickly reprinted by other American newspapers, appeared in several European journals, and elicited almost universal praise as "the richest legacy of a father to his children." Washington's basic purpose was to announce that he would not stand for reelection as president. But he also meant the Farewell Address to be his political testament—a valedictory enunciating the principles that should guide Americans in their political relations with each other and with the rest of the world. Washington had issued a similar document in June 1783. The last of his circular letters to the governors of the thirteen states during the Revolution, it was known at the time as Washington's legacy and was widely celebrated throughout America. Being of the same genre and responding to similar rhetorical situations, the legacy and the Farewell Address evinced similar patterns. Both began by announcing Washington's retirement—the former from the army, the latter from the presidency—and by characterizing the advice to follow as the unbiased counsel of a parting friend. The bulk of both texts explained the great "pillars" of American liberty and how to save them from ruin. In the Farewell Address, Washington sounded two major themes. The first, which had also received attention in his legacy, admonished against "the spirit of party" that threatened to destroy America's fragile union by sacrificing the good of the whole to local prejudices and policies. The second, which had not appeared in 1783, urged America to "steer clear of permanent alliances with any portion of the foreign world." Although Washington would be widely misquoted in later years as cautioning against "entangling alliances" (a phrase from Jefferson's First Inaugural), his advice soon became a maxim of American foreign policy and was cited as a persuasive justification for isolationism well into the twentieth century.

The reverence accorded Washington's Farewell Address as a personal legacy to his countrymen helps explain the furor that arose in the nineteenth century when the public learned Alexander Hamilton had been its principal author. In fact, almost all of Washington's speeches, during both the Revolution and his presidency, were composed with the assistance of ghostwriters. Burdened with a staggering load of official duties and insecure about his use of language in public documents, he relied heavily on Hamilton, Joseph Reed, Robert H. Harrison, David Humphreys, Timothy Pickering, Jonathan Trumbull, Jr., William Jackson, Edmund Randolph, James Madison, and others. But while Washington's aides and associates were responsible for much of his prose, he so thoroughly superintended the composition of his major speeches that they unquestionably bore his personal stamp.

His typical method of speech preparation as president was to begin by soliciting suggestions from his cabinet as to what topics should be discussed. Sometimes he would give those suggestions directly to the person responsible for drafting the speech. Or, working from the suggestions, he would draw up a list of main points, with notes as to how they might be treated. From these materials one of his associates would prepare a draft, in which they usually had wide latitude to exercise their rhetorical prowess. Washington would then review the draft, making suggestions and corrections as to the ideas and their manner of expression.

At some stage, he would circulate the draft among his cabinet. If further drafts were necessary, the process would continue until Washington had a text with which he was fully satisfied. At times he would write out his speaking copy in his own hand, all the while smoothing, refining, and amending. Consistent with Washington's thorough and cautious approach to decision making in general, it was a time-consuming operation designed, as he said of his eighth annual message to Congress, so that "the whole may be revised again and again before presentation."

Although we can assume Washington took as much care with the presentation of his speeches as with their preparation, his impact on audiences was due more to the drama of the occasion and the power of his presence than to his skills of delivery. He was, from all accounts, considerably less than dynamic on the platform. Uncomfortable when called upon to speak impromptu, he preferred to read his speeches from manuscript. As president, he usually wore his spectacles while speaking so he could see the text clearly. He spoke rather slowly—probably at about one hundred words a minute—in a flat, hollow, undistinguished voice. His articulation was precise and distinct, despite his ill-fitted and uncomfortable false teeth. He seldom gestured while speaking, and when he did, the movements seemed stiff and awkward in comparison to those of a practiced orator.

But little of this seemed to matter. Washington was a charismatic leader, a towering figure whose hold on the imagination of his contemporaries is almost impossible to recapture today. Over 6 feet tall and weighing more than 200 pounds, he had a personal magnetism belied by the stiff portraits, the marble monuments, and the moralistic biographies that have shaped his popular image. Considered by Jefferson to be the finest horseman in America, he had a strong, finely proportioned figure, moved with athletic grace, and seemed uncommonly majestic in bearing. Gilbert Stuart, who studied his features most closely, thought they were "indicative of the strongest passions." "Had he been born in the forests," Stuart said, "he would have been the fiercest man among the savage tribes." Combine the content of Washington's speeches, his heroic reputation and commanding physical presence, and the kinds of historic, emotionally charged occasions he faced when addressing the officers at Newburgh, resigning his commission, and inaugurating the presidency, and it is not hard to understand why he was able to move audiences despite his rather ordinary delivery. There must have been many listeners who responded to Washington's speeches as did James McHenry to his 1783 Annapolis address. "So many circumstances," McHenry reported, "crowded into view and gave rise to so many affecting emotions. The events of the revolution just accomplished; the new situation into which it had thrown the affairs of the world; the great man who had borne so conspicuous a figure in it, in the act of relinquishing all public employments to return to private life; the past, the present, the future, the manner, the occasion—all conspired to render it a spectacle inexpressibly solemn and affecting."

As a speaker, then, Washington was effective far beyond the sum of his oratorical gifts. For a man whose "colloquial talents," to borrow Jefferson's

words, were "not above mediocrity," Washington achieved some stunning rhetorical successes. Nor can his achievements as a speaker be attributed solely to
his ghostwriters or to his charismatic presence. Washington managed his rhetorical capital with extraordinary vision. Keenly aware of the importance of
uttering the right words at the right moment, he chose both his words and his
moments for public utterance with great care. "He is a man of very few words,"
said Charles Wilson Peale in 1775, "but when he speaks it is to the purpose."
Washington would have been pleased with Peale's description. When his nephew
Bushrod Washington was elected to the Virginia legislature in 1787, Washington
advised him to "speak seldom, but to important subjects," to make himself
"perfectly master of the subject," and to "submit your sentiments with diffidence." Consistent in this, as in all other matters, Washington followed his own
advice throughout his military and political careers. Regarded in Europe and
America alike as the greatest man of his age, he exemplified John Adams's
observation that "eloquence in public assemblies is not the surest road to fame
and preferment . . . unless it be used with great caution, very rarely, and with
great reserve."

INFORMATION SOURCES

Research Collections and Collected Speeches

The great bulk of George Washington's surviving papers are in the Library of Congress,
where they comprise over 400 volumes of manuscripts. The standard published collection,
Fitzpatrick's *Writings of Washington*, includes all of Washington's major speeches, though
it omits most of the ceremonial addresses he delivered on such occasions as his 1789
inaugural journey from Mount Vernon to New York, his 1790 New England tour, and
his 1791 circuit of the southern states. This shortcoming will eventually be remedied by
The Papers of George Washington, a comprehensive new edition under the general
editorship of William Abbot. Until that project is completed, however, the other works
listed below will remain important published sources for Washington's speeches.

A Compilation of the Messages and Papers of the Presidents. Edited by   CMP
    James D. Richardson. Vol. 1. New York: Bureau of National Lit-
    erature, 1897.
Henderson, Archibald. *Washington's Southern Tour*. Boston: Houghton Mif-
    flin, 1923.
Monaghan, Frank. *Notes on the Inaugural Journey and the Inaugural Cer-
    emonies of George Washington as First President of the United
    States*. New York: Privately printed, 1939.
The Papers of George Washington. Edited by W. W. Abbot et al. 9 vols.
    to date. Charlottesville: University Press of Virginia, 1983-.
The Writings of George Washington. Edited by John C. Fitzpatrick. 39 vols.   GW
    Washington, D.C.: Government Printing Office, 1931-1944.

The Writings of George Washington. Edited by Worthington Chauncey Ford.   *GWF*
14 vols. New York: Putnam's, 1889–1893.

The Writings of George Washington. Edited by Jared Sparks. 12 vols. Bos-   *GWS*
ton: Little, Brown, 1855.

Selected Critical Studies

Gilbert, Felix. *To the Farewell Address: Ideas of Early American Foreign Policy.* Princeton: Princeton University Press, 1961.

Kohn, Richard H. "The Inside History of the Newburgh Conspiracy: America and the Coup d'Etat." *William and Mary Quarterly* 27 (1970): 187–220.

Lucas, Stephen E. "Genre Criticism and Historical Context: The Case of George Washington's First Inaugural Address." *Southern Speech Communication Journal* 51 (1986): 354–70.

Morgan, Edmund S. *The Genius of George Washington.* New York: Norton, 1980.

Paltsits, Victor Hugo. *Washington's Farewell Address.* New York: New York Public Library, 1935.

Stein, Nathaniel E. "The Discarded Inaugural Address of George Washington." *Manuscripts* 10 (1958): 2–17.

Washington's Farewell Address: The View from the Twentieth Century. Edited by Burton Ira Kaufman. Chicago: Quadrangle, 1969.

Wills, Garry. *Cincinnatus: George Washington and the Enlightenment.* New York: Doubleday, 1984.

Selected Biographies

Alden, John R. *George Washington: A Biography.* Baton Rouge: Louisiana State University Press, 1984.

Cunliffe, Marcus. *George Washington: Man and Monument.* Boston: Little, Brown, 1958.

Fitzpatrick, John C. *George Washington Himself: A Common-Sense Biography Written from His Manuscripts.* Indianapolis: Bobbs-Merrill, 1933.

Flexner, James Thomas. *George Washington.* 4 vols. Boston: Little, Brown, 1965–1972.

Freeman, Douglas Southall. *George Washington: A Biography.* 7 vols. New York: Scribner's, 1948–1957. Volume 7 completed after Freeman's death by John Alexander Carroll and Mary Wells Ashworth.

CHRONOLOGY OF MAJOR SPEECHES

See "Research Collections and Collected Speeches" for source codes.

Speech accepting appointment as commander in chief, Philadelphia, June 16, 1775; *GW*, 3: 292–93; *GWF*, 2: 476–81; *GWS*, 3: 1–2.

Speech to the New York legislature, New York, June 26, 1775; *GW*, 3: 305; *GWF*, 2: 500–02; *GWS*, 3: 13.

Speech to the officers, Newburgh, New York, March 15, 1783; *GW*, 26: 222–27; *GWF*, 10: 170–74; *GWS*, 8: 560–63.

Circular letter to the governors of the thirteen states, issued from Washington's headquarters, Newburgh, New York, June 8, 1783; *GW*, 26: 483–96; *GWF*, 10: 254–65; *GWS*, 8: 439–52.

Speech resigning commission as commander in chief, Annapolis, Maryland, December 23, 1783; *GW*, 27: 284–85; *GWF*, 20: 338–39; *GWS*, 8: 504–05.

First Inaugural Address, New York, April 30, 1789; *GW*, 30: 291–96; *GWF*, 11: 381–86; *GWS*, 12: 1–6; *CMP*, 1: 43–46.

Second Inaugural Address, Philadelphia, March 4, 1793; *GW*, 32: 374–75; *GWF*, 12: 265; *CMP*, 1: 130.

Sixth Annual Address to Congress, Philadelphia, November 19, 1794; *GW*, 34: 28–37; *GWF*, 12: 491–98; *GWS*, 12: 44–54; *CMP*, 1: 154–60.

Seventh Annual Address to Congress, Philadelphia, December 8, 1795; *GW*, 34: 386–93; *GWF*, 13: 140–45; *GWS*, 12: 56–63; *CMP*, 1: 174–78.

Farewell Address, September 17, 1796, released to the public through *Claypoole's American Daily Advertiser*, September 19, 1796; *GW*, 35: 214–38; *GWF*, 13: 277–325; *GWS*, 12: 214–35; *CMP*, 1: 205–16.

DANIEL WEBSTER
(1782–1852), defender of the Union

CRAIG R. SMITH

Daniel Webster was one of the most prolific and effective public orators in American history. His addresses of note are not limited to one genre but span the rhetorical spectrum. His forensic pleadings changed the course of constitutional law. His epideictic efforts reveal a mastery of style and form perhaps unsurpassed in American rhetorical literature. And his deliberative addresses are an integral part of the history of the nation. Webster not only provided creative vehicles for his arguments, he lifted the standard of American public address to new heights.

At Phillips Exeter Academy, he was less than secure about public speaking. In fact, in his first year he was so distressed at being away from home that he often found himself unable to stand before the class and wept in his room over his plight. He learned Latin from a tutor in order to meet the entrance requirements of Dartmouth College. During his studies, he became familiar with ''Cicero's Select Orations,'' and at Dartmouth his talent was refined by classes in oratorical composition and delivery. These classes, under the direction of Professor Haddock, were perhaps some of the most rigorous in the new nation and included instruction on all of the elements of rhetoric, with special emphasis on logic, the emotions, stylistic commonplaces, and organization. Webster was required to take courses in public address every year he attended Dartmouth, culminating in legal and deliberative oratory in his senior year. He was chosen to be one of the commencement speakers in 1801, but he turned down the opportunity because he believed he was not placed prominently enough in the program. Instead, on graduation day, Webster spoke before the United Fraternity on the subject of ''Opinion.''

Webster took up the study of law on his own at age nineteen. But because of his father's financial difficulties, young Webster was forced to teach school and delay his entry into the bar. In 1802, he returned to Salisbury, New Hampshire, and began an apprenticeship in the law under Thomas Thompson, a graduate of Harvard. On July 17, 1804, Webster moved to Boston to tutor his brother Zeke in Greek and Latin and was accepted as an apprentice by the great Christopher Gore, a famed Federalist, commissioner, and lawyer. Webster rifled Gore's incredible library, and worked diligently at improving his use of the English language.

Webster was admitted to the bar in March 1805 and began practicing in Boscawen, New Hampshire, where he became an instant success. Although he never stopped learning, Webster's entry into the bar marked the end of his formal training and the beginning of his illustrious career.

DANIEL WEBSTER AS JUDICIAL PLEADER AND CEREMONIAL ORATOR

Webster excelled in forensic speaking, and his training in the law was prodigious. From his first case, Webster was unusually successful, especially before the Supreme Court, presided over by fellow Federalist John Marshall. In fact, it is said that Marshall often had his decisions ready before Webster presented his oral arguments before the court because Marshall was so impressed with the briefs Webster filed. More than likely, however, Marshall was delighted to use Webster's unionist arguments to inculcate the Constitution with Federalist dogma. With Marshall as chief justice, Webster usually won his cases. When Marshall was replaced by Democrat Roger Taney in 1835, Webster's winning percentage began a decline that would eventually put his lifetime average before the Supreme Court at 48 percent.

Perhaps the three most important Supreme Court cases Webster argued were *Dartmouth College v. Woodward*, decided in 1819, *McCullough v. Maryland* also in 1819, and *Gibbons v. Ogden* in 1824. Each of these cases set precedents that affect the American jurisprudential system to this day.

As a graduate of Dartmouth College, Webster had a particular interest in seeing that the institution carried the day. The state of New Hampshire had ousted Dartmouth's president and placed the college under the jurisdiction of its board of trustees. However, Dartmouth had obtained a royal charter prior to New Hampshire's becoming a state. Webster argued that contractual obligations were based on natural law and were therefore immune to man-made law. A right, such as the charter of Dartmouth, once invested, became a natural right and could not be divested through legislation.

The Supreme Court agreed with Webster that the original charter had been violated. Chief Justice Marshall, writing for the majority, held that the charter was a contract; therefore the covenants in the charter were inviolable. To be fair, Webster used arguments developed earlier in the case by associates; but his brilliant presentation of these arguments, in conjunction with his famous phrase, "It is, sir, as I have said, a small college. And yet there are those who love it," was credited with making the landmark decision possible. It also made Webster's reputation as a constitutional lawyer.

McCullough v. Maryland was a very different kind of case. Here Webster was defending the constitutionality of the Bank of the United States. A second bank had been chartered by President James Madison to deal with the economic woes caused by the unfortunate War of 1812. Many states were opposed to the national bank because it preempted their ability to operate banks and tax revenues. Maryland was one of those states. Webster represented the national bank before the Supreme Court. His position required the widening of the scope of the government's power. He argued that the necessary and proper clause of the Constitution established the legitimate role of the federal government in dealing with national problems.

The Supreme Court accepted Webster's argument and held the Maryland tax to be unconstitutional. It noted three distinct areas of federal power: the federal government draws its authority from the people, not the states; the necessary and proper clause gives Congress broad powers to implement the enumerated powers of the federal government; and any state legislation that interferes with the existence of legitimate federal powers is invalid.

As in the previous two cases, Webster's arguments in *Gibbons v. Ogden* stretched the powers of the federal government by extracting implicit meaning from explicit language. In this case, the commerce clause was the issue. Robert Livingston and Robert Fulton had been granted exclusive rights to operate a steamboat line on New York waters. In the absence of a federal law to the contrary, no action was taken to restrict that license. Livingston and Fulton sold their rights to Ogden. Gibbons, however, operated a steamboat between New York and New Jersey and refused to stop when Ogden claimed Gibbons was stealing his business. Gibbons argued that his license under the Federal Coasting Act justified his action and negated the monopoly granted to Fulton by New York. Ogden sued Gibbons for encroachment.

With the talented William Wirt at his side, Webster argued Gibbons's case. He said that congressional regulatory power in commerce was complete and exclusive, that the Coasting Act was commercial regulation, and that the state of New York was in conflict with this power. He went on to argue that interference with this form of transportation would occur unless the Court remedied the situation. Again Marshall sided with Webster, as did the majority on the Court. Congress had the power to regulate "that commerce which concerns more states than one." Therefore New York could not limit the scope of the federal powers by creating a state monopoly over an interstate waterway since that would effectively render the federally conferred license useless.

Webster argued over twenty cases before the Supreme Court from 1819 to 1824. The important ones strengthened the hand of the federal government and further confined the power of the states to regulating their own internal affairs. Thus Webster's forensic position complemented the political position he would espouse as a senator. In both the courts and the Congress, Webster stood for the Union.

In the years that followed these cases, he argued many others before the Court that had important impact, including *Ogden v. Saunders*, which established the states' power to pass bankruptcy laws. In this case, Marshall again agreed with Webster but found himself on the dissenting side for the first and only time as chief justice. These and other cases demonstrate Webster's mastery of argumentation. His appearances in criminal cases, however, demonstrate his ability to produce enormously persuasive narratives.

Perhaps the most famous criminal case Webster argued was the Knapp-White case of August 1830. Captain Joseph White, a well-to-do entrepreneur, was found murdered in his bed on April 7, 1830, in Salem, Massachusetts, and panic swept the town. Eventually the police apprehended three men: Richard Crownshield, Joseph Knapp, and Frank Knapp. Under questioning, Joseph Knapp, who was married to White's niece, admitted to hiring Crownshield to commit the murder in order to gain White's inheritance. Crownshield then committed suicide in prison, and Knapp quickly retracted his confession.

Because of the fervor in the community, the prosecution invited Webster to represent their interests in the trials that followed. Several were necessary because of the complexity of the indictments and an early mistrial. To a packed courtroom, Webster performed well. The Knapp brothers were convicted and publicly executed, and Webster's legend grew.

Webster's success in this forensic effort resulted in part from his ability to recreate scenes before the jury. He played on their powers of imagination by building a coherent scenario of the crime. This stratagem was essential because one of the problems in the case was proving that both brothers were involved in the conspiracy. By recreating scenes in the mind's eye of the jurors, Webster was able to sustain the claim that the brothers were in league with the murderer. Furthermore, playing the scene helped incite the jury against the murderers since the victim was eighty-two years old and helpless. The following passage reveals Webster's strength at narrative:

The deed was executed with a degree of self-possession and steadiness equal to the wickedness with which it was planned. The circumstances now clearly in evidence spread out the whole scene before us. Deep sleep had fallen on the destined victim and on all beneath his roof. A healthful old man to whom sleep was sweet, the first sound slumbers of the night held him in their soft but strong embrace. The assassin enters through the window already prepared, into an unoccupied apartment. With noiseless foot he paces the lonely hall, half lighted by the moon; he winds up the ascent of the stairs, and reaches the door of the chamber. Of this he moves the lock by soft and continued pressure, till it turns on its hinges without a noise; and he enters and beholds his victim before him.

Early in 1830, Webster had gained national attention with his "Reply to Hayne." Now in August, his reputation as a criminal lawyer swept Massachusetts.

Webster eventually argued before the Supreme Court 168 times and held forth before many juries. His forensic powers not only served him well, they helped strengthen the young Union and set a model for criminal prosecution.

Daniel Webster's ceremonial addresses are some of the most sophisticated ever delivered. They have elements from the other forms of public address within them allowing Webster to reinforce deliberative policy or forensic judgment in the guise of an epideictic effort. For example, in 1820, when Webster delivered the Plymouth Address, not only did he invoke American values, he condemned slavery and suggested a course for the future. He thereby concealed deliberative and forensic arguments inside the ceremonial shell.

On June 17, 1825, in his first Bunker Hill address, Webster argued for Greek independence and speculated on South American revolutions. Seven years later in "The Character of Washington," Webster used an ostensibly epideictic occasion to attack John C. Calhoun's doctrine of nullification. In his "Reception at Madison" address, Webster argued for western expansion, the American system (introduced by Henry Clay to expand roads, railways, and canals), and nationalism. Furthermore, Webster hoped the speech would enhance his presidential candidacy.

The cloaking of one strategy in another is evident in every major ceremonial speech of Webster. The "Completion of the Bunker Hill Monument" address was an occasion for Webster to stir support for nationalism. Delivered just before the hostilities that led to the Mexican-American War, this speech allowed Secretary of State Webster the opportunity to rationalize manifest destiny, though he opposed the acquisition of the barren lands of the Southwest. Even his last critically acclaimed speech, "Addition to the Capitol," which he gave in 1851, is full of deliberative recommendations and forensic deprecations of slavery.

Webster's most acclaimed ceremonial speech was his "Eulogy to Adams and Jefferson." It, above all others, reveals his skill in employing the epideictic form. On July 4, 1826, exactly fifty years after the Declaration of Independence, Thomas Jefferson and John Adams died. On August 2, 1826, Daniel Webster accepted an invitation to speak of this event and about the lives it concerned. The dual deaths not only captured the national imagination but seemed marked by providence; a mystique grew around the occasion.

The task of speaking about this event was doubly difficult because Jefferson and Adams represented very different personalities and political philosophies. Webster overcame this problem with a diverse set of rhetorical strategies. First, the speech was almost perfectly proportioned. The introduction, body, and conclusion discussed and developed the lives and accomplishments of Adams and Jefferson in almost fugal form; first one of the founders was discussed for a few paragraphs and then the other. And with each new mention of the former presidents, the information about them was extended, as were the themes Webster wished to develop. The introduction described the event that had brought the audience together. Webster not only met the expectation present in the audience but elicited an expectation of what was to come. The parallel lives of the two patriots were generally explored as a kind of preview of what was to come. In the introduction, Webster created a pattern that would guide him through the speech. The audience would be involved in the speech by references to the occasion. Then the occasion would be explored by references to the parallel lives of the two patriots. Anecdotes from the lives of the subjects would be woven into the values Webster wanted to reinforce in his audience at Faneuil Hall, Boston. He also worked hard to unite his subjects and then to unite them with the audience. For example, Jefferson is said to have received the highest honors at William and Mary College; Adams is said to have argued before his state's supreme court at the early age of twenty-four. Jefferson is pictured as just in representing his constituents; Adams is portrayed as devoted to justice. Webster's reconstruction of Jefferson's involvement with the Declaration of Independence was not a difficult image to sustain. After all, at the time, Jefferson was thought to have authored the document by himself. But with Adams, he faced a larger challenge. Though no record of the debates was extant, Webster contended that Adams's debating skill was crucial to the passage of the Declaration. Webster reinforced this judgment by inventing a speech for Adams. The strategy worked because the *ghosting* was dynamic and well fashioned, and it riveted the audience:

Sink or swim, live or die, survive or perish, I give my hand and my heart to this vote. ... Why put off longer the Declaration of Independence? That measure will strengthen us. It will give us character abroad. . . . But while I do live, let me have country, or at least the hope of a country, and that a free country. . . . Independence now, and Independence for Ever!

Afterward many said they felt Adams presence in the hall as Webster delivered the famous ghost speech.

Webster's approach to narrative material was equally adept. Adjusting to his Massachusetts audience, he consistently spent more time in each unit on Adams than he did on Jefferson. But in each case, the story was interrupted in order to secure the audience's attention with new argumentation on some moral question. Once the separate treatment of each subject was complete within a unit, Webster united his subjects through some anecdote and then tied both of the founders to the present audience: "Both had been presidents, both had lived to great age, both were early patriots, and both were distinguished and ever honored."

In his conclusion, Webster argued that the United States was a model for the world, that it embodied a new approach to government, that its citizens must preserve its institutions, and that all must be guided by God. Webster's vindication of Jefferson and Adams was part of an overall strategy to reinforce present values so that future policies would be improved. Though more subtle than in other ceremonial speeches, the invocation of a deliberative policy seemed natural to Webster's conclusion.

In 1808, Webster wrote a treatise on interposition that would later come back to haunt him. In it he argued, much the way John C. Calhoun would twenty years later, that the federal government could not place a tariff on imported goods. The treatise served as the basis for Webster's stirring Rockingham memorial address to the assembled members of the dying Federalist party. The speech led to Webster's selection to the Massachusett's state senate. His credible and winning performance there led to his election to the House of Representatives, where he served from 1813 to 1817 and again from 1823 to 1827. During this time, Webster steadily moved from being a New England Federalist with parochial interests to becoming a Whig with national interests. The circle was completed in 1827 when he was put in the U.S. Senate by cotton and wool mill owners who favored a tariff. Thus began one of the most illustrious careers in the history of the U.S. Senate.

While the tariff would fade into the slavery and states' rights issues, all were founded on the question of how much power would be accorded the states in a federal government. These issues had surfaced in 1820 and been resolved in Clay's ingenious compromise. In 1830, they reached another crisis point when Robert Y. Hayne of South Carolina rose to defend his state's right to ignore the federal tariff. He argued that the federation was a "compact of states." Webster entered the Senate and listened patiently through Hayne's presentation.

The Webster-Hayne debate consisted of three exchanges. But it was Hayne's bitter second attack on Webster that provoked one of the most famous moments in the history of the Senate. Hayne attacked Webster's inconsistency, condemned

Massachusetts for the use of slum labor, and defended his own state's slavery. Hayne's speech was cheered, and many thought at that point that he had won the debate. He had thrown Webster's 1808 position in his face. Undaunted, the great Massachusetts debater turned the tables and argued that Hayne had plagiarized Webster's early position (and not very well at that) and that was too bad because Webster had been wrong when he articulated it. Webster's second reply, delivered from twelve pages of notes on January 26 and 27, was extemporaneous, dramatic, and overpowering. Webster claimed that "we, the people" not the states, formed the Constitution, and thus, nullification was not an option open to the states:

The people, then, Sir, erected this government. They gave it a Constitution, and in that Constitution they have enumerated the powers which they bestow on it. They have made it a limited government. They have defined its authority. They have restrained it to the exercise of such powers as are granted; and all others, they declare, are reserved to the States or the people.

Webster went on to explain that if each state could nullify what it did not like, the Union would fall into chaos. The country was no longer in the ratification phase of the formation of the Union. The phase passed when a sufficient number of states ratified the Constitution to make it the supreme law of the land. At that point, the states had given up their primacy to the new federal government. To Hayne's "liberty first, Union afterwards," Webster dramatically responded, "Liberty and Union, now and forever, one and inseparable!"

The 30,000-word speech was widely praised and circulated as a pamphlet after Webster revised it. Webster became a national figure of great stature. His second victory over the South came in 1833 when Webster defeated Calhoun in a debate over the force bill. Calhoun, the only person in U.S. history to serve as a vice-president under two presidents from different parties, had resigned after splitting with President Jackson and had taken a seat in the Senate to represent South Carolina's interests. He resurrected his position on concurrent majorities and states' rights. But Webster dispatched Calhoun with more ease than he had Hayne. Calhoun and his allies deserted the floor of the Senate, and Webster carried the vote thirty-two to one.

By 1836, Webster was a contender for the presidential nomination, but in that year, as in several others, he was not to be the choice of his party. He would serve several times as secretary of state with distinction for Whig presidents. From 1841 to 1844, he helped negotiate difficult treaties with England. He resigned when he broke with President Tyler over annexation of Texas. From July 1850 until his death, he ran the State Department for his friend, President Fillmore. Yet his most important achievements would result from the speeches he gave in the Senate, and the best of these were given during the Compromise of 1850 debates. They reveal not only Webster's masterful use of audience adaptation but his mature understanding of style, argument, and credibility as persuasive forces.

As the 1850 session got underway in January, 55 percent of the Senate was Democrat, 42 percent Whig, and 3 percent Free Soil. The Senate was divided evenly between slave and free state senators, as was each party. But the issue was more complicated than that because some senators from border states, fearing that war would tear their constituencies apart, hoped for a compromise.

The causes of the crisis of 1850 were no less complex. President Taylor, a hero of the Mexican-American war and a southern slaveholder, surprised many senators by calling for the organization of Deseret (now Nevada, Utah, and parts of adjoining states) and New Mexico as free territories and for the admission of California on the same basis. This cheered hard-liners like William Seward, who had supported the ill-fated Wilmot Proviso, which would have precluded slavery from the territories acquired from Mexico at the end of that war in 1847. But it bothered Webster and other moderates who thought the president's action was precipitous, and it infuriated southerners, who saw the move as a threat to their power in the Senate. They knew the population was rapidly shifting to the North and West, thus depriving them of the White House and control of the House of Representatives for the foreseeable future. The Senate was the last refuge of the South, and now in 1850 the president was threatening the balance there.

While Clay and Webster worked for compromise, Calhoun at one extreme and Seward at the other argued for their moral imperatives. Webster's first great speech in the debates came on March 7, four days after Calhoun's defense of the South. It is clear that Webster was trying to set out arguments that would mollify the northern audience, which he knew was moderate at heart. They had not supported the Free Soil party in the droves some had predicted, and even those who did were motivated more by a desire to keep western lands open than by a desire to free slaves in the South. Webster also knew that the compromise was crucial to the settlement of the Texas border, debt, and bond situation and that many of those bonds were held by northern Whigs. Thus, in the March 7 speech, Webster set out lines of argument by which he hoped to ensnare public opinion in the North in support of the Clay omnibus bill.

The speech had limited success. Although hard-line abolitionists, including Emerson, condemned Webster, most newspapers supported his position. The speech was revised, published, and reissued several times to meet the large demand for it throughout the country, much to the horror of northern abolitionists and southern fire-eaters.

But Webster must have known he could not produce immediate compromise in the Senate for several reasons. First, the president opposed the plan. He wanted to extend the Union of states to the Pacific by converting California to statehood and organizing the New Mexico and Deseret territories. Second, the young lions, like Foote of Mississippi and Seward of Pennsylvania, had not had their say. An event beyond Webster's control also stymied attempts at compromise. When Calhoun died on March 31, it reminded southerners of his moral defense of their culture and increased southern obstinancy. Thus, a legislative interregnum was necessary. Clay became so despondent he left the Senate for his Kentucky home. But Webster remained active, debating small parliamentary matters and keeping pressure on the business community.

Fate rescued the situation. On the Fourth of July 1850, a very hot day, President Taylor, who was fond of eating cherries soaked in bourbon and cream, over-indulged and contracted an intestinal disorder. He died a few days later and was succeeded by Millard Fillmore, a Webster ally. Fillmore asked Webster to become his secretary of state. Webster accepted and used his farewell address to the Senate on July 17 as a platform for a final appeal for compromise.

The speech succeeded for several reasons. First, it provided an effective counterpart to Webster's March 7 speech. While that speech prepared the northern audience for the compromise, the July 17 address prepared the Senate. Second, Webster raised those issues where there was agreement among his colleagues to a transcendent level and reduced their differences to the pragmatic. Third, his enormous credibility at this point in history was brought to bear on the situation as he attempted to get a majority of his colleagues to form a core in favor of compromise. Finally, Webster developed a powerful argument in a progressive form that worked to coalesce a majority of the Senate into supporters of the compromise. The argument began by discussing how the compromise would benefit first Massachusetts, then the North, and then the nation as a whole. Then Webster turned to his southern colleagues and selected Maryland to demonstrate the point to the South. He showed how the compromise would help Maryland, the South, and then the country as a whole. Then he reinforced the structure of this argument by showing how much each state, each region, and the nation would lose if the compromise failed. The parallel structure of this argument from consequences is compelling and at times overwhelming.

The evidence is strong that the strategy worked. Debate became less acrimonious. A majority opposed to divisive amendment held through several crucial votes. In August, Webster's hand-picked candidate for Congress, Samuel Elliot, defeated the abolitionist Charles Sumner in Boston. And most important, Senator Stephen Douglas began using the strategy Webster had recommended in his speech to achieve consensus—that is, to pass each piece of the legislative package separately as opposed to Clay's omnibus approach.

In September, the various compromise bills passed the Senate, and when the House passed them, joyous Washingtonians took to the streets in wild celebration. Webster, in ill health, had to be carried to his doorstep to wave at parade goers and to speak to unruly gangs of admirers because they refused to disperse until he came out to receive their adulation. Webster had the satisfaction of knowing that his last deliberative speech in the Senate had helped shape the strategy that would preserve the Union beyond his lifetime. More important, his legend would reinforce the virtues of freedom of expression in a democratic republic.

Webster's ability to use all of the available means of persuasion to obtain support for his policies was supported by his intimate and sophisticated use of rhetorical form. When pleading a case, he not only understood the importance of evidence and argument, he understood the importance of associates on the bench, the scene of the crime, and the imagination of the jury. When speaking at a ceremony, he knew that the audience had to be involved in the speech if they were to be persuaded to the values it endorsed. And when addressing the Senate, he knew that the issues had to be reconfigured so that his colleagues could transcend their division and unite behind his proposals.

Like the best speakers in ancient Greece, Webster recognized that the stronger illusion would prevail over the weaker and that the closer one approximated the truth in the mind of listeners, the more one was likely to gain the adherence of those listeners. Like few other speakers in U.S. history, Webster was able to appeal to the actual consciousness of the audience in terms of their needs and desires while appealing to their innate potential consciousness in the values he espoused. Perhaps that is why he has played such a large role for such a long time and is ever ingrained in the rhetorical literature.

INFORMATION SOURCES

Research Collections and Collected Speeches

The almost 2,000 documents that make up the papers of Daniel Webster written prior to 1820 are located in the Baker Library, Dartmouth College, Hanover, New Hampshire. This collection includes a draft of Webster's argument for the *Dartmouth College* case. Available on microfilm, the forty-one-reel microfilm edition was published in 1971. The most relevant reels for rhetorical scholars are numbers 30 through 37, the congressional documents. Selected libraries usually have the documents under this listing: *Guide and Index to the Microfilm: Microfilm Edition of the Papers of Daniel Webster*. Edited by Charles M. Wiltse. Ann Arbor, Mich., 1971. Another 2,500 items can be found at the New Hampshire Historical Society, Concord. Of most importance to rhetorical scholars are Webster's outlines for the reply to Hayne (January 1830) and for the March 7 address of 1850.

Congressional Globe.	CG
Register of Debates in Congress. Edited by Gales and Seaton.	RD
Works of Daniel Webster. Boston: Little, Brown, 1877.	WDW
National Edition of the Writings and Speeches of Daniel Webster. Edited by James W. McIntyre. 18 vols. Boston: Little, Brown, 1903.	NEWS

Selected Critical Studies

Arntson, Paul, and Craig R. Smith. "The Seventh of March Address: A Mediating Influence." *Southern Speech Communication Journal* 40 (1975): 288–301.

Black, John W. "Webster's Peroration in the Dartmouth College Case." *Quarterly Journal of Speech* 23 (1937): 636–42.

Foster, H. D. "Webster's Seventh of March Speech and the Secession Movement, 1850." *American Historical Review* 27 (1922): 245–70.

Howell, Wilbur S., and Hudson, Hoyt H. "Daniel Webster." In *A History and Criticism of American Public Address*. Edited by William Norwood Brigance and Marie Hochmuth. New York: Russell and Russell, 1960.

Selected Biographies

Bartlett, Irving H. *Daniel Webster*. New York: W. W. Norton, 1978.
Current, Richard N. *Daniel Webster and the Rise of National Conservatism*. Boston: Little, Brown, 1955.
Fuess, Claude M. *Daniel Webster*. Boston: Little, Brown, 1930.

CHRONOLOGY OF MAJOR SPEECHES

See "Research Collections and Collected Speeches" for source codes.

"First Settlement of New England," Plymouth, Massachusetts, December 22, 1820; *NEWS*, 1: 181–226.

First Bunker Hill address, Charlestown, Massachusetts, June 17, 1825; *NEWS*, 1: 235–54.

"Eulogy to Adams and Jefferson," Boston, August 2, 1826; *NEWS*, 1: 289–324.

Reply to Hayne, U.S. Senate, Washington, D.C., January 26–27, 1830; *RD*, vol. 6: p.1, 58–93.

Argument on the trial of John Francis Knapp, Salem, Massachusetts, August 6, 1830; *NEWS*, 11: 51–105.

"The Character of Washington," Washington, D.C., February 22, 1832; *WDW*, 1: 219–33.

Debate on the force bill, U.S. Senate, Washington, D.C., February 16, 1833; *RD*, 9: p. 1, 553–87.

Reception at Madison, Madison, Indiana, June 1, 1837; *WDW*, 1: 401–09.

"The Completion of the Bunker Hill Monument," Charlestown, Massachusetts, June 17, 1843; *NEWS*, 1: 259–83.

March 7 address, U.S. Senate, Washington, D.C., March 7, 1850; *CG*, 31st Cong., 1st sess., p. 1, pp. 476–83.

July 17 address, U.S. Senate, Washington, D.C., July 17, 1850; *CG*, 31st Cong., 1st sess., p. 2, pp. 1266–70.

"Addition to the Capitol," Washington, D.C., July 4, 1851; *WDW*, 2: 595–620.

GEORGE WHITEFIELD
(1714–1770), itinerant evangelist

———————————————————————— EUGENE E. WHITE

George Whitefield was the son of a Gloucester, England, inn owner. Educated at St. Mary de Crypt Grammar School, Gloucester, and at Oxford University, he was ordained a deacon in the Church of England in 1736 and a minister in 1739. He made his first trip to America in 1738 as chaplain to Frederica, Georgia, and, after being appointed chaplain to Savannah by the trustees of Georgia, he made a second trip (November 1739-January 1741) at the time of the Great Awakening, the wave of religious emotionalism that between 1739 and 1745 swept over New England, the Middle Colonies, and, to a much lesser extent, South Carolina and Georgia. Whitefield spent the next thirty years itinerating over the British isles and visiting America five more times. He died September 30, 1770, at Newburyport, Massachusetts.

WHITEFIELD: GRAND ITINERANT AND CATALYST OF THE GREAT AWAKENING

All great persuasion is a fitting response to a provoking social urgency. Both audiences and communicators are creatures of that urgency. The way listeners and readers react to persuasion is conditioned by their readiness to respond, which in turn stems partly from their anticipations concerning the persuader and from their relationship to the urgency. The communicators draw the thrust of their message partly from their identification with the urgency and from the perceptions they have of the listeners and readers as fellow participants in the urgency. In the middle years of the eighteenth century, a series of great religious revivals, called by some the Second Reformation, stirred Great Britain, various countries in Europe, and the English colonies in North America. Although circumstances differed in the particular countries, the urgency was everywhere a protest against rationalism and formalism in religion. It was the need felt by great numbers of people to reinvigorate Protestantism through a more popular, more affecting, and more individualized mode of worship.

Through his sensational field preaching, Whitefield became a major catalyst of the forces generating the Second Reformation. For thirty-four years (1736–1770) he followed the biblical prescription: "Go ye into all the world and preach the gospel to every creature." Traveling by horseback, schooner, and even canoe, he sought converts in England, Scotland, Wales, Ireland, Bermuda, Gibraltar, and colonial America. The out of doors was often his chapel; and a mound, tombstone, tree stump, hogshead, or horse's back served frequently as his pulpit. In his constant itinerating, Whitefield sometimes preached more than forty hours a week and eventually delivered 18,000 sermons to some 10 million auditors. Along with John Wesley, he introduced field preaching in England in 1739 and spearheaded the Methodist revival in England, as well as the evangelical movement within the Church of England, during the 1740s, 1750s, and 1760s. Perhaps his greatest contribution, however, was to precipitate the Great Awakening in this country.

In the fifteen months (October 30, 1739-January 24, 1741) that Whitefield remained in America during the Great Awakening, he delivered over 500 sermons as well as several hundred "exhortations" to small groups in private homes. In evangelizing from Boston to Savannah, he traveled more than 2,000 miles through the colonial wilderness and over 3,000 miles by boat. Most of his sermons were delivered in repeated visits to the large cities of Boston, New York, Philadelphia, and Charleston or on tours between them, with only a limited number being presented at his Savannah parish.

The effectiveness of his speaking is evinced by the tremendous audiences that gathered to hear him. Inasmuch as many of his sermons were given outside, it may appear that a large congregation could not hear distinctly. However, Benjamin Franklin in his *Autobiography* estimated that the evangelist could be understood by 30,000 persons and explained that he "might be heard and understood at a great distance [because] his auditories, however numerous, observ'd the most exact silence." Unfortunately, the colonial literature of the period recorded only generalized estimates of the size of Whitefield's congregations. Innumerable citations in newspapers, journals, letters, pamphlets, and the *Christian History* (the first religious magazine in America, published 1743–1745) referred to audiences of many thousands. For example, various newspapers reported that over 23,000 persons attended Whitefield's valedictory sermon on the Boston Common and that 20,000 came to one of his sermons on Society Hill in Philadelphia. (These were the largest crowds to hear a speech in America prior to Daniel Webster's first Bunker Hill address in 1825.) Such figures may seem unreasonably high in view of the scattered population of the colonies, the frequent disparity in estimates of particular audiences, and the fact that estimates were usually made by friends of the revivalist.

Although the exact size of Whitefield's audiences cannot be determined, he obviously addressed immense congregations. Not one of hundreds of newspaper articles, pamphlets, and published sermons challenged either the printed estimates of the size of his auditories or the alleged effectiveness of his oratory. Indeed, even his enemies acknowledged his power over the emotions of the masses and admitted that thousands followed him from place to place to hear him preach.

Whitefield's preaching was the catalyst of the awakening because it answered the yearnings of great numbers of people frustrated by the prevailing formalism and rationalism in religion. Hence it served as the instrumentality to set into motion and to shape the expression of previously prepared forces of revivalism. The Great Awakening was not an impromptu phenomenon; quite the contrary, conditions in the colonies were conducive to a general revival.

For many years New England had grieved over the falling away from the ideals of the original Puritan settlers. In the eyes of the pious there was a "*great decay of Godliness* in the lives and conversations of people both in town and land from what they had seen in the days of their fathers." Ministers "mourned" in their sermons and public prayers the indifference to matters of the soul and set aside special fast days to pray for a "general revival of religion." Occasional localized revivals, such as Solomon Stoddard's five "freshlets" in Northampton and Jonathan Edwards's widely publicized Northampton revival of 1734–1735, gave promise for a universal awakening.

In the Middle Colonies for two decades prior to the Great Awakening, Theodorus Frelinghuysen, the Dutch Reformed minister of the Raritan Valley in New Jersey, the German sectaries, and William Tennent, Sr.'s, log college evangelists had been planting the seeds of revivalism. Gradually, as a result of their joint efforts, a spirit of militant evangelism spread over much of New York, Pennsylvania, and New Jersey. Great segments of the population were stirred by the quickened religious tempo of the times. Sporadic revivals occurred; discontent with the formalism of the churches became widespread.

If the colonies in 1739–1741 were the right place and the right time for an outburst of religious fervor, Whitefield was eminently the right person to provide the necessary stimulus. Without suitable leadership, the sluggish forces of revivalism would not have developed into a social movement. A prophet was needed under whose banner of salvation could be aroused an army of the pious and devout. The circumstances of the times required a new voice, a fresh personality, and an unorthodox approach. No colonial minister—not even the great Jonathan Edwards—could fit the role. Whitefield supplied the necessary leadership partly because he was the most widely publicized and most lavishly praised clergyman in the colonies and probably in the Protestant world; his constant itinerating was spectacularly unique; his theology, while familiar, provided a dramatically fresh emphasis; his sermon methodology and delivery exploded conventional pulpit practice.

Almost incredible stories of Whitefield's ministerial success in England began to arouse attention in the colonies early in 1737. Such a flood of reports was printed about the size of his congregations, the amount of his collections, and the innovation of his preaching in the streets and fields on weekdays that, upon his arrival in Philadelphia in the fall of 1739, his name was a household word. According to historian Ola Winslow, the colonies were so favorably predisposed toward him that he "did not even plant; he merely put in his sickle and claimed the harvest." The advance publicity was especially effective in New England. So laudatory and so abundant was the propaganda printed prior to his New England tour in 1740 that the minds of the people were "greatly prepossessed" in his favor as a "wonder of piety, a man of God, so as no one was like him."

During his stay in America, Whitefield's activities were widely publicized throughout the colonies. Newspapers frequently devoted front pages and sometimes almost entire issues to him; preachers generally eulogized him, though in Charleston and the Middle Colonies some conservative ministers condemned him; and numerous pamphlets were printed about him. Whitefield and his traveling companion, William Seward, were skilled propagandists. They sent to newspapers and to influential persons frequent letters containing accounts of his ministerial activities. They inserted in newspapers the location and dates for the delivery of his sermons. This was something new to the colonists and created considerable excitement. Another method the evangelist used to attract attention was the printing and wide distribution of his voluminous journals, tracts, and sermons. Many of these writings were injudicious and later weakened the influence of his preaching, but at the time they stimulated the curious as well as the pious to attend his sermons. As a result of the great amount of publicity afforded the preacher, he was probably the best-known person in North America and the only person who was known in all the colonies.

Frequently in his letters, Whitefield recorded that he was never so contented as when in the saddle seeking fresh harvests of souls. By moving almost constantly from place to place he brought the revival to tens of thousands who could not have been reached otherwise. As various contemporaries noted, his riding from place to place, frequently in the company of numerous horsemen, provided exciting pageantry and a valuable analogy to Christ and his prophets. Never before in the colonies had a minister itinerated in such a fashion to preach out of doors or at meetinghouses of any denomination. With criers and newspaper bulletins preceding him, Whitefield drew crowds of almost unbelievable size whenever he reined in his horse. Historian Perry Miller has described his sweep across Massachusetts and Connecticut in this way: "We must go to such analogies as Peter the Hermit or Savonarola, or possibly the Pied Piper, to grasp what this triumphal progress was like: a whole society was stricken and convulsed."

At the time of the Great Awakening, the general emphasis on formalism and rationalism in sermons left great numbers of persons emotionally unsatisfied. First, the stiff and restricting skeletal sermon structure, which had been evolved by William Perkins, John Udall, and other English theologians in the late sixteenth century, was retained throughout the seventeenth and the first half of the eighteenth century, even by the major homiletic innovators—Solomon Stoddard, Cotton Mather, and Jonathan Edwards. In this disposition, the major parts (Laying Open the Text, Doctrine, Reasons or Propositions, and Application or Uses) were characterized by a formal profusion of divisions and subdivisions, each one of which was baldly stated and its relational position in the overall structure clearly identified.

Second, the emotional response of parishioners was further restricted by the tendency of ministers to follow traditional ideas about human psychology, the morphology of conversion, and the duty of ministers and the end of listeners. Traditional theory ran something like this: God had created humans in his image as rational beings and had designed their nature so that it recognized and responded to the world through a sequence of faculties, the most important of which were the Understanding (the King of the faculties—the capacity of judging), the Will (the Queen of the faculties—the capacity of embracing or rejecting), and the Affections. Because of Adam's fall, the individual faculties and their sequence were spiritually paralyzed for all members of succeeding generations—that is, except for elected persons, upon their experiencing a new birth. The route by which God enabled the elect to perceive that they were saved followed roughly the arch of the faculties and consisted of several clearly identifiable steps. Knowledge and understanding of biblical truths always came first; then came conviction of conscience, fear or despair that one can do nothing to improve one's spiritual state, true humiliation in which one sorrows for one's sins and prostrates oneself before God, and, finally, apprehension and ecstasy of faith. The duty of the minister was to teach or advise by means of information and logical analysis in the first three parts of the sermon; emotional coercion was not required at this stage because any point of doctrine, once understood, should be believed by the Understanding and accepted by the Will. By this appeal to the Understanding and the Will, all persons—the elect and the nonelect alike—could be guided through the first two stages of conversion: knowledge and conviction. The end of the listeners in attending to these first three parts of the sermon was to make a logical judgment. The duty of the minister in the final part of the sermon, the Application, was to appeal especially to the Affections and thereby to encourage the elect to experience the ecstasy of realizing that one possesses faith. The end of the auditors in listening to the Application was to strive actively for grace or the assurance that they already possessed grace.

Although Whitefield substantially adhered to the skeletal structure of the traditional sermon, he modified the function of the parts, ignored conventional concepts of human faculties and the morphology of conversion, and drastically altered the prevailing views of the duties of the preacher and the ends of the listeners.

Whitefield designed the entire sermon—not just the Application—to be an emotional exhortation. The beginning, which was more informal than was customary, consisted of an opening statement, explanation of the Text, and a mention of the affecting truths suggested by the Text he was going to discuss. The function of the main portion of the sermon (which corresponded to the Reasons segment) was not to teach or advise but to stimulate the listeners to the point that they would surrender to his entreaty in the close. One of the chief methods the evangelist used to develop this part of the sermon was to present a vivid dramatization of a biblical narrative, such as Abraham's offering up his son Isaac for the sacrifice, the marriage of Cana, or the return of the prodigal son. His method in presenting the narration was to weave a story from the appropriate verses in the Bible. For instance, he began his discourse on the sacrifice with the first verse in Genesis 22, where, as the narrative goes, God directed Abraham to sacrifice his son. Then he took up the next eleven verses in turn, interpreted them, invented dialogue among the main characters, and pictured the emotions of the father, the son, and their two servants on the three-day journey to the mountain where Abraham was to kill Isaac. This dramatic material, as well as others Whitefield used, was extremely clear and impelling narration.

Another method Whitefield used to develop the main part of the sermon was to analyze the text under three or four well-organized contentions. This organizational procedure was similar to traditional practice; Whitefield's development of this sermon part was greatly different, however, because he used intensely emotional material to make his points.

The ending of Whitefield's sermons, which occupied about one-fourth of the total length of his printed sermons, invariably consisted of a passionate appeal to "come to Christ." Usually he directed his exhortations to the "sinners," with contrasting allusions to the "fortunate believers." At times he spoke to different segments of the audience. In "Persecution Every Christian's Lot," he addressed those who were about to accept Christ, those who already believed, the ministers, himself as a person who had experienced persecution, and the "persecutors."

At times, the evangelist personalized his message by posing as a divine emissary sent by God to bring sinners "home to Christ." He offered to meet his hearers at Judgment Day, when he would intercede for them with God. He promised that believers would sit with him on the right hand of God and talk with the prophets and apostles for all eternity. However, with stern visage and ringing voice, he also threatened that he would appear before God and help condemn hardened sinners to hell forever. Although his printed addresses contained only a few allusions to his personal experiences, contemporaneous reports show that such references formed a fairly important part of his preaching.

Whitefield's sermons made little appeal to the reasoning of his listeners. He not only tacitly rejected the division of man into faculties, with the Understanding being the superior faculty, but he also often ridiculed the power of "natural logic" as being "carnal and at enmity with God and religion." Whitefield believed that his only duty was to lead sinners to Christ. Listeners, he thought, did not need to get their "head stored"; their only end in listening to his sermons was to seek union with Christ. He never plied his listeners with rational, logical evidence, or complicated systems of thought but reduced his theology to the simplest terms of sin, faith, hell, and heaven.

A basic emotional premise of his preaching was that all persons, having shared in Adam's original sin, were vile creatures totally incapable of spiritual "good works." He was fond of comparing his listeners and himself to "vile worms," "dung and dross of creation," and other evidences of opprobrium caused by Adam's sin. He spoke of the "rightness" of their eternal damnation. They could not escape damnation by listening to conservative ministers who were not only going to hell themselves but were leading their followers to the same place. Salvation was possible only when "divine revelation" revealed that they were born again in Christ and that their sins were forgiven. According to Whitefield, a spiritual rebirth required a physical and spiritual alteration of the entire being— a complete metamorphosis from a worldly to a spiritual attitude. Because grace was irresistible, regeneration could happen in "the twinkling of an eye"; it did not require a protracted morphology of steps to conversion or a prior rational commitment. Without the idea of instantaneous conversion and without Whitefield's apparently throwing open the gates of heaven to all eager seekers, mass conversions would have been impossible, and there would have been no Great

Awakening. The only way to attain a new birth was through complete faith in the righteousness of God; good works, pious deportment, or intellectual beliefs could not help in this effort.

The most important emotional element of his sermons was his emphasis on the delights of conversion and God's love for the regenerate. Much of the winning, persuasive quality of his speaking came from his mystical portrayal of the eternity of rest and peace that awaited the converted in heaven. In glowing terms he described how the children of God would gather about His throne on Judgment Day to be "blessed for evermore." He also dwelt on the great love God had manifested by sending his only Son to suffer and die upon the cross. The evangelist dramatized in vivid word pictures his conception of how Christ looked, how he felt, and what he thought and said during the crucifixion. Although some ministers like Cotton Mather had referred on occasion to the person of Christ, Whitefield's personification of Christ was sensationally novel.

Almost every contemporary reference to Whitefield's oratory commented on the effectiveness with which he delivered his sermons. Unlike the typical minister who read or memorized sermons, Whitefield needed no notes or manuscript, and his eloquent simplicity of delivery could stir the learned as well as the unlettered. In a widely disseminated pamphlet, the conservative Episcopal minister Alexander Garden said this about the popular response to Whitefield's preaching: "Such effects . . . are very plainly owing to . . . his *talent of delivery*, or voice and vehemence in speaking, adapted to take the ear and excite the passions of his hearers. I bid him only to put the *same* words, which from his mouth produced the boasted effects, into the mouth of an *ordinary* speaker, and see whether the *same* effects would be the consequence." The friends of the evangelist found his dynamic activity when speaking "beautiful" and "magnetic." The *Christian History* reported that "he uses much gestures, but with great propriety: . . . every motion of his body speaks, and [is] natural and unaffected. If his delivery is the product of art, 'tis certainly the perfection of it, for it is entirely concealed." The evangelical preacher Josiah Smith asked the rhetorical questions: "How awfully, with what *thunder* and sound did he discharge the artillery of heaven upon us? And yet, how could he soften and melt, even a *soldier of Christ*, with the love and mercy of God?" In the estimation of the objective Franklin, "Every accent, every emphasis, every modulation of voice, was so perfectly well turn'd and well plac'd, that, without being interested in the subject, one could not help being pleas'd with the discourse; a pleasure of much the same kind with that receiv'd from an excellent piece of musick."

In February 1741, as the *Minerva* pushed its way slowly through the cold Atlantic waters toward England, George Whitefield labored in the cabin, recording the context of the sermons he had preached during the Great Awakening. Cast adrift from the spell of his oratory, the revival moved toward emotional excesses under the emulators of the English evangelist. By the latter part of 1742, the climax had been reached; increasing numbers began to question the divine motivation of the turmoil. Gradually the revival lost its unity and disintegrated into quarreling factions and eddies of local fervor. Out of the upsetting of the old decorum there emerged new religious and social patterns. These patterns assigned to the common person a somewhat greater share in the shaping of affairs of church and state, accelerated the growth of various evangelical denominations, and eventually contributed to religious liberty and the disestablishment of religion. From the awakening a recurrent revival tempo flowed into the mainstrem of the emerging American community, and a greater sense of empathy for unfortunates seemed to characterize society. A final consequence of the awakening is the resultant long-lasting division of American Protestantism that redefined the duties of the preacher and the end of the listeners: conservatives endorsed a rational intellectual religion with special reliance on the written word, while Calvinist evangelicals preferred to have their "hearts touched" by the spoken word of an affecting religion. There can be little doubt that the preaching of George Whitefield in the Great Awakening made him one of the most important figures in the history of modern religion.

INFORMATION SOURCES

Research Collections and Collected Speeches

Every major university library has in its holdings the Early American Imprint series that contains a microprint copy of the complete text of all existent books, pamphlets, and broadsides printed in the United States from 1639 to the end of 1800. The titles are keyed to Charles Evans's *American Bibliography* and its supplements. Title cards, which accompany each item, correct the numerous errors in Evans's *Bibliography*. The entire collection is indexed by author and title. Thus, the large number of imprints written by or about Whitefield and the Great Awakening are readily available. Whitefield's preaching and other happenings of the Great Awakening were given intense coverage in newspapers, such as *American Weekly Mercury, Boston Evening Post, Boston Gazette, Boston Weekly News Letter, Boston Weekly Post Boy, New York Gazette, New York Weekly Journal, Pennsylvania Gazette, South Carolina Gazette*, and *Virginia Gazette*.

Many of Whitefield's sermons that were delivered during the Great Awakening were published individually and/or in collections. Below are representative citations.

Whitefield, George. *The Eternity of Hell Torments*. Boston, 1740.	EHT
———. *Five Sermons*. Philadelphia, 1740.	FS1
———. *Five Sermons*. Philadelphia, 1746.	FS2
———. *The Marks of the New Birth*. New York, 1739; Boston, 1740.	MNB
———. *The Marriage of Cana*. Philadelphia, 1742.	MC
———. *Nine Sermons*. Boston, 1743.	NS
———. *The Prodigal Son*. Boston, 1742.	PS

Selected Critical Studies

Davies, Horton. *Worship and Theology in England: From Watts and Wesley to Maurice, 1690–1850*. Princeton, N.J.: Princeton University Press, 1961.

Kenney, William H. "George Whitefield, Dissenter Priest of the Great Awakening, 1739–1741." *William and Mary Quarterly* 3d ser., 26 (1969): 75–93.

King, C. Harold. "George Whitefield: God's Commoner." *Quarterly Journal of Speech* 29 (1943): 32–36.

White, Eugene E. "Decline of the Great Awakening in New England: 1741 to 1746." *The New England Quarterly* 24 (1951): 35–52.

———. "George Whitefield and the Paper War in New England." *Quarterly Journal of Speech* 39 (1953): 61–68.

———. "The Protasis of the Great Awakening in New England." *Speech Monographs* 21 (1954): 10–20.

———. *Puritan Rhetoric: The Issue of Emotion in Religion.* Carbondale: Southern Illinois University Press, 1972.

Selected Biographies

The best way to follow Whitefield's life and career through the Great Awakening is to consult installments of his accounts and journals. His entire autobiographical narrative is contained in the following individual publications: *A Brief and General Account of the First Part of the Life of the Reverend Mr. George Whitefield, from His Birth, to His Entering into Holy Orders* (Boston, 1740); *A Further Account of God's Dealings with the Rev. Mr. George Whitefield from the Time of His Ordination to His Embarking for Georgia* (Philadelphia, 1746); *A Journal of a Voyage from London to Savannah in Georgia*, 5th ed. (London, 1739); *A Continuation of the Reverend Mr. Whitefield's Journal, from His Arrival at Savannah, to His Return to London*, 2d ed. (London, 1739); *A Continuation . . . During the Time He was Detained in England by the Embargo*, 3d ed. (London, 1739); *A Continuation . . . from His Embarking after the Embargo, to His Arrival at Savannah in Georgia* (London, 1740); *A Continuation . . . from a Few Days after His Return to Georgia to His Arrival at Falmouth, on the 11th of March, 1741* (London, 1741).

Dollimore, A. A. *George Whitefield.* London: Banner of Truth Trust, 1970.

Henry, Stuart C. *George Whitefield: Wayfaring Witness.* New York: Abingdon Press, 1957.

Tyerman, Luke. *The Life of the Rev. George Whitefield.* London: Hodder and Stoughton, 1876–1877, 2 vols.

CHRONOLOGY OF MAJOR SPEECHES

See "Research Collections and Collected Speeches" for source codes.

Whitefield delivered each of the following speeches several times during the Great Awakening. He also presented them elsewhere, in one form or another, both before and after his American tour.

"Abraham's Offering Up His Son Isaac," *NS*.

"Directions How to Hear Sermons," *FS1*.

"The Conversion of Zacchaeus," *NS*.

"The Eternity of Hell Torments," *EHT*.

"The Gospel Supper," *FS2*.

"The Lord Our Righteousness," *NS*.

"The Marks of the New Birth," *MNB*.

"The Marriage of Cana," *MC*.

"Persecution Every Christian's Lot," *NS*.

"The Prodigal Son," *PS*.

WILLIAM LOWNDES YANCEY
(1817–1863), lawyer, politician, diplomat, secessionist

——————————————————————————— HAL W. FULMER

The first half of the nineteenth century was dominated by the question of the Union's stability and future. One group of southerners, the fire-eaters, preached a doctrine of sectional separation for over forty years prior to Fort Sumter. Chief among this group was William Lowndes Yancey.

Yancey was born in Georgia but was reared in New York as the stepson of Nathan Beman, an abolitionist clergyman. He attended Williams College from 1831 to 1832. While at Williams, he was a leader of the literary society and in it defended Andrew Jackson's presidential campaign. As a result of these debates, he was asked to stump the region for Jackson and the Democratic party. He was briefly the editor of a unionist newspaper in South Carolina and was an anti-nullifier in the crisis of 1832. He studied law in Greenville, South Carolina, and settled in Alabama as a genteel planter in 1835. Four years later, his slaves accidently poisoned and his fortunes dissipated, he returned to the full-time practice of law. He won election to the Alabama Congress in 1841 and 1843, championing the need for public education and women's rights. He was elected to the U.S. House in 1844 and, despite reelection, resigned in 1846. He would hold no public office for sixteen years.

He offered the Alabama platform to the state convention in 1848. Introduced as a minority report, the platform was nonetheless carried, binding the delegates to the national Democratic meeting to support only proslavery candidates. He was the leading figure in the Montgomery Commercial Convention in 1858. Yancey was instrumental in the division of the national Democratic party in 1860, leading a walk-out by southern delegates after the rejection of the Alabama platform. He campaigned in the South and North for John Breckenridge in 1860 and took part in the Alabama secession convention following Lincoln's election. He served briefly and futilely as an ambassador to England, seeking diplomatic recognition for the Confederacy. He ended his public career with a term in the Confederate Senate from March 1862 until his death in July 1863.

WILLIAM YANCEY AS THE ORATOR OF SECESSION

In the truest sense of the word, William Yancey was a demagogue, a "voice of the people." Although he did not hold public office for almost two decades, he was one of the most important oratorical figures of the antebellum South. He was in demand throughout the region for a variety of occasions from political rallies to barbecues. His power was not in his voting record or patronage but in his oratory. He was the legacy of John Calhoun's complex constitutional theories, and his greatest achievement was popularizing Calhoun's tenets. He translated the abstract notions of state sovereignty, nullification, and secession into the public forum. His incessant calls for southern secession were the region's best response to the abolitionists' demands for immediate emancipation.

Yancey's rhetoric of the two decades before the Civil War was dominated by four aspects. First, he saw all issues as sectional ones between a minority South and majority North. Throughout his speeches ran a two-pronged rhetorical theme: attack the North and defend the South. Following his election to the U.S. House in 1844, Yancey wasted little time in establishing his presence as a champion of southern rights. In his maiden address on January 7, 1845, he argued in favor of annexing Texas. His major arguments in that speech formed the foundation of his rhetorical invention for the ensuing two decades. According to Yancey, the North had "forgotten their fathers" and had abandoned the principles of the American Revolution; slavery was essential to the South's survival; the founding fathers had been slave owners; a strict interpretation of the Constitution was required; the issue of honor was paramount; and political parties were to be viewed suspiciously. Included in his speech was a foreshadowing of his major rhetorical thrust as the orator of secession. Defending Texas's right to declare itself free of Mexico, Yancey said: "They had here learned that every nation had the right to dissolve the bands which bound them, when [those bands] became subversive of their liberty." In his Alabama platform of 1848, Yancey vowed "our unalterable determination, neither to recognize as Democrats or to hold fellowship or communion with those who attempt to denationalize the South and its institutions." On the stump against the Know-Nothing party in 1855, Yancey claimed the South and its institutions were at risk: "The institution of slavery . . . is essentially sectional . . . and now in the hour of its greatest peril, assailed by the great Northern antagonistic force, it must look to the South alone for protection." In his opening address to the delegates of the Montgomery Commercial Convention on May 10, 1858, Yancey suggested the South was a legislative minority and that the majority North had "fastened the shackles upon us, and will not loose them! But let us stand up and resist them like men." The overarching issue for Yancey was southern self-preservation, of which slavery was only a part. Yancey's speeches were frantic calls for the South to see the enemy as the North and to save itself by seceding from the Union.

Second, Yancey maintained a religious fervor for the Constitution. More than the Protestant Bible, the Constitution was Yancey's sacred text. Not unlike the fundamentalist religious groups of the antebellum South, Yancey called for a literal interpretation as the exegesis of his text. His primary supporting material throughout his speeches was the citation of various parts of the Constitution. As the evangelical called sinners to repent with "The Bible says . . . ," so Yancey challenged his southern audiences to save their region with "The Constitution states . . . " From his entry into the U.S. House to his final days in the Confederate Senate, Yancey built his rhetoric on a foundation of a strictly interpreted Constitution. In 1846, despite his early role as an antinullifier, he defended the group's actions, suggesting "they rallied in defense of the Constitution. Their's was, indeed, a noble object. . . . The people of that noble little state [South Carolina] were unanimously battling for sound constitutional principles." At the

Democratic national convention on April 27, 1860, Yancey defended his region by suggesting, "And thus planting ourselves firmly upon the Constitution . . . we ask [the North] to read that compact and see whether we do not rightly interpret our rights and obligations." Following the convention's rejection of the southern proposals, Yancey withdrew and led most of the southern delegates away with him. The convention split into the National Democrats of Stephen Douglas and the Constitutional Democrats of Yancey and Breckenridge. In Baltimore a month after the split, Yancey followed the nomination of Breckenridge with a disclaimer that their group were disunionists. The issue, he contended, was not the Union but the protection of and duty toward the Constitution. Foreshadowing the coming conflict, Yancey appealed to those "Lovers of Truth, Justice, and the Constitution," advising the benefits of martyrdom for such a duty: "Whosoever bears that banner in the field, although borne down, will find a consecrated grave." Such a use of the Constitution aided Yancey in his efforts to attack the North and defend the South: those who maintained a strict interpretation of the Constitution were friends of the South, and those who did not make such an interpretation were its enemies.

Third, Yancey maintained a consistency of theme regardless of the occasion. Congressional debates, campaign speeches, or ceremonial addresses were all agencies for Yancey to spread his gospel of secession. For Yancey, the South was at peril because the North no longer honored the Constitution as a covenant among the states. The South's only hope, according to Yancey, was to preserve itself by withdrawing from the Union. Six years before Fort Sumter, Yancey suggested a fitting response to northern aggression. The government "will then have become centralized and no longer subserves the end for which it was created, withdraw from it!" To accomplish such a task, Yancey warned his listeners to avoid party factionalism and "rely upon one party, and that must be the men of the South for the sake of the South." Yancey used the occasion of an address to the Mount Vernon Association on February 23, 1858, to promote the southern cause and educate the audience in their constitutional right of secession. Despite the ceremonial nature of the occasion honoring George Washington's birthday, the speaker charged the North with unwarranted aggressions against his region. He challenged his listeners to "pledge to each other your lives, fortunes, and sacred honor in imitation of [Washington's] illustrious example. 'If this be treason, make the most of it!' [Loud and continued applause]." At the Commercial Convention in Montgomery, May 10, 1858, he ended his address to the delegates by calling for another American Revolution and asking his audience: "Are you ready, countrymen? is your courage up to the highest point? . . . If you are, I am with you; if you are not, I am not with you." The night after Lincoln's election in November 1860, Yancey openly called for his state to leave the Union, wrongly assuring his listeners that the South would be allowed to leave in peace. He urged his audience to follow his defiant stand, again calling for martyrs to the southern cause: "I would in the cause of my state, gather around me some brave spirits, who however few in number, would find a grave, which my countrymen—the world and all future ages should recognize as a modern Thermopylae!''

Finally, the fourth aspect of Yancey's oratory was that it constituted a rhetoric of unbending defiance. He was unwilling to compromise any of his views on the relationship between South and North; his speeches clearly reveal the sharp line of demarcation he drew between the two regions. He rhetorically pushed the South toward sectionalism and isolation. Despite his occasional disclaimers about not being a disunionist, Yancey never retreated from his rhetorical position, advocating secession in his twenty years of public life. Again, with almost religious zeal, he rejected compromise as tantamount to a loss of salvation. For Yancey, compromising the Constitution through liberal interpretations meant the destruction of the South, and compromising his personal advocacy on behalf of the South meant loss of honor and dereliction of duty. For Yancey, *compromise* was the ultimate devil term. To the delegates at the national convention at Charleston in 1860, he drew a sharp distinction between South and North, claiming: ''Ours is the property invaded, ours are the institutions which are at stake; ours is the peace that is to be destroyed.'' At this same convention, with clear and abrupt language, Yancey defied the North to disturb the South or slavery: ''It does not belong to you to interfere with our institutions. You must not touch them. You are aggressors if you do.'' With vivid imagery, Yancey suggested that the South would not be moved on the issue: ''Let the thunders roll and the lightening, and paint out the dark cloud to your countrymen [the North], and let them know there is earnestness and meaning in the Southern words.''

This unwillingness to compromise the Constitution or his beliefs and his singleness of purpose to preserve the South characterized Yancey the fire-eater. Many scholars have debated what constituted the essence of these southerners, of whom Yancey was most prominent. Their repeated calls for secession and self-preservation certainly set them apart from other contemporary groups wrestling with the questions of Union. Their style could be dramatic. Yancey thundered to the northern factions at the 1860 convention, ''We hold that Constitution up against your orgies of passion.'' However, their rhetorical stance, more than their style or even their invention, suggests the defining characteristic of a fire-eater. Yancey and the others would not be moved on the need for secession. The fire-eaters assumed such a stance years before the election of Lincoln and the secession conventions, and they would not compromise their position. Across time, location, and occasion, Yancey returned to his themes of an aggressive North, a minority South, and secession for self-preservation.

Another aspect of Yancey's oratory deserves comment. Not willing to issue his challenges from the confines of the South, he embarked on a speaking tour of the major northern cities in the fall of 1860. Labeled the ''Prince of the Fire-Eaters'' by the northern press, Yancey nevertheless stumped for Breckenridge in New York, Albany, Cincinnati, Boston, and Washington, D.C. The tour was remarkable for several reasons. Yancey had attacked the North for years but from afar; now he was actually entering the enemy's territory with his oratory. The speeches, however, were given to large audiences and often to cheers and applause. The tour also revealed Yancey's unwillingness to compromise his stand even when facing potentially hostile audiences. In a speech at Cooper Institute on October 10, 1860, just nine months after Lincoln's famous address there, he pleaded for a hearing from the northern audience: "I trust, fellow citizens, that an Alabamian may yet speak to the citizens of New York in the language of fellowship." On the explosive issue of slavery, he suggested that the institution was vital to the South's economy and that the founding fathers had been slave owners. He used humor in an effort to conciliate his listeners: "Our forefathers were not only slave-owners but imported slaves from Africa. Virginia wished to suppress that trade, but Massachusetts and other states wished it to be carried on [Laughter]." In Albany, he declared himself a strict constitutionalist and challenged Republican editor Thurlow Weed on the issue: "I recommend Thurlow Weed . . . to kiss this book [the Constitution] [laughter], and if he does, he will have more of the Constitution on his lips than he has ever had before [laughter and applause]." Yancey alleged that Weed's historical knowledge was extremely weak: "Thurlow Weed only made a mistake of *thirty years* [laughter]. . . . But this is a fast age. We have the telegraph and railroads now, and truth travels faster than it used to." This mixture of bulldog defiance and humor was obviously well received.

In addition to humor, Yancey used strong ethical appeals throughout his northern tour. He presented himself to the crowd in Washington in this way: "I am no party man, and I do not address you as a party man to-night. I come before you this evening as the friend of the Constitution and the Union under the Constitution." Moments later, he attempted to shed the popular perception of his disloyalty: "I tell you, gentlemen, my disunionism consists in this: I stand by the Constitution." He urged reconciliation between the sections in an effort to restrain "that unworthy part of our natures which would make us grapple with each other." Such moderation on Yancey's part was intermixed with his familiar themes of constitutional rights, southern self-preservation, and northern aggression. "All that we of the South have ever asked of the government," he told one audience, "is to keep its hands off of us and let the Constitution work its own way! [applause]." Yancey even broached the issue of secession with his northern listeners: "The Constitution itself reserved certain rights to the states . . . that when the Government was oppressive they should have the right to form new governments. . . . [The South] must and she would have a recognizable equality in the Union, else she would take it out of it [renewed applause]." This mixture of humor, reconciliation, and defiance in the northern tour was an unstable rhetoric at best, suggesting Yancey's tedious effort at identifying with his audience and remaining true to the positions he had held for two decades.

Yancey's efforts on behalf of Breckenridge were to no avail. Only five months after his northern tour, he was in Montgomery to welcome the provisional government of the Confederate States of America. The high point of Yancey's secessionist zeal was realized when he introduced Jefferson Davis, provisional president, to the crowd in Montgomery. Just prior to Davis's inauguration, Yancey claimed for himself and his region that "the man and the hour have met." Ironically Yancey's hour was past. Feared as a radical, he was not invited to take part in the new Confederate government. Disagreements with Davis led the president to send Yancey abroad as an envoy to England, seeking diplomatic recognition for the new nation. Yancey's was the voice of the stump and the convention, not the diplomat. His mission a failure, he returned home and was elected to the Confederate Senate in 1862. He spent the last eighteen months of his life battling against the need for Confederate conscription and the justification for a Confederate Supreme Court. Both issues, he declared in a familiar theme, were unconstitutional.

In conclusion, what might be offered as an evaluation of Yancey the orator? The majority of the South did not heed his calls for secession until his life was almost over. He was, however, an immensely popular figure throughout the region in great demand as an orator. He was invited to speak at a variety of key events over a twenty-year period. Despite not holding public office, he dominated state, regional, and national gatherings chiefly through his reputation and his abilities as a speaker. Transcripts of his speeches reflect repeated interruptions of applause and laughter. In his own time, secession was not unthinkable, and the American Revolution, not quite eighty years past, offered at least some justification for the idea. What Yancey seemingly wanted was to actuate the theory of secession as found in historical precedent and the Constitution; he wanted to put the theory to a test. He believed that secession could occur peacefully. By 1860, he was not alone in such beliefs. Ethically he was committed to his own people, and he placed his region above party and nation. His consistency of theme suggests a concern for his region that Yancey could not put away. Ultimately he was a tragic figure, who finally rallied the South to secession and then was rejected by his region as too radical for the newborn Confederacy. As an uncompromising fire-eater, he helped lead his region out of the Union. In accomplishing this task, he appealed as much to history, the Constitution, and his own character as to sheer emotionalism.

As many commentators suggest, had the South been successful, Yancey's radicalness, like that of Patrick Henry, would have been overlooked or softened through the ensuing historical scholarship. The South's failure, however, left him with the epithet: the Orator of Secession.

INFORMATION SOURCES

Research Collections and Collected Speeches

The William Lowndes Yancey papers are in the Alabama Department of Archives and History, Montgomery. This collection includes drafts of speeches, pamphlets, scrapbook collections of newspaper clippings, and letters, which cover most of Yancey's career. The archives also contains a large holding of Alabama newspapers from the Yancey period, which include accounts of and commentaries on many of his speeches. The papers of John W. DuBose, Yancey's only biographer, are also in the archives at Montgomery.

John W. DuBose. *The Life and Times of William Lowndes Yancey.* New   *WLY*
York: Peter Smith, 1942.

Library of Southern Literature. Edited by E. A. Alderman and J. C. Harris.   *LSL*
Atlanta: Martin and Hoyt, 1908–13.

The South in the Building of the Nation. Vol. 9. Edited by Thomas E.   *SBN*
Watson. Richmond: Southern Historical Publication Society, 1909.

Southern Historical Society Papers. Vol. 46. Richmond: William Byrd,   *SHSP*
1928–1930.

Selected Critical Studies

Brown, William G. "The Orator of Secession." In *The Lower South in American History*. New York: Macmillan, 1902.

Eaton, Clement. "The Voice of Emotion." In *The Mind of the Old South*. Rev. ed. Baton Rouge: Louisiana State University Press, 1967.

Hayes, Merwyn A. "William L. Yancey Presents the Southern Case to the North: 1860." *Southern Speech Journal* 29 (Spring 1964): 194–208.

Huddleston, Bill M., and Sidney R. Hill, Jr. "William L. Yancey: A Patriotic Anomaly." *Pennsylvania Speech Communication Annual* 40 (1984): 21–26.

Mitchell, Rexford S. "William L. Yancey." In *A History and Criticism of American Public Address*. Vol. 2. Edited by William N. Brigance. New York: McGraw-Hill, 1943.

Oliver, Robert T. "William L. Yancey: Apostle of Disunion." In *History of Public Speaking in America*. Boston: Allyn and Bacon, 1965.

Perritt, H. Hardy. "The Fire-Eaters." In *Oratory in the Old South*. Edited by Waldo W. Braden. Baton Rouge: Louisiana State University Press, 1970.

Selected Biographies

DuBose, John W. *The Life and Times of William Lowndes Yancey*. New York: Peter Smith, 1942.

CHRONOLOGY OF MAJOR SPEECHES

See "Research Collections and Collected Speeches" for source codes.

"Annexation of Texas," maiden address, U.S. House of Representatives, Washington, D.C., January 7, 1845; *Congressional Globe* 14 (1845): 100–2.

"Alabama Platform," resolutions and address to the Alabama state convention, Montgomery, Alabama, January 3, 1848; *WLY*, pp. 212–14; *SBN*, pp. 339–41.

"Stump Speech against the Know-Nothing Party," Columbus, Georgia, 1855; *WLY*, pp. 297–310.

"Washington's True Legacies," address to the Mount Vernon Association, Mount Vernon, Virginia, February 23, 1858; *LSL*, pp. 6027–33.

"Opening Address and Debate over African Slave-Trade," Montgomery Commercial Convention, Montgomery, Alabama, May 10, 1858; *DeBow's Review* 24 (June 1858): 583–601.

Address to the National Democratic Convention, Charleston, South Carolina, April 27, 1860; *Charleston Daily Courier*, April 30, 1860.

Address to the Constitutional Democratic Convention, Baltimore, Maryland, June 23, 1860; *WLY*, pp. 480–84.

"Equal Rights in a Common Government," Washington, D.C., September 21, 1860; *LSL*, pp. 6033–39.

Address at Cooper Institute, New York, October 10, 1860; *New York Times*, October 11, 1860.

Address to the people of Montgomery, Alabama, November 10, 1860; *WLY*, pp. 539–40.

"The Exemption Bill" (debate on conscription), Confederate Senate, Richmond, Virginia, September 10, 1862; *SHSP*, pp. 89–91.

BASIC RESEARCH SOURCES IN AMERICAN PUBLIC ADDRESS _____

The Information Sources, which conclude each essay in this book, list the pertinent books and articles about the speaker and where texts of the speaker's most important speeches may be found. As one begins the study of the history and criticism of American public address, however, it is also helpful to know something about the standard works in the field, where to begin research on orators, and where in general to find texts of their speeches.

A milestone in the scholarly study of public address is *A History and Criticism of American Public Address*, published in three volumes. William Norwood Brigance edited the first two volumes (1943) and Marie Hochmuth (Nichols) edited the third (1955). The complete work stands as a monument to American oratorical criticism and remains one of the standard sources for the criticism of America's leading political orators. These volumes are often cited in the Information Sources for orators discussed in this book. Although *A History and Criticism* contained critical essays on orators, it did not offer any speech texts. That void was filled with the appearance of two books that collected important speeches.

Wayland Maxfield Parrish and Marie Hochmuth (Nichols) published a collection of speeches, *American Speeches*, in 1954. This book was an archetype for future collections of speeches because it prefaced the text with biographical information, the occasion of the oration, and information about the nature of the original source of the speech text. Hochmuth's essay on Lincoln's First Inaugural is a classic in the field of rhetorical criticism, and Parrish's "The Study of Speeches" informed much of the rhetorical criticism published for a decade. The other important collection of speech texts is A. Craig Baird's *American Public Addresses, 1740–1952* (1956). Like Parrish and Hochmuth, Baird added a seminal ingredient, his chapter, "The Study of Speeches," in which he answered the important questions of why one should study political oratory and how one should study speeches.

Succeeding books on the criticism of American oratory seemed to follow these early examples. Several successive works served the needs of students and critics by supplying collections of significant public addresses. Ernest J. Wrage and Barnet Baskerville edited *American Forum: Speeches on Historic Issues, 1788–1900* (1960). They expanded the kinds of speech texts offered by including less significant but nevertheless important figures in American politics and culture. Lesser-known figures such as Lyman Beecher,

Henry George, and Thaddeus Stevens assumed their rightful places alongside the Lincolns and Websters of the period. *Selected American Speeches in Basic Issues (1850–1950)* (1960), edited by Carl G. Brandt and Edward Shafter, Jr., contains some useful texts for important nineteenth-century speakers.

Slavery and the Civil War generated, and was generated by, much rhetorical discourse, and two books are especially helpful to students of that era. *The Anti-Slavery Argument* (1965), edited by William H. Pease and Jane H. Pease, presents a number of speeches, often in a pro and con format, by important orators and by lesser-known ones, such as James G. Birney, Amos Phelps, and Gerrit Smith. For a wider treatment of the period, students may consult *Democracy on Trial: 1845–1877* (1966), edited by Robert W. Johannsen, which contains speeches delivered by the standard figures of the era, such as Lincoln's last public speech, as well as speeches by such orators as Thaddeus Stevens against presidential reconstruction and Clement Vallandigham against Lincoln's policy in the Civil War.

For the study of female oratory, one may advantageously turn to Judith Anderson's *Outspoken Women: Speeches by American Women Reformers 1635–1935* (1984). Anderson has included hard-to-find texts of speeches by women orators and has oriented critics of feminist rhetoric with a fine historical overview of the role and successes of American women on the political platform. *The World's Great Speeches*, edited by Lewis Copeland and Lawrence Lamm, contains the texts of many lesser-known speakers in addition to the standard ones on a wide range of interests and topics, from legislative to courtroom to after-dinner speaking.

Robert T. Oliver wrote *History of Public Speaking in America* (1965) as a comprehensive study of speech making in the United States through the end of the nineteenth century. To date, it stands alone as an excellent storehouse of historical information, rhetorical criticism, and bibliographical sources. On a more specialized level, *Oratory in the Old South*, edited by Waldo W. Braden, commends itself to students of southern rhetoric before the Civil War. The book contains essays on topics such as the fire-eaters, southern moderates, and southern unionists. J. Jeffery Auer assembled twenty-three essays from leading scholars of the era in *Antislavery and Disunion, 1858–1861* (1963). Among the noteworthy contributions are Robert Oliver's essay on William Seward's "Irrepressible Conflict" speech, Kenneth Stampp's piece on the Republican National Convention of 1860, and Marie Nichols's criticism of Lincoln's first Inaugural Address. On the subject of the Lincoln-Douglas debates, one can consult Saul Sigelschiffer's *The American Conscience: The Drama of the Lincoln-Douglas Debates* (1973), which contains texts of the seven debates as well as critical commentary.

Researchers of religious rhetoric should examine DeWitte Holland's edited volumes, *Preaching in America* (1971) and *Sermons in American History* (1969). *Preaching* is an excellent source for essays that place in perspective the theological issues of the times and the responses of various orators-preachers to religious and political concerns. *Sermons* contains, along with brief biographical materials, important historical sermons on a wide variety of topics by America's leading preachers. Holland serves readers and critics well by including pro and con sermons on important religious issues.

Students interested in the rhetoric of the American revolution will want to investigate a series of bicentennial monographs published by the Speech Communication Association. Barbara Larson's *Prologue to Revolution: The War Sermons of the Reverend Samuel Davies* (1978), Kurt W. Ritter and James R. Andrews's *The American Ideology: Reflections of the Revolution in American Rhetoric* (1978), and Ronald Reid's *The American*

Revolution and the Rhetoric of History (1978) provide stimulating and insightful analyses of the rhetoric that helped give birth to a nation.

General readers may find Karl Wallace's *A History of Speech Education in America* (1954) a helpful overview of the educational and cultural heritage in which the study of oratory has flourished in American colleges and universities.

The study and criticism of American political oratory is ongoing, and the productive results of scholarly research are published in a variety of scholarly journals. *Presidential Studies Quarterly*, under the auspices of the Center for the Study of the Presidency, increasingly devotes space for critical essays on all aspects of presidential rhetoric. Book reviews on topics of rhetorical transactions are also included. The Speech Communication Association publishes several significant journals that regularly treat American political oratory: *Quarterly Journal of Speech, Communication Monographs*, and *Critical Studies in Mass Communication*. Regional speech associations routinely publish articles on political oratory: *Southern Speech Communication Journal, Western Journal of Speech Communication, Central States Speech Journal*, and *Communication Quarterly*. All of the speech journals are indexed in *Index to Journals in Communication Studies through 1979* (1980) compiled by Ronald J. Matlon. The Matlon index is a good beginning point for research on American public address. Articles contained in the speech journals are also listed in the bibliography published annually in *Communication Monographs*.

CHECKLIST OF BASIC RESEARCH SOURCES IN AMERICAN PUBLIC ADDRESS

Collections of Speech Texts

American Forum: Speeches on Historic Issues, 1788–1900. Edited by Ernest J. Wrage and Barnet Baskerville. New York: Harper, 1960.
American Public Address: 1740–1952. Edited by A. Craig Baird. New York: McGraw-Hill, 1956.
Amercian Speeches. Edited by Wayland Maxfield Parrish and Marie Hochmuth. New York: Longmans, Green, 1954.
Outspoken Women: Speeches by American Women Orators, 1635–1935. Edited by Judith Anderson. Dubuque: Kendall/Hunt, 1984.
Selected American Speeches on Basic Issues (1850–1950). Edited by Carl G. Brandt and Edward M. Shafter, Jr. Boston: Houghton Mifflin, 1960.
Sermons in American History. Edited by Dewitte Holland. Nashville, Tenn.: Abingdon Press, 1971.
The World's Great Speeches. Edited by Lewis Copeland and Lawrence Lamm. 3d enl. ed. New York: Dover, 1973.

Collections of Speeches and Critical Essays

The Antislavery Argument. Edited by William H. Pease and Jane H. Pease. Indianapolis: Bobbs-Merrill, 1965.
Democracy on Trial. Edited by Robert W. Johannsen. New York: McGraw-Hill, 1966.
Sigelschiffer, Saul. *The American Conscience: The Drama of the Lincoln-Douglas Debates*. New York: Horizon Press, 1973.

Collections of Critical Essays

Antislavery and Disunion, 1858–1861. Edited by J. Jeffery Auer. New York: Harper & Row, 1963.

Preaching in American History. Edited by DeWitte Holland. Nashville, Tenn.: Abingdon Press, 1969.

Larson, Barbara A. *Prologue to Revolution: The War Sermons of the Reverend Samuel Davies*. Annandale, Va.: Speech Communication Association, 1978.

Oratory in the Old South 1828–1860. Edited by Waldo W. Braden. Baton Rouge: Louisiana State University Press, 1970.

Reid, Ronald F. *The American Revolution and the Rhetoric of History*. Annandale, Va.: Speech Communication Association, 1978.

Ritter, Kurt W., and James R. Andrews. *The American Ideology: Reflections of the Revolution in American Rhetoric*. Annandale, Va.: Speech Communication Association, 1978.

General Sources, Index

A History and Criticism of American Public Address. 2 Vols. Edited by William Norwood Brigance. New York: McGraw Hill, 1943.

A History and Criticism of American Public Address. Vol. 3. Edited by Marie Hochmuth. New York: Longmans, Green, 1955.

A History of Speech Education in America. Edited by Karl R. Wallace. New York: Appleton-Century-Crofts, 1954.

Index to Journals in Communication Studies through 1979. Compiled by Ronald J. Matlon. Annandale, Va.: Speech Communication Association, 1980.

Oliver, Robert T. *History of Public Speaking in America*. Boston: Allyn and Bacon, 1965.

Journals

Central States Speech Communication Journal.
Communication Monographs.
Communication Quarterly.
Presidential Studies Quarterly.
Quarterly Journal of Speech.
Southern Speech Communication Journal.
Western Journal of Speech Communication.

GLOSSARY OF RHETORICAL TERMS

actio   the art of delivering the speech with effective voice, gestures, eye contact, and so on.

ad hominem argument   "to the man or person"; an appeal to prejudices or character assassination rather than to reason or intellect.

ad libitum   "as one desires or wishes"; to insert or delete words from a prepared speech text; slang is ad-libbed.

affirmation by denial   a rhetorical technique wherein the orator affirms a point by ostensibly denying it, as in, "I have not allowed myself, Sir, to look beyond the Union, to see what might lie hidden in the dark recess behind" (Daniel Webster, reply to Hayne).

after-dinner speech   a humorous speech, usually with a serious thought ensconced within it, delivered after a festive or ceremonial dinner.

analogy   a form of argument in which it is advanced that if two things agree with one another in some respects, then they will probably agree in other respects as well.

anaphora   parallelism, the beginning of successive phrases or sentences with the same words or words, as in "we can not dedicate—we can not consecrate—we can not hallow this ground" (Abraham Lincoln's Gettysburg Address).

anecdote   a brief, interesting, and often amusing story or event used for humorous effect in a speech or for support of some persuasive point.

antithesis   an opposition of ideas emphasized by the positions of the contrasting words, as in, "Nothing can be nobler than a nation governed by conscience, nothing more infamous than power without pity, wealth without honor and without the sense of justice" (Robert Ingersoll, Decoration Day address).

argument from authority   occurs when a speaker offers evidence from accepted experts to substantiate a point.

argument from definition   occurs when a speaker employs legal or moral meanings to formulate an appeal, as in, "Plainly, the central idea of secession is the essence of anarchy" (Abraham Lincoln, First Inaugural Address).

audience   the person(s) assembled to hear a speech; can also denote the reading person(s).

audience adaptation   how the speaker adjusts the style of word choice, the kind of
gestures, the nature of the reasoning and analysis, the impact of emotional appeals, and
so on in order to meet the needs of a given audience or for different audiences.

auditor   the person(s) who hears a speech; synonymous with *audience*.

ceremonial speeches   addresses, often in an elevated style, delivered on formal occasions such as inaugurals, eulogies, dedications, and commencements. See *epideictic
oratory*.

chiasmus   the inversion of parallel phrases or words.

Ciceronian speech pattern   an organizational pattern for the development and arrangement of a speech, discussed in Cicero's *De Inventione*; consisted of an *exordium* or
introduction; a *narratio* or narration of the events under consideration; the *partitio* or
division of the main points in the speech; the *confirmatio* or arguments that support the
orator's thesis; the *refutatio* or refutation that addressed arguments from the opposition;
and the *epilogus* or conclusion that summarized the points of the speech.

classical canons of rhetoric   codified by Cicero in *De Inventione*; consisted of *inventio*
or invention, the art of discovering arguments to persuade an audience; *dispositio* or
disposition, the art of arranging and organizing the arguments in the speech (see *Ciceronian speech pattern*); *elocutio* or style, the art of selecting language effectively; *pronuntiatio* or *actio* or delivery, the art of delivering the speech with an effective voice,
gestures, and so on; and *memoria* or memory, the art of recalling or remembering the
speech at the time of its delivery.

deduction   a reasoning from known or accepted principles or premises to a specific
conclusion. See *induction*.

deliberative oratory   delineated in Aristotle's *Rhetoric*; consisted of political speaking
in legislative bodies, toward action or nonaction in the future, aimed at expediency. See
epideictic oratory; forensic oratory.

discourse   denotes formalized speech making, the words of the speech, the complete
speech as delivered.

disjunctive syllogism   See *method of residues; syllogism*.

dispositio   the ancient art of arranging the speech for maximum persuasive appeal.
See *Ciceronian speech pattern; classical canons of rhetoric*.

elocutio   the ancient art of selecting the right words for the speech. See *Ciceronian
speech pattern; classical canons of rhetoric*.

emotional appeal   a rhetorical or persuasive argument that stirs the audience's emotions—love, hate, anger, fear—as in, "We profess to have no taste for running and
catching niggers—at least, I profess no taste for that job at all" (Abraham Lincoln, joint
debate at Alton, Illinois, with Stephen Douglas).

enthymeme   a rhetorical argument; occurs when the speaker bases an argument on
generally held beliefs without expressing the premises, as in "War and dissolution of
the Union are identical and inseparable" (Henry Clay, Compromise of 1850 speech).

epideictic oratory   expounded in Aristotle's *Rhetoric*; consisted of ceremonial speaking before the people, toward establishing honor and virtue through praise or blame,
while focusing on the present. See *deliberative oratory; forensic oratory*.

epistrophe   the ending of successive clauses, phrases, or sentences by the same word or words, as in, "that government of the people, by the people, for the people, shall not perish from the earth" (Abraham Lincoln, Gettysburg Address).

ethos   one of the three rhetorical appeals adduced in Aristotle's *Rhetoric*: the speaker's character or goodwill, good sense, and good moral character are judged by the audience in terms of the audience's foreknowledge of the speaker's credibility and how the speaker utters the address. See *logos; pathos.*

eulogy   an instance of epideictic oratory; a speech of tribute in which the orator praises in elevated language the decedent's past life as an exemplar for the living. See *epideictic oratory.*

exordium   the introduction of a speech in which the speaker tries to make the audience receptive to the speaker and to the cause. See *Ciceronian speech pattern.*

extemporize   to deliver a speech with little preparation or notice; also to speak without memorizing the address; *extempore remarks* usually denotes a speech drawn from the immediate time and occasion; *extemporaneous speaker* usually indicates a speaker, who with little or no prior preparation, delivers a speech. See *impromptu speaking.*

forensic oratory   expounded in Aristotle's *Rhetoric*; consisted of legal courtroom oratory, toward establishing justice, with regard to the past. See *deliberative oratory; epideictic oratory.*

genre   a kind of oratory or speech in which similarities and differences distinguish certain speeches from others; for example, within the genre of epideictic oratory are eulogies, inaugurals, and commencements.

imagery   descriptions and figures of speech, as in, "Cast down your bucket where you are" (Booker T. Washington, Atlanta Exposition address).

impromptu speaking   occurs when a speaker delivers an address with no preparation or deliberation. See *extemporize.*

induction   reasoning from particular examples to a general conclusion. See *deduction.*

irony   a rhetorical method by which words are used in an opposite sense to their intended meanings or in a manner not expected or usually appropriate, as in, "Faith that can be unsettled by the access of light and knowledge had better be unsettled" (Henry Ward Beecher, "The Two Revelations").

jeremiad   a kind of speech, with religious overtones, that condemns a social evil as a crisis and proposes a solution by returning to traditional values held by the audience as a chosen people.

logical appeal   a rhetorical argument based on statistics, testimony, facts, and so on that appear rational and reasonable to the audience as proof for the speaker's claims. See *emotional appeal.*

logos   described in Aristotle's *Rhetoric*; the persuasive arguments and materials presented by the speaker in the speech to prove a truth or an apparent truth. See *ethos; pathos.*

maxim   a statement of a general truth or rule of conduct, used rhetorically to display the speaker's possession of good judgment and character.

memoria   the art of recalling and remembering the speech at the time of delivery. See *classical canons of rhetoric.*

metaphor   a figure of speech implying comparison by a word or phrase of one meaning applied to another, as in, "What does he do—this hero in gray with a heart of gold?" (Henry Grady, "The New South").

method of residues   a rhetorical application of the disjunctive syllogism (either A, B, or C; not A, not B; therefore, C) in which the speaker systematically eliminates alternatives until the audience is logically left with only the speaker's alternative (Patrick Henry used this method in "Give Me Liberty or Give Me Death").

oral outlining   a rhetorical technique in which the speaker indicates the structure and organization of the speech.

orator   denotes from times past a practiced, accomplished, and eloquent speaker; synonymous with *speaker*.

parallelism   See *anaphora*.

pathos   one of the three rhetorical appeals postulated in Aristotle's *Rhetoric*; a persuasive means by which the orator stirs the emotions of the audience in order to persuade them, appeals to the heart. See *ethos; pathos*.

peroration   the conclusion of a speech; usually connotes one of high artistry or exceptional elegance and force.

persona   the rhetorical role and language assumed by the speaker for a persuasive purpose, as in abolitionist, secessionist, fire-eater, unionist, and so on.

pitch   the musical-like tone or note level at which an orator speaks, usually varied within a range for vocal emphasis and variety.

pronuntiatio   the pronunciation and delivery of the speech. See *classical canons of rhetoric*.

proof, artistic and inartistic   from Aristotle's *Rhetoric*; artistic proofs or appeals were generated by a knowledge and application of the art, such as how to make oneself appear credible to the audience; inartistic proofs—contracts, wills, evidence, and so on—existed before the speech and were used by the speaker as proof for an argument.

rate   refers to the words-per-minute (wpm) in a spoken discourse; an average rate is around 125–175 wpm.

reductio ad absurdam   a rhetorical argument in which the orator takes a premise, usually an opponent's, and extends the premise to an absurd conclusion, thus negating the premise, as in, "It should not be denominated a Constitution. It should be called, rather, a collection of topics for everlasting controversy; heads of debate for a disputatious people" (Daniel Webster's reply to Hayne).

rhetor   from the Greek, meaning "to speak"; denotes one who is knowledgeable in the art of persuasion and skilled in the practice of speaking persuasively; synonymous with *speaker* and *orator*.

rhetorical genre   the different kinds of speeches—forensic, deliberative, and epideictic. See *genre*.

rhetorical question   a question asked for persuasive effect; ordinarily the speaker phrases the question to elicit the desired response from the audience; occasionally the audience may respond vocally, but usually the audience members mentally supply the answer to themselves, as in, "Are we disposed to be of the number of those who, having eyes, see not, and having ears, hear not, the things which so nearly concern their temporal salvation?" (Patrick Henry, "Give Me Liberty or Give Me Death").

satire   a rhetorical use of ridicule and sarcasm to attack persons or objects, as in, "Men pretending to be ministers of God, with all manner of grimace and shallow ridicule and witless criticism and unproductive wisdom, enact the very feats of the monkey in the attempt to prove that the monkey was not their ancestor" (Henry Ward Beecher, "The Two Revelations").

speech writer   a person who writes, usually for hire, speeches or who extensively helps the employer to compose addresses.

syllogism   in rhetoric, the arguing from the general to the specific; for example, "All rhetors are successful speakers; X is a rhetor; therefore, X is a successful speaker." See *enthymeme*; and *method of residues*.

volume   the loudness level at which an orator speaks, usually varied for emphasizing points and stressing ideas.

vox populi   Latin for "voice of the people"; in rhetoric, denotes an orator who speaks on behalf of the people.

SUBJECT INDEX _____

Page numbers of actual entries appear in **boldface**.

Abolitionist rhetoric: Adams, John Quincy, 7–13; Channing, William Ellery, 79–86; Douglass, Frederick, 139–45; Garrison, William Lloyd, 183–89; Giddings, Joshua Reed, 190–96; Lincoln, Abraham, 259–70; Phillips, Wendell, 316–24; Sumner, Charles, 364–70; Truth, Sojourner, 385–90

Adams, Abigail, 31

Adams, Charles Frances, 166

Adams, John, **1–6**; Franklin, Benjamin, 180; Jefferson, Thomas, 4; Otis, James, 301, 304–05; presidential speeches, 2–3; views on oratory, 2–3

Adams, John Quincy, **7–13**; abolitionist rhetoric, 9–10; *Amistad* case, 11; Benton, Thomas Hart, 51; Boylston Professor of Rhetoric, 7; epideictic oratory, 8; gag rule, 10; Giddings, Joshua, 190; Jackson, Andrew, 243; *Lectures on Rhetoric and Oratory*, 7; presidential addresses, 8–9; Webster, Daniel, 420

Adams, Samuel, **14–21**; Committees of Correspondence, 15; mediocre speaker, 15; rhetorical strategies, 18–19; sarcasm, 18; taxation without representation, 15–17; use of Edmund Burke, 20

Addresses, *See Speaker and Speech Index*

American Anti-Slavery Society, 342, 359

American system, 213

American Whig Society, 278

American Woman Suffrage Association, 359

Ames, Fisher, **22–27**; Calvinism, Toryism, and Federalism, 22–23; compared to British orators, 25; delivery, 24; epideictic oratory, 25–26; Essex Junta, 23; irony and sarcasm, 24

Amistad case, 11

Anthony, Susan B., **28–34**; compared to other suffragists, 32; delivery, 32; feminist organizations, 28; friendship with Elizabeth Cady Stanton, 29; interruption of Centennial celebration, 31; lecture circuits, 29; logical argumentation, 30–31; Stanton, Elizabeth Cady, 341; wit, 32

Armstrong, Samuel C., 399

Atlanta Constitution, 197

Augusta Exposition, 198

Austin, James T., 318

Beecher, Henry Ward, **35–46**; ad libitum remarks, 41, 43; Corwin, Tom, compared to, 102; Darwinism, 41; delivery, 42–43; Ingersoll, Robert G., 229–30; lectures, 36; Lowell, James Russell, compared to, 274; Plymouth Church, 36; speech preparation, 40–41; Stone, Lucy, 359; Talmage, De Witt, compared to, 371; theology vs. religion, 41; Mrs. Tilton, 43–44

SPEAKER AND SPEECH INDEX

CONTRIBUTORS _____

J. JEFFERY AUER is professor emeritus of speech communication at Indiana University, Bloomington. He has taught courses in the history of American public address and, especially, in contemporary political communication and presidential rhetoric. Among his books are *Antislavery and Disunion: Studies in the Rhetoric of Compromise and Conflict, 1858–1861* and *The Rhetoric of Our Times*.

WILLIAM L. BENOIT is assistant professor of speech and dramatic art at the University of Missouri, Columbia. He teaches courses in rhetorical theory and criticism, argumentation, and persuasion. He has published on Nixon's Watergate rhetoric and judicial rhetoric.

HAL W. BOCHIN is professor of speech communication at California State University at Fresno. He teaches courses in rhetorical criticism and the history of American public address. He has studied Joshua Giddings's leadership of the antiwar movement in the House (1846–1848) and has described Giddings's relationship with the antiwar protesters Thomas Corwin and Caleb Smith in articles for *Ohio History* and the *Indiana Magazine of History*.

WALDO W. BRADEN is Boyd Professor Emeritus of Speech at Louisiana State University, Baton Rouge. He taught and directed graduate study in American public address. He has published numerous articles in speech and history journals on William E. Borah, Abraham Lincoln, and Franklin D. Roosevelt. From 1970 to 1980 he edited *Representative American Speeches*. His latest book is *The Oral Tradition in the South* (1983).

BERNARD L. BROCK is professor of speech communication at Wayne State University, Detroit, Michigan. He teaches courses in rhetorical criticism, political communication, and contemporary public address. He is coauthor of *Methods of Rhetorical Criticism: A Twentieth-Century Perspective*.

FERALD J. BRYAN is assistant professor of speech and theatre arts at Mount Union College, Alliance, Ohio. He teaches courses in the history and criticism of American public address and in communication theory. He is a native southerner and has delivered convention papers and published essays on southern oratory and the rhetoric of the populist movement.

CARL R. BURGCHARDT is assistant professor of speech communication at Colorado State University, Fort Collins. He teaches courses in critical methodology and the history and criticism of American public address.

RONALD K. BURKE is associate professor of speech communication at Syracuse University, Syracuse, New York. He teaches a course in the history of American public address and has published articles on antislavery activists. He is compiling data for a book on black abolitionist Samuel Ringgold Ward.

RICHARD J. CALHOUN is Alumni Professor of English at Clemson University, Clemson, South Carolina. He has published numerous articles on contemporary American literature, southern literature, and literary criticism. He has written and edited four books; the most recent is *James Dickey* (1983).

KARLYN KOHRS CAMPBELL is professor of speech communication at the University of Minnesota, Minneapolis. She teaches courses in rhetorical theory and criticism, political communication, and in the rhetoric of early and modern feminism. She is the author of essays analyzing feminist rhetoric and speeches by women and of *Critiques of Contemporary Rhetoric* and *The Rhetorical Act*, and she is coeditor of and contributor to *Form and Genre: Shaping Rhetorical Action*.

MICHAEL CASEY is assistant professor of speech communication, University of Maine, Orono. He has taught courses in rhetorical theory, public address, and argumentation theory. His primary research interests are political and religious rhetoric.

DANIEL ROSS CHANDLER is minister at United Methodist Church, New York. Since 1976, he has held assistant professorships in speech communication in the state and city universities of New York and at Rutgers University. His published books are *The Reverend Dr. Preston Bradley* and *The Rhetorical Tradition*.

CELESTE MICHELLE CONDIT is assistant professor of speech communication at the University of Illinois, Urbana. She teaches courses in public address and rhetorical criticism and has published articles in these areas.

HOWARD DORGAN is professor of communication arts at Appalachian State University, Boone, North Carolina. He teaches courses in the history of American public address and in southern oratory and has published numerous articles in the fields of southern rhetoric and Appalachian studies. He is the current executive secretary of the Southern Speech Communication Association, a past editor of the *Southern Speech Communication Journal*, and coeditor of and contributor to *The Oratory of Southern Demagogues* and *Public Discourse in the Contemporary South*.

BERNARD K. DUFFY is professor of speech at Clemson University, Clemson, South Carolina. He teaches courses in rhetorical theory and American public address. He is the author of articles and essays on rhetorical theory and political rhetoric and is editor with

Halford R. Ryan of *American Orators of the Twentieth Century: Critical Studies and Sources* published by Greenwood Press.

KAREN A. FOSS is associate professor of speech communication at Humboldt State University, Arcata, California. She teaches courses in women and communication and rhetoric and is coeditor of *Women's Studies in Communication*, the journal of the Organization for Research on Women and Communication.

HAL W. FULMER is assistant professor of communication at Mississippi State University, Starkville. He teaches courses in public speaking, rhetorical and communication theory, and persuasion.

G. JACK GRAVLEE is professor and chair of speech communication at Colorado State University, Fort Collins. He teaches courses in the history and criticism of American and British public address and in contemporary American television. He has contributed essays to *America in Controversy* and *The Oratory of Southern Demagogues*.

CHARLES J. GRIFFIN is assistant professor of rhetoric and communication at Kansas State University, Manhattan. He teaches courses in the history and criticism of American public address, and his research interests include American religious oratory.

J. JUSTIN GUSTAINIS is associate professor of communication at the State University of New York at Plattsburgh. He teaches courses in rhetorical theory and rhetorical criticism.

DAVID HENRY is professor of speech communication at California Polytechnic State University, San Luis Obispo. He teaches rhetorical theory, public address, argumentation/critical thinking, and public speaking. His research is primarily in the criticism of political discourse.

ANTHONY HILLBRUNER is professor of rhetoric and American studies at California State University, Los Angeles. He teaches rhetorical theory and criticism. He has published over forty scholarly articles and was a visiting scholar in residence at Cambridge University in 1972 and at Oxford University in 1979. He has contributed to several books and is the author of *Critical Dimensions*.

LAWRENCE W. HUGENBERG is associate professor of speech communication at Youngstown State University, Youngstown, Ohio. He teaches courses in historical and critical research, political communication, American public address, and rhetorical criticism. He received the Youngstown State University's Distinguished Professor Award in 1983 and the Central States Speech Association Outstanding Young Teacher Award in 1984. He is editor of *Studies in Rhetoric Honoring James L. Golden.*

SANDRA SARKELA HYNES is assistant professor of speech/communications at Jefferson Community College, Louisville, Kentucky. She teaches courses in public address and communication theory.

JAMES JASINSKI is assistant professor in speech communication at Southern Illinois

University, Carbondale. He teaches courses in public address and rhetoric in American society and rhetorical theory and criticism. He is researching different visions of the American public in the ratification debate of 1787–1788.

LOCH K. JOHNSON is professor of political science at the University of Georgia, Athens. He teaches courses in American government, specializing in executive-legislative relations and national security policy. He is a former American Political Science Association Congressional Fellow and author of *The Making of International Agreements: Congress Confronts the Executive* and *A Season of Inquiry: The Senate Intelligence Investigation*, winner of the 1985 Certificate of Distinction of the National Intelligence Study Center.

WILLIAM LASSER is assistant professor of political science at Clemson University, Clemson, South Carolina. He teaches courses in American politics and public law. His publications include articles in the *Journal of Politics* and *Technology Review*. He is completing the manuscript for a book on the Supreme Court in periods of crisis.

DALE G. LEATHERS is professor of speech communication at the University of Georgia, Athens. He contributed an essay on Billy James Hargis to *American Orators of the Twentieth Century: Critical Studies and Sources*.

THOMAS L. LESSL is assistant professor of speech communication at the University of Georgia, Athens. He teaches courses in communication theory and in rhetorical criticism and theory.

JOHN LOUIS LUCAITES is assistant professor of speech communication at the Univesity of Alabama. Tuscaloosa. He teaches courses in Anglo-American political discourse, rhetorical criticism, and the relationship between rhetoric and social theory. He is coauthoring a book (with Celeste Michelle Condit) on the black American rhetorical tradition.

STEPHEN E. LUCAS is a professor of communication arts at the University of Wisconsin, Madison. He teaches courses in the history of American public address. His book *Portents of Rebellion: Rhetoric and Revolution in Philadelphia, 1765–1776* (1976), was nominated for a Pulitzer Prize and received the Speech Communication Association Golden Anniversary Award. He is working on a comprehensive study of George Washington's public discourse.

DAVID A. MCCANTS is professor of communication and chair of the department of communication and theatre at Indiana University-Purdue University at Fort Wayne. He teaches courses in the history and criticism of American public address and in major American controversies.

JANIS CAVES MCCAULEY is professor of English at Bob Jones University, Greenville, South Carolina. A specialist in Renaissance literature, she has also published articles on several nineteenth-century literary and cultural figures. She is currently writing a monograph on the sermons of John Donne.

MICHAEL DENNIS MCGUIRE is associate professor of rhetoric at the University of

Georgia, Athens. He teaches courses in the history of rhetoric, rhetorical theory, rhetorical criticism, and international rhetoric.

CALVIN MCLEOD LOGUE is professor and head of speech communication at the University of Georgia, Athens. He teaches a seminar in rhetorical criticism. He contributed to *Oratory in the New South* and edited with Howard Dorgan *Oratory of Southern Demagogues* and *Public Discourse in the Contemporary South: A New Rhetoric of Diversity*. He received the Creative Research Medal from the University of Georgia Research Foundation for his continuing criticism of southern discourse.

WALDO E. MARTIN, JR. is associate professor of history at the University of Virginia at Charlottesville. He teaches courses in the history of black people and race relations, modern black consciousness, and the 1960s. He is the author of *The Mind of Frederick Douglass* (1984) and "Frederick Douglass: Humanist as Race Leader," in Leon F. Litwack and August Meier, eds., *Black Leaders of the Nineteenth Century* (forthcoming).

ALLEN H. MERRIAM is associate professor of communications at Missouri Southern State College, Joplin. He teaches courses in public speaking, political and social communication, and international communication. He contributed a chapter on feminist rhetoric in India to *Women in Politics; Studies in Role and Status* (1974). He is also the author of *Ghandi vs. Jinnah: The Debate over the Partition of India*.

JOHN W. MONSMA is professor of speech communication at Northern Arizona University, Flagstaff. He has taught courses in rhetoric, public address, and debate. He has published articles on debate and the teaching of communication to Native Americans.

ALEXANDER MOORE is assistant editor of the Papers of John C. Calhoun at the University of South Carolina, Columbia.

MICHAEL G. MORAN is associate professor of English at the University of Rhode Island, Kingston. He teaches courses in composition and rhetorical theory and directs the university-wide writing program at the University of Rhode Island. He has coedited and contributed to *Research in Composition and Rhetoric* and *Research in Technical Communication* and is writing a book on eighteenth-century scientific and technical discourse.

THOMAS H. OLBRICHT is chairman of the religion division and professor of religion at Pepperdine University, Malibu, California. He has published articles and chapters in several books on preaching and biblical studies in the United States and is writing a book on the history of biblical studies in America.

JAMES S. OLSON is professor of history at Sam Houston State University, Huntsville, Texas. He is the author of twelve books, the most recent of which are *Catholic Immigrants in America* (1986) and *Saving Capitalism* (1987).

MICHAEL RICCARDS is president of St. John's College, Sante Fe, New Mexico. His main areas of interest are the American presidency, political theory, and political behavior. He has been a Fulbright Fellow to Japan, a National Endowment for the Humanities Fellow at Princeton University, and a Henry Huntington Fellow at the Huntington Library in California. He is the author of *The Making of the American Citizenry: An Introduction to Political Socialization* and *A Republic If You Can Keep It: The Foundations of the American Presidency* and has completed a historical survey, *The Uncertain Consul: The Presidency and the American Republic*.

RONALD F. REID is professor of communication studies at the University of Massachusetts, Amherst. Most of his teaching and writing is in the history and criticism of American rhetorical discourse and rhetorical theory, especially colonial and early nineteenth-century rhetoric. He is the recipient of several awards from the Speech Communication Association, including the James A. Winans/Herbert A. Wichelns Memorial Award for Distinguished Scholarship in Rhetoric and Public Address.

HARRY W. ROBIE is assistant professor of English at Berea College, Berea, Kentucky. He teaches courses in interpersonal communication, public speaking, oral interpretation, and persuasion. His research interests include native American oral performance and cross-cultural communication.

LLOYD E. ROHLER is assistant professor of communications at the University of North Carolina, Wilmington. He teaches courses in the history and criticism of rhetoric and rhetorical theory. He is the editor of and contributor to volume 1 of *Great Speeches* (1986).

HALFORD R. RYAN is professor of speech, Washington and Lee University, Lexington, Virginia. He teaches courses in the history and criticism of American public address. He researched the Beecher Family Papers, Yale University, New Haven, Connecticut, on a Washington and Lee University Glenn Grant.

EDWARD L. SCHAPSMEIER is distinguished professor of history at Illinois State University, Normal. He teaches a course in great figures of American history and has written articles relating to the political career of Alexander Hamilton.

JO BOLIN SHIELDS has taught classes in classical and modern rhetoric.

RONALD E. SHIELDS is assistant professor of theatre at Bowling Green State University, Bowling Green, Ohio. A specialist in performance studies, he has published in *Literature in Performance*.

CRAIG R. SMITH is president of Freedom of Expression Foundation, Washington, D.C. He has taught rhetorical theory and criticism and American public address and has published numerous articles on Daniel Webster's speaking and a book on the Compromise of 1850.

STEPHEN A. SMITH is associate professor of communication at the University of Arkansas, Fayetteville. He teaches courses in the history and criticism of American public address, political communication, and freedom of speech. His articles on the history and theory of the First Amendment have received the H. A. Wichelns Memorial Award and the J. William Fulbright Research Prize in Communication Studies.

HERMANN G. STELZNER is professor of communication at the University of Massachusetts, Amherst. He has been editor of *Communication Quarterly* and *Quarterly Journal of Speech.*

BETH M. WAGGENSPACK is assistant professor of communication studies at Virginia Polytechnic Institute and State University, Blacksburg, Virginia. Her teaching encompasses the field of rhetoric and public address, particularly in the areas of persuasion and rhetorical criticism. She conducts research into the rhetoric of the women's movement, impression management, and political rhetoric.

EUGENE E. WHITE is professor emeritus of speech communication at Pennsylvania State University, State College. He is a frequent contributor to scholarly journals and is the author or editor of ten books, including *Puritan Rhetoric: The Issue of Emotion in Religion* and *Rhetoric in Transition.* He is a recipient of the Winans/Wichelns Award for Distinguished Scholarship in Rhetoric and Public Address and the Speech Communication Association Golden Anniversary Prize Fund Award.

MARK R. WINCHELL is associate professor of English at Clemson University, Clemson, South Carolina. A frequent contributor to scholarly journals, he is also the author of books on Joan Didion, William F. Buckley, Jr., and Leslie Fiedler and monographs on Horace McCoy and John Gregory Dunne. At present he is doing research for books on the contemporary novelist William Humphrey and former Georgia senator Herman Talmadge.

THOMAS D. WORTHAM is professor of English and American literature at the University of California at Los Angeles. He is editor of James Russell Lowell's *The Bigelow Papers* and the letters of William Dean Howells and the author of articles on Lowell, Howells, Oliver Holmes, and the fireside poets, among others. The editor of the journal *Nineteenth-Century Literature*, he is currently at work on a book on Howells's early writings and a new edition of Ralph Waldo Emerson's poems.

DAVID ZAREFSKY is professor of communication studies and associate dean of the School of Speech at Northwestern University, Evanston, Illinois. He teaches courses in American public discourse, historical and contemporary, and in theories of argumentation. He has researched the papers of Stephen A. Douglas in several manuscript collections. He has written several articles on the Lincoln-Douglas debates and is preparing a book on the debates.